Peter Hook was born in Salford in 1956. He was a founding member of Joy Division and New Order and now tours both bands' music with his new group, Peter Hook and the Light. He also DJs, and promotes Fac 51 The Haçienda and The Haçienda Classical concerts around the world. Peter lives in Cheshire with his wife, Rebecca, and children, Heather, Jack and Jessica, and their dog, Bo.

Further praise for *Substance*:

'The 768 pages will delight both New Order-ites and general rock readers, revealing the astonishing human bathos behind this group's godly future-rock . . . The way Joy Division and New Order combined high art with base behaviour is well established but this book rides that tandem to new dimensions . . . but there's much more than carnage'

Mojo

'Set against a lurid backdrop of orgiastic tours, awash with drink, drugs, and a debauched retinue of dealers, hookers and mad roadies, Hook drawing from a seemingly bottomless well of outrageous anecdotes, many of them hilarious and told with the same droll voice that delighted readers of *The Haçienda: How Not to Run a Club*' ***Uncut***

'If you think you know all about sex, drugs and rock 'n' roll, think again. There are stories here that make Ozzy Osbourne look like Mother Teresa. A bloated behemoth of a book, it includes details of the tours and fights and drugs, as well as the most comprehensive archive of track listings, record releases and concert dates ever produced . . . Hook lures us into his eventful, colourful story' ***Sunday Express***

'At times, *Substance* ... becomes as debauched as the notorious biography of the 70s rock decadents Led Zeppelin ... Rock writing rarely tells us properly what a band treading water or in slow decline feels like from the inside. Hook does so memorably ... For all his boisterous indestructability, this book often has a haunted quality, and is all the more powerful for it' ***Guardian***

'Epic rock tale of sex, drugs and jealousy ... A must for fans, it's wildly funny and revelatory' ***The Sun***

'It's been nine years since Peter Hook left New Order and his new book *Substance* chronicling the original four-piece's history is as mammoth and downright idiotic as the band deserves ... something hilariously daft happens on nearly all of *Substance*'s 750 pages' ***Classic Pop***

'You don't have to be an ardent fan of Manchester music to enjoy this doorstopper ... engrossing' ***Cheshire Life***

'A rollicking read' ***Record Collector***

SUBSTANCE

Also by Peter Hook

The Haçienda: How Not to Run a Club

Unknown Pleasures: Inside Joy Division

SUBSTANCE

INSIDE NEW ORDER

PETER HOOK

SIMON & SCHUSTER

London · New York · Sydney · Toronto · New Delhi

A CBS COMPANY

First published in Great Britain by Simon & Schuster UK Ltd, 2016
This paperback edition published by Simon & Schuster UK Ltd, 2017
A CBS COMPANY

1 3 5 7 9 10 8 6 4 2

Simon & Schuster UK Ltd
1st Floor
222 Gray's Inn Road
London WC1X 8HB

www.simonandschuster.co.uk
www.simonandschuster.com.au
www.simonandschuster.co.in

Simon & Schuster Australia, Sydney
Simon & Schuster India, New Delhi

A CIP catalogue record for this book
is available from the British Library

Paperback ISBN: 978-1-4711-6971-7
Ebook ISBN: 978-1-4711-3243-8

Typeset in the UK by M Rules
Printed and bound by CPI Group (UK) Ltd, Croydon, CR0 4YY

MIX
Paper from responsible sources
FSC® C020471

Simon & Schuster UK Ltd are committed to sourcing paper
that is made from wood grown in sustainable forests and support the Forest
Stewardship Council, the leading international forest certification organisation.
Our books displaying the FSC logo are printed on FSC certified paper.

Rest in peace: Jean Jackson, Billy 'Blue' Hook, Wilma 'Tinks' Hook, Rex Sargeant, Annik Honoré, Paul (Twinny) Bellingham, Michael Shamberg, Jack Bruce, Steve Strange, Anne Kirkbride, Ben E. King, BB King, Joe Moss, Pete de Freitas, Errol Brown, David Bowie, Tony Warren, John Rhodes (Rhodesy) and Paul Kershaw of the Stockholm Monsters, Kirsty Howard, Harold Moores, Paul Massey, Vinegar Vera, Natasha Wise, Alan Wise (Impressario Extraordinaire), Howard Marks, Caroline Aherne.

This book is the truth, the whole truth,
and nothing but the truth … as I remember it!

Note to Readers

Some readers may find discrepancies in the running times of New Order recordings when checked against those found on numerous websites. The timings listed in this book are to the best of my knowledge correct as the tracks were recorded at the time.

CONTENTS

Contents

INTRODUCTION

When I started my first book about the Haçienda, I knew that if I ever got round to telling the New Order story it would be the most difficult by far. In twenty-six years of New Order there were some wonderful moments, but there was also a lot of pain and heartbreak, self-doubt, frustration and annoyance. It's a wonder any of us got through it.

If Joy Division defined my life, New Order shaped it: a fascinating story of sex, drugs and (indie) rock'n'roll; of art, money and crass stupidity, blind faith and amazing good luck – backed by a soundtrack of truly great songs written by wonderful musicians.

Ten things you should *always* do when you form a group

1. Work with your friends
2. Find like-minded people
3. Have ultimate self-belief
4. Write great songs
5. Get a great manager
6. Live in Manchester
7. Support each other through thick and thin
8. Realise no one person is bigger than the group (thanks to Gene Simmons for that one)
9. Watch where the money goes
10. Always get separate legal advice for everything before you sign; failing that, ask your mam and dad

PROLOGUE

1985

© Kevin Cummins

'Turned out his cure for jetlag was the biggest line of coke I'd ever seen.'

Let's start with a story. It's the only one in the book that includes a Hollywood actress, Orchestral Manoeuvres in the Dark and a mushroom vol-au-vent, so it's unique in that regard. On the other hand it's got a few other themes that'll be cropping up as we go along (girls, cocaine, Barney being a twat …) so it's a good one to set the scene.

It starts in 1985 when New Order were told, firstly that John Hughes was using two of our songs for his new film, *Pretty in Pink*, and secondly that he wanted a new track written especially for the movie to replace them.

So that was good. Unfortunately, somebody came up with the bright idea of getting the new song produced by John Robie and, oh man, back then I hated John Robie with a passion. He could sometimes be what you would call a very interesting/difficult character. We'd met him on the 'Confusion' session with Arthur Baker in New York. But, as my roadie mate Twinny said, 'He's not one of us, Hooky.'

When we were mixing his version of 'Sub-culture' at the Village Recorder, a studio in Santa Monica, California (where Fleetwood Mac had recorded *Tusk*, the most expensive album ever made, costing over $1 million dollars, although we would eventually eclipse that with one of our own), he had impressive bravado when it came to girls, something I could only dream of. He would approach girls in restaurants, clubs etc., offering them the chance to do some backing vocals on a track he was recording with 'New Order, a group from Eeengerland'. They always said yes, so every night we'd have a studio full of giggling airheads, with certain members of our entourage (a phrase you shall be reading a lot during this book) all over them like a cheap suit.

Not only that, but it was my belief that in one fell swoop Robie had helped destroy a huge part of the magic of New Order, simply by telling Bernard, 'You do realise this song's not in your key, don't you?'

Of course Bernard didn't realise the song wasn't in his key. None of us did. We didn't know anything about stuff like that. We always wrote the music first, and what I'd always loved about Barney's vocals was the unintentional strained quality as he tried to fit into the track. Like Ian, he wasn't blessed with the world's best singing voice, but it had emotion, passion, and to me the struggle in Bernard's voice was a major part of the band's appeal. (I agree with David Byrne, who said, 'The better a singer's voice, the harder it is to believe what they're saying.')

Not after Robie. After he piped up, we always had to write in Bernard's key. Not only that, but it marked a new awakening. Suddenly Bernard was thinking, *Oh, there's a right way of doing things? A proper way of doing things?* and over time it got so that not only were we writing everything in the same one or two musical keys, but every song had to have a vocal verse, a vocal bridge, a vocal chorus, a vocal middle eight (that was different) and finish with a vocal double chorus. To me that went against everything we'd ever set out to achieve. We were about tearing up and rewriting the rulebook, not consulting it every five bloody minutes; we were punks, rebels.

If you ask me, the rules ended up blanding us out. They took us from writing great songs like 'Blue Monday', where we were building the sound we wanted – a unique sound, nine minutes long, and if anybody had told us, 'You can't do that,' we would have told them to fuck off – to formulaic songs like 'Jetstream'.

Anyway – spit – back to the winter of 1985, and because the rest of the band loved him, and he and Bernard were *proper* buddies, Robie flew over for the *Pretty in Pink* sessions at Yellow Two in Stockport, right across the road from Strawberry Studios. There, Robie spent his days pissing me off by removing my bass from 'Shellshock' and putting the line on strings instead. 'You understand don't you, Hooky,' he'd smirk, while in the late evenings he swanned around the Haçienda.

We'd introduce him to girls then stand there aghast as he came out with lines like, 'Oh, you've got a face like Botticelli's Angel.'

'Fuck off,' they'd say.

In America he had women queuing up for him, but God bless those Manchester girls for giving him short shrift.

Robie had a strict studio routine. Every night at 8 p.m. he'd go upstairs to eat his pre-ordered Chinese takeaway. He'd sit in this funny little chair, all tied together with webbing, watch a bit of telly, eat his meal, and then return to the job of ruining New Order. One night the band were sitting upstairs after dinner and laughing about Robie always sitting in that particular chair when Barney suggested undoing the webbing, so it would collapse with him in it when he next sat down.

Brilliant, we thought, *that'll be funny*.

So he did it and it was. It was really funny. But of course Robie had sussed that I didn't like him, so when he fell through the chair and ended up with his Chinese all over himself, he blamed me. No matter how much I insisted I was an innocent bystander, he said he was going to get me back, get his revenge.

'You wait, Hooky … You wait!' he'd drawl, all New Yorky.

But he didn't. Not during that session anyway. We finished 'Shellshock', gave it to John Hughes, and the next thing you know it was early 1986, and we were rolling up to the premiere of *Pretty in Pink* in Los Angeles at the Chinese Theatre. Psychedelic Furs were there, OMD, Echo and the Bunnymen, Suzanne Vega (who burst out crying because you could barely hear her track), loads of bands. Rob Gretton couldn't come. There was the small matter of a cocaine-induced psychosis keeping him in a mental hospital. So it was me, Terry Mason, Steve and Gillian – and Bernard, who went with Robie, because you couldn't get a cigarette paper between them by then; they were a right pair of bosom buddies, almost an item.

First up, we all watched the film, which featured 'Thieves Like Us' and 'Elegia' but only a six-second clip of 'Shellshock'. John Hughes hadn't replaced the old tracks. He obviously didn't think 'Shellshock' was good enough, which I thought was hilarious and made a mental note to rag Robie about it later. Afterwards there was a nightclub reception where I got chatting to OMD, who I had not seen since their old Factory days, and I was complaining I felt jetlagged.

'Come with me,' came the invitation from one of their entourage. 'I've got just the thing.'

Turned out his cure for jetlag was the biggest line of coke I'd ever seen, then another and another, until I was completely fucked. I'd not had much coke before, so the feeling was very strange. It was also before I drank a lot so there was nothing to lighten the load. It did have the desired effect of keeping me awake but had the undesired side-effect of turning me into a teeth-clenched twat. I felt like I had a very stiff pole stuck up my arse. It made me very quiet and starey. In no way did I deserve what happened next, as there was absolutely no provocation on my part.

What did happen next was that I was sitting opposite Molly Ringwald, staring, having a drink with Steve, Gillian and Terry, stiff as a pole (see above) when out of the corner of my eye I see Barney a few feet away, sort of sniggering. I was just thinking, *Oh yeah, what's that twat cooking up?* when the next thing I knew, Robie was in front of me going, 'Hey, Hooky, you remember that chair in Yellow Two?' And he shoves a huge mushroom vol-au-vent right in my face.

I was in shock. Him and Barney walked off laughing and I just sat there as it dripped slowly down my face.

Now I had dressed up for the evening: a Crombie with a nice shirt and tie, very smart for me, and a face full of mushroom vol-au-vent was not exactly what I wanted to complete the look. It was one of those really creamy ones, all hot and sticky, and it got everywhere. As Steve, Gillian and Terry helped clean me up, I was still in shock and thinking, *That was bang out of order. What Barney did was in the middle of Stockport, with only us lot there. And Robie goes and does that to me at the premiere of* Pretty in Pink, *right in front of Molly fucking Ringwald.*

They all agreed. They were going, 'Yeah, he's a disgusting little twat. You should fucking hammer him, Hooky,' and me all full of coke, was going, 'Right, right, I'm going to fucking have that twat,' and them, all three of them, were going, 'Yeah, have him, have him.'

So by then I was wound up, right up, and the red mist descended. I was really on the warpath, and said, 'Right, where is the little cunt? I'm going to *fucking do him.*' I set off down the stairs to find him. Halfway down I spy Robie and Barney at the bottom, chatting up a couple of girls, going, 'Oh, you two look like you could be backing singers ...'

'Hey you, y'twat,' I said, and then, when he turned around, I nutted him. *Bang.* Right between the eyes, or so I thought – turned out it glanced him more on the cheek than anything else. But anyway, down he went like a sack of fucking spuds.

Oh my God. Total pandemonium. Psychedelic Furs legged it, OMD legged it, Suzanne Vega burst out crying again, and the two girls ran off screaming. The whole area cleared. Only Barney standing there, his jaw on the floor, then going, 'You shouldn't have done that, Hooky. That's fucking disgusting, that is.'

'And you, you twat,' I said, 'you say one more word and you'll be fucking next!' And I slowly turned – with Terry holding my coat like a butler gently putting it back on my shoulders – as we returned upstairs, where news of my exploits had spread. I spent the rest of the night shaking hands with people congratulating me on giving Robie exactly what he deserved. I was buzzing off my tits, feeling ten feet tall. A proper, coked-up little hard man. *Yes.*

Then, next morning:

Oh God, what have I done!

Terry came to my room, early. He had this habit of pulling at his wattle when he was nervous. 'Bernard wants a group meeting, Hooky,' he said, pulling at the wattle for all he was worth. 'He's not happy!'

Sure enough, Barney wasn't happy. He was sat there in the beautiful Sunset Marquis Hotel with a face like a smacked arse, going, 'It's terrible what you did. It was disgusting. How could you, how could you?'

But I'd been getting phone calls all morning, notes pushed under my door: *great news about Robie*, inundated with people thanking me for nutting the twat. I was starting to feel a bit more vindicated and, instead of just sitting there taking it, I was like, 'Listen, he's a twat. He shouldn't have done that to me anyway, putting a vol-au-vent in my face at a movie premiere in front of Molly fucking Ringwald when it was you who did the jape at Yellow Two in the first place, you twat.'

'Well, it's still disgusting,' he said, all prim and proper. 'You should go and apologise to him. You must apologise to him or I'm leaving the band.'

I said, 'Apologise to him? I'll rip his fucking head off.'

The trouble was, they all thought we needed Robie because he was still producing 'Shame of the Nation' and 'Sub-Culture' and without Rob Gretton we were a bit leaderless and worried about the American record company finding out about his nervous breakdown. So, for a quiet life, I agreed to say sorry, and went off to his room.

He opened the door, looking a bit bruised and very hangdog.

'Oh, it's you,' he said.

'Yeah,' I said. 'Listen, I came to say sorry about last night.'

'OK,' he nodded, 'come in and sit down.'

I sat down. He looked at me, little wounded soldier. 'What you did was really low, Hooky,' he began.

And, oh Jesus, it was like being back at school. I felt the beginnings of a new anger brewing as he started laying it on thick about what a dirty, lowdown dog I was, calling me cowardly even, hitting him with a sucker punch – until I couldn't take it any more, and exploded.

'Listen. You showed me up at a red-carpet premiere in front of Molly fucking Ringwald, right. As far as I'm concerned, that's fucking assault with a deadly weapon, mate.'

He went, 'Well you did that chair to me. You did that chair …'

I said, 'I didn't fucking *do* the chair, you fucking bald dwarf. I didn't do the chair. It was Barney that did the fucking chair. Jesus!'

He was angry now. 'Well, anyway, I think you're an asshole, and it was really low what you did.'

I said, 'Right, you fucking twat. Come on, outside now, I'm going to smash your fucking teeth in. In the corridor, now!'

He didn't move. I'd blown it again.

I stormed out, slamming his door, kicking the walls, absolutely seething. I returned to my room and hit the minibar with all the force of a mini-hurricane. I decided that was it. I'd had enough of the band, because this was as bad as it was going to get. I was leaving. I went to tell Steve and Gillian. They said they were leaving too!

Fuck me. Surely *this* was as bad as it was going to get?

Oh, how wrong I turned out to be.

PART ONE

Movement

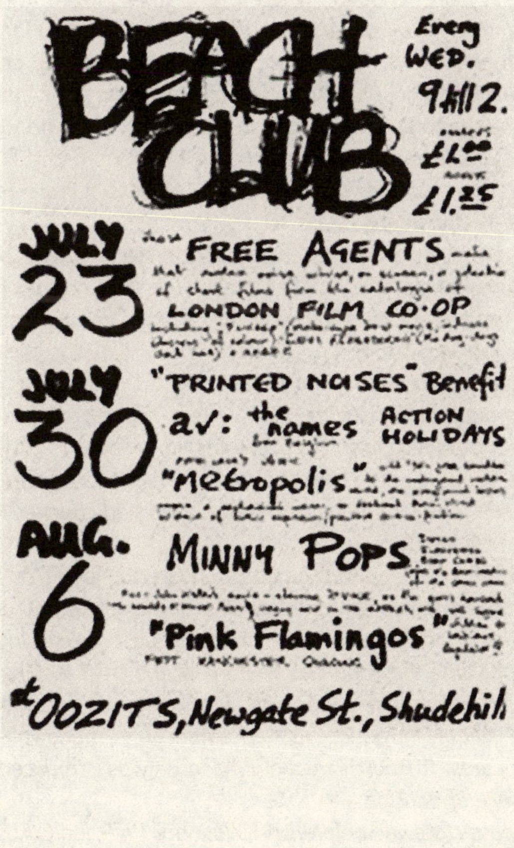

'One genius and three Manchester United supporters'

It was hearing 'Sebastian' by Cockney Rebel on a holiday in Rhyl in North Wales in 1973 that truly ignited the young Peter Hook's passion for music. He and schoolmate Bernard (Barney) Sumner were already attending gigs regularly when Hook read about the emerging Sex Pistols and immediately felt a connection with this bunch of 'working-class tossers'. Sure enough, when the Pistols played Manchester's Lesser Free Trade Hall on 4 June 1976 (50p a ticket) Hook, Sumner and schoolfriend Terry Mason were among the audience and, like the majority of those who also attended (Mick Hucknall, Mark E. Smith and Morrissey among them), they decided to form a band. One visit to Manchester's legendary Mazel's music store later, and Sumner and Hook were the proud owners of lead and bass guitars respectively (Mason briefly the singer).

Quickly becoming familiar faces on Manchester's growing punk scene, Hook and Sumner met Ian Curtis at the city's Electric Circus venue. 'He had "Hate" written on his jacket,' remembers Hook. 'I liked him immediately.'

A paragraph in Sounds *on 18 December 1976 was the first press notice for the 'Stiff Kittens'. A short time later, Curtis joined as lead singer, before the group abandoned the 'Stiff Kittens' name ('too cartoon punk') and became Warsaw. Drummer Steve Morris joined and played his first gig with the band at Eric's, Liverpool, on 27 August 1977, completing the musical line-up, and by January 1978 the band had changed their name again, becoming Joy Division.*

In May 1978 local DJ and promoter Rob Gretton joined as the group's manager, and the following month Joy Division were featured on the compilation album Short Circuit – Live at the Electric Circus. *In a relatively short space of time they had become one of the city's leading post-punk bands. In short order came a landmark appearance on* Granada Reports, *where Tony Wilson introduced a performance of 'Shadowplay' and the world – or at least the north-west of England – was introduced to Curtis's distinctive style of dancing.*

More releases followed before, on 13 January 1979, Ian Curtis appeared on the cover of the NME*. A few days later, however, the troubled singer was diagnosed with epilepsy. Things began to move fast. Recorded with mercurial producer Martin Hannett, debut album* Unknown Pleasures *was released to great acclaim in June. The band spent the rest of 1979 consolidating their success with gigs and TV appearances. It was an exhausting schedule that took its toll on Curtis, who by then was a new father, leading to several instances of on-stage fitting, as well as self-harming episodes.*

In March 1980, the band convened to record their second album, Closer*, with Hannett. However, the following month Ian, who had by then embarked on an intense love affair with Belgian journalist Annik Honoré, attempted suicide. A little later, Debbie Curtis, sick of her husband's infidelity, announced her intention to begin divorce proceedings.*

Then, on 18 May 1980, Joy Division ended. With a new album, Closer, and single, 'Love Will Tear Us Apart', recorded and ready for release, singer Ian Curtis committed suicide days before the band were due to embark on a US tour. The three surviving members, bassist Peter Hook, drummer Stephen Morris and guitarist Bernard Sumner, reconvened and decided to carry on, starting with the two songs left by Ian and Joy Division – 'Ceremony' and 'Little Boy' (later to be renamed 'In a Lonely Place'). In the meantime, plans were made for the trio to play live; and Ruth Polsky, the promoter of the aborted US Joy Division tour, booked a series of American dates.

Do we need to go into the circumstances of Ian's death?

Not really; they are well documented and I've already done that in my Joy Division book and, anyway, all the books are about Ian's death in a way. We were very young. I was just twenty-four and, looking back now, in my early sixties, shockingly young to have to deal with any of it. We were now very, very nervous. What would happen? Would we succeed in any way now Ian had gone? Were we good enough on our own ... without him? We were scared. We never talked about it in depth. Never analysed any of it. We just scratched the surface with pithy comments. Getting strength from togetherness that ended up, in a true northern English fashion, with us taking the piss both out of Ian and each other. We never confronted the grief. No one around seemed to know what to do or say. Maybe it was just too shocking for everyone, so it was much easier for family and friends to ignore it and let us get on with it. I would say looking back I was very proud of all of our immediate circle: Tony Wilson and Alan Erasmus of Factory, Rob and Pete Saville. None of them ever said it was over. The encouragement was always positive and about carrying on, as if this was just a hiccup on our upward trajectory. I thank them for that.

As a group we became very insular. I don't remember any of our peers saying anything much to us. Maybe they did to Tony and Rob, Bono being the notable example, I suppose. We did receive a lot of letters from fans, expressing their shock and grief – some lovely and some even written in blood. At the time, I was so pleased to finally have a home phone of my own I even (stupidly or like a true punk) put my name in the phone directory and had some really weird stuttering phone calls that lasted for months. Finally I had to give in, change my number and go ex-directory.

Sadly this was also where my relationship with Debbie and her daughter Natalie and Ian's parents finished too. I was embarrassed and ashamed, and I dealt with it by hiding away from them. Iris, my then-girlfriend, kept in touch but I suppose they had more in common. My relationship would only be rekindled years later when Debbie contacted me to help intervene in her business affairs with Rob. She was finding it very difficult dealing with him and I was delighted to help and since then we have had a good on-off relationship.

So this is, if you like, the story of a long and drawn-out grieving process that begins just a few days after his inquest when me, Barney and Steve, our manager Rob Gretton, and faithful helpers Terry Mason and Twinny, gathered at our rehearsal room next to Pinky's Disco in Salford. And while them three sat around making tea and smoking dope and feeling sorry for themselves, us three did the only thing we could. We started playing, jamming, writing songs again.

Why not? After all, we were still professional musicians and had been for six months. And what professional musicians do when they're not touring, making records or head-butting producers is hang around practice rooms waiting for inspiration to strike. So even though Pinky's was a freezing cold pit with a dangerous hole in the floor, we took solace in it and our work. Besides, we had Tony Wilson and Rob on our backs. Rob in particular was like a lunatic, literally ordering us to play. It was like a mantra with him. 'Write, come on, write. The best song you're ever going to write is your next one, so come on. Chop chop.'

He was convinced that if he kept us behaving like musicians then, after a while, we'd return to being just that. In hindsight, of course, he was right and that did eventually happen, but at the time we were thinking, *What are you going on about, mate? It's fucked. It's all over. Ian's killed himself.*

But if Rob told you to get your finger out and write, that's what you did – or tried to do. We had 'Ceremony' and 'Little Boy' on tape already, and to work out the lyrics we had to listen to them over and over again, and hearing Ian's voice like that it was almost like he was back with us in Pinky's again. Weird.

And then it would hit you that he wasn't.

The problem was that in Joy Division, he was our ears, he was the conductor, the lightning rod, and the majority of the songs happened through the process of him picking out the good bits as we played. Every now and then he'd stop us jamming and go, 'That was a great bit. Play that again.'

Not any more. We were looking for him but he wasn't there. Like twats we'd play for hours and nobody said a word. Not Rob, Terry or Twinny. Not me, Barney or Steve either. We'd lost him and we'd also lost our confidence.

We started recording the jams on our new four-track tape recorder so we could listen back and try to do what Ian had done. That worked, after a fashion. Trouble was, nobody wanted to do the vocals, so we ended up with loads of instrumental songs with titles like, 'Idea No. 1', 'Idea No. 2' and 'Guitary one', scrawled on the wall. But none of us could sing and play at the same time anyway, so we just played. Rob even had a go at some lyrics and titles, God bless him.

Meanwhile, the long-awaited 'Love Will Tear Us Apart' single came out, but we hardly noticed. I remember hearing it on the radio when I was driving to the post office. The DJ said it had come straight in at number 13 in the charts. I just turned it off and went in to tax my car. When *Closer* came out we didn't promote it at all, didn't even read the reviews. Why bother? It was over and done with. We were much too focused on trying to cope without him.

We discussed getting another singer. The three of us had played on a Kevin Hewick track called 'Haystack' for Factory Records, but talk of recruiting Kevin for vocals came to nothing.

It's a myth that Bono approached Tony to offer his services. We wouldn't have wanted him anyway, not because it was Bono or that we hated U2 ('Them Irish twats,' as Rob used to say), it was just that we didn't want an established vocalist to come in and change how we worked. We wanted a singer; we didn't want an Ian replacement. However, Tony did tell us later that Bono had come to his office in Granada, saying that Ian was the best of his generation and promising to carry on in his memory and achieve the success he felt Joy Division deserved. For Tony, U2 accomplished that at Live Aid, where he said Bono showed himself to be the only frontman with the charisma of Ian.

There was only one thing for it.

One of us lot would have to be the singer. To work it out, Rob thought it would be a good idea to put us in the studio with Martin Hannett, with Hannett in the Simon Cowell role and the three of us auditioning like a kind of post-punk *X-Factor*. It was a terrible idea, though. Martin had idolised Ian. Of everybody in the Factory family he was hit the hardest, and we entered the studio to find him medicating his depression in the usual way, with dope and coke. It didn't exactly help matters that he'd always had a fairly low opinion of me, Steve and Barney anyway: 'One genius and three Manchester United supporters' was what he'd called Joy Division. Even though that's not strictly speaking true, because Steve supported Macclesfield Town, but you knew what he meant. Being Martin Hannett, he wasn't exactly backward when it came to telling us what a poor substitute we made for Ian's genius.

'Oh, you're all shocking,' he'd say, listening to the playback, head in hands. Fair enough, we *were* a bit shocking – I mean, none of us was under any illusions when it came to our singing – but we weren't *that* bad. Pretty early on it became clear that Martin wasn't bemoaning our presence so much as Ian's absence.

Despite the fact that Steve, to say the least, wasn't keen on singing, he still tried out, and so did me and Barney. I think secretly both of us fancied being frontman. But we were all shit according to Martin. At one point in Strawberry Studios we were recording 'Ceremony' and Martin had decided to use all our three vocals mixed together in the track at the same time. 'The best of a bad bunch!' he cried. Then he started cackling. But then Bernard insisted on having 'just one more go', and in doing so used up mine and Steve's tracks, wiping them, so by the time Martin finally threw up his hands and told us to fuck off, Barney's was the only vocal left on tape. Which is pretty much how he became our singer.

But even I have to admit it worked out well. Barney improved quickly and became a good vocalist. Also, the fact that he couldn't sing and play at the same time helped us to develop a more unique sound, with the songs always picking up when he stopped singing and started hammering away at the guitar, as if he was taking out all of his vocal inadequacies, frustrations and grief on his poor old Gibson copy.

One gig is worth ten rehearsals. That's what Rob used to say. He was desperate to get us gigging again, so when the Names, a band from Belgium, pulled out of a Factory Records night at the Beach Club in Manchester he decided we should do it as 'The No Names'. He thought that was hilarious. Come the night and the audience didn't know, the other bands didn't know, the promoter didn't know. Nobody knew it was the ex-Joy Division. The surprise on people's faces as we set up and played was priceless, and A Certain Ratio were amazed. All I can remember of it was being terrified, setting up and playing, and me operating our trusty tape machine with all the keyboard parts on a backing track, and us doing a seven-song set where Steve sang three, and Bernard and I sang two each …

And not being bottled off. Now that was the most important thing. Not being bottled off.

So that was it. We'd popped our gig cherry as a trio. Rob decided we needed more and proposed getting in touch again with Ruth Polsky in America. 'Right,' he said, 'we promised her we were going to go as Joy Division. That twat killed himself. But we promised her we were going. So we're fucking going.'

His idea was not to have the pressure of playing in Manchester, or anywhere in England come to that, so we'd be a bit more relaxed. His other idea involved the equipment. Rob reasoned that as we were already a bit on the shaky side, not having our own gear would only make us shakier, so he made the decision to fly it all over to America.

To give us the comfort of what we knew best, to sound exactly how we wanted to sound: that was the plan. We'd lost our lead singer and our confidence, but at least we had great gear. So why not take it with us?

What could possibly go wrong?

'This is New York'

There was this tiny, and I mean *tiny*, pub near our practice room at Pinky's, called the Dover Castle. One dinnertime, Rob presented us with a load of ideas for band names that he'd got out of that week's *Sunday Times*.

'Let's get it over with,' he said.

Bearing in mind we were still in our early twenties and I was reading *2000AD* and Sven Hassel books, him reading the *Sunday Times* seemed pretty radical. Very grown-up.

'Right,' he said. 'Khmer Rouge?'

No, too terrorist.

'The Shining Path?'

That was too terrorist as well. Sounded like an LP title. Me and Barney hated that one.

'Are they all terrorist names?'

'No, don't think so,' said Rob, continuing. 'Mau Mau, the Immortals, Fifth Column, Theatre of Cruelty, Year Zero, Arab Legion ... oh, maybe they are?'

There were loads of them, all of which we hated.

'You've got to fucking pick one,' said Rob. 'Now!' As ever, he made it sound more like a threat than a request.

Rob and Steve decided on the Witch Doctors of Zimbabwe. Me and Bernard wanted New Order, which had begun life as 'The New Order of Kampuchean Rebels' (we gave the spare 'The' to Matt Johnson, and dumped the Kampuchean rebels). For a while there was a tense stand-off, with Rob and Steve saying New Order was a shit name and me and Barney threatening to leave the band if it was called the Witch Doctors of Zimbabwe.

We got our way. It was sorted and Rob sent the name off to Ruth. And I must say that never at any point did any of us consider a certain Mr Hitler and his bloody *Mein Kampf*, honest! Shows you how daft we were. We just thought it summed up our new start perfectly.

Then we went into Western Works, Cabaret Voltaire's studios

in Sheffield, and recorded and wrote a couple of tracks with them, one featuring Rob on vocals. We also played gigs in Liverpool and Blackpool, and carried on writing and rehearsing. By the time we left for New York, as well as 'Ceremony' and 'In a Lonely Place', we had 'Dreams Never End', 'Procession', 'Mesh' and 'Homage', plus the obligatory 'new one' (an instrumental in this case). Also a song called 'Truth' – our first to feature a drum machine, later a vital part of our arsenal.

Geek Alert

Dr. Rhythm DR-55

Released by Roland in 1980, the Doctor Rhythm offered three drum sounds, Kick, Snare and Hi-hat, as well as an Accent sound and a limited number of programmable patterns. Using active tone generation circuitry, its sounds were analogue, crisp and punchy; a balance knob altered the level of the Kick, Snare and Hi-hat while a separate Accent knob controlled the amount of emphasis to accented steps. It also featured a simple-step programmer with alternating button presses for notes and rests, and there was a 'tap write' programming mode, which lacked a metronome click for time-keeping. A volume control affected the overall level of both the main and headphone outputs, and the main output was mono. There was also a separate trigger facility, which emitted a pulse for every accented step in the pattern. The patterns were organised into banks, with A and B being programmable, and C and D presets. Each pattern could be switched between 12 or 16 steps, for 3/4 or 4/4 time signature, and two songs could be programmed, each containing a maximum of 128 bars.

The Boss Doctor Rhythm, bought and programmed by Steve, became a herald for a new age. Both he and Barney had flirted with electronica in Joy Division, Barney building from scratch a Transcendent 2000 synthesiser (given away in kit form with *Electronics Today* magazine), and Steve using a Synare I drum synthesiser. Their enthusiasm for all things electronic would grow and grow. The drum machine would also be used live as a backing track for the song 'Procession' so Steve could sing and play keyboards (obviously it was impossible for him to play the kit at the same time).

So, with our tried-and-trusted Velvet Underground 'Sister Ray' cover version, off we went.

Things started badly. We landed and British Airways had lost our cases. Fly the flag and lose your bag, eh? There were seven of us on the trip: me, Steve, Barney, Rob, Terry, Twinny and Dave Pils, and four of our cases went missing. Barney, who could fall into a vat of dog shit and still come up smelling of roses, was unaffected, and stood there, sympathetic as ever, saying, 'Right, I've got my case, let's get off then, shall we?' smirking while those of us who'd lost them, including yours truly, had to hang around waiting for all the bloody forms to be filled in.

New York was wonderful, everything I'd hoped it would be. It was enjoying an Indian summer and it was as hot as hell, which wasn't so bad if you had a change of clothes, but a disaster if you'd arrived from Manchester wearing jackboots, a thick coat and fucking British Airways had lost your bag.

It didn't turn up for five days, that bag, and you don't want to know how badly I stank by then.

But still. We were in New York. *Finally* we'd made it. And even though touring Manhattan felt sad because we'd catch sight of places Ian would have loved, like CBGB's and Max's Kansas City, it was still fantastic to be there, especially when we made it to our hotel and it turned out to be the infamous rock'n'roll joint the Iroquois on West 44th Street, second only to the Chelsea on West 23rd Street.

Why? It was even sleazier.

The Clash were staying there, too, and they were at their height, in between *London Calling* and *Sandinista!* But even though they were the Clash, and Paul Simonon was one of my bass heroes, there was an instant hatred between the two camps. Whether it was because they were Cockneys and we were Mancs, and they took themselves very seriously and we were shambolic, I don't know, but there was an intense rivalry right from the word go. Every day at 5 p.m. the hotel offered free hors d'oeuvres (or as we used to call them, 'horses' doovres') in the bar, and every day at 5 p.m. New Order and the Clash would be waiting for, then scrapping over them, grabbing the chicken wings and the loaded potato skins, both of which seemed exotic at the time, before the barman had even put them down, us going, 'Fuck off, y'Cockney bastards,' and them going, 'Ah fack off, ya Manc twats.' I knew that New Order were skint – we were on $3 a day 'per day' money – but I was surprised that the Clash were as hungry as we were.

(Incidentally, Rob's book claims he allowed $700 per day money for the trip but I can guarantee we never saw that much.)

'Per day' or 'per diem' money is a charming old rock'n'roll custom where the band or crew member is given cash for everyday expenses on top of their wages. Essentially a bonus, the money is usually spent on drugs and goes undeclared either to the wife or taxman. It was supposed to be receipted-for in records but when New Order were investigated by HMRC in 1985 and Rob referred to the receipts, most were signed M. Mouse or W. Churchill etc., and so the band were fined for poor accounting practice (though the crew got away scot free). These days the practice must be included as a personal gain on a P11D personal tax declaration form.

One time, me and Barney shared the hotel lift with Joe Strummer, who got in with piles of dandruff all over the shoulders of his black coat, holding on tightly to some American girl.

As we alighted at our floor Barney turned round, smiled and said to him, 'Is it snowing outside?'

'Fack off!' he snarled, as the doors shut.

Meanwhile, every time Rob saw Bernie Rhodes, their manager, he'd call him a cockney bastard, shouting it straight across the bar.

You could understand the friction. We weren't exactly at our most endearing.

So anyway, having made enemies of the Clash it was decided to hire a couple of vehicles: the U-Haul van for all the gear and what's called a shooting brake for us, the musicians, to travel in. It was a light-blue Buick eight-seater with rear-gunner-style seats in the back. If you've read the Joy Division book you'll know how bad Steve was at driving, and Barney had only passed his test the week before, so had no confidence at all, so it fell to me to drive. Trouble was, I'd forgotten my licence, so we cooked up a plan where Barney was going to hire the car, and then as soon as we were out of the hire place, we'd swap seats and I'd drive for the rest of the trip.

All Barney had to do was drive out of the hire place. That was all, a thirty-foot drive.

Fuck me, it was hair-raising. It was an automatic, which he'd never driven, so I sat beside him going, 'Just relax, be calm. I'll take over as soon as we're out on the street. Now take your foot off the brake and gently press the accelerator ...'

'Aaaaarrgggh!' six Mancs screamed in terror, as the car began to violently kangaroo towards the busy street, Barney alternating his foot from brake to gas. He was gripping the wheel, face and knuckles white with fear as we headed to the exit.

'Bernard, brake,' I said. 'Brake, mate. Brake, for fuck's sake!'

And he did, just in time, and six Mancs sighed with relief as Bernard came to a screeching halt and just avoided hitting a car, the car in question being a hearse, complete with coffin. You should have seen their faces in the hire office. We then started to have some fun driving round Manhattan in the shooting brake shouting things like, 'Hello girls, we're in a band!' when Barney spotted a pair of skis in a dustbin and made us stop so he could grab them.

'These are great!' he said, except they weren't really. They were horrible old plywood things, black with paint peeling off.

Later we pulled up at some lights and Twinny jumped out of the car. We were like, 'Hey, what's going on now?'

We looked over to see him taking a pair of shoes off a tramp who was passed out on the street. He left his own shoes with the guy and got back in the car, we were all, 'What the fuck?'

'Fuck off!' he says, 'they're Kickers. These are brand new and mine have got holes in!' You can take the boy out of Salford, eh?

Meanwhile, vehicle number two was the U-Haul van. Driving that was Terry, who was a good driver but nervous, and became even more so in the very busy New York traffic. For our first gig at Maxwell's, New Jersey, him, Twinny and Dave Pils had to pick up the gear from the airport, bring it back to the hotel and then take it to the gig the next day.

Now, when it came to the van, we had our gear insured with the Co-operative Insurance Services in Manchester. Rob in particular was very diligent about things like insurance: 'I worked for Eagle Star for two weeks in the 1970s!' Anyway, the policy stated that the van had to be alarmed or the gear wasn't insured. The one we'd hired wasn't alarmed, so for security, I told Terry to remove the high-tension lead (ask your dad) and bring it into the hotel. First night we were there I'd said to Rob, 'I bet you that fucker hasn't taken off the H-T lead,' went out, popped the hood, checked, and sure enough the dozy twat had left it on, so I took the lead off, all covered in oil and grime, found Terry sound asleep in his room and draped the cable across his face, giving him a lovely Mexican Zapata oil-moustache in the process. Thinking that would teach him, I left it at that.

The next day we were all very excited and the boys set off for the gig with us following a few hours later. However, when we arrived at Maxwell's there was no sign of the van or Terry, Twinny and Dave. After a while they drove up, all as white as sheets and screaming blue murder. Terry had managed to crash the van twice on the way. He'd hit a bus and the side of the Jersey tunnel. Plus they'd had a puncture.

Still, nobody had died, and we started unloading the gear, including a transformer – a bit of kit we needed to cope with the voltage difference between our English gear and the output in the US.

Only, Terry had hired this particular bit of kit on Rob's orders, and neither of them knew the first thing about stepping up voltage. So on the basis that if you had a big transformer you couldn't go wrong, Rob had told Terry to hire the biggest he could find (this would become a habit of Rob's).

He had, and it was huge. Terry had actually hired Pink Floyd's transformer and they were playing stadiums at the time. It weighed a ton – two tons in fact. A 250-kilowatt transformer. God knows how they got it in the van. It took six of us to lift it out. We plugged it in at Maxwell's and I swear the lights dimmed in Manhattan as it powered up.

Turned out to be a great gig. I mean, it was only our fourth as a three-piece but it felt like we'd got some of our mojo back, and with all three of us sharing vocals we began to think we might be able to pull this off. Maybe there really *was* life after Joy Division.

Back at the hotel all of the band were on a high, but Terry, Twinny and Dave Pils had topped their nightmare journey to the venue with a just-as-white-knuckle drive back. Finally arriving at the hotel hours after us, then parking right outside on 44th Street, they were way too frazzled to do anything but crawl to bed.

The next morning I was on Terry's back about moving the van so we wouldn't get a parking ticket. Off he trudged to do the deed – only to return a few minutes later, looking very sheepish.

'Umh,' he said, pulling on the wattle. 'Van's gone.'

'You what?'

'Van's gone.'

'Van's gone?' I said. 'How the hell has the van gone? Don't tell me you forgot to take off the . . .'

Great.

Even so, we came to the conclusion that the van had been towed away for a traffic violation and spent the rest of the day scouring Manhattan for it. After the umpteenth pound had told us that, no, they hadn't seen a van full of musical gear, a very heavy transformer and a pair of old wooden skis, we finally faced up to the fact that our van and all our equipment had been stolen.

Shit!

So, me and Rob hotfooted it to the local police station. I marched straight up to the desk sergeant and, adopting my best Hugh Grant voice, said something along the lines of, 'Excuse me, my dear fellow, we seem to have had some of our property stolen, old boy.'

But instead of despatching Kojak and issuing APBs, he said in a very broad New Yawk accent, 'Sit down oveh dere!' and pointed at a bench.

I was aghast. 'My dear fellow, you don't seem to understand. I am English and I will call the British Embassy if ...'

Before I could finish he repeated himself, much louder this time, giving me a proper Alex Ferguson hairdryer, with his hand on his gun for good measure. 'Sit down oveh fuckin' dere!'

Me and Rob did as we were told, trembling like two naughty schoolboys.

Later, what seemed like *much* later, he gave us a piece of paper, and told us to fill it in. It was awful. If we were scared before we were terrified now. The gear was gone and it seemed like no one, not even the police, was going to help.

We filled in the form as best we could and returned it to the cop, who didn't even look up. Then, as we went to leave, he said, 'Hey!' We turned back, smiling, full of hope that he was going to help after all. Hooray! Rob and I beamed at each other, then at him. 'Welcome to New Yawk!' he grinned, then looked down again.

Outside, full of righteous indignation, we phoned the embassy and asked to speak to the ambassador. He would help, surely? We were taxpayers after all. When we explained to the receptionist what had happened she just told us to go to the cops. Then hung up.

Double shit!

We hit on the idea of phoning the insurance company, so Rob got on the blower at the hotel and, I kid you not, this is how it went.

'Hello, yeah, Rob Gretton here. We're New Order; we've got an insurance policy with you. Number so and so. Right, that's right ...'

We were all looking at each other. The guy must have gone off to find the details. Rob gave us the thumbs up. *Don't worry, lads, it's all being sorted.* Guy comes back to the phone.

'Right,' said Rob, 'you've got the policy. Great. We've had all the gear stolen. Well, it's covered isn't it?' Pause. 'Yeah, great,' another thumbs up, pause. 'Was the van alarmed? No it wasn't. Hello ... Hello? He's hung up.'

Our mouths dropped open in disbelief and as Rob, with a 'that's torn it' expression, realised what he'd done, we all exploded into a big shouty mess, our anger directed at our stupid manager: ten thousand pounds' worth of gear gone, never to be replaced. There might not be any point in crying over spilt milk, but we did it anyway. Tony Wilson, who was in New York at the same time recording A Certain Ratio's second album, said, 'It's so poetic, darling. It's the perfect ending!'

We seethed silently.

Next step, tell Ruth, who had kittens but begged us to carry on. We decamped to her office in Danceteria and hit the phones to hire gear, while Rob made amends by making me and Barney use our credit cards to pay for new equipment. A trip to Manny's, a huge Aladdin's Cave of a music shop on 48th Street yielded, for Barney, a nice Yamaha guitar combo and a Gibson 335 with 'second' stamped on the back of the headstock (although none of us could see why, but it was cheap at $550 so we kept schtum). I got a Yamaha BB800 for $431 but had a problem replacing my Shergold six-string bass. There was no equivalent in America. And no matter how much I tried, the only one I could find to hire was a Fender version, which I had to go and pick up from downtown Manhattan. There, I literally bumped into Liza Minnelli coming out of her room. 'Liza! With a Zee!' I blurted, without really thinking about it.

'Fuck off,' she drawled in return.

Charming!

So nothing was getting any better. We'd lost our gear and I'd been told to fuck off by Liza Minnelli with a Zee, and the only real respite from the misery was when Rob and I were in Times Square and came across a stall where you could print up your own *New York Times* front cover. I mocked one up that said, 'TERRY & TWIN IN $40,000 ROAD CREW FOUL-UP – ROB AMAZED', took it back and showed it to the high-tension-lead twins, who freaked, thinking they'd made the daily papers.

Apart from that, it was blood, sweat and tears: me, Barney and Steve sitting in a room at the Iroquois having to relearn and rewrite all the songs.

Geek Alert

Fender Baritone Bass Guitar

The Fender Baritone Bass Guitar is a six-string electric bass guitar made by Fender. It debuted in 1961 and differed from the previous Fender Precision Bass by having six strings with lighter gauges, a shorter scale and a mechanical vibrato arm. As with most Fenders then, it had a 7¼-inch fingerboard radius. The original Bass VI had three Stratocaster single-style coil pickups, controlled by a panel of three on/off slider switches instead of the more common three-position switch. The Fender Baritone bass guitar is tuned a fourth lower than a normal guitar to BEADFB, whereas the Shergold six-string bass guitar is tuned to concert pitch at EADGBE.

The hire guy had warned me. 'This is a baritone,' he kept saying.

'I don't care. It's not singing, mate, it's just playing!'

Back at the hotel I tuned it up to *EADGBE*, overtightening the strings, and breaking them one by one, bending the neck like a banana. I was lucky I didn't lose an eye. It was useless. This led to me having to relearn all the six-string songs on the four-string in a blind panic, with Steve banging along on phone books beside me. There is definitely a special kind of camaraderie that comes from being thrown against the ropes, and we all pulled together, and even forgave Terry and co.

So anyway, we managed to do the rest of the gigs. And I suppose if there's one thing to be said for having most of your gear nicked it's that it liberated us from the responsibility of looking after it, and we ended up partying harder than we would have done otherwise. Every cloud, and all that.

Then, on returning to New York, there was a message for us – the cops had found the van.

'It was in the middle of the Brooklyn Expressway,' we were told. The crooks had dumped it on the central reservation with the doors open and the engine still running.

We hardly dared ask. 'Is there anything still in it?'

The cop nodded confidently. 'Yeah, man, there was stuff in it. If you go to the pound you can get it back.'

We were literally dancing in the police station, over-fucking-joyed, singing, 'The stuff's in the back, the stuff's in the back,' and all but floated on a cloud of optimism to the pound, where a city employee led us to our long-lost van, removed the new padlock and opened the rear doors with a flourish.

'There you go,' he said, 'there's your stuff.'

In the back was the transformer. And the fucking skis.

'Brilliant!' said Barney. He clambered into the van and retrieved the skis, happy as Larry. The rest of us looked at each other, mouths open in disbelief.

The transformer would have been worth a fortune if they'd sold it for scrap because there was so much copper in it, but they couldn't lift it out of the van. Thank God for small mercies, at least we didn't lose our deposit on it. Otherwise, it was all gone. We'd lost our singer, lost our gear, our insurance cover and, thanks to Rob choosing the 'Something to Declare' route at the airport on the way back, ended up spending six hours and getting stung for a load of import tax on the gear we'd bought in New York.

And yet it hadn't been a disaster. In fact, it had been a hell of a first tour. I mean, what an adventure. Did I mention us touring all the great clubs in Manhattan, with Rob going, 'Look how simple this place is. It's just painted black with a PA in one corner. Brilliant!' (and the idea for the Haçienda was born).

There were some great adventures. One night a member of our entourage shagged Ruth. Talk about every dog having his day. Delta 5, a group from Leeds, were playing in New York at the same time and one of them nearly had a fight with Ruth over who was going to sleep with him. Ruth won but said to her the next day, 'You can have him. He kept his Y-fronts on the whole time!' Another member of our entourage – the jammy bastard – became very friendly with Beth, the gorgeous singer.

On the last night a member of our entourage was desperate to get a blow job off a hooker and went out, doing the dirty deed in an alley near the hotel at a cost of $15, a bargain! Rob was so excited by this that he persuaded the guy to go out and sneak the hooker back in so she could give us all a blow job. 'I'll pay for everyone!'

So our guy went back out, but got caught bringing her in by the night watchman. He panicked and handed the guy a $20 bribe.

'You limeys are amazing!' he laughed. 'I normally get paid to throw them out!'

I went first, and then we sniggered uncontrollably as we peeped round the corner to watch Rob, fascinated by his toes, which were doing the weirdest things, clawing and curling up like you wouldn't believe. Lucky for him we didn't have camera-phones in those days.

It was a wild, eye-opening time and I loved every second of it. I remember being in the taxi on the way to the airport at the end, as we drove over the 41st Street bridge, looking over my shoulder and seeing the whole of Manhattan lit up so beautifully, like a huge Christmas tree, and being so dog-tired that I could hardly keep my eyes open. It seemed like an amazing hallucination. I tried to rouse the others, but none of them would, or could, wake up. Then I fell asleep myself, and was shaken awake by the cab driver when we arrived, stumbling through the airport onto the plane and falling asleep again straight away.

Everybody slept the whole flight back, only waking when it touched down in Manchester. We were that exhausted. I remember getting home and Iris saying, 'Well, what was it like then?' and me going, 'Quiet. You know ...' and sloping off to bed to recover.

That tour, so full of ups and downs, did a lot to dispel the unhappiness around Ian dying. It was the first time – and now, in retrospect, one of the only times – we'd been a real band in the true sense of the word. There were no diva tantrums and, because we were sharing singing duties, there was no 'pecking order' bullshit either. The ups and downs of the tour brought us together. They made us tighter. I'm not sure we would have continued but for that tour.

And those skis, by the way, never did make it back. Me and Twinny chucked them in the bin, and Barney's never forgiven us. Never stopped going on about them.

EXTRA

THE DAILY TRIBUNE

FINAL
WALL STREET
CLOSING
COMPLETE SPORTS

TERRY & TWIN $40,000 ROAD CREW FOUL UP - ROB AMAZED

Panic In New York;
Menagerie Breaks Loose

New York State Theatre

Building Boom
Of Roaring '20's
Biggest of All

English Sailor
Set Mark for
Marathon Walker

BROADWAY
HEART-BEAT

PERMANENT LANDMARK

'This is a rock band, let's stick with the guitars and drums'

Martin Hannett was in the US at the same time as New Order, brought over by Tony Wilson to record A Certain Ratio's To Each *album at the Eastern Artists Recording Studio (EARS) in New Jersey. It was also there that New Order completed work on their first single, 'Ceremony', first released in March 1981, then later re-recorded with Gillian Gilbert and re-released in September of the same year. Meanwhile came the job of replenishing kit stolen in New York …*

Returning to our practice rooms after the tour we had literally nothing – two little amps, Barney's guitar, my bass and a snare drum, that was it. It was like there was somebody up there who didn't like us. As though Ian was in heaven surrounded by our gear, laughing his dogs off.

But in a funny way this is where it gets interesting, because although we could borrow equipment from A Certain Ratio, we still needed gear of our own, and went cap in hand to Tony for cash to buy more. The upshot was that Barney and Steve got a bit more ambitious when it came to new gear. Mr Rock'n'Roll here was all, 'What are you doing? This is a rock band, let's stick with the guitars and drums,' but the other two had eyes as big as saucers – Steve looking at new Pearl syndrum kits, and Barney eyeing up bigger synthesisers and sequencers. The real transition from the Joy Division sound to the New Order sound was about to begin.

And there would also be another reason we would end up going 'more synthesiser', but we'll come to that later …

The other major moment here was Barney becoming the singer. I've racked my brains but I cannot remember how it came about. It seemed like one minute it was all three of us and then it was just him. I think, on the American tour, Rob had spotted that all of us doing something new was making the band different, but not as good. It was changing the sound too much and taking us out of our comfort zones. As far as Rob was concerned it wasn't rocket science: keep the world-class rhythm section the same, make Barney sing and bring someone else in to play guitar and keyboards. Simples. The songwriting dynamic would be unchanged: music first, vocals later.

Rob suggested Gillian Gilbert, firstly because she'd played with us before (when Barney had injured his hand at Eric's in Liverpool), and was already in a group, the Inadequates; secondly because she was Steve's girlfriend, therefore she was a known quantity; and thirdly because she wasn't very experienced and probably wouldn't change our style and sound. Secretly, I thought he fancied her.

As far as Barney and I were concerned, I can't remember either of us having any particular objections. As long as it wasn't my girlfriend hanging around with us, then it didn't matter to me. Gillian was quiet, and although you couldn't have much of a crack with her, she was easy to ignore. You knew she wasn't going to join the band and start telling you what to play and trying to change your style of music. As with the lead singer, that was important. I remember having a conversation with Rob sat on his office floor – he had no chairs – and him saying we'll try her out and sort out the publishing later. I nodded in agreement, thinking to myself, *What's publishing?* (And that ignorance has cost me millions.)

Payment for written music is usually divided into two parts. There is one pot for the writers, i.e. publishing (usually achieved by *radio* play or film or advert/film soundtrack use and still very lucrative now), and one pot for the performers who record it, called performance royalties (usually achieved by record sales, downloads, streaming etc., not very lucrative these days mainly due to the internet making it very easy to share music without permission or purchase).

When a song is written, depending on who wrote what, the percentage split between the writers and performers must be agreed. In a democracy, e.g. New Order, it was all split into quarters, 25 per cent each, and the same for the performance royalties. This stayed the same up until *Republic*, when Barney decided he wanted more, and truth be told, he deserved it. He was doing two jobs.

'I had a stalker'

In our early days, no matter how much we insisted to promoters that we were New Order, they'd bill us as Joy Division, ex-Joy Division or 'used to be Joy Division'. Looking back, you had to feel sorry for our audience: those poor people who had supported Joy Division and then turned up to find that 'New Order' were using them as guinea pigs to test our new songs. 'Challenging them', we called it at the time.

What followed were our Spinal Tap 'Jazz Odyssey' days, with punters looking at each other nonplussed, thinking, *What is this?* or shouting out for Joy Division songs, or showing their displeasure by launching glasses at our heads.

You couldn't blame them. They didn't know the songs because we hadn't recorded them yet. Plus we were a bit of a liability live in those days. We felt exposed without Ian there, that figurehead to hide behind. The thing was, Joy Division had a perfect balance, the four of us were each fantastic at what we did, but New Order had weak links: Gillian, because she couldn't play very well; and Barney, who was, shall we say, having trouble adjusting to the frontman role, and whether it was nerves or the first flowerings of a full-on prima-donna personality I couldn't say, but it made him difficult to be around, smashing stuff up, medicated off his face on Pernod most of the time. It was a big change to his whole persona in Joy Division: cool, quiet and aloof. It was a shock. So we felt a bit wobbly, and while some of the gigs were good, a lot were bloody awful. Our reputation as being a bit hit-or-miss was becoming too well deserved.

On plenty of occasions, fights and mini-riots broke out, especially when it became evident that we were only playing a very short set, twenty to twenty-three minutes. Ironic, eh? They didn't like the material but wanted more of it. Tossers!

It was a nightmare at first. But we soldiered on, as we always did. One thing you'd have to say about us is that right through our career we were very bloody-minded and stubborn. We believed totally in the music. That it would always prevail. Nothing else mattered. So initially we would carry on as we did in Joy Division. We wouldn't put singles on the albums, wouldn't appear on the covers, wouldn't make videos, wouldn't do merchandise. We would be evasive, unpredictable and difficult with the media ... We would stick to our guns, because we were still young and idealistic, and wanted to prove ourselves as a new group. The only problem was, we hadn't recorded any New Order songs.

Yet amazingly Rob decided to reward us. He phoned me up and said, 'What you need is a new car.'

'What?' said I.

'A new car, knobhead. I'm going to buy you a new car.'

And he did. Our budget was £5,000 each, which me and Barney broke straight away, both spending £5,012. It was incredible. The world was our oyster. We convened immediately, debating which vehicle to buy. It was so exciting, forgetting about our money problems at home. Me and Barney were rattling off the sports car names, ever practical. Eventually we asked Steve, 'What car are you going to get, Steve?'

'A Volvo,' he said. 'It's boring and dependable, like me.'

I opted for an Alfa Romeo Sprint Veloce in black. A beauty. The only problem was the insurance. For some strange reason musicians are treated like lepers when it comes to insurance and still are. It's never changed. We're 300 per cent loaded. It always used to amuse me when you went into Salford Van Hire to hire a van and there in huge letters above the desk was warning number one: 'NO HAWKERS. NO GYPSIES. NO MUSICIANS.' We moved a lot of furniture for friends, I can tell you.

The first quote, from Cloverleaf Insurance, which specialised in high risks and young drivers, was £5,000 fully comprehensive, a whole £12 less than the car cost to buy.

I remember picking up the car at Bauer Millett on Deansgate. I was beside myself. The salesman took me out to the road. 'There she is,' he said, 'what a beauty!'

But there were two of them. Same model, even the same interior. I was puzzled. Then who should come waltzing round the corner but Barney.

'Hello,' he says, smiling away. 'I've bought the same car as you.' And he had. My registration was NBU 140W and his was NBU 141W. I had a stalker.

TIMELINE ONE
APRIL–DECEMBER 1980

© Peter Gruchot

April 1980

Joy Division: 'Love Will Tear Us Apart'
(Factory Records FAC 23)

Seven-inch track list:
'Love Will Tear Us Apart' 3.25
'These Days' 3.25
Run-out groove one: *Don't disillusion me*
Run-out groove two: *I've only got record shops left*

'The run-out groove messages were our way of tantalising the listener with a little puzzle or lyrics from the song that was coming next, inspired by Porky Prime Cuts, a mastering plant in London. Porky (George Peckham), a record cutting engineer, was famous for scratching little missives into the run-out groove of his mastered records.'

Recorded in Strawberry Studios, Stockport, Manchester, and Pennine Sound Studios, Oldham.
Engineered by Chris Nagle and John Needham.
Produced by Martin Hannett.
Designed by Peter Saville.

18 May 1980

The day before Joy Division are to leave for America, Ian Curtis commits suicide.

23 May 1980

Ian Curtis is cremated. Factory Records hold a wake at Palatine Road and screen the Sex Pistols film, *The Great Rock 'n' Roll Swindle*.

'This was a truly miserable affair. I called in after we had been to the funeral and everyone was smoking dope, so I left.'

13 June 1980 (a Friday)

The inquest into Ian's death is held at Macclesfield.

'I remember Debbie's father saying, "He was on another plane!" and me thinking, *I know what plane he should have been on.*'

16 June 1980 (a Monday)

The band convene at Pinky's

19 and 20 June 1980

'The JDs' (Peter Hook, Stephen Morris, and Bernard Sumner) record with Kevin Hewick at Graveyard Studios, Prestwich, with Stewart Pickering engineering. Of the two songs recorded, 'Haystack' is released later that year on the compilation *A Factory Quartet* while 'A Piece of Fate' is reworked by Hewick into 'No Miracle' in 1993.

> **'This was a nice session, with everyone being very helpful and enthusiastic, even Barney. Kevin was very excited, a lovely boy. Stewart Pickering and his lovely family now run a deli in Cheshire, called the Yard. I get cheap meat. Top One.'**

20 June 1980

Joy Division: 'Komakino'
Free giveaway
(FAC 28)

Seven-inch flexidisc track list:
'Komakino' 3.40
'Incubation' 2.50
'As You Said' 1.55
Recorded in Strawberry Studios, Stockport, Manchester.
Engineered by Chris Nagle.
Produced by Martin Hannett.
Initial pressing: 25,000 copies in a plain white sleeve (second pressing of 25,000 copies, 18 November 1980).

> **'Great songs and a great shame to leave unreleased. "As You Said" was mainly Martin's work; loops and drums he had done on the ARP sequencers as he produced the album *Closer*, edited together to form a track. It sounds very current production-wise even today, although you can clearly hear the timing glitches. This was our altruistic phase. The record shops were instructed to give the flexidisc to the fan on their purchase of the LP. Some did, some didn't. Some even sold it separately, while some shops just gave them away to anyone – good boys.'**

27 June 1980

Joy Division: 'Love Will Tear Us Apart', twelve-inch
(FAC 23.12)

Twelve-inch extra only:
'Love Will Tear Us Apart' (Pennine version) 3.14

Run-out groove one: *Spectacle is a ritual*
Run-out groove two: *Pure spirit*

Entered UK chart on 28 June 1980, remaining in the charts for 16 weeks, its peak position was number 13.

Recorded in Strawberry Studios, Stockport, Manchester, and Pennine Sound Studios, Oldham.
Engineered by Chris Nagle and John Needham.
Produced by Martin Hannett.
Designed by Peter Saville.

> **'Martin was never satisfied with the mix of 'Love Will Tear Us Apart', hence the appearance of the Pennine version. He would redo the mix every time he could. It ended only when Tony Wilson told all the studio owners in England that he would not pay for any more mixes done on that song, anywhere.'**

18 July 1980

Joy Division: *Closer*
(FACT 25)

Track list:

'Atrocity Exhibition'	6.05
'Isolation'	2.52
'Passover'	4.45
'Colony'	3.53
'A Means to an End'	4.06
'Heart and Soul'	5.50

'Twenty Four Hours'	4.26
'The Eternal'	6.04
'Decades'	6.08

Run-out groove one: *Old Blue?*
Run-out groove two: n/a

Recorded in Britannia Row Studios, London.
Engineered by John Caffey, assisted by Mike Johnson.
Produced by Martin Hannett.
Designed by Peter Saville, Martyn Atkins and Chris Mathan.
Photograph by Bernard Pierre Wolff.

> **'One of my favourite albums of all time, to play it in 2011 with my band the Light was such a thrill.'**

Entered UK chart on 26 July 1980, remaining in the charts for 8 weeks, its peak position was number 6.

30 July 1980

New Order play the Beach Club, Manchester; first live appearance.

> **'About 1990 the Doves bought Cheetham Hill, our rehearsal room, from us. Later, Jimi Goodwin got in touch with me. 'I've found a bag of your tapes. Do you want them?' And lo and behold in this bag was the very backing tape we'd used at the Beach gig. Must get it baked (i.e. using an oven to heat it up and reactivate the glue that joins the brown magnetic particles to the clear tape beneath, to stop it flaking off) and transferred.'**

2 September 1980

Joy Division: 'She's Lost Control'
(FACUS2/UK)

Twelve-inch track list:

'She's Lost Control'	4.45
'Atmosphere'	4.10

Run-out groove one: *Here are the young men*
Run-out groove two: *But where have they been*

Recorded in Strawberry Studios, Stockport, Manchester.
Engineered by Chris Nagle.
Produced by Martin Hannett.
Sleeve photography by Charles Meecham.
Typography by Peter Saville.

4 September 1980

New Order play Brady's, Liverpool, supported by Skafish; 'Ceremony' has vocals by Stephen Morris.

5 September 1980

New Order play Scamps, Blackpool.

7 September 1980

New Order work in Western Works Studio, Sheffield, with Cabaret Voltaire, recording demos: 'Dreams Never End', 'Homage', 'Ceremony' (featuring Stephen Morris on vocals), 'Truth', 'Are You Ready for This' (co-written with Cabaret Voltaire and featuring Rob Gretton on backing vocals).

September 1980

New Order embark on a short North American tour.

20 September 1980

New Order play Maxwell's, Hoboken, New Jersey.

21 September 1980

New Order's van is stolen from outside the Iroquois Hotel on West 44th Street, New York.

22–23 September 1980

New Order enter the Eastern Artists Recording Studios in East Orange, New Jersey, to finish the single versions of 'Ceremony' and 'In A Lonely Place', produced by Martin Hannett.

26 September 1980

New Order play Hurrah, New York City, supported by A Certain Ratio.

27 September 1980

New Order play Tier 3, New York, supported by A Certain Ratio.

30 September 1980

New Order play the Underground, Boston.

24 October 1980

Factory becomes a formal limited liability company: Factory Communications Ltd (FCL); directors Wilson, Erasmus, Saville, Hannett and Gretton each take an equal shareholding of 20 per cent.

> **'Supposedly the shares were for us but Rob put them in his name, saying, "If we don't get paid we will still have had something out of Factory." It would soon become a bone of contention. In legal terms it's called a "conflict of interests". Be warned.'**

24 October 1980

New Order play the Squat, Manchester, their first gig featuring Gillian Gilbert.

> **'Must have been very nerve-wracking for her. A very short set. Twenty-one minutes with no encores. Nowadays it beggars belief to think that you'd go anywhere to play for twenty minutes. Saying that, apart from "Homage" that was all the songs we had.'**

November 1980

From Brussels with Love
(TWI 007)

Track list of various artists including:
'Haystack' by Kevin Hewick '& a few musicians' 3.35

Recorded in Graveyard Studios, June 1980.
Written by Kevin Hewick.
Recorded by Martin Hannett.

The original cassette booklet says, 'Kevin Hewick -Haystack- / An experiment at Graveyard Studios. June 1980. Kevin plays with a few musicians. Recorded by Martin Hannett'. The 'few musicians' were Bernard, Peter and Stephen, who became New Order.

24–28 November 1980

New Order enter Cargo Studios, Rochdale.

'This was to demo some of the songs and to start to work primarily on the vocals, that many did not yet have.'

December 1980

New Order enter Strawberry Studios to re-record 'Ceremony' with Gillian Gilbert.

> **'Rob's idea to fully integrate Gillian into the group turned out to sound very similar and you can't really discern much difference, maybe a little faster. The main difference was the different sleeve.'**

13 December 1980

New Order play Rotterdam Hal 4, organised by Mike Pickering, an old friend of Rob Gretton.

Ten things you should *never* do when you form a group

1. Work with your friends (they won't be for long if you do)
2. Let the singer do his own backing vocals (this is a great opportunity for the band to pull together – ignore it at your peril; see also 'narcissism')
3. Have a couple in the band (they will always conspire against you)
4. Listen to an A&R man (apart from Pete Tong, everyone I have ever met has been an idiot)
5. Let your manager open a club/bar (see *The Haçienda: How Not to Run a Club*)
6. Let the publishing/performance split go unspoken (sort it out as soon as the recording is finished and put it in writing; this is the worst thing you will ever have to do, but the most important, and usually splits most bands before they even start)
7. Get off the bus (Fatty Molloy did this once and has regretted it ever since)
8. Think one member is bigger than the group (courtesy Gene Simmons again)
9. Sign anything that says 'in perpetuity' (that means forever, even you won't live that long)
10. Let your record company owe you money (see Factory Records)
11. Ship your gear – always hire (a very famous sub-dance sub-indie outfit once phoned their manager after they'd split and said, 'Hey, where did all the money go?' See above!)
12. Interfere with another group member's sleep (they will turn very nasty and may call the police)
13. Interfere with another group member's girlfriend/wife (this will always end in violence)
14. Never have a party in your own hotel room (always go to someone else's)

. . . Oh shit, way too many. I'll stop now.

'Anything to keep Rob happy . . .'

In May 1981 the group gave their first-ever New Order interview to Neil Rowland of the Melody Maker. *As well as a somewhat tense encounter with the band's bass player, 'Pete Hook', who is described as 'refusing to take anything seriously, twiddling with his bass to avoid a face-to-face discussion', it features what would be recurring themes throughout the band's career: accusations of fascism 'suggested by their name', a preoccupation with the legacy of Ian Curtis, and an interest in the band's live form ('New Order gigs have the electricity of, say, Floyd's days at the Roundhouse').*

On the home front, Iris and I were getting used to having only one income. She was working as a clerk for the Manchester office of the Co-operative Insurance Services (the very same company that refused to pay out for our gear).

By this time we were living in an almost empty house in Moston. The only furniture we had was two deckchairs, a mattress, oh, and a beautiful white kitten called Biba, happily pissing everywhere. The girls were ganging up on me. They were getting accustomed to me being away a lot and coming back to recover. I was regularly 'playing away from home', shall we say.

We started 1981 with a flurry of gigs, keen to get more experience under our belts and prove to ourselves that we still had a chance in music. The reputation we were acquiring when it came to gigs meant that people were coming along in a state of higher-than-usual expectation, knowing that something – it might not always be good, mind you, but *something* – was going to happen. Firstly, would we really ignore Joy Division and play all new material? As I said, I'm sure that at first most of our fans must have been coming out of pure curiosity.

Take the set list, for example. If you look at any from that era (and, to be fair, from more or less any era until 1987, when Barney started to put his foot down), you'll see that they were constantly changing. One reason was because we'd have Rob lying in the dressing room, pushing his glasses up his nose and shouting at us: 'Hey, fucking hell, what's that fucking song? What's that song you play that goes, "in this room, in that room", play that,' and we'd go, 'Oh, we haven't played that for ages. Not rehearsed it.'

'Oh go on, play it. Play "Homage", that's it, "Homage".'

So fuck it, we'd play it, anything to keep Rob happy. But of course we'd all be struggling to remember the riffs and the order, and Barney the lyrics, and for every night we took a chance and caught the magic there were two other nights we sounded like crap. Sure, it was a bit hit-and-miss, but it was never *boring*. We were still punks and were happy to go along with it.

I remember years later we were in the US when I saw Bruce Springsteen play two different cities on the same tour. Not only did he play the same songs in the same order for hours, but he actually said the same things in between the songs in the same order. I was amazed that people did that much preparation. How professional.

Then there was also the fact that generally we only played for about twenty to thirty minutes max. We did that because it felt long enough. Our excuse was to stop the crowd getting bored. How considerate were we? I think we were still glad to get the gig over with, to be honest. But some would reward our thoughtfulness by getting angry and rioting. Ungrateful bastards.

So we had a reputation: you might have a shit night at one of our gigs, or you might have a great night, there was no way of telling. The only thing you could be certain of was that you were going to have a memorable night. People came away with many tales to tell.

We embarked on a European tour in May, playing France, Belgium, Germany, Denmark and Sweden. It was a great tour. When Barney wasn't moaning about how hard it was to be the singer he wasn't averse to using his frontman status to ingratiate himself with certain fans. The gigs were very small – shit dressing rooms, four cans of pale ale and a pickled herring, if you were lucky – but they were good, the kind of gigs you could only look back on with great fondness. Paying-your-dues sort of thing, you know?

In short succession New Order released the 'Procession' single in September 1981 and the Movement *album in November, followed by a twelve-inch of 'Everything's Gone Green' on Factory Benelux in December. Originally the*

B-side of 'Procession', 'Everything's Gone Green' was the most electronic of New Order's singles up to that point, marking a new direction.

Our writing method stayed pretty much the same for all our records, up to and including the songs on *Technique* in 1989. For the acoustic songs we would jam as a three-piece and pick out the best bits to build a rough structure. Barney would add some keyboard parts, one of us would supply a vocal line, and then we would work on the lyrics together – a nice collaboration. The electronic, sequencer-based songs we would program first and then jam over.

The plan was to make a new album with Martin Hannett in Strawberry Studios, but he was in full-on arsehole mode by then. In the studio he'd say, 'Right, I'm going to the tape store,' and he'd sit in there to read and do drugs while he listened to what we were playing on a little Auratone mono speaker rigged up by Chris Nagle, the engineer.

'If I hear anything I like, I'll come out,' he'd say.

He never came out.

Most of the time we would just hear the front door slamming as he left for home or to score more drugs. Occasionally, when he did come out, he would remind us how crap we were without Ian, like he couldn't stand us being there, these poor substitutes for the real genius. Having him behave that way was heartbreaking.

Ours was a journey that had begun by seeing the Sex Pistols then meeting Ian, and then Rob, and then Tony Wilson, and finally working with Martin. Of all those guiding lights, Ian and Martin had shone the brightest, but now one of them was dead and the other hated us; couldn't even stand to be in the same room as us, we felt. With hindsight I suppose you could blame some of his behaviour on the drugs, but at the time it was crushing.

One night in Strawberry, the band talked, just the four of us and Rob. It was always freezing in Strawberry because the storage heaters hardly ever worked and it felt especially cold that night as we brooded downstairs. We opened up about how we felt. One of the only times we've ever done it. We all ended up crying. Not hugging each other or anything like that. Just sort of crying, each in our own little world. I suppose it was a bit of a blood-letting. Why? Maybe because those pent-up emotions had to come out sooner or later, and a band meeting in a freezing-cold studio was as good a place as any. Or maybe it was because the situation with Martin had got so bad and we were mourning the fact that we were losing him as well as Ian – Ian to the rope, Martin to the drugs.

We'd managed to complete the album recording in Strawberry in early 1981, so now came the task of mixing it.

Strangely enough, Tony and Rob were happy with the way the recording had gone. There was certainly no panic about the new material, vocally or musically, or, for that matter, Martin's behaviour. That gave us a lot of heart. It was soon to change.

We moved to a new recording studio called Marcus Music in Kensington Gardens Square, London (Martin thinking it a good idea to get away from Manchester, for a while at least). We were glad of the change of scene too. We were staying in a hotel round the corner and working, again at night. This time it worked out well because you'd have breakfast at dawn on Queensway and go to bed about 8 a.m. and the hotel would be dead quiet because everyone else was out sightseeing. When they came back we would get up and go to the studio like indie vampires.

On the first day, as we walked in, Martin demanded a gram of coke before he'd start work. We all looked at him in utter disbelief. At that time we didn't know much about coke, certainly not where to get it, not to mention the fact we were in London and didn't know anyone. It was a Mexican stand-off at first. We thought he was joking and tried remonstrating, tried reasoning, but after an hour or so it was obvious he meant it. We were aghast. So Rob started phoning round while Martin and Chris Nagle sat there like a pair of malevolent Buddhas, with Martin refusing to do so much as twiddle a knob. A genius, sure. But what a prat.

And then, when he finally got his drugs a couple of hours later, he gave them to Chris, chuckling, saying, 'Sort that out, Christopher, and we shall begin.'

He did eventually knuckle down and mix some tracks, but we as a band weren't happy with them at all …

Hold up. What? *We weren't happy with them?* That was new. Normally it was a case of whatever the wizard-genius wants he gets, because whatever the wizard-genius does works. But suddenly we – by which of course I mean Barney and I – were disagreeing with him. We'd been looking over his shoulder during the making of *Closer*, eager to learn the ropes for ourselves, and even chipping in with the odd idea and suggestion, and now we had opinions of our own and they were beginning to find a voice.

The main thing we asked for on *Movement* was more drums. Martin was still up to his old tricks of distorting everything, recording everything through the Marshall Time Modulators and then putting them back, audio completely mangled, high in the mix. But *we* wanted the sound to be cleaner and more powerful, a little less feathery. Making *Unknown Pleasures* we would never have dared ask for more drums; making *Closer* we might have been brave enough to *suggest* it; now, making *Movement*, we were demanding it. What's more, we now had Rob backing us as opposed to backing Martin. For the first time we knew what we were talking about, and now Rob was siding with us rather than the coke-addled prima donna in the producer's chair. He mixed them all, but on reflection at home we felt a few could do with being harder, again less ethereal. We were starting to enjoy standing up for ourselves.

After Marcus Music we moved to Trevor Horn's Sarm West Studios in Notting Hill (where the tape operator was none other than a lovely young lad called Flood, who would later become very famous for making records with U2, but at this point was more famous for making tea), the idea being to remix the tracks the band didn't like. Here, Martin's 'erratic' (i.e. twattish) behaviour continued. We were still chipping in with ideas, but if Martin didn't like them he'd simply walk out saying, 'Christopher, I'm going for a walk round the block, you do their mix while I'm gone,' so we'd get Chris to turn up the drums, make it bassier, fatter, ballsier, which he'd do very reluctantly, because Chris was nothing if not totally loyal to Martin, and then Martin would return and say, 'Have you done it?' and we'd go, 'Yeah,' and he'd go, 'Right, on to the next track.'

Not interested in hearing what we'd done at all. Didn't want to know.

God, we had some fights with him. The two that we argued over most were 'Truth' and 'Everything's Gone Green'. On both we wanted the drum machine and synthesisers strong and loud. (Incidentally, these were our first two 'electronic' tracks: 'Truth' the first to use a drum machine, then 'Everything's Gone Green' with drum machine and pulsed synthesisers.)

Then there was 'Procession'.

Yellow Two Studios one night: me, Martin and Barney were re-recording the vocals.

After the first take, Martin on the talkback: 'That was crap. Do it again.'

Barney, in the booth, did it again.

'Crap. Again.'

Martin punishing him over and over again. *Punishing him for not being Ian,* I thought.

'And again.'

By the fifteenth or sixteenth time, I was trying to reason with him. 'Martin, come on,' I said, 'we've got some good ones, we can drop them in.'

'No, no,' he snapped, 'I want a full take. It's got to be a full take.'

Then he made Barney sing it again.

'Again.'

And again …

I counted. Barney sang it forty-three times until, at last – and you've got to give it to Barney, he had a long fuse in those days – he eventually freaked and the session came to an abrupt end as we stormed out.

The whole thing was bullshit. Martin had always been a handful but his madness had usually had a method that was sorely lacking here. Before, he was experimenting, but he was happy, and he would *never* have made Ian sing something forty-three times. Now we felt he was winding us up, exercising his producer power in a cruel way just to piss us off rather than trying to get good results. 'Procession' was a good song and Barney was doing a good vocal. The only problem in the studio that night was Martin.

The music recording was a little easier. Later Martin still thought Barney's vocals were weak and needed augmenting and asked Gillian to do backing vocals. I have never been a fan of girly backing vocals, dinosaur that I am. I was outvoted.

And then we stuck 'Everything's Gone Green' on the reverse, which, considering it went on to become a benchmark for electronic music, and the first of a holy trinity of electronic singles (followed by 'Temptation' and 'Blue Monday'), was a bit of a perplexing move.

But that's hindsight for you, 20/20, as well as being a good case of the band maybe being too close to the material, or even false modesty. Fortunately we had Factory Benelux to thank for recognising the song's true potential.

Factory Benelux had been set up by Michel Duval and Annik Honoré (Ian Curtis's mistress) in 1980, and in a funny way was even wilder and freer-thinking than Tony and Factory at home in Manchester. It was they who gave us the opportunity to do a longer twelve-inch version of 'Everything's Gone Green', which came out in December 1981, finally giving the song the prominence and aural impact it deserved. On the Factory single it was edited and marked as the B-side inadvertently.

By now we were using drum machines, triggers, pulses and synthesisers – no sequencers yet though. These things may have sounded great but they took a long time to set up, and for me this period marked the start of that interminable sitting around that any acoustic player in an electronic band has to do, while the rest of the band program the drums and synths.

I like to be doing stuff. I had no interest in the programming. I thought it was just boring, not a means to an end. I was going, 'Why can't we just fucking *play*? We're a band. We've written hundreds of fantastic songs. Can't we just *play*?'

The other guys were busy reinventing pop; me, I liked pop just fine the way it was.

But – before you go thinking I'm some kind of King Canute – it was my stance against programmed music that made our sound the way it was (even if I do say so myself), keeping it a hybrid of rock and dance: the sound of the future. Instead I decided to bury myself in the recording process, becoming the band's recording engineer.

The final nail in the coffin for Martin was when it came to mastering the album. Martin would master his mixes only, whether or not the band wanted to use them. He wouldn't listen to our mixes, he outright refused to even have them on his acetate or test pressing.

Geek Alert

An acetate is a lacquer-coated metal disc that mimics the properties of vinyl and is used in studios for aural approval before pressing to vinyl. For a test pressing the master tape of the song is used by the recording plant to make a metal 'mother' from which several test records, a limited run for quality purposes, are made. If these are accepted the larger batches of records are then produced.

By the end of the session there were two versions of the album on acetate and test pressing: Martin's version, with the mixes he liked (i.e. his mixes) and the band's version, which had the mixes we liked, some of which were his – which meant that he never actually heard the version of the album we cut, the final version of an album he'd produced.

That was it. We knew it was over.

And then we went back to America.

'Feels like I've been here before'

More than any other song, 'Everything's Gone Green' made Martin Hannett a thing of the past as far as his association with New Order was concerned. After we'd recorded that track, me and Barney were flushed with new-found confidence. We felt we could be just as good without Martin; in fact, I'll go one further and say we thought we could be *better* without him.

So we told Rob, Tony, Steve and Gillian that we weren't going to use him any more, and that was that. He was sacked, and we went to America feeling like a new band.

Once again, Ruth Polsky promoted our tour, and she and I began an affair. It didn't make any sense to me; after all, she ran Danceteria and Hurrah, two of the hottest clubs in New York, and was one of the coolest, best-connected people on this musical planet, and I was just a dick from Salford. But there you go. Was it my amazing prowess as a lover (I wish), or just my lack of Y-fronts? Or was it to do with the fact that she was a complete coke fiend?

As I said, I had no experience with drugs back then. I never accepted it when it was on offer (high on life, me), even famously doing the Woody Allen gag in Ruth's apartment one night, and blowing eight lines all over her floor. But on the other hand it didn't bother me to wake up and see her doing a couple of lines in the morning. I was puzzled, but all I knew was that it made her horny, and bearing in mind that I was in my early twenties and like a flagpole most of the time, her being horny suited me down to the ground.

Which is not to say her habit didn't have its downsides. After all, it was because she was off her head that she left the band's money, $10,000, in a hotel safety-deposit box in San Francisco, only realising after we'd flown to Toronto. When she returned to pick it up, she'd lost the key as well, so they had to drill it open. Add in the cost of her travel and it cost thousands of dollars. But we just laughed. It was only money. So, a little thing like that was a small price to pay for having a permanently horny, great-fun girlfriend, who was also amazingly well connected and very well respected.

Ruth was feisty. She had been with so many people in bands that her plan was to write a book called *Under the Stars* and out them all. Several years after she died I used the title as a Monaco track in tribute. She was a fabulous lady. I broke her heart but I miss her still.

One night she took us to the Ritz in New York to see a band, Bauhaus or someone like that. Rocking up on the night we'd assumed it'd be like a normal gig, with sticky floors and people treading on your toes, but we couldn't have been more wrong. It turned out we were sitting on a private mezzanine floor along with a load of other reserved tables, complete with our own bar service, and not like in England where you'd have the rest of the punters looking at you, going, 'Fuck off, who do you think you are?' but everyone giving it the proper star treatment. 'Right this way, sir.' Wow! We felt like Billy Big Bananas. Bring it on. One of those moments where you'd pinch yourself and go, 'Is this for real?'

God Bless America.

Trouble is, that kind of stuff can turn your head if you're not careful. Years later I was queuing for a London club, seOne, with Terry Mason. Standing in front was the singer Ben Volpeliere-Pierrot from Curiosity Killed the Cat, the twat with the beret, who was giving it all, 'Don't you know who I am?' to the doorman. They were big at the time.

But the doorman didn't care, saying, 'You're not on the list, so do one.'

We were laughing our dogs off behind him, and he kept turning round and scowling, until at last he took the bouncer's advice and fucked off, to assorted catcalls, curiously, from us.

Me next. I step up. Say to the bouncer, beaming, 'Peter Hook, New Order, mate.'

He looks down his list.

'No Peter Hook down here, no New Order either, mate.'

Everyone else in the queue laughing their dogs off at me.

Oh shit.

So there you go, kids: karma. It'll get you every time.

Anyway, back to America in November 1981, and another thing contributing to the band's new-found sense of purpose and confidence was meeting Michael Shamberg.

Michael, who was struck down by mitochondrial disease in 2006, and sadly died in 2014, was a wonderful man. And even though he and his girlfriend Miranda didn't make a great success of running the American arm of the label, Factory USA, Michael certainly excelled in helping shape New Order's international image via our fantastic music videos.

Michael had a great eye for up-and-coming video/film directors, and it was he who brought in Jonathan Demme to direct 'the Perfect Kiss', Kathryn Bigelow for 'Touched by the Hand of God', Robert Longo for 'Bizarre Love Triangle' and Philippe Decouflé for 'True Faith'. In many ways he came to represent our video image in much the same way as Peter Saville did our graphic image. We gave him total freedom and complete artistic control. In other words, we couldn't be bothered to have anything to do with them. We thought they were fucking boring. They also cost a fortune and put us in heavy debt with the record company, but that was another lesson we learned the hard way. Not only that, but Michael was also responsible for putting us in touch with Arthur Baker and John Robie (well, no one's perfect) at Shakedown Records.

Something else that happened on that tour, way more important than Ruth, Michael or getting the star treatment at the Ritz: I had my first experience of pizza. It was after a gig at I-Beam in San Francisco when I was so hungry I thought I was going to die.

I'd got talking to this girl. 'I must get something to eat,' I gasped. 'Are there any fish and chip shops round here?'

She said, 'Huh? How about some peeezza?'

I was like, *You what?* (Different times, remember, different times.) 'What's a peeezza? What the hell's in it?'

'Cheese and tomato,' she said, and I was like, 'Oh, I don't like tomato,' so she rolls her eyes and says, 'Tell you what, I'll get you one,' and thank God she did because, oh my days, it was like a slice of heaven on a plate. *Whoa*. My culinary education, having been introduced to curry by Cabaret Voltaire, was now complete and the world was my oyster. I remember walking down Haight-Ashbury later that night feeling very, very, cosmopolitan and very, very, happy and looking round at the streets buzzing and thinking, *How does a fucking tosser from Salford end up eating peeezza in a place like this with a beautiful girl called Gianna Sparacino?*

Luckily Ruth didn't find out.

We were staying in Chinatown in a hotel that must have been a knocking shop. Why? Because it had vibrating beds, obviously. You put a quarter in the slot on the headboard and the bed shook for about thirty seconds and then stopped until you fed in more coins. Fuck knows what good it did, but it was great fun and Rob in particular loved it. He was phoning everyone all the time, going, 'Quarters? Have you got any more quarters, I've fucking run out of 'em.'

Another night we went out for a Chinese meal and Rob was showing off that he knew all about the food, which was pretty impressive back then – especially if you'd only just had your first slice of peeezza – asking the waiter, 'Have you got any Chinese wine, mate?'

To us he was winking and going, 'Fucking Chinese wine. It's brilliant. You'll love it.'

So this guy said, 'I have special wine for you. Special wine ...' and off he goes, returning with what turned out to be a bottle of 'Foetus of Running Deer wine' – complete with the foetus in the bottle. We were all gagging at the sight of it, but of course Rob, being Rob, ended up drinking it, because he was a bull-headed bastard at the best of times, and when he was pissed it was even worse.

I remember another time years later in London where the Greek promoter, a right canny little bastard called Petros Moustakas, said to Rob, 'I'm going to place a fifty-pound note on the back of your hand, put a lit cigarette on it, and if you can hold it there until the note burns, it's yours.'

Rob, pissed as a fart, goes, 'Fucking no problem, Petros. Fucking put it on.' So the guy lays the £50 note on the back of his hand and applies the cigarette.

Rob was like, 'Go on, fucking burn, burn,' but it wouldn't burn. The restaurant began to fill with the smell of what I now know to be burning flesh. Meanwhile Rob sat there grimacing with what must have been extreme pain until at last he couldn't take it any more, and whipped his hand away to reveal a huge blister on the back of it.

Petros says, 'Oh, bad luck, Robert. Do you want to try the other hand?'

And Rob, belligerent and pugnacious as ever, pushes his glasses up his nose and says, 'Yeah, go on, then, yer twat.'

Everyone was going, 'Oh, Rob, stop, no, no,' holding their hands over their noses to ward off the stench of burning Rob.

He just laughed, 'Again!' The only thing he said to Petros. 'Again!'

What none of us apart from Petros knew was that the paper used for £50 notes is a very good heat conductor. Rather than burning the note, the heat was being transferred to Rob's hand. Our stubborn manager ended up with two holes in the backs of his hands that stayed with him for the rest of his life. Stigmata, like he'd been crucified.

At the end he looked at Petros and just said: 'Fuck off.'

Rob was tough when he wanted to be. He was hardcore, without a shadow of a doubt.

Movement came out while we were away. The reviews were OK, and though I grew to like it more and more as the years went by, we weren't especially happy with it at the time. When we listened to the finished product what we heard was the sound of a band whose producer had lost faith. You could hear it. The album had ended up sounding like a Joy Division album with New Order vocals.

Saying that, these days I really like the production. It might have been a bit of a weird push-and-pull group effort but it sounds good. Not a classic, and we certainly bettered it with *Power, Corruption & Lies*, but still – a good album. The lyrics aren't very profound (we certainly missed Ian on that score). But the music's great. These days I wonder what Ian would have done on 'Dreams Never End' or 'I.C.B', or can you imagine what he might have come up with for 'Blue Monday'? It's a mind-boggling idea. It would have been so wonderful to find out.

MOVEMENT TRACK BY TRACK

'Dreams Never End': 3.13

No escape for so few in fear …

The first bass riff after Ian's death, and my first vocal line after 'Novelty'. It never felt good doing them alone and I soon lost heart. Quite prophetic that it starts the album. The six-string Shergold bass guitar really comes into its own. On the record you can hear Martin struggling with my vocals, mixing a low take in with a high take. Recorded 'as live', the three of us play up a storm. Strangely, Martin didn't completely deconstruct the drum kit on this song. He allowed us to play together and used the best take. He later overdubbed hi-hat, both closed and open. A classic 'New Order' rock tune. I remember our sound guy Ozzy once saying to me, 'After that intro it was all downhill for you lot!'

'Truth': 4.37

The noise that surrounds me …

Our first drum-machine song on record. Very atmospheric. The ARP Omni strings are especially haunting. Barney also using the melodica to great effect. We had great sonic hopes for this song but the battle with Martin left it smack in the middle of the dispute. Reminiscent of Joy Division's 'Insight'. A chilling dystopian vision of … a new world order.

'Senses': 4.45

No reason ever was given …

The core of this song is the interplay between the three of us – it being all-important. Great use of the Joy Division-esque sliding of song parts over each other to create a new third part. Steve's syndrums and

Martin's time modulation of the tom-toms give it a very modern feel. Martin's least favourite song, he struggled to understand it. Also my first attempt at overdubbing bass, two of them playing different parts at the same time, four- and six-string.

'Chosen Time/Death Rattle': 4.07

Believe in me …

The laid-back vocal disguises this dark, brooding song. The six-string bass melodies are very strong. The first New Order track to have a separate bass synth line taken from an early acoustic bass part, with great guitar work by Barney. Steve's syndrums sound fantastic and, together with the Powertran synthesiser, swamp the track at the end to great effect. Martin's idea. A classic recording done live. Hardly any overdubs.

'I.C.B.': 4.33

Manna falls from heaven …

This track was started by Joy Division but never finished, and in my opinion sounds the most like JD. Martin's electronic treatment of the tom-toms electrifies the track in a wonderfully modern way. Laid-back vocal by Barney again suggests a lack of confidence that would soon be rectified. Excellent build-ups with space sound syndrums suggesting Steve was a Clangers fan.

Interesting to hear me backing Barney with a low vocal.

'The Him': 5.29

Reborn so plain my eyes see …

I love this bassline. Bauhaus ripped it off for 'Bela Lugosi's Dead' (I take it as a compliment, lads, don't worry). Fantastic live, with a dark and magnificent false ending. Barney's layering of the ARP Omni strings is very effective. My low vox backs him again at Martin's insistence. When he sang this live the end refrain was particularly plaintive for our overworked singer: 'I'm so tired, I'm so tired, I'm so fucking tired,' he used to sing.

'Doubts Even Here': 4.16

Collapsing without warning …

My favourite track on the album, with vocals written by Steve, who then didn't have the confidence to sing it. Barney didn't like it so it was given to me. Fantastic melodies and tom-tom riffs. I came up with the vocal end-piece, and Martin overdubbed Gillian reading 'The Lord's Prayer'. The syndrum end gives it an apocalyptic feel.

'Denial/Little Dead': 4.20

It comes and goes and it frightens me …

Another song with the interplay and drop-outs being very important. This track has the most overdubs, low bass keyboard, high strings, snare drum, toms etc. Later, live, Steve had two snare drums, one placed behind him, which when he hit it, on the rolls, was fantastic to witness. I was very impressed. The vocal sounds drunk, sadly.

One night, shortly before the album came out, I got a phone call off Rob. 'You've got to go down to London!'

'Eh?'

'Pete Saville's got a migraine. He can't finish the sleeve. You go down and do it!'

'Migraine?'

'Get it finished, Hooky!'

Peter Saville was working at Dindisc Records, an offshoot of Virgin in London, for a very feisty young lady called Carol Wilson. I think the pressure of working for a normal record label was getting to him, and he started suffering from debilitating migraines under pressure. I was elected to be the cavalry. So, clutching my aspirins, I went down to mop his fevered brow.

Peter had been asked to do two covers, one for 'Procession/ Everything's Gone Green', our double-A-side single, and the LP *Movement*. Rob was desperate to get the records out, as they were our first, so was pushing Peter more than usual.

When I got there on the train he was not well at all, and I had to gently lead and cajole him to show me what he was working on. With his head in his hands he explained his ideas. Inspired by the Italian

Futurist movement of 1909, he was exploring graphic images relating to the markers of modernity of the industrial city, machines, speed and flight. Futurism exalted the new and disruptive.

Blimey, I thought, *it's no wonder he's got a bloody headache.*

So I was presented with several books on *arte meccanica* (machine aesthetics). I stared blankly. An hour or so later, with Rob's words ringing in my ears, I pointed out two designs, one for *Movement* saying, 'Can't you just replace the words on that one, Pete?' and another nice strong design for the single. He said, 'OK. Leave it with me. I feel a bit better now. I may change the colours.'

Later he took me for dinner to his private club, the Zanzibar (the forerunner of the Groucho Club in Soho, which will be getting its very own chapter later). There he regaled me with tales of his life in London, at one point saying, 'Do you know how hard it is living in London, Hooky? I have to pay six hundred pounds for a pair of trousers!'

'Fuckin' hell, Pete, I'm only on thirty quid a week. How would I know?'

I was glad to get to Euston.

Thinking on, it must have been very difficult for Rob to juggle the finances. He was running a group, New Order, which had absolutely no income. We were touring but buying piles of equipment to replace what had been stolen in New York – all using Joy Division's money. Rob had a great way of accounting. If anyone questioned it he would always say, 'I have two pockets. The left one is the group's and the right one is mine and I never get them mixed up!' and patted them both for effect. Strangely, at the end of the night buying drinks etc. for everyone, he never seemed to keep a note of which pocket he was delving into. We were happy about that. It was mainly us he was buying drinks for, so as long as there was something in one of them, we never cared.

Having been released as New Order's producer, Hannett's woes increased when his objections to the Haçienda club fell on deaf ears. As a Factory director he had wanted to use profits on what he considered to be the most important aspect of the label, the music. He wanted a recording studio, or if not then at least a new Fairlight CMI Series II synthesiser, the same model used by Kate Bush, Jean Michel Jarre and Martin's arch-rival, Trevor Horn.

Sure enough, shortly before the club was due to launch, Factory's musical magician filed a lawsuit against the label he'd helped create, attempting to prevent the opening and claim more money from his stake in the company. It was the beginning of the end for his relationship with Factory . . .

Martin wanted Factory to buy a recording studio because he said that with one album it would have been paid for, and then all the rest of our records would be recorded for free. You know what? He was absolutely right. The most idiotic thing for a record company to do was to invest in a club. So many times afterwards, when the Haçienda was losing money hand over fist, Tony would sit there with his head in his hands, going, 'Oh, we should have listened to Martin Hannett . . .'

What could Martin have done with a Fairlight? Could he have made his *Hounds of Love* or *So*? We'll never find out. All we know is that Martin took the hump and the rest of the Factory board voted against him. They ostracised him. Ironically, exactly what 'the others' would do to me in 2011.

They voted him a total buyout of £25K, and stipulated that it included him giving up his album points on all recordings for all Factory acts including Joy Division and New Order, which over the years would have been worth millions – all for £25K.

In March the following year he issued a writ against Factory – they gave it its own catalogue number, taking the piss – but it didn't do him any good. Poor old Martin just didn't have the money to fight the case when it was referred to the High Court. He needed £8,000. His drug addiction came back to haunt him.

With hindsight, it was disgusting, highway robbery. We knew nothing about it and I never would have done if his girlfriend Suzanne hadn't told me about it when it happened to me with New Order. No matter how we felt about Martin when we parted, we knew that without him we would never have achieved the lasting effect we've had, particularly with Joy Division. So to take those points off him and buy him out was merciless, especially when you consider that he was right. He didn't say *never* open a club, he said don't open it now. Do a studio first and *then* do a club. Probably the only sensible thing anyone ever associated with Factory suggested, and he was shouted down. Tony had it right. We should have listened to Martin.

Geek Alert

My Equipment List

By this time I had replaced my stolen gear with a much better version of roughly the same set-up – as used by Martin Hannett when he was a bass player. For the more technically minded among you I was using a Yamaha BB1200S four-string and a Shergold six-string bass guitars, both fed into an Alembic stereo valve pre-amplifier, each channel with separate EQ, then mono-ed into a Roland Sip-301 pre-amplifier with two internal effects sends, one for the Electro-Harmonix Clone Theory pedal and the other for a Yamaha analogue delay unit. The Roland mono output was then bridged into a stereo Amcron DC300A solid-state stereo amplifier (1,200 watts per channel rms = LOUD) into two custom-built flight-cased cabinets each containing two fifteen-inch JBL 4560 1000-watt bass speakers ...

It was awesome!

I was ecstatic. Thank you, Martin.

One other very important piece of equipment for any bass player is the strings he uses. I have used many different kinds in my time, with varying degrees of success, but settled very early on for Elite bass strings from the Bass Centre in London – my first and only sponsor, come to think of it. The strings are very bright and very strong, so very reliable. A normal bass guitar is tuned E A D G with string gauges 105, 80, 60, 45 on average. This wasn't good enough for me! Again very early, I realised because I was playing mainly the high strings D G, I needed more low-end frequencies to make them sound fatter, so I started using 105 85 65, 65, which gave me problems because that last string would be stretched so tight to get the pitch, it was prone to snapping, and when it did snap it could cut your bloody head off. So I soon went down to 60s for the G string, which worked better with less snapping, and I still use them now. Really makes your fingers hard.

My record for breaking strings at a gig was three at once. I hit the guitar so hard it snapped three strings, the A D and G. That of course was in my younger, very punky days, when you played every gig as if your life depended on it. Heady days! These days I just stick to snapping one at a time.

TIMELINE TWO
JANUARY–DECEMBER 1981

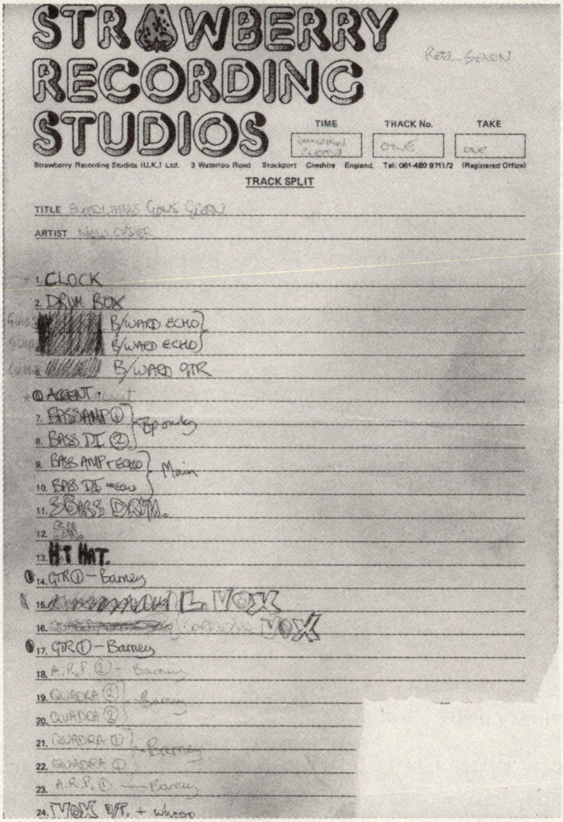

STRAWBERRY RECORDING STUDIOS

REEL SEVEN

TIME | TRACK No. ONE | TAKE ONE

Strawberry Recording Studios (U.K.) Ltd. 3 Waterloo Road Stockport Cheshire England. Tel: 061-480 9711/2 (Registered Office)

TRACK SPLIT

TITLE

ARTIST NEW ORDER

1. CLOCK
2. DRUM BOX
3. B/WARD ECHO
4. B/WARD ECHO
5. B/WARD GTR
6. AGENT
7. BASS AMP ①
8. BASS DI ②
9. BASS AMP + ECHO } Main
10. BASS DI + ECHO
11. BASS DRUM.
12. SN.
13. HI HAT.
14. GTR ① – Barney
15. L VOX
16. VOX
17. GTR ① – Barney
18. A.R.P. ② – Barney
19. QUADRA ②
20. QUADRA ② – Barney
21. QUADRA ①
22. QUADRA ① – Barney
23. A.R.P. ① – Barney
24. VOX D/T. + whoop

2 January 1981

New Order play Porterhouse, Retford.

3 January 1981

New Order play the Tatton Community Centre, Chorley. Organised by Rex Sargeant, his group PR5 supported.

> **'A fan from early Joy Division days (there is even a letter from him to Ian in *So This is Permanence*), Rex committed suicide by hanging in 2010.'**

4 January 1981

New Order play the Fan Club (Brannigan's), Leeds.

> **'This was where Rob fell in love with Mandy H, the DJ on the night. She was a very well-respected punk DJ and it seemed to be love at first sight, with him ending up following her around all night like a lovesick cow. That was a good gig, that one. We always had good gigs in Leeds.'**

12 January 1981

New Order play Eglinton Toll Plaza, Glasgow, supported by Bombers Over Vienna and Positive Noise.

14 January 1981

New Order play Plato's Ballroom (Mr Pickwick's), Liverpool.

21–23 January 1981

New Order enter Cargo Studios in preparation for recording their first album – they would be working on the album for the next seven months.

'We had most of the *Movement* songs written but Rob thought it a good idea to demo them. We chose Cargo for two reasons, because we got such a great sound there, and John Brierley was such a fantastic engineer, and our practice place was such a shithole we just had to get out. Three reasons!'

22 January 1981

New Order: 'Ceremony'
(FAC 33)
Seven-inch track list:

'Ceremony'	4.34
'In a Lonely Place'	4.35

Run-out groove one: *Watching forever*
Run-out groove two: *How I wish you were here with me now*

Twelve-inch track list:

'Ceremony'	4.34
'In a Lonely Place'	6.12

Run-out groove one: *Watching love grow forever …*
Run-out groove two: *How I wish we were here with you now*

Recorded in Strawberry Studios, Stockport, Manchester.
Additional recording EARS, Trenton, New Jersey.
Engineered by Chris Nagle.
Produced by Martin Hannett.
Designed by Peter Saville.
Entered the UK chart on 14 March 1981, remaining in the chart for 5 weeks, its peak position was number 34.

26 January 1981

New Order record their first John Peel session at BBC, Langham 1 Studio, Maida Vale, London.

John Peel track list as recorded

'Dreams Never End'	3.13
'Truth'	4.21
'Senses'	4.25
'I.C.B.'	5.19

Engineered by Dave Dade.
Produced by Tony Wilson (a different Tony Wilson).

> **'This was a great compliment, and these were great to do. There was literally "no messing about", you would be booked in for a maximum three hours, which included setting up, miking up and soundchecking. It produced a pretty straight, i.e. live, version of the songs, fuelled by adrenalin. Much truer versions. They literally threw you out when your time was up. Great canteen.'**

February 1981

New Order enter Britannia Row Studios, Islington, for overdubs on 'The Kill' and 'The Only Mistake' to be included on the upcoming Joy Division album, *Still*.

> **'This felt very strange. Not only to be back in Britannia Row after *Closer* but working on Joy Division songs too. A weird, out-of-body feeling. It was lovely to hear Ian's vocals in those surroundings again, and it brought back some nice memories. Strange being back with Martin, but we kept it professional.'**

6 February 1981

New Order play Comanche Student Union, Polytechnic, Manchester, supported by Stockholm Monsters and Foreign Press.

It's also where Rob first met Howard 'Ginger' Jones, who was virtually hired on the spot, with absolutely no qualifications, to scout locations for what would become the Haçienda. Eventually they settled on a former boat showroom and New Order had to sign huge personal guarantees for the loans to build the club. They took a lease for twenty-five years on the building.

7 February 1981

New Order play Roadmenders, Northampton, supported by Stockholm Monsters.

9 February 1981

New Order play Heaven, London, supported by Section 25 and Stockholm Monsters.

> 'Rob hired the Pink Floyd-devised quadrophonic PA system from Britannia Row for this show, as well as persuading Martin Hannett to mix the sound. Quadrophonic is in effect two stereo systems joined together by a joystick controller: a normal stereo set-up in front of the audience and another normal system behind. The joystick allows you to pan sounds at the sound guy's discretion, right round the four stacks and around the building. Unfortunately, no one took into the account the shape of Heaven. It was not square. Also no one took into account the shape of Martin Hannett, who was also not square. He was off his rocker when he arrived – after the soundcheck and just before the doors opened. Martin seemed to enjoy himself but the reports were of a "very confused" sound, with effects flying all over the place and drowning out the group. We would go on to use this system with much better effect later in our career.'

14 February 1981

Peter Hook interviewed on BBC Radio 1's *Walters' Weekly*.

16 February 1981

New Order's first Peel session broadcast.

17 February 1981

New Order play Rock Garden, Middlesbrough.

'I do remember the Hell's Angels that worked there laughing when we arrived. There were no steps up to the back entrance; they'd hidden them and were taking the piss, going, "Hope you don't scrape your shoes, nancy boys," as we clambered inside. At least the skinheads from the Warsaw days had moved on.'

10–13 March 1981

New Order record 'Procession' and 'Everything's Gone Green' with Martin Hannett in Strawberry Studios and Yellow Two.

21 March 1981

New Order play the Boys Club, Bedford, supported by Section 25 and ICI. The gig is organised by long-time supporter and author of *From Heaven to Heaven: New Order Live: The Early Years*, Dec Hickey.

22 March 1981

New Order play Jenkinson's Bar, Brighton, supported by Section 25.

'This was a tiny basement pub near the seafront in Brighton. They gave us the snooker room as a dressing room. About thirty people turned up. I love Brighton.'

27 March 1981

New Order play Trinity Hall, Bristol, supported by Tunnelvision. This is the first New Order gig to appear on a vinyl bootleg, *The Dream*, about a year later, then a great compliment.

8 April 1981

New Order play Rock City, Nottingham, supported by Minny Pops.

'We always made sure we had Factory bands as support wherever possible. The Minny Pops were from Holland. A nice group, especially Wally, their lead singer. I loved their single "Night Train" and went on to produce them.'

10 April 1981

New Order play Cedar Club, Birmingham, supported by Minny Pops.

17 April 1981

New Order play St Andrews University, Fife, supported by Foreign Press.

> **'Payback. We used to borrow Foreign Press's PA a lot when we were skint. So we gave them a few gigs. And used their PA again! A double-edged-sword payback, eh?'**

18 April 1981

New Order play Victoria Hotel, Aberdeen, supported by Foreign Press.

19 April 1981

New Order play Valentino's, Edinburgh, supported by Visitors.

22 April 1981

New Order play 'Atmosphere' (Romeo & Juliet's, Sheffield), supported by Tunnelvision.

> **'Annik came to this gig and it was lovely to see her. She also attended the following evening. I loved Tunnelvision. Martin Hannett produced the first single and I ended up doing their second one, as well as some production work after that. This really was the start of a period where me, Barney and Steve would all be meeting bands and getting into producing them. Barney did Section 25, Happy Mondays. Steve and Gillian produced Thick Pigeon (who, incidentally, were Stanton Miranda, Michael Shamberg's girlfriend, and Carter Burwell, who later made his name scoring films for the Coen Brothers).'**

23 April 1981

New Order record Granada TV's *Celebration*, performing two sets. First Set: 'Truth', 'Procession', 'Ceremony', 'Doubts Even Here', 'Truth', 'I.C.B.', 'Chosen Time', 'Digital' (instrumental), 'Chosen Time', 'Denial' (titled 'Little Dead'). Second Set: 'Dreams Never End' (various attempts), 'The Him', 'Procession', 'Senses', 'I.C.B.', 'Denial' (titled 'Little Dead'), 'Ceremony', 'In a Lonely Place' (part). The show was broadcast on 18 June 1981 with only these songs: 'Truth', 'Ceremony', 'I.C.B.', 'Chosen Time', 'Denial', 'Dreams Never End'.

> **'You weren't allowed to touch the sound desk, as it was union-controlled. Rob wanted Chris Nagle to do the sound, so not for the first time we had a massive stand-off with Rob threatening repeatedly to pull the gig, literally banging heads with the union rep. The rep won. This led to a very uncomfortable programme, mainly caused by Dec Hickey's dancing (watch it on YouTube and you'll see why).'**

24 April–4 May 1981

New Order enter Strawberry Studios to begin work on their debut album, *Movement*, with Martin Hannett, then move to Marcus Studios at Kensington Gardens Square, London, and Sarm West, Notting Hill, London, for mixing.

6 May 1981

New Order play Forum Ballroom, Kentish Town, London, supported by Tunnelvision and Safehouse.

> **'This was the first New Order gig to be promoted by Final Solution, a promotion company set up by Colin Faver and Kevin Millins. They used to love doing wacky things in really wacky places. It was the precursor to the rave thing, raves without rave music – the idea being that they'd bus people into strange places for the gigs. They would become close friends.'**

7 May 1981

New Order play Talbot Tabernacle, London, supported by Tunnelvision.

> **'We'd sold out the Forum so they added the Tabernacle, which was a lovely venue, but tiny. It was almost like a secret gig so the atmosphere was incredible.'**

8 May 1981

New Order play University Student Union, Reading, supported by Section 25.

> **'This might be New Order's first-ever encore. It was suggested by Section 25's Larry Cassidy and we thought, *Why not!* We got on really well with all of Section 25, a really underrated band in my opinion.'**

13 May 1981

New Order begin a European tour, playing Palais Des Arts, Paris, France, supported by Malaria.

> **'Malaria were an all-girl group, which was great because we copped off with most of them. We also had the New Order bootlegger with us, Duncan Haysom. We had met him in England and he tagged along, becoming Barney's first-ever cabin boy. Barney loved to have an unpaid slave.'**

15 May 1981

New Order play L' Ancienne Belgique, Brussels, Belgium, supported by Malaria. The show is promoted by Annik Honoré. Performances of 'Truth' and a debut performance of 'Everything's Gone Green' are later used on *The Factory Complication.*

> **'Odd being back. Brought back many memories of Ian and Joy Division. Their ghosts lurked everywhere and sent shivers down my spine.'**

16 May 1981

New Order play Markthalle, Hamburg, West Germany, supported by Malaria.

> **'This gig was crazy. The audience was composed of loads of staunch, far-right skinheads. We got the shock of our lives when we came on. They hated us, and I got hit on the head by a wooden knuckleduster almost straight away. Bottles were flying about liberally all over the stage. We bombed, so thought we'd get our own back at the end by playing 'Everything's Gone Green' over and over again. Don't ask me why. It went on for about twenty-five minutes. We bored them into submission. When we went back in the dressing room afterwards the skins were sat there drinking our rider. We got them out then realised they'd stolen all our bags. He who laughs last, eh?'**

17 May 1981

New Order play Saltlagaret, Copenhagen, Denmark, supported by Before and Basement Level Sounds.

> **'The promoter here was lovely; he did the whole Scandinavian tour. He taught me to juggle, saying, "You must have a big set of balls, Peter!" Luckily, mate, I have!'**

19 May 1981

New Order play Roxy, Stockholm, Sweden, supported by Malaria.

22 May 1981

New Order play Lobo Disco, Gothenburg, Sweden, supported by Malaria.

25 May 1981

New Order play Chateau Neuf, Oslo, Norway, supported by Cosmic Overdose and Basement Level Sounds.

27 May 1981

New Order play the SO36 Club, West Berlin, supported by Malaria.

> **'Possibly the first time Bernard did a "Whoo!" Another famous vinyl bootleg.'**

June 1981

Ben Kelly pays his first visit to Whitworth Street to survey the Haçienda building.

> **'Rob and Tony had asked Peter Saville to design the Haçienda from scratch. The idea scared him to death so, searching for a way out, he suggested Ben Kelly, who he'd met at the Dindisc offices in London when they collaborated on an award-winning Orchestral Manoeuvres in the Dark sleeve. Ben, though initially daunted by the task, grasped this fantastic opportunity with both hands . . . to Saville's audible sigh of relief, no doubt.'**

18 June 1981

Celebration screened, New Order's first-ever TV appearance. Songs broadcast: 'Dreams Never End', 'I.C.B.', 'Chosen Time', 'Denial', 'Ceremony', 'Truth'.

20 June 1981

New Order play Glastonbury Festival.

> **'We played before Hawkwind on a co-headline. Very open post-apocalyptic festival vibe, full of bikers and hippies. Very easy-going, completely unlike now. Drugs openly on sale all round the site. This would be our first of three headline appearances at Glastonbury.'**

July 1981

The finishing touches are made to New Order's debut LP. Meanwhile, the lease on the Haçienda building on Whitworth Street is signed.

> **'An important occasion in our downfall. The lease offered was twenty-five years, an obscene amount of time, and the cost and responsibility was enormous. Rob and Tony asked for a shorter term, but the owner did a fantastic double-bluff, saying, "We've got someone else interested now," so they panicked and signed.'**

September 1981

New Order: 'Ceremony II'
(FAC 33)

Twelve-inch track list:

'Ceremony'	4.22
'In a Lonely Place'	6.12

Run-out groove one: *This is why events unnerve me*
Run-out groove two: *How I wish you were here with me now*

Recorded in Strawberry Studios, Stockport, Manchester.
Engineered by Chris Nagle.
Produced by Martin Hannett.
Sleeve design Peter Saville.
Second release, this one featuring Gillian Gilbert; twelve-inch with a different sleeve. Notably not much difference, slightly faster.

> **'A valiant effort by Rob, to finalise her place in the band.'**

11 September 1981

New Order: 'Procession'/'Everything's Gone Green', double A-side
(FAC 53)

Seven-inch track list:
'Procession' 4.04
'Everything's Gone Green' 4.25

Run-out groove one: *Soft*
Run-out groove two: *Hard*

Recorded at Strawberry Studios, Stockport, Manchester.
Mixed at Sarm West, Studios, London.
Engineer Chris Nagle.
Produced by Martin Hannett.
Design: Peter Saville.
Entered UK chart on 3 October 1981, remaining in the charts for 5 weeks, its peak position was number 38.
Available in nine different-coloured sleeves: black, red, blue, brown, yellow, orange, green, aqua and purple, on grey 'chipboard' cardstock.

'"Procession" was a complete contrast to "Ceremony": Steve had written the lyrics and the vocal hook, and it sounded very poppy and immediate. It also helped us find a great use for that Yamaha amp we'd bought in America that cost us a fortune in import duty. It had a reverb spring in it, and when you shook it, it made a great noise. So we shook it like hell, recorded it and featured it in the song.'

19 September 1981

New Order play Kulttuuritalo, Helsinki, Finland. First outing for 'Temptation' live.

'"Temptation" was an instrumental because the vocal hadn't been written yet. In those days the vocal/lyrics were a group effort, but Barney would improvise "live" if he was drunk enough. When we first started playing "Temptation" he used to sing, "I've got a cock like the M1," and things like that.

'Section 25 supported, with Paul the guitarist travelling overland to the gig; it took him a week to get there and a week to get back. At the gig, Barney got caught with a bottle of vodka in

his pocket, and was arrested by this little old bloke. As he was led away I was pissing myself, thinking it was absolutely hilarious. Turns out the liquor laws are very stringent in Helsinki and alcohol is not allowed on public show. I went to tell Rob, thinking he deserved to join in on the merriment, but his face drained and he ran off to spring him. "We've got a bloody gig to do," he screamed, running through the crowd.'

23 September 1981

New Order play Phoenix Hall, Sheffield Polytechnic, Sheffield, supported by Section 25, Stockholm Monsters.

25 September 1981

New Order play the Assembly Rooms, Walthamstow, supported by Airstrip One, Doctor Filth.

26 September 1981

New Order 'Mystery gig', Bodiam Castle, Kent. Cancelled because of flooding.

'This was a Final Solution production and coaches were supposed to leave from Speakers' Corner, Marble Arch, the idea being that nobody knew where they were going. They'd pick people up and drive them to the gig and then back again. Shame the weather put paid to this one. The location was beautiful and we had spent a lovely afternoon there earlier. As a bonus, ticket-holders were given free entry into Heaven, the gay nightclub that Kevin Millins ran in London. I believe a few of our fans reached an epiphany with that freebie.'

October 1981

Work begins on the Haçienda. Fact 51 Limited created: half of the shares held by FCL, half by Gainwest, New Order's new limited company.

'This was a big deal for us. The initial estimate for the build was £70,000; that soon rose to £144,000, finishing at £550,000. Why we weren't alarmed I'll never know, but we should have been. It was obvious it was already out of control. Trouble was, we had no personal money whatsoever. There was nothing to relate it to. The whole thing seemed ridiculous. We were earning thirty pounds a week. But I must say the idea of your own club with free entry and free drinks to me, a musician, seemed insanely attractive. I was bewitched. What a sucker.'

8 October 1981

Joy Division: *Still*
(FACT 40)

Two x twelve-inch track list:
'Procession'

Disc One:

'Exercise One' (*Unknown Pleasures* session)	3.05
'Ice Age' (Oct/Nov 1979, Cargo Studios)	2.22
'The Sound of Music' ('Love Will Tear Us Apart' Session 1)	3.53
'Glass' (Factory sample)	3.55
'The Only Mistake' (*Unknown Pleasures* session)	4.15
'Walked in Line' (*Unknown Pleasures* session)	2.46
'The Kill' (*Unknown Pleasures* session)	2.14
'Something Must Break' ('Transmission' Sessions)	2.47
'Dead Souls' ('Licht und Bleinheit'/Sordide Sentimentale)	4.52
'Sister Ray' (Live at Moonlight Club, 2 April 1980)	7.34

Disc Two:

'Ceremony'	3.50	Live at Birmingham University, 2 May 1980
'Shadowplay'	3.54	Live at Birmingham University, 2 May 1980
'A Means to an End'	4.01	Live at Birmingham University, 2 May 1980
'Passover'	5.05	Live at Birmingham University, 2 May 1980
'New Dawn Fades'	4.01	Live at Birmingham University, 2 May 1980
'Transmission'	3.33	Live at Birmingham University, 2 May 1980
'Disorder'	3.20	Live at Birmingham University, 2 May 1980

'Isolation'	3.05 Live at Birmingham University, 2 May 1980
'Decades'	5.22 Live at Birmingham University, 2 May 1980
'Digital'	3.53 Live at Birmingham University, 2 May 1980

Run-out groove one: *The chicken won't stop*
Run-out groove two: *The chicken won't stop*
Run-out groove three: *The chicken won't stop*
Run-out groove four: *The chicken stops here*

> **'[The run-out is] a reference to the film Ian reportedly watched before he committed suicide: *Stroszek* by Werner Herzog (the scene where the chicken dances on a hot plate). Maybe a metaphor for how he felt.'**

The final Joy Division album, a double LP comprising songs never readily available and some formally unreleased; it also includes a live recording of their final concert.

The first 5,000 came with a collectors' hessian cloth cover.

Recorded and mixed at Strawberry Studios, Stockport, Manchester, and at Britannia Row Studios, London.
Engineered by Chris Nagle.
Produced by Martin Hannett.
Designed by Peter Saville.
Entered UK chart on 17 October 1981, remaining in the charts for 5 weeks, its peak position was number 5.

23 October 1981

New Order play Bradford University, supported by Crispy Ambulance.

26 October1981

New Order play the Ritz, Manchester, supported by Beach Red.

> **'Notable for the first appearance of "Hurt", our first fully programmed sequencer song. We jammed it as an instrumental, hoping that after a few drinks Barney would be inspired enough to try a vocal.**

'This ended up a terrible concert, which was awful for a home-town gig. Gillian played "Senses" completely out of tune. She probably knocked the modulation wheel and didn't know what to do about it.

'We hated playing in Manchester. Everybody has a great time except you, and you end up running round like a lunatic, looking after all your mates who disgrace themselves, drink the dressing room dry, and end up fighting with the doormen. I've got a feeling that Rob promoted this gig himself. His idea being that if we promoted it, we kept all the money. But he spent it all on a huge PA that nearly blew the bloody roof off!'

6 November 1981

New Order play Perkins Palace, Pasadena, California.

'It was great to be back in America. We went for a walk as soon as we arrived and got stopped by a motorcycle cop for jaywalking. We thought we were crossing the road. He let us go when he discovered we were limeys.'

7 November 1981

New Order play Market Street Cinema, Los Angeles, California, supported by Simple Minds.

'Simple Minds were supporting us but came up with that old trick of delaying their appearance so they seemed like the headline band. Terry and I rumbled it pretty quickly but our lot were at the hotel so, without back-up, we stormed their dressing room, kicking hell out of the door shouting, "Come out, you fuckers!" They were screaming like little girls inside. We carried on kicking until they came out and went on. We'd fallen for it once with Fast Breeder in Manchester (see *Unknown Pleasures*), never again. It was a sparsely attended gig, although legend has it both bands played well. We had a much better night at the I-Beam.'

9 November 1981

New Order play I-Beam Club, San Francisco, California.

> **'One of my favourite gigs in the whole wide world; real, funky place full of history.'**

10 November 1981

New Order play Berkeley, California.

> **'I don't think this gig happened.'**

15 November 1981

New Order play the Masonic Temple, Toronto, Ontario.

> **'Our first time in Canada, a lovely place. The food was excellent, just like home but with a French accent.'**

17 November

New Order play the Channel, Boston, Massachusetts.

18 November

New Order play the Ritz, New York.

19 November

New Order: *Movement*
(FACT 50)

Track list:

'Dreams Never End'	3.13
'Truth'	4.37
'Senses'	4.45
'Chosen Time'	4.07

'I.C.B.' 4.33
'The Him' 5.29
'Doubts Even Here' 4.16
'Denial' 4.20

Run-out groove one: *If I hear anything I like …*
Run-out groove two: *… I'll come out!*

Recorded at Strawberry Studios and Yellow Two Studios, Stockport, Manchester, Marcus Music Studios and Sarm West Studio, London.
Engineered by Chris Nagle, assisted by John and Flood.
Produced by Martin Hannett.
Designed by Peter Saville and Grafica Industria.
Entered UK chart on 28 November 1981, remaining in the charts for 10 weeks, its peak position was number 30.

Tony Wilson describes the chart position as 'extremely poor'. OMD, the Human League, Heaven 17 and Depeche Mode all release albums in the autumn that chart higher.

'We weren't that bothered. We always expected a post-Joy Division backlash. We were enjoying ourselves so just got on with it.'

19 November 1981

New Order play the Ukrainian National Home, New York.

'It wasn't a great gig. I remember the hall being so big and noisy; it ruined everything. It was quite a restrained performance, as I'm sure you'll agree when you watch the video. Filmed and edited by Michael Shamberg, it became our first New Order video release, *Taras Shevchenko*, eventually released on Factory and Factory USA nearly two years later.

'It was the last gig on that US tour and recorded at a Ukraine National Home, not a normal gig venue. Michael liked that. After the show Ruth and I were standing outside. It was an early show, so it was still light, and I was standing on the bottom of the ramp

at the back of the truck, waiting to get a taxi. Then, all of a sudden, I flew high up in the air and landed on the floor.

'I was like, "What the fuck happened there?" and what had happened was, they'd put a bass bin in the truck and hadn't flipped it off its wheels. The truck must have been on a slight incline, so when they went to get another bass bin, the fucking bass bin rolled out, came flying down the ramp, hit me and sent me flying in the air. BANG! It's amazing how rubbery you can be when you're not expecting something.'

21 November 1981

New Order play Trenton, New Jersey. Set list: 'The Him', 'Dreams Never End', 'Procession', 'Truth', 'Senses', 'Chosen Times', 'Denial', 'Ceremony', 'In a Lonely Place'.

22 November 1981

New Order play the Peppermint Lounge, New York.

'That's where a certain member of our entourage copped for a girl who wore Rupert the Bear trousers. We used to follow them, going, "Rupert, Rupert the Bear. Everyone knows your name." The guy dumped her as soon as he'd slept with her, and she got really upset and started following us around like a stalker. It got him in a bit of trouble, that attitude.'

Mike Pickering returns from Rotterdam with a brief to book bands and acts for the Haçienda. The opening date is set for 21 May 1982.

'The construction of the Haçienda was marked by many problems, the first of which was when they tried to use the original wooden balcony, and spent a lot of money on it – even trying it in three different positions – only to get it condemned by the fire brigade who refused to issue a certificate of "fire worthiness". They had to build a new one from scratch, made of concrete. Tony and Rob argued about where the stage should go. Rob wanted it at the end. Tony wanted it in the middle. Tony won and it was built

in the narrowest part of the club, creating terrible sound and bad sight lines.'

December 1981

New Order do not appear on a Granada TV special, despite rumours they were there, dressed as Santa Claus.

'There might have been a load of Santa Clauses on it and Tony's gone, "Here's New Order dressed up as Santa Claus!" We didn't do it. I would remember that. Imagine Barney dressed up as a Santa Claus. He's more like fucking whatshisname, the other one . . . Scrooge.'

19 December 1981

New Order: 'Everything's Gone Green'
(FBNL8)

Twelve-inch single:

'Everything's Gone Green'	5.33
'Cries and Whispers'	3.25
'Mesh'	3.00

Run-out groove one: *Why did Regulus go back to Rome?*
Run-out groove two: *To reach the other side.*

Recorded at Strawberry Studios, Stockport, Manchester.
Mixed at Sarm West Studios, London.
Engineered by Chris Nagle.
Produced by New Order.
Designed by Peter Saville.

Martin Hannett instructs his lawyers to begin proceedings against Factory.

TEN BEST BASS RIFFS (ACTUALLY, THIRTEEN)

1. 'Age of Consent'
2. 'Leave Me Alone'
3. 'Recoil'
4. 'Waiting for the Sirens' Call'
5. 'Krafty'
6. 'Shine' (Monaco)
7. '60 Miles an Hour'
8. 'Regret'
9. 'Vicious Streak'
10. 'Primitive Notion'
11. 'Someone Like You'
12. 'Too Late'
13. '14K' (Revenge)

'Lead us not into temptation, but deliver us from evil' (Matthew 6:13)

New Order's technical revolution occurred over the course of four tracks: 'Truth', where we blooded our Boss Dr-55 Doctor Rhythm; 'Everything's Gone Green', where we created the first post-punk rock/dance track by any Manchester group, using pulsed synthesisers for the first time; and then 'Temptation' and 'Hurt'.

We always went through the same process when we started to write: what kind of song do we want? Fast, dancey, powerful, catchy? It never changed. Fast dancey tracks were always the most difficult to write, and were very few and far between. Meanwhile, we started to experiment by triggering the synthesisers with control voltage from the outputs on the drum machine, programing different rhythms until we got something we liked. It didn't take long: it was so new that everything we did sounded fantastic. 'Temptation' quickly followed, no pun intended, with the pièce de résistance being the first fully programmed sequencer song, 'Hurt'.

Recorded for a clean start at Advision Studios in London, 'Temptation' and 'Hurt' were not only our first tracks without Martin Hannett and our debut as producers, but the ones on which we used the lessons learned on 'Truth' and 'Everything's Gone Green' to take yet another huge leap forward.

They were also the tracks on which we channelled a love of Kraftwerk and Giorgio Moroder. Ian Curtis had first introduced us to the icy Germans, and that was quickly followed by an even greater admiration for Moroder, particularly his work with Donna Summer on 'I Feel Love' and his production of the wonderful Sparks track 'Number One Song in Heaven'. His solo record *E=MC²* became a big inspiration and definitely led us into 'Temptation'. All we had to do was work out how they bloody did it.

But we did and, looking back now, those four tracks were a milestone, if not for everyone, then certainly for us. For New Order they heralded a completely new way of writing, recording and performing – a unique blend of the science-fiction futurism of Kraftwerk and the unpolished edge you could only get from a Factory band.

For example, if you listen to 'Everything's Gone Green', all through the song there is a variance to the pulses that defies logic but sounds great. Also the twelve-inch of 'Temptation' is riddled with mistakes, programmed and acoustic, again to great effect. It sounds like we had something fantastic in our hands that we were struggling to express and contain. It was true. The songs sound much more fragile, approachable and human because of it.

The Advision session went well. Our aim was to record and finish off 'Temptation' and 'Hurt' (initially 'Cramp'). Barney and me very much took command, organising the recording and the overdubbing. The keyboards and drum machine were recorded and the acoustic instruments layered on top until we were happy with the amount of melodies and the song structure. Vocals would also be jammed, having already been tried out – aided by the demon alcohol – 'live' at gigs by Barney, with the best bits refined in the studio. He also developed a method technically known as 'dah dee deeing' where he would hum, whistle, and scat-sing etc. over the backing track to see whether it suggested a vocal line or not. This led to some wonderful moments, the 'Oohs' on 'Temptation' being the first. I can safely say, without hesitation or fear of contradiction, that my basslines would often be used as an inspiration for a lot of the vocal lines throughout our career, something I was very proud of. Barney called me 'Mr Melody' in his lighter moments, of which sadly there weren't many.

'Hurt' was an entirely different matter; here we had New Order's first sequencer song. This was achieved by recording the analogue monophonic bassline into our first sequencer.

Geek Alert

Sequencers

An analogue sequencer is a device that can record and play back music programmed into it. It achieves this by handling the note and performance information in several forms, typically voltage/gate and trigger information using analogue electronics. The sequencers were designed for both composition and live performance for what was generally thought of as repetitive music such as that by Kraftwerk or Giorgio Moroder, music with a trance-like feel enhanced by repetition. The programming was done in steps. On 'step sequencers', notes are rounded into equal time intervals of different durations: 32's, 16's, 8's, 4's. Sequencers had no swing sound, or what we call 'real feel'. This would be offered later.

The sequencer gave a very stiff, precise and robotic output, exactly what Barney wanted. If I remember rightly, this first way of programming was called binary code, a combination of ons and offs, and this was how he programmed the first home-made sequencer using Powertran parts he had built for us by Martin Usher, his own resident electronic genius. This was joined by a custom-built adaptation of a Clef band box, which was the drum machine included in many home organs that Martin bastardised for us, converting it into a programmable drum machine with separate outputs for each drum sound (Martin Hannett had 'drummed' this into us as being absolutely vital for the best spatial recording and audio separation). Martin was a lovely man who accompanied us on our first tour of Australia just to keep our ramshackle collection of keyboards in working order.

Our initial foray into electronica, defined as music created using electronic instruments (synthesisers, drum machines and, soon, samplers etc.), but being dominated by an electronic sound was bringing its own brand-new, inherent set of problems.

Both drum machine and sequencer were rack-mounted and looked good but were very unreliable. The sequencer could only play one song at a time.

At the end of the session we were both very happy with the finished tracks. Well, me and Barney were. It would be years later when Steve would tell us how unhappy he was with 'Temptation'. It seemed the snare drum was panned over to one side, which he hated, but he chose not to tell us until nearly twenty years later, typical Steve. At the time we obviously took his silence as approval.

The engineer, Peter Woolliscroft, finished our technologically revolutionary EP off perfectly by using and mastering with one of the first-ever Sony PCM 1610 digital editing systems available in the UK. This was very much in keeping with our new forward-looking attitude. We were persuaded to record a shorter, seven-inch version at the same time. We weren't that keen but Tony Wilson said it was imperative. He thought it needed to be heard on the radio, this being, he felt, the first song Barney had written in his own voice as opposed to aping Ian. Ironically we would emulate the seven-inch version for gigs not the twelve-inch version.

It reached number 29 in the UK charts. Not bad for a first effort. It was also our first success of note in America. An FM station, WLIR in New York, championed it and turned it into a regional hit. We were absolutely oblivious.

I had heard that some people felt these 'electronic ideas' had been suppressed in Joy Division. This was not the case at all. It was a natural learning curve afforded by using new technology as it became readily available.

This newly available equipment was very impressive and expensive (the ARP Quadra and Pro One collectively cost £3,000 in 1982), and led to the creation of a lot of awful white middle-class synth boybands, they being the only ones who could afford this new technology. It would be years before the equipment to make this kind of music would be readily available to the working class, leading thankfully to another revolution: acid house. But Rob never had trouble finding the money for any of it. As far as he was concerned, the more futuristic and expensive the better. Interestingly we were using the funds of a rock band – Joy Division – to go synth.

'TEMPTATION' EP TRACK BY TRACK

'Temptation': 7.26

Oh, you've got green eyes ...

Fast, dancey, simple. 'Temptation' became the one song we would always try to copy but never could. A complete one-off.

A truly mad love song. The strained vocal chorus is oh-so plaintive. The whoop early on in the track was where me and Rob, spotting it was snowing outside, snowballed Barney while he was doing the main vocal. The 'eyes drop', as it became known, would melt many a young girl's heart and was used many times in the dressing room after the show. What an opening line. 'Oh, you've got green eyes?' – especially if they had.

'Hurt'/'Cramp': 8.13

I am the boy you will enjoy!

1 ... 2 ... 3 ... 4 ... Right from the vocoder intro you know this track is different. A much more adult/sophisticated song, the slow start built to a double-time break, the melodica and first verse then slowing to another drop. The Pro One sequencer was perfect for this as it had an A-to-B switch with a different sequence on each. Gillian flicked it live: sometimes well, sometimes badly.

In March 1982 we were doing a tour with Stockholm Monsters, which I loved because I was their soundman. I got to set up the New Order gear, soundcheck, then do the Monsters' soundcheck, then do their gig, and then go and play with New Order and finally strip our gear down. So my night was very full – my whole day was full, to be honest, which was mega. What's more, I loved the Monsters. I loved their attitude; they were all like me: working class and very down to earth, north Manchester boys and girls from Moston and Blackley in Manchester.

Sure enough, the tour was great – right up until Rotterdam, where the first thing that struck me was the lack of security men, just one big fat bloke, and the second thing that struck me was the height of the average Dutch person. They seemed very, very tall.

A lack of security men and a larger-than-usual-sized audience: both things that proved to be a big factor in what happened next . . .

We played, went off, end of gig as far as we were concerned. But instead of the usual drill, which was the audience shouting for a while, getting bored and then drifting off – we did no encores, you see, it was against the punk rulebook – they just stood there and kept yelling for more, bellowing at the empty stage.

We thought thirty-odd minutes of concert was perfectly adequate, but they obviously didn't, and weren't prepared to shift until they'd got their money's worth. Or maybe they just loved us?

By now the house lights had gone up, which is usually the signal to leave in any language, but they still weren't shifting, and with no security on hand to herd them out they remained rooted to the spot, loudly demanding more New Order. Our lads went on stage to clear the equipment – still the punters weren't having it, shouting at the stage, the tension building palpably in the room.

You can tell when things are going to go off at a gig. There's a certain point at which the hostility levels spike, and it's usually a few seconds before people start throwing things. Sure enough, a bottle came sailing over the crew's heads – *bang* – smashing on the stage and sending our guys scurrying for cover.

Another bottle and then another smashed on the stage, and the lads had to get off and take cover in the wings. Watching their retreat, the Monsters, who were helping, became wound up: 'Come on, we'll go on and fuck them off,' they were shouting, and that's exactly what they did, snatching up bits of wood for weapons and running out to scream at the audience: 'Go on, fuck off, the lot of you.'

In return the Dutch were all like, 'Hurdy, hurdy, hurdy, blah, blah, blah,' still booing and still chucking stuff.

'Fuck off.'

'Hurdy, hurdy, hurdy,' etc.

Leading the charge from our side was Slim, the Monsters' roadie, who then went on to become our roadie and these days still runs the door at the Manchester Academy. Right by his side was Ozzy – as in Oz PA, who supplied and ran our sound system – who was worried about his equipment. Rightly so! They had reclaimed the stage, but Ozzy was getting more and more wound up. Down at his feet was a Dutch guy hoisting a bottle like he was about to throw it, and Oz shouted at him, 'If you fucking throw that, you twat, I'll fucking do you.'

It did no good. He obviously didn't speak 'fucking English'. The Dutch geezer slung the bottle and Ozzy retaliated by diving off stage, grabbing this kid by the collar and proceeding to kick seven shades of shit out of him. Or at least trying to.

Other crew members waded in, diving off the stage like cowboys in a saloon fight: Slim, the Monsters and Rob were there, too. Barney had disappeared, of course, and so had Steve and Gillian, but I was in the wings watching, and to be honest had no intention of joining in because our lot were doing really well.

Until all of a sudden it went wrong. By now the Monsters had retreated, and this kid fighting Ozzy had turned him over, and his mate was about to kick him in the head.

I thought, *Oh fuck, I can't have that,* so I dived off, grabbed hold of the kid and punched him as Ozzy pulled himself to his feet behind me.

Just as all that happened, I heard a shout go up. *'Hij is uit de fooking band! Grijp hem!'*

I wonder what that means, I thought.

Oh, shit. They all dived on me. Being from the band, I was the grand prize – or prize turkey more like – and they all wanted a shot. No sign of any of our lot by this stage, just a sea of angry, tall Dutch fuckers laying into me. One of them punched me right on the nose, sending me flying backwards, and that was it. I banged my head really hard on the wall and I was out. Sparkled. Never been unconscious before or since, but I was out like a light.

Now, I was unconscious, so I didn't see any of this, but what happened next was that Slim and Dave Pils came wading back into the melee and charged to where the Dutch audience were still giving me a shoeing. Slim came out waving a dustbin and he was a big lad, Slim, you wouldn't want to get in the way of him wielding a dustbin. He was using it like a cross between a shield and a battering ram, Dave Pils

© Bart Plooij

© Bart Plooij

by his side, kicking out and twatting them, eventually grabbing hold of me and literally dragging me out from under the barrage of boots and fists. You ask me, they saved my life.

But like I say, I didn't know any of that at the time. I do remember sitting on a flight case backstage and someone asking me, 'Hooky, Hooky, are you all right?' and me replying, 'Can I have some more milk on me cornflakes, mam?' and I actually saw flying pink elephants, them lot saying, 'What's he going on about? He must have concussion.'

I just remember coming round, shouting at anybody and everybody: 'Where were you, y'bastards? While I was getting the shit kicked out of me, you fucking twats.' Barney, we found out later, was actually hid under a piano on the balcony. Wouldn't come down. Right shithouse. Steve and Gillian were actually sitting down on the balcony too, watching. Cheers, fellow bandmates.

Oh, my poor face. Big bruise-eggs all over it. Eyebrows stuck out like Frankenstein's monster. Nose stuffed full of drying blood. It's one of the few times I've ever come off worse, to be honest.

You'll never guess who made an appearance next? Only the big fat bouncer, followed by an irate promoter who uttered those immortal words: 'You'll never play in this town again! It's your fault, you play too short and no encore.' I was ready for round two but Rob packed me off.

I wish I had a pound for every time I would hear those words in my career.

'It's all over!' he spat, and he threatened to pull the tour. To appease him we promised to play for longer next time. We added one song.

He had A4 printouts done and distributed them at the gigs saying, 'Be warned, this band only play for 23 minutes and do not play encores!' In Dutch, of course.

It was a lie. We played for at least half an hour, the bloody cheek.

'The noise attracted scumbags like a magnet'

To me, the period I'm talking about now – 1982–84 – was a golden period, the time when I really enjoyed being a part of New Order and one I look back on with great fondness.

For a start the rehearsal room issue had been sorted at last. As Joy Division we'd practised at T. J. Davidson's old draughty warehouse on Little Peter Street in Manchester until it closed. From there, with its memories of Ian and filming of the 'Love Will Tear Us Apart' video, we'd moved to Pinky's, next to Broughton Baths in Salford, sharing a room alongside A Certain Ratio. Pinky's was scummy, filthy and cold, and when Rob announced plans for us to leave we were overjoyed.

God knows how he found it, but Rob got us this old Gas Board building used for reconditioning gas cookers next to a graveyard in Cheetham Hill. Perfect.

He then got Mike (Corky) Caulfield (our new roadie) and Terry to supervise renovations. Corky was an old friend of Rob's from Wythenshawe, who now worked as a builder, and Terry was certainly a willing apprentice. He also brought in Peter Tattersall from Strawberry Studios to advise on noise reduction, and they transformed the place, with three-foot padded walls and triple-glazing gracing the nine skylights. It even boasted central heating and a fully fitted kitchen. This was luxury. OMG! Fully carpeted. All we had to do was nick some tables and chairs.

The day we moved out of Pinky's we bought A Certain Ratio a sheep's head. (We left the eyes in to see them through the week, something for them to remember us by.) The trouble was the butcher had cut it into four and we had to stick it back together with gaffer tape to get it on the bloody microphone stand for when they came back in on Monday at the earliest. A whole weekend to ripen, lovely!

Also known as gaffer's tape, gaffa tape or just gaffa, gaffer tape is a strong, tough, cotton-cloth pressure-sensitive tape with very strong adhesive properties, used in theatre, film, television and rock'n'roll. It is the most used item in rock (not, as is commonly thought, cocaine or bullshit, although those two do go together very well). From tying down a cable or tying up a miserable lead singer, to holding up backdrops or holding up pissed drummers (I have seen more than one taped to his seat), as well as being used for the bandaging of open wounds and the decoration of a consenting groupie, this is a truly miracle product. It has a light side and a dark side.

Barney reckoned it was the sacrificing of that sheep that led directly to us writing 'Blue Monday' and even said so in the documentary *The New Order Story*. What is it about guitarists and black magic?

One of the first things we did there was record the first version of '5.8.6.', which didn't work out well for me. We had been asked by Jon Wozencroft if we would supply a piece of music to be given away free with a fanzine he was doing called *Feature Mist*. The others had started programming an opus, led by Barney, that turned into '5.8.6. Instrumental' (the song title came from seeing the order of the tune written down; the first part of the song is five bars long, the second eight bars and the third six bars, hence '5.8.6.'; this was unusual, normally they are all even numbers. Unless it's a programming error, of course, but in this case it was intentional).

The three of them spent ages clustered round the sequencer and the drum machine like witches at a cauldron. There was literally no room for four. So I thought I would take the opportunity to go home early, thinking, *Brilliant. I'll wait until they've finished and then put the bass on.* The normal way we did things. They programmed it for a while, mainly at night, until they were happy and when it was finally pronounced finished, I said, 'Right, I'll put the bass on!'

Cue horrified looks all round. Then stutteringly they all said, almost in unison, 'We ... we think it ... it's good enough ... good enough ... as it is ... just as it is, no ... no bass.'

NO FUCKING BASS!

I was shocked, absolutely devastated. I felt betrayed, like I'd had a knife through my heart. The first one of our songs ever not to have the bass on. The others weren't bothered how I felt. They had obviously talked about it when I'd gone home early.

Rob shrugged. 'You can't complain about what happens if you're not here!'

Jon fucking Wozencroft! I blamed him. Never liked him. Never would.

It made a wonderful difference to be in a proper rehearsal space. It was dry. It was warm. And for the first time we were able to practise and play in comfort. However, I did wonder if the music would suffer.

Meanwhile, Rob had spent a fortune on the soundproofing but it didn't work and the noise attracted scumbags like a magnet. The problem was that for true soundproofing you need isolation. The only medium sound does not travel through is a vacuum. Even Rob couldn't achieve that, and Tattersall was, in my opinion, a bit of a bullshitter. So even though the lads nailed three feet of Rockwool on the wall in a lovely wooden frame, with plasterboard over and then painted, the sound just went straight through to the outside, attracting said scumbags like zombies in a scene from *The Walking Dead*.

Basically we kept getting burgled and ended up having to tarmac over all the skylights so it ended up looking and feeling like an armoured bunker, all four-inch tarmac and solid steel doors, and no windows at all. Before the fortifications, there was a tiny music shop in the shopping precinct next door that occasionally boasted some of the most up-to-date and expensive gear in the world, as owned by New Order. Every time we were robbed I'd pop round and get the stuff back. The guy would go, 'Hi, Hooky, yours? Thought so. Didn't know what it was? Can I get back the tenner I paid for it, please?' That item in question being a £3,000 Yamaha sequencer for sale in a Cheetham Hill precinct music shop. But we didn't mind all that much because Cheetham Hill was a nice place to hang out then, and it boasted the first Spud 'U' Like in Manchester.

Spud 'U' Like is a British fast-food restaurant specialising in cheap and nutritious baked potatoes (known commonly as 'spuds' in colloquial English), complete with a wide range of fillings. Founded in Edinburgh in 1974, it went on to have branches all across Britain.

We would try and maintain a schedule (it didn't last, but we'll come back to that) working from 11 a.m. to 6 p.m.-ish and, just as we had in Joy Division, we wrote by jamming the songs, the difference being that now we were putting some of the ideas into a sequencer. Bernard and Steve did the programming while yours truly would put them on tape to be jammed over later.

I became a recording whiz, using our new eight-track recorder and an Amek Tac16 mixing desk to great effect. It was my job to set up, operate the equipment and record all our ideas.

So we had a base, a decent base, at last, and if we weren't rehearsing or writing or touring, we were doing production work. So yeah – all of us threw ourselves into it like it was a vocation, delighting in using our state-of-the-art gear on all these new songs. So much better than what it became, when we used to spend months in one studio working on one track.

What I liked about the lifestyle then was being busy all the time, and doing it for the love of music. Money never came into it. Probably why my relationship started to get a bit rocky. Iris couldn't bear to leave me in bed on those cold, dark, wet Manchester mornings and more than once I'd be shaken awake with, 'I've missed the bus, you'll have to take me in!' Shit, that was my money for the week gone.

Back then my car (pre-Alfa) was a Jaguar 420G, a real gas guzzler, (KFR 666F), that I kept running only with great difficulty. It was only doing six miles to the gallon. Money was still a big problem personally. Years later Iris admitted to doing it on purpose so I'd have to get up. Women, eh?

I can remember being at the Gas Board when Rob suggested the band go on more money than the crew, and the crew going on strike at the thought of it. Rob had to patiently explain that we wrote the songs and without the songs none of us would be there. But we never asked for more money. Our previous pay rise from £30 to £70 had been for us all. It was Rob's idea to go from £70 to £100 a week, but the crew really got the hump about that, because until then the whole operation had been run like a co-op. We even all roomed together: I roomed with Dave, Rob was in a room with Barney (him ending up in the bath all the time because of Rob's snoring). We all shared and stayed in the same hotels.

There was no us-and-them division (great name) in those days.

In fact, it wasn't until we were in America in 1988 – a big band by then – that we resigned ourselves to staying in different hotels to the crew. That was down to the American crew members saying, 'We can't afford to drink in the Four Seasons, man! Days Inn, pleeeese!' Before that, Rob insisted on keeping us all together, and thank God he did because I had some great laughs with the crew.

It was on tour that I really came alive. Fuck sitting around watching other people program sequencers. Fuck that for a game of soldiers. I wanted to be out on the road. Out there I'd be planning things with the roadies, lugging gear, setting up the sound. After the show the others would be in the dressing room drinking and I'd sit for a minute and then go, 'Right, let's do the gear then,' get back out and do it. I didn't want to be in there doing nothing. It was probably just to do with being young and being hyper and having loads of energy. I've mentioned before that in Joy Division I used to get so wound up before a gig that I'd have to go for a run just to get rid of some of the excess energy. But that's the way it was back then. Everything we did was new and great, and I loved it. I loved driving the lorry with the gear across huge continents. It was like being a pirate. Like being a Viking. The world, and everything in it, was our plaything.

Including the fanmail. Right through the band I loved writing back to the fans. The others were never interested. I thought it was wonderful that people took the time to write to you. Some were mad but they were all interesting. To me it was good manners to reply. I did it even when the band were really big. My mother taught me well; it was a pleasure. I used to take it all with me on planes and do it at 30,000 feet in the air, posting them when I got back to England. I mean, I'll be honest, my letters weren't exactly long, heartfelt missives. They were more a case of me scrawling, 'Send an SAE next time, dickhead! We're not made of money,' and moving on to the next one. But even so, if

I had a quid for every time I've had a fan come up to me and tell me he got one of those letters – 'You once wrote to me and told me to fuck off!'– I'd be a rich man by now. You reply to a fan, you get a fan for life, Rob would say. I should put that in my rules for a group, really. The rest of the band were completely mystified by my interest. Only Tony Wilson and Rob acknowledged the commitment involved in answering every letter.

Incidentally, Barney even had a rubber stamp made with his signature on so I wouldn't bother him. He hated doing it that much. Fucking misery guts. All the same, I had to admire the sheer cynicism of it.

But anyway, that was later, when we were big. Back in the early 80s, I'd still be out front talking to fans when I was doing the gear – I loved being in a group so much.

There are a million reasons why things went wrong for me in New Order, and we'll be covering a fair few of them, don't you worry about that. But one of them is the fact that the more successful we became the less I could muck in, and the less I mucked in, the less busy I was. And you know what they say: the devil makes work for idle hands …

'But then twatto returned . . .'

Looking back with the great benefit of hindsight I can see where things started to go wrong quite clearly.

Firstly, there were the big things, like us bankrolling the Haçienda.

For the opening night me and Iris got an invite through the post just like everybody else. I had been down once before the build and once during it but I hadn't taken much notice. It was all too big for me to grasp.

On the opening night I gawped and gasped, just like everyone else, oohs and aahs coming from all sides. I was absolutely blown away. It was a great night with free drinks for everyone. The place was packed, every ligger in Manchester out in full force. Tony swanned around for all he was worth. Vini Reilly and A Certain Ratio performed. It was a great night. But it didn't feel in any way mine. Not yet anyway.

But in a way, it was the little things that were more damaging. Things that gradually moved the band away from being the democracy it had been to the dictatorship it would become.

There was an example during the Peel session we made that June. We were recording in Revolution Studios in Cheadle. While recording the track 'Too Late' Rob had an idea for a backing vocal. Barney was out for a butty or something so I sang it. We recorded it and thought it was really good.

But then twatto returned and the first thing he said was, 'What's that – that vocal?' Screwing up his face like he'd smelled something nasty. 'I don't like that.'

The rest of us all thought it was good and, remember, up until that moment New Order, like Joy Division, had been run as a democracy, the will of the majority, which would have meant the vocal staying on the track. But Barney had screwed up his face so much and, to make his feelings completely plain, turned on his heel and left the studio on the pretext of 'going for a walk', leaving us to stew.

We all looked at each other like naughty schoolkids.

Steve and Gillian liked it but sat on the fence (as ever) and Rob said nervously, 'Oh well, if he's not happy, maybe we should take it off, you know.'

I said, 'Fuck him. Tell him to fuck off, the knob.'

Normal Peter Hook mode.

We took it off. Barney got his own way for the first time and, I tell you what, it was downhill from there on in. Next thing you knew – and this was on the same session – Barney was insisting on doing all his own backing vocals.

That's a cardinal sin. In my rules of a group: never let the singer do his own backing vocals. To me it sounds weird. When Ian was alive he made sure that the other members had a go because that's what you do in a group. It's a *group*. Not just a bunch of musicians backing the singer. But Barney always did his own from that moment on. He had a wonderful sense of humour and could be great company, but in situations like this he had a seriousness and ruthlessness that I was definitely lacking.

From that session we never properly recorded 'Too Late'. Barney decided he didn't like it. So that was the end of that.

June took us off to warmer climes. Italy was a great tour and we loved it. What a beautiful country. It was the only place Barney seemed to like. We were always puzzled for years because we never went back. The audiences were very intense and there were a couple of banners at every gig along the lines of 'Fuck off Nuovo Ordine, vogliamo Joy Division' but even that wasn't enough to dampen our spirits, because aside from that it was dead sunny and every gig was great, the hotels were wonderful and the beaches were brilliant. One of the gigs was in Taranto, in the south of the country. We were staying right on the beach and we literally dumped our clothes in a pile and legged it to the sea where we were entertaining the promoter's rep, Marina. My God, she was gorgeous! Bronzed, bikinied, slim, beautiful and Italian. She had a bigger stacking circle round her than Heathrow airport. She needed her own air traffic control, this girl. We were all trying desperately to impress her, to get her attention. Human pyramids, push-up contests, arm-wrestling, the lot. Nothing worked.

The gig was in a hotel outbuilding on the beach where, literally, as the sun went down these strange figures all wearing black appeared in dribs and drabs until eventually there were hundreds of them. Goths. We were amazed, and it was a great night.

After the show, Marina was down to two suitors. Guess who? Yep, me and him. Waiting until he went to the toilet, I pulled her outside and, giggling, we ran away, ending the evening with a wonderful kissing session in the moonlight on the beach. Then she disappeared into the night, just like Cinderella. I clutched the glass slipper. I was in heaven.

He wouldn't speak to me or even look at me at breakfast or all the next day.

It was during that tour that I also ended up meeting this gorgeous older woman who introduced me to some, shall we say, *interesting* practices involving the minibar champagne and unusual receptacles, and who spent the whole time we were together lounging around my room in stockings and suspenders, being all exotic and, again, Italian.

I remember she went out on the balcony for a cigarette and Corky, who was in the room next door, started chatting her up. I could hear him going, 'I'm with a band, you know, I'm a technician,' etc. etc., and I walked out and put my arm round her. He jumped. 'You jammy bastard!' he spat, and retreated back into his room.

The next day, when we were leaving, I thought, *Oh, there's still a load of stuff left in the little fridge. Might as well have that*, and emptied it all in my bag, thinking that it came with the room. It was the first time I had ever seen a minibar.

Later I arrived in reception to find Rob having some kind of meltdown. 'Hooky, Hooky,' he said, as soon as I appeared, 'what have you done, you twat?'

'What?'

'Look at this bill here,' he said. 'You've had everything out of the fucking minibar.'

And I went, 'Yeah, so? It's free, isn't it? They give it you with the room.'

'No, you daft twat, you're supposed to pay for it when you drink it.'

Oops.

I had to get it all out of my bag and put it on the reception desk under the withering gaze of the receptionist. 'Right', says Rob, 'the only thing that's missing is the champagne. Where's the champagne, dickhead?'

Double oops.

*

Next we went to Greece, the first time I ever got drunk on ouzo and also the first and last time that Nick Cave turned into a bat and flew into my room.

It was a three-day event in Athens billed as 'The Festival of Independent Rock and Roll', the first in Greece since a new democracy was declared in 1980. Run by a delightful guy, Dimitri. It featured the Birthday Party first night, the Fall the second and booby prize (according to Mark E.) us last. It was big news and we got the biggest headline for our night, '**ΟΙ ΦΑΣΙΣΤΕΣ ΕΠΙΣΤΡΈΦΟΥΝ**' or, for the less well-educated among you, me included, 'THE FASCISTS RETURN'! The build-up was getting quite intense. All three bands and crew were there for five days, enjoying a little holiday, and it turned into quite a party, with all three bands socialising very, very well on the hotel's rooftop terrace. Terry Mason even fell in love with the Fall's manager Kay Carroll and was doing the usual lovesick-cow routine, following her round even though she was Mark's girlfriend at the time. Wow, she was a character, to say the least. Very manly, a real ball-breaker.

So anyway, the Birthday Party did their gig – and we got the shock of our lives to find that despite the fact that they were like wild animals onstage they just sat around beforehand reading books and playing chess, the complete opposite of their stage persona. In a way they were like the mirror image of us: we were dead wild off stage, very composed on it.

It was a good show and the audience were hungry for it and loved the aggression. In a way, it was their first-ever punk gig. There was a lot of missile-throwing and fighting in the crowd.

'I'm doubling the security tomorrow,' said Dimitri.

The Fall were next and, despite the security increase, there were more missiles and violence in the crowd. I'm not surprised, though, because the Fall were crap. I felt like throwing things at them myself (only joking, Mark).

'I'm doubling the security tomorrow,' said Dimitri.

Later that night this sorry tale begins in a nightclub where the whole touring party, that's New Order, the Fall and the Birthday Party, are celebrating. Quite a gathering, as I'm sure you can imagine, and we were all getting absolutely twatted on free ouzo. And I mean completely wasted. Every time you went to the bar and asked for a drink, no matter how many you ordered, they would not let you pay. This was fantastic. This club had swimming pools inside and was open-air, absolutely beautiful. Yours truly had spent the night talking to the girl who did sound for the Birthday Party, a real character, a bit of a tomboy and a great friend of Ruth Polsky's. So it was hardly surprising that by the end of the night, we were so trolleyed that we were heading back to the hotel together. We staggered out of the club and she tells me she is dying for a wee. I push her next to a taxi and she drops 'em and starts to wee, then the bloody taxi drives off and there she is in all her glory at the front door of the club.

Full fucking moon.

I got her in another taxi and she had her feet out of one window and I had my head out of the other, spewing. I was giving the driver garbled directions in between pukes, going, 'Hotel! Hotel!' and him driving me to about four different ones all over Athens, picking my head up to look at it, me going, 'No! No!' until eventually we made it back to the right one, and I crawled up the stairs and into the lift, where she made a drunken dive for me.

And then, all of a sudden, as I pulled myself up, I got an attack of guilt. I know. It was ironic considering I had a girlfriend back home, but she was a mate of Ruth's, you see, and although Ruth and I were in a sort of lull by then, long-distance relationships etc., that didn't make it any easier. So the only thing I could think to do was get rid of her. I ended up pushing her out of the lift, my hand full in her face.

I know, I know. Not exactly the most gentlemanly behaviour. But I was so drunk and, believe me, I paid for it, spending the next few hours in a nauseous ouzo haze, lying on the cold tiles on the floor of my bathroom, unable to even move until about 5 a.m. when I at last managed to crawl into bed. Having found sanctuary at last, I was just drifting off when I became aware of something happening on my balcony, then the curtains opening and something I took to be a giant bat entering my room.

Except it wasn't a giant bat. It was much worse than that.

It was Nick Cave, the ghost of Christmas Goth, come to get me, Scrooge Hook.

'What the fuck are you doing?' I screamed, sitting up, clutching at my bedsheets like a Hammer Horror heroine.

'Where is she?' he demanded, in his Aussie-Goth accent.

'What are you talking about?' I said, gathering my wits. 'I don't fucking know. Get out of my fucking room, you twat.'

By this time I'd got out of bed and was feeling less like a Hammer Horror heroine and more like a very drunk and pissed-off bassist, so I grabbed hold of him and propelled him back towards the balcony, where the curtains swished behind him as he turned back into a bat and flew away. I hoped. Didn't fancy cleaning him up off the pavement.

Anyway, Nick seemed infatuated with the gorgeous tomboy sound engineer. So thank God I'd left her in the lift, because otherwise, having climbed over the balcony to reach my room, Nick Cave would have drunk my blood for sure!

When I crawled down to breakfast, I was again sick as a dog after wolfing endless glasses of water – turns out ouzo is like its close cousin, Pernod. It crystallises in your stomach as you dehydrate and then, when you have another drink, rehydrates – *Boom* – you're pissed again. (See Bernard Sumner Detroit gig cancellation 1988.)

Then, to add insult to injury, Rob shouts, 'Hey, Romeo, here's you and your girlfriend's bill from last night!'

Turns out the reason they wouldn't take any money was because they were running a tab. She'd gone by now so I had to pay for it all. Bollocks.

We were on that night. The papers had done the usual Nazi-sympathising stitch-up on us, so a bunch of right-wing nutters had come down to see us, as well as a group of left-wing anti-Nazi types.

Needless to say, it all started getting a bit heavy, and we were pleased that the promoter had doubled the security. What we needed was a line of hard-nut bouncers right across the front of the stage.

It was a bit of a shit atmosphere, to be honest. Shit vibe, shit gig. Loads of missile-throwing, chanting and fighting before we even went on. The roadies went and armed themselves with sticks and poles, fearing the worst, and what really didn't help matters was that someone was being a bit of a twat. For a start, he was drunk. It wasn't unusual for him to be drunk, and I don't mean that in a critical way: he needed his Pernod to work up the courage to sing, something that probably any frontman can identify with. However, the trouble with using booze to calm your nerves is that it can so easily go wrong, and this was one of those nights when he'd drunk too much and gone over the edge from blissed-out to pissed-up, which probably explains why he did what he did on 'Truth', which was open his eyes (in those days he usually sang with his eyes tight closed), put his melodica down, pick up an apple that was on top of his amp and fling it high into the air. He then closed his eyes again.

My first thought was, *Christ, it's going to hit someone*, and sure enough as I watched it arc through the air, I saw it heading towards a big group of Greek kids, most of whom were looking at it – all of them, in fact, apart from one guy, the guy who got hit by the apple on the back of the head. Crunch! Golden Delicious.

Barney had quite a throw on him because this poor apple kid was quite far back. And I'm not kidding. It sparkled him. There was blood everywhere and, of course, this being a New Order gig, the fact that a kid had been hit with an apple signalled the outbreak of a huge fight, so the next thing I knew there was a melee by the mixing desk, with our soundman Ozzy nutting all these crazy Greek kids before the bouncers piled in to stop the fighting and they carted the poor kid off in an ambulance. Barney hadn't even noticed. An apple a day, eh?

I was glad when it was all over. It was bedlam.

'I wish I had doubled the security,' sighed Dimitri.

In stark contrast, the next day he took us on a day trip to a gorgeous island off the coast. The water was crystal-clear and I was enjoying snorkelling until an octopus swam past me and looked straight at me. I swear it even winked. It was huge. I flew out of the water and wouldn't go back in. This was like being on your holidays.

Meantime, same jaunt, last story. Barney had gone off with the Birthday Party's tour manageress, a Balinese princess called Minu. She was the actual daughter of a Balinese king and had taken to hanging out with him. Because of a coup on her Indonesian home island of Bali, she told us she had no nationality and just constantly travelled, owning three passports.

Oh, and she was lovely, and we were all dead jealous. So of course we were coming up with all kinds of plans to get him back.

Now, the toilets in this particular hotel were terrible. I was sharing a room with Dave, who kept warning me to be careful because it wouldn't flush.

'Why don't we just deck over into Barney's room and use his toilet?' I said. So for two or three days, while Barney was off on a social whirl with his Balinese princess, we were shitting in his toilet and, oh man, it was getting more and more ripe in there, hilariously so. It was like 100-degree heat and the room had a 'Do Not Disturb' sign on the door, so by the third day it was honking.

So Barney comes back and swans straight into the hotel bar to rub our noses in what a great time he'd been having with his princess before declaring, 'Right, I'm just going up to my room.'

We were like, 'Oh yeah, we'll come up with you,' and followed him, with him going, 'What are you two bastards doing?' We were acting a little suspicious.

'Nothing, nothing, we're just making sure you're all right,' we said, laughing behind our hands.

We watched as he opened the door to his room, went inside.

All we heard was, 'Oh, you dirty bastards,' followed by the sound of Barney spewing all over the floor.

Poor lad. He always did have a bit of a delicate constitution.

Next stop, Britannia Row. New Order had our second album to make.

'Marooned in the middle of puke'

More little signposts, more nails in the coffin of the band. Like a difference in working hours that might have been brewing for a while but really became apparent when we decamped to Britannia Row in Islington to make *Power, Corruption & Lies*.

'Four hundred pounds a day,' Rob says, 'So get on with it!' We booked a month.

The recording got off to an inauspicious start when, on the first night, me, Rob, Steve and Gillian went to see ABC with Mike Johnson, our new sound engineer for the album (he would end up engineering four albums and nine singles in total for us). Martin Fry was a big mate of Mike Pickering, so Rob said we must say hello.

Now, this gig was somewhere in Essex, and I was driving, sober as a judge, but that lot got royally pissed, and I'm talking absolutely trashed. At one point Rob had disappeared. I found him in a stairwell, head in his hands, sat in a huge pool of vomit. He'd been spewing so hard his false teeth had come out and were marooned in the middle of puke. I ended up having to pick them up for him – all the time with him telling me to fuck off, mind you, which was typical Rob – and put them in his pocket. The things you do.

Next, I bumped into Steve, who was going mental, because he couldn't find Gillian.

You see, it hadn't exactly escaped my notice that Mike had taken a shine to Gillian, and was making his feelings known. 'What the fuck?' I told him, 'her and Steve are together.'

'You're joking,' he slurred.

'No, you knobhead, they're a fucking couple.'

He went, 'Oh my God. Do you know what? I never got that impression ...'

By the time I'd got the lot of them back in the car, they all sat in complete silence, mortified, pretending to be asleep, for what became a very long drive back to London, with a month-long recording session ahead of us.

*

Still, it went well, all things considered. Britannia Row was pretty much how I remembered it, a plush studio where they still served sandwiches in the afternoon, and although I wouldn't say the group were getting on famously, we were rubbing along OK.

Our accommodation was a flat at the back of Harrods in Knightsbridge (Flat 6, 15 Basil Street, to be precise), which was lovely. But this was where I first noticed the big difference in the hours. We'd go into the studio at midday and finish at 2 a.m., but when we arrived home I'd go to bed while that lot stayed up for hours, smoking dope and watching videos of *The Old Grey Whistle Test* or *2001: A Space Odyssey*. Steve had a huge collection of them and, even though they were all unmarked, he knew exactly what was on each, one of those strange, uncanny things about Steve. He was weird.

And then, in the morning, oh, fuck me. Muggins here had the job of getting the whole lot of them out of bed, and while Barney, Steve and Gillian were difficult enough to shift, they were nothing – *nothing* – compared to Rob Gretton. They were like three willing puppies compared to our comatose manager.

Getting him out of bed was just the beginning. After that he wouldn't budge from the flat until he'd had a fag, then a bowl of Coco Pops, then another fag and then a shit, and it had to be in exactly that order, and we'd all have to sit there and wait for him to do it because we were all in one car, Steve's Volvo. Me and Barney had left our cars at home for our wives.

Of course, we should have said, 'Fuck you, we don't need you, you're not even in the band, we're going in the car, you get the Tube.' Whatever.

But we didn't because ... well, I suppose that looking back he was being a bit of a bully, wasn't he? Intimidation in the workplace they'd call it now, nothing too overt though. Ever since we met Rob he had come and done everything with us, everything. His thing was, right from the start, we are all in this together. One for all, and all for one. Even though for him it was mainly a fantastic holiday.

While we were in the studio, a representative of the Australian touring company brought in a contract to be signed, for our forthcoming tour with John Cooper Clarke. The company had the very grand name of Eddie Zimblis & Co, and we were to be paid £800 per gig. Something to look forward to.

In the studio, Bernard had found this old white lab coat on the back of a door that he insisted on wearing while he worked. 'I look like a mad scientist,' he said. Every day he took tiny little slivers of an acid tab that he said 'opened him up'.

I had never taken acid and didn't notice much difference in him, to be honest, so I was like, 'Yeah, whatever floats your boat, mate.' To me he looked like a white-coated lackey from an old Bond movie. Later I discovered that the lab coat belonged to Mike Johnson. It was his uniform when he worked on the Kit Kat production line at Rowntree's in York (have a break, eh?).

So we settled into a sort of recording split, where I'd sit with Mike Johnson doing the nuts and bolts of it all, and they'd come in, record their parts, bugger off, and then later, when we were mixing the tracks, come in again and pass judgement.

During the mixing Rob would usually say, 'Just make it go FUCKIN' WOOMPH!' He even jumped on the desk naked just to hammer the point home. That really was his sole contribution to the recording process after the Coco Pops, fag and shit debacle of the mornings. He would come in handy on the lyric-writing and song title collaboration at the end, though, usually clutching his latest copy of the *Sunday Times*.

There was no schedule and we just sort of made the day up as we went along. We had a list of songs and ideas and just worked through them.

There was a lot of downtime sitting by Mike, so I read. I had a little table on which I had my pile of books and, by the end, they were nearly as high as the studio ceiling. I used to get all the song titles from them. Even the album titles, as it turned out, because 'A startling tale of power, corruption and lies' was a review quote from the *Daily Telegraph* on the back of *1984* by George Orwell. 'Leave Me Alone' came from *Tender Is the Night* by F. Scott Fitzgerald, and 'Ultraviolence' was from *A Clockwork Orange*, to name but a few.

Meanwhile, Steve was being Steve, a genius of the drums, while Bernard played the guitar and keyboards and programmed the sequencer (fantastic synth lines – you've got to hand it to him, he really did revolutionise indie music with that record). Obviously I did the bass and we then worked on the vocals and lyrics together.

Next came the making of what would be our signature tune and to this day the biggest-selling twelve-inch of all time, 'Blue Monday'.

Our synthesiser line-up had been joined by what would soon become one of Bernard's favourites, a Moog Source, designed by keyboard legend Robert Moog, who was the inventor of best synthesisers in the world. We used it for the bassline of 'Blue Monday', sequenced with one of Barney's home-built Powertran sequencers. He said he was channelling Sylvester's 'You Make Me Feel (Mighty Real)' and Kraftwerk's 'Uranium', while he tried to show his love for the production of Klein + M.B.O.'s 'Dirty Talk' by putting it on the record player umpteen times during the mix, desperately trying to influence the sound of the song. Every single time he put it on he'd say, 'It should sound more like this!' but the fact was that 'Dirty Talk' never sounded anywhere near as good as our mix. Me and Mike were delighted.

We had also acquired our first Sequential Circuits Prophet 5, while another very important acquisition was an Emulator I, one of the first sampling keyboards, on which you could sample/grab a sound and play it across the keyboard in different pitches. It also came with a small library of sampled sounds on the new floppy disk format. We had great fun with this machine, and all of us would be fighting over it when it came to our later production duties. Once you got past the novelty of sampling various bodily functions it became a very valuable tool. We would smash a huge piece of glass outside the practice place for use on 'Blue Monday' (muggins here was stuck with clearing up the mess) and sampled all sorts of other noises for inclusion on many of the tracks.

We had also moved up to an Oberheim DMX Mk I drum machine, which was so easy to use it was ridiculous. I remember being in the practice room watching Steve program it. He had it on the floor between the legs of a chair. Asked why, he said it was because the only mains lead he could find was a short kettle lead from the kitchen. Hence our new £2,000 drum machine was stuck on the floor right next to his overflowing ashtray.

Steve was always doing weird stuff like that. It came as no surprise to me that after spending days programming our magnum opus 'Blue Monday', using every trick this wonderful machine could provide, the mains lead popped out of the back, the machine dumped all its information, and the first incarnation of 'Blue Monday' was lost.

Steve said he was backing up the memory to cassette when it

happened, but I'm pretty sure you couldn't dump a Mk I to cassette. I thought that came in with the Mk II model, which was radically different (See New Order gig, Zurich 84), and anyway, the first thing Steve did was get a longer plug lead, not a new cassette player.

The upshot was we had to hurriedly recreate all these fantastic drum beats, rhythmic punctuations, fills and drum stops we'd stolen from the songs we'd heard in New York clubs, as quickly as possible before they disappeared into the ether.

It took a long time to recapture them, and the lingering doubt that we had lost the best version still haunts me now.

Production-wise, Barney and I were using little tricks we'd nicked off Martin Hannett, like putting a speaker into the live room, feeding it sounds, recording it back to the desk through another microphone, and then mixing the result in with the tracks. They had this wonderful tiled room in the basement at Britannia Row, almost purpose-built for doing that. Its ambience suited the tempo of 'Blue Monday' in particular.

The song was turning into a monster and was occupying a large amount of our studio time. Barney was obsessed with catching the disco-pulse sound of Giorgio Moroder's electronic music, the alternating octaves of the bass sound that normally a disco bass player would play. He had already experimented with the effect on '5.8.6.', taking ages to get it just right. 'Blue Monday' had been selfishly written to start with, the idea being that we could play an encore without having to go back on stage and do it ourselves. The machines would play it as we relaxed and put our feet up while Terry prepared the 'headaches'.

It was very much a studio song, and Mike Johnson had to improvise on the old mixing desk to get exactly the effect we wanted. We'd gaffer-tape drum adjustment keys to the pan knobs in order to do really quick left-to-rights of the whooshing noises that you couldn't do otherwise. We fabricated huge tape loops that ran suspended from microphone stands all round the studio. It was very exciting.

I remember Gillian doing a long list, like a colouring-in chart, of the 'Blue Monday' sequences in case the sequencer fucked up, so we could reprogram it if needs be. All the program information was laid out in binary form. She spent hours colouring it in, like being at a really long meal in Pizza Hut with the kids.

Meanwhile, I put the six-string bass on the track, and afterwards Bernard felt inspired enough to try a vocal. And then it became a song. Not a great song, in my opinion, but something a bit different – nearly eight minutes long, no chorus, more rhythmic than melody-driven – a song we thought we'd want to release quietly as a single.

Little did we know, eh?

On Test

The DMX

Oberheim Electronic's Programmable Digital Drum Machine

I'll always remember the first drum machine that I ever saw. It was a toy-like box with three buttons marked Bossa-Nova, Foxtrot and Rock. The actual sound was very mechanical, and each variation had a single drum pattern which lasted a solitary measure and repeated indefinitely. Within half a minute, anyone playing along with it would scream from boredom. Thankfully, drum machines have progressed greatly since that time, which brings us to the DMX. This is no toy, but a very complex microcomputer based tool. The sounds themselves are real recordings of drums converted into a digital format and programmed onto integrated circuit chips called EPROMs (Erasable Programmable Read Only Memories).

My first experience with this unit was through a practice amp which was lying around the magazine office, waiting to be reviewed. I listened carefully to each of the sounds and to tell the truth, I wasn't impressed at all. My reaction was that they (Oberheim) should have hired me to record the drums, as I felt that I could have done a much better job. I forgot about the DMX itself for a couple of days, but continued to dwell on what type of sound I'd go for if I was to do a recording for this type of unit. The sound couldn't be too stylized, as it might be used for any type of music. Therefore all the fundamental frequencies of each particular sound would have to be present in order to lend themselves easily to equalization, for the purpose of pulling out those frequencies which are characteristic to any particular style. Then it dawned on me. The DMX's drum sounds were just that, completely neutral.

Sure enough, when I brought it into the studio and hooked it up through the board (there are individual outputs for each sound card) every type of sound that I could want could be obtained via equalization. The DMX comes from the factory with the following voices and variations:

Bass — bass drum at three volume levels

Snare — snare drum at three volume levels

Hi Hat — with a closed and an accented sound, plus a longer "open" sound

Tom 1 — with three individual pitches

Tom 2 — lower in pitch than tom 1 also with three individual pitches

Cymbals — a ride which can be played with or without an accent and a crash

Percussion 1 — tambourine with accent at two volume levels and rimshot.

Percussion 2 — shaker with accent at two volume levels plus hand claps.

All these make up a total of 24 sounds, and each is controlled by a correspon-

Continued...

IM&RW October 1982 87

'She went off like a firework'

We ran over on the album. It took seven weeks from start to finish (quite a contrast with the six days spent on *Unknown Pleasures*) and suddenly that exciting Australian tour seemed less exciting. We literally finished recording at Britannia Row, drove home, repacked our cases and went to the airport, back on tour.

In those days I'd lost count of the amount of times I'd come home off tour and my missus would say, 'Good tour? Anything happen?'

And I'd think about us being up all night for days on end, running riot in cities all around the world, off my face, a different girl in every port, and then I'd say, 'Oh, quiet, you know?'

God, the duplicity! The lies! The roadies had the bare-faced cheek to manufacture big rows with their girls when they got home so they wouldn't have to sleep with them until they could get to the VD clinic. They'd all meet at St Luke's, hoping for the all-clear. The double life we were leading was becoming very set and entrenched, one of the bad things we had brought with us from Joy Division.

Australia was another one of those tours. It was the best place I'd ever been to in my life and the only place I've ever considered relocating to. It's like England except with sun and beaches.

And spiders.

There was one particular occasion when Mike Johnson, who we had drafted in to do sound for the tour, pointed out a spider in his room in the Bondi Beach Hotel.

'Hooky, come and check this out!' he said. It was huge, a bird-eating huntsman spider. It had fangs and, I'm not kidding, this thing was as big as my hand.

So here's me, shit-scared of spiders, ever since I was a nipper living in Jamaica and we were invaded by them, demanding that Mike did something about it. It wasn't in my room but I was next door and definitely not far enough away. He just laughed and said, 'Bollocks to that! I'm going out for a drink.'

I was brooding and when we returned to the hotel I refused to go to bed or let him or Dave Pils go to bed until the spider was dealt with. The very thought of the furry beast was driving me crazy. So finally I'm in Mike's room demanding to see it again, and, oh fuck, it had gone.

That was it. No chance of me leaving Mike's room until I found the bloody thing. After a while Mike found it. 'Here she is, the little beauty,' he says. 'She must be looking for a phone number.' And there it was, so big it was straddling the phone book.

In the end, with me threatening to scream the place down if *one of you bastards doesn't do something about that fucking spider*, Dave grabbed the shoebox that I used for carting my tapes around, tipped out the cassettes, used the lid to calmly brush the huntsman into the box and then replaced the lid.

You could hear it scampering around in there, loud as a hamster and a lot angrier, as we took it down to reception. Dave (the bastard) then chased me down seven flights of stairs waving the bloody box. Then we got to reception and I hid in the corner of the room.

'Excuse me, daaahlin', apples an' pears etc.,' says Dave Pils in pure cockney, 'I've got a single room, but there's two of us in it.'

'Oh,' she said, 'we'll soon put that right. Who's the other guest?'

'Him,' said Dave, and put the spider out on her desk.

She went off like a firework, leaping onto her chair with a scream, while I was doing exactly the same in the opposite corner.

Dave was laughing his dogs off. 'You pair of ponces,' he said. Then, scooping up the spider, he puts it back in the box.

With me following a discreet distance behind, shouting instructions like, 'Just you make sure you get rid of it, throw it in the traffic, across the road,' he left reception and deposited the spider right outside.

Not nearly far enough away for my liking.

'It'll come back,' I bleated, looking forlornly at the short distance from where he'd left it to the doors of the hotel.

'It'll be all right,' said Dave, and that was it. I didn't sleep a wink that night.

For the Australian tour we were supporting John Cooper Clarke.

I love John Cooper Clarke. Not only is he influential as a poet but he's a great bloke to boot. For all his ups and downs – and God knows there's been enough of both – you never hear anyone say a bad word about him. Not that many people can be so off their cake and still remain nice, but he could, and it's good to see someone like myself go through hell and come out the other side.

So anyway, he turned up in Melbourne with a girlfriend in tow. They were both addicts. They had gone cold turkey on the plane, and they were fucked. I was amazed they got through immigration or customs. As soon as they got in their hotel room they refused to come out until we got them some smack. This wasn't really our problem and was more amusing than anything else; we just passed his request on to the poor promoter.

Whatever happened, John made the gigs and it was a good bill. Then, for some insane reason, he decided to come to New Zealand, to support us when we popped over mid-tour to play some dates there.

There we found the audiences full of skinheads, every town we played. It was intimidating but they turned out to be quite friendly to us, and John even had these skinheads serving him up. Unfortunately, smack was something like NZ$1,000 a gram and over the course of the four gigs he'd run up quite a bill, which he couldn't pay, so he had to stay in New Zealand and work for the skinheads to pay off his debt.

We were glad to see the back of him at that point. What a shit drug. It kills so many people. I can never see the allure.

The skinheads took us to a party one night. We didn't realise that they were gatecrashing it. They all stormed into this house and before we knew it this poor kid came flying over the balcony from the first floor. The skins were laughing and hanging over the rail. 'Watch out for the flying Abo!' they yelled. We just picked the poor bugger up and legged it.

On the last night in Perth, we had an end-of-tour barbecue. The last night of a tour is always funny. Everybody's a bit pissed off. Whether it's because they've had enough and can't wait to get home, or whether they don't want to go home, it's always a strange atmosphere, and for this reason most of our end-of-tour parties were a bit sour.

Not that that would ever stop us. Our Perth motel was right on the beach and had an open area for barbecuing, so we commandeered it, bought a load of stuff from the supermarket and away we went.

Everyone started drinking early doors. Me and Ozzy were cooking prawns on the BBQ. Then it started to go a bit tits-up. The whole crew were pissed as arseholes, badly drunk. Everyone was milling around in Steve and Gillian's room on the ground floor, and Steve was off his face. When he was drunk he had a habit of pretending to be a black dude, which was really strange, because he was usually dead quiet. But when he was drunk: 'I'm the black dude now. I'm the geezer from the Bronx. I'm a pimp.' What's more, he was playing this game where he had a carving knife in each hand and was jumping at the glass patio windows of the room and bouncing off.

Meanwhile, Gillian had been giggling with a couple of the roadies, loads of doe-eyes and looking under her fringe and fluttering her eyelashes in a way that always reminded me of Princess Diana.

Next thing I knew, she'd disappeared. I thought, *Uh oh! What's going on here?*

Then, to cut a long story short, I ended up finding her in another party, looking sheepish.

'What's going on here then, eh?' I said, 'Steve's down there, waving two carving knives about, jumping into the fucking window. Gillian, you'd better get down there and sort him out.' And she stood up in her long maxi dress, and nearly fell arse over tit – almost as though her ankles were tied together.

It calmed down a little after that, and I stopped drinking. I felt a bit weird. Later, when I went to bed, I just started throwing up and it was like Mount Vesuvius. I was so ill I couldn't move. It was coming out with such force that it burned my throat and sinuses.

I was in agony. I never made it out of the bathroom all night. I couldn't even cry for help. I've never had food poisoning like that before or since.

The next day the doctor came. 'Yeah, yeah, you've got food poisoning – you had a barbie or something? Funnily enough, Mr Liddle has the same thing ...'

Our resident lighting genius, Andrew Liddle, had joined us straight from the theatre at eighteen, and fitted in very well. Now in his second year, he was as mad as a hatter, but became a great mate.

Rob was having kittens. 'How are we going to get these two home?' The answer came when they took us to the airport, flat on our backs in the van, wheeled us in on a trolley to check-in, where the British Airways guy takes one look and says, 'They can't travel like that, they're too poorly.'

And Rob going, 'Oh God, when's the next flight?'

'In a week.'

I looked at Liddle and even at death's door you could see he was thinking the same thing as me, which was: *Result! Another week in Perth!*

'Well, let me have a word with the captain and see what I can do for you,' said the check-in bloke, and he only got us on the bloody plane, the bastard. So weak we were just about holding each other up, just. Stumbling along the plane. The flight was full apart from two rows of seats and they put Liddle in the middle of one and me in the middle of the other, and we got to fly all the way back to England with five seats each to ourselves. Magic!

I would have loved that extra week. What a beautiful place Perth is. On the way home we stopped in Bangkok for nine hours and every one was gagging to get to the city to see what it was like.

By now I was feeling well enough for some sight-seeing. We left the airport and got some dodgy taxis into the centre, but instead of taking us to the city, the driver took us to his brother's bar, which was full of girls, very attentive girls. The roadies loved it. Needless to say, it wasn't long before two of them disappeared with a pair of girls. When they reappeared they were a little crestfallen that they had to pay, and one of them said, 'I thought they fancied us.'

On that I note we went for a walk round the local area and soon attracted a large crowd, or rather Gillian did. I don't think they had ever seen someone so white before, especially so Gothic. Her and Steve couldn't shake off the hundreds of admirers and when Gillian started to get upset they had to go back to the bar.

Back in the safety of the airport we boarded and settled down, only to be rudely awoken by screams coming from the toilet in the plane. On investigation it was one of our crew; the other roadies had told him that if he poured aftershave down his Jap's eye he wouldn't get a dose, and then sat back to enjoy the show. And what a show it was. This guy was in agony for the whole trip.

In the New Year I heard a shocking story. It seems the other roadie had gone home and settled down with his missus for a lovely Christmas. On waking on Christmas Day he had tried to sneak out of bed to get her presents, but it seemed she had hold of his knob and wouldn't let go. In the end he had to put the light on and actually realised his knob was stuck to the bedsheets by a bright-yellow discharge that had dried in the night.

She looked at him. He looked at her, grimacing, 'Merry Christmas.'

Turns out he had a strain of tropical gonorrhoea that took three months to get rid of. Needless to say, she didn't like her present that year.

'What did she get you?' I asked.

'You won't believe it . . .' he said. 'Aftershave.'

POWER, CORRUPTION & LIES TRACK BY TRACK

'Age of Consent': 5.13

I've lost you, I've lost you, I've lost you, I've lost you …

The recorded version is different to the live version. In those days it was too difficult to change the song once it was recorded and on tape. A great bassline, even if I say so myself, changing subtly throughout. Barney's plaintive vocal reaching and searching for the key gives it a lovely edge. A keyboard low bass note overdub on the chords gives it strength. Beautiful guitar motifs, both lead and rhythm. The long drop-down to build tension leads to one of Barney's best melancholic string endings, Steve's syndrum dropdown being the first of our many dub breaks to come, one of our greatest 'live' songs. The title came from a *Sunday Times* article about children having sex younger and younger, leading to a call for a reduction in the 'Age of Consent', something, as a father, I am completely against.

'We All Stand': 5.13

Three miles to go, we've got three miles to go …

A more complete contrast is hard to imagine. For the low line, my first use of a fretless bass, with an overdubbed six-string playing a chord-like figure. It would be sequenced 'live'. The use of mainly 'real' instrumentation, piano, oboe etc., completes the change in feel, unusual so early in a record. Steve obviously draws from 'The Sunshine Valley Dance Band' for the jazzy drums. A story of isolation and fear in war, Barney being quite fixated on soldiers and warfare early in our career, a theme that would recur many times.

'The Village': 4.36

Our love is like the flowers, the rain, the sea and the hours …

Our first sequenced love song, the story of a doomed relationship, and we wax very poetic. A magnificent hybrid song, of rock and dance (soon to be our speciality). Sometimes delivered very aggressively, belying its pop song appearance. The name came from the cult TV show *The Prisoner* starring Patrick McGoohan.

'5.8.6. Intro': 1.44

A wonderful piece of music: mean, moody and magnificent. Originating from hearing a slowed-down version of the main song and deciding to overdub the bass and keyboards to form an intro. Mistakenly labelled as part of the main song.

'5.8.6.': 5.44

Heard you calling, yes, I heard you calling …

Our earlier dispute over the bass guitar seemed to have been forgotten for the LP version, with Barney enthusiastically helping me do a disco number on the bass guitar. A veritable *tour de force* of great keyboard overdubs and sounds, and Steve works very hard on both drum machine, Simmons SDSV and 'live' drum overdubs, conjuring up a fantastic atmosphere.

'Your Silent Face': 7.31

A thought that never changes remains a stupid lie …

Another sequencer *tour de force* by Barney, ripped off a Kraftwerk tune, which I cannot remember for the life of me, hence the working title 'K.W.1' (at least we were honest). For the vocal line Barney suggested using the bass riff from a mistake I had made on another song. He'd seen a live video of a Toronto gig where I had played the wrong riff to a song, but he loved it. Seeking out the video, sure enough it was great, and became the vocal line (that acid seemed to really make him appreciate me more; I must try some). The use of the traditional oboe sample perfectly balances the ultra-modern sound of the synthesisers.

'Ultraviolence': 4.52

Who felt those cold hands …

Written with the working title 'Who Killed My Father', this track has a real Joy Division feel to it, great bass riffs. The melody in the middle was written on the fretless and is sort of in between two notes, so live it never sounded as good as it does on the record. Great Simmons sounds by Steve.

A simple and effective song, dark and mysterious. The lyrics are obtuse and exact. Perfect.

'Ecstasy': 4.26

Touch my soul …

What I used to love about 'old' New Order was the willingness to experiment. This instrumental was only ever meant to be just that, an instrumental. Later, if Barney couldn't get a vocal the track would be changed, sometimes out of all recognition, to facilitate the vocal, robbing us of great moments like these, which to me speak more than a thousand lyrics ever could. A great dance tune. Top drum riff and melodies.

'Leave Me Alone': 4.40

A thousand islands in the sea …

One of my favourite tracks of our career.

An achingly melancholic bass riff, which summed up perfectly the book I was reading at the time, *Tender Is the Night* by F. Scott Fitzgerald. The recording lasted the full length of the book and as the track built with Barney's beautiful guitar lines taking it to perfection, my heart was ripped asunder as the marriage of Dick and Nicole Diver disintegrated. The will-he-won't-he affair with Rosemary had me shouting, 'No! No! No!' in my seat. His problems with alcohol would even echo my own in later life. An 80-millisecond delay on the snare drum makes the track swing gloriously.

TIMELINE THREE
JANUARY–DECEMBER 1982

© Marc Tilli

4 January 1982

New Order appear on BBC2 Arts programme *Riverside* to perform 'Chosen Time', 'Temptation', 'Procession', 'Hurt' (instrumental), 'Senses', 'Denial' and 'In a Lonely Place'. Only the first two are broadcast.

> 'January 4th is Barney's birthday. My wife always says to me, "It's sad how you remember that. You're obsessed." Anyway, we turned up to the Riverside and were amazed to find that Jimmy Pursey from Sham 69 was dancing in a ballet there.'

5–10 January 1982

The band record 'Temptation' and 'Hurt'/'Cramp' – the first track to feature a sequencer.

> 'In Advision was a video edit suite. Me and Dave Pils were always rooting around and managed to power up the edit suite. Lo and behold we got the whole bloody lot up and running. Luckily for us they were editing a *Playboy* video, so me and Dave sat there watching all these girls come on and introduce themselves and then strip off – it was very soft porn, don't worry. Then this one girl comes on and says, "Hi, I'm Chenille from Essex." I could see Dave stiffen (body language, I mean), staring intently. I said, "You OK, Dave?" He had gone white. "Dave?" He turned to me and said, "Fucking hell, that's my girlfriend!" and ran out. We didn't see him for ages. Turns out they'd just met, had a couple of dates, and she'd never mentioned being an, "ahem", glamour model. How weird is that?'
>
> 'I've heard that you're supposed to be able to listen to the seven-inch and twelve-inch versions of "Temptation" together, put them together to make one big song, but that's a myth.'

22 January 1982

New Order play the North London Polytechnic, supported by Stockholm Monsters.

'Apparently, with the help of Stockholm Monsters, I stopped a fight but laid out a bloke who later went on to become a member of The Men They Couldn't Hang. The gigs were rough in those days. I'm sure he deserved it.'

23 January 1982

New Order play the Imperial Cinema, Birmingham, supported by Stockholm Monsters.

'Our first meeting with Les Johnson, who would go on to promote many of our gigs and later manage the Wonder Stuff. A truly nice bloke.'

26 February 1982

New Order play Trinity Hall, Bristol, supported by the Wake (which at this point includes Bobby Gillespie on bass).

'Trinity Hall was in a pretty wild part of Bristol, with a large Rasta community. There was always a very "special" atmosphere at these shows.'

3 March 1982

New Order play the Blue Note, Derby, supported by Stockholm Monsters. At this gig the band first meet Paul Mason, the manager of the Blue Note, who would later manage the Haçienda.

'Rhodesie, the Monsters' guitarist, was nuts. He had a Ferrari in the front room of his house. He'd nicked it and didn't know what to do with it, so he knocked down the wall of his council house, pushed the Ferrari in, bricked it back up and then him and his missus used to sit in it and eat their tea watching the telly through the windscreen.'

5 March 1982

New Order play Sir Francis Xavier Hall, Dublin. This is followed by a terrible radio interview with Dave Fanning.

> **'When we got there, Dave was very, very serious and we reacted accordingly, becoming a tad annoying to say the least, bloody-minded, giving him the sullen one-word-answer treatment and generally taking the piss and acting up, our punk credentials right to the fore.'**

9 March 1982

New Order play Tiffany's, Leeds, supported by the Thunder Boys.

10 March 1982

New Order play Tower Cinema, Hull, supported by the Things.

11 March 1982

New Order play Soul Kitchen at the Mayfair Suite, Newcastle, supported by the Wake.

16 March 1982

Martin Hannett issues a High Court writ against FCL. It gets its own catalogue number: FAC61.

8 April 1982

New Order play Glazenzaal, Rotterdam, Netherlands, supported by Stockholm Monsters.

> **'. . . and I almost died!'**

9 April 1982

New Order play Meervaart, Amsterdam, Netherlands, supported by Stockholm Monsters.

10 April 1982

New Order play Stokvishal, Arnhem, Netherlands, supported by Stockholm Monsters.

11 April 1982

New Order play Muziekcentrum, Utrecht, Netherlands, supported by Stockholm Monsters.

12 April 1982

New Order play Staargebouw, Maastricht, Netherlands, supported by Stockholm Monsters.

14 April 1982

New Order play Lido, Leuven, Belgium, supported by Stockholm Monsters.

15 April 1982

New Order play L' Ancienne Belgique, Brussels, Belgium, supported by Stockholm Monsters.

17 April 1982

New Order play Le Palace, Paris, supported by Stockholm Monsters.

> **'For some strange reason New Order never had a good gig in Paris, right up until 2000. Tonight was no different. Parisians in general can be a very tough audience and on this occasion were far from impressed. There was virtually a dead silence between**

songs and as one particular song died, a voice in the audience cried out, "Ay!" We all looked round and the guy carried on, saying, "Ze zound, she is a sheet!" We were speechless.'

19 April 1982

New Order: 'Temptation'
(FAC 63)

Seven-inch track list:
'Temptation' 5.14
'Hurt'/'Cramp' 4.42

Run-out groove one: *Try listening to the Twelve-inch …*
Run-out groove two: … *now listen to the Seven-inch*

Twelve-inch track list:
'Temptation' 7.26
'Hurt'/'Cramp' 8.13

Run-out groove one: *What do you think?*
Run-out groove two: *Thought so …*

Recorded at Strawberry Studios, Stockport, Manchester.
Mixed at Advision Studios, London.
Engineered by Pete Woolliscroft.
Produced by New Order.
Designed by Peter Saville.
Entered UK chart on 22 May 1982, remaining in the charts for 7 weeks, its peak position was number 29.

The first New Order recording made without Martin Hannett. About fifty seconds into the twelve-inch version you can hear someone screaming.

21 May 1982

The Haçienda opens.

'What happened then was, anybody you met who you became friendly with, and most of the groups on Factory, would end up working there; 52nd Street all worked at the Haçienda, as did Stockholm Monsters, as well as any City fans Rob met, so our whole world became one big family.'

24 May 1982

New Order play Pennies, Norwich, supported by 52nd Street and the Flamingos.

'A very small gig, which we will have done just for fun. Interestingly, we played "The Passenger" by Iggy Pop as an instrumental. That was 52nd Street's first support gig. Barney would go on to produce them, with his co-producer Donald Johnson from A Certain Ratio. Lovely guy, Donald, very broad shoulders.'

25 May 1982

New Order play Kilburn National Ballroom, supported by 52nd Street and Send No Flowers.

1 June 1982

A second John Peel session is broadcast, recorded not at Maida Vale but at Revolution Studios in Cheadle, Manchester.

John Peel track list:

'Turn the Heater On'	5.00
'We All Stand'	5.15
'Too Late'	3.35
'5.8.6.'	6.05

'"Turn the Heater On" was Ian Curtis's favourite reggae song, where he got the idea for using a melodica. If you listen to "Too Late", Barney's only playing guitar at the end, after he's stopped singing. That became the whole template for the band.'

5 June 1982

New Order play Provinssirock Festival, Seinäjoki, Finland.

16 June 1982

New Order play Tenax, Florence, Italy.

> **'The wonderful Italian tour, never to be repeated.'**

17 June 1982

New Order play Piper, Rome, Italy.

18 June 1982

New Order play Tur Sports Centre, Taranto, Italy.

21 June 1982

New Order play Palasport, Bologna, Italy.

22 June 1982

New Order play Rolling Stone, Milan, Italy.

> **'This gig was famously captured for a bootleg album. The Sparks cover was done for fun, the pulses being very much like "Temptation", and hurriedly programmed by a mischievous Barney, obviously enjoying himself. Wonderful to hear Ozzy going mad, "dubbing" it up heavily with a Roland "555" Space Echo we used. Rob loved it when he did that. Sounds like I got pissed off after ten minutes by launching into "Ceremony" then leaving.'**

26 June 1982

New Order play the Haçienda, supported by Swamp Children.

'Incidentally we never got paid for playing here. Rob always convinced us to put the money straight back in the Haçienda coffers.'

18 August 1982

Joy Division: *'Here Are the Young Men'*
(FACT 37)
A Factory records video.

30 August 1982

New Order play the Venue, Blackpool, a gig promoted by label mates Section 25, supported by them and Kevin Hewick.

11 September 1982

New Order play Futurama Four, Queensferry Leisure Centre, Deeside.

19 September 1982

New Order play Sporting Arena, Athens, a three-day festival including the Birthday Party and the Fall.

'An apple a day does not keep the doctor away.'

October and November 1982

New Order are at Britannia Row recording *Power, Corruption & Lies* and 'Blue Monday'.

15 November 1982

Mixing of 'Murder' and 'Leave Me Alone'.

16 November 1982

Mixing of 'Only the Lonely' (working title for 'Ecstasy') and 'We All Stand'.

17 November 1982

Mixing of 'We All Stand' (continued), 'The Village' and 'KW1' (working title for 'Your Silent Face').

18 November 1982

Mixing of 'Age of Consent' and '5.8.6.'.

November 1982

New Order EP
(Factus 8)

Twelve-inch track list:

'Temptation'	8.47
'Hurt'/'Cramp'	8.03
'Everything's Gone Green'	5.30
'Procession'	4.27
'Mesh'	3.02

Run-out groove one: *A brave New World …*
Run-out groove two: *… a brave New Order!*

Designed by Peter Saville
Painting by M. J. Ladly (Martha Ladly of Martha and the Muffins, and Peter Saville's girlfriend at the time).

> **'A compilation of early New Order singles especially for the American market.**
>
> **'We did not know anything about this. I think Tony Wilson collated it in an arrangement with Rough Trade America, a sort of New Order sampler.'**

25 November 1982

New Order play Palais Theatre, Melbourne, Australia.

27 November 1982

New Order play the Seaview Ballroom, Melbourne, Australia.

29 November 1982

New Order play Capitol Theatre, Sydney.

> **'There is some debate as to whether this gig happened. But I seem to remember us agreeing to do an encore with John Cooper Clarke playing 'Lady Godiva's Operation' by the Velvet Underground, badly as I recall. Not that John would have noticed.'**

3–4 December 1982

New Order play Mainstreet, Auckland, New Zealand.

> **'Back then New Zealand looked like a small town, full of old English cars, Morris Oxfords and 1000s. It actually looked like Altrincham. It was a really strange place.**
>
> **'If you want to hear how difficult it was to get our equipment to work then listen to the tape of this gig. Our rendition of "K.W.1" is actually painful. The drum machine starts wrong, the synth is out of tune, out of time, and the acoustic players don't do much better. It just sums up aurally what we were trying to achieve and how easily it could go wrong. It would drive us all insane nearly every night. But it took balls . . . I thank you all.'**

4 December 1982

Feature Mist

Track list:
'Prime 5.8.6. (pt 1)'
'Prime 5.8.6. (pt 2)'

Between 1982 and 1986 Jon Wozencroft's audio-visual outfit Touch released a series of 'cassette magazines', the first of which, *Feature Mist,* included original music from New Order, Simple Minds, Tuxedomoon, Soliman Gamil, the Death and Beauty Foundation, Flesh, Eric Random and Shostakovitch, alongside excerpts from an interview with Robert Wyatt and other works from Vladimir Mayakovsky and Hans Eisler.

6 December 1982

New Order play Victoria University, Wellington, New Zealand.

8 December 1982

New Order play Hillsborough Hotel, Christchurch, New Zealand.

10 December 1982

New Order play Selinas Hotel, Sydney, Australia.

11 December 1982

New Order play Manly Vale Hotel, Sydney, Australia.

14 December 1982

New Order play Old Melbourne Hotel, Perth, Australia.

24 December 1982

New Order: 'Merry Xmas from the Haçienda'
(FAC 51B Flexidisc)

Seven-inch track list:

'Rocking Carol' (We Will Rock You)	3.33
'Ode to Joy'	3.55

These two songs were part of the *Granada Reports* TV programme (background music only) broadcast on 23 December 1981. Released in a limited edition of 4,400.

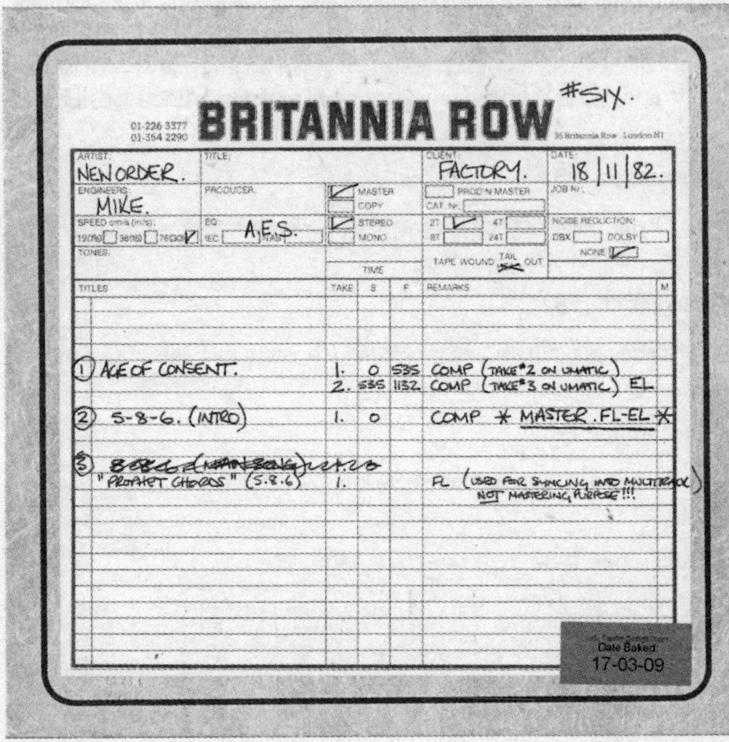

#SIX.

01-226 3377
01-354 2290
BRITANNIA ROW
36 Britannia Row · London N1

ARTIST: NEW ORDER. | TITLE: | CLIENT: FACTORY. | DATE: 18 | 11 | 82.

ENGINEERS: MIKE. | PRODUCER: | [✓] MASTER [ ] COPY | [ ] PROD'N MASTER | CAT. Nr. | JOB Nr.:

SPEED cm/s (in/s): 19(7½) [ ] 38(15) [ ] 76(30) [✓] | EQ: IEC [ ] A.E.S. NAB [ ] | [✓] STEREO [ ] MONO | 2T [✓] 4T [ ] 8T [ ] 24T [ ] | NOISE REDUCTION: DBX [ ] DOLBY [ ] NONE [✓]

TONES: | TIME | TAPE WOUND TAIL ~~HEAD~~ OUT

TITLES	TAKE	S	F	REMARKS	M
① AGE OF CONSENT.	1.	0	535	COMP (TAKE #2 ON UMATIC)	
	2.	535	1132	COMP (TAKE #3 ON UMATIC) EL	
② 5-8-6. (INTRO)	1.	0		COMP * MASTER. FL-EL *	
③ ~~[illegible] (MAIN SONG) [illegible]~~ "PROPHET CHORDS" (5.8.6)	1.			FL (USED FOR SYNCING INTO MULTITRACK) NOT MASTERING PURPOSE!!!	

Date Baked:
17-03-09

TEN BEST HOTELS IN THE WORLD (ACTUALLY, ELEVEN)

1. Sunset Marquis, Hollywood
2. Hotel Adlon, Berlin
3. Midland Hotel, Manchester
4. W Santiago, Chile
5. Zero 1, Montreal
6. Four Points, Mexico City
7. Farmer's Daughter, Los Angeles
8. The Landmark, London
9. Faena, Buenos Aires
10. Hyatt on Sunset (the Riot House)
11. Delano, Miami

'Arthur was fucking bonkers ... I loved him.'

It was Michael Shamberg's idea to record with producer Arthur Baker in 1983. Initially he approached Arthur for a remix of '5.8.6.' or 'Blue Monday', but Arthur declined in favour of writing something new.

'Arthur is changing the world! Like you!' Michael yelled at Rob. 'You should do a song together.'

New Order were making what you might call white dance music, but Arthur Baker, with Afrika Bambaataa and Planet Patrol, was making much more, dare we say, dark, dance music, a lot funkier. He was pioneering the use of the Roland 808 drum machine, and we didn't have one of those yet, but we really liked the sound of it; we were still using the Oberheim DMX. He was also using sequencers in a similar fashion, so there was a big crossover, a lot of common ground, and I could see why Michael, Rob and the others were dead excited about it.

Me?

I'd rather have stayed at home and rocked. I was very set in my ways when I was young. We'd written *Power, Corruption & Lies*, *Movement*, *Closer* and *Unknown Pleasures* all on our own, why did we need anybody else?

What's more, we didn't have any new material and we had never before done anything with no song idea, completely unprepared.

Through Michael, Arthur suggested we start work at Fred Zarr's studio in Brooklyn, and get a track going. This was the first time we'd ever done anything like this, we simply didn't know what to do, and we were scared. We presumed that Arthur would be there with us and we could do our usual thing of jamming while he picked out the bits he liked – our idea of 'getting a track going' was Arthur fulfilling the all-important Ian Curtis role.

We got to New York, went in the studio. No Arthur. He was busy finishing off a track with another English band, Freeez, the track being 'I.O.U.', which was to become a huge hit for him.

OK, fine. So we did what we always did when we wrote. We jammed. We jammed and we jammed and we jammed and we jammed, and the tower of tapes was getting higher and higher and higher and higher, and all the time we were wondering when Arthur was going to arrive so he could listen to them. *Poor bastard*, we thought.

For two or three days we did that, until at last he turned up, breezing in like a huge grizzly bear, long dark hair, long beard, every inch the New Yawker he is.

Now, I know Arthur well, still do, and he's never changed from that day to this. The only difference is that he now has a bit more grey in his hair, but otherwise he's the same larger-than-life character he's always been, a wonderful guy. I love him to death.

So he comes in, takes over. 'How's it going, man? How's it going? I'm Arthur, Arthur Baker. What's happening? What have you got for me?'

Proud as punch, we pointed at our tower of tapes.

He looked at it. And the bit of him you could still see between the beard and the hair went pale as he looked at these hours and hours of New Order jam tapes – at which point it became clear that our idea of 'getting a track together' and his idea of 'getting a track together' were two entirely different things. No doubt he was as 'Confused' as we were, ha! But you had to hand it to him. He was very decisive. Straight away he said, 'Right, OK, forget that. We'll go straight in the studio and we'll write something there.'

So that's what we did. And it was wild.

The thing was that in those days all the studios in America were running twenty-four hours a day, especially in New York, and were booked solid in eight-hour sessions. So we'd literally be trooping up the stairs while a bunch of guys, in our case James Brown, were coming down having just finished their session. Once inside, it was just Arthur and his engineer, who had the biggest eyes I've ever seen – huge, bulging, scary eyes, they were.

What I soon realised about Arthur was that the way he recorded and produced was very 'punky'. He'd sit at the desk and everything would be zero, infinity at unity level.

But two minutes later it was all up to full. It was like him putting his foot down in a car and not stopping for anything. He didn't seem to know what he was doing, but he was just going to do it anyway. He was really enjoying himself and it was infectious.

Then, when Arthur ran out of steam, he'd be sitting there sweating like he'd just run a marathon, and the engineer would back everything down again. So scary eyes had the job of turning it all down when it got so massively distorted that you couldn't hear anything. Then Arthur would start again, searching for the perfect mix.

To put it another way, Arthur was fucking bonkers.

Tell you who wasn't so keen, though: Steve. Arthur had his TR808 drum machine going and Steve couldn't get near it. It was like Arthur had sharpened elbows keeping him off that thing, meaning that Steve – the band's drummer – didn't get a look-in, didn't get to play any of the drums on 'Confusion'. Arthur did the lot.

Steve was really, really upset about it and even slunk off at one point. But of course, the devil in me was going, 'Ha! Well now you know what it was like for me when you three did '5.8.6.', y'twat!' It really is dog eat dog in a group.

Meantime, Arthur was working out great for me. I was in the studio playing with all the gear they had in there – loads of keyboards, set-ups for both bass and guitar, all of it live and plugged in – and I was playing a sort of one-fingered bassline that Arthur heard and went, 'That's good, that's good. Give me that, give me that.'

He took it off me, programmed it and, lo and behold, it became the bassline to 'Confusion'.

The next minute you know we've got this bass synth going and Arthur was doing loads and loads of different rhythms on the 808. I played a melody line on the keyboard and he took that as well and programmed it up, then Bernard got some more keyboard lines, using some as ideas for the vocal. Then, at Arthur's insistence, we all chanted 'Confusion' then, 'ratatatatatatatta hey!' with great gusto, even Rob. Then me and Bernard swapped so I played guitar on the track and he played bass. Then I added another 'Hooky bassline' on at the end, again at Arthur's absolute insistence, with him saying, 'That's New Order to me, man!' And that was it.

That was 'Confusion'.

It had bags of me on it. It was fantastic. I was delighted. It was fun working with other people. Who'd have thought it?

When he finished recording for the night, Arthur would take a tape over to a club called the Fun House, where they had a tape machine, so, as well as playing records, the DJs could play studio mixes. What him and the club's resident DJ John 'Jellybean' Benitez used to do was sneak early mixes of their production work into the set to gauge the effect it had on the crowd. If it worked and people dug it, they knew they were on to something. If it didn't work, and everyone started drifting off, they knew the track needed attention.

He did it with 'Confusion', and by all accounts it tore the roof off. After that we all agreed – even Steve – that the recording had been a great success.

We'd done well with 'Confusion' and Arthur wanted to do one more track. One night he was on his way to the studio and saw the words 'Thieves Like Us' sprayed on a wall in Brooklyn, which he really liked as a title. We had an eight-bar idea but we never got the time to work on it because 'Confusion' took so long. So 'Thieves Like Us' would have to wait for another time.

We ended up staying in New York for about three weeks – including the recording. We were in the Iroquois again and even had our own rooms, no crew with us this time, you see, which was great because I was back to having a full-on love affair with Miss Polsky, living it up at Danceteria and Hurrah every night, straight in, no queue, free drinks tickets once we got inside, cock of the walk.

Then, next thing you knew, it snowed. Three feet of snow in Manhattan and the whole city ground to a halt. The place was like a surreal alien landscape undisturbed by anything that normally moved. It was great. You just slipped your way round Manhattan from coffee shop to hotel to nightclub. We were marooned, with Arthur, Michael and Ruth keeping us entertained, living it up every night and sleeping during the day.

Interestingly, in the Red Flame on 44th Street (our coffee shop of choice) we had noticed something strange was happening to our bills. We would all ask for separate bills and they would often read $4.38 or $5.15 but when we went to pay it would be $5.38 and then $6.15. We were very puzzled but, being English, with that famous reserve, it took us a while to work up the courage to mention to the girl on the till. It fell to Barney, tight-arse being the most perturbed.

'Excuse me, miss, there seems to be a mistake on the bill. It's for a dollar more.' She looked him up and down and said, 'Listen, you guys are so mean we've taken to putting our tips on your bill. OK? There ain't no way you miserable limeys are gonna pay it otherwise, is there?' she snarled.

We had to agree there. Ah, those infamous cultural differences.

I remember being taken to an Afrika Bambaataa gig somewhere on Times Square and it went off with all the gangs fighting inside, a really heavy scene, and we were going, 'Fucking hell, this is a bit heavy, Arthur,' and he went, 'Oh man, it's always like this. This is what it's like. This is New York.' Strangely, something else we would be enjoying, against our will, in the Haçienda very soon.

It was a great time and a wonderful place to be. The atmosphere was fantastic.

Back on tour in Sweden that February, our Salford Van Hire Transit van developed a fault. I couldn't figure out what it was. The clutch linkage seemed broken, but it was beyond my expertise. It needed to go into the garage. We were staying in a very strange guesthouse on the outskirts of Stockholm, in what seemed like a sanatorium. We could see patients being walked round the grounds in their pyjamas. Barney wanted to do his laundry and asked to be taken to a launderette. I explained about going into town later to drop the van off at the garage and suggested he do it after that.

He was accompanied by Duncan Haysom, the New Order bootlegger he had taken under his wing, who was accompanying us on the tour. We set off and, as we got in the centre and the traffic got heavier, the van was becoming harder to drive. Rob was screaming at me to keep going, smoke everywhere. As we stopped at a set of lights Barney shouts, 'Look, a launderette,' and promptly opened the door to get out.

I was going, 'Eh! Eh! Don't get out. Do it after the van. We can't stop,' but he ignored me and disappeared, closely followed by Duncan.

Rob was screaming, 'Drive! Drive! We'll get him later.' So I did just that and we limped through the centre and on to the garage. We swapped the van but when we got back to the centre we couldn't find the launderette or either of the likely lads.

After a couple of hours we gave up. Remember, there were no mobiles or sat navs in those days, and began the long drive back to the sanatorium. There, Twinny said to me, 'Come on, let's jape Barney's room,' so we all went in his room, moved his bed out on the balcony, took out the light bulbs and suspended a bucket of water over the door for when they returned.

Then we went to Rob's room next door to wait. Five hours later and it was going dark and still no sign of them. Then it struck us we were in the middle of nowhere, they didn't speak Swedish, how the hell were they going to get back?

Another couple of hours passed and a cry went up, 'They're here!' We heard them come up the stairs, gripped by excitement. As they went in their room we heard the splash of the bucket falling, closely followed by, 'You bastards.'

Then Rob's door was kicked open and with a blood-curdling scream Barney dived full length, and landed on Rob with his hands round his throat. Oops, we didn't bargain for this. Rob kicked him to the opposite wall, next to the sink, where Barney slid to the floor. Still screaming, he reached over and grabbed a big bar of soap off the basin, took a massive bite then spat it out and sat on the floor blowing bubbles.

I turned to Twinny and said, 'Let's leave these two lovers alone, eh?'

Turned out him and Duncan had ended up getting a train from Stockholm then walking for hours to the sanatorium. I have to say his clothes were immaculate and he smelled and looked lovely.

The next day we found an open-air swimming pool that was full of topless women.

What a lovely afternoon. A rather dishevelled-looking English group enjoyed an afternoon's swimming and sunbathing. Even Barney cheered up. Although the strange sight of Steve and Gillian, both dressed head to toe in black, sat on the terrace in the sunshine with their cases like two out-of-place bats, will live with me forever.

We returned home, tired and happy, for the release of 'Blue Monday'.

It came out without much fanfare. No promotion by us at all. Radio I wouldn't consider it. At nearly eight minutes and in twelve-inch format only, they wouldn't even listen. It was just too long.

'Cut it down to three minutes,' they said, 'and we'll think about it.'

'Piss off!' we said.

We were happy to try anything in those days. For example, when it came to mastering 'Blue Monday' we took our 1610 U-matic cassette to Strawberry Mastering Studios in Victoria, where we told the engineer, Ravi, that we wanted it to sound like 'Cocaine' by Dillinger. Ian loved that track – we all did – especially the sweet distortion on it. 'That's how we want it to sound, all distorted like that,' was what we told Ravi, who did everything he could to persuade us otherwise. Put it this way, there was quite a lively atmosphere that day. And what do you know? It sounded shite. Meanwhile, Ravi had brought the fader up too late on the twelve-inch version and missed off the first drumbeat. Being a democratic organisation, we took a vote on whether the mistake should stay and the 'Yes' vote prevailed, which is why the run-out grooves are 'Outvoted' and 'Fac 73 1A'.

Incidentally, both 'Blue Monday' and the album were pressed at MVS (Record Pressing Ltd) in Islington. Even though Factory had a stake in MVS they were still in debt to them, and financing the pressing was a typically cap-in-hand affair.

But we did it. 'Blue Monday' came out, and at first the only plaudits we received were via stories told to us about other bands. Such as, Kraftwerk being so impressed with the song that they turned up at Britannia Row to record *Tour De France* because they wanted to achieve the same sound we'd got on 'Blue Monday', even going to the lengths of booking Mike Johnson as engineer. They took one look at the 60s décor and equipment, turned on their heels and left. They didn't believe we could have recorded it there. They even accused Mike of lying.

The other story I heard was about the Eurythmics being in a cab on the way home from the studio, having just finished their new album. On hearing 'Blue Monday' on the radio, Dave Stewart ordered the taxi driver to pull over, then listened very carefully to the whole track. Putting his head in his hands, he ordered the taxi back back to the studio saying, 'Oh God. We're going to have to start it all again.'

Neil Tennant also tells a story in the *The New Order Story* about hearing 'Blue Monday' for the first time and it breaking his heart, it being the very track he wanted the Pet Shop Boys to make: '"I'm Keeping My Fingers Crossed", it was called,' he said. Too late, Neil.

We loved the idea of not compromising, of being told that it was commercial suicide to release records like that. Tony and Rob were right behind us. When we were informed that it had no chance in the charts or radio play anywhere in the world we just laughed. But exactly the opposite happened: it reached number 12 in the UK charts on 19 March 1983 and descended quickly, but stayed in the top 100 for another seventeen weeks.

Otherwise, not too much of a splash. (Although in 1998 an American metal band called Orgy had such a huge hit with it that we were sent awards which said: Congratulations on writing 'the most played song of the year on US radio'.)

It did well among our new fans, as we'd hoped, but staunch Joy Division fans were a bit mystified, calling it too much of a change in direction. There was some international chart action, but it wasn't really what you'd call a big hit anywhere.

But we did get asked to play on *Top of the Pops*. Well, I say play, more mime in fact, and we did not mime so we said no. We will only play live.

They said no.

They asked again the next week, same reply both ways.

Then they asked a third time and said yes, you can play live. We were delighted. Regardless of what most musicians say, *Top of the Pops* in England was pretty much the Holy Grail. Everybody watched it, all the people that mattered, your mates and your family. We were hoping to be like the Sex Pistols Mk II and blow everyone away.

It didn't work out like that.

For *Top of the Pops* you had to be there at eight o'clock in the morning to set up your gear, and then you had to break for lunch and do an afternoon soundcheck before the first rehearsal.

It was a long day and it was particularly hard for us because, firstly, they weren't set up to do live sound, and secondly, the BBC crew, in true television fashion, were a right bunch of jobsworths. A group like us arrives, anti-miming, and you could see their faces drop, like, 'Oh bloody hell, look what the cat's dragged in,' but we were at our ornery, cantankerous young worst and we felt miming was wrong, very wrong, and we weren't about to surrender our principles to anyone, and that's why we were playing live. (Surrendering our principles came later, when, after years of holding our noses in the air and saying, 'Keep music live,' we got offered to do a broadcast in San Remo, with a guaranteed audience of fifty million. 'But you can only do it if you mime,' they told us, and we went, 'Oh well, shall we mime then? Does it matter, really?' And we did. We got pissed up, had a right laugh, mimed, made a complete bollocks of it and nobody noticed and nobody cared. Least of all us.)

Either way, we were doing it live and, on the plus side, I looked good, because I was wearing a new shirt. A new shirt for me, that was. I'd found it in the dressing room beforehand, last week's band must have left it – top. But on the minus side, as everyone who saw it then or has seen the YouTube clip since knows, it sounded bloody awful.

It's no secret that our single went down ten places in the charts the week after our performance, which was practically unheard of. A slot on *Top of the Pops* usually guaranteed you a ten-place increase up the charts. But we were delighted about the drop because we'd achieved our objective – the objective being to be as awkward and truculent as possible, to everyone. So what if the record went down and we didn't achieve anything apart from devilment? The important thing is to do what you do and believe in what you're doing and why you're doing it.

The great thing about playing *Top of the Pops* – apart from the subsidised canteen – was that you got paid for it, and you even got what they called porterage for supposedly carrying in your own instruments. Plus they sent you a cheque to your home address. They sent it to you personally rather than to the group so Rob couldn't get his hands on it.

We were still only on £100 a week. So that was mega.

What wasn't mega was going back to my mum's, full of myself, only to be greeted by her saying, 'How could you?' as she cuffed me round the head. 'How could you show me up in front of the neighbours?'

I went, 'What?'

She went, 'You were chewing, chewing on bloody *Top of the Pops*. I've never been so ashamed. What will the neighbours say?' And she wouldn't talk to me for weeks.

Top of the Pops aside, 'Blue Monday' went on to be our biggest-selling single ever, still is. Even so, it was never that special to us and, to be honest, I thought 'Thieves Like Us' was a much better song.

Besides which, I've got mixed feelings about 'Blue Monday' now. When you have a hit like that you start getting the kind of royalties that make it less important to keep working. You can sit there doing nothing and the money keeps rolling in. The success of the back catalogue means there's less pressure to come up with new wage-earners. There's artistic pressure, but no financial pressure.

When we bumped into Errol Brown of Hot Chocolate in Advision Studios in 1987 someone asked him if he was doing new material. 'My dear boy,' he said, 'why should I? I earn enough on the songs I've written.'

And eventually that made it particularly hard for me for two reasons:

first, I like to work. I like to be kept busy. Second, I'm shit with money. The other two were careful – in Barney's case, *very* careful. But not me. I throw it away like a man with eight arms. So in a way, 'Blue Monday' became another nail in the coffin.

The sleeve was magnificent. Peter Saville had come on a rare trip to the practice place in Cheetham Hill and had been intrigued by all our new equipment. As we very proudly showed him our new Emulator keyboard he was fascinated by the fact that the sounds were stored on these …

'Floppy disks?' he said. 'It looks like a little miniature LP sleeve!' he giggled. 'How cute.'

Should have been no surprise to us when he later presented his interpretation of it as the sleeve for the twelve-inch, the idea being to 'emulate' the disk. We had made remarkable use of the Emulator on 'Blue Monday' so it seemed very fitting.

There were many production problems to be sorted out in using the floppy disk design for a sleeve, though, the first being the cut-outs. There were three. To copy this for the sleeve each one had to be done separately by hand through a machine press, once for each hole. With an initial pressing of 50,000 copies, this became a considerable outlay of time and money. Next, we didn't want our name or any information about the song on the sleeve. The same way we acted in Joy Division, not even the song name.

Let the music speak for itself.

Peter was still very intrigued by this attitude and he came up with a great idea. He was fascinated by the data held on this little blank disk with no information on the surface but everything coded onto the disk. He liked the idea of coding the information onto his version of the disk, the record sleeve, using the tools of his trade, colours and ink. He came up with his infamous coloured alphabet, each colour representing a letter. This became a design puzzle for the fans. You could decipher the colours using the pinwheel code on the sleeve itself. All the information was there to read, once you worked it out. His own musical Enigma code.

The initial pressing soon sold out and a delighted Tony told us he'd ordered 100,000 more. We weren't that bothered … we had the rest of the United Kingdom to terrorise: Scotland and Ireland and Wales soon fell under our spell. Then it was back to America.

'OK, pizza'

Bands touring outside the United Kingdom were obliged to detail every item of their equipment on a document called a 'carnet', then pay the value of it upfront as a bond to HM Customs. The band's carnet would be stamped on each exit and entry point of the different countries on the tour, and when the band arrived back to Britain they presented the completed document and were refunded the money. If there were any mistakes on the form the bond was forfeit and prosecution considered. This was supposedly to stop the illegal importing of retail goods into America ...

As ever the tour got off to a shambolic start, not just me and Ruth splitting up and then her being on the whole tour with us. No, it being the US, the cock-up involved our gear.

Before we'd set off, I'd told Terry, who had by now been promoted to tour manager, that he had to be extra careful with the carnet because there was no margin for error. The problem was that if you made a mistake, like if you missed out a bit of equipment, or mislaid or had an item of equipment stolen, and you couldn't account for it when you were travelling, you risked getting your gear impounded and losing your money at home.

So anyway, me and Terry arrived at Atlanta airport to reclaim our gear after the flight, where we were dealing with this really sweet customs guy, who didn't want any hassle. Like us, he just wanted to authorise the carnet and get on with his day.

'What's your name, son?'

'Peter.'

'OK, Pizza,' he said to me,

'No. Peter,' said I.

'Pizza?' *One last try*, I thought.

'Peder!' says I again.

'Oh. Peter!

'OK, Peter, I just need to check it. What I'll do is pick one piece of equipment, you show it to me and we'll sign off the whole goddamn thing.'

I went, 'Right, OK,' thinking, *Great*. (So much better to do it this way than go through the entire ten pages of kit.) One piece of equipment – Wow! That was all he was going to pick in order to pass the whole bloody carnet.

He cast his eye down the list to pick something out at random.

'OK, Peter,' he said, 'why don't we try this Boss Dr Rye Thim?'

I swallowed. 'Er, Boss Dr Rhythm?'

'Yup,' he said, 'that's what it says here. The Boss Dr Rye Thim. Let's have a look at that, shall we – see if the good doctor is in?'

He chuckled at his own joke as Terry and I looked at each other, both knowing – a kind of telepathic knowing – that Terry had already dropped an enormous bollock. The Boss Dr Rhythm was the drum machine we used when we started in 1980, but we didn't use it any more. Not on tour anyway.

But Terry had forgotten to take it off the carnet from the last time we came to America. And now the fucking Dr Rhythm was in – in our practice room in Cheetham Hill with its feet up laughing its dogs off.

The customs guy looked at us expectantly, pen hovering over his clipboard. 'OK, Peter, have you got it so I can sign this?'

'Sure,' I said, 'I think I know where it is.'

Inwardly cursing, Terry and I started searching through the cases, eventually picking out an old ugly hand-painted black plug-board complete with inbuilt trip switch and a dirty long lead on it – literally the only thing in all of our cases without a brand name on it.

'Here!' I said. 'This is the Boss Dr Rhythm DR55!' producing it like a magician's assistant would, complete with arm flourish.

I looked at him, rictus grin, thinking inwardly, *Please believe me! Please believe me! It's a Boss Dr Rhythm. Please believe me!*

He looked back at me. I smiled harder. Then, at last, he seemed to decide.

'OK, Peter,' he said, and ticked it off.

You've never see two people move as fast as we did then. Packing all the gear in the van in record time, waving goodbye to the guy and wiping lines of nervous sweat off our brows, I turned to Terry and said, 'You fucking twat!'

A very, very lucky escape.

But the carnet escape wasn't the main reason I remember that particular American tour. It wasn't even what happened in Washington (which we'll come to). No, it was the girls.

That tour of America in 1983 was when New Order discovered groupies.

We'd heard that American women were mad for it, and we couldn't wait. But after the gig in Atlanta we all sat in anticipation of our post-gig bounty and nobody came in the dressing room at all. Nobody. Certainly none of the gorgeous girls we'd seen in the audience. What's wrong, Atlanta?

So anyway, the next gig, Austin, was a great gig, Club Foot, run by Kerry Jaggers, who would become one of our oldest friends and colleagues. It was a wonderful venue situated downtown near to our hotel. We'd been out into the audience and it was full of Texan women and they were gorgeous. Hundreds of them, there were. I thought I'd died and gone to heaven, I really did.

So anyway, after the gig, we were backstage rubbing our hands, twiddling our imaginary moustaches, all sat there going, 'Right, come on, Terry, get the headaches ready, this is going to be mega, this.'

HEADACHE or HEADACHES:

A drink or drinks containing:

- Pernod (LARGE amount)
- Orange juice (small amount)
- Sparkling white wine (LARGE amount)

Another name we considered was 'knicker-loosener' but we preferred to keep it subtle. I mean, you really couldn't shout, 'Terry! Do us another knicker-loosener, mate!' across the dressing room, could you? They'd think we were up to no good! Interestingly, you would be using the name again the next morning, as in, 'I've got a right fucking "headache" this morning! Never again!'

But again, not a soul came back.

Oh man, this was fucking ridiculous.

We said, 'Terry, you're the boss, get out there and find out what's happening.'

Five minutes later he returned with a hangdog look and, pulling at his wattle, said, 'Bad news, lads. Ruth's told security not to let *anyone* backstage.'

Fuck that. We weren't having that. Rob got hold of this security guy and pushed twenty dollars in his hand. 'Listen, mate, anyone, and I mean ANYONE, who wants to come backstage, you send them in, especially if they're female. All right?' Then I went to tell Ruth what I thought about her, too. I cringe now, thinking what a bastard I was. But no lie, within about twenty minutes, the dressing room was full of people, mainly female, and me and Barney were soon doing our best Terry-Thomas impressions, 'Hel–lo. Ding dong. What's your name? Let me get you a drink, my young lady, do you come from around here? Ooh, you're gorgeous!'

And that was it. That was our downfall sealed. From that moment on, every gig was full of girls backstage, loads and loads of them. You could literally take your pick. It was incredible.

American women. God love them. Back in England it still felt like you had to be engaged and have a bottom drawer (ask your mum) before you could have sex with the girl of your choice. English girls held on to their virtue like it was a prize. Which it is, of course. Now that I'm older, I realise that. But when you're twenty-seven, it's a pain in the arse, because all you want to do is get your end away.

Not in America. American girls were all, 'Hey, man, I love your accent, let's go out!' Their attitude to musicians, especially English musicians, was wonderful, so welcoming and friendly, and we were like pigs at a trough. Next thing you knew the crew were getting in on the act and everyone was just taters.

It was brilliant, completely at odds with our dour, arty image, but still brilliant.

It was at Austin that I met a girl wearing a Soviet red banner flag as a dress. She was a schoolteacher – we used to attract a lot of teachers, funnily enough – and we, er, 'got on' so well that she decided to fly to join us when we reached New York.

Great. Trouble was that by the time the band arrived in New York, I'd already met another girl in Toronto, and she'd decided to come to New York as well. So, when I arrived in the Big Apple, I had two girls coming to see me, plus Ruth, as we had taken to rekindling our liaison occasionally.

So when the girl from Austin turned up I had to tell the girl from Toronto that she was my girlfriend who'd come over from England to see me, and moved her out to stay with Dave Pils, after which I spent my time flitting between the two rooms, entertaining both girls. God forgive me ... but it was mega.

Oh, my giddy aunt. No wonder I earned myself the nickname Brian Rix from Steve and Gillian. I mean, I'm not proud of it (not much) and I know it doesn't cast me in the most gentlemanly light, but you've got to look at it from my point of view. For me, it was like rags to riches. Years and years of near-famine and then suddenly feast. Fantastic.

This was a very eventful tour and we even managed to squeeze in filming a video for 'Confusion' with Arthur after our gig at the Paradise Garage, New York. It was produced by Charles Sturridge, a friend of Alan and Tony. Charles actually lived at 89a, Palatine Road, the Factory office in Manchester, when he was directing episodes of my favourite soap opera, *Coronation Street*. He was also famous in England for directing eleven episodes of Evelyn Waugh's *Brideshead Revisited* in 1981, and won many awards.

The idea for the video came from Arthur, and revolved around two great dancers he had befriended in the Fun House. The idea was to show their daily lives up to and including getting ready to come to the club. A nice concept, and as it didn't entail much work on our part we liked it. They used footage from our Paradise Garage soundcheck and then filmed us walking around both the Paradise Garage and the Fun House (the walking-round concept that Electronic would use to great effect in all their videos later), with some footage recorded in the DJ booth with Jellybean too.

It went well. The night flew by and, before we knew it, it was finished and as we were getting ready to leave the club about half past seven in the morning somebody says, 'Oh, where's Arthur? Is Arthur not coming with us?'

'No, no, he's gone with his missus.'

We went downstairs and just as we were getting in the cab, I looked across the street to see Arthur and his missus parked up in his car, and they were arguing like fuck, really going at it.

Arthur was driving, but he was parked in a really tight spot. As they argued he was ramming the car behind and then the one in front, trying to get out of the space.

They never missed a beat. I couldn't hear what they were saying but certainly got the gist. And then, as the whole street watched them, he screamed off up the road.

What a guy.

Then came the flight from New York to Washington.

What happened was that, as per usual, everyone got up late. Because me and Steve were driving the two hire cars the idea was that we'd drop everyone off at the departures gate, then return the cars to the rental office and come back in the bus to the terminal.

I said to Steve, 'Put your foot down, mate, or we'll miss the flight!'

We'd screwed the cars so much on the drive to the airport that the disc brakes were glowing red but, for the next leg of our journey, Steve seemed to lose any sense of urgency, drove like an old granny and made us so late that the plane with the heavy sleepers had left, and only Rob was there waiting for us.

'You fucking daft pair of bastards,' he said, 'you've missed the flight. We've got another one in three hours ...'

So we went to the bar, where they were offering breakfast for $1.99, or a double Midori cocktail, which is a melon-based vodka drink, for $2!

We looked at each other. 'One cent difference? Oh, fuck it, shall we get a drink?'

We had three double Midori cocktails for breakfast, me, Steve and Rob – amazing start to the day.

Then Rob went, 'Shall we have another?'

So we did, then another. Until we must have had about ten doubles each.

I don't remember getting on the plane, but I remember being in a middle seat, and seeing double, and then seeing treble, and then beginning to throw up.

The passenger next to me was a large black lady and she started screaming until a stewardess came along, hauled me up and deposited me in the toilet. It's only a short flight from New York to Washington, but I spent most of it sitting on the toilet with my head in my hands, groaning, wanting to die. Then, just as the plane began its descent ready for landing, I fell off the toilet (eat your heart out, Elvis) and got jammed in between the toilet compartment and the wall, my feet stuck against the door.

The stewardess pounded on the door. 'Sir? Sir? Come out, we're landing.'

I groaned so she tried the door but couldn't open it because my feet were up against it. There was no way, in fact, that they were going to open the toilet door. So instead I just stayed in there, in flagrant contravention of just about every flight regulation in the book, while they landed, waited until everybody else had got off and then, with the help of Rob and Steve, I was coaxed/dragged out of the toilet.

I was still seeing three of everything. Even by the time we got to the gig venue, the Ontario Theatre, where they laid me out under a table, hoping I'd recover in time for the gig.

Which I did, sort of. I stayed under the table, sparkled, for the whole soundcheck, but then at about six or seven o'clock, I woke up, thinking firstly that I felt like shit, and secondly that I needed something to eat.

'Have I got time to eat before the gig?' I said to Ruth. (She was talking to me at this point, but not for much longer ...)

She went, 'Yeah, OK, no problem, go and get something to eat. Quando Quango are playing first.'

'Quando Quango? How did they get here?'

Ruth said, 'Ask Rob, he's paying!'

So anyway, I went to get something to eat at a burger place near the venue where I got talking to a fan, a lovely girl, and I chatted to her as I ate, just about beginning to feel human again, when I was surprised to see this guy come running over.

'Hey, are you out of the band?'

I went, 'Yeah.'

He said, 'They're on stage, man.'

'Nah,' I said, 'they can't be on stage, not without me,' thinking I'd only been gone a few minutes, but not factoring in that while I may have been on the road to recovery I was still technically pissed as a fart. Not only that, but I'd been doing the old Hugh Grant bit on the girl fan for ages.

Next thing you knew, Ruth came barging in, screaming, 'WHAT THE FUCK ARE YOU DOING? YOU'RE SUPPOSED TO BE ON STAGE, YOU ASSHOLE! AND WHO THE FUCK IS SHE?'

Then, looking at this girl, and looking back at me, something obviously snapped. She'd had enough of my antics. She yelled, 'YOU FUCKER!' and gave me a mighty right-handed slap, then grabbed my arm, pulled me off my seat and dragged me back to the venue. I have to say, I fully deserved it.

Right through the front door we went, there was no one about, and straight into the hall where, sure enough, the band were playing 'In a Lonely Place'.

As we ploughed through the audience towards the stage I thought how weird it was, watching my own band play (a bit like it is now, to be honest). It was like a dream because Rob was up there, playing the cymbals that I normally played.

I staggered on, not knowing what to do or say because all the rest of the group were looking at me and the audience were gawping too. So I just said the first thing that came into my head.

Which was, 'Hello, shitheads.'

The audience didn't like that. Tempers were already frayed. A few missiles were thrown and the bad atmosphere almost developed into a riot, and once again, at the end of the gig, I heard those immortal words, as the promoter strode up to me, jabbed a finger in my chest and announced, 'You'll never play in Washington again.'

We were back on the next tour.

Not long after that Anton Corbijn turned up. Anton is a photographer with whom we'd had a long association; his pictures of Joy Division in the Underground in London are legendary and he would eventually go on to direct the film *Control* about Ian.

Anton, who is a very nice bloke indeed, turned up to do photos of the band, while a guy from *Sounds* did the interview. We had a great time, with three days of sitting around, drinking, partying and generally chewing the fat – until we got to Trenton, New Jersey, where Anton had to say goodbye. We were sat outside on the grass and it was a lovely sunny day. Anton had packed away his gear and put it in a car bound for the airport, and he was just waiting for his journalist to arrive when suddenly he said, 'I've forgotten something. What have I forgotten? I've definitely forgotten something. What is it? Shit!'

It was really bugging him.

We were puzzled. What could it be?

And then the blood left his face. He looked like Terry and I must have looked when the customs guy asked to see the Boss Dr Rye Thim. And he said, 'I've forgotten to take any pictures.'

Oh.

Not only that, but his cameras had gone, so it was indeed panic stations. You've got to hand it to him, though, what he did was go straight to the garage across the street, buy two disposable cameras, each with twelve shots, then take us to a nearby funfair, did the pictures, and ...

They turned out great, some of my favourites of the group in fact. I wish more photoshoots could be like that. Done in five minutes before you run to catch your plane home instead of the hours it normally takes of setting up lights and screens and taking Polaroids and all the other shit they normally do.

And that was it, we got our plane, I arrived home, collapsed onto the sofa, and my missus said to me, 'How was it, then?'

'Oh,' I said, 'you know ...'

'Go and have a holiday, Judas'

Years later, Barney and I were talking to one of our many financial experts, complaining about our constant lack of money.

'Isn't it funny,' says this guy, smiling, 'how in groups, the members never have any money, but the person who holds the chequebook always has loads of it?'

It's true. The fact is there is a certain amount of mismanagement in all groups. How are the managers able to do it? Because musicians are the mugs who let them.

I live a very comfortable life, and have done for a number of years, so don't get me wrong. But I couldn't stop working now even if I wanted to. Not if I plan to maintain the comfortable life I have worked so hard for. And I have to admit, it's galling to see people who have been in far less successful bands than I have who seem to have done much better financially.

One reason for that, among other things, is Rob controlling our income and ploughing it into the Haçienda. Another reason is our total obliviousness, because when you're out in America or Australia, and you're taters, and you're having a great time, you don't think to ask Rob, 'Eh, Rob, how much did we get for that gig? How does it balance against the costs? Have we made sure everything is running efficiently?' You just don't do it.

As far as we were concerned – or at least, as far as I was concerned, because I can't speak for the others – our money was being earned and was accumulating somewhere for when we needed it. The first part was right, at least.

As for the second part . . .?

It's called sticking your head in the sand, and because I did that I lost millions of quid and still don't have financial security now, even after forty years of being in the music business, the co-writer of 'Blue Monday' and 'Love Will Tear Us Apart' and many successful albums. At the end of the day I've only got myself to blame for said actions and for never raising my voice against signing daft agreement after daft agreement, that signed away 30 per cent of my earnings *in perpetuity* and all my rights to publishing and song royalties to erroneous partnerships and companies I have absolutely no control over. It's unbelievable to me now.

I'll tell you a story. In 1985 I needed thirteen grand to help buy my studio, Suite 16, so I went to Rob, cap in hand, to borrow the money – which, don't forget, was *my* money.

He sat there practically making me beg for it. At one point he even called to his partner Lesley, 'What do you think? Should we give it him?' he sniggered. 'OK,' he said, after keeping me hanging on for ages. I was delighted. Freedom at last. I would be able to do something on my own. Then, just as I was being shown out the door, he added, smirking, 'But I'll have to ask the others first!'

Just to complete the humiliation. I never quite forgave him for that.

That kind of thing was characteristic of his manner. He had this way of making you feel either silly or guilty for asking about your own money. He'd be patronising or he'd chuck money at you – literally throwing it at you, and go, 'Here's a grand, go and have a holiday, Judas.'

It was one of those nails in the coffin I keep talking about. Because Rob wasn't just managing the band, he was managing us as individuals, and when your manager is also your personal assistant and he's telling you what to do in all aspects of your life, the dynamic begins to change. That, as we'll see, is exactly what happened to New Order, because in later years, when Rob was a much-reduced force, Barney basically started managing the band.

Not only that, but we had the conflict of interest that occurs when three of the four band members are using the management for personal services, but not the fourth, me.

So that was brewing. Next thing we knew Rob came to us one day around 1982 or 1983 and said to us, 'We're having trouble getting money out of Factory. They can't pay us what they owe us, so they've offered us a twenty per cent share of the company.'

So we said yes to that, same way we said yes to everything.

He said, 'All right, then. What I'll do is, I'll put the shares in my name but split the money I get with you lot.'

Of course, it should have been four per cent each, split five ways, to make that twenty per cent. But we didn't do that.

He was also registered as a director, so the first directors' remuneration he got, he split with us, because were all in it together. Great.

The second one, he said, 'We need a good record player so we can listen to test pressings, so I'll use the directors' remuneration to buy that, all right?'

We said yes. The great new record player was stored at his house.

The next time, he never mentioned the directors' remuneration, and one of us must have brought it up, because his answer was, 'Well, I'm doing all the fucking work, not you lot. Why the fuck should you get any?'

That was the last we ever heard of that remuneration. I mean, let's be fair, Rob was right. He was doing all our work in Factory, and he did have all the associated stress and worry. But those were his terms, he was holding the shares for us, so if the company was sold we would get our money back, money that we were owed by them.

Plus, what we didn't realise was that even more trouble was just around the corner. Somewhere along the line, Rob had been developing a taste for cocaine.

So after another successful year, business gripes aside, we had the added bonus of the resurgence of bloody 'Blue Monday'.

Unbeknown to us it had inadvertently opened us up to a new market, the club DJs, who were about to give us considerable mainstream success. That summer a lot of holiday DJs had picked up on the record. It became a resort floor filler, one of those summer hits that everybody wanted to hear on their holidays and then again when they got back, to remind them of what a great time they'd had.

Tony Wilson heard about this because somebody had said to him, 'Have you heard this new song by the group Blue Monday – 'New Order'? Isn't it on your label?' All of a sudden in September there was a huge upsurge in interest. It went up in the charts again and we were even invited to play it on *Top of the Pops* again. We turned it down because they wanted us to mime and there was no way we were miming, not after last time.

Tony of course was delighted, saying, 'Darlings! I am going to order another 100,000 to celebrate!'

'Good for you, Tony,' said us.

TIMELINE FOUR
JANUARY–DECEMBER 1983

© Kevin Cummins

4 January 1983

Mixing of 'Ultraviolence'.

5 January 1983

Mixing of 'Ultraviolence' (continued) and 'Blue Monday'.

6 January 1983

Mixing of 'Blue Monday' (continued) and 'The Beach'.

7 January 1983

Editing for album and singles begins at Advision in Fitzrovia, London.

26 January 1983

New Order play a sell-out gig at the Haçienda, Manchester.

29 January 1983

New Order play Great Hall, Student Union, Cardiff, supported by the Wake.

3 February 1983

A Radio Lancashire interview with Hooky is broadcast.

February 1983

New Order fly to New York to record with Arthur Baker and stay for three weeks, writing and recording 'Confusion'.

25 February 1983

New Order play Kolingsborg, Stockholm, Sweden.

26 February 1983

New Order play Kolingsborg, Stockholm, Sweden.

7 March 1983

New Order: 'Blue Monday', twelve-inch
(FAC 73)

Track list:

'Blue Monday'	7.29
'The Beach'	7.19

Run-out groove one: *Outvoted!*
Run-out groove two: *Fac 73 IA*

Recorded and mixed at Britannia Row Studios, London.
Engineered by Mike Johnson, assisted by Barry Sage and Mark Boyne.
Produced by New Order.
Designed by Peter Saville.
Entered UK chart on 19 March 1983, remaining in the charts for 38 weeks, its peak position was number 9.

The titles came courtesy of Fats Domino and the B-side title from a wonderful 1959 film about the end of the world, *On the Beach*.

11 March 1983

New Order play the Ace, Brixton, supported by Stockholm Monsters.

Band do interview with Richard Skinner for Radio 1's *Rock On*, broadcast the following day.

12 March 1983

New Order play Recreation Centre, Tolworth, Kingston-upon-Thames, supported by Stockholm Monsters.

> **'Here it was proved that every group is exactly the same. The Monsters imploded. They were all drunk and speeding like crazy. Chop the guitarist went for his brother the singer, swinging the guitar at his head and (luckily) missing. Lita, a grade-eight piano player, was so drunk she couldn't play. "Fookin' hell," says Barney, "she's playing the keyboards like Gillian. Like she's using a fuckin' orange!" Kersh, their new bass player, collapsed and had to be helped/dragged off stage. (Years later Kersh, lovely Moston boy, died after an unsuccessful attempt to beat heroin. RIP, mate.) Me and Andy Fisher, their new manager, hid under the mixing desk we were so embarrassed, telling the PA guy to give us a shout when it was all over.'**

23 March 1983

New Order play the State, Liverpool, supported by James.

> **'Great group, James. Their original drummer, Gavin, was one of the best drummers in Manchester. I think, him, Reni and Steve Morris definitely Manc Top Three. We played two nights, sold out the first one. Good gigs. Liverpool audiences have always been good to us, ever since we played there as Warsaw.'**

24 March 1983

New Order play the State, Liverpool.

31 March 1983

New Order appear on *Top of the Pops* for the first time, playing 'Blue Monday' live.

> **'All the other bands, who were miming, were in the bar getting drunk.'**

1 April 1983

New Order appear on *Switch* programme, Channel 4. They play 'Age of Consent' and 'Blue Monday'.

> **'Typically Channel 4 were a bit more free-thinking and the set-up and sound was a lot better.'**

11 April 1983

New Order play Coasters, Edinburgh, supported by the Wake.

12 April 1983

New Order play the Assembly Hall, Edinburgh, supported by the Wake.

'I remember their bass player (Bobby Gillespie) saying he'd had his six-string bass stolen and could he borrow mine? I wouldn't normally consider it but I took pity on him and he borrowed my bass for the show.'

13 April 1983

New Order play St Andrews University, Stirling, supported by the Wake.

14 April 1983

New Order play Tiffany's, Glasgow, supported by the Wake.

'Wild gig. Glasgow has always had a wonderful affinity with Manchester. This gig, right on Sauchiehall Street, was very busy and raucous right from the start. The coppers always walked round in threes. There was a lot of missiles and spit coming from the crowd and I remember one black-haired punk with fingerless black gloves on being a real pain. As the gig ended there was much gesticulating from us on the stage to the audience. Suddenly, Slim went down through an opening in the flight-case wall, striding through it like Leonidas in *300*, the leader of the Spartans. All the audience fell back as he screamed, "I'm sick of this! I'll have the lot of, you Scottish bastards!" and you know what? They stopped. What a standoff. Slim v. Glasgow. And you know what? Slim won. They backed off, exiting outside to carry on fighting in the street. As we left we could see people putting their chips down, running into the melee, throwing a few punches and then coming back, picking up the chips to continue eating. Weird and wild. I love Glasgow.'

15 April 1983

New Order play Orient Cinema (moved to Ayr Pavilion), Ayr, supported by the Wake.

'Ayr was much more refined.'

22 April 1983

New Order play Savoy, Cork, Ireland, supported by Porcelain Tears.

> 'In the hotel lobby after the show we were chatting and an old woman was walking past. On hearing our accents she shouted, "You English?" I go, "Yeah, Manchester, darling." And she came and spat on my shoes then walked off swearing. I was shocked. I didn't even see her at the show.'

23 April 1983

New Order play Aula Maxima, University College Galway, supported by New Testament, All Cats Are Grey.

> 'There was a lot of spitting on this tour and by the time of Galway we had had enough. We took an empty bottle of Paul Masson wine, pissed in it, gobbed in it, put loads of green un's in, cigarette butts and all sorts of shit in it, and we decided, "Right, if anyone fucking spits tonight, they're getting this on the head."
>
> 'We went on and, of course, they were all spitting again, and there was one kid in particular who took great delight in singling me out. So, anyway, I got the Masson bottle, went over to him and he thought it was wine. I'm smiling away and so is he, still thinking it was wine as I poured it in his mouth. Then all of sudden he goes green and he realises that something very, very nasty indeed has been poured straight into his mouth. We are laughing but the crowd get upset and start throwing more things at us and, like a dickhead, I go to the microphone and say (are you ready for this?), "Listen, if you fucking thick Irish bastards don't stop throwing things ..." and as soon as the words were out of my mouth I thought, *I shouldn't have said that*, and sure enough an avalanche of bottles came flying over and I ducked and one of them hit Steve right on the side of the head. Knocked him right off his seat. Sorry, Steve. It was another wild gig.'

24 April 1983

New Order play Rose Hill Hotel, Kilkenny, Ireland, supported by Porcelain Tears.

> **'I have a theory: lovely hotel, shit gig. And this is where it started. We were treated like kings in the hotel, given the run of the restaurant and the bar by the owner. It had a swimming pool as well. We all got absolutely trashed and useless on the night. Unfortunately, the gig was being recorded for Radio 1, Richard Skinner's programme. Oh, and it was dreadful, truly shocking performance by us, with an audience of about fifteen.'**

26 April 1983

New Order play Sir Francis Xavier Hall, Dublin, Ireland.

2 May 1983

New Order: *Power, Corruption & Lies*
(FACT 75)

Track list:

'Age of Consent'	5.13
'We All Stand'	5.13
'The Village'	4.36
'5.8.6.' Intro'	1.42
'5.8.6.'	5.47
'Your Silent Face'	5.58
'Ultraviolence'	4.48
'Ecstasy'	4.24
'Leave Me Alone'	4.38

Run-out groove one: *Where's Murder?*
Run-out groove two: *I said where's Murder?*

Recorded and mixed at Britannia Row Studios, London.
Engineered by Mike Johnson, assisted by Barry Sage & Mark Boyne

Produced by Be Music (New Order).
Designed by Peter Saville (Roses: Fantin-Latour).
Entered UK chart on 14 May 1983, remaining in the charts for 29 weeks, its peak position was number 4.

It sells 75,000 copies in the UK in its first two months of release. Unlike *Movement*, reviews are very good.

'The cover artwork was reputedly Peter Saville's favourite. He borrowed an image of *Roses* by Henri Fantin-Latour from the National Gallery. When Tony Wilson asked for permission to use the image it was denied and Tony was also told that the picture was out on loan somewhere, anyway. Tony got very upset, arguing that the British taxpayer owned the painting and, therefore, we not only had a right to see it but also the right to use it as we deemed fit. Amazingly, the gallery complied, calling back the picture and giving permission. So we were able to present the wonderfully inspired juxtaposition of a classic still-life oil painting with Saville's colour wheel giving the album details in code.

'By mistake Peter used the working titles of two songs, listing "Your Silent Face" as "KW1" and "Ecstasy" as "Only the Lonely".

'Barney said in an interview that the whole album was a "pounds, shillings and pence LP, if you know what I mean, wink, wink," a reference to his taking of acid while making and recording the album. A silly comment, that to me really downplays the amount of ground-breaking and innovative work he did on the record.'

9 May 1983

New Order play Tower Ballroom, Birmingham, supported by James.

10 May 1983

New Order play Victoria Hall, Hanley, supported by James.

20 & 21 May 1983

First-birthday party celebrations at the Haçienda.

'The club, at this point, was losing £10,000 a month, and we were earning £103 a week (our pay rise plus £3 to cover National Insurance). We were blissful in our ignorance but it was a great night. I think there was only me and Barney who went. It was around about this time that Steve and Gillian came to the club one night and were turned away, which pissed them off so much they never came back. Me and Barney were losing four grand a month between us, but at least we were getting some drinks out of it.'

27 May 1983

New Order appear on *Veronica's Countdown*, Dutch TV.

17 June 1983

New Order play Club 688, Atlanta, Georgia.

'This was a fantastic club. Iggy Pop's set list from the previous night's gig was scrawled on the wall by the stage, close to a Ramones set list of – we counted – seventy-three songs. A gorgeous lady brought lunch in for us, telling us that the last English band she'd served was the Sex Pistols, complete with Sid Vicious. "Lovely boys, they were! So polite," she drawled. We were absolutely spellbound.'

19 June 1983

New Order play Club Foot, Nightlife, Austin, Texas, supported by Almost Anyone.

21 June 1983

New Order play Florentine Gardens, Los Angeles, California.

23 June 1983

New Order play the Fantasy, Fullerton, California (a venue also known as the Billy Barty's Roller Rink), supported by Pompeii 1999 and Saccharine Trust.

'We had a food fight in the dressing room and Barney clobbered Andy Liddle with a fairy cake. In retaliation Andy dumped a huge pot of coleslaw on Barney's head while he was in the shower. Barney couldn't get the oil and smell out for days. After the show we met Mark Williams, who would later become a great friend and an A&R man at Virgin. He had two girls with him who looked like they'd just stepped right out of a poster for *One Million Years B.C.* – they both looked like Raquel Welch. Me and him were like the cat that got the cream. One of them went on to become Bob Dylan's girlfriend, so Mark told me later. "They met at a party," he said. "She thought he was a tramp that had wandered in."

'The only other thing of note was Terry Mason getting so sunburned that when he dived in the pool the next day, his top layer of skin parted company with his bottom layer and filled up with water, and as he got out of the pool it was leaking like he'd been peppered with bullets. Everyone around the pool ran away screaming.'

24 June 1983

New Order play Echo Beach, San Francisco, California.

'Far away in time . . . Later we would meet the lovely Martha Ladly of the Muffins and "Echo Beach" fame when she became Peter Saville's girlfriend, and I would do my first bass session gig for her in 1982, playing on her track "Light Years" and getting paid the princely sum of £125 in cash. I was delighted.'

25 June 1983

New Order play I-Beam Club, San Francisco, California.

'My favourite concert venue in all of America, until I got to Red Rocks. It was in Haight Ashbury, such a funky district, and had a great vibe. Tonight we debuted "Thieves Like Us".'

27 June 1983

New Order play the Commodore, Vancouver, Canada.

29 June 1983

New Order play First Avenue, Minneapolis, Minnesota.

> 'We are asked by the manager of the club if we want to go to the club owner's house after the show and maybe jam in his home studio. "He supports young musicians. It's called Paisley Park. Everything's purple!" he explained. "Tell the old pervert to fuck off," we said.'

30 June 1983

New Order play the Metro, Chicago, Illinois.

> 'One of the hottest gigs I have ever done. It was so hot the fold-back engineer went out and bought a thermometer to measure it – 118 degrees Fahrenheit! The thermal cutouts on my Amcron DC330A's amplifiers (set at 120 degrees) kept shutting down and turning themselves off and on. My belt and shoes went instantly wet. Even Gillian was sweating. The owner Joe Shanahan promised us he would fit air-conditioning in for the next time we played and he did.'

2 July 1983

New Order play St Andrew's Hall, Detroit, Michigan.

5 July 1983

New Order play the Spectrum, Montreal, Canada.

7 July 1983

New Order play Paradise Garage, New York, supported by Quando Quango.

'Paradise Garage was the best club I had ever seen. It was huge and it had three stereo sound systems hanging from the roof, six stacks! Each one was independent, which meant the DJ could do some amazing effects, dubbing them up, cutting the bottom end then the treble etc., bringing them in and out. Most club PAs in England are mono, sadly. I remember the owner of the Paradise had two Dobermann pinschers that followed him everywhere, just two steps behind, stopping exactly when he did. He'd had their ears gaffer-taped up, because that's how you make their ears stand up. They flop naturally if you don't, but you can train them to stand up. I swear I'll get a pair when I retire. Dogs that is, not ears.'

8 July 1983

New Order play Ontario Theatre, Washington.

'Yes. Not exactly my finest hour.'

9 July 1983

New Order play City Gardens, Trenton, New Jersey.

'Barney had got into the habit of wearing these tiny, skin-tight white shorts on stage and it was a very bad look. It annoyed me. I thought they looked shit, and at this gig there was a young lady at the front of the audience shouting at him about his shorts all through the gig, which amused me greatly. After the show Barney walked out on the stage and was talking to Terry at the front when this girl appeared again, shouted, "Oh, those fucking shorts!" grabbed them and yanked them right down to his ankles. He, like me, never wore underpants so the sight of his big white arse waddling off the stage with these tight shorts stuck round his ankles will stay with me forever. Thanks very much, Vanessa.'

20 July 1983

New Order play the Haçienda, Manchester.

August 1983

New Order: 'Confusion', twelve-inch
(FAC 93)

Track list:

'Confusion'	8.13
'Confused Beats'	5.19
'Confused Instrumental'	7.33
'Confusion Rough Mix'	8.04

Run-out groove one: *Tim Tom Cbs!*
Run-out groove two: *Not the way I Would've done it!*

Recorded at Unique Studios, New York.
Written by New Order and Arthur Baker.
Produced by Arthur Baker and New Order.
Engineered by F. Heller and C. Lord.
Mixed by Arthur Baker and John 'JellyBean' Benitez at EARS, New Jersey.
Mix engineer: John Robie.
Designed by Peter Saville.
Entered UK chart on 3 September 1983, remaining in the charts for 7 weeks, its peak position was number 12.

27 September 1983

Tony Wilson appears on Channel 4's *Loose Talk* with A Certain Ratio to defend their use of Nazi imagery. Tony also received his first newspaper front page with this controversy, and was delighted. The *Jewish Chronicle* in Prestwich, Manchester, ran a big piece on the Haçienda and Claude Bessy's use of German propaganda videos on the screens in the club.

18 October 1983

Taras Shevchenko video (IKON 4) released. Video recorded at the Ukrainian National Home, New York.

Track list:
'I.C.B.' (actually 'Chosen Time')
'Dreams Never End'
'Everything's Gone Green'
'Truth'
'Senses'
'Procession'
'Ceremony'
'Little Dead' (actually 'Denial')
'Temptation'

Sound: A Be Music Productions
Image: Rebo Associates
Computer graphics: Carter Burwell from photographs of Ronny Kienhuis
Construction: Shamberg / Rebo Partner

> **'Taras Shevchenko was the Ukrainian minister of something. Torture, probably.'**

October 1983

A Factory Outing video released, featuring a variety of Factory bands. New Order contributed '5.8.6. (Prime 5.8.6.)' and 'Your Silent Face'.

10 October 1983

New Order interviewed on BBC's *Riverside*.

31 October 1983

Howard 'Ginger' Jones sacked from the Haçienda.

> **'We didn't know much about this. We weren't informed and weren't even asked our opinion. It was just something that they did. I think they needed a scapegoat.'**

30 November 1983

New Order perform 'Thieves Like Us' for a pilot of a show called *DJ*, hosted by Kid Jensen.

1 December 1983

New Order play the Academy, Brixton, supported by James and the Wake.

> **'We always treated our support bands very well. We had been horrified by the way we were treated when we were supporting people. We swore to break that vicious circle, live and with the Haçienda. We always made sure they were paid, got a rider and a decent soundcheck with good-length set, often at our expense.'**

2 December 1983

New Order play the Town Hall, Bournemouth, supported by James and the Wake.

3 December 1983

'Thieves Like Us' live on *DJ* broadcast.

TEN BEST NEW ORDER SONGS

1. 'Thieves Like Us'
2. 'Leave Me Alone'
3. 'Homage' (unreleased)
4. 'Too Late' (John Peel session)
5. 'Someone Like You'
6. 'Ruined in a Day' (K-Klass Remix)
7. 'Every Little Counts'
8. 'Age of Consent'
9. 'Temptation'
10. 'Elegia'

'Love is the air that supports the eagle ...'

New Order began 1984 on a high, with the success of 'Blue Monday' and the release of 'Thieves Like Us' in April. Behind the scenes, Factory Records resolved a legal dispute with Martin Hannett who, having stepped down as director the previous June, accepted a one-off payment of £25,000; Factory, meanwhile, enjoyed the reflected glory of an episode of The Tube, *which was broadcast from the Haçienda in January.*

The 'Thieves Like Us' graffiti may well have been spotted by Arthur Baker in New York. But it was actually a 1937 novel by Edward Anderson and later, in 1974, was made into a film by Robert Altman. On record, of course, we remained a perfect cerebral proposition, beloved of intellectuals everywhere. In real life, however, we continued to lay waste to that image wherever we went.

I was very happy with this recording, thinking 'Thieves Like Us' a far superior song to 'Blue Monday'. Electing to record again in Britannia Row with Mike Johnson as engineer, we finished this session quickly, in four days. Barney and Steve had programmed a keyboard and drum masterpiece, and the bass guitar riff came with a little help from Hot Chocolate's 'Emma'. Lyrically it was very evocative, a real love song, and the words flowed easily too. The B-side was 'Lonesome Tonight', our homage to Elvis.

Barney had been obsessed with a 'live' recording he had where Elvis is obviously totally pissed and just cannot stop laughing to sing, 'Are you lonesome tonight.' He keeps messing up the song and it is very funny. Barney suggested one night we jam it on stage, saying, 'It's easy, just C and F!' This was the result, a glorious tune even though it's nothing like Elvis's, given away in true New Order fashion as a B-side. The dropdown is wonderful and I must admit the awful noise at the end was inspired by my cold, which was dreadful at the time. When Barney heard me hawking up the phlegm into a handkerchief he suggested we put it on the end because the contrast between something so beautiful and something so awful might be interesting. He was absolutely right.

Pete Saville's cover design was based on a metaphysical painting, *The Evil Genius of a King* (1914–15) by Giorgio de Chirico. The numbers around the central image had been taken from an eighteenth-century board game for which the rules had long been lost. It turned out to be called 'The Jew's Game'. Peter's numbers were completely random and every effort was made to exclude numbers that could in any way relate to the record. Peter and Trevor Keys (the photographer) hoped that some arcane or sinister message would be read into them, which of course is exactly what the music press did.

We were still gigging everywhere we could in England and outside, and embarked on our first German tour, putting the lessons we had learned in America to good use, like in Düsseldorf, where we met a couple of lovely girls after the first gig. At first it seemed we were doomed to remain friends with them. They didn't speak much English but were very cute and we retired to a room for a goodnight drink. I was happily chatting (as best I could) on the bed with mine, and A. N. Other was at the foot of the bed with his. I was resigning myself to an early night alone when he suddenly announces loudly he's going for a piss in the en-suite. I did have a feeling it was some kind of signal, but wasn't sure, so the remaining three of us carried on in our broken English when all of a sudden the toilet door burst open and a totally nude man jumped over our heads with gay abandon, landing on the poor girl sitting on the floor. I grabbed my shocked belle and we retreated into the toilet, where after an uncomfortable coupling on the tiles, we lay on the floor waiting for the grunting next door to stop. Afterwards I took the girls out and they went home. Trouble was, they were none too happy when we decided to, shall we say, 'move on'.

New Order's next gig was in Frankfurt, and the girls turned up at soundcheck. It was nice to see them, but my mate would have nothing to do with them, blanking them completely. It was quite embarrassing and his girlie was getting really upset. I made my apologies and got ready for the gig.

So, later, there we were, playing our little hearts out on stage, Barney as detached as ever, and me keeping my watchful eye out on the crowd, when suddenly I spied the same two girls marching through the audience and right to the lip at the front of the stage.

Uh-oh. They were holding out a piece of paper. Barney, oblivious as ever, was off in his own little world of Pernod-induced self-medication.

The fact that they were being ignored only made them angrier, and they started shouting and gesticulating. The whole sorry scene was beginning to seriously cramp my style.

I ambled over, grabbed the note, and said, 'Please stop, we're trying to play a concert here.' Which, having delivered their missive, is exactly what they did.

At the end of the gig I unfolded the note. It read, 'You two are a pair of English bastards.'

I couldn't disagree with that. They were exactly right. Thing is, we were a right 'love 'em and leave 'em' lot. Our roadies were very much in the habit of passing themselves off as members of the band. The amount of times I'd discover some girl trying to kick in a hotel room door, screaming, 'You're a bastard, Barry Summer!' or just standing there, clutching their empty purse and bawling their eyes out. I quickly lost count of the occasions I had to give one of their cast-offs, or cast-outs, money for a taxi home. I never got it back.

Best one was the time in America in some hotel when I could hear one of the roadies through the wall, singing an *a cappella* 'Blue Monday'.

'How does it feel ...'

'What was that all about?' I asked him the next day at breakfast.

'Oh, bloody hell,' he said shamefaced, 'I got her stripped off on the bed and was just about to dive in when she put her hands between her legs, clamped 'em tight shut and said she wouldn't until I sang to her. In the end I had to.'

How does it feel indeed!

On this particular German tour we were being supported by Shark Vegas, whose manager was a bit older than us (a totally ancient thirty-five or something) and utterly gorgeous. One night after dinner in Berlin she stood and said, 'Right, I'm going home now. Peter, you will be coming with me.'

I went, 'You what?' and nearly choked on my sauerkraut.

'Come with me, Peter, come on ... *schnell, schnell!*'

So I did, and it was great.

The morning after, I said, 'Er, shall we go and get some breakfast, then?'

'No,' she said. 'You will go now,' and she threw me out. Unceremoniously, just like that. She gave me the address of the hotel and sent me off in a taxi. Fair enough, I suppose. If you dish it out you have to be prepared to take it in return. At least I knew how Barry's girls felt. A little dirty and used, as you asked.

So it was a pretty good tour. Or rather, it was great until our esteemed lead singer decided to start throwing his weight around – the continuation of a worrying new trend.

One of the things I always felt about Barney: if he's in a strop, everyone knows about it, and they all get it in the neck. Put it this way, as my dad used to say, 'If I'm suffering you're all suffering.' So when Barney was unhappy, we all had to be unhappy. I'd known him longer than most; after all, we'd started the band together, so in those days if he tried it on with me, I'd tell him to fuck off. But that didn't stop me suffering indirectly. When he was pissed off – which, as New Order went on, was most of the time – it was like a huge black cloud that followed him into the room, and whether you were the target for his ire didn't matter; it settled over everyone, and you just had to put up with it, same as everybody else. I've met lead singers that were stroppier than Barney – Ian McCulloch, John Lydon and Billy Corgan to name a few – but it didn't make it any easier to put up with.

One particular night in Copenhagen he had a right cob on. He was knackered, which was fair enough; after all, he was our frontman and, as we all know, it's a tough job being frontman, because they keep telling you so. The problem is when you start taking out your exhaustion on other people – and of course he was a dab hand at that. He can be a vindictive so-and-so, can Barry Summer.

The long and the short of it was that in Copenhagen he stormed off at the end, no thought of an encore. He was gone, leaving Rob worried there'd be another riot if we didn't go back on. The minutes ticked by until we formulated a plan to go out and play the song, only with Slim on vocals, and we managed to pull it off, and because he'd gone, everyone relaxed.

Even so, we'd got a taste of what it was like when Barney pulled a strop, and it was something that was to become more and more common as the band went on.

Fortunately, the black cloud that followed him into rooms also followed him out again, and another thing that started around that time was people cheering and the party starting as soon as they heard the news that Barney had left.

He'd leave and we'd go, 'Hurrah!' and reach for the champagne and Twiglets.

But sometimes he'd come back in. 'Forgot me jacket ...'

Freeze frame. The room held its breath in case he decided to stay.

He'd leave again.

'*Hurrah!*'

Poor old Barney has no idea how many rooms full of people have celebrated his departure over the years.

'One look at the books was all it took'

Like many a tale of woe, the story of New Order's tax problems began at the Haçienda. We were due a PAYE inspection, so management had said to the girl on the door, 'The guy from the HM Customs is coming. When he arrives, give him that set of books, there. Whatever you do, don't give him this set of books, here, because they're the cash books.'

> Cash books documented a practice that involved paying some employees in cash, on a casual basis, as opposed to putting them on the books as salaried employees with the associated extra liability. This was basically to swindle the taxman out of the PAYE and National Insurance payments due, thus saving the company a lot of money and form-filling and the casual employee a large amount of tax. A dubious but popular practice in the 1980s.

So, the guy came to the door and said, 'Hi, I'm from the PAYE and I've come for the books,' and she went, 'Oh yes. Here you are,' and gave him the cash books.

That was what started it all. One look at the books was all it took for the taxman to start investigating the Haçienda, and with the club being so badly run, he found one thing after another until he rubbed his hands together and decided to investigate the rest of the operation into the bargain: Factory Records, New Order, Joy Division and all of us as individuals.

From there, it went from bad to worse, because if the taxman was hoping that having uncovered a disaster area of accounting at the Haçienda, then our other affairs might be equally haphazard; well, we were happy not to disappoint him.

It all started to get very technical, because the first thing they tried to do was make us pay tax on earnings before we'd even been paid by Factory. So if the label had £100,000 and half of that was owed to us, Her Majesty wanted the tax – *our* tax – from Factory there and then, before it was paid to us. This was unique even for HMRC and took some fighting.

Next thing was a bunch of missing forms. Or, to be more accurate, forms that had never been filled in.

It turned out that a P11D was something you were supposed to fill in to declare to the taxman that you're using, say, your company car for the odd bit of shopping or the company phone. The taxman doesn't mind you using company-owned materials for personal use as long as you don't take the piss. It's called a 'benefit in kind' and all they ask in return is that you fill in a P11D form and pay the extra tax due.

We never had. Not for years. In fact, not since we went legit.

When we asked our accountant why we hadn't been filling in P11D forms, he said, 'I thought you were doing it.'

We said, 'No, we're musicians, you're the bloody accountant.'

We were fined for that, too, for eight years' non-filling-in of P11D forms.

Next under the spotlight was Factory's fraudulent habit of putting money – Joy Division's and New Order's money – into the Haçienda without it going into our limited company first. Rob had no idea it was illegal. They'd done it twice, both times when New Order had been abroad and they'd urgently needed money to keep the club open. Rob had told Tony to do it, we just didn't realise the ramifications. We weren't trying to hide it.

Now, you might wonder why our manager wasn't on hand to stop the money matters going astray? The answer is that Rob was always with us. As I said earlier, he didn't need to be. Recording and playing live were the two things we didn't need help with. He should have been back in Manchester, manning the office and making sure we weren't accidentally making white-collar criminals of ourselves.

Upshot: eventually, among other things, we would get done for two counts of fraud in a limited company.

We got called in for a meeting with the taxman in his office near Deansgate. So we all trooped along. Terrified, we were herded into an office. The five of us sat down, Rob in the middle. On the other side of the table sat the two taxmen, one a very dour Scot and the other a more nerdy, bespectacled clerk. A typical bad cop / good cop situation, it seemed.

When they were ready the Scot said, 'Can I get ye some tea?'

We said yes. Before long a full china tea service with pretty pink flowers had appeared, and so began a rather bizarre tea ceremony.

Scotty decided to serve us, starting first with our venerable manager.

'Tea, Mr Gretton?' he growled.

'Er … yes, please.'

'Milk and sugar, Mr Gretton?' he then purred.

'Er … just milk, ta.'

Then Scotty poured, milked and then passed Rob the cup and saucer. Now, Rob was shaky at the best of times (we would find out why later), but as he reached out even we could see his hand start to tremble; he responded by reaching with both hands.

Us four were gripped watching this spectacle unfold, and as the cup and saucer were passed to him, Rob's eyes started to bulge in concentration, and as Scotty handed the tea over it began jumping around in mid-air, tea slopping everywhere, including all over Rob as he pulled it down to his lap.

We looked up to see Scotty turn to his fellow taxman and nod slowly and wisely. Guilty before we'd even started, betrayed by a bloody cup and saucer. And even worse, no biscuits.

The rest of the meeting went from bad to worse. All our shortcomings were paraded before us along with threat after threat ranging from fines to imprisonment.

Then came a rather surreal exchange about Joy Division T-shirts, with us proudly proclaiming we did not sell merchandise because we didn't believe in self-promotion of any kind, preferring to let the music speak for itself.

'Rubbish,' boomed Scotty. 'How come wherever I go I see Joy Division and New Order T-shirts, worn and for sale, eh?'

Now, we had no idea where he was going to see these things, but we were all speechless anyway.

He continued, 'I don't believe you, and will be fining you accordingly.'

So we would get fined £10,000 for not doing our own T-shirts.

In truth, we wouldn't do our first proper deal for Joy Division T-shirts worldwide until 2012. Beam me up, Scotty.

We were all broken by the end, and as we slumped out of the office and trudged dejectedly towards the exit, Scotty appeared behind us again shouting, 'Stop! Wait!'

Oh my God! What now? What else could he possibly have found out? We turned around and he was beaming. 'You can't go, you haven't signed my LPs yet,' he said. And you know what? Like kittens, we all meekly signed them, with him adding, 'Can you make it to Stuart, best wishes, please?' Fucking hell.

We were later told you never have to meet the taxman. It seems it's the one thing they can't make you do. They can just deal with your accountant. Unfortunately, we went on our own.

Another time I had the tax gimps turn up at my house in Moston to go through all my stuff, counting my cutlery, poking their beaks into the garden shed and inspecting my spanners, until at last when they were leaving one of them turned to me smiling and said, 'Where did all the money go, Mr Hook?'

'Eh? You what?'

'Well, you've got hardly anything in your house, and yet you've earned hundreds of thousands of pounds. Where's it all gone?'

At the time I just thought he was being a cheeky bugger and ushered him out with as much indignation as possible. But now I wonder, yeah? Where *did* all the money go? And why did none of us ever ask what was going on? Idiots!

Why hadn't Rob been diligent? Why hadn't he been looking after the money we were earning? Truth was, he was too busy having a wild time with us on tour, and I have to say that was how we preferred it at the time. Because when it came to slugging your way out of a gig riot, Mr Gretton was very handy to have around.

That particular encounter with Her Majesty's revenue collectors cost us around a million pounds in fines, as well as the unpaid tax we had to stump up, and of course none of it was tax deductible. It was the highest tax fine of any pop group in the United Kingdom ever, we were proudly informed.

It was also the first time we became aware how badly things were unravelling, how the apple had a rotten core. There was the sudden realisation that maybe some of these people in charge – i.e. Rob and Tony – didn't actually know what the fuck they were doing.

But if it was a lesson, then it wasn't a hard enough lesson, because we reacted to it by doing nothing.

At this point in 1984, when not New Ordering, everybody in the group was out doing a lot of production work for other groups, mainly on Factory, under the credit 'Be Music'. This was Rob's idea. He wanted us to be seen as one entity. As if he was worried about one or more of us making a name for ourselves outside of New Order. At the time we didn't care so went along with it out of respect. It was his way of trying to keep everything part of the group. You can see the familiar dynamic, the pattern, can't you? We're pulling one way, apart. Rob pulling us back. And it stayed that way until at last one of us – Barney – insisted that we had our own name on productions, and the policy was dropped.

We had been approached to do a benefit concert for the National Union of Mineworkers led by Arthur Scargill. The production company that was making *Play at Home*, our TV programme for Channel 4, was in charge. We said yes. It was terrible what was happening, with twenty mines closed that year alone and plans to close seventy more. Thousands of people had lost their jobs. We weren't very political as a group but we were glad to help on this occasion. Margaret Thatcher was a scary woman, and to us in the North she was becoming a bit of a bogeywoman. It was very easy for us in this situation and we got to do something we enjoyed while helping.

There was a march planned that was ending in London; our gig was the payoff. The gig was free for the marching miners – just what a bunch of hairy-arsed miners needed after a long walk. The line-up was us; an up-and-coming young comedian called Keith Allen; John Cooper Clarke, who seemed in much better health than when we had last seen him, and a new Factory band, Life.

At that time Keith was billing himself as a 'Northern Industrial Gay' and specialised in opening for punk bands. Terry Mason tried to throw him off the stage when he appeared smothered in baby oil in his peaked cap and studded jockstrap (Terry thought he was a stage invader) but I rescued Keith and made a friend for life, like finding a lion with a thorn in its paw. Wonderful. We little realised what he would come to mean to us and what a huge part he would play in our lives.

Another notable meeting at this gig was the first appearance of

Tom Atencio, formerly of MCA Records, who would soon become our America manager and another dear friend.

Tom had been in phone contact with Rob, proposing the idea of both Joy Division and New Order being signed to an American label owned by Quincy Jones, called Qwest Records and distributed by Warner Brothers. This was very exciting, and he seemed a really nice guy.

To record our next album we went back to Britannia Row in London and the band division that had first arisen making *Power, Corruption & Lies* once more raised its ugly head. We were getting in from the studio at 1 a.m. and I was doing the big cartoon-yawn off-to-bed bit while they were all skinning up and firing up the toaster for a heavy session of dope, toast and *2001: A Space Odyssey* or whatever.

In the morning, it was the same story. I'd go for a run or do weights (I'd brought my own with me) on the roof of the apartment while they slept in. Every day I'd be banging on their doors, 'Come on, we said we were leaving at ten. Come on!'

I just couldn't see the point of working all day and night and then coming back and staying up watching fucking stupid videos, *Eraserhead* and stuff like that, into the early hours. I'm sure they probably thought the combination of films and dope was very inspiring, but as far as I could see all it inspired them to do was hang around in bed until midday.

Besides, as someone who's taken more than their fair share of drugs, I've never bought into all that about them being a creative tool. Not unless you think that spending all day under the duvet crying is especially creative.

Now don't forget, I wasn't forcing them; they would say to me as I went to bed, 'Make sure you get us up for a ten o'clock start.' In the end I was like, 'Right, if you're not ready I'm going without you.' Mike Johnson, who was staying elsewhere, would already be at the studio, twiddling his knobs. So I'd be the first to arrive, wound up after another fruitless morning of trying to get my reluctant bandmates out of bed, not to mention the bloody manager, and I'd get on with stuff myself. Do overdubs, tidy stuff up.

This was a problem, not a huge problem yet, but it continued on *Low-Life* and then became a problem with rehearsals back in Manchester, where for me it was exacerbated by the pressures of my home life, what with my missus, Iris, constantly mithering me about the hours I kept. It was a situation that got even worse the following year, 1985, when my beautiful daughter, Heather, was born. You're a new dad, you want to see your child; you don't want to be needlessly stuck in the studio. I mean, our rehearsal room was next to a graveyard in Cheetham Hill; at night it was pitch-black, so it can't have been any fun for Steve and Gillian to finish at one, two in the morning and then have to drive an hour home to Macclesfield every night, but it never stopped them.

I used to say to the rest of them, 'Can't we start at eleven and finish at six? Then we could do other stuff – I could see my kid, we could go out with mates, have dinner with the missus?' Everybody would grudgingly agree it was a great idea. We might even stick to a schedule for a day or so – before slipping back. Iris would pick me up from the rehearsal room at seven in the evening and them lot would be looking at their watches and thinking, *Oh, off already, are we?* Them three didn't seem to have a life outside the group. But I'd think, *Well, yes. We agreed we'd finish on time, so fuck ya!*

So they'd write without me. I'd come in the next day and find a new song on the table, get my bass out ready to play on it, and then watch the atmosphere darken, them obviously thinking but never saying, *But this one sounds better electronic …*

'You know what our problem is?' Barney used to say to me. 'You're a lark and I'm a nightingale.'

'No,' I'd say back, 'you're not a nightingale. You're a twat who can't get to work on time!'

It was him who had suggested the time in the first place but he was still always late. He said he was allergic to being on time. It had started to get worse around then and continued all the way through New Order, right up until we split in 2006. You'd arrange to rehearse at one for a couple of hours, tell your missus you'd be home about five, and Barney wouldn't roll in until four.

I'd go, 'What time do you call this?'

'Oh,' he'd say airily, 'you're such a clock-watcher, you are. I can't do that. I'm too much of a free spirit.'

'Be a free spirit on someone else's time, you selfish bastard. At least you could have phoned?'

'Oh, you're a right bastard, Hooky. Always on my case.'

*

Meanwhile, back at Britannia Row, we settled into a nice routine, including a weekly Monday shopping trip for me, Steve and Gillian down the King's Road, taking in all the wackier shops. We were getting fashion conscious and it was a lovely way to start the week. Barney never went ... he was too scared of the moths escaping from his wallet. We were actually getting on and working together quite well.

I'd like to say that Gillian really came into her own on this record but, sadly, I can't. In my opinion she didn't add much musically, just taking Barney's riffs off him as he wrote them for both keyboards and guitar. We still split the publishing equally, with neither me nor Barney wanting to confront that little problem ... yet.

When we finished at Britannia Row and moved to Jam Studios things started to get really raucous. Jam Studios had a very good reputation and famously starred in the Rolling Stones film about the recording of 'Sympathy for the Devil'.

We had only been there a few days when Kevin Millins decided to take me and Barney out on the town, where we promptly bumped into the studio manageress, Helga, who was of Scandinavian extraction and a huge presence in all ways – a no-nonsense lady who in my opinion would have been better off running a high-security prison than a recording studio. But here she was, and definitely the worse for wear, with the drink making her very smiley and friendly, if a little unsteady on her feet. Barney rushed to her rescue and, emulating his hero Terry-Thomas, said, 'Come here, my lovely. I'll look after you.'

And that was the last we saw of them. *What is it?* I thought, *about the start of these album sessions that sends everyone mad?*

Really that was just the beginning. During the next day or so, on answering a knock on the studio's front door, I was confronted by Denise and Cheryl of a burgeoning Manchester girl band – one of those who never even got to the name stage – making a guest appearance.

'Surprise!' they shouted. 'We missed you!'

They both jumped round my neck. These two were wild. They started the day by putting on faux-lesbian shows for roadies, sitting on either side of the hapless victim and kissing while groping his thighs, driving him mad. They then moved into the flat with us. I was sharing a room with Andy Robinson, then our keyboard roadie, so when we got back from the studio Cheryl and I would retire for a while, then she'd get up again and ended up sleeping on the floor in the single room with Denise and her beau, usually tickling their toes with a huge pink vibrator she'd brought with her. Her beau then took to hiding it under everyone's pillows along with last night's used johnnies. You'd go for a shit and reach for toilet paper only to find one hidden in the roll. He had some stamina, that lad. They were everywhere.

We used to go out a lot with Kevin Millins, who took us to the Kit Kat Club in Notting Hill and Taboo in Leicester Square, introducing us to Steve Strange, Leigh Bowery, Marc Almond and all that lot.

We also spent a lot of time with Rusty Egan, former Rich Kids drummer who ran and DJed at the Embassy Club, where we hung out with Richard Jobson from the Skids, Killing Joke and their roadies, as well as the Banshees and all their roadies.

I remember one night the girls dancing and ended up snogging outrageously lying in the middle of the dancefloor, while everyone stood around, shocked, with people going, 'Oh my God, they're with New Order. From Manchester! Look at them!'

The rest of them were mortified. Me and A. N. Other thought it was hilarious, even swapping the girls for snogging sessions by the toilets. Until someone overstepped the mark and that was the end of that. The girls hung round for quite a while though. I even took to leaving them in my flat while we went to the studio, wondering what they did all day.

We got the answer to that question years later when this guy started talking to Barney in a club about some hookers he'd met in London in 1984 who said they were living in New Order's flat. Barney was shocked. The guy said they were touting for business in the street then taking the lucky punter upstairs before despatching them with a toss or a blow job. The guy said, 'I went back a couple of times. They were wild!' They certainly were, God bless them.

I wasn't drinking much then. In fact, I used to drive us all around.

I was at my sober bad-boy worst at that point, and had about seven girls on the go at once. I got a call from one of them, saying she'd caught the clap off the bass player for a well-known, uncompromising indie band – a band that I'd annoyed at the Haçienda (what a way to get your own back!) – so I had to come clean to them all. Now, one of my girlfriends, Gill Smith, who wrote for *Record Mirror*, was also a dominatrix, and was not at all impressed. She ended up leaving me for

Billy Mackenzie out of the Associates. He was a lovely man, who later killed himself, although she swore to me it wasn't connected. Gill was always trying to get me into this sub-dom stuff. She'd go, 'I'll get me whip out,' or, 'Let me get my paddle and try it on you.'

I'd be, like, 'You get your paddle out and it's going straight through that window, love. Followed closely by you!'

I did like the fashion that went with the scene, but not that arse-slapping side of it. Poor old Gill, it was very frustrating for her. She was a dominatrix who wasn't allowed to dominate. Still, she had other outlets for her interests. She used to model for *Skin Two*, the magazine version of a club we were introduced to, again by Kevin Millins. As a matter of fact, we'd been to the very first one in 1983, and what an eye-opener that had turned out to be. Barney and I had rocked up with Kevin in our leather jackets and motorbike boots but were underdressed compared to the leather and rubber gear on everyone else. There were guys with their arses hanging out; girls squeezed into rubber dresses with the boobs cut out. You name it. Clubbers were fucking each other in plain sight. At midnight they would put on Gregorian chants and the dominatrices would take to the stage and proceed to whip the fuck out of some ecstatic gimps while everyone stood around and watched as though they were enjoying highbrow performance art. It was great.

One night I nudged Barney and pointed. 'You see him over there? Hiding in the corner. He's a dead ringer for Pete Saville.'

Turned out it *was* Pete Saville, standing there all in black, with his polo-neck jumper on looking very intellectual, ever-present cigarette in hand, and when I crept up and surprised him, he was mortified that we'd caught him here, at this arse-slapping club.

'I . . . I . . . I . . . just like the fashions!' he stammered.

We laughed. 'So do we!' we chorused.

He didn't stay embarrassed for long, though, and soon the whole lot of us were going back every week. At first, Steve and Gillian found the whole thing excruciating. Gillian even burst into tears when some guy licking a dominatrix's boots stuck his hairy arse in her face. But they soon developed a taste for it, and with us all going it became a big thing back home. We'd ring Manchester and tell our mates, 'Bloody hell, you should see this club. You get to see all these birds getting their arses smacked,' and before you knew it, all the Manchester lot led by infamous Manchester promoter Alan Wise were coming down, just to get a look at the wild goings-on: 'Rubbernecking', you might say. Ha-ha.

In the end Skin Two had to put a block on people coming in unless they were very much dressed for the occasion, and our lot weren't about to squeeze into rubber basques (apart from Rob, of course, who one night did just that, pouring himself into a black plastic dress of Gillian's so as not to be refused entry), so that was the end of that.

Anyway, apart from the hours, and despite – or maybe because of – the debauchery in the flat and the nocturnal exploits, *Low-Life* was a good recording experience – one of the best, if not *the* best – and the finished product, which I think is probably my favourite of our New Order albums, speaks volumes about the group dynamic at the time. The combination of the sequencers and the rock side was perfectly balanced. We were very much together.

Just listen to the songs: 'Love Vigilantes', 'The Perfect Kiss', 'This Time of Night', 'Sunrise', 'Sooner Than You Think', 'Sub-Culture', 'Face Up' – they're all real *band* songs. And apart from 'Love Vigilantes' we were still writing the lyrics by committee, the three of us with Rob chipping in. 'Love Vigilantes' Barney did alone. (This process didn't change until Barney announced in 1987 that he now wanted to write all the lyrics and vocal lines by himself for *Technique*.) He did a great job and I was blown away when I heard it. A lyrical masterpiece that is still one of our most popular songs.

The album was recorded normally using a 24-track Studer tape machine and our own great collection of equipment, using pretty much the same stuff we used on *Power, Corruption & Lies*. The only big differences here were the adoption of MIDI technology and the use of SMPTE Timecode. Deep breath ...

Geek Alert

SMPTE Time code and clock

The Society of Motion Picture and Television Engineers devised SMPTE (the time code that bears their name) initially to synchronise soundtracks to films, so that separately recorded dialogue could be added (dubbed on) later.

It was discovered that SMPTE time code was also a useful way of synchronising not only live sequencers from a tape machine, but also one tape machine to another. Both machines carry a track of code, and a synchroniser box compares the time positions of the two codes. If the codes are not identical, a control signal is derived which changes the speed of the slave tape machine, forcing it to move back into sync with the master machine. In the case of the sequencer the synchroniser box reads the pre-recorded code off the master tape machine, then sends out a midi clock telling the sequencer/drum machine where to stop and start for overdubbing or replacing parts or sounds.

Initially, such SMPTE systems were very complicated and expensive, but now SMPTE systems are cheap enough to use in studio applications. The code is based on real time, measured in hours, minutes and seconds, with further subdivisions to accommodate individual frames of TV and film material. This is in direct contrast to MIDI Clock, which is a direct multiple of tempo. Because SMPTE is independent of tempo, a whole tape must be recorded or 'striped' with code before any recording or programming starts.

When using SMPTE to sync a MIDI sequencer to tape, the SMPTE code is normally recorded on the highest-numbered tape track, and the track output fed back into the converter box. Noise reduction should be avoided if possible, because it can introduce errors into the code. Because sequencers can't read SMPTE directly, a conversion has to be done somewhere along the line, to generate a data format the sequencer can understand. This could involve a conversion to MIDI Time Code (MTC).

However, it is necessary to convert the SMPTE time information into musical tempo, by a dedicated SMPTE-to-MIDI sync box. The initial tempo of the piece of music and the SMPTE location of the song start, plus the degree and location of any subsequent tempo changes, are stored in the form of a 'tempo map', which must be created before the sequence can be sync'ed to tape.

The Roland SBX-80 was our synchroniser of choice.

The SBX-80 was a powerful link in syncing our drum machines and/or synthesisers to tape. To make the most of the SBX-80 you must use a Midi-clock-based drum machine and/or sequencer. It is capable of performing a multitude of syncing tasks, but the best is enabling you to expand the number of tracks of your tape recorder. This is accomplished by syncing your midi-clock-controlled drum machines and sequencer/controlled synthesisers with the twenty-three tracks on the tape. If your drums and synthesisers are not on tape but are synced up and running live, you have a lot more tracks available for recording acoustic instruments or voices on the tape machine. This means you will have more control over the balance of all the parts when it comes to mix, also less tape wear on the sounds. It is also easier to add/change drum fills and synthesiser parts later. It is a little risky, but worth the reward.

The SBX-80 can also generate midi-clock as well as the standard Roland sync (via five-pin DIN plug). The SBX-80 has a built in recorder that can read SMPTE and a quarter-note click and stores it as a song. Its display shows SMPTE in hours, minutes, seconds, frames and bits. It also shows measures, beats per measure and tempo. It is actually an SMPTE to beat-per-measure converter. The SBX-80 generates midi clock with 'midi note pointer' also.

The first step in recording is to decide on a tempo. You will not be able to change tempo once the SMPTE is recorded. If it ends up being incorrect the whole song may have to be re-recorded at the new tempo. You type the tempo in from the SBX-80's numeric keyboard. Then connect the drum machine and/or sequencer up to the SBX-80's clock outputs so that you can hear the patterns you have already programmed to be sure that your tempo selection is absolutely correct. You are now ready to begin recording.

MIDI Connection

Musical Instrument Digital Interface was invented in the early 1980s by two sound engineers, Dave Smith and Ikutaru Kakehashi.

Originally conceived as a way to pass digitally encoded information about a performance between different synthesisers, the protocol quickly expanded to include other music-related functions. Synchronisation was, and is, one of those functions. The MIDI 1.0 Spec includes several important messages that allow communication of synchronisation signals over a MIDI connection.

The main use in a studio format is connecting synthesisers and sound modules together. MIDI uses a sixteen-channel frame, so up to sixteen devices can be operated from one master keyboard. This is very useful in a studio format and once your equipment is connected together, in and out with the special MIDI leads, you have a fully integrated easily switchable system enabling you to change between different instruments easily and to experiment quickly, with many different sounds.

It also incorporates a MIDI Beat Clock, which was a system message in the original MIDI spec so that you could get your drum machine to play in time with your sequencer or arpeggiator. MIDI Beat Clock is meant to address the dimension of speed/tempo. The Beat Clock succeeds in doing that, to the point that if you change speed (tempo) in the master device, the slave devices will follow along in real time and play along at the new speed. But strictly speaking, Beat Clock only communicates speed. Beat Clock operates at twenty-four pulses per quarter-note (tied to musical tempo), but aside from having a first pulse and a last, it does not by itself include a stop or start message. Beat Clock is what we call a 'dumb sync'.

Speed – Yes.

Transport and location – No.

The revolutionary aspect of SMPTE code enabled the recording artist to overdub the drum machines and sequencers to a tape machine at any time. In our recording of *Power, Corruption & Lies*, once the sequencers and drum machines were on tape and you had started adding the acoustic tracks and vocals, there was no efficient or easy way of re-recording, replacing or altering (for whatever reason) these recorded parts. Not a bad thing, I must admit, because musicians are prone to procrastination and now they had the freedom to change everything whenever they wanted.

Some cynical people might say that all this technology was invented by studio owners just to waste time and make them more money. That wasn't true. But the by-product of having much more choice and flexibility in recording was that things started to take much longer to finish (remember this was way before computers in music came along – musicians say that computers were 'definitely' invented by studio owners to make more money).

We then decamped from Jam back to Britannia Row to mix, where we again reverted to the Transdynamic (see ebook of paperback edition for details) to enhance our sonic assault on your senses.

I actually kept a little diary here of how long it took us to mix the songs from start to finish, which makes very interesting reading.

On mixing 'The Perfect Kiss', we were told we had to do several versions. Rob wanted a dub (his constant mantra being 'Dub it up'), a twelve-inch and a seven-inch version, the first time our single would be on the LP. The times they were a-changing. It took us nearly forty-eight hours to mix the three versions, one after the other. Me and Mike Johnson stayed awake the whole time. On the first evening Rob had come in with champagne to celebrate because it was the last track of the album. Then they all got pissed and passed out before going home to sleep, leaving me and Mike to it. They came back the next day and chipped in with a few suggestions then went back to sleep again. Mike and I laughed. We were very happy knowing that we'd made something very special together.

To record 'Elegia', our Ian Curtis tribute, we had taken advantage of an offer of free studio time at CTS Studios in Wembley. They offered a day, meaning ten hours, which we took to mean twenty-four. We had cut/mastered many of our records there with a really wacky bloke called Melvin, who was quite old, and he was desperate to get us into the attached studio to impress the owners, his bosses. He was hoping we'd like the studio so much we'd come back for a proper session.

We spent the session whizzed off our tits on speed, and although he assumed it was going to take around eight hours, instead we spent ten just programming the sequencer, then putting the bass and guitar down and the drum effect overdubs, even at one point bringing Melvin's nephews, who called in from school in the afternoon, onto the track and recording them saying their names, 'Ben and Justin', over and over again. (It was the working title for a while.)

It was a great day. Barney, released from the pressure of singing, was really relaxed. He wrote and played all the keyboards and layered them onto the track. We ended up recording an epic 17-minute, 32-second version of it.

The whole process, start to finish, took twenty-four hours. The next group were due in at ten the next morning and we left about 9.30 a.m. Melvin was ga-ga with lack of sleep. Rob was impressed. 'Now that's what I call value for money,' he chuckled. 'Free!'

I remember as we were leaving, clutching our finished tape of 'Elegia', Melvin said, 'You will come back, won't you, to use the studio properly?'

'Yes, mate, no problem,' we said, but we never did.

Salford Van Hire were right. You should never trust a musician.

Peter Saville was given the job of finding a sleeve and he racked his brains. Tom Atencio had been on at him since they met to 'Pleeeezze, Peter, put their fucking faces on the cover!' so I think the idea of doing it felt quite natural.

Pete concluded, 'He was right. I felt it was time!'

But he spent so long deliberating that a panicked Tony Wilson and Rob Gretton made a special trip down to London to ask what was taking so long. As Pete explained his idea, Tony went silent, lost in thought, while Rob was open-mouthed in shock. Tony then decided it was a great idea too. Rob was still open-mouthed.

'We won't tell the band,' said Pete. He then persuaded us to come down separately, for a promotional photoshoot to be used, he said, 'after the record is released'.

He knew if we came together we would never take it seriously. Trevor Key took the photos using a completely new camera film called Polaroid roll. Pete stopped the individual session when he saw the shot he wanted to use. He then decided to treat the photos using a technique (no pun intended) called 'New Computer Reprographics', which allowed for the landscape-shape oblong/rectangle of the photograph to be treated and compressed into a square using a new computer called a Scitex machine and, in his words, 'make you look weirder'.

Peter felt that Stephen Morris's picture had turned out the strongest so decided to use it as his number one. But he also felt very strongly that if he featured anyone's picture too much, either by putting it on the front or putting the title or song credits on it, it would be going against his feeling that everyone in the band was equal, i.e. there was no band leader.

To further compound this he decided to wrap the whole sleeve in tracing paper (stealing the idea from a volume on his bookshelf) and seal the package so it had to be torn to be opened.

He said, 'I felt much better further obscuring your faces.'

Factory and Rob loved the sleeve. But when we finally caught up with him at the Cambridge Ball in 1985, me, Barney and Steve rounded on him as one, screaming, 'You bastard! You lied to us.'

It *is* a great sleeve. Two great ideas, one to obscure our faces to intrigue people further and the other one (which Peter loved) was the idea of you having to destroy the tracing-paper cover to get to the record. Another bonus was many fans buying two copies, one to play and one to save unopened.

'He went absolutely berserk when he saw the video'

By now New Order had achieved the holy grail of chart success, artistic independence and critical acclaim, and were continuing to attract the attention of more mainstream media outlets. The band were asked to participate in a Radio 1 event, Rock Around the Clock, *as well as being one of several major groups given the opportunity to make their own documentary for Channel 4's* Play at Home *strand. The resulting film was an extraordinary glimpse into the chaotic world of Factory Records, as members of Durutti Column, A Certain Ratio and Section 25 demand to see accounts from Tony Wilson, who is later interviewed naked in the bath by Gillian Gilbert. Meanwhile Rob Gretton interviews himself and Peter Hook interviews Alan Erasmus on the back of a motorbike.*

Alan was always the most enigmatic figure in the Factory Records story, still is. Like the Scarlet Pimpernel, you seek him here, seek him there, but really, he could be anywhere, and no one really knew what it was he did exactly, but it was nice he was there.

He'd always turn up at the most unlikely moments, say something to make his presence felt in some strange and surreal way, and then disappear again.

That was Alan. Always was, always will be. Our section of the *Play at Home* documentary was filmed at his girlfriend's farm, which was where we also stored the Factory boat. Yes, we had a Factory boat, an 'investment' of course, which as far as I can tell is what you call any ill-advised purchase.

No prizes for guessing what happened to it. That's right, it sank. Alan took us to see it while we were filming at the farm; it was on/in the river opposite. We all stood there laughing. Really, we should have been alarmed at the metaphor.

We did have a Factory car, too, an old Daimler that Alan had also bought, again as an 'investment'. That completely disappeared. Nobody knew where it went until years later when they tore down the Haçienda building and discovered that it had been bricked up in one of the renovations, next to a huge pile of over-ordered T-shirts. There it had stayed for years, rusting and gathering dust until the building was finally sold.

We had a great time filming the documentary, and being involved in the writing. As for Tony's infamous nude interview with Gillian in his bath, he got a warning off Granada TV (his day job) for showing his winkle. Rob decided to interview himself, which was surreal. He said he was the only man up to the job, fair enough. Barney's interview with Pete Saville was another highlight, along with Steve's surreal chat with Martin Hannett, who insisted on a real gun being available for the interview. He eventually agreed to a blank firer. I think it must have puzzled any viewer more than answered their questions, but hey-ho.

For Rock Around the Clock, *an event to be broadcast simultaneously on BBC2 and Radio 1 – part of a 24-hour fundraising telethon – New Order were booked to play in the basement studio at BBC's Broadcasting House. Produced by Mark Radcliffe, the session was marked by bad tempers and fiery playing, and featured 'Sooner Than You Think', 'Age of Consent' 'Blue Monday', 'In a Lonely Place' and 'Temptation'.*

Well, it was a complete fuck-up.

What happened was that we'd played in St Austell on 23 August, and the *Rock Around the Clock* thing was on the 25th, giving us plenty of time to make our way from Cornwall to London – in effect, a day off between the two gigs.

Although not for me and Slim. I was doing the sound for a Stockholm Monsters gig in Bournemouth the night before, the 24th. A girlfriend, Kim, was promoting the gig so I told her we'd come from St Austell to Bournemouth, see her, do the Monsters, then go on from Bournemouth to London, a much shorter journey than St Austell to London. That was my timetable and meant my time was pretty much accounted for.

As for the rest of the band and crew, they decided that because the hotel in St Austell was so nice, they'd spend the intervening day there and drive to London the next day. 'Don't worry about it, Hooky, don't worry about it, we'll be fine, we'll be fine,' said Rob when I raised concerns. 'We'll see you there at eleven.'

But Rob must have put the phone down and then rejoined the rest of the band at the bar, because by all accounts they spent their day off, not to mention the ensuing evening, getting absolutely hammered.

Their intention was to leave at seven the next morning to reach London, but even if they could have got up for seven (and, as it turned out, they couldn't) they still wouldn't have made it.

The journey from St Austell to London is five hours at least, and that's with a good tailwind, no traffic delays and no stops for petrol or crisps to keep hungover band members from losing their minds.

Meanwhile, Kim very kindly drove me and Slim from Bournemouth to London and we were at Broadcasting House for 11 a.m., like good little boys.

No sign of the band.

Of course not. They were on their way. No mobile phones in those days. We just had to sit tight and wait.

Which is what we did. We waited. New Order weren't on until five, so there was still plenty of time. No need to panic just yet.

The guy arrived with the foldback system and I got him to set it up. The extra mixing desk arrived too, same thing.

FOLDBACK SYSTEM

When you see a band perform live, the black speaker boxes facing the musicians at the front of the stage are called 'fold back'. Folding back the music to the performers, so each musician can hear what they're playing on stage.

Then we waited some more. Time ticking on now. Lunch came and went, and there was still no sign of the Cornish contingent.

About three o'clock, Ozzy, Terry, Dave Pils and Corky arrived with the gear, looking a bit sheepish and full of tales about the terrible traffic. Did they know where the rest of the band were? Did they fuck. It was a hot day. I was starting to sweat. We set up as much as possible: my rig, the guitar rigs, drums and sequencers.

Shitting it by now.

At last, at twenty to five, we still weren't ready when the band arrived. The BBC crew were going absolutely mental, they were all still flying around the place trying to plug in our very complicated drum and sequencer set-ups when at last I got to find out what had happened. Sure enough, they'd all got up that morning, all with stinking hangovers, had a bit of breakfast, and then set off around nine-ish, hoping the journey from Cornwall to London would take them about a couple of hours.

It had taken them nearly eight.

So they were wrecked. Stressed, and hungover, and very hot and bothered – and none more so than our illustrious lead singer, who was doing the now-familiar routine of spewing into a plastic bag then taking out his bad fortune on everybody else. He was as miserable as sin and, if you watch the footage, you'll see he spends half his time gesticulating at the poor sods in the control room, tearing off his headphones, kicking stuff, swearing, red-faced and angry, even yelling at Steve at one point to go faster on the only slow track we played. Eddie of Oz PA was doing foldback and had plastered a sticker saying 'Gay Sperm' onto his amp. But even that did nothing to lighten his mood. Watching it I am at a total loss as to what the tosser is mad at ... himself? The BBC, the traffic, those bloody awful shorts? It really is a mystery. It was definitely more like 'Rock Around the Cock'.

But you know what? It ended up being a unique performance, and I loved it. There was no doubt that Barney was like a kid having a tantrum and it wasn't pretty to see but, even so, you had to hand it to him, he played like a demon, and the fact that the whole thing was teetering on the edge of catastrophe from start to finish just added to our punky, anarchic allure as far as I was concerned.

Yes, so it must have cost us a few favours at the BBC, the old 'you'll never work at this radio station again'-type thing, but it was great. It was what we were all about. The way we saw it was, ah, fuck it, just move on.

Which is what we did. We moved on, and in December of that year signed a licensing deal with Qwest, Quincy Jones's label in America. Rob Gretton, unbeknown to us, had in all his negotiations with any American label insisted that any deal would only be for one record. Presumably this was to safeguard against us getting stuck for, say, a five-album deal, to a bad label. Quite why he was so careful about this territory and so gung-ho about Factory and England we will never know. Maybe he wanted to redress the balance? But this fact and this fact alone, of one album, was enough to put off any blank-cheque-waving American record company, and left Tom Atencio with a problem: how could he convince any 'decent' record company to take us on, with such a short contract on offer?

For accomplishing that we had Tom to thank, and thank him we did mainly by making his life a misery and frustrating him at every turn.

Poor old Tom, he's so American, it's not true: LA through and through, and I mean that in a loving way. He is all about hard work and your talent being well rewarded. And we drove him mad because he wanted us to be huge in America, like Bon Jovi or something, and while of course we would have loved to be big in America we also wanted to do things on our terms.

So, say with *Low-Life*, which was where Tom first came on board as our US manager, we'd all sit round and he'd say, 'What we need to do, man, is we need to get a single from the record, make sure the single is on the record, then we need to remix it, give it to college radio ...'

And Rob would push his glasses up his nose and interrupt him: 'Fuck off, will you, you boring bastard. Fuck off.'

They were at war, those two, practically from the moment they met.

It used to drive Tom insane. He hated that we didn't put the singles on the albums. He hated the fact that we didn't do interviews and if we did we were rude to the press, also the fact that we never appeared in our videos. In fact, he made it his mission to get the band in a video so MTV would play it. When at last we appeared in the video for 'Touched by the Hand of God' in 1987 MTV still wouldn't play it because the director, Kathryn Bigelow, had inserted a grisly car-accident scene, so he was foiled again.

Years later, when we made the 'Regret' video in Cannes in 1993, Tom was as usual desperate for us to appear and, if you see that video, we do indeed feature. Blink and you miss us, but we are in there.

Knowing full well that our blink-and-you-miss-us appearance was going to send Tom nuts, Rob took great delight in playing him the video. Perfect for a rock'n'roll manager. He went absolutely berserk when he saw it. So nuts that he physically jumped on Rob and started shaking him, trying to get his point across.

Tom deserved better, of course, as he did a brilliant job, but the real reason we got big in America was nothing to do with appearing in videos. It was because we had great songs and we started small, built a following and kept going back. Loyalty.

And the reason we kept going back? Well, I'm afraid to say that's because we were such fanny rats. After that gig in Austin, when we discovered that we had sexual as well as musical pulling power, it was America, Land of the Free, for us from then on. We'd sit down and Rob would say, 'Do you want to do a tour of Europe?' and we'd say, 'What, Europe? Fuck that, let's go back to America!'

It was such a great place to play. The treatment (not just the girls) beat the shit out of anywhere else in the world.

Sorry, Europe. I love you, I really do. And now that I'm a happily married man in my sixties who doesn't touch drink or drugs, I can say hand on heart that I don't discriminate between the continents. Back then, though, for a stupid, easily led, randy 28-year-old, in love with being a rock star, it was America all the way.

And Tom Atencio, God bless him, was doing his very best for us against terrible, occasionally insurmountable odds, trying to turn us into huge U2-style stadium-filling megastars. He eventually did, but our awkwardness was unique and we definitely stood out among all the other acts.

Signing the licensing deal with Qwest/Warner Brothers was a huge feather in his cap, of course. When he presented the idea and got interest at the record company, it was passed to business affairs where David Burman, the head, sent a letter back saying, 'No!' to the very start of the deal adding, 'This will ruin us. If we set a precedent like this Warners will be finished.'

But Tom persevered, working not only on Quincy Jones but also on Mo Ostin, the head of Warners, until they agreed, and he sweetened the deal by giving them Joy Division and *Movement* and *Power, Corruption & Lies* to distribute.

Factory were paid $250,000 upfront for the licence for *Low-Life*, split 66 per cent to us and 33 per cent to them, with a commitment from Warners to contribute 50 per cent to our video budgets. We were now in a different league, with great bargaining power. To get a licensing deal for one record was exactly what we wanted, because we didn't fancy an American record company sticking their oar in and making us do the crap we usually went out of our way to avoid. (Having said that, years later we were being presented with cassette copies of *Power, Corruption & Lies*, only to discover that Qwest had added 'Blue Monday' and 'The Beach' anyway, naughty.) So the idea of signing a licensing deal with Qwest was that we maintained our independence, our uniqueness, but were able to take advantage of better distribution muscle.

There were many people at Warner Brothers who would become very important – instrumental in our success, if you like: Karen Berg, Steven Baker and Craig Costage, to name but a few.

Financially, I'm not sure if it helped. Nearly all our money was going into the Haçienda by then anyway, but in terms of recognition, it was a great boost. Qwest and Warner Brothers were hot on promotion, and because Barney hated promotion, and Stephen and Gillian just picked and chose what they wanted to do, yours truly handled the bulk of the PR. I'm not complaining – it suited me fine. Rather than hang around my hotel room, bored, I'd go to radio stations and be rude to interviewers, get a load of free T-shirts, a load of girls' names for the guest list later, get taken out by these gorgeous people who worked in the different territories for Warners. It was great. What a life.

LOW-LIFE TRACK BY TRACK

'Love Vigilantes': 4.16

You just can't believe the joy I did receive …

Described by Barney as a redneck tune, but influenced by the Falklands conflict in 1982. At the time Barney even thought of joining up, going so far as to ask, 'Do you get per-day money in the army? Do they mind if you don't get up early?'

Starting from a bass and drum jam, a great 80-millisecond snare delay leads into a gritty and frightening song, charting the futility of war, complete with corny country-and-western ending.

'The Perfect Kiss': 4.51

My friend he took his final breath …

This track took even longer to program than 'Blue Monday', nine months from start to finish, and went through many incarnations. At several points I thought we'd never finish it. A true story of an acquaintance who was shot and killed in Moss Side, Rob hated the lyrics on the chorus, saying, 'It sounds like "I gnaw". Get rid of it.' A track of many moods and intoxicating builds. The frogs were an old Emulator sample we had. I only ever think of it in its true twelve-inch version. I suppose this is what you would consider a taster. Great intro.

'This Time of Night': 4.45

What good's a lie when you've nothing to hide …

A very dark song, influenced by our nights at Skin Two, it should definitely have been used in the *Fifty Shades of Grey* film, I thought. A great hybrid rock/dance tune. We were getting very good at this. Barney's piano playing is a highlight. Dual basses drive it along and the combination of 'live' drums and drum machine are excellent. A welcome return of very rare, band backing vocals (reminiscent of *Movement*).

'Sunrise': 6.01

You gave me a gift that you then took away ...

This track always reminds me of *Blade Runner*. The ominous synth line sets just the right atmosphere. A fantastic bass riff with 'The Cramps'/ Ennio Morricone-like rhythm guitars. Originally called 'The spaghetti western one'. We worked really hard to get a fantastic lead-guitar sound, taking Barney's strings off and placing small metal washers on the strings at the bridge end to get a killer metallic sound. I was very flattered when Barney took the end bass riff and made it the third verse.

'Elegia': 4.56

My name is Ben, my name is Justin ...

A beautiful instrumental, and very moving in the full-length seventeen-minute version. This remixed edit brings together all the best bits. There were many timing errors in the long version that we never had time to correct. Sadly, Ben and Justin never made the final mix.

'Sooner Than You Think': 5.12

We had a party in our hotel last night ...

Written after a party in our hotel one night. A very unusual tune, showing exactly why I used to love New Order. We were so versatile. The LPs were so exciting because you never knew what kind of track was coming next. Oh, I'm getting all melancholy. We were thinking about an Irish tour when we wrote it.

'Sub-Culture': 4.58

I sit around by day tied up in chains so tight ...

The second of our Skin Two commentaries. I remember Barney being captivated by this beautiful blind girl there one night. She was dressed in a skin-tight black rubber dress. A lovely girl, I would like to dedicate it to her. It suffered from five o'clock in the morning lyrics when we couldn't think of anything else for the chorus apart from the 'shaft' bit. So we shafted you with bum lyrics, hee-hee. Walking bassline stolen from Michael Jackson's 'Beat It'. Complete with 'doped-up' vocal and sampled sexual grunts.

'Face Up': 5.02

With your long blonde hair and your eyes of blue …

A track in two halves with the soundtrack-like intro inspired by *Caligula*. Which could have easily been another song. Another great hybrid with my favourite 'knicker-loosener' dropdown ever. Well done, Barn, fantastic live.

TIMELINE FIVE
JANUARY–DECEMBER 1984

©Trevor Watson

10–15 January 1984

'Thieves Like Us' is recorded at Britannia Row, Islington.

27 January 1984

The Tube's Haçienda edition is broadcast, featuring the Factory All Stars, an interview with Tony Wilson and Paul Morley, the Jazz Defectors, Marcel King and the Breaking Glass Dance Troupe. Also featuring an unknown Madonna on her first visit to the UK.

19 March 1984

New Order play Caesar's Palace, Bradford.

30 March 1984

New Order play Uni-Mensa, Düsseldorf, West Germany, supported by Shark Vegas.

31 March 1984

New Order play Haus Nied, Frankfurt, West Germany, supported by Shark Vegas.

April 1984

New Order: 'Thieves Like Us', twelve-inch
(FAC 103)

Track list:

'Thieves Like Us'	6.36
'Lonesome Tonight'	5.11

Run-out groove one: *Melvin says …*
Run-out groove two: … *Watch*

Recorded and mixed at Britannia Row Studios, Islington, London.

Engineered by Mike Johnson.
Written by New Order and Arthur Baker.
Produced by New Order.
'Lonesome Tonight' written and produced by New Order.
Designed by Key/PSA (Peter Saville Associates).
Entered UK chart on 28 April 1984, remaining in the charts for 5 weeks, its peak position was number 18.

2 April 1984

New Order play Volkshaus, Zurich, Switzerland, supported by Shark Vegas.

> **'Everything went wrong at this gig. The DMX went down and the promoter had to get us another one as we had no spare. He turned up with a DMX Mark 2 and it was completely different to a MkI so Steve couldn't program it in time for the gig, or properly, and it showed. The audience got really pissed off, booing us, throwing things and doing Nazi salutes. But the one thing I'll never forget was that it cost nine pounds for a bowl of cornflakes! I nearly choked on them. That was three days' money. Three days' per-day money for a bowl of fucking cornflakes and they weren't even Kellogg's!'**

5 April 1984

New Order play Alabamahalle, Munich, West Germany, supported by Shark Vegas.

6 April 1984

New Order play Wiener Arena, Vienna, Austria, supported by Shark Vegas.

8 April 1984

New Order play Metropol, West Berlin, supported by Shark Vegas.

10 April 1984

New Order play Saga Cinema, Copenhagen, Denmark, supported by Shark Vegas. Hooky and Slim sing 'Blue Monday'.

> **'Afterwards I went to the infamous "Spunk Bar", an old Hell's Angels hangout, and bought a T-shirt with Slim to celebrate his debut, XXXL.'**

12 April 1984

New Order play Trinity Hall, Hamburg, West Germany, supported by Shark Vegas.

> **'What a night!'**

15 April 1984

New Order play Galactica, Luneburg, West Germany, supported by Shark Vegas.

16 April 1984

Musik Convoy: New Order and Depeche Mode

> **'We took a rainy day out to play on a German TV show with Depeche Mode, and the differences between us couldn't have been more apparent. They mimed, all dressed up to the nines, and we ambled in scruffy and played a storming version of "Thieves Like Us". They looked embarrassed, prancing around to a backing track, and rightly so.'**

May 1984

New Order are faced with an Inland Revenue tax investigation.

1 May 1984

New Order: 'Murder', twelve-inch
(Factory Benelux FBN 22)

Track list:

'Murder'	3.55
'Thieves Like Us' (instrumental)	6.57

Run-out groove one: *where you're flicking ...*
Run-out groove two: *that ash*

Recorded and mixed in Britannia Row Studios, Islington, London.
Engineered by Mike Johnson.
Produced by New Order.
'Thieves Like Us' written by New Order and Arthur Baker.
Designed by Peter Saville Associates.
Photography by Trevor Key.

3 May 1984

Top of the Pops appearance playing 'Thieves Like Us'.

> **'This whole episode was much easier, there being little or no resistance to us playing live. Interestingly, the contrast came from the other groups on the episode. Orchestral Manoeuvres in the Dark, U2, Kajagoogoo etc., they all came to us and apologised for miming. Bono said, "There was a tricky harmony on the chorus ..." I got a few complaints because my bass was making the cameras shake and rather naughtily put feedback all the way through OMD's dreadful offering, "The Locomotion", meaning they had to mime again. That'll teach them for nearly killing me at the premiere of *Pretty in Pink*.'**

14 May 1984

New Order play an NUM benefit gig at Royal Festival Hall, London, supported by Keith Allen, John Cooper Clarke and Life.

17 May 1984

New Order play Paradiso, Amsterdam, Netherlands, supported by Quando Quango.

> **'As a gig the Paradiso is very interesting. I have been booed off there in four groups and started four riots: Joy Division, New Order, Revenge and Monaco. Is that a record?'**

21 May 1984

New Order play Palais, Leicester, supported by Life and the Flamingos.

> **'Terry fell in love with the Flamingos' lead singer because she would cover herself in yoghurt and roll about on the floor as she sang.'**

21 May 1984

Haçienda second birthday party.

25 May 1984

Pop Elektron, Belgian television. New Order play 'Thieves Like Us'.

> **'We had become a little more in demand on the continent and now had access to all these TV shows. They never had a problem with us playing live at all, happily agreeing. A nice edit with some great "Oooohs".'**

3 June 1984

New Order play Powerhouse, Birmingham, supported by Stockholm Monsters.

> **'This was a strange night, not many people and a weird atmosphere. We were a bit down in the dressing room afterwards, when these two girls appeared, first of all asking for autographs**

on paper then suggesting we sign their breasts and then their bottoms with biro. Needless to say, someone soon got caught with one of them in the toilets by the cleaner, and we laughed as she chased them off with her mop. When I arrived back at the hotel I could see everyone else settling in for an all-night drinking session. I retired. In the morning, a very drunken Dave Pils, my roommate, appeared. He said, "Why is there biro all over my bed?"'

4 June 1984

New Order play the Palais, Nottingham, supported by Stockholm Monsters.

5 June 1984

New Order play Studio, Bristol, supported by Stockholm Monsters.

'This gig started well, with Ozzy being offered some help loading in by a bunch of guys who were waiting at the front door. Ozzy said, "It was going great and the van was nearly empty in no time, but when I went into the venue to set it up there was nothing there. I looked through a door at the side of the stage and saw the guys running off. They had been busy loading the stuff into another van out the back door. We were lucky I didn't wait until it was empty." The gig finished with a riot in the street as the crowd had things thrown at them from the roofs of the houses opposite.'

27 June 1984

New Order play Mayfair Suite, Southampton.

1 July 1984

New Order play Roskilde Festival, Roskilde, Denmark.

4–5 July 1984

New Order play two nights at the Rock-Ola, Madrid.

6 July 1984

New Order play Palma Club, Valencia, Spain.

7 July 1984

New Order play Studio 54, Barcelona, Spain.

10 July 1984

New Order play Marbella Estadio Municipal, Marbella, Spain.

> **'This gig was very undersold so the promoter arranged for a load of English 18–30 kids in coaches to turn up. They were so pissed they just stumbled around, completely oblivious to us.'**

12 July 1984

New Order play Pacha Auditorium, Valencia, Spain.

11 August 1984

New Order play De Panne Seaside Festival, De Panne, Belgium.

> **'Playing at a festival was very new still and enjoyable for it. Fad Gadget were playing and I loved them. I was perched by the side of the stage and Fad himself was having a bad gig and ended up throwing his guitar at the bass player's head, who just ducked and carried on. I had to be restrained from going on and punching him. Bloody lead singers!'**

12 August 1984

New Order play Inside Festival, Luik (Liège), Belgium.

> **'We had a great game of football in the afternoon with the Bunnymen, even Mac and Barney played. We beat them 5–2. Then we both got together to do "Sister Ray".'**

15 August 1984

New Order play the Mayfair Suite, Sunderland.

16 August 1984

New Order play City Hall, Hull.

19 August 1984

New Order play Leisure Centre, Gloucester.

20 August 84

New Order play Winter Gardens, Margate.

21 August 1984

Play at Home, 'The Story of Factory Records', Channel 4. Interviews with Tony Wilson, Rob Gretton, Martin Hannett and New Order. New Order recorded live at the Haçienda (20 July 1983): 'Lonesome Tonight', 'Temptation', 'Thieves Like Us'.

> **'It was nice to watch it on TV; it all seemed very positive. Our troubles were just about to begin really.'**

22 August 1984

New Order play Goldiggers, Chippenham.

23 August 1984

New Order play Cornwall Coliseum, St Austell, supported by Cabaret Voltaire.

25 August 1984

Radio 1 Saturday Live. New Order appear on BBC2's special *Rock Around the Clock.*

> **'When planning a long journey or setting off for an important meeting, always plan well ahead, taking into account possible traffic problems and other delays. You wouldn't want to be caught out, would you?'**

26 August 1984

New Order play Guildhall, Portsmouth.

> **'We were driving back from here when I noticed a car behind following us from the gig. I just burned them off, but we had Kevin Millins following us and he disappeared. We turned round to find him and noticed he had pulled over on the hard shoulder of the motorway. We came back and parked behind him. Then he told us he'd seen the car full of kids go spinning off the motorway and down the embankment. As it span, one of the kids had been thrown out of the window and fell into the central reservation and another kid fell out on the slope. They were hurt but not badly injured.**
>
> **'"Hello, mate," I said to the first one, who was pissed as a fart, "You all right?"**
>
> **'"Well, I was asleep in the back. So I don't know what happened. The next thing I knew, I woke up in the central reservation."**
>
> **'"How many of you were in the car?"**
>
> **'"There was three of us," he said, and I thought, *Shit, where's the other one?* Turns out we'd got the driver, we'd got the kid that was in the back, but we hadn't got the kid that was in the passenger seat.**

'I went into the hedge by the motorway and I came across this kid in the bushes, shirt ripped off him. He must have gone right through the hedge and he was just lying there. I was worried; he looked in a bad way.

'"Are you all right, mate?" I said, and he went, "Top gig tonight, Hooky. 'Sunrise' was excellent."

'Turned out they'd stolen their dad's car to get to the gig, then written it off. Luckily, because they were pissed they'd had the windows open, which was how come they'd all been thrown out. Must have had concussion though, we hadn't played "Sunrise" that night!'

©Kevin Cummins

27 August 1984

New Order play Heaven, London.

19 October 1984

Nude Night begins at the Haçienda.

October, November and December 1984

New Order record the album *Low-Life* at Jam, with mixing at Britannia Row Studios.

TOP TEN BEST PEOPLE I NEVER GOT TO PLAY WITH, SADLY (BUT WAS ASKED)

1. Denny Laine
2. John Lydon
3. Iggy Pop
4. Duffy
5. Mike Skinner
6. David Guetta
7. Robbie Williams
8. Johnny Marr
9. The Rolling Stones
10. Ian Brown

'Take us back to Hong Kong, Pedro'

On 2 March 1985 I became a father for the first time when my daughter, Heather Lucille, was born in St Mary's Hospital in Manchester. This was a wonderful moment and everything went well with the labour. I'm not too sure I could say me and Iris were getting on famously beforehand, but in the true tradition of most couples, we thought a child would help bring us together. I had always wanted children and coming from a biggish family, two brothers, was looking forward to being a hands-on dad. Ironically, as we were celebrating her birth, Rob was planning one of our most travelled years ever, taking us all round the world and me away from the pair of them for a long, long time.

Also putting a weak fool, me, in temptation's evil way.

The strange thing about having a child is that you cannot for the life of you remember what it was like before you had one. Seeing how beautiful our newborn baby girl was I couldn't believe there would ever be any problems. As I drove home that night down Oxford Road in Manchester, I sailed past Whitworth Street. I was so emotionally drained I couldn't even consider a night out in the Haçienda.

I must have been knackered.

In terms of the band this made things more difficult. I was the first one to have a child, and if I wasn't on tour then I wanted to be with the baby, and that created yet more working-hour friction.

We were working steadily, with Rob accepting whatever gigs we were offered in England, wherever they were. I suspect we needed the money. But when the offer of a Far East and Australian tour came up we couldn't resist it. The fees were low so there was no way we could afford to freight the gear. So we decided to only take the specialist items we needed in our luggage. This worked quite well apart from it being a complete ball-ache, especially when you were tired, plus it meant a lot of wear and tear on the gear. We were now using Voyetra-8 synthesisers that were rack-mounted with an external keyboard. Much more portable than the Prophet 5s.

Barney loved the Voyetra but they ate studio time/money like a hungry monster. They were just about portable. We looked like a retreating army carrying what we could rescue on the way out. And believe me, getting this lot to work when you arrived at the gig was no mean feat. Most of the soundchecks were spent fixing the drum machine and synth/sequencer set-ups. It was a nightmare and completely draining. No one apart from Barney knew what the hell was going on. Later we would have a trained keyboard/programmer roadie but at the moment we were just soldiering – and soldering – on.

The problem was that the equipment was intricate and our roadies weren't. Our roadies were our mates who didn't know their arse from their elbow and had even less idea about how to set up a sixteens pulsing keyboard. To try and get round that problem, Barney came up with a unique colour-coding system: 'Right, what you do is, you have a green sticker on the input here. You have a green sticker on that lead, then a yellow sticker and another on the output …' etc., etc.

Trouble was, he forgot that gigs are dark. Terry wore glasses and on the night, as soon as the stage lights came up and the beers started to go down, all the colours changed …

Most gigs Terry just looked completely terrified and confused, grabbing at his wattle, while Gillian usually stood there with tears in her eyes.

I think it's probably time to analyse what exactly New Order were doing with all this stuff and why.

The equipment kept breaking down. Why? Because most of it was in its infancy and had not been thoroughly tried and tested by anyone for anything. This stuff was meant for a high-tech studio environment, not sweaty gigs with even sweatier roadies throwing it haphazardly in the backs of lorries.

Barney always said that the manufacturers should pay us as guinea pigs with all this stuff. It was built then sent to us half-finished, and it was mainly Barney and Steve's feedback and critiques that made the Mk II versions tougher and more reliable than the Mk I. These companies were profiting from our agony.

We ran all the keyboards and drum machines live. And why? Because we were mad. No, scratch that, we did it because we were being true to ourselves, trying to distance New Order from groups like Depeche Mode, who put everything on a backing track and mimed, which we thought was the work of the devil. No pain, no gain, eh? The synths and drums were playing 'live' even though they were 'programmed'. Like the difference between vinyl and CD it added a warmth and richness to the sound. It also made each night different, sometimes slightly, sometimes drastically. Add in the chances of them going wrong completely and it certainly upped our edge factor and made us 'special', as they say in school. 'Ooh, little Hooky, he's very special, isn't he?'

Later we gave in and started using sixteen separate digital backing tracks, compared to most people's stereo output. It meant the sound engineer could make allowances for acoustic problems, but you still sounded different at every gig. Every gig would be different balances and equalisation, essentially a live remix. Which we felt was important, and, while that made things a damn sight easier, it still wasn't the end of our woes; you needed someone who knew what they were doing to work the gear and, as I said before, in our band when it came to anything other than bass or drums, that someone was Barney. He'd have to run over from singing to figure out the problem, which could be any number of things: the synthesisers had got too hot, they'd dumped the programs, the tuning had wandered, the drum machine had stopped or dumped its memory.

Or, the player/roadie was pissed. If it could go wrong, mechanical or human, at some time it would go wrong. Our nerves were frazzled at nearly every gig.

The Emulator I, in particular, was a real troublesome bit of kit, and as often as not would simply refuse to load the samples from the floppy disks. I remember one soundcheck us desperately trying to get it to load. Our soundman Ozzy called, 'Hang on, I've got an idea!'

We were very intrigued. We'd tried everything, switching it on and off, cleaning the disks, cleaning the disk drive, trying other disks, button combinations etc. etc. We patiently waited for Ozzy to walk from the mixing desk to the stage, climb up, walk over to the Emulator, pick it up off the stand and throw it on the floor. BANG!

'Try it now,' he said, walking off laughing, and fuck me it worked. It loaded up a treat. We later worked out it did the same thing if you hit the left-top leg with a hammer, saving Ozzy the walk.

Word got round about that. Erasure phoned us up. 'We've heard you get the Emulator I to work by hitting it with a hammer. Where did you hit it exactly?'

Gradually we built up a vast supply of spares, at one point running five Prophet keyboards and three poly-sequencers with two spare DMXs as well. It cost a bloody fortune. It was definitely the Haçienda of equipment. But again we soldiered – and soldered – on for ourselves, and the audience, feeling it enriched all our lives in one way or another.

So by the time we arrived in Hong Kong in April we were expecting a battle and must have looked like a squad of well-equipped hardline troops, like a musical SAS, prepared (or not, as the case may be) for anything the Far East could throw at us. Having spent the first part of the year in the UK, which was great for the music – home crowds and all that – but not so great when it came to a spot of rest and relaxation afterwards, we were dead excited about what was ahead of us.

We were right to be. Hong Kong was absolutely brilliant – I fell in love with the place straight away. So busy, so vibrant. It looked just like *Blade Runner*. An assault on all the senses.

At our first gig of the tour we met up with Gillian's cousin, a young squaddie stationed in Hong Kong. Loud and brash, this guy was the complete opposite of Gillian. He and his mates made up half our audience and his mates spent the evening sniffing dried lizard brains, so it looked like a leery night was guaranteed for all. At the gig I met an English girl, a part-time music journalist who worked and lived at the British embassy. She was lovely, and accompanied us on a tour of Hong Kong's seedier clubs, where we got very drunk. Later she asked if I'd take her home.

'I will … as long as I get a Ferrero Rocher,' I said.

She laughingly agreed so we sneaked away from the rest and got a cab,

'**我阿爸每個禮拜都會俾啲零用錢我,我就會攞啲零用錢去買漫畫睇同埋買雪糕食**!' she said to the driver, which I hoped translated as, 'Take us to the British embassy, driver, and don't spare the horses, this guy is an absolute Adonis! HURRY. HURRY!'

I had no idea what she really said but off we sped. As we wound up the hills it was a beautiful warm night and the view was amazing, so things swiftly became very romantic in the back, when we shuddered to a bumpy halt. The driver got out, leaving us alone in the cab, which seemed like too good an opportunity to miss, and before long we were, what can I say … at it.

Unfortunately, just as we were reaching a climax, the driver started banging on the window and screaming in Cantonese, '你想去野生動物園就搭五號巴士啦!' Which sounded like, 'You dirty English fuckers, car going to fall off jack!'

It turned out we'd had a puncture and he'd just got the car jacked up and ready for the spare, when it started rocking violently, hee-hee. I gave him a big tip.

'Get some Finilec, mate! That'll sort you out,' I shouted as he roared off.

She offered to show me the sights of Hong Kong the next day, and I was more than happy to accept; the band had two days off before making our way to Japan, what better way to spend it?

Until I remembered a prior commitment.

'Oh, bollocks, I can't,' I told her. 'We're supposed to be spending the day with the promoter in China. He's taking us to some beautiful seaside resort he reckons is the dog's bollocks. Wang Chou or something?'

'Ew,' she said.

Now, when the promoter had proposed this, we'd all thought, *Yeah, why not? Sounds interesting.* But by now we were having such a great time in Hong Kong, we were collectively wishing we could stay put. But still, you know what it's like. The guy was really insistent, and he was dead nice; he'd planned this trip to China, so it seemed rude to refuse.

The next day we got up and, after a long breakfast, fourteen of us piled into a bus that took us across the border into China, at which point the promoter, our tour guide, told us that it was a journey of forty kilometres to our destination – this 'beautiful seaside resort'.

What struck us right away was the vast difference between Hong Kong – dazzling, hospitable, New Order-loving Hong Kong – and China, which to our eyes looked like a Third World country. We saw old, dilapidated buildings and shacks crowded one on top of another and teetering on the banks of rivers. As for roads, forget it. Our driver had to thread his way across a pothole-strewn terrain that seemed to stretch from the border right up to our destination, avoiding suicidal motorcyclists/cyclists the whole way.

As a result, the forty-kilometre journey from the border to the 'beautiful seaside resort' took us the best part of five hours, and by the time we turned up it was 9 p.m. The fact that the 'beautiful seaside resort' was nothing of the sort, and was just as deprived-looking as the various shanty towns we'd passed on our journey, took a distant second place to the fact that we were absolutely starving and mithering our host for something to eat.

'OK, I take you, I take you!' he said, and he gabbled something to the driver, who drove us to a restaurant.

Once there we disembarked, the promoter telling us, 'This is the best restaurant in town,' with a grand wave of his hand.

Like everything else we'd seen since entering the country it looked like a broken-down relic from another decade. What's more, I was looking at it thinking that the owner must have an awful lot of pets, because they were all kept in cages outside the restaurant: puppies, lizards, snakes, cats, you name it.

'Are you sure this is the best restaurant?' we asked him once we'd passed the cages and got inside, because God, if it was then we didn't want to see the worst. It was an absolute shithole.

One of the crew went to the toilet and returned with the news that there wasn't a toilet as such, just a hole in the floor right next to the kitchen. Other customers were staring at us open-mouthed, this group of Mancunians in leather jackets and biker boots, with Gillian getting most of the boggle-eyed looks.

We sat, ordered, then the food started coming out – first some chicken, and oh, my godfathers, it was dreadful, absolutely rotten. It was chicken that looked like it had been run over by a lorry and then cooked. Then we had the snake. At least you didn't have to pick your own snake. It was horrible. Full of tiny little bones. Fucking awful. Next the owner came out and said, '如果有任何您想去外面和你的狗.'

'What did he say?'

'He said, do you want to pick a dog?'

And we were like, 'We're not going to take a dog home, mate. What are you talking about? Fuck off. Listen, we need to get to the hotel,' thinking they might have something to eat and drink there.

The promoter said, 'OK, we go hotel. Bus driver back before lights go out,' and we were like, 'Hang on, what does that mean? "Before the lights go out?"'

We soon found out. Leaving the restaurant for a walk around the beautiful seaside resort, bemoaning our luck, unable to believe we'd left Hong Kong for this absolute shithole of a place, the lights went out and the entire town was plunged into total darkness.

Half of us were in the bus, but I was with the other half who spent an hour or so plunging around the place in the pitch-dark, falling over, turning our heels in potholes, eventually arriving back at the bus bedraggled and limping and covered in mud.

There the beaming promoter assured us that we were going to the best hotel in the area, but you can imagine that by now we didn't have a lot of faith in his ability to distinguish between 'the best' and 'an absolute dump', so it wasn't like we breathed a sigh of relief at this point. Sure enough, after another pothole-ridden journey across town we arrived at the best hotel, the nicest hotel in this part of China, and of course it was shit.

Three of us to a room, and the beds were damp. It was a horrible place; me, Slim and Dave Pils in one room, where I carefully unfurled the mosquito net that was over my bed.

'This is quite cosy,' I said, climbing beneath it. 'It's like being in a tent. It's like camping.'

But Dave was going, 'Fuck off, Hooky, I'm not sleeping in no tent,' really pissed off. Slim joined in with a big 'Me neither!'

We had a terrible night's sleep. Of course. During the night, they held the Chinese National Indoor Door-Slamming Competition, so no one got a wink of sleep. Every time you dropped off, the sound of doors would jerk you awake again. In the morning we pulled ourselves from our damp beds.

'Shall we go and get some breakfast, then?' I said.

'You go ahead,' said Dave from the other bed, sounding very sorry for himself, 'I think I've been bitten.'

I got a look at him. He wasn't kidding. Overnight he'd been transformed into the Elephant Man, with lumps all over his face, all over his body. We started to count the bites and gave up at fifty-seven. Meanwhile Slim had been bitten too, about fifteen. Me, I was all right. I'd used the mosquito net.

We met up with the rest, the whole lot of us praying for a decent breakfast.

It was fried locusts, snake or whatever. Nothing that looked remotely edible. By this point you had fourteen people going absolutely nuts, sick to the back teeth of this place, desperate to leave.

Our host waltzed in, fresh as a daisy, looking as though he'd had the best sleep of his life, clapped his hands together and said, 'How is everybody? Looking forward to coach trip into mountains?'

That was the last straw.

Tired, hungry and no way prepared to get back on the bus if it meant another long, and no doubt highly dangerous coach trip, I grabbed him by the lapels. 'Listen, mate, if you don't take us back to Hong Kong now, we're going to fucking kill you.'

He swallowed. 'OK, OK, we go back Hong Kong. Now! Now!'

We all jumped in the bus. 'Get to Hong Kong, Pedro. Take us to Hong Kong now. Step on it.'

No, wait, first we had to have something to eat.

'Take us to a restaurant. Somewhere that serves rice.'

I can't remember who said that, but it was a genius idea. At least if they had rice we could eat the rice.

So anyway, the bus took us to this restaurant just on the outskirts of our beautiful seaside resort where we stumbled off, raced inside and at last – *at fucking last* – we had something to eat, a bit of fried rice and meat, and it was actually OK. I mean, it was very brown, but compared to everything else that had been put in front of us in the last twenty-four hours or so it was definitely OK, and everyone tucked in.

'What meat is this?' somebody asked.

'Oh that, it's common meat. Common meat.'

So we carried on eating. Finally sitting back smiling, hands patting our full bellies, then someone said, 'What kind of common meat is it, Pedro? Which common meat? Was it beef?'

'No, it not beef.'

'Was it lamb?'

'No, not lamb.'

'Well, what was it then?'

'It dog.'

Poor old Gillian threw up right there and then, right next to the table. The rest of us headed towards the exit as quickly as we could, pale-faced, cheeks blowing out as we clambered back onto the bus, dragging the promoter along with us and whipping the bus driver back into action again. 'Hong Kong, Pedro. Now!'

'Excellent,' he said. 'When we get back to Hong Kong I take you for monkey brains too!'

We arrived at the border. Of course, it took us fucking *hours* to get through immigration back into Hong Kong; literally there were blokes holding two live chickens in each hand in front of me, and by the time we got back it was in the wee small hours.

I phoned up my girl, who said, 'I can't come now, Peter, it's three in the morning. I've got to work tomorrow,' so that was yet another grievance to add to the list.

But our host still had another trick up his sleeve.

'Make a mistake with plane,' he said, ashen-faced in the hotel lobby.

'What you mean? What do you mean, "make mistake with plane"?'

'Plane I thought seven o'clock at night. It seven in morning.'

So that was it. Any chances I had of seeing the embassy girl were again scotched, and instead we were due at the airport straight away, the one and only silver lining of that particular fuck-up being that at least we didn't have to spend any more time with this dickhead.

I mean, he was a lovely bloke, but the whole thing had just been a complete nightmare from beginning to end, and we were young and horrible, and so as we were leaving we were taking the piss, really laying on the Manc accent, talking dead fast, going, 'See yah, knobhead,' knowing full well he wouldn't be able to understand what we were saying. 'We've had a fucking shit time, you ruined it for us, see you later, you cock.'

Oblivious, he was beaming, waving goodbye, when suddenly he said, 'I have present for you all.'

'Present for us all?'

Remember, we were laden down with gear, more stuff than we could carry, but that didn't matter to the promoter. He excused himself to the coach and then returned to where we were waiting to go through immigration, carrying fourteen boxes piled high.

They were tea sets that he presented to every single one of us. 'A little memento of your trip,' he said as he bowed.

I'm afraid to say that some of those tea sets got left there and then in immigration. Dumped. Me, I kept my tea set. I took it halfway round the world, lavishing much care and attention on it and then, much later, lost it when Iris and I split up. I was gutted because I'd gone through hell and high water, not only to get it, but then keep hold of it. I say lost it – I mean I couldn't catch it when she threw it at me. Ah well. Easy come, easy go?

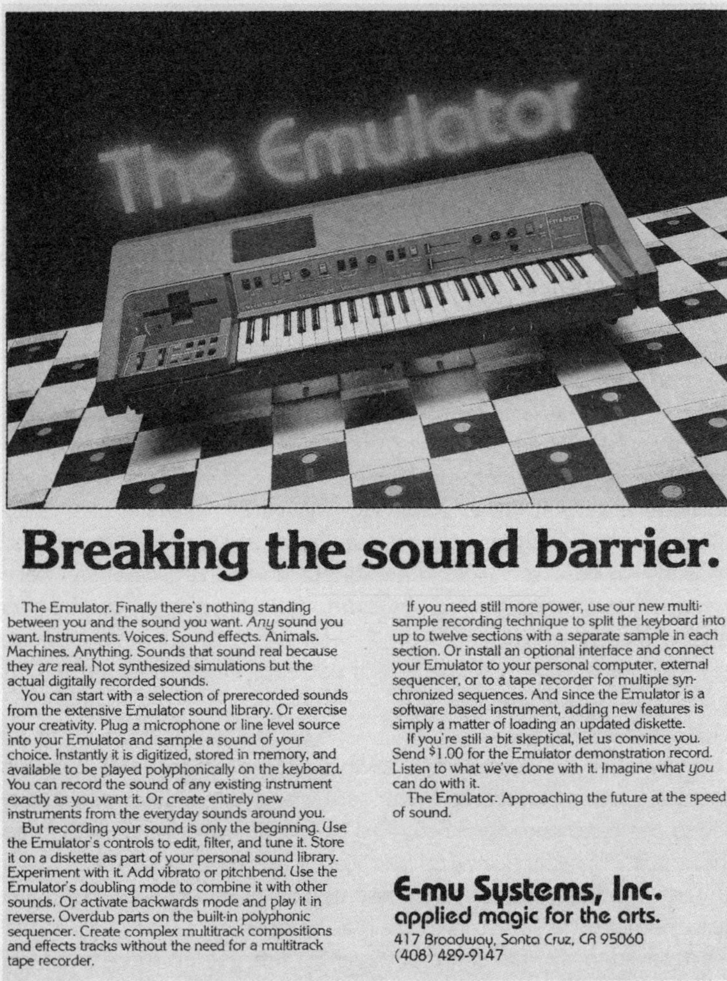

'It was the highest room-service bill in the history of the hotel'

We loved Japan. In Japan in those days you got looked after like nothing we'd ever experienced before, treated like little gods. We made it through immigration, picked up our bags, and then as we entered the arrivals hall, an army of Japanese kids ran forward to grab them off us. It was nearly a riot.

We were like, 'Hey, what are you doing!?' but soon twigged they were trying to give us a proper Japanese welcome by carrying our bags for us. *Great*. This was the life. Then we looked round and saw Gillian still struggling with hers. Turns out that in this culture they don't help a woman. We got her a trolley.

Then Tony Wilson appeared. He had been scheduled to come to film a gig video, which would later become *Pumped Full of Drugs*.

His arrival came as a shock, because we knew that back at home his wife Hilary had been attacked and slashed across the face by a woman who was stalking Tony. She'd even been sleeping in his garage. Hilary had warned Tony that someone was hanging around but he did nothing. One day the woman had knocked at the door while Hilary was alone with their infant son, Oliver, asleep upstairs. The woman asked for Tony, and when Hilary said he wasn't there she slashed her across the face, right on the doorstep, pulling her outside and then going in the house and closing the door behind her, leaving poor Hilary bleeding on the ground.

Hilary obviously went hysterical, crying for help. When people came to her aid and finally entered the house the woman was arrested, and would eventully end up in Broadmoor. Meanwhile, after making sure Oliver was safe, Hilary was taken to hospital. And yet, after all of this, Tony still chose to fly out to Japan and leave them both at home.

'I'm filming, darling. It's my job,' was the only thing he said. Well, we supposed it was his business. Whatever was going on at home, he was just his normal self. 'Hello, darling!' to everyone, while he flounced around slinging the saddlebags that he carried everywhere with him.

Our hotel was the Tokyo Prince. It was beautiful, thirty-odd floors of absolute luxury. As a gift, the record company had left us a brand-new CD player on each of the band members' beds. They weren't even out in England yet, and it's a measure of how spoilt we were getting that I was gutted to get a black one when the others got red, and protested loudly. When we came home there were hardly any CDs available to buy anyway.

Later on, as we ambled round the shopping district, we realised they had no staff in the shops. You had to ring a bell for service. Once the crew realised this they were soon togged out head-to-toe in designer labels. They never rang the bell. 'Couldn't find it!' they said, like butter wouldn't melt.

We also learned about Japanese girls, who were so accommodating it was unbelievable. They used to hand out business cards saying things like:

Suki;)
Satisfaction Guaranteed
To ALL travelling Musicians
Multi-Orgasm to your pleasure.

I never had the pleasure, but heard that they'd treat you like a lord – tidy up, straighten your clothes and polish your shoes, even packing your bag for you, so Andy Robinson said. Nobody could decide if they thought it was nice or a bit creepy.

Our first night there, Rob called my room.

I said, 'Rob, what the fuck? It's four in the morning.'

'Yeah, but one of our guys is on the roof.'

It was true. Bored and jetlagged, this bloke had got out of his window and was edging along a ledge, making his way around the building and spying in the windows, like a hairier version of King Kong.

I was waiting for the Sopwith Camels to arrive and shoot him down. Security had spotted him and called Rob. They were panicking, running round, garbling into walkie-talkies. Then, as me and Rob were looking up watching the drama unfold, Rob suddenly announced, 'I'm going back to bed. Fuck him.' And he did. (Not fuck him, went back to bed.)

I shrugged my shoulders and followed suit. 'Let him get on with it . . .'

The next day we were soundchecking and trying to cobble together the gear for the show. I gave the promoter a shopping list of stuff we needed – important stuff because the next day's show was being filmed by Tony.

Sadly, we were a man down. Slim had caught a virus that Westerners are particularly susceptible to in Japan. Years later, I'd catch it myself.

Anyway, Slim couldn't move at all and spent the whole five days we were there in bed, sweating cobs.

I kept saying to him, 'Order what you want to eat off the room-service menu. Make sure you eat and drink.'

But when me and Dave Pils went to check on him later we could tell he hadn't.

'What's going on, Slim? Why haven't you eaten?'

'It's too expensive, Hooky. Have you seen the prices? They're ridiculous,' he groaned.

You can take the Manc out of Manchester but you can't take Manchester out of the Manc, eh? Saying that, he did lose two stone; he was delighted. Every cloud ...

Back at the gig the promoter was still on the case, getting us our equipment.

'Hey, Taka, can you get us a Vox UD30?' I asked, as a joke (it's one of the rarest amps in the world).

'Maybe, Mr Peter,' he said, nodding furiously.

It wasn't the answer I was expecting.

'Really? You sure? They're rarer than rocking horse shit.'

'Maybe, Mr Peter.'

More nodding.

I said, 'All right, can you get a Vox two-by-fifteen bass cab?'

Nodding. 'Maybe, Mr Peter.'

I had a long list. He said 'maybe' to everything on it and, frankly, I was amazed. I was going to our lot, 'It's brilliant. This guy thinks he can get us loads of vintage gear.'

Later on in the day, I said to the promoter, 'Hey, where's that gear? It's getting a bit late,' and he was still replying, 'Ah, maybe, no problem, no problem,' but no gear was materialising.

In the end I grabbed the translator and said, 'Listen, we're waiting for all this vintage gear he said he could get, and it's not turned up and we need to set up now.'

'Oh, Peter, I am so sorry.'

'What? What are you sorry about?'

'Well, in Japan, they don't have a word to say to a Westerner that means no. It brings shame on you if you have to tell somebody you can't do something, so what he meant was, no, he can't get that, but he didn't have the word to say it.'

'You what?'

We ended up having to cobble together a load of old crap to play the gig.

We played, and there was no atmosphere whatsoever. Songs would be met with polite clapping, perhaps a bit of appreciative murmuring if we were lucky. There was such a general lack of enthusiasm that we came off stage calling them all the names under the sun.

The promoter was there. 'Mr Peter, you do encore?'

'Do encore? For them fuckers? No chance.'

'You mean close show?'

'Yeah, I mean close fucking show. We're off, mate, we're out of here. Fuck that.'

But after a minute or so we'd cooled down a bit, and Barney said, 'Come on, let's go back on and give them loads of feedback and "Sister Ray".'

So we came out of the dressing room to find the crew going, 'What are you doing?'

'Come on, we're going back on just to piss them off.'

We arrived back on stage as the audience were leaving. However, by now the security had departed and suddenly the kids still inside the hall were a different crowd; this meek and mild-mannered bunch were transformed into a marauding horde, charging to the front and throwing themselves about like it was Pearl Harbor all over again.

We looked at each other. Talk about going from the sublime to the ridiculous: twenty minutes ago we could hardly rouse them from their torpor. Now they were flinging themselves around with all the wild abandon of six-year-old kids on Haribo.

Next thing we knew, a bunch of them had climbed up and started charging around the stage banging on the drums. In an instant the stage was overrun. Our crew came hurtling on to try to stop them, instruments were kicked over and we were smack in the middle of yet another non-crowd-control situation.

Needless to say, we abandoned our hilarious feedback-drenching antics in favour of a speedy retreat, and were scuttling off at the same time as the security reappeared, took to the stage themselves and a full-scale riot broke out.

It turned out that the reason they'd been so quiet in the first place was that in the seated auditorium they had a security man at each end of every row, and a metal barrier between every two seats. Fair enough, it was a safety measure after a stampede at a concert in the 1970s killed several people, but it wasn't exactly conducive to a rocking night out.

'You will never play in Japan again,' said the promoter backstage, screaming at me as we listened to the sounds of battle from out front.

'Oh, put a lid on it,' I told him. 'If I had a yen for everyone who's said that to me . . .'

Japan was wild. We were taken to a wonderful club in the Rippongi District called 'Lexington Queens', a handwritten sign on the door proudly proclaiming, 'Western Models and Rock Group Members Free! Free Drinks Too! No Beer!'

This was our sort of gaff, and inside it was indeed full of models of both sexes, all impossibly beautiful. According to our interpreter the only crime in Tokyo was among these Western models all stealing from each other.

I was having a wild time quaffing free drinks and dancing on the podiums with the models, when Ozzy beckoned me to the bar and ordered a treble vodka and orange. 'Check out the barman,' he said.

I watched, and although the barman grabbed a bottle of vodka he didn't add any to the orange juice. Instead, he wiped what turned out be a vodka-soaked rag on the rim of the glass before handing it to Ozzy.

So that's how they did it. Ah well. We had a great time anyway. Everyone was high on life. I met a wonderful, dark-haired American model who came back to my hotel. She must have had nursing ambitions, because she said, 'Lie down and take off your clothes. I'm going to give you a bed bath.'

Blimey, I must get these leather pants cleaned, I thought.

But she carries on and it was glorious and so relaxing that the next thing I knew I was waking up the next morning. Fortunately, we made up for it.

At lunch I found out that Terry Mason had got arrested the

previous night for the heinous crime of carrying a walkie-talkie near the American embassy. We'd bought a couple of cheap Radio Shack walkie-talkies, and Terry loved carrying his around. It had a massive extendable aerial, which he found many uses for. Some Japanese policeman had decided he was a spy and arrested him outside the embassy.

Terry said, 'It was hilarious. He tried to put me in his sentry box and the roof was really low, I'm six-foot-four and I was bent double. It felt like *Alice in Wonderland*. In the end I just pushed him away and walked off.'

The next day it was time to leave. Now, at the start of the week, Rob had said to everyone, 'Eat and drink whatever you want. We can't afford per diem so I'll pay it.'

We'd been quite restrained, apart from the spring rolls and Japanese beers in the bar, practically living off them.

As we were preparing to depart Rob said to me, 'Right, Hooky, you go down and get the bill for the room service, I'll pay it on me American Express.' All we had to pay was the room service and other extras. The promoter was footing the bill for the rooms.

I ambled down, asked the receptionist for the bill, hanging out in reception as they got it ready.

Gradually I became aware that firstly the bill was taking a long time, and secondly there was a lot of whispering and conferring behind the desk.

'Is everything all right?' I asked.

The girl said. 'I have to go and get superior.'

'Really? Can't you just give me the bill?'

'I must get superior.'

She toddled off. The receptionists wear ceremonial dress in the Tokyo Prince and she looked beautiful.

Next thing, a deputation of them arrived and a more senior-looking woman said, 'Who will be paying the bill? Who is the boss?'

I said, 'Mr Gretton. He will be here in a minute.'

'OK, we have the owner of the hotel here, the general manager, and the room-service supervisor.'

They were all bowing like there was no tomorrow. Whatever was wrong, it was serious.

I phoned upstairs. 'Rob, you'd better get down here. Something's wrong. They won't give me the bill.'

Eventually he appeared, and they presented him with the bill, bowing and backing off at the same time.

He looked at it. Pushed his glasses up his nose. 'Oh my fucking Christ,' he said, blood draining from his face. 'It's over ten grand.'

'What?'

We'd managed to spend two grand a day on room service. Most of it on the bloody spring rolls, as it turned out. Fair go, they were lovely, but we'd assumed they were on the house, being such tiny little things.

It was the translator who put us straight. It was the highest room-service bill they'd ever had in the history of the hotel. Rob was delighted, another first for New Order.

After Japan we moved on to Australia and New Zealand. The group's tour was to coincide with the creation of Factory Australasia, with *Low-Life* being its inaugural release. Andrew Penhallow was the boss and such a nice guy. His house on the cliff overlooked Bondi Beach, where his kids took me crabbing in rock pools. What an idyllic life. We only did four gigs – Perth, Melbourne, Brisbane and Sydney – but got a great response. If I say so myself, the set list was great.

We moved on to Auckland where we met a lovely young lady. She took us for a meal before disappearing into the night with one of our entourage. It was a day off the next day and it did nothing but rain. It poured down. We were stuck in the motel in the middle of nowhere. In the evening a few of us ventured out for a beer, and who should we bump into almost straight away? The lovely lady from the night before.

I made a beeline for her, and we got on famously, and ended up spending the night together. In the morning she dropped me off at the motel. 'I'm off out now with your friend,' she told me, 'I've promised to show him the sights.'

I thought, *He's going to be delighted.*

Later Rob had a meeting with one of the local crew and couldn't resist telling him, 'Bloody hell, you know that bird? She's been through two of our lads already. One of them had her the first night, then she went with Hooky, and now she's back with the first lad. She's fucking mad for it.'

The guy had said, 'That's my fucking sister, you bastards,' and stormed off.

Rob reckoned it was the single most embarrassing moment of his life.

Luckily the gig went well, with no sign of the guy or his sister.

One morning I went for a crap and saw blood in it. I was thinking I must be dying, until gradually it dawned on me that everybody else on our coach was as subdued and thoughtful as I was.

A few minutes into the journey Eddie blurts out, 'I think I might be dying.'

'What?' we all said.

'Well, I went for a crap this morning and there was loads of blood in it.'

It was a real 'I'm Spartacus' moment, except with blood-soaked stools instead of rebellious slaves.

'I had blood in my poo.'

'Yes, I had blood in mine too.'

Anyway, the promoter was on board the bus seeing us off. He turned slowly around to this bunch of ashen-faced people all thinking they were dying and said flatly, 'It was the beetroot you had last night for dinner, you daft bastards.'

I got the feeling he was very glad to see us go. We made one more stop in Hawaii, which was a very strange gig to play. I cannot for the life of me figure out why we did it – apart from it being Hawaii and us getting a week off, of course. I had the worst sunburn ever. It felt like I had two teams of wild horses pulling my face apart. I remember it rained every day at 3 p.m. out of a clear blue sky. We must have lost a fortune. The equipment was awful and hardly anyone turned up. Tom Atencio joined us, and one of the crew was mugged on a drug deal by two rickshaw-riding ex-soldiers. Meanwhile, Slim copped off with the hotel owner's daughter (a spoilt heiress who took to driving him round in her brand-new soft-top Camaro, both of them completely trollied; talk about every dog having its day). Eventually, she was kidnapped out of Slim's room by two armed security men. An intervention, they called it. Dave was delighted, saying, 'If I'd had to watch them at it one more night, I would have jumped out the fucking window myself.'

Later Eddie managed to get deported because he didn't have an American visa, although I doubt that lying full-length in the check-in queue nursing a massive hangover and a beer bottle on his chest helped.

'I'll be writing about that in me memoirs'

The touring came thick and fast. Back in America that August and life was great again. In Oakland, one of the roadies counted how many girls we had in our huge dressing room and gave up at two hundred. I met some amazing girls: teachers, ballet dancers, blonde twins, oh my God, and a gorgeous girl who gave up a modelling career. She'd cut off her hair with nail scissors just to spite her parents, who desperately wanted her to be a model. It was a cosmic conversation.

By this time we were getting so many girls that I just decided to go for the prettiest in every dressing room. With the allure of being in a successful group I was suddenly in their league. My first question was usually, 'Do you come from around here?' and then the classic, 'What do you do for a job?' Pretty standard fare.

One girl replied, 'I mekochinirdseeders!'

'Eh?' I replied.

'Imeakmachinmerdreaders!'

Blimey. I leaned closer saying, 'Eh?' again.

She was getting exasperated, 'Imemeekmoctincirdkneeders!'

Oh shit. I was seriously in danger of blowing it here. Too much rock'n'roll had wrecked my ears. Thank God her friend took pity on me, saying loudly, 'She makes mocking-bird feeders! You know, for in the cages?'

When I took her home she did indeed have a mocking-bird, complete with feeder. In the morning she left for work saying, 'You know where you're going, yeah?'

'Me, I'm an intrepid traveller. I've been everywhere. Don't worry about me.'

Later I showered and left. As the front door slammed shut behind me I gulped. I was in the middle of suburban Denver with houses stretching for miles and miles. It took me three hours to find a diner. When I walked in dressed in leather pants and biker boots, I swear I had the same effect a little green man would have.

I finally got a cab, reaching the hotel in time to meet one of our roadies coming out. Turned out he'd spent the night with a mate of the girl who made mocking-bird feeders, and he looked like he'd been assaulted by a mountain lion. Covered in scratches and bites all over.

I went, 'What the fuck?'

'She was wild,' he said, looking very pleased with himself.

'But what are you going to do when you get home?'

He hadn't thought of that. Reality hit him. We were going home in just over a week and he was ripped to ribbons.

'Oh my God, what am I going to do?'

We were laughing, like we normally did. 'You daft bastard.'

This guy was a great character but he was mental and a right scrapper, a ball of pure aggression when he got going, not somebody to take shit from anybody. These days you'd get three months for nutting a member of the audience, but back then it was fine. The only person who could control him was our monitor guy.

Then he had a lightbulb moment. 'I know what I'll do,' he said. 'I'll start a fight to cover it up.'

I had an idea who was in his sights. He and one of the local promoters had been at each other's throats since we started touring America and it was a wonder they hadn't already kicked off. Things were about to come to a head in Santa Monica in more ways than one . . .

Something else was reaching the boil. In my opinion, Barney had been getting more and more frustrated with Gillian. Now, whatever else I may say about Barney – that he was a moody, tight-fisted bastard who made our lives a misery – I want to be clear that I understood the pressure he was under. Of us all, he did the most work. Steve and I did bass and drums, of course, and we worked on the lyrics and vocal lines together, but Barney ended up doing most of the keyboards and guitars himself.

I know he found it hard being frontman. He liked being first to get wrecked and having the attention of beautiful girls backstage, mind you. There were no complaints about being frontman then. But generally speaking, he found it hard, and he wasn't backward when it came to letting you know about it.

We'd talk about getting Gillian to write more. 'Don't *you* do it,' I used to say to Barney. 'If you don't do it, then she'll *have* to have a go.'

'Oh,' he'd say, 'I couldn't do that to Steve.'

Which is why you should never have a couple in the band.

I don't think he was a fan of her guitar work either, and later began to refuse playing the songs on which it featured, making us even more electronic. Over time we ended up neglecting greats like 'Sunrise', 'Age of Consent', 'Broken Promise', 'Way of Life', 'Love Vigilantes' and so on. Very frustrating for me.

So, Santa Monica. The day began badly, with our roadie and the promoter getting right on each other's tits, our guy winding him up something rotten – this was wrong, that was wrong – and the poor guy getting more agitated in return. 'Fuck you, man, get off my case,' little knowing what we knew, that our guy had an agenda. He needed an excuse for his ripped-up back.

It wasn't fair because the promoter was a lovely bloke; he certainly didn't deserve what was coming. But once our guy put his mind to something… Physically they were evenly matched so the outcome was up for grabs, but it was definitely going to happen.

We did the gig. Barney was drunk and, while we were playing, some guy tried to get up onstage and I put my foot on his head and – well, I wouldn't go as far as to say I kicked him off, it was more of a gentle push really, but you know, maybe some of the audience got the wrong idea and thought I'd actually kicked the gentleman in question, perish the thought, and started booing.

Next they started throwing things. After that the songs began falling apart, and at the end I looked across the stage to see that Barney was going psycho on Gillian's gear.

He had kicked her amp over, grabbed her effects pedals and thrown them out into the audience, closely followed by her guitar. When we got backstage the group was in full-on *inquireeey* mode (see Timeline, 2 August 1985). Gillian was very upset. She was screaming and crying, with both Steve and Rob trying to placate her.

Rob was puzzled. To be fair, we never told him how we felt and he probably thought she did as much as we did.

Well, this might bring things to a head, I thought. Only, it didn't, because Barney backed down, probably feeling guilty because he'd made her cry. We missed our chance to voice our opinions. Again.

We had our opportunity to say it, and perhaps we could have put a few things straight, but like everything else – management, money, working hours, all the things that spent years simmering beneath the surface – it was a toxic issue that was allowed to keep on simmering.

So Barney apologised. Put the whole episode down to the stress of being frontman, and we hit the drink.

Next thing, the fight broke out. That's right, the promoter had finally snapped, our guy's goading had at last pushed him over the edge, and he'd had enough and thrown the first punch.

He was, of course, playing right into the hands of our roadie, who responded in kind. My God, what a fight it was. This wasn't the most vicious fight I'd seen but it was one of the most evenly matched, and because of that it was one of the longest.

When it first broke out we tried to part them. Impossible. So we stood around watching, like you do, but after a while we got bored. It just went on and on. They were grappling and rolling about on the floor for around thirty minutes and after a while the PA guys were stepping over them to load the gear, until at last two warriors stood panting, bleeding but, hopefully, cooling down. It was a draw.

'Right,' said our guy, seeming to have regained his composure at last, 'job done.'

And with that he shook the promoter's hand, turned on his heel and went back to work.

The funny thing is, I've worked with that same promoter many times since. He's a lovely guy. Of course, he gradually became aware that he had been used in order to help out in a tricky domestic situation, but to tell the truth I don't think he really minded. It was such a memorable tussle that I think he was quite chuffed to have taken part in it. For years afterwards he would say to me, 'Hey, do you remember that massive fight I had with your guy? Tell him I said hello.'

'Are you joking?' I'd tell him. 'I'll be writing about that in me memoirs.'

Over the course of the tour we'd noticed we weren't getting a great reaction from the front rows. It was unusual for America and we were scratching our heads about it. The people at the back were into it, same with the sides. It was just this front-row business.

Then Terry Mason sussed it. 'It's their guest list,' he said. 'They're all too cool for school.'

We investigated and it turned out to be true. The venues were taking 500 tickets right at the front, just for all these spoilt bastards to basically ignore you.

It affected our performance, so we insisted it change. They could still have tickets but not at the front; that was for paying fans only.

Unfortunately, the directive hadn't filtered down by the time we played Irvine Meadows and when Terry saw what was happening he went down with some of the boys and cleared the whole of the front rows out, letting the paying audience in.

God bless him. Except the record company people complained to the venue, who then got the police to arrest Terry and throw him in the holding cells (which they had backstage for unruly clients). It took Tom Atencio ages to negotiate his release, but on his return he was treated like a hero.

So because of that I wasn't too bothered to be stood there with the promoter screaming in my face, 'You'll never play in California again!' after our refusal to do an encore had sparked a stage invasion that resulted in the gear being smashed, the PA tipped over, security beaten, you name it.

But of course we did play Irvine Meadows again. Of course we did.

And that was it. Another brilliant, riotous tour of America, the band almost at their peak, great music, plenty of laughs, plenty of back-biting, but lots of love. What more could a boy from Salford ask for?

Needless to say, we returned home and were delivered into yet another shitstorm.

'Go on, go on holiday, you twat'

Arriving back in Manchester in August 1985 we discovered that our tour of America had earned us the grand total of £8,264 each, a lovely cheque made out to each of us personally. It was the first money we'd ever earned from a tour and we had to meet in our accountant's office and sign our cheques straight over to 'Fac 51 The Haçienda' and we were devastated. Absolutely gutted.

I mean, in a way, you never miss what you've never had, so it was bearable, but Iris wouldn't let up about it, saying, quite rightly, 'You go away for months on end and don't even get paid. You don't even come back with some magic beans, you idiot. What's going on? What hold has he got on you?'

She was right, and although the double life I was leading away from home might have been the carrot, I had to agree it was ridiculous.

If we moaned about it, then Rob would pick us up for the moaning. He'd say, 'The trouble with you is ...'

That's how he used to begin every dressing-down. 'The trouble with you is ...' and you'd know you were in for a penetrating audit of your shortcomings. The Haçienda was burning through thousands of pounds of the band's money every month and you couldn't pay your bloody gas bill but complain about that and you got called a moaning bastard. 'The trouble with you is, you're a twat. You don't listen to me. When you start listening to me then everything will be all right,' Rob would say.

He'd shout for his chequebook and give you money to go on holiday. You'd be standing there aghast, you were being spoken to like a schoolkid in short trousers but with a cheque for £2,000 in your hands.

'Go on, go on holiday, you twat.'

So, having to give away that eight grand didn't really hurt the way you might think. It hurts more now than it did at the time.

And anyway, regarding Rob, things were about to change. Drastically. The coke was creeping up on him.

*

What happened to Rob was like a series of events that eventually built up into one big one. His behaviour was becoming more and more outlandish, but, in a way, you began to think it was just normal. Like him taking his clothes off. He had a habit, especially when he was drunk, of completely disrobing and marching around the studio or backstage stark bollock naked. He just started doing it more often.

Another thing he used to do was summon you to his house. You'd get a call, be told to come over, then arrive and find yourself on the receiving end of one of his 'The trouble with you is ...' bollockings.

He used to do it to our lighting guy who lived in Leicestershire. Poor geezer had a two-hour drive from Leicester to Manchester to get a bollocking. 'The trouble with you is ...' then have to drive home again.

It got worse. Earlier in 1985 was a planned birthday party at the Haçienda. All our American pals were coming, including Ruth, Michael Shamberg, Frank Callari and Mark Kamins (Kamins had discovered Madonna), and Rob said he was going to order all the drugs for them so they didn't have to scrabble around for it – thirty grams of it.

Later the night was cancelled and no one came, so Rob was stuck with the gear. You can guess the rest.

By the time of our next European tour he was in a state. Not only was he taking loads of coke, but he was becoming a real liability to have around.

The band had a brand-new Audi 200 Turbo Quattro. Rob had told me to go and buy him the best and fastest and most expensive car available. 'It'll be the group car but I'll keep it,' he said. We were wasting a fortune on cars. Rob already had a Ford Granada 2.8 Ghia that I'd imported for him from Germany, but it had to go because even though he'd had specialist security locks fitted, kids just smashed the windows and climbed in to steal it. We lost a fortune on it.

By now Barney had a Mercedes sports car and I was driving a Toyota Supra 2.8i Mark I (A513 NVU), Steve another Volvo, and Gillian a Fiat 500 (I am not joking).

Anyway, the idea was that when we toured we took Rob's car and for a time we did travel together in the car. However, Rob being late every day forced me – the nominated driver – to drive like a maniac in order to make it to the next venue on time.

The others hated that. I can't say I blamed them. It's one thing driving like a maniac, quite another being driven around by one. The car had a top speed of 140mph and was the fastest road car for sale in England at the time. Rob was always sat in the passenger seat going, 'Faster! Faster!' I was happy to oblige. But it was scary and draining and even I was worn out.

After a few days the others decided to go in the bus with the rest of the crew. Not only did this mean they missed out on my white-knuckle driving, but they also dodged the responsibility of pulling Rob out of his pit every day.

For them, win-win. For me, lose-lose.

So anyway, Rob at last out of bed, moaning and grumbling, would handle his coke comedown with a bit of breakfast and then by smoking spliff after spliff, one after the other all the way through my drive to the venue and then at the venue right up until soundcheck, when out came the coke again.

He would be chopping out the lines, and ready to start on the booze too. Sure enough, a couple of hours later our manager was fully juiced once again, ready for a night spent partying with the crew. They seemed to know the best drug dealers and they'd stay up all night every night, with me wondering naively how they did it.

About seven o'clock one morning there was a knock at my hotel room door and, when I opened it, who should be standing there but Rob, bleary and red-eyed.

'Rob, what are you doing?'

'I need you to take me to an optician,' he said, and though he was a man who'd obviously not had a wink of sleep, that still didn't account for the fact that his eyes were bright red. I mean, *bright red*, like devil's eyes.

What he'd done was try to take his contact lenses out, but because he was so off his head he'd accidentally pushed them round the back of his eyes. I had to take him to an optician who used a pair of tweezers to go behind his eyeballs and fish out these contact lenses. Unbelievable.

Another night, on that same tour, some kid came backstage in Holland telling us he had a load of duty-free diamonds and would we like to invest in them?

'I am a reputable dealer. This is a once-in-a-lifetime opportunity,' he said.

Only Rob, who was completely off his head, thought it was a good idea.

'Let's get all the gig money from the tour and buy these diamonds,' he was saying, virtually foaming at the mouth.

'You don't even know this guy,' we were saying. 'You don't even know if they're fucking real. Are you mental?'

'Yeah, they're diamonds, look at them, they're diamonds,' he was saying.

'Pack it in, Rob, will you? Shit.'

'No, this is a great deal for the band. You leave it to me. I'm doing a great deal for you lot. The trouble with you is you don't know a good deal when you see one. You're idiots.'

The whole time this diamond trader was egging him on, clearly knowing a coked-up mug when he saw one. We had to throw the bloke out before he got his way.

By the time we reached Rotterdam Rob had a new bee in his bonnet. His major worry was that the same kids who had started the Rotterdam riot in 1982 would return to batter us now that we were back a full three years later. His idea was to hire a hundred Hell's Angels for security, just like Rolling Stones at Altamont.

Which of course turned out so well for them.

We talked him out of that idea as well, but when we got to play the gig I looked down to see Rob crouched by the drum kit with an open penknife in his hand, looking wide-eyed and delirious, scanning the crowd for the Rotterdam skinheads he was convinced were out to get him.

Things got worse after the Leuven gig on the last night of the tour, when Rob decided he wanted to go to a reggae club he'd heard about. He did love his reggae, did Rob. The other three had had enough of him and returned to the hotel but even though I was knackered I thought I'd keep an eye on him so decided to go.

By now Rob's eyes were wide as saucers. He was completely off his face, even more so than usual. Meanwhile the club was full of huge and scary-looking Dutch geezers, with really heavy dub being played through a massive sound system. You could feel your entire chest vibrating from the bass. I love bass, of course, but the whole thing – Rob's state, the other clubbers, the whole dark vibe of the place – was giving me the creeps, and I was desperate to leave from the moment we arrived.

'I don't like the look of this, Rob,' I was telling him.

'I fucking like it,' he insisted. 'The trouble with you is you don't know good music when you hear it. Fuck off if you don't want to be here.'

I wanted nothing more than to fuck off, but couldn't leave Rob alone, so hung around for a bit until, suddenly …

Oh God, where was Rob?

He'd disappeared. One minute, he'd been standing with me as we wandered around the club, me feeling knackered and not just knackered but bored shitless; him stumbling around, giving out bug-eyed stares and getting angry glares in return. The next minute, he wasn't there, and now I was knackered, bored shitless *and* worrying about Rob.

At least I had a new purpose. I started searching for him until, eventually, I came across him, and my God, he was in a state.

He'd found an alcove and had wedged himself into it. His shoulders were up by his ears. From somewhere he'd found a small white towel, only it wasn't white any more, because he'd been chewing his tongue, chewing it like it was a dummy, chomping down on his coke-anaesthetised tongue, which was bleeding so profusely that it had turned the white towel almost completely red.

'Christ, Rob, what are you doing?'

He never stopped chomping down on his tongue. Between everything he said he kept on chomping.

'Shut up, you twat.'

'Look, mate,' I said, 'we've got to go. I'm knackered and you're in a right state. We've got to get out of here.'

'Well fuck off, fuck off then,' he chomped.

I hold my hands up now and say I didn't know what to do. Rob was hardcore. He could be a bully. Even in this state – maybe *especially* in this state – he was an intimidating and overbearing presence. Plus all he was doing was swearing at me. Maybe something inside you snaps and you think, *Why the fuck should I have to take this? Why the fuck should I stand here and listen to this twat with his self-inflicted problems slag me off to high heaven?*

'Come on, Rob.' I tried one more time, one last time.

'Shut up and fuck off, you cunt!'

Right, fuck you.

I left him to it.

*

As it was my job to ferry him around in the group car, I had to take him home to England, which on one hand was a pain in the arse because of his increasingly weird behaviour, but sometimes I was still enjoying driving.

The other three went home on the crew bus. They had definitely had enough by now. With them gone at least there was no one to tell me to slow down and be careful. Rob just sat in the passenger seat rolling spliffs and managing that day's coke comedown, insisting I go faster. We set off for Calais.

'I've run out of dope,' he said.

'Yeah? So what?'

'You'll have to catch the bus so I can get some more.'

Them lot had left ahead of us.

'But the bus set off ages ago.'

'I don't fucking care when the bus set off, I want you to catch it. Now put your foot down and stop fucking moaning.'

We were on the next ferry, an hour behind the band. Once we were back in the UK it was dark and I was on the motorway, reaching stupid, crazy speeds trying to catch the group's bus. I was doing 140mph, with the Audi flat out, with Rob skinning up what was left of his dope by my side, when I spotted a flashing blue light on the horizon in the rear-view mirror. I slowed down to the speed limit and waited for it to go past.

Only, it didn't. A Jaguar V12 in full police livery flashed past then jammed on the brakes, screeching all over the motorway before slowing down and pulling us over to the hard shoulder.

I remembered reading somewhere that coppers prefer you to step out of the car when they pull you over. Like they get narked if they have to speak down to you or something, so I told Rob to stay put and got out.

'Excuse me, officer, is there something wrong?'

I was met by a red-faced copper. 'Yes, there's something wrong,' he said, poking me in the chest with his index finger. 'I'll tell you what's wrong. It's you, you bastard.'

Bloody hell, I thought. *Bit strong.*

He said, 'I've been chasing you for twenty minutes, you little get,' looking me up and down. 'See this car, this Jag? It needs a service, but if it had been on song, I'd have fucking caught you.'

Well, I thought, *you wouldn't have, because the top speed of a Jaguar XJ12 is 136mph, and the top speed of an Audi 200 Turbo Quattro is 140mph*, but I didn't say it.

He was still poking me. In those days coppers were much more physical than they are now.

'Who does the car belong to?'

I said, 'It belongs to my boss.'

'And what would your boss say if he knew you were driving it like a twat?'

I thought, *Well, you could go ask him if you like, because he's in the car, only he's stoned out of his gourd*, but decided against saying anything again.

'Right,' said this outraged copper, 'I'll tell you what you're going to do now, sonny Jim. You're going to get on the wet floor, on all fours, and inspect your tyres.'

So that's what I did. As tyrant number one, Rob, sat in the car, and tyrant number two, the copper, stood over me, I had to get on the wet tarmac to inspect the Audi's tyres for stones or nails, one by one, every single tyre.

When I'd finished, the copper gave me all sorts of shit about how if he ever saw me on 'his' motorway again, he was going to do me, and how I was lucky he didn't tell my boss what I'd been up to. Again, I thought to myself, *If you want to have a conversation with my boss you're more than welcome to do it, mate, best of luck*, but I kept it zipped until at last the copper grew tired of being red-faced and indignant, got in his Jaguar and left.

I took my seat back in the Audi and set off much more slowly. Beside me, Rob sat watching me with dark, suspicious eyes.

He was giving me the creeps. 'What's the matter?' I asked him.

In a low, ominous voice he replied, 'You told him I had dope.'

'You what?'

'I was reading your lips. You told that copper I had dope.'

I said, 'Rob, fuck off.'

But he fixed me with his beady stare, pushed his glasses up his nose and pointed an accusing finger at me. 'You told him I had dope, Judas. You fucking dobbed me in it.'

It was one of those moments – one of those real eye-opening moments where I thought, *You have truly lost it, mate.*

He ordered me to keep driving. My policeman friend must have told all his mates about us, because there was a copper in the slip-road exit of every service station from there to Manchester. I had to do the speed limit all the way, with Rob calling me Judas the whole time. 'The trouble with you is ...'

I've never been so happy as when I dropped him off on Whitworth Street and at last he could get on the fucking bus.

'Merry Christmas, Rob!' said I. He just turned, gave me the V-sign and disappeared into the coach.

Phew. What a life.

TIMELINE SIX
JANUARY–DECEMBER 1985

26 January 1985

New Order play King George's Hall, Blackburn.

> 'Barney was beginning to dislike playing, especially in England, and sometimes he had a point: it was a completely different proposition to playing abroad. Abroad, for example, our audience was a fifty-fifty split male and female, but in the UK it was 90 per cent male and of those a lot seemed to be gagging for a fight. Here there was a mini football riot outside the gig with two sets of rival supporters fighting in the street. One side had been throwing half-bricks and someone on the other side had been hit on the head and sadly died. We didn't find out until the next day. The thrower, as it turned out, a New Order fan, got life. I met him many years later. He still regretted it. Rightly so.'

27 January 1985

New Order play Tiffany's, Leeds.

28 January 1985

New Order play Finsbury Park, Michael Sobell Sports Centre, London.

5 February 1985

New Order play Caley Palais, Edinburgh.

6 February 1985

New Order play Barrowlands, Glasgow.

> 'Barrowlands was one of my favourite gigs to play ever. It just had a great atmosphere every single time we played there. The owner was a wonderful old gangster who always looked after you so well.'

2 March 1985

Peter Hook's daughter, Heather Lucille, is born.

'What a beauty.'

14 March 1985

New Order play Lancaster University, Lancaster.

9 April 1985

New Order play the Tower Ballroom, Birmingham.

10 April 1985

New Order play the Mayfair, Swansea.

17 April 1985

New Order play the University, Salford, supported by Happy Mondays.

18 April 1985

New Order play Rotters, Doncaster.

19 April 1985

New Order play the Leisure Centre, Macclesfield, supported by Happy Mondays.

26 April 1985

'Shellshock' recorded at Yellow Two Studios at the request for a new track for *Pretty in Pink* by writer John Hughes. John Robie produces, Julia Nagle engineers.

26 April 1985

New Order play Canton (club), Hong Kong, China.

May 1985

New Order: 'The Perfect Kiss'
(FAC 123)
Twelve-inch track list:

'The Perfect Kiss'	8.45
'The Kiss of Death'	7.00
'The Perfect Pit'	1.23

Run-out groove one: *All these crabs ...*
Run-out groove two: *are making me itch!*

Seven-inch track list:

'The Perfect Kiss' (edit)	3.47
'The Kiss of Death' (edit)	3.00

Run-out groove one: *That's Soul Folks!*
Run-out groove two: *I feel it's a Hottie!*

Recorded and mixed in London, at Jam and Britannia Row Studios.
Engineered by Michael Johnson.
Produced by New Order.
Designed by Peter Saville.
Entered UK chart on 25 May 1985, remaining in the charts for 4 weeks, its peak position was number 46.

> **'We had wanted to use a final sample to finish the twelve-inch track off, "That's All Folks!" from the Warner Brothers cartoons. But we were quoted $30,000 for one use. And we were on their label. Just shows you ... no favouritism.'**

1 May 1985

New Order play Koseinenkin Kaikan Hall, Tokyo, Japan.

'あなたは再びこの町で遊ぶことは決してないだろう！'

2 May 1985

New Order play Koseinenkin Kaikan Hall, Shinjuku, Tokyo, Japan.

This Japanese gig results in the *Pumped Full of Drugs* video, directed by Tony Wilson and released in 1986.

3 May 1985

New Order play Club 'D', Shibuya District, Tokyo, Japan.

> **'This was a complete contrast to the other two gigs. It was a small club with no stage and about 200 capacity. They all went nuts. It was great.'**

4 May 1985

New Order play Koseinenkin Kaikan, Osaka, Japan.

13 May 1985

New Order: *Low-Life*
(FACT 100)

Track list:

'Love Vigilantes'	4.18
'The Perfect Kiss'	4.48
'This Time of Night'	4.43
'Sunrise'	5.58
'Elegia'	4.53
'Sooner Than You Think'	5.11
'Sub-Culture'	4.54
'Face Up'	5.03

Run-out groove one: *The girls are here, there ...*
Run-out groove two: *and everywhere! Thank God!*

Recorded and mixed in London, at Jam and Britannia Row Studios.
Engineered by Mike Johnson.
Tape operators: Mark, Penny and Tim.
Produced by New Order.
Designed by Peter Saville Associates.
Photography by Trevor Key.
Entered UK chart on 25 May 1985, remaining in the charts for 10 weeks, its peak position was number 7.

15 May 1985

New Order play Canterbury Court, Perth, Australia.

17 May 1985

New Order play the Powerhouse, Melbourne, Australia.

18 May 1985

New Order play Selina's, Coogee Bay Hotel, Sydney, Australia.

> **'Coogee Bay was gorgeous and this pub was huge, two thousand capacity. The doors opened at 6 p.m. and we weren't on till 1 a.m., so I asked the promoter why was there such a long gap. "Aussies like a lot of drinking time, mate!" And sure enough they did, the place was full by 7 p.m. and everyone was completely pissed by the time we went on. We went down a storm, but it was so hot on stage that Dave Pils had to go and get two jugs of iced water to put down my leather trousers. I was in danger of keeling over. My boots filled up and held it all in ... bliss.**
>
> **'After the show the promoter, Ken West, had noticed my growing hair and said, "Here, let me put that in a ponytail for you, at the back." So began my glam rock phase. Thanks, Ken.'**

20 May 1985

New Order play Easts Leagues Club, Brisbane, Australia.

'We got bullied by the first fifteen. The hulking brutes kept calling us whingeing Poms and laughing at our clothes, boo hoo.'

23 May 1985

New Order play Logan Campbell Centre, Auckland, New Zealand.

27 May 1985

New Order play the Wave, Honolulu, Hawaii.

14 June 1985

New Order play the Pink Punk, Pimm's Event, New Hall College, Cambridge.

16 July 1985

New Order play the Haçienda, Manchester.

20 July 1985

New Order play the WOMAD Festival, Mersea Island, Essex.

'We turned up early in the afternoon and there was nothing in our tent/dressing room apart from a scraggy donkey tied to the central pole. So anyway, the Pogues dressing room was next door and they were laughing, going, "Hey, you fucking Manc bastards, like your donkey!" When they left we went for a mooch round, and their dressing room was all done out like a palace with food of every description and tons of drink like a banquet. So we helped ourselves then went and got the donkey and tied it up in their tent. It ate everything, destroying the rest and shitting everywhere. We pissed ourselves, saying, "Them fucking Pogues, the cheeky bastards, that'll teach them to take the piss out of us." When they came back they went fucking berserk, it was handbags at dawn. The gig was awful. It rained while the Pogues were on, they were great, and half the audience disappeared to change, then it rained again, and a third disappeared, then it rained again and no one moved. By the time we came on everyone was soaked and miserable and we responded in kind. I remember Barney getting really upset about a review we got for it and me saying, "I thought you didn't read reviews?"

'"Oh yeah," he said.

'I'll never forget that donkey. I think it's gone solo now.'

1 August 1985

New Order play Felt Forum, New York, supported by A Certain Ratio.

2 August 1985

New Order play Opera House, Boston, supported by A Certain Ratio.

'There was a huge riot after this gig. We had finished the gig and retreated to the dressing room as usual. But this time it was miles away from the stage, a real Spinal Tap moment. We were right in the gods. We just sat there blissfully unaware that downstairs the audience had got upset because we hadn't come back for an encore, so they smashed up the seats then invaded the stage and smashed the equipment. It then became a massive battle that spilled out onto the street. In the end, they had to call the mounted riot police. It went on for ages but the first thing we knew about it was when one of the roadies came in all bloodied and battered about twenty minutes later. We wondered where they were. So we had to stay in the gig for our own safety. Outside, our crew bus driver was desperately trying to keep the bus from being damaged. He was a Vietnam vet and he had to chase loads of kids away. His catchphrase was, "There's going to be an inquireeey!" And when we came out later, when it had all quietened down, that was the first thing he said, "There's going to be an inquireeey, Peter! There's going to be an inquireeey!"

'So we got in our small van to go back to the hotel. As we started to drive off, someone began throwing stones. I looked round to see about five kids, two girls and three boys.

'The driver stopped and we got out, going, "What are you fucking doing, you cheeky bastards?" and they were going, "Fuck you, man, you assholes, you didn't do an encore, you caused a riot, fuck you."

'This girl threw another stone, and a certain member of our entourage, for some insane reason, which is not like him because he's such a shithouse usually, started running after her. He had a half-empty bottle in his hand and was chasing this girl, waving it over his head.

'I took off after him and after a few yards caught him up, just as he went to swing the bottle at her head. I managed to grab his coat and pull him back and it missed her by a whisker. We stopped and she carried on. When we got back to the van, the promoter had come out, and guess what he said . . .'

4 August 1985

New Order play International Centre, Toronto, Canada, supported by A Certain Ratio.

5 August 1985

New Order play Agora Theatre, Akron, Ohio.

'This was where one of our roadies was having sex with a girl on the bus. A member of our entourage, who was handy with a video camera, had noticed a gap in the curtains. Getting the lads to bring some flight cases out of the gig, he built himself a platform and filmed the happy couple inside. He still shows it to anyone who asks.'

6 August 1985

New Order play Bismarck Theatre, Chicago, Illinois, supported by A Certain Ratio.

9 August 1985

New Order play Warner Theatre, Washington DC, supported by A Certain Ratio.

11 August 1985

New Order play Fox Theatre, Atlanta.

12 August 1985

New Order play McAlister Auditorium, New Orleans, Louisiana, supported by A Certain Ratio.

14 August 1985

New Order play City Coliseum, Austin, Texas, supported by A Certain Ratio.

16 August 1985

New Order play Rainbow Music Hall, Denver, Colorado, supported by A Certain Ratio.

17 August 1985

New Order play the Coliseum, Utah State Fairgrounds, Salt Lake City, Utah, supported by A Certain Ratio.

> **'It was the first time we'd played in an amusement park. It was great, because they took us on the rides and you'd go straight to the front of the queue (one of the perks of being in a band, that was). The trouble was, when you came off, and tried to buy your picture, the punters had bought them all. This gig was funny for me. Terry had been driving them lot back after soundcheck and got lost, turning up nearly an hour late. Barney was in a foul mood, even fouler than usual.'**

20 August 1985

New Order play Henry J. Kaiser Convention Center, Oakland, California, supported by A Certain Ratio.

22 August 1985

New Order play Civic Auditorium, Santa Monica, California, supported by A Certain Ratio.

> 'Tony made a surprise appearance here, and what was even more surprising was that he had a girl in tow. He introduced her as Debbie Diamond. "Wow," I say, "what a name." "It's my porn star name," she said. I laughed, thinking she was joking, and then it turned out she was one of America's biggest porn stars, star of *Debbie Does Dallas*. Along with her co-star Ron Jeremy she was a legend. What the fuck Tony was doing with her was anyone's guess. Pete Saville was well impressed.'

23 August 1985

New Order play Irvine Meadows, Irvine, California, supported by A Certain Ratio.

> 'That morning I had woken up early to sunbathe by the pool in the Sunset Marquis. It was almost empty apart from a young couple and their toddler daughter close by. It was a beautiful morning, clear blue sky and not a breath of wind. The pool looked like a huge mirror. So I was sat there and the couple had breakfast delivered and while they were busy moving everything round on the small pool tables the toddler went to the edge of the water and was looking at her reflection. Next thing I knew she stepped straight in and without a sound disappeared into the pool. I jumped up and just as her ponytail was disappearing, grabbed it and pulled her out, carefully putting the suspended toddler back facing her mum and dad. She stood stock still for a minute, then burst out crying.
>
> 'You need eyes in the back of your head as a parent, don't you?'

22 October 1985

New Order play the Guildhall, Preston, supported by Section 25.

> 'Preston Guildhall. Fucking hell. Well I can safely say that there were no beautiful ex-models who made mocking-bird feeders and no ballet dancers. There was fuck all in Preston Guildhall bar a bunch of twats throwing beer.'

25 October 1985

New Order play University of London Union, supported by James and Grab Grab the Haddock.

> 'Tonight's message on my cabs read "Gary R.I.P." for Gary Holton from the Heavy Metal Kids who had just died. A great character. I loved him in *Auf Wiedersehen, Pet*.
>
> 'Barney was a bit squiffy and made some very witty comments, but the pièce de résistance was his X-rated version of 'Love Vigilantes' where he changed the lyrics:
>
> When I walked through the door,
> My wife she lay upon the floor,
> Sucking cocks there were four,
> And I said you dirty whore,
> What are you doing on the floor?
> Sucking big fat cocks o'fuckin' hell.
>
> 'I nearly wet myself. He could be very funny.'

26 October 1985

New Order play Octagon, Sheffield University, Sheffield.

November 1985

New Order: 'Sub-Culture'
(FAC 133)

Seven-inch track list:

'Sub-Culture'	3.25
'Dub-Vulture'	3.34

Twelve-inch track list:

'Sub-Culture'	7.26
'Dub-Vulture'	7.57

Twelve-inch track list USA:

'Sub-Culture' (remix)	7.26
'Dub-Vulture'	7.57
'Sub-Culture' (original LP version)	4.57

Run-out groove one: *The trouble with you is . . .*
Run-out groove two: *you're a twat*

Recorded at Village Recorder, Santa Monica, California.
Written by New Order.
Produced by New Order.
Remixed by John Robie.
Engineered by Michael Johnson.
Typography by Peter Saville Associates.
Entered UK chart on 9 November 1985, remaining in the charts for 4 weeks, its peak position was number 63.

'I did not like this at all. I thought the off-time bass synth too loud and distracting and there were too, too many edits, and the girly backing vocals, oh God. I thought John was just showing off. We are friends now and even he admits, like we all do, how stupid and annoying we could be. I wasn't alone in hating it. Pete Saville disliked it so much he refused to do a sleeve for it, and it went out in a plain black sleeve, "a mourning sleeve", he said. We were in a studio that Fleetwood Mac had built. It was done out like an English stately home, all wood-panelled, like an old baronial hall with special lights for morning, afternoon and night. The owner was telling us that they came in with a three-year booking, if he built them a studio of their own. It was the best favour they could have done him.

'He said, "I borrowed the money, built it and they paid for it five times over. Sometimes, they'll come in just for half an hour." It was him who told us the urban myth about Stevie Nicks having a girl who blew coke up her arse because her nose was so fucked. I wondered what her job description would have been.'

8 November 1985

New Order play Pavilion, Hemel Hempstead.

10 November 1985

New Order play Hammersmith Palais, London, supported by A Certain Ratio.

3 December 1985

New Order play the Haçienda, Manchester (first set matinee), supported by Happy Mondays.

'This was done as a "homage" to Roger Eagle to emulate the matinees he used to do at Eric's in Liverpool, the idea being kids could come to this one as they weren't allowed in if you were selling alcohol. It went well. This was filmed for BBC's *The Old Grey Whistle Test*. "As It Is When It Was" and "Sunrise" were both shown live on the programme.'

3 December 1985

New Order play the Haçienda, Manchester (second set).

5 December 1985

Proposed Haçienda party for Ruth Polsky's birthday cancelled.

6 December 1985

New Order play Central London Polytechnic.

'Some dirty bastard got me right on the head with an empty beer can. Find a bin next time, knobhead.'

7 December 1985

New Order play Thames Hall, Fulcrum Centre, Slough.

10 December 1985

New Order play El Dorado, Paris, France, supported by Quando Quango.

'This was a bus tour, and when we arrived the night before in Paris we got the bus driver to park on the Rue St Denis right in the heart of the red-light district. Within an hour seven of us had been with hookers. Naughty boys. Later we went to see Spandau Ballet and got lost backstage. We stumbled across their dressing room, stole all the beer and trashed the room. Ludicrously drunk, we returned to the auditorium and ended up on the balcony, where a certain member of our entourage took the opportunity to have a piss on the crowd and band below.'

11 December 1985

New Order play Salle Villar, Maison de la Culture, Rennes, France, supported by Quando Quango.

12 December 1985

New Order play Exo 7, Rouen, France, supported by Quando Quango.

13 December 1985

New Order play Salle du Baron, Orleans, France, supported by Quando Quango.

15 December 1985

New Order play Rotterdam Arena, Rotterdam, Netherlands, supported by Quando Quango.

'Diamonds are a manager's best friend.'

17 December 1985

New Order play Manhattan Club, Leuven, Belgium, supported by Quando Quango.

'Our manager crashes and burns.'

'The trouble with you is . . .'

Though 1986 would be one of New Order's most tumultuous years, it was also one of the group's most successful periods, bringing the release of the three singles 'Shellshock', 'State of the Nation' and 'Bizarre Love Triangle', as well as appearances on the soundtracks of two hit movies, Pretty in Pink *and* Something Wild, *both key films of the 1980s. Meanwhile, the group would record their fourth album, Brotherhood, on which a clear split between the more rock-orientated sound of side one and the electronic-based direction of side two was apparent.*

A new year brought no end to Rob's strange behaviour. In fact if anything it got worse.

The Haçienda was still in trouble and the idea of the 'Management Co-operative' had not worked out. They just voted to keep everything as cheap as possible for the punter, with us ending up with the glorious accolade of selling the cheapest beer in Manchester. The lunatics really were running the asylum. (See *The Haçienda: How Not to Run a Club* for detail.)

So Rob and Alan Erasmus had headhunted a man who'd impressed us running a couple of venues we'd played at, the Blue Note in Derby and later Nottingham Rock City. Paul Mason came in just as Rob was going completely bananas. At his interview he reported that Rob spent the whole time throwing chips at Tony until Tony got so annoyed that they ended up rolling about and wrestling on the floor. Definitely the funniest interview story I ever heard since my last interview in 1976, when the boss at AFA-Minerva had asked me why I had applied for the position and I truthfully said, 'Because it's more money, duh.' Needless to say I was not asked back.

The craziness continued. The lectures continued. He took to bringing us carefully cut-out newspaper articles in the practice room, handing them out to band members and crew. 'RIGHT, THIS IS FOR YOU, HOOKY!' he'd bellow, and give you an article with random words circled, underlined or crossed out, complete with pictures. You'd be looking at it, turning it over, wondering what it all meant.

And a bit like with Ian – no, a *lot* like with Ian – none of us ever said, 'You need help, mate.' It was a gradual escalation and the difference with Rob was that he'd created his own climate of control tinged with a little fear. He was obviously in charge, so you didn't offer help. You just did as you were told. We were too nervous to even suggest it.

One night, with us sat round the big practice-room table – the group, Terry, a couple of the roadies – Rob marched around it giving us one of his famous scoldings/pep talks. He started by tapping his temple: 'The trouble with you lot is you think I don't know what you're planning,' walking round and round the table like an evil sergeant major, like Robert De Niro in *The Untouchables* just before he bludgeons a minion to death with a baseball bat. Barney giggled once and Rob was right in his face. 'Don't you laugh. Don't you fucking laugh. I know what you're thinking. You're thinking, *How can we get rid of Rob? How can we get someone better?*'

This particular night, I had to leave. My daughter, Heather, was in the Monsall Isolation Hospital diagnosed with lactose intolerance. Iris was with her, one parent being allowed to stay, but I had to get there and say goodnight before they turned off the lights at 9 p.m. I managed to excuse myself from the scolding, which wasn't easy. I put my hand up, explained the situation and was allowed to leave.

Or so I thought. Because you know when you get that feeling you're being followed? It plagued me on the short journey from the practice rooms in Cheetham Hill to the hospital just down the road. As I pulled into the car park I found out why. None other than Rob squealed in right behind me.

I got out just as he did the same, but I could tell from the look on his face that I was in for another bollocking, a continuation of the same bollocking, in fact.

Sure enough, Rob started laying into me. Right there in the middle of the car park, telling me what my trouble was, going on about how New Order were going to be bigger than U2 – and how the Haçienda was going to be the biggest and best nightclub in the world. We were all going to be rich. And of course he was shouting, right at the top of his voice, effing and jeffing, and if you think I swear a lot you should have heard Rob when he got going. Which meant that everybody could hear him. In the hospital buildings around us, lights were going on one by one.

'Rob, pack it in, will you?' I tried to say, but there were already a couple of security guards making their way across the car park towards us. Then suddenly he jumped back in his car, saying as he did, 'I'll fucking see you, Hooky, don't you worry. You haven't got away with this ...' and screeched away.

Bloody hell.

My favourite story of this rather sorry little episode was, 'The Invisible Shirt'.

There was a clothes shop in Manchester called 'L'Homme' run by a very interesting man, Richard Creme. He was about seven feet tall and a real character. His was an expensive, very classy and intimidating shop frequented mainly by footballers and other very rich people. Rob had taken to shopping there. Now Richard could sell 'sand to the Arabs' and I have a very expensive (and grotesque) pair of Vivienne Westwood jeans to prove it. Rob had fallen for one item that he couldn't resist telling us all about, a see-through shirt or, as he called it, his 'invisible shirt'. Said shirt cost a fortune, completely validating it according to Rob. He'd grin and say, 'And you can't even see it!' He thought it was fantastic. We were slightly less impressed and one crack by Barney had us all in stitches (ironically, lacking in Rob's shirt), which I wish I could remember. Rob turned on Barney. 'You, you're a selfish little toad, aren't you? You're a stuck-up cunt. You're an unenviable little twat. Do you know what the trouble with you is?'

Fucking hell, I couldn't wait.

It led to the longest and most sustained 'the trouble with you is ...' tirade we had seen yet.

Looking back, Rob must have been up to his eyeballs in coke, but other than what I've already described we never actually saw him do it; it wasn't like he was chopping out lines in the practice room. But he must have been doing it somewhere on the quiet because it caused him to have what can only be described as an extended nervous breakdown. A cocaine psychosis, they called it.

There had to be a breaking point. And there was. I'm only glad I wasn't around to witness it.

I heard all about it, though. It was a weekend that began with Rob and Lesley accompanying Mike Pickering and his missus to London, the idea being that they'd watch Manchester City play Tottenham Hotspur. Rob had insisted on Mike booking them the best and most expensive hotel in London, which Mike duly did, getting them rooms at Blakes. Checking into their rooms, Rob insisted on taking a bath right away, blasting his head with the shower for hours, then refusing to get out, just asking when his mum was going to arrive. He'd already been behaving in what you might call an erratic and worrying fashion on the journey down, kicking and punching the car, so his behaviour when they reached the hotel proved to be the last straw. After six hours in the bath the other three decided to call it quits, forget about the match, bundle Rob back into the car and get him home.

The return journey proved to be a bit more of a white-knuckle ride, with Rob staging a repeat of the car assault from before, except even more viciously as his condition worsened, with strange echoes of Ian's ill-fated car ride back from London in 1978.

Once back in Chorlton, our manager darted out of the car and into his house, crashing up the stairs and locking himself in the office at the top. Next thing they knew, files and sheaves of paper came flying out as Rob began trashing his office, pulling open filing-cabinet drawers and chucking the contents out of the window. Mike and co. implored him to stop, before spending the rest of the day scrabbling around trying to pick up Joy Division's and New Order's business affairs from the back garden (probably in better order than they had ever been in his office).

Meanwhile, Rob had been coaxed out of his office and into the front room, whereupon he declared, 'I want something to eat, Mike.'

'Right,' says the future leader of M People, 'what can I get you, Rob?'

'I want an Indian.'

'Right. OK. You want an Indian. What do you want from the Indian?'

'I'm not going to tell you.'

'Well then, how are we going to get your food if we don't know what you want?'

'I want you to guess. I want you to guess what I want from the Indian, and if you get it wrong, you're in trouble.'

So Mike ordered everything on the menu. Every main meal, every sweet, every single item, Mike ordered the lot. When it arrived it took three Indian guys ages to bring it all in, in relays.

'I don't want it now,' said Rob.

And with that, he legged it, leaving Mike, Lesley and whoever else was nursemaiding him at the time with a house full of Indian food and the huge worry that Rob was going to do himself a serious mischief unless they did something drastic.

They began combing nearby streets for him with no luck. Returning to the house Lesley received a phone call from a local corner shop. 'Your husband's in my shop, and he's acting very strangely. He keeps saying he wants something but won't tell us what it is. He says we have to guess.'

They hotfooted it to the shop and managed to persuade Rob back to the house. But the fun was still not over. Rob was very agitated. A big bloke, remember, and in a rage there was no way they could control him, so they called the police.

The police arrived.

The police called a doctor.

The doctor, seeing that Rob was in the grip of a huge psychotic episode, called another doctor, because you need two doctors for a committal.

Which is what they did. They committed Rob. Took eight police to get the backwards coat on our poor manager, and then they carted him off to the nuthouse.

With Rob in the hospital New Order did what we always did. The same thing we did when Ian was ill. We just carried on writing, rehearsing and even gigging. Financially Phil McIntyre, a local promoter, came to our rescue by organising some gigs for us. These days Phil is a big name in the comedy world, but back then he promoted rock shows and he'd had a great, if somewhat strange, relationship with New Order and Rob himself. For instance, whenever he was doing gigs with us, Rob would delight in giving him weird challenges, like, 'Right, Phil, can you get me tea and toast for four people now?' and even though it was one o'clock in the morning and we were in Wolverhampton, Phil would trot off and return twenty minutes later with tea and toast for four. The man was a bloody marvel.

When Phil discovered we were having difficulties, he set up three gigs for us in the North, paying us £10,000 in cash upfront. So we had some money for the time being. Apart from that we had no money and no access to the group's bank accounts.

Lesley Gretton came with Mike Pickering to the practice room to talk to the group.

'Listen,' she said to us, 'please don't sack Rob. If you sack him it'll finish him off. Please wait.'

Up until then it hadn't even occurred to us to sack him, but after she'd left we began to think it over. After all, we really didn't know what was going to happen. What if he never recovered? We were scared. We discussed what to do. Who to ask? It was Tony, in the end, who approached Tom Atencio, our American manager, to manage us, telling him the group was skint. Tom declined, saying the long distance between us would make it impossible. In the end we decided to be loyal and hold on for Rob. We'd just have to muddle through as best we could.

Stories began to emerge from Rob's stay in hospital – how true they were no one knew: how he'd been phoning up Gillian and asking her to run away with him, saying they were destined to be together and how in his partner Lesley he'd got the wrong Gilbert (they both had the same surname, weirdly enough); that he'd been raving about how Tony Wilson was the real father of his son, and how Tony's son, Oliver, was the spawn of the devil; how he, Rob, was the baby Jesus; how one day in the hospital he decided that he could help City win their next game, and he'd dress all in green so no one could see him on the pitch, so he went round the wards nicking everybody's green clothes and then put them on. Except he couldn't find any green shoes, so he just went out in his socks and set off from Cheadle Royal Hospital walking to City's ground before the staff finally found him walking on the A34 and managed to grapple him back to the ward.

No wonder Lesley warned us off going to see him. In the end it was months before I next laid eyes on him. He had come to my house in Moston for Heather's christening party, and I was shocked by his appearance. He looked like a little old man. He had lost five stone and was shaking uncontrollably, and talking very slowly. Everything about him that had once been big, brash, loud and overbearing was suddenly small, quiet and withdrawn. He was diminished in every way. The drug had crystallised in his brain, sending it haywire.

*

It turned out that before he was sectioned, Rob had been doing ten grams of coke a day, a daily habit of £500, £3,500 a week. He did nothing by halves. God only knows how he found the time to do it all. In the heyday of my addiction I was doing an eight-ball a day (3.5 grams) and it seemed to take forever just to chop it out, nearly a full-time job.

The doctors were worried that it may have injured his heart too. It was all very sad.

Anyway. Diminished or not, Rob returned as New Order's manager. In the wake of his drug consumption, he began drinking quite heavily and, although he wasn't supposed to, smoking dope, and though he at least put on some weight, he never regained his previous stature. From then on Rob was a shadow of his former self.

People used to comment on the two films: 'How come the Rob in *Control* is the complete opposite of the Rob in *24 Hour Party People*?' That was why.

A classic 'before and after' tale.

Thus began a new chapter in our story. Barney, like all of us, had felt the sharp edge of Rob's tongue on many occasions and I guess he felt it was time for a bit of payback, because he started giving back as good as he'd ever got.

What was happening, I realise now, was that Barney was making his bid for leadership of the group. Maybe he thought it was his turn. Me and him had started the group together but when we recruited Ian, it was Ian, because of his ambition, drive and sheer talent, who became our leader. Then Rob came on board and when Ian died, he took the wheel. And whatever you think of Rob's style – some said it left a lot to be desired – there was no doubt that New Order were totally in his hands. He browbeat us, but he also protected us. He steered us.

Now, although we still needed a manager for the day-to-day running of things, again (in my opinion), Barney decided he wanted to be in control.

Or maybe not! Let's give him the benefit of the doubt here. Maybe he didn't consciously *decide* he wanted to be the leader. Maybe he just realised that without Rob's hand on the tiller he could get away with being a proper little prima donna, a much more likely scenario.

And that is exactly what happened. As well as being hard on Rob he started to throw his weight around in other ways. The first thing to happen in earnest was that he began being late all the time; before it was some of the time, now all. Suddenly we were always waiting on Barney for everything from his physical presence to his metaphysical decisions.

That was the first thing. But it was by no means the last.

© Kevin Cummins

PART TWO

Brotherhood

'Just a gnat's whisker'

While Rob was in hospital we had a tour of Ireland to undertake. This was something that fell to Terry as our stand-in manager to organise. His career was going up and down like a bride's nightie. He started by ringing the promoters, trying to salvage the tour and find out the details. They smelled a rat almost instantly. 'Why aren't I talking to Rob? Where's Rob? What's going on?' Terry would try and reassure them that everything was OK. But Rob was the only one who knew the deals for the tour, the only one who knew how much we were getting paid for each gig, and they seemed to sense it, leaving Terry to try and bluff it out of them by pretending he knew what was going on when in fact he knew nothing of the sort. Realising that Rob was no longer in the saddle I think they sensed an opportunity to take advantage and bring the prices down. Who can blame them? This was before computers, and all the information was in Rob's notebooks or diaries, and God knows where they were. Probably still in his back garden.

In a way, though, the subsequent Irish tour brought us all together. Something about stepping into the breach, I suppose. We had to go ahead with it to keep the wolf from the door and, after all, we've always been at our best with our backs against the wall, so off we toddled.

We hired a Ford Granada in Dublin for the Irish jaunt, and every time we opened the boot the bloody alarm went off, but apart from that it was fine. We took it all round the country, ending up in Belfast, and don't forget this was in 1986, at the height of 'the Troubles'. We arrived at the border to find the checkpoint staffed by a crowd of really young-looking squaddies. I mean, we were young – still in our late twenties – but these guys looked like schoolkids to us. I'd been saying, 'It'll be fine. We're all English, we're New Order, they're going to love us,' but these squaddies were far more concerned about being blown up or shot to be impressed by a pop group turning up at the crossing, even if we had been on *Top of the Pops*.

So we drove up and they were like, 'Shut up, show us your passport. Shut it,' even though we hadn't said anything yet.

And I said, 'Listen, I've got to tell you something …'

'Just shut your fucking mouth and show us your passports.'

We gave this kid the passports. He looked them over then tossed them back at us. 'All right, now open the boot.'

'Well, that's what I needed to …'

'Just shut your mouth and open the fucking boot,' he said. I could see his finger twitching on the trigger of his gun.

'There's a problem …' I said again.

'JUST OPEN THE FUCKING BOOT!' he roared.

Oh shit!

So I did. I bit my lip, screwed up my courage and opened the boot, the alarm went off straight away and I watched as all the soldiers in the immediate vicinity hit the deck in a sweating panic, screaming and pointing their guns at everyone and everywhere. I cringed. The others in the car had their heads in their hands, convinced they were going to die.

'I tried to tell you …'

'Just fuck off!' he said.

We made it past the border in one piece and went on to Belfast. Our hotel, the Europa, had been bombed so many times it was deemed one of the safest in the city. It was a tall and very striking building, and quite glamorous, but to reach it you had to pass through a fortified security area, which didn't do a lot to calm our already battered nerves. Maybe coming to Belfast in the midst of such turmoil was a bad idea, we thought. Maybe this trip was going to finish us off.

Instead, quite the reverse happened. We had an absolutely storming gig, the best of the tour. A great unified audience. It was a bit weird to see how the crowd segregated as they left the venue, and we had the shock of our lives later, when we went out to try and get something to eat – just seeing how barren and war-torn the place looked. But despite that, or maybe even because of it, we had an awesome gig, and drove away from Belfast raving about what a great place it was.

All apart from Barney, who next morning on the way to the airport was saying how he hated it and would never come back.

As far as I know, he never has, because one thing you have to say about Barney, he's a man of his word.

*

We soldiered on through the first part of the year without Rob. I know he was still in the hospital around the time we went to the *Pretty in Pink* premiere, but I'm pretty sure he was back by April, when we finished preliminary work on the album that would become *Brotherhood* at Jam Studios in London and then decamped to Windmill Lane studios in Dublin. I remember him being in the studio, sitting on the sofa, drinking tea and toast and smoking dope. The same as ever, except slower and less bombastic.

The Jam sessions went well and the atmosphere was OK. We had a huge flat in London near Hyde Park. Next door, we believed, was Princess Anne's house. The flat was very old and had an Arabian flavour but was run-down. It was certainly a lot quieter than recording *Low-Life* had been. Both Rob and Gillian wanted to get fit. They were still burning the midnight oil and I was going to bed. On waking in the morning I'd go for a jog round Hyde Park and one or both would try to join me. It was hilarious. Sometimes Rob would just drop on the grass when we entered the park and I would go right round and he'd still be there when I got back.

There was only one mad night I can remember, when one of our road crew had come down and we'd gone to the Embassy Club. Rusty Egan, the then-owner, and our old mate from the Rich Kids, had given us a crowded lift home in his beautiful Mercedes 190 SL. As we pulled up at the flat we saw an old British Leyland Mini with four girls snorting drugs inside. We could see them at it through the steamed-up windows. So we knocked and asked if they wanted to come in to our flat for a drink. Turned out they were off-duty hookers. They welcomed our invitation. You couldn't see Rusty for dusty. Once he found out they were hookers, he was off like a frightened rabbit. Inside, we negotiated a deal. Me, I politely declined, but the girls charged me £10 to stay in the room. It was wild. Soon one of our blokes had two of them on the go: him flat on the floor, one on his cock, the other on his face, very surreal, while the other bloke cavorted in the shower with his girl.

The fourth girl then dragged me off for a freebie. Things then took a turn for the worse as one of my mates started complaining he'd been diddled. He'd paid £20 and only been entertained by one of the girls. 'You owe me a tenner, Hooky,' he said.

'Fuck off, mine was a freebie,' said I, laughing.

The girls then upped and scarpered, leaving us all there arguing. One of my mates put his used johnnies all over the stairs like dirty banana skins. It was definitely time to head for Ireland.

Originally we had planned to record at Jam in London and mix in Dublin but, as per usual, we'd overrun and still had loads of recording left to do and were forced to continue recording in Dublin. The Dublin studio, Windmill, had a good reputation but was pricey – £60 an hour. So in an effort to keep us aware of that fact, I marked the studio Ampex clock with £5, £10, £15, £20 etc. for every five minutes.

Of course it had no effect whatsoever; we ran well over the allotted time, despite the fact that we'd already done a lot of recording in Jam. It was an expensive session, especially when you factored in the accommodation and travel on top.

Meanwhile, the stylistic divide continued to worsen. It was here that the rock/electronic split began to surface. Ever the punk at heart, I loved the guitar-based material and loved it when we played together. But the others preferred the more sequencer-led tracks, and niggles again began to occur about the amount of bass on some of the songs. On 'Bizarre Love Triangle' we'd had one of our first arguments about the level of the bass guitar. Our engineer Mike Johnson had insisted to the others they were wrong to suggest turning it down. 'It's a great counterpoint,' he'd said. 'That's what New Order is all about.'

On *Brotherhood* there was a slider marked 'Hooky's Bass' on the desk, and I'd see Barney's hand inching towards it.

'The bass is a bit too loud,' became his constant refrain. 'Ooh, let me take it down a notch, Hooky, just a tiny bit, just a gnat's whisker. There, isn't that better?'

You might think this would get on my nerves. Luckily it didn't, because I was very good friends with Mike, freelance by now, who rigged up the desk so the slider Barney was constantly moving did nothing, wasn't even connected. Thanks, Mike. How's that for a gnat's whisker, eh? You need them ears syringing, mate.

In the end the divide was so pronounced that we ended up having the guitar-based songs on side one, and the more electronic songs on side two. When I listen to it now I'm positive that side one has weathered the years far better than side two, but the songs on side two are now my favourites.

Accommodation-wise, we stayed at Blooms Hotel in the centre for a few nights before moving to the countryside well outside the city, into a gorgeous house near a place called the Devil's Kitchen. Perfect for us.

The others stayed in the newer main house while me and Andy Robinson billeted in an old self-contained cottage attached on one side. Here at last we had the luxury of two cars, one for the larks and one for the nightingales. Every morning me and Andy would start the day by playing *Please* by the Pet Shop Boys at full volume and make breakfast together like Morecambe and Wise in that famous sketch. Then, we'd meet Mike in Windmill Lane about midday to start work and the others would turn up any time before midnight. At this point Andy was our keyboard roadie. He was very good with keyboards and computers later, too, becoming invaluable to us in all aspects of our music. Many years after, he'd turn his back on me, but now we were as thick as thieves and had many great adventures together. We were very close.

Now, when we were here, in Devil's Kitchen miles from anywhere, you'd think the opportunities for night-time mayhem would be few and far between. Not the case at all. We were taken to many clubs by a very good friend of ours, Dennis Desmond, our Irish promoter who lived in Dublin. Our favourite club was one called the Pink Elephant, where supposedly married women who wanted a fling hung out. We gathered that, because every time you got a lift home the car always had baby seats in the back and they'd always say, 'It's my sister's car.'

This was where Barney met an incredibly beautiful young model called Katrina. I ended up with her friend, who played so hard to get that I gave up in the end. She was also a model, 'for Toby Jugs!' so Barney said.

I remember driving back to the house one night from the club, the four of us, with my lady next to me in the front. We were getting on fantastically and I was thinking tonight might just be the night. So there we are, me bombing it down this narrow, pitch-black country lane, one hand on the wheel, showing off, when suddenly in front of the car up pops this beautiful white baby rabbit, big eyes shining, completely dazzled by the headlamps. I braked ... but too late, BANG! The rabbit disappears under the car, banging its way down the chassis. Shit. She turned her head away and never spoke to me again. Barney and Katrina were pissing themselves. 'She's a big animal lover, Hooky,' said Katrina by way of consolation. Ah well.

Dublin, however, couldn't have been better. The bars and clubs were great and later you could decamp to certain places that stayed open all night. Although they couldn't serve beer, you could drink spirits, wine or pre-mixed cocktails.

Around the same time, a mate of mine, the son of a very famous Radio 1 DJ, got in touch because his friend, 'Mad Tee', needed help. Turned out Mad Tee had been exposed in the *News of the World* for being a high-class hooker and drug supplier to the kind of judges and MPs who enjoyed having their arses smacked. She had to come and live with us in Devil's Kitchen for a while, which was dead exciting, and even though I spent the entire time getting knocked back when I tried to get off with her, it was good fun having her around. She seemed so intensely exotic.

We'd booked the house for a month, thinking we could finish the album in that time. Wrong. Despite my idea with the studio clock, and despite the fact that Rob would point at it constantly, going, 'Come on, you lot, get a fucking move on!' We were trying, but when it came time to record the vocals Barney began another new ritual, which was the 'I can't sing in . . .' (insert your own conditions here).

So, for example: 'I can't sing in daylight.' 'I can't sing facing west.' 'I can't sing sober.' 'I can't sing with rubber-soled shoes on.' 'I can't sing with you/him/them in the room.' Etc., etc.

Yes, I'm making some of those up, but not all of them. Believe you me, it was getting tough. Obviously we sailed past the deadline and were forced to vacate our gorgeous countryside digs and relocate back to Blooms Hotel in the city. Andy Robinson got really friendly with the manageress, which meant the group had the run of the place.

Still, all that fun had a knock-on effect when it came to mixing the album, and at Windmill Lane we had one of the biggest rows we've ever had. Once again the problem came down to differences in working hours.

During the day we'd start mixing the tracks, getting a great balance, and then at night they'd come in and fuck it up. So began this weird little dance, with me on one side fighting, not only to finish the bloody record but also to keep my bass on the electronic tracks, and them on the other, changing everything late at night and trying to either turn the bass down or take it off some tracks completely. On *Brotherhood*, and then for every album after that, the fastest way to clear the control room was for me to pick up my bass. I'm telling you, the room would magically empty. Me and Mike used to laugh about it.

I had a suspicion that this was how it was going to be from now on, this constant fight … heartbreaking. For them to even think this track would sound better without me on it, and to be made to feel unwelcome every time you picked up your instrument, was a real kick in the bollocks.

I'd fluctuate as to how I dealt with it. One morning I'd be, like, 'I'm splitting the band. Fuck it. Who gives a shit?' The next day I'd come into the studio determined to stand my ground. A lot would depend on how hungover I was.

And it was funny, because much later, when Bernard went off to do Electronic with Johnny Marr, I'd hear that he was doing the same to Johnny. Barney had one of the world's best guitarists on board and he'd layer hundreds of keyboards and sequencers on the songs, mixing them and filling all the tracks up and leaving Johnny just one track for his guitar.

Arthur Baker told me that story to try to make me feel better, and in a funny way it did the trick, because I realised that while Barney might have been a twat, at least he was a consistent twat. He wasn't just victimising me; it was just Barney being Barney, looking after number one.

So anyway, back to Dublin, we were mixing 'Broken Promise' and me and Mike had already been at it for nine hours when them lot turned up.

Mike was at the desk, me sitting to his left, my stack of books at hand, and we played them our work.

'Oh no, I don't like that,' came this voice from behind us. 'I've been thinking about what I'd like to do to this track, and I'd like to pump the whole track through the monitor speakers in the studio [we were still using Martin Hannett's best trick] and mix it in stereo like that.'

Now don't forget, the early start had been agreed by everyone the night before, as it was every night, and only me and Mike had stuck to it and now after nine hours' hard work Barney wanted to do something that I knew would sound shit. I kicked off, roaring, 'You fucking what? We've been doing this all day and it sounds great. There's no way I'm fucking it up for that.'

The argument raged until I ended up storming off. Mike tried to play peacemaker and they attempted Barney's idea, which took the rest of the night and ended up making the track sound just as crap as I'd predicted. What did they do? They reverted to the way we'd been mixing it all day, the one you can hear on the album. I suppose the problem was the two shifts. It just did not work. I do remember Barney suggesting once that as we kept such different hours why didn't I work with Mike from 10 a.m. to 10 p.m. and he would work with him from 10 p.m. to 10 a.m., problem solved.

'When would I sleep, Barney?' asked Mike.

Apart from that, Ireland was great, and what with the Morecambe and Wise breakfasts, the Pink Elephant and Blooms, and the various restaurants and bars we frequented, I had a rare old time and was sad to say goodbye. I even had one lovely girlfriend who'd wake me up every morning on her way back from work at a local burger bar. She smelled lovely and I always woke up with a huge appetite.

We had some tidying up to do, which we did in Amazon Studios in Liverpool, and it was nice to be home-ish. When we arrived we got several warnings about not talking if we went into the village nearby, and having to be accompanied at all times by an employee, them saying that they couldn't guarantee our safety if anyone heard our Manchester accent. That very old 'healthy' rivalry between Liverpool and Manchester was still in place. Me and Mike ended up living in a lovely farmhouse together, just down the road from the studio, while the others commuted.

When we got there Echo and the Bunnymen were in the next studio recording their fifth album. We knew the lads of old, and while socialising we hatched what we thought would be a great plan, a scheme to co-headline a tour together. The reasons? They're not very edifying, I'm afraid, but here we go: we'd worked out that while headlining the big gigs we were now doing was very prestigious, by the time you came off, everybody had left and all the fun had gone with them. The idea of touring together was so that we'd headline on alternate nights, and the band that was on first would get the party going and make sure it was still in full swing when the headline band came off. Simples.

We ended up doing it, too, in 1987, which we'll come to, but the planning didn't go too smoothly. In the gap, Mac of the Bunnymen had changed his mind and decided the Bunnymen should headline every gig, he just chose not to tell us. That information kept coming through first from their agent and then their management. Every time it surfaced I'd phone Mac up and say, 'Hey, mate, your agent/manager says you want to headline every gig?' and Mac would go, 'Fucking hell, Hooky, you know me, I'd never say that. That agent/manager is a fucking idiot. Tell him I said that.'

So I'd phone back. 'Listen, I've just spoken to Mac and he says you're a fucking idiot and it's *you* who wants the Bunnymen to headline.'

He'd say, 'Hooky, look, I'm telling you. Every time I say to Mac that we're co-headlining, he says, "No way are the Bunnymen going on before those Manc bastards."'

It was then I realised who was lying.

Then it changed to the Bunnymen must headline big cities and New Order would do the small cities. It was doing my head in. What a load of shit. Every time I'd phone Mac he'd deny it.

And so it went on; we got our way in the end and tossed for who started the tour. Then one drunken/druggy night, much later on that tour, Mac admitted that it was him who'd been causing all the trouble. He just laughed his evil little cackle. That's Mac for you, and you've got to give it to him, he's a right bastard, but he was fighting for his group and it reminded me of what Ian would have done for Joy Division.

Frontmen, see. They're all fucking nuts.

At some point around the making of *Brotherhood* we returned to Japan, where we did some work on mixing the *Pumped Full of Drugs* video, as well as recording 'As It Is When It Was' and 'Shame of the Nation'. The idea was to make a Japanese-only EP, which never came out, but we found homes for the songs anyway. 'As It Is When It Was' on the album, and 'Shame of the Nation' on the B-side of 'State of the Nation', a newer version, so all's well that ends well.

It turned out to be a wild week. When we got there we discovered that our Japanese contact in the record company had organised such a full timetable of studio and promotion that he hadn't allowed us any time to sleep. He'd scheduled us to work through the night and then go straight to the company in the day to do the promo.

'No sleep,' he said tersely, when we queried it. 'No sleep for week! And I will stay awake with you,' said Taka.

Sorry, mate, but bollocks to that. We bailed out of the promo straight away, so at least the group got some kip, but the record company man felt he had to honour the agreement, so he and the engineers worked through the night and day as well. They had other sessions booked in.

We were very excited to be recording in Japan. The Japanese were getting a fantastic reputation at the time for innovative recording products and we were going to be recording in Nippon Columbia's new flagship studio using the prototype of the much-anticipated Mitsubishi X-850 32-track digital recorder, the first of its kind in the world. This machine would later go on to be used by industry heavyweights like Prince, Quincy Jones and George Martin, but here they were trying the prototype on little old us. God bless them. They were in for some trouble.

The digital recorder would give us many problems while we were recording and was constantly being fixed. The biggest issue was its inability to handle fast short duration sounds like a rimshot. The machine processors simply could not handle the sound being so sharp and fast. Every time you tried to record one it sent the channel completely crazy, to the consternation of the engineers, and the amusement of us.

In England we had recently switched to Japanese products, trying Yamaha keyboards and sequencers such as the DX7, DX5 and DX1 keyboards. We also had a rack-mounted TX816 tone generator and the smaller TX81Z, again the first of its kind, as well as a QX1 sequencer with both RX1 and RX5 drum machines. The prices were never questioned – a considerable investment by Rob on our behalf. Yamaha's reputation for reliability and construction quality was second to none. Finally we were able to rest some of our unreliable Prophets etc., and have a little more confidence about shipping the equipment around the world.

These Yamaha products were very good but difficult to program, with some of the equipment not being very musician-friendly at all. They certainly didn't share our musical language. After a request from Andy Robinson the Japanese record company had arranged for the main designer and programmer of the equipment to join us in the studio for a brainstorming session.

Something to look forward to, eh, readers?

Bazinga!

When the designer turned up *she* was lovely, but not a musician at all, so did not understand musical notation, a strange oversight. Andy really went out of his way to educate her until he ruined it by insisting they had dinner back at the hotel. That was the end of *Miss Yamaha 1986*.

The first day went well, with us all trying each other out, *Madchester v. Japan*. Both of us jockeying for position, setting up and wiring in our own equipment and mating it with theirs, a nice easy night. But by the time we arrived in the studio for our second night of recording these guys had been working for two days straight, and things were starting to come apart at the seams. We couldn't understand them anyway but now even the Japanese translator said they were talking gobbledegook. And then it got worse. They began walking into walls, spontaneously falling asleep on the toilet, even on the control desk, then waking up with a start with the imprints of the knobs on their faces. It was hilarious at first. We were mixing the video soundtrack in one studio, and recording the new tracks in another studio next door; them doing their best to stay awake as they went between the two.

We were unhappy with the acoustics in the live rooms of the studios. They were very well built and expensively finished but, as was the fashion at the time, very dry-sounding, very dead. There was no reverb, no ambience, no life at all. So we told them the only thing we could do was set up the drums in the stairwell and record them there. Being used to the laid-back style of English and American engineers we didn't think it was a big deal, but these guys seriously freaked. The translator was saying to us, 'But we have studio built here, cost many yen, built by specialists from California. They feel insulted.'

'Well, they've been robbed because it sounds terrible. Did they do the sound system in the Haçienda as well, by any chance? Probably a get-back for Pearl Harbor, love!'

They did not find any of that funny at all. It was like they were all on drugs. Out of their minds with fatigue, tired and wired, trying to accommodate what they thought of as our crazy demands. It was bedlam. Hilarious bedlam. It was a hell of an achievement that we got anything done. The translator wasn't a musician either, so God only knows what some of the stuff we were asking for was translated to. Even the trip to the studio could be an education in cultural differences.

One day me and Barney decided to walk from the hotel, as it wasn't far. On the way Barney was eating an apple and threw the core in the gutter. Honestly, the Japanese people were so shocked at this they gasped. Then huddled in conversation discussing what the 'round eye' had done. Outrageous. Amazingly, they even had ashtrays at the traffic lights too. We laughed as we walked through the exquisite Japanese garden outside the studio. We really felt like square pegs in round holes.

At one point the head of Nippon Columbia came to see us. With him came a load of lackeys/assistants and three huge ceremonial plates of sushi. It was the most fantastic sushi you've ever seen. But this was 1986 and sushi hadn't reached Salford yet, so as these trays were being carried in we were looking at them sideways, thinking, *What the bloody hell is that?* then recoiling when the translator told us it was raw fish.

Raw fish? Ew, you dirty bastards!

These guys from the record company were laying it out like the wonderful feast it so obviously was, but like a bunch of philistines we'd scuttled into a corner to hold our noses and make fake puking sounds. When they'd left we asked the translator to find us a McDonald's and donated the sushi feast to the engineers, who pounced on it like starving men. We were like, 'Shut the door, mate, it stinks.'

'我々は再び東京を満たすまで'

On 7 September 1986, our great supporter and my former lover Ruth Polsky set out to attend an Aids benefit in New York. It was the first-ever Aids fundraiser in the world and Ruth had already seen the havoc this disease was wreaking among many of her friends in New York clubland. She was very serious about it, and so 'the Queen of New York City', who had never paid to get into a club in her life, did something she'd probably never done before. She queued up proudly outside the Limelight to get in – her way of respecting the gravity of Aids and making a strong statement.

However, as she waited, a driver ran a red light and crashed into a taxi, which hit the kerb, took off into the air and landed on the pavement in front of the club, scattering everybody but her, and killing her instantly.

Rob went to her funeral alone, on our behalf. Truth was, we couldn't all afford to go; we just didn't have the money, still suffering the fallout from our tax debacle. Instead we'd pay our respects when we next went to the US, which was towards the end of that year, a mammoth tour. Of course the preparations were tinged with sadness, because as our US fixer and agent Ruth would have been responsible for the tour, and as well as being our biggest yet it would have been her biggest production too. The fact that she was unable to see it through when it was something she'd begun – something she'd been a part of since the very beginning, since before Ian died – was very, very sad indeed. On that tour – overseen by Tom Atencio in place of Ruth – there was a sense that we were doing it for her.

The idea was to capitalise on our growing US popularity, which we did. We wanted to behave like a regular band by doing a regular long tour, and indeed it would turn out to be the zenith of our touring career.

The other three hated it, of course; they despised the very idea of it, six weeks away. The question of lengthy tours would be a thorny issue from then on. I never got why this one was different.

Me, I loved it. For the first time we introduced merchandising; we had run out of excuses not to. Tom Atencio described it as the life-blood of touring in America and it ended up being very profitable; also, for the first time we were being driven around – in limos, no less – so yours truly no longer had to worry about ferrying everybody around (or staying sober, which, as will soon become clear, was very much another part of my downfall). In addition, we took a lot of drugs. If Ruth was looking down on us, she would have loved it.

'We weren't really a *Smash Hits* kind of group'

We were in LA, again staying at the Sunset Marquis, the rock'n'roll hotel, and having a wild old time. Terry was made up because Roy Scheider (of *Jaws* fame) was living in one of the coveted corner rooms reserved for very big stars. Cozy Powell was living there too at the time and had his collection of hot rods parked downstairs in the basement car park. That day we were due to leave for a gig in Santa Barbara when who should turn up but the Scarlet Pimpernel himself, Alan Erasmus, with a journalist in tow, Sylvia Patterson.

We are all a bit surprised and puzzled, especially when Alan, having only been in the US a matter of hours, told us the trip had been arranged and paid for by Factory, and that Sylvia would be staying with us for a while, doing a big article for some magazine (he didn't say which). He then departed for the airport and home, leaving Sylvia with us, who then told us the article was for teeny-boppers mag *Smash Hits*.

Completely nuts.

It was typical Alan/Factory but to us seemed like a waste of time, money and effort.

Travelling to the gig we remained puzzled and confused. We weren't really a *Smash Hits* kind of group. Or, shall we say, we didn't like to think of ourselves as a *Smash Hits* sort of group. So for that reason we had a bit of a downer on Sylvia Patterson. Another reason we had a downer on her was because we felt that having a female journalist on board was going to be cramping our style a bit. Basically, you get two different sorts of journalists: type one, who mucks in, has a laugh and almost becomes part of the crew (Miranda Sawyer, say, who whenever she appeared became one of the lads) and type two, who lurks on the sidelines, looking on, making you feel like they're not a fan of the music, or like they're judging you.

Sylvia Patterson seemed to be the second type. So even though she was given a backstage pass and was free to come and go as she pleased, I'd have to hold my hands up and say she probably wasn't made as welcome as she could have been. Terry, in particular, took an instant dislike to her, and when he saw her take a couple of beers off the rider – hardly the world's worst crime, and in fact not really a crime at all for an invited journalist – needed no further excuse to ban her from the dressing room altogether.

It transpired she was holding out for an interview with Barney. *Heh*, I thought, *that's going to be interesting.*

Things went from bad to worse. Unable to enter the dressing room, poor old Sylvia was forced to lurk in the corridor outside. Every time I caught sight of her she had a face like a smacked arse, and who could blame her? After the show Tom Atencio had invited Santa Barbara's most gorgeous women into our dressing room. He opened the door with a flourish, declaring, 'Look what I've found!' as he ushered them in. Santa Barbara's women are some of the most beautiful on the planet. It was as though a dozen Raquel Welch lookalikes had entered the inner sanctum – and soon we were busy metaphorically twirling our moustaches, dishing out Pernod and Asti Spumante, the complete Terry-Thomas effect. Inside the dressing room it was a colourful, bubbly riot; while outside stood Sylvia Patterson, face like thunder. The door would open to allow another Raquel Welch in or out, and in that brief period the door was open I'd see her peering inside.

The whole time, Rob and Terry were mithering Barney to do this interview. 'Fuck off,' he said. No doubt she was mithering them, they were mithering him, and he was putting it off, having far too good a time for any of that. I already had a girlfriend with me so I was pretty restrained that night, but Barney was having a great time and ended up taking a load of people back to his room for more partying.

As bad luck would have it, in the room next door, without doubt hearing the sounds of said party, was poor old Sylvia.

Two particular girls had zeroed in on Barney. They were friends and got everybody else to leave in order to enjoy his company in a more intimate setting.

Next thing, there's a knock at the door. It's Rob, and he's insisting Barney does the interview.

Furious at being interrupted, Barney bundled the two girls into a wardrobe, told them to be quiet and allowed Sylvia in the room, beginning the interview by telling her that if she mentioned anything she saw or heard that night, he'd break her legs.

As you can imagine, after that opener the interview was short and bad-tempered, and as soon as Barney got Sylvia out of the room he resumed the evening's entertainment. God only knows what she heard through the walls that night. I dread to think.

The next morning, after the bleary-eyed group had posed for photos by the pool and then left for the next venue, Sylvia and her photographer encountered the two girls leaving Barney's room. The girls had taken his pair of leftover shorts as a souvenir and, to add insult to injury for Barney, found $200 in the pocket (ouch!) so Sylvia got the photographer to take a picture of the two girls holding shorts and money aloft. Now, I know what will have hurt Barney the most, and it wasn't losing the shorts.

No doubt when Barney went home his missus would ask him what the tour was like and he'd say, 'Oh, quiet, you know?' just like the rest of us, when in fact the truth of it was the exact opposite. Our illustrious lead singer had certainly come to terms with the pains of being front man.

Now, fast-forward a load of gigs, and I think we were in Boulder, Colorado, by the time the news filtered back from home that the current issue of *Smash Hits* featured the New Order interview, complete with the headline: 'Ask us anything horrible and we'll break your legs!' and a picture of the two girls holding up Barney's shorts.

Swizzing around the West Coast of America in search of New Order, Sylvia Patterson encounters an ill-tempered fellow who says...

"Ask us anything horrible and we'll break your legs!"

continued...

▲ Two American foxtresses pilfer Barney's "shorts" and have a birrova laugh!!

boring job – a postman or something – and he kept on having to do all these really boring post jobs until *one* day (*dramatic pause*) he got this job flying parcels over a *shark infested* sea – and one engine on

Considering what it was that he'd really said, and what had really gone on, *Smash Hits* had let us off quite lightly. Even so, it was still incriminating stuff, especially the bit about the two girls giggling in his wardrobe while Barney did the interview.

Anyway, back to the gig, and first was the problem of how, what or when to tell Barney. Me, I must admit, I was loving it. I was in that rare and privileged position of having a front-row seat without being involved. Being one of the few people in the company who would stand up to Barney then, I had nothing to fear from him; all I needed to do was sit back and enjoy the fireworks.

Sure enough, Rob and Terry agonised over when to tell him. They reasoned that if they told him before the show, then he'd make it a terrible show; he was prone to doing that for the smallest of reasons anyway. But if they waited and told him afterwards then he might be even more angry.

In the end they chose to tell him beforehand, against my better judgement, and it was indeed a crap gig. Like I say, Barney is one of those who if he feels shit, then everybody else has to feel shit, too, and it was like a dark cloud came over the entire backstage area, infecting the dressing room, the performance, everything. He came off stage and started hitting the Pernod hard, and you could tell that he was in a very dark place. He had been well and truly caught with his pants down. Or rather, aloft.

Like everybody else, I escaped the dressing room, leaving our singer to brood and drink alone. What a difference to Santa Barbara …

In the corridor outside I encountered Tom Atencio, with the local Warners rep.

'Hey, Peter,' he said brightly, 'could I bring someone to meet you guys?'

I said, 'Aw, mate, you couldn't have picked a worse time. Who is it?'

'Oh, it's this guy who runs three record shops in the area. He's a great guy, big in A&R for A&L at A&M, gets us lots of exposure. He's here with his girlfriend and I'd be so happy if you could just meet him, give him an autograph, sign his records?'

'All right, bring him through. I'll do it,' says I.

There was a seating area outside the dressing room. Low table, drinks machine nearby, that kind of thing. There they introduce the record-shop guy, who was a short bloke in spectacles, quite nondescript, with a girl in tow, and a bunch of New Order records tucked under his arm.

He walked up to where I was standing, tossed the records onto the table and, looking away, said, 'Sign my records.'

I had that weird moment of not being able to believe what I'd heard.

'You what?' I said.

He went, 'Sign my fucking records, man.'

I looked at him. Then, giving him back the records, I said, 'Come with me. I've got someone I want you to meet.'

I led the guy and his girlfriend to meet Barney, and they followed me into the dressing room, where I entered to find our singer in the process of pouring himself another Pernod.

In we went: me, the record-shop guy and his girlfriend.

I said, 'Barney, this guy wants to meet you.'

Barney looked around, putting the top back on his Pernod bottle, eyebrows raised.

The guy said, 'Sign my records,' throwing them again on the table in the dressing room.

Barney looked at him.

'You what?' he said.

'Sign my fucking records, man.'

It went off, as I knew it would. Barney grabbed his bottle of Pernod by the neck and looked like he was about to swing it at the guy, who ducked out of the way, at the same time as his girlfriend screamed, 'Don't you do that!' and dived forward to protect him.

Barney never missed a beat, started screaming at the girl – at both of the poor sods – unmentionable, unprintable things, while I stood there laughing my dogs off. As the two visitors recovered their wits and started screaming abuse back at him I could see his knuckles whitening on the neck of the Pernod bottle and decided to step in before he did any real damage.

I grabbed the guy with one hand, his girlfriend with the other and bundled them out the door, slamming it shut just as Barney reached it on the other side.

The door shook as Barney tried to open it but I held it shut. He started kicking it but I kept it closed.

'I think you'd better go, knobhead,' I said to the record-shop guy.

'But nobody's signed my fucking records, man.'

'That was how I ended 1986'

The record-shop guy threatened to go to the police but nothing ever came of it.

And the tour rumbled on, with plenty of great gigs and lots of great parties to show for it. Returning to New York, we played a benefit concert for Ruth. The fact that it was a benefit for Ruth, not to mention the manner of her passing, was obviously lost on Billy Idol and his mates, who all tried to get in for nothing, the freeloading bastards. It wasn't even that expensive. Thinking about it now though it was probably someone using his name, happens to me all the time. It was sold out.

Around the same time we decided to go and pay our respects at Ruth's grave, only them lot wouldn't get up in the morning, so I ended up going alone. Or rather me and Julie Panebianco (a lovely girl and, before you ask, I didn't, she was too nice) from Warners took a cab to Ruth's parents' home on the outskirts of New York, where we met her mum and dad. They were an elderly Jewish couple who were very pleased to see us and said they'd heard all about New Order and then, after a cup of tea, offered to drive us to see Ruth's grave.

Her mum stayed at home so her dad drove, and fuck me, this guy was the worst driver I've ever seen. He drove through give-way signs, across red lights, pulled out into traffic. It was like he was determined to commit every traffic violation in the shortest possible time at full speed. Julie and I sat screaming, fingernails dug into the plastic like Steve Martin in *Planes, Trains and Automobiles*.

By some miracle we arrived at the cemetery in one piece, where we stood at Ruth's grave and paid our respects before attending to the business of whether or not we dared get back in the car with her dad. If we did, it seemed like there was every likelihood we'd be joining Ruth sooner rather than later.

We contemplated doing a runner from the graveyard. That would have been a first. The problem was we were in the middle of nowhere, Hoboken or something, so in the end we decided we had no choice but to risk it and got back in the car with him, only to endure more death-wish driving all the way back to their house. Pinned to our seats with fear, we closed our eyes and prayed either we'd get home or the end would come quickly.

Eventually we arrived back. Not long after we got there, and while we were still shaking from the ordeal, Ruth's brother arrived.

'Where have you been?' he said.

'We've just been to see your sister's grave.'

He looked at us, face pale. 'You didn't get in the car with my dad, did you?'

Turned out the poor guy had Alzheimer's.

After a show in Tampa towards the end of the tour, everybody else was off to an aftershow party at some club, but I was feeling knackered. Our tour DJ, Frank Callari, chopped me out a line of coke. 'Have that, brother, you'll be fine.'

I hadn't had any since the *Pretty in Pink* premiere and I thought, *Why not? What the hell?*

So I did. I had the line and pretty much right away, after a crap, was hot to trot. I must admit over the length of this tour I had got heartily sick of sitting in rooms listening to this lot come out with a right load of boring old shite, with their coke-induced revelations and truths, refusing to go anywhere, just sitting there with their noses in the trough. I suppose it was 'if you can't beat them' etc. 'So, let's get to the party.' Amazingly we all did. We went to whatever club was holding it, and there I got approached by a girl. She was lovely, but I'd decided I wasn't interested in copping off, because – and I know how awful this sounds – I wanted a night off. This is how it got on tour; it was so easy to cop off with girls that you'd literally be doing it for the sake of it. I lost count of the times I fell asleep on the poor girls, and I mean, literally, *on* them.

So anyway, I was chatting away with this girl, a fan, and I was just being myself, not bothering with the Terry-Thomas routine, flying high on this line of coke, having a pretty good time, when she excused herself to go to the toilet.

I sat there watching the world go by, waiting for her to get back, when this kid slid into the seat beside me. 'Hey you, motherfucker.'

'You what?'

'That's my fucking sister, you don't fuck with her.'

With that he left, and I sat there, a bit puzzled. Shortly after, the girl returned, we continued chatting, and for one reason or another I didn't mention this brother figure lurking around. Then she went off again, this time for a dance to a song she liked, and once more this American kid takes a seat next to me. 'I'm telling you, motherfucker, I'm watching you, and if you fuck with my sister, I'll kick your ass.'

I don't like being threatened, but fair enough, the kid was only looking out for his sister. So I said, 'Look, mate, I've got no intentions towards your sister, all right? Now fuck off.'

He did.

The girl returned, flushed from her dance.

I said to her, 'Listen, I'm not being funny, but your brother's getting well irate over there. He's really worried about you.'

She looked confused. 'Brother? I haven't got a brother.'

Right.

I got up, stormed across the club, grabbed hold of the kid by the lapels, nutted him, threw him on the floor, put my foot on his throat and was calling him a lying twat until the doormen dragged me off and – one of the perks of being in the group hosting the aftershow party – threw *him* out.

Now, I remember that incident well, because after that I started taking coke all the time. It was a combination of factors: no longer doing the equipment, no longer doing any driving, doing a lot of partying. After that, coke became a habit.

And that was it. That was how I ended 1986.

I was a cokehead.

BROTHERHOOD TRACK BY TRACK

'Paradise': 3.48

When I looked into your lifeless eyes …

Our homage to Dolly Parton, Barney still being a bit obsessed with country music lyrically. The sound of Jam Studios' live room on the drums takes me straight back there. An unusual song, structure-wise. Six-string bass parts too quiet. Too many lead/backing vocals. The fight began here.

'Weirdo': 3.51

It's a life that's made for me …

I felt the backing vocals on this record were doing nothing for the track, and me and Barney were nose to nose over the mixing desk. Great bass riff with a super break.

'As It Is When It Was': 3.43

I bang my head against the wall …

A proper New Order song, recorded in Japan. Ruth Polsky's favourite, she loved that the 'Love Will Tear Us Apart' bass riff was used again. With a magnificent soaring chorus and break, this track really shone live. A vision of Manchester at its bleakest.

'Broken Promise': 3.44

Every time I see you, you shout at me …

This track feels almost *Movement*-era to me. A great vocal line delivered very passionately. This song soon lost favour. It had too many guitars and just could not be delivered in the same way live.

'Way of Life': 4.03

A failure of your moral code ...

We were trying to emulate 'Age of Consent' so I just played the riff backwards and *voilà*. Me and Mike came up with the idea for the reggae drop in the studio, and to get the bass sound for the intro overloaded the input of the studio cassette deck to get just the right distortion. Terry Mason's favourite song. To me this side of the album was what the band was all about, and the second side complemented it very well.

'Bizarre Love Triangle': 4.20

Shot right through with a bolt of blue ...

We were still writing the lyrics together here, and I'm pretty sure Steve came up with the above. In fact *only* Steve could have come up with it. This song has no key change but the chorus jumps out on its own. A great pop tune, driven by Barney's wonderful string riffs. It started life in a different key, which to me sounded much better. I had a great open-string bass riff which we lost on the key transition. I must go through those old cassettes. Time ... the enemy of the people.

'All Day Long': 5.09

This is a song about an innocent ...

The only song about child abuse you can dance to. Dark, dark lyrics. Barney once drunkenly told me this was the only bass riff of mine he hated. Personally I think he got it mixed up with 'Angel Dust', but it hurt nonetheless. Very powerful live, with a sharp contrast between the synths and the orchestral overdubs. Great guitar work by Barney.

'Angel Dust': 3.40

I fear you will betray me ...

Barney had brought in an old album of Eastern prayer calls to sample. It's embarrassing now to think how negative I was to all his ideas. I regret that. The fear of being sidelined made me hostile. We worked hard in Jam to get the guitar lead lines as 'Ennio Morricone' as possible, and even threaded metal washers on the strings to give us a more metallic sound, like we did with 'Sunrise'. Barney worked on the mix of these four tracks in Amazon Studios harder than I have ever seen him work before. He wanted the production to be just right. He pushed me and Mike very hard, very hard indeed. I resented that too. The underwater Lexicon reverb effect alone took ages. Worth it though, they sound superb. Well done, Barn. Sorry, mate.

'Every Little Counts': 4.25

I think you are a pig, you should be in a zoo …

A victim of five o'clock in the morning lyrics. When you're so tired anything seems perfect. In Windmill Lane we were pissing ourselves. It was nice to hear Barney enjoying himself too. You can hear us commenting in the background. Rob and Mike hated it. Looking back now it stops the track being timeless and I'd say they were right. But live, people love it. The keyboard effect at the end was done on the Emulator II, with Barney holding *all* the keys down at once, using both arms. My second rip-off Hot Chocolate 'Emma' bassline.

TIMELINE SEVEN
JANUARY–DECEMBER 1986

21 January 1986

New Order play Galway, Ireland.

> **'On this tour the promoter decided we needed security and provided us with this tall thin dude who was like Jason Bourne. It was a bad time again in Ireland and there had been some threats against English groups. He even had a gun, which we badgered him to show us, but he wouldn't; ironic, because we'd soon be seeing so many in Manchester that we would be heartily sick of them.'**

23 January 1986

New Order play Connolly Hall, Cork, Ireland.

> **'Here I had the dubious honour of being spat at by an old lady because I was English. I was really shocked. Our security guy told us, "For fook's sake keep yeer traps shooot!"'**

24 January 1986

New Order play Sir Francis Xavier Hall, Dublin.

25 January 1986

New Order play Sir Francis Xavier Hall, Dublin.

27 January 1986

New Order play Queen's University, Belfast.

February 1986

Pretty in Pink by John Hughes released.
Featuring, by New Order:
'Elegia'
'Thieves Like Us'
'Shellshock' 6.04

The first two tracks were not included in the movie soundtrack.

8 February 1986

New Order play the Royal Court Theatre, Liverpool. This benefit for Derek Hatton's Liverpool City Council was billed as 'With Love from Manchester'.

> **'We'd played with the Fall before on the closing night of the Electric Circus, so Mark E. Smith was an old adversary, but we'd never played with the Smiths, who were very big by then, so there was a lot of competitive pressure. Rob and Tony liked Derek Hatton because he was all about shaking up the establishment, and was becoming a very strong character in Liverpool politics. Tony used to work in Liverpool, so I suppose he had a political interest, even though everyone hated him there. He was always getting his Ford Escort Mexico stolen and dumped there. Famously on one day it was stolen twice, and the second time left on bricks with no wheels. 'Fucking Scousers got my car . . . again!' he'd say sadly.**
>
> **'Rob liked Hatton because he liked rebels, and he said to us we should just do it for the rider, so we put in for a rider that came to £65 and the Smiths did it for a rider plus expenses which came to about £600, and we were going, 'Fucking tight bastards,' until we found out that Mark E. Smith had charged them a grand to do the gig, plus rider, plus expenses. Good old Mark. I've still got the poster.'**

27 February 1986

New Order play Civic Hall, Wolverhampton, supported by Life.

28 February 1986

New Order play St George's Hall, Bradford.

1 March 1986

New Order play Spectrum Arena, Warrington.

21 March 1986

New Order: 'Shellshock'
(FAC 143)

Seven-inch track list:

'Shellshock'	4.19
'Thieves Like Us' (instrumental edit)	3.55

Twelve-inch track list:

'Shellshock'	9.40
'Shellcock'	7.31

Run-out groove one: *So Hip it Hurts!*
Run-out groove two: *Watch Out for the Dwarf!*

Recorded in Yellow Two Studios, Stockport.
Mixed at the Village Recorder, Santa Monica, Los Angeles.
Engineered by Julia Nagle and John Robie.
Produced by New Order and John Robie.
Designed by Peter Saville Associates.
Photograph by Geoff Power.
Entered UK chart on 29 March 1986, remaining in the charts for 5 weeks, its peak position was number 28.

27 March 1986

New Order play the Apollo Theatre, Oxford.

28 March 1986

New Order play Brighton Centre, Brighton.

29 March 1986

New Order play Poole Arts Centre, Poole.

April, May, June 1986

After sessions at Jam Studios in London, New Order go into Windmill Lane Studios in Dublin to record *Brotherhood*, finishing up at Amazon Studios in Liverpool.

14 June 1986

New Order play City Hall, Sheffield.

21 June 1986

New Order play Loughborough University, Loughborough.

29 June 1986

New Order play Greetings 4, Valdarno, San Giovanni, Italy.

19 July 1986

Festival of the Tenth Summer, Manchester Exhibition Centre (G-Mex), Manchester.
(FAC 151)

Featuring: A Certain Ratio, New Order, the Fall, Cabaret Voltaire, Pete Shelley, the Worst, Wayne Fontana and the Mindbenders, the Smiths, OMD, the Virgin Prunes, Sandie Shaw, Howard Devoto, Happy Mondays, Durutti Column, James.
Special guests: John Cale, John Cooper Clarke, Steve Diggle, Margi Clarke, Steve Naïve.
Comperes: Bill Grundy, Paul Morley.
DJ: Jerry Dammers.

The Festival of the Tenth Summer, held to celebrate ten years since the Sex Pistols played at the Manchester Lesser Free Trade Hall, included a concert and a book by Paul Morley and Jon Savage. Promotional materials, including a set of postcards designed by by Peter Saville Associates around the theme of the numbers zero to nine, and an exhibiton at the City Art Gallery included various number-related artworks, while posters advertising the event also incorporated the motif.

> 'The Festival of the Tenth Summer was set up to mark a decade since punk changed all our lives, forever. It was a proper Manchester occasion and a great gig. Rob was there, so he must have been feeling a hell of a lot better and on the road to recovery. I have lots of fond memories of that gig. Got a really bizarre VHS video shot by IKON with a still camera from out front. There's a bizarre moment with legendary Manchester city councillor Pat Carney and a little Peruvian woman doing an appeal for her lost son with the crowd all shouting at her. I went to Pete Saville's exhibition earlier in the day and the exhibits were wonderful. Peter arrived fashionably late, when everyone was already there, and started going mad about one number, '7' I think, which was made of small stones arranged to look like a number 7. Turned out Oliver Wilson, aged four, had been doing his own design work and no one noticed, thinking it was Pete's. I remember Terry Mason bagged the number '8', which was huge and made out of aluminium, for his house in Swinton saying, 'It was perfect for hiding the bins behind.'

August 1986

Pumped Full of Drugs video (IKON 17 /FACT177) released. Video recorded at the Shinjuku Koseinenkin Kaikin Hall, Tokyo, Japan, 2 May 1985.

Track list:
'Confusion'
'Love Vigilantes'
'We All Stand'
'As It Is When It Was'
'Sub-culture'
'Face Up'
'Sunrise'
'This Time of Night'
'Blue Monday'

TIMELINE SEVEN JANUARY–DECEMBER 1986

Prime mover: Rob Gretton
Director shoot: Anthony Wilson
Director edit: Hidetake Ogo
Technical director: Naru Yanagihara
Typography: Chris Mathan for Peter Saville Associates
Photography: Trevor Key

16 August 1986

New Order play Valby, Copenhagen, Denmark.

7 September 1986

Death of Ruth Polsky, New York.

10 September 1986

New Order play Mayfair, Newcastle.

11 September 1986

New Order play Playhouse Theatre, Edinburgh.

12 September 1986

New Order play Barrowlands, Glasgow.

13 September 1986

New Order play Caird Hall, Dundee.

> **'One of our roadies (who shall remain nameless) got hand relief off a lovely young girl in a club after the gig. Then she spent the whole night chasing him round screaming at him because her watch had come off during the deed and she couldn't find it. She was demanding he pay for a new one. Twinny was very embarrassed.'**

22 September 1986

New Order: 'State of the Nation'

Seven-inch track list:
'State of the Nation' 3.28
'Shame of the Nation' 3.33

Twelve-inch track list:
'State of the Nation' 6.32
'Shame of the Nation' 7.54

Run-out groove one: *Hail Mary!*
Run-out groove two: *Lucky Johnny!*

'State of the Nation'
Written and produced by New Order.
Recorded April 1985 in Tokyo, Japan.
Engineered by Michael Johnson.

'Shame of the Nation'
Written and produced by New Order and John Robie.
Recorded October 1985 to April 1986 in Manchester, New York and LA.

Designed by Peter Saville Associates.
Photography by Trevor Key.
Entered UK chart on 27 September 1986, remaining in the charts for 3 weeks, its peak position was number 30.

22 September 1986

New Order: 'Peel Sessions 1982' EP released.
First transmission: 1 June 1982.

Track list:
'Turn the Heater On' 5.00
'We All Stand' 5.15

'Too Late'	3.35
'5.8.6.'	6.05

Recorded at Revolution Studios, Cheadle Hulme, Manchester.
Engineered by Andy MacPherson.
Produced by New Order.
Designed by Wyke Studios.
'Turn the Heater On' written by Keith Hudson.

Entered UK chart on 27 September 1986, remaining in the charts for 1 week, its peak position was number 54.

> **'When I listened to this for the re-releases of *Low-Life* and *Brotherhood* in 2014 I cannot for the life of me think why we never recorded "Too Late" properly. Barney must have hated it. As I mentioned previously, "Turn the Heater On" was Ian Curtis's favourite reggae track. We did it to celebrate his life.'**

29 September 1986

New Order: *Brotherhood*

Track list:

'Paradise'	3.48
'Weirdo'	3.51
'As It Is When It Was'	3.43
'Broken Promise'	3.44
'Way of Life'	4.03
'Bizarre Love Triangle'	4.20
'All Day Long'	5.09
'Angel Dust'	3.40
'Every Little Counts'	4.25

Run-out groove one: *See An Old Soldier Right*
Run-out groove two: *More Juice Please*

Recorded at Jam Studios, London, and Windmill Lane Studios, Dublin, Ireland.

Mixed at Amazon Studios Liverpool.
Engineered by Michael Johnson.
Produced by New Order.
Designed by Peter Saville Associates.
Photographed by Trevor Key.
Entered UK chart on 11 October 1986, remaining in the charts for 5 weeks, its peak position was number 9.

September 1996

Joy Division: 'First Peel Session' EP released.
Recorded: 31 January 1979
First transmission: 14 February 1979

October 1986

Something Wild by Jonathan Demme released, soundtrack includes 'Temptation' by New Order.

2 October 1986

New Order play Tower Ballroom, Birmingham.

3 October 1986

New Order play Winter Gardens, Malvern, supported by Happy Mondays.

4 October 1986

New Order play Town & Country Club, London.

6 October 1986

New Order play Royal Albert Hall, London.

13 October 1986

New Order play the Haçienda, Manchester.

29 October 1986

New Order play the Mesa Amphitheatre, Phoenix, Arizona.

31 October 1986

New Order play San Diego State University Open Air Theatre, San Diego, California.

1 November 1986

New Order play Irvine Meadows, Irvine, California.

4 November 1986

New Order play Cow Palace, Hollywood, California.

> **'Frank grabbed me after this gig and said, "There's a party in Bel Air, stick with me." Sure enough, after the show we ended up in a car with some very, very attractive people and a very familiar male driver, who I thought I knew, on our way to the elite Bel Air, California. We arrived at this beautiful mansion only to be dumped while the kids went out hunting for beer. Frank and I sat on the upstairs landing outside the toilet doing "bumps" of coke, waiting for our hosts, where, bizarrely, we were joined by Marc Quinn, an old friend from Groucho's. Marc is now famous for making a bust of his own head, out of his own blood, then freezing it. He was as puzzled as we were. As we chatted our eyes alighted on a melted statuette, all blackened and burned. Marc as a sculptor was most intrigued, but one thing we all agreed on was that it was a weird ornament to have at the top of your stairs. Our host returned looking as familiar as ever and we couldn't resist getting the history of the statuette.**

'"It's my dad's," he says. "The house burned down in 1983 and that was the only thing saved."

'*Oh*, we thought, none the wiser as to the importance, and we must have looked very puzzled as he elaborated: "Gene Kelly's my father. It's his honorary Oscar."

'"Singin' in the Rain",' the three of us chorused.

'Turned out we were in Gene Kelly's house in Bel Air with his son, Timothy, entertaining us, on 725 North Rodeo Drive.

'Blimey! Not bad for a tosser from flabbergasted.'

5 November 1986

New Order play Palladium, Hollywood, California.

5 November 1986

New Order: 'Bizarre Love Triangle'
(FAC 163)

Seven-inch track list:
'Bizarre Love Triangle' (edit) 3.40
'Bizarre Dub Triangle' (edit) 3.23

Twelve-inch track list:
'Bizarre Love Triangle' (full) 6.39
'Bizarre Dub Triangle' (full) 7.06

Run-out groove one: *MPO.*
Run-out groove two: *MPO2.*

Recorded in Jam Studios, London, and Windmill Lane Studios, Dublin, Ireland.
Engineered by Mike Johnson.
Written and produced by New Order.
Remixed by Shep Pettibone for Mastermix Productions.
Remix engineered by Steve Peck.
Edit by Shep Pettibone and the Latin Rascals.
Designed by Peter Saville Associates.

Photographed by Trevor Key.
Entered UK chart on 15 November 1986, remaining in the charts for 2 weeks, its peak position was number 56.

'The first remix to feature no bass guitar; thanks, Shep.'

7 November 1986

New Order play Arlington Theatre, Santa Barbara, California.

8 November 1986

New Order play Berkeley Community Theatre, Berkeley, California.

'I had arranged for Tasha from San Diego to join me here. I had never flown anyone in before and it was so easy. Unfortunately, just before she arrived I discovered I had caught an STD. I was devastated but thought that I would come clean, so to speak. When she arrived I fessed up and she simply said, "You probably got it from me. Let's go to the hospital." Which we duly did, and were examined, had blood tests, and were given prescriptions, then the drugs, and then the one thing I had completely forgotten about, the bill. Three hundred and fifty dollars . . . each. Shit. I broke out in a cold sweat. I did not have the money in cash and if I used my credit card the missus would see it.

'"Pay at the cash desk at the entrance to the hospital," the nurse said.

'As we walked down the corridor I came clean again – about my lack of money this time.

'She laughed and said, "You didn't give them our names, yeah? This way then." And she kicked the fire escape doors open and we escaped into the gardens, legging it back to the hotel. Now that's what I call a health service.

'After the gig Johnny Marr turned up at the hotel with his wife Angie; everyone was pretty clattered, but in a room later, with him and a few of the crew, he asked me if I fancied doing a record with him. I was really flattered. Johnny is a great guitarist, not as good as Barney in my opinion, but a great guitarist nonetheless.

He said very seriously, "The best guitarist in Manchester should do a record with the best bass player in Manchester."

'I didn't forget about it, but in the cold light of day was a little embarrassed. My heart lay in New Order and I was happy, even with all the little foibles, so I never followed it up with Johnny. Later, when Barney went off to form Electronic with him, I mentioned it to a journalist and was accused of lying – as though I'd made it up to be spiteful, just to rain on their parade. Me and Johnny have never spoken since, but hand on heart, it happened.'

10 November 1986

New Order play the Coliseum, Utah State Fairgrounds, Salt Lake City, Utah.

11 November 1986

New Order play CU Events Center, Boulder, Colorado, supported by Love Tractor.

14 November 1986

New Order play Maceba Theatre, Houston, Texas.

'Me and Frank decided to drive for a change, so we hired a big old Lincoln Continental for old times' sake. These cars had fantastic sound systems, and after a long enjoyable drive we arrived in Houston just as the sun was setting and the city lights started to flicker on. Frank said, "I have the perfect tape for this!" and put on Tangerine Dream. It was a gorgeous memory of a gorgeous man. The pair of us sat there grinning from ear to ear, high-fiving, so happy with our lot. Frank went on to manage many great groups but died in 2007, aged fifty-five. Sorely missed.'

15 November 1986

New Order play Bronco Bowl, Oak Cliff, Dallas, Texas.

17 November 1986

New Order play City Coliseum, Austin, Texas.

20 November 1986

New Order play Oriental Theatre, Milwaukee, Wisconsin.

21 November 1986

New Order play Aragon Ballroom, Chicago, Illinois.

22 November 1986

New Order play Fox Theatre, Detroit, Michigan.

24 November 1986

New Order play Congress Centre, Ottawa, Canada.

26–27 November 1986

New Order play Massey Hall, Toronto, Canada.

30 November 1986

New Order play McMaster University (Ivor Wynne Centre), Hamilton, Canada.

1 December 1986

New Order play unknown venue, Buffalo, NY.

2 December 1986

New Order play Syria Mosque, Pittsburgh, Pennsylvania.

4 December 1986

New Order play Irvine Auditorium, University of Pennsylvania, Philadelphia, Pennsylvania.

5 December 1986

New Order play 1018 Club, New York.

> **'Benefit gig for Ruth Polsky. God rest her soul.'**

6 December 1986

New Order play the Orpheum, Boston, Massachusetts.

7 December 1986

New Order play Opera House, Boston, Massachusetts.

8 December 1986

New Order play Constitution Hall, Washington DC.

9 December 1986

New Order play Felt Forum, New York.

12 December 1986

New Order play Fox Theatre, Atlanta, Georgia.

13 December 1986

New Order play Tampa Bay Theatre, Tampa Bay, Florida.

> **'A few complaints at this concert. One minute Steve was playing the drums and then he wasn't but the drums carried on. People spotted it and complained at the box office. Americans were still**

getting used to the concept of pre-recorded parts being played by performing groups. A disclaimer would be put on the tickets for the next tour.'

15 December 1986

New Order play Knight Center, Miami, Florida.

TEN BEST PEOPLE I DID GET TO PLAY WITH (IN NO PARTICULAR ORDER)

1. Primal Scream: 'Untitled' and 'Atmosphere'
2. Perry Farrell: 'Wishing on a Dog Star', 'Kinky'
3. Hybrid: 'True to Form'
4. Martha Ladly: 'Light Years from Love'
5. Liela Moss (Duke Spirit): 'Second Chances'
6. Inspiral Carpets: 'The Way the Light Falls'
7. Jaz Coleman and Geordie (Killing Joke): various
8. Vini Reilly (Durutti Column): 'Hooky's Tune'
9. Nick Hussey: 'Salty'
10. Gwen Stefani: 'The Real Thing'

'My knee was in the video'

In Japan again, at the beginning of 1987, and we were introduced to two new wonderful things: kimonos and Kobe beef.

See? Our palates, along with our waistlines, were expanding, both physically and metaphysically. No doubt we were attracted by the fact that in order to make Kobe beef, the cows were massaged daily with beer – supposedly to make the meat very tender. We liked the idea of that and were happy to be plied with the stuff.

Trouble was, in Japan you got such small portions. So we'd be banging on the tables, 'Bring us more beef, Pedro, bring us more beef!'

Everybody else in the restaurant, these quiet, retiring Japanese types – and I'm telling you, I've never seen so much bowing in all my life as I did on that tour – would be staring at us, open-mouthed, like we were arrivals from another planet, and because they stared at us, we played up to it and our manners got even more coarse and rough.

I remember this particular night when we'd finished our Viking feast of Kobe beef and had been hitting the saki hard. Rob in particular was absolutely bladdered. Now our promoter again on this tour was a venerable older gentleman (let's call him Taka), who came across like someone out of an old Japanese gangster movie and Rob was fascinated by his hair, which was always creamed down smooth, with a mirror-like finish, like mine at the time. Suddenly Rob stood up, grabbed the poor bloke in a headlock, went, 'Ah, you're all right, you,' and knuckled his head hard.

When Rob at last let him go Taka was very flushed and his hair was sticking out in all directions. We laughed but we soon realised that all the other Japanese were looking at Rob like he'd just stuck a knife in the bloke. It turned out that in Japan, men never touch each other, it is frowned upon; apart from a handshake it's completely forbidden. So it was that shocking to them – seeing their boss treated like that, his hair sticking up all over the show – they literally nearly fainted.

What with stuff like that and our hosts' inability to say the word 'no', we actually found it a little bit difficult to work in Japan, and it was a bit of a relief to move on to Australia again, where support for New Order had always been very solid, and our promoters Vivien Lees and Ken West would soon be going on to much bigger things (i.e. promotoing the Big Day Out festival).

Our lives were entering a sort of treadmill stage, repeating in a wonderful pattern. We would go to Japan/Australia one year, the next year would be America and Europe, bit of a break to record or write an album, then back on the treadmill again. Working like this and being looked after so wonderfully made the years fly by.

Our 1987 tour of Spain was slightly different. It was organised by Andy Fisher (ex-Stockholm Monsters manager) in his new guise as an agent. It also featured, for the first time, my new bass roadie Jane Roberts. Dave Pils had shocked us all by handing in his notice and leaving after eight years. Dave was a great guy and a very good friend. He was vegetarian and when Rob asked him why, he said in his Bow Bells cockney accent, 'You just cannot get a good cut of meat these days.' Dave I would sorely miss too.

Jane and I had been introduced at the Haçienda. Standing five-foot-ten in Doc Marten boots, she was attractive in a grungy kind of way and very confident. She marched up to me, poked me in the chest and said, 'I should be your roadie,' then walked off. I was intrigued. I talked it over with Andy Robinson and we decided to go for it.

We arrived in Spain and the first thing we realised was that the promoter was an arsehole. He was a round, squat little guy who just didn't seem to know what was going on. Rob was still struggling to regain his lost leadership role and together they made quite a pair. The first day we were there he took us to a funfair and insisted Rob join him on this big-wheel thing where they promptly got stuck in their seats right at the top. Rob was terrified of heights, and always had been. He started screaming and then this Spanish guy joined in.

'Quite a sight,' said Denny Laine, who was standing next to me.

I had to agree. Turned out that Denny Laine (ex-Moody Blues/Wings) was Pedro's best mate and had joined us on the tour. A nice bloke as it goes, and he kept saying to me, 'We are destined to work together.'

We weren't, as it happened.

The first gig was in a bull ring and our dressing room was right next to the bull's dressing room. Which, surprisingly, Barney found quite funny.

Terry had developed an obsession with Dead or Alive from Liverpool, and played 'You Spin Me Round (Like a Record)' on his Walkman, constantly. Even when you tried to talk to him he wouldn't turn it off, mouthing the lyrics in your face. Some kind of surreal protest, I thought, like Dave's departure had unsettled him.

I also discovered something else going wrong: me and Jane were flirting like crazy and it was getting worse and worse. After the gig, back at the hotel, one of Pedro's oppos had turned up on a Yamaha V-Max, a beautiful, very high-powered motorcycle. Jane admired it. 'Take it for a spin, señor,' the guy said, as he tossed me the keys. Jane was grinning from ear to ear and I couldn't back down, sensing a way to impress her. So I got on and raced off, slipping and sliding my way through the Madrid traffic, with no helmet on.

This thing was a monster and it was one of the most terrifying rides of my life, fighting my way through the traffic in the busy centre, I thought I was going to die. Every time I changed gear, the back tyre locked up, squealing, and I had to kick the behemoth back up again. Having got lost, when I eventually arrived back at the hotel they'd retired to the bar. I parked and fell on the floor, shaking. When I had sufficiently recovered I went in, tossed him the keys back and said, 'Thanks, off to bed. I'm tired.'

This girl is trouble, I thought, as I lay in bed, still shaking.

The next gig, at Mollerussa Pabellon, was probably the worst we ever did. It was terrifying for a number of reasons. First of all, no one had any idea where the place was or why we were playing there. It was a tiny town with a population of only 15,000. It didn't make sense.

We arrived to find the venue was a big metal-roofed cowshed, and the acoustics were awful. The dressing room had been built out of plywood in a corner of the room by one side of the stage. But it had no roof.

'No time to build roof,' we were informed by Pedro. We were also informed there was no security.

'They no turn up,' he said, but assured us everything was '*bueno*' because he had drafted in two of the local Catalan rugby teams to do security.

Now these men were seriously huge and there was a lot of them. I think they were all up for a paid night out and had turned up in their droves. Unfortunately they were also bitter rivals and spent the soundcheck charging each other in scrum-type formations across the shed. To say we were worried would be the biggest understatement of our entire career. On returning for the gig it had quietened down and the audience had at least separated the warring teams, for a while. We went on … it started to go wrong immediately. The audience began to divide into factions, too, and we were being drowned out by the chants of both sides. *Shit.* Barney just did what he normally did in situations like this, closed his eyes and sang. One of the rugby players working behind the barrier at the front, who had already been laughing at my ripped jeans, threw a full glass of beer over Barney.

I thought, *Right, I've had enough*, and went to put my guitar down to go and nut this bastard. Jane grabbed me. 'Stop. Look, there's too many of them.'

I looked. There was. At least ten of the big bastards at each end of the barrier. This little one was obviously on the wing. I bit my tongue and smiled at Jane.

Shit! I was really starting to like her … a lot.

We finished and sought refuge in the tiny dressing room, where we swore there would be no encore. But then, as if on cue, it started raining bottles and glasses. The bastards had spotted the dressing room had no roof and found our weakness. We bolted out, with Rob screaming, 'Do a fooking encore! Now!'

I said, 'Make sure you get the money, Rob.'

'I will after this debacle!' he shot back.

We encored, tore the gear down and loaded out while it seemed like half the crowd were still kicking the shit out of the other half.

I had never been so glad to escape to a bus in my life. Once there, Jane sat next to me. We both laughed with relief as the lights went off and we drove away, and then she leaned forward and kissed me full on the lips. Double shit.

I did not know what to do. This was different from all the one-night stands. We parted and studiously ignored each other for the rest of the evening.

In the morning, as we left for the airport, Rob was really hungover. 'Did you get the money, Rob?' asked Andy Fisher.

'Yes. Ten grand in potatoes,' and pulled a massive wad out of his pocket, waving it around. At the airport Pedro turned up and took Rob to one side, pulling him over to some seats away from where we were checking in. We could see Pedro gesticulating fiercely, spouting off passionately then getting down on one knee. Weird. Was he going to propose? Then we all watched as Rob reached into his pocket and pulled out the wad of potatoes and handed them back to Pedro. Rob shrugged. Me and Barney screamed, 'NO!' and legged it across to where they were, but Pedro had a speed that belied his shape and was gone in an instant, running outside and jumping into a car that I'm sure was driven by that bastard Laine. We stormed back to see Rob.

'What happened?' we demanded.

'I felt sorry for him. He was going to lose his house.'

'What about our fucking houses!' we chorused.

It was a quiet flight back.

We returned to a freezing-cold UK to prepare for the release of what would go on to become our biggest-selling album, helping us to finally crack America: *Substance*.

It started with a little acorn. Tony Wilson came to tell me he was thinking of getting a new car. He didn't need my permission, but he always asked my advice on which car to buy and I'd picked his previous one, a Mercedes 190E 2.3-16 valve, a beautiful car but very small inside, and Tony had had a child in the meantime so he wanted something bigger.

I suggested he got a Jaguar XJ6 Coupé, which he duly did, then had it modified to look like Steed's Jaguar out of *The Avengers*. It was a beautiful, beautiful car – the best car Tony ever had; plus, it came with a CD player, and in those days, to have a CD player in your car made you Mr Fancypants right from the word go.

So now he had this amazing car complete with CD player, and what Tony wanted to do was play the New Order singles in his car, only our singles had never been released on a CD. We still had a policy of not putting the singles on the album, and it was way before the days of CD singles. Ours had only ever come out on vinyl. So what Tony suggested to Rob was that we do a CD compilation of singles, so he could play them in his car. Not only that, but Tony had an idea how to clear our debts too. Every idea Tony ever had was a way of clearing our debts. Each album we made would clear our debts. Every club night we tried would clear our debts. Each gig we did at the Haçienda would clear our debts, he said.

At this point in time the situation was getting pretty dire. This was before the days of Madchester and the Happy Mondays' and the Haçienda's heyday. Factory depended on New Order to keep it afloat – so it could keep on putting out records by the likes of Shark Vegas and Kalima. The trouble was that New Order was having a problem getting the money from our records' successes out of Factory and the bill was getting bigger and bigger. As a Factory director, Rob was compromised. Tony was spending money like there was no tomorrow. On cars, see above, and business-class flights. Around that time he was given some kind of award for being the most-travelled record company executive in the world. They totted up that one year he spent something like £300,000 on travel alone. He liked nothing more than flying to New York in business, to talk business to somebody about some fanciful deal they may do with Factory – deals that never, ever came off. He certainly was a social animal. I remember Rob sitting there once, at a meeting, with Tony telling us about it and saying, 'And you know what he's fucking achieved in all that time? Ask him, ask him ... Fuck all.'

So what Tony did was suggest to Rob that we release *Substance* at a more favourable rate of 25/75 in Factory's favour, the idea being that it would recoup more quickly and Factory could pay New Order the money they owed from the other records. Tony always had a bee in his bonnet about our deal with Factory, telling Rob time and time again that it wasn't 50/50; that because Factory paid the mechanical royalties to the BPI it was 59/41. Rob wouldn't entertain it.

> The term 'mechanical' has its origins in the 'piano rolls' on which music was recorded in the early twentieth century. The concept is now primarily oriented to the sale of records or compact discs, but has grown to include internet downloads. The scope is wide and covers any copyrighted audio composition that is rendered mechanically (stamped, pressed or copied); that is, without human performers. Basically, every time a song is manufactured (in whatever format) to be sold or downloaded, the writer is owed a 'mechanical royalty'. That royalty is roughly equal to 9.1 per cent, regardless of whether the manufactured items are sold or not. The internet download rate is usually lower. The record company is generally the payer.

So I suppose it was karma that *Substance* would then turn out to be our biggest-selling album ever; we gave away our biggest-selling record to the record company at a reduced cost – for no reason other than they couldn't pay us for the other ones at the full rate because of bad management.

I remember bumping into the guy who played 'Gordon the Moron' when Jilted John appeared on *Top of the Pops* once and him saying to me, 'Why do people say Factory were a great record company? They couldn't even pay their artists. I would think that's a prerequisite for any great record company.'

That, right there, ladies and gentlemen, was an example of Factory logic. In other words, no fucking logic at all.

In the meantime, it was decided we would re-record two of our singles for the compilation: 'Confusion' and 'Temptation'.

Not a great session. My nemesis John Robie had given Barney this idea about singing in his key and, having listened to 'Confusion' with his new cultured ear, Barney decided he wanted to have another go at it. Personally I liked the song the way it was and thought the re-recording in a different key made it sound sad – not sad as in bad, but a melancholy key (have a listen) – an argument that would end up raging from that day to the day we split in 2006.

'It's just the same,' he'd snap, 'only different.' Thanks for the technical description, Barn. 'Temptation' was the same idea and we used the opportunity to bring it in line with how we played it 'live', but again, to my mind it didn't sound better than the original. The use of the Yamaha synths and huge snare sound made it sound too hard to me.

Either way, we re-recorded at Yellow Two; and, as I said, it was a pretty un-joyous experience.

To finish off *Substance* we were sent to Advision Studios in London to record what would become 'True Faith' with Stephen Hague. Tom Atencio had been pressing for us to write a straightforward pop hit – something purposely commercial and transatlantic – and he thought that if anyone could deliver his beloved 'breakthrough single' it would be Stephen Hague, who at the time had a great reputation as a pop producer.

*

By the time he commenced a long association with New Order in 1987, producer Stephen Hague already had a reputation for crafting lush, intelligent pop music, having produced OMD's 1985 album, Crush, and then gone on to breakthrough work on the Pet Shop Boys' debut album, Please, *producing the hits 'West End Girls', 'Opportunities (Let's Make Lots of Money)' and 'Suburbia'. After producing 'True Faith' for New Order, Hague continued to work with the band as well as the Pet Shop Boys and Erasure, producing their massive-selling* The Innocents *album, plus production work for Electronic, the Communards, Pere Ubu, Holly Johnson and Public Image Ltd.*

What we didn't realise was that Stephen specialised in co-writing with the artists, which wasn't something we wanted. Not only that, but the session came with a serious deadline – our first. Factory had gone all-out to coordinate a simultaneous release of *Substance* throughout all the licensees in Europe and America. Very ambitious. We had ten days to write and mix the two tracks, and no longer. The pressure was on.

During the first few days of the session, Hague and Barney worked on the chord sequencing. We'd turned up without much in the way of ideas, a bass/snare pattern and a half-written low bass riff Barney had nicked from a song he'd heard on Kiss FM in New York, and a two-chord change suggesting possibly a verse/chorus transition.

After a few days we began to get a bit bogged down, but my suggestion that we jam ourselves out of it was met with a lack of interest, even from Hague. He had a very rich sound, much richer than what was then the 'traditional' New Order sound. I had a feeling that when I came to work on it there would be so many riffs on the record that there wouldn't be any room for me to add anything. Hague was oblivious, and even suggested that Barney work on the vocal melody before the tracks were fully formed. I understood that from his point of view as a pop producer – the old adage that it's all about the vocals – but this was not how New Order worked. Barney was a very reluctant lead singer, still giving the impression that he didn't want to sing at all. Early in the session Hague was recording tracks of vocal ideas and lyrics, recording track after track, which he would happily work on for hours collating into a 'master' ideas track.

Barney would be doing a fair bit of drinking to lubricate himself while doing these vocals, which would wipe him out for the next day on a couple of occasions. After one particular night of singing he decided to stay in bed the next day and 'work on the vocals' while the rest of us returned to the studio to watch Hague program the drums on his Emu SP12 drum machine.

Steve Morris was the next band member to suffer from the not-so-warm shoulder. Steve didn't get to play on either track apart from some live hi-hat and cymbals at the end of the session.

As luck would have it, that day we had also managed to lock Barney in the flat, deadlocking the front door so escape was impossible. All he had for company was some mouldy cheese and daytime TV.

Amazingly, when we returned that evening he had managed, probably out of sheer boredom, to nearly finish the lyrical ideas for both tracks. We showed solidarity by staying up all night suggesting changes and finishing off the lyrics. It was nice to be included at last. Although Barney was pretty pissed off, you couldn't help thinking some kind of proper imprisonment was the way forward for the next LP.

There was a small taste issue with regard to the drug reference in the second verse – small boys growing up and doing drugs – with Hague worrying about the radio reception of what would surely be our next single.

Rob was very defensive of it, suggesting it reflected the culture of the time. Rob was right but we were being very, very naive, which now is frankly embarrassing. We went with the headmaster's recommendation, changing it back as soon as he left the room for 'live'. This was one of just a handful of what you might call 'cultural differences' between the ex-punks from Manchester and the pop producer from Portland. Even so, Rob and I worried it might lead to accusations of a sell-out. Were we selling our soul to the devil with Stephen Hague as the salesman?

That aside, the session progressed well from a work point of view, with the vocals on the tracks improving them immensely and the next few days spent augmenting them with more keyboard overdubs.

I could hear time running out for me. Stephen had earmarked the last three days to mix. So finally, on the evening of the day before mixing, it was time for yours truly to step up. One of the things I'd always liked about Hague's way of working was his early finishes, rarely working past nine most evenings. Tonight it looked ominous.

We started with '1963', its title now taken from Barney's lyrics, and as I suspected there was nothing for me to play on the track. The only sound was people leaving the room as I picked up my guitar. I was really struggling, getting nowhere, and I could see what 'the others' would be thinking again: *Why can't we have one without him on it?*

So there were no cheerleaders, no one saying, 'Go on, Hooky, go for it, Hooky.' My neurosis and paranoia were the only things keeping me company tonight. Don't worry, I'm not after sympathy, I'm just telling you what happened.

Hague tried to help in his own way, getting me to double the sequence bass, play the low notes of the chords on the bridge and chorus, but it wasn't very satisfying. It certainly wasn't me. I tried 'True Faith' and couldn't get much on it either. There were a few OK-sounding bits, and I tried, I really did, maybe too hard, but I felt I was getting nowhere and then, on the dot of nine o'clock, just as I was thinking, *Fuck it, if that's what they want*, Hague piped up with, 'That should do it! I think that'll be enough.'

I gave up. I left the control room and moped around, thinking that them lot had beaten me; that I was surplus to requirements at last. Hague just carried on 'finishing off', as he termed it, and we called it a day.

Then Tom Atencio appeared.

'Hey, Hooky,' he said to me, 'what the fuck are you doing, man?'

'What do you mean?' I bleated.

'Where's the fucking bass? I don't hear you on this fucking track?'

'I can't get anything, Tom. I just can't get anything. I can't get any bass on the tracks. I can't play on these songs,' I wailed.

Tom had this habit of calling me 'you fucking fucker' when he got angry.

'Come on, Hooky, you fucking fucker. You've got to be on the tracks. Now get back in there and fucking, fuckering do it.'

'No, Tom, you don't understand. They don't want me on the track. The producer hates my guts. Them lot don't care. They've written me out, mate.'

'Right, you fucking fucker, wait there, I'll be back.'

Tom stormed into the control room, and of course I wasn't there, but I hope it went along the lines of: 'You bunch of fucking fuckers, you've got to put Hooky on this track, man, come on. He's got to be on this record. Hooky is the sound of New Order.' Going absolutely mad. That was what I was hoping.

As far as Hague was concerned, he'd finished the track. He didn't give a shit that one of the band members wasn't on it. The other three – they didn't give a shit either, and that's what really hurt at the time and still does.

I wondered then and wonder now if I was reaping what I'd sown – for being too loud and obstreperous, for not being 'electronic' enough? Or if I just deserved it. I don't know. It didn't seem to bother Steve Morris.

But anyway, Tom came back out, told me to stop being such a fucking soft fucker, and pushed me back in the control room to do my bass again.

Really nervous now, I returned. It was uncomfortable but I started playing again and at last it began to come – on 'True Faith' I got the intro part, then the ascending bits, then the bridge, the break bit, the end bit. '1963' followed, not as strong as the other song but a great outro and loads of bits in between.

In the end, I was really proud of the bass on both, and I thought the tracks stood up as proof that I was indeed intrinsic to the New Order sound, just as Tom had said I was – the only person in our immediate circle ever to admit it.

Listen to Stephen Hague's pop mix and the bass is so low you can barely hear it, and now even he admits that was a mistake. To my mind, Barney loved that mix and that was what he was aiming for from that moment on. Low bass or no bass at all.

I think the B-side, '1963', holds the record (no pun intended) for the longest time before you actually hear any bass on a New Order track. Five minutes odd, sadly.

I got a little 'revenge' when Arthur Baker did a remix of '1963' and included all the bass melodies Hague had rejected.

'True Faith' ended up being a big song for us, no doubt about it. The title I got from a book I was reading at the time, James A. Michener's *Texas*, which talked about Catholicism being the only 'True Faith'. Rob liked that. Here's a little-known fact: Barney and I were the only two Protestants at Factory; nearly all the rest were Catholics. Read into that what you will.

I didn't think 'True Faith' was that much better than anything we'd done in the past, but it certainly eclipsed our previous work in terms of sales and international exposure on *Substance*. I have to say '1963' was a beautiful song, even if I'm hardly on it. Well done, Barney. To further compound any ill-feeling I held towards the record, they cut me out of the video as well. Well, my knee was in the video. Should have been my arse, really.

Geek Alert

Recording 'True Faith'

Advision Studio One was state-of-the-art and had a first-generation SSL mixing board and Urei Time Align studio monitors. In terms of digital processing units, Advision sometimes obtained and used prototypes of units before they were even marketed. The studio had previously been used by Stephen Hague to mix Malcolm McLaren's 'Madam Butterfly'. The house engineer was David Jacob, who had worked with him on the McLaren mix.

SSL mixing consoles: 4000 series desk

Founded in 1969, SSL was a digital audio pioneer company that designed high-quality mixing desks with high-bandwidth performance as standard.

Most consoles came with a 'Total Recall Facility', enabling settings (and mixes) to be recalled with a high degree of accuracy. This was felt to be important to most producers and record companies, enabling 'mistakes' to be easily and quickly remedied. However, in practice this rarely happened as a lot of the outboard equipment, reverbs and effects had to be re-set by hand.

The development of converter technology for the transforming of analogue signals into digital signals had created a variety of supporting technical developments. DSP or Digital Signal Processing technology had led to the advent of digital mixing desks. This technology had created both a cheaper and lower-maintenance alternative to the old analogue mixing desk. SSL digital audio consoles would now become the first choice for most studios around the world.

Personally I was never convinced, and thought that the SSL desks had a bright, tinny sound, but there was no doubting their usefulness. The recording medium was to be two Sony 3324, 24-track digital recording machines linked together. The Sony 3324 was a 'Dash' recorder with a 16-bit resolution and a 44.1kHz or 48kHz sampling rate, and required the use of half-inch metal-particle formulation magnetic tape. All 'Dash' recorders primarily use the SDIF-2 (Sony Digital Interface Format -2) and were completely compatible with SSL mixing desks. These early machines would soon get a reputation for being brittle at the top treble frequencies and there was much resistance to the recording of 'rock' music on them, but it wasn't apparent on this session. Hague reckoned this was the perfect set-up for our music. The connecting software enabled the machines to lock and run together in perfect sync, or the machines could be offset against each other to a predetermined value. Based on the tempo of the track you worked out a SMPTE-to-bars formula for how much one machine could be offset. The computer would read the number of bars in SMPTE code and enter it into the remote of the slave machine. The machine could then rewind or wind to the point stipulated, e.g. eight bars ahead or behind the master machine. You were also able to make digital copies of the master reel on the slave machine, and then offset it by a set amount of bars forward or backward, enabling you to move sections of music around, doing major structural edits to the songs. There was also a rehearse-mode facility on the master machine that you could practise/listen to, previewing the results without actually going into record on the slave machine. You could then elongate or copy any of the recorded elements by bouncing the parts between machines. You were still susceptible to crinkling and shedding of the tape and bad edits, things you would normally associate with analogue machines, but it was much easier to make safety copies, with these usually being produced at the end of each day's session. Because of the high specification of the conversion cards, several transfers could be done between the two machines with no deterioration of signal. Even working digitally there could be a difference after a few bounces, mainly depending on the source material. You would have to listen carefully for deterioration of live kit sounds and possibly certain elements in the low end. Even now you could not just bounce back and forth endlessly. Syncing up the tape machines with the 'live' equipment was still in its infancy. A spec for MIDI Time Code would not actually appear until late 1987, so there was no MIDI clock/MIDI Time Code at this time. There was an external box that was attached to the serial port of the computer that could read and generate SMPTE, setting the tempo on it and recording the SMPTE to one track of the tape machine then routing the same track back to the reader.

Our Yamaha QX1 sequencer was used along with a Yamaha DX5 for bass sounds (basically two Yamaha DX7s in one) along with the Octave Voyetra 8, polyphonic synths, and an Akai S900 sampler. It was very early days for this machine and there were not many library sounds for it yet. Many would be amassed throughout the session. We also used an Emu Emulator II sampler, using five-inch floppy disks, which came with a large library of sounds.

Two CV-to-MIDI converters were used – the idea being that you could link the Midi and non-Midi keyboards together and play them at the same time (you can hear this technique in a lot of 80s records, some using very complex sounds – this was long before layered pre-sets and Roland's LA Synthesis was developed). There was always a certain amount of excitement generated by connecting all the boxes together just to see what would happen, *à la* 'Temptation'. The pad sound on 'True Faith' and all the chord changes were a combination of an Emu II sample and the live Voyetras.

MIDI was used extensively to connect the set-ups together. A Macintosh SE30 computer – running Performer (written especially for the Macintosh) – ran the sequencer patterns, which were copied from our QX1. A pattern-based, non-MIDI Emu systems

SP12 drum machine was also used to program the drums. The computer was clocking the SP12, and drum tracks on both songs were written in real time. Neither 'True Faith' nor '1963' would feature real drums. Live hi-hat and cymbals would be integrated later into both songs, with the use of close-microphones for the hi-hats and stereo overhead microphones for the cymbals.

Work on 'True Faith' and '1963' was taking place simultaneously, with the band and producer sometimes bouncing back and forth between the two tracks on an hourly basis.

Schedule

Day 1: Set-up.
Day 2: Recording both sequenced backing tracks.
Day 3: Overdubbing keyboards and drums with song structure of '1963'.
Day 4: Overdubbing keyboards and drums with song structure of 'True Faith' plus vocal try-outs both tracks.
Day 5: Overdubbing keyboards and drums both tracks.
Day 6: Vocals both tracks.
Day 7: Vocals, backing vocals plus guitars and bass both tracks.
Day 8: Set up mix.
Day 9: Mix 'True Faith'.
Day10: *Mix* '1963'.

Vocals were sung in the control room into a hand-held Beyer M88 microphone, the idea being to make face-to-face communication the most important thing. We had been doing this with Barney for some considerable time. It was difficult but made for no isolation, in a working context that always comes from having a singer 'isolated' in a vocal booth. Martin Hannett had shown us the problems with that. There was no discernible loss in quality by not recording the vocals in isolation, and it made for a much better work environment; problems with sibilance or popping were dealt with as they appeared.

Later that year we returned to Glastonbury for the second of what would eventually be our three headline visits. It turned out to be something of a transitional year for the festival and we couldn't get over the difference between the two-hippies-in-a-field of 1981, when we played with Hawkwind, and the muddy roadblock of six years later. There were so many people there and so much traffic around the site that we literally couldn't get in. We were staying in a hotel nearby but when it came to arriving onto the site to play we just couldn't get through, so Rob bribed a guy offering helicopter rides to take us in. Christ, this thing was like a flying motorcycle. I was shitting myself. It felt like it was going to drop out of the sky at any second; it was the first and only time that Gillian ever touched me, gripping my hand like a vice, convinced we were going to die. But it did beat the three-and-a-half-hour traffic jam to get on the site. Luckily we were able to drive out.

The first time we played Glastonbury we had used the Eavis farmhouse as a dressing room, and I remember getting there early and Michael teaching me how to make toast in an Aga cooker (the first time I'd ever seen one) while Emily played with her dolls at our feet. (Michael's cooking tip: you put the bread on a metal plate then put it on the highest rack right at the top of the Aga. It makes beautiful toast, but make sure you keep an eye on it as it also makes beautiful charcoal.) I distinctly recall sitting there, eating delicious home-made marmalade on toast, as delightful and rustic a scene as you can possibly imagine – then to be confronted with the mayhem outside.

Like everything else, the dressing room had changed since the last time we were there. The farmhouse was no longer being used; it was all a bit more rock'n'roll and we were in a big static caravan. I remember seeing Michael later walking around carrying black bin liners full of money. The event had exploded. It had in the space of a couple of years gone from being a small (well, smallish) cottage industry to a vast, gargantuan exercise. With the popularity and money had come an almost complete breakdown in security. There were people clambering over walls and pulling the fences down. But even so it still made an absolute fortune.

I think it was the last one they did for CND. I remember feeling very guilty because by rights we should have done it for free – correct me if I'm wrong, but I think that for years bands played Glastonbury for expenses only and all the profits went to CND – but Rob had insisted we got paid. Quite a lot too, £10,000 if memory serves. Sorry, Michael. Ironically, we must have blown that tenfold by bringing in Philippe Decouflé to film us playing 'True Faith' live on stage. The American record company had been protesting about the lack of the band in the videos, which usually resulted in them getting dropped from MTV every single time. Everyone loved Philippe's video for 'True Faith' and the only concession Warner Bros demanded was refusing to pay for their share of the video costs unless the group were included. Filming at Glastonbury was deemed the solution. Typically, in the video there was my leg for a second, if that? I protested but 'the others' obviously loved it and voted for that edit. I was really starting to feel victimised.

It was a great gig though. Out of our touring career, my three highlights are the three times we played Glastonbury. I love it there and it can come in quite handy. I remember having a race in my car with some bloke in the tunnels under Manchester airport (the ones where all the footballers crash) and he beat me hands down. As we pulled up at the lights at the end I wound the window down and shouted, 'You might have beat me but I've headlined Glastonbury three times! Beat that? Ha!'

That showed him.

In June we played a jazz festival in Denmark (the precursor to the Aarhus Jazz Festival which would start in 1989), another Alan Wise gig, but he didn't tell us until we got there that it was a jazz festival. God knows what possessed him, the money probably. A very peculiar place for us to play; I know we'd had some pretty wild performances but . . . ironically, this would prove to be our wildest. It was a lovely day and a lovely hotel. It just went downhill when we got to the gig and realised everyone and every band, apart from a comedy German group and us, were jazz aficionados. One look at the age of the hepcats in the audience and we knew it wasn't going to go well.

But every cloud has a silver lining and ours, on this particular day, was Elephant beer by Carlsberg, 7.2 per cent. It was very strong but surprisingly drinkable. So we settled down watching Miles Davis's antics. This guy really was a cool cat and everywhere he went at the festival he was escorted by about twenty security men, which was funny because the audience were a real bunch of geriatrics. The stage was entered from the back by a raised wooden walkway, about 3ft high and 100ft long. As we were preparing to go on it was just getting dark and Terry mustered the troops by the entrance of the walkway while the comedy German group did a 'Madness'-type walk back from the stage. As they got off we got on and we set off, everything seemed normal. But when we got to the stage, Steve went, 'Where's Gillian?' Looking round, there was no sign of her. She had been her usual quiet self all day, so nothing unusual there.

One of the roadies tore down the walkway to see if she'd gone for a piss but came back with no sighting. Now, this was worrying, where had she gone? I can't remember who it was, but a shout of 'Here she is!' brought us halfway along the walkway to where she had fallen off and lay flat out on the grass. Everyone was very worried but as we pulled her up we noticed her eyes rolling, and that she was pissed ... as a fart! The bloody Elephant beers had struck. We dusted her off and got her to the stage where she slurred, 'I'm all right. I'm all right.' And then went on to play the keyboards with what Barney once again described as 'A BLOODY ORANGE!'

The noise was terrible. Steve grinned and bore it, but at one point it got much too much for me and I had to go and hide behind my bass cabs, it was so embarrassing. Everything was way, way out of tune (which fortunately may have worked in this jazz setting). The roadies all had their hands over their ears, and believe you me they'd heard a few dodgy 'uns in their time. At one point I even pushed Barney out as he tried to join me behind the cabs, with him shouting, 'No, no, let me in.'

I'd like to say the set flew by, but I can't, it was excruciating, and at the end me and Barney stormed off, leaving Steve to escort the inebriated Gillian.

We didn't watch Miles Davis, preferring to go and drown our sorrows in the hotel bar with our new friend 'The Elephant'. The next morning as I lay in bed with a throbbing head I could hear shouting outside. I looked out of the window and there was Alan in his underpants, gesticulating to two blonde girls who were riding horses in the surf on the beach; both girls by this time had very wet T-shirts on and he was shouting, 'Come up here. Come up here. Fifty Kronkers the pair of you!' I laughed, typical Alan, then as I turned round I realised someone was in my bed.

Jane.

The bloody Elephant beer had struck again.

Damn you, Carlsberg.

Also around this time we were approached by Michael Shamberg to write songs for the director Beth B, who was making a film called *Salvation!* We had a few riffs knocking around so we jammed a bit and came up with 'Skullcrusher', 'Sputnik', 'Let's Go' and a couple of others, including 'Touched by the Hand of God'.

'Touched' came from a bass riff I'd done on the sequencer, which pleased Barney no end, because using sequencers wasn't something I made a habit of, and it was the only proper song we got out of the session. The rest of the songs were more like little snippets, or 'stings' as I now know to call them, thanks to the *Mrs Merton Show*.

Everybody loved 'Touched', and Tony and Rob both wanted to do it as a single, so for its release we got Arthur Baker to remix it, and before leaving for our tour of America we recorded another video.

Recommended again by Michael Shamberg, the director was Kathryn Bigelow, who's since won an Oscar for *The Hurt Locker*, and of whom I remember two things very distinctly: first that she had a daughter the same age as my own daughter Heather, who sat with us in a restaurant eating tzatziki and taramasalata. I remember being amazed at how cosmopolitan this kid was, comparing her to my own, who lived on a diet of fish fingers, baked beans and the like. The second thing was that it looked to me as though Pete Saville had fallen for Kathryn, big-time. It looked like he fancied the pants off her.

In the restaurant Rob said, 'Are we gonna get some wine or what?' and Pete asked for the wine list, which I think was the first time I'd seen anybody do that. For me, back then, drinking was about drinking to get pissed, not the flavour, the bouquet or whatever other delights the wine list held. But Pete made this big song and dance about ordering the wine, like, 'Do you want a Zinfandel or should we go for a Chardonnay? A Sauvignon Blanc or Pinot Noir. Oh yes, it's a good year for Pinot Noir ...' All that lot.

The wine arrived, the waiter poured it out, just a little bit, and Pete swilled it around his glass, sniffed it then had a taste, all the time behaving like he was the most sophisticated man on the planet. Doing all but drumming our fingers on the table, we waited, wishing he'd get the whole charade over with, all gasping for a drink. But

Pete wasn't happy. He asked the waiter for the cork, which he sniffed and then, pulling a face, said, 'Oh no, it's corked. I'm going to have to send it back.'

We were all going, 'Send it back? What? We're gagging for a drink here.' But with a look at Kathryn as though to apologise for his uncultured companions, Pete insisted on sending it back, and we had to go through the same rigmarole again.

He returned two more bottles before he finally got one fit for Kathryn Bigelow to drink. I don't think it worked, as far as I know, although it did cross my mind that I must try that sometime; it seemed like a very Terry-Thomas thing to do. I liked it.

I think it was Barney who came up with the idea to do a spoof heavy-metal video, to parody all the glam-metal groups of the period, Mötley Crüe, Def Leppard etc. So we hired Brixton Academy and we even hired a heavy-metal dresser because, yes, there are such things as people who 'dress' heavy-metal videos, and then we gave the footage to Kathryn. Back then she was much less well known, having only directed a vampire film called *Near Dark* and a movie called *The Loveless*. They're both highly regarded cult film nows, but neither were massive hits so you could say we got Kathryn at an advantageous rate, Michael Shamberg recognising her potential.

She ended up using one of the *Near Dark* stars, Bill Paxton, in the 'Touched by the Hand of God' video, which she filmed around Battersea, stopping traffic for him to run across Battersea Bridge. The idea was to have the 'love scene' movie bits intercut with the 'concert' bits, so that it looked like one of those typical 1980s movie tie-in music videos, also parodying the typical glam-rock music videos of the era, over the top and over-budgeted. And if you think about that – how we originally recorded the song for a movie, but then paid a Hollywood director to make a spoof movie for the song's video, well that might make your head hurt a bit.

The other thing about this video was that 'we' wanted to feature the group in it this time, even if we were obviously miming, wearing wigs and lots of daft leather costumes (we must have been mad). Prior to that, as I said, MTV had always resisted playing our videos because we never featured and it was one of their things at the time: band must be in video. Tom Atencio, in particular, was always on at us to appear in the videos, and I've told you the story of the 'Regret' video, as well as what happened here, which was that despite New Order's starring appearance in the video, Kathryn Bigelow's movie-style footage was considered too gruesome for MTV, the car crash particularly, and actually was also banned by English daytime/Saturday morning television, which was very important for a group's videos at the time, so it *still* didn't get played. Oops.

We actually had a great time doing it and enjoyed the dressing up and play-acting. When Barney put 'Ace' in white tape (don't ask) on the back of his jacket, it felt like the crowning touch. We thought there was no way you could not get the gag.

But when we next went to America in 1988, the record and video had been a hit and loads of people came to see us expecting to see a heavy-metal band, then asking for their money back when it turned out we were four scally Mancs playing sequenced pop music.

First, though, we had our 1987 American tour to negotiate.

5) FACILITIES continued

c) The aforementioned rooms must have easy access to the Stage without having to walk through the audience. All rooms must be lockable and the key/s must be delivered to the Artistes Tour Manager upon his arrival at the venue on the day of the performance. Should the rooms have no key/s, then security guards must be provided at the doors of each room whilst the Artiste is on the premises. The Promoter will indemnify the Artiste against the loss of any personal belongings or equipment resulting in lack of security.

..................(Please initial here)

d) REFRESHMENTS

The following is to be provided in the Artistes Dressing Room, at least one hour(1) prior to their arrival at the Venue.

2 Bottles of Pernod (1 Litre by volume each bottle)

2 Bottles of Vodka (1 Litre by volume each bottle)

3 Bottles of medium White Wine.

4 Bottles of local Champagne

24 Cans of San Miguel.

24 Cans of Heiniken.

24 Cans of Holsten Pils.

48 Cans of Pepsi-Cola.

12 Cans of Seven-Up.

12 Litres of Fresh Oranage Juice.

4 Litres of Sparkling Mineral Water.

2 Litres of Still Mineral Water.

A selection of, Fruit, Nuts, Snacks and Sweets.

A plentiful supply of Glasses, Ice and Openers.

The following is to be provided for seven(7) Road Crew on arrival at the Venue and during Load In.

Fresh Sandwiches (Cheese, Egg, Meat)

Coffee and Tea and Fresh Milk.

Fresh Oranage Juice.

Pepsi-Cola.

Mineral Water.

General selection of Soft Drinks.

....................(Please initial here)

Continued/...

'Make-up-wearing, miming bunch of flouncing jessies'

Prior to the band's US tour with Echo and the Bunnymen came the release of 'True Faith'. New Order's fourteenth single was also the band's breakthrough. Benefiting from being released in multiple versions, not to mention a BPI-award-winning video from director and choreographer Philippe Decouflé, the single not only climbed to number 4 in the UK charts, but became the first New Order single to crack the US Hot 100, eventually rising to number 32.

I forget why, but for some reason – probably because it was my nefarious plan in the first place – I'd become involved in planning this supposedly co-headlining tour of America with the Bunnymen and, as I've already said, there was a lot of horse trading that went on: Mac telling me the agent was talking out of his arse, the agent telling me that Mac was leading me up the garden path. Back and forth it went for months.

Gene Loves Jezebel were on the tour as well, as the support. Us and the Scousers had no idea who they were and didn't even see them perform until about the third show of the tour. Then Tom Atencio had to endure both me and Mac going mental about them: 'Who put those make-up-wearing, miming bunch of flouncing jessies on our bill?'

Their place in the hierarchy as far as their on-stage times never changed: they were always a lowly number three. Except you wouldn't have known that from the amount of gorgeous groupies they had hanging round. We would all stand in our dressing room areas staring enviously across at the Gene Loves Jezebel area, which would be stuffed full of girls. We were like, 'They're only the support band and they all wear make-up. What the fuck is going on?' We didn't do too badly, mind, but in comparison to them we were beginners. They got so many girls it was unbelievable.

As for their entourage – you would not *believe* what dirty bastards they were. They were giving out backstage passes in return for blow jobs, shocking to us, and we didn't shock easily. I mean, Terry may have gone out and asked girls if they fancied coming backstage for a drink, but he wasn't demanding blow jobs before he let them in. The Gene Loves Jezebel guys even made a helmet for the girls to wear while they were in the process of earning their backstage pass. It had a drinks holder and ashtray on top so the guys had somewhere to put their fag and their drink while the blow job was in progress. God knows how that worked; it can't have been a very vigorous blow job, but – hand on heart – that's what they used to do.

So anyway, you'll just have to imagine all of that going on in the background as this tour progressed. And progress it did – a bit of a juggernaut.

The days of roughing it in vans and cars were way behind us now. We went by air and for every gig we had the limos all booked.

Meantime, it was very musically rewarding as well. What happened was that a kind of healthy competition grew up around New Order and the Bunnymen, with each band wanting to blow the other off stage every night, and as a result the performances got better and better.

We played amusement parks. Got to the front of all the queues (Hurrah!) only to find that fans had bought all our photos at the end again (Boo!). We played the Red Rocks Amphitheatre in Denver, which has to be one of the most beautiful gigs in the world, with a stunning, stunning vista. The music was good, the gigs were great. What more could you ask for?

I remember at San Diego, Mac's wife Lorraine, who I knew from Pip's in Manchester from the old Roxy room days (in 1974 Barney and I had at last one night plucked up the courage to ask her and her mate to dance but they turned us down – your life could have been so different, Lorraine) turned up and saw me with a girl. The next gig she said to me, 'Hooky, who was that girl you were with last night?'

'Oh, it was a friend of mine, actually, my cousin.'

I stood there hoping I wouldn't break down under questioning.

'Oh, I see, your cousin. Does she live over here?'

'Yes, yes, they emigrated and she lives over here. She's lived over here for a long time now.'

'Oh, what does she do?'

'I think she's in real estate.'

Beginning to sweat now.

'Oh, right, where does she live?'

'Oh, I'm not sure.'

This questioning went on – I'm not kidding you – for about twenty minutes, with me desperately fielding the questions, telling more and more outrageous and unbelievable lies until at last, Lorraine said to me, 'Hooky, if she was your cousin, why were you kissing her?'

I was speechless.

'Well,' she sniffed, 'I hope Mac's not like that.'

'Oh no, Mac's not like that at all,' I said, like butter wouldn't melt.

Oh, I tell you, Mac is a devil, he really is, and I mean that in the nicest possible way. He made Barney looked like Snow White by comparison. He used to drive everybody mental. Lead-singer syndrome (LSS) forbids me making a comparison, but let's just say that Mac was even worse than most I had to deal with; he could smell somebody opening a wrap from a quarter of a mile away. I'm not kidding, the slightest rustle from your wrap and there at your left shoulder was Mac. 'Y'all right, Hooky?'

Equally, Barney, for all his diva strops and unreasonable demands, was mainly passive-aggressive, whereas Mac was just aggressive. He'd have huge punch-ups with the Bunnymen's bassist Les Pattinson and with his guitar roadie, Curly Jobson, Richard Jobson's brother.

One night, Curly walked on stage to take Mac's guitar for tuning, and for some reason Mac turned round and kicked him, so Curly put his foot through Mac's amp and kicked his guitar off stage. They were a feisty bunch. Mac just loved causing trouble. What a character. I'm not sure I could have put up with being in a group with him, but touring with him was great fun.

Me, Mac and Andy Liddle were in the bar one night with the Bunnymen's sound guy, who looked really miserable. I said to Mac, 'What's the matter with him?'

'Oh, his wife's left him, la, ran off with his bestie. Best leave him alone.' We did and all sat there in silence, then the sound guy puts his glass down on the bar, not too heavily, but enough for the barman to go, 'Hey, motherfucker, watch my fucking bar top.' Oops.

The soundman goes, 'Bar top? Watch this ...' and picks up his stool and demolishes the whole bar: optics, glasses, bottles, everything, and finally bounces the stool on the bartop, several times. Then he says, 'Room 1024. Send me the bill.' And goes to bed.

Andy Liddle said, 'You know what that reminds me of? That reminds me of the dwarf on Ozzy Osbourne's *Speak to the Devil* tour. He did that. Ozzy used to hang him every night at the end of the show but he had to drop it because people were saying it was dwarfist and the poor guy was gutted, kept saying he was on a thousand dollars a night and how was he supposed to feed his kids now? Ronnie, he was called, lovely little fella. He smashed the bar up and it cost him five grand. Luckily he couldn't reach the top bit. I reckon that's gonna cost that fella ten thousand!'

In Salt Lake City we nearly got our comeuppance. We were running out of drugs. By that I mean everyone was down to their last eight-ball or something. One of our guys panicked and phoned his girlfriend's brother, a dealer in LA, and asked him to drive up with two ounces of Columbia's finest.

Unfortunately the guy had been picked up by the police on the freeway for speeding, and they found the drugs, along with two loaded guns. He'd phoned his sister to tip her off and the news spread through us like wildfire. Everyone was either up there – paranoid – coming down – paranoid – or somewhere in-between and paranoid. We were all convinced we were going to be raided and then banged up. We were wondering who'd be wearing the dress on Saturday night.

So there was only one thing to do ... and I know you're thinking, yes, get rid of it all. But that's not what drug-fiend Mancs do. Someone came up with the bright idea of putting it all together, all labelled up with everyone's name on, and getting a friend to drive it down to San Diego for us. Only a maniac would have thought this a good idea (confession: it was my idea). The dealer had just been caught driving and here was our mate being asked to do the same thing for hundreds of miles, again with it all conveniently labelled. Luckily for him there was one sane member of the party, his girlfriend, who just said, 'No!' and gave me the huge bag back. Shit. There was only one thing for it ... we'd have to do it all in the crew bus. We started with great gusto chopping through piles and piles of it. Everyone was cock-a-hoop but within an hour we were all strung out to fuck, with me and roadie Jonny Hugo leading the charge. Then the others started to crawl off to bed one by one and I'd say there were five of us left, the real hard core, when the driver let out a scream of, 'Oh, fuck, the police!' Blue flashing lights suddenly surrounded the bus. Everyone panicked like mad; it was like *The Banana Splits*, all the others jumping out of bed and joining in, throwing drugs and drug paraphernalia everywhere. Planting it in other people's beds, even. We were all terrified.

Then the lights disappeared ... they had driven past, no doubt on their way to a real emergency. How's that for guilty consciences? The relief was palpable. It was very subdued from then on. Me and Jonny carried on all the way to San Diego and when we arrived ours were the only rooms not ready. So we had to sit guiltily for what seemed like forever in reception. I eventually passed out, but Jonny carried on, slowly working his way through everybody's drugs, even making it to the gig the next day with no sleep at all. Eventually he fell asleep/passed out in a bowl of cornflakes with everyone laughing round him, until one of the catering girls said, 'Isn't he drowning?' then pulled him out and gave him the kiss of life, which luckily brought him round. Typically, later, when everyone had had a drink, they all wanted their drugs back, to no avail. Between me and Jonny we'd done the lot.

Either way, it was a great tour. The Bunnymen were enjoying it so much that they decided to stay on in America without us, possibly thinking that they would still be attracting the same crowds of three to four thousand we were getting every night. They were probably a little bit surprised and disappointed when, without us, their audiences went right back down again.

But, yes, a great tour – until we got to Irvine Meadows.

'I want to work with other people'

Well, it wasn't like it spoiled the tour or anything, but I suppose you'd have to say that it opened a new chapter of the story, because at Irvine Meadows, just outside LA – one of my favourite venues – Barney made his shock announcement.

To be precise, it was *before* the gig. There was a Factory meeting in a hotel nearby. Typical Tony. Typical Factory. He flew over, of course, as well as Alan Erasmus and a couple of accountants, spending thousands upon thousands of pounds in order to talk about how much debt Factory was in; how much money the Haçienda was losing, all the usual kind of shit.

Barney must have been gearing himself up to say something because he'd sat on the windowsill for the duration of the meeting, as though he was too nervous to join the rest of us at the table, and then, at some point, he just said it. He just sort of blurted out that he wanted to work with other people. I think we were talking about future plans for the next record or something.

It certainly cast a cloud over the gathering, I can tell you that much. Every meeting we had in those days was about how we would be saving something or someone, all sorts of pie-in-the-sky projections that even if you knew weren't going to come off were at least grounded in one definite reality – which was that we were going to be making another record together.

Suddenly, we might not be making another record together, because Barney wanted to work with other people. History tells us that he went off to do Electronic with Neil Tennant and Johnny Marr (who maybe approached him on that 1986 tour, after he'd approached me – who knows?), and that New Order would reconvene for several more albums. But you've got to remember that at the time we didn't know that. All we knew was that Barney wanted to work with other people. On the face of it, it sounded quite reasonable, because he'd no doubt learned lots of tricks from producers like John Robie and Stephen Hague, and he'd been feted by his peers – the Pet Shop Boys, for example – as one of the driving forces in synthpop, and when you look at it like that, you can hardly blame him for wanting to stretch his wings and escape the group dynamic.

But I didn't see it like that. I saw it like, 'He wants to work with other people. Which means he doesn't want to work with me.'

We'd all had our little musical holidays before. I remember being pleased as punch to earn £150 for playing on one of Martha Ladly's solo singles, 'Light Years from Love'.

Martha Ladly, of Martha and the Muffins, has something of a walk-on part in the New Order Story. Having left the group, she began a short-lived solo career; at the same time she lived and worked with Peter Saville, one of her paintings being used on the sleeve of the NewOrder EP 'Factus 8 – 1981–1982'. After two decades in Britain, Ladly returned to Canada and is currently a professor of design at the Ontario College of Art and Design.

The story of New Order is in some senses the story of a coup: how a band went from being a democracy to a dictatorship, and of course, it was a typically Barney, bloodless, passive-aggressive coup, in that it happened bit by bit, brick by brick, decision by decision.

It looked obvious, the elbowing me aside in the recording studio, the bullying of Rob, the time-keeping ... and now this. Barney was throwing his toys out of the pram one by one. Maybe he assumed we'd all be waiting for him when he decided to return. Maybe we would. He played the irreplaceable-frontman card and won the hand. From that moment onwards we were wondering what Barney might do next, whether we were surplus to requirements, and it cast a pall of doubt and uncertainty over the whole band from then on. You might even say it was the moment we stopped being a 'group' in the proper sense of the word.

After the meeting we got in our separate limos to go to the gig. I remember being absolutely gagging for a drink and stuck in traffic all the way to Irvine Meadows and being a right obnoxious brat and kicking off, going, 'This is bloody stupid, all this traffic, ridiculous, nah nah nah.'

The driver had been getting more and more nervous, shifting in his seat, until at last the divider slid down. He turned around and said, 'Man, these cars you're complaining about are all your fans. They're coming to see you.'

He was right. It was a sell-out gig and I'm kicking off in the car because of it. I couldn't explain it then and I can't explain it now but it was a very, very strange feeling indeed.

After that Barney was constantly on the phone, making arrangements. Once, he left his Filofax open in the kitchen area of our practice room and, well, you've got to look, haven't you? Lo and behold, there on the opening pages were all sorts of plans for the people he wanted to work with, Stephen Hague featuring prominently. There was even a section marked 'touring' full of the places he wouldn't play with us. It was absolutely heartbreaking.

But at the time? Guess what we did. That's right. In time-honoured tradition, we ignored the discontent festering at our core and we just carried on.

Cue *Dad's Army* music. 'Don't tell them your name, Pike!'

With the tour drawing to a close in California, we stayed at the good old Sunset Marquis, and I whiled away many a happy afternoon shopping on Melrose Avenue, where all the shop assistants were beautiful, mainly out-of-work actors and actresses.

In one particular vintage store I'd spotted a beautiful 1960s James Dean-style leather jacket. It cost $675. A lot of money. I had been to see it about three times, and as we were preparing to leave for the airport, I could no longer resist. I said to Terry, 'I've got to go and get that jacket. I'll see you at LAX,' and tore down to Melrose.

When I got to the shop the jacket was still there. It was meant to be. I took it to the counter. It was getting seriously close to my departure time but there was only one guy in front of me, a short dude clutching an old pair of cowboy boots. He offered them to the shop assistant, who said, 'That'll be seventy-five dollars, please.'

'Oh, man,' the short dude said, 'they're really battered. How about I give you forty-five?'

'Sixty-five,' the shoppie countered.

Oh shit.

I was getting really fidgety. They were going backwards and forwards for what seemed like hours, in increments of five dollars. I was at boiling point and was going to offer to buy the fucking boots myself when at long last they settled on $50.

The guy paid and, as he turned round clutching his new 'old' boots, he barged into me … it was fucking Bruce Springsteen, the tight bastard.

He then got on a customised Harley outside that must have cost a fortune. I was so shocked I forgot about my flight for a moment. Then, coming to, I paid and legged it. I just made it. Terry was sweating even more profusely than usual when I got there and had to give me a bump in the security queue to get over it.

As we flew home I regaled them all with my tales of meeting Brucie, and even the air stewardesses, who we knew quite well by this time, were joining us in the toilets for a little Brucie bonus. It made the flight fly by, if you'll forgive the pun.

The year ended nicely, with a request from Tony to record the music for a new TV football show featuring George Best and Rodney Marsh, the imaginatively titled *Best & Marsh*. It was a nice bit of synchronicity for me as I'd got George Best's job at the Manchester Ship Canal company way back in 1973 (see *Unknown Pleasures*). To make the tune we wangled a free afternoon at Granada TV's studio. Merry Christmas.

TIMELINE EIGHT
JANUARY–DECEMBER 1987

FACTORY (COMMUNICATIONS) LIMITED

MODIFIED COMPANY BALANCE SHEET AS AT 30 JUNE 1987

	Notes	1987		1986	
		£	£	£	£
FIXED ASSETS					
Tangible Assets			17783		13705
Investments			2		2
			17785		13707
CURRENT ASSETS					
Stocks		177950		92174	
Debtors		856348		779730	
Cash at Bank & in Hand		25445		4993	
		1059743		876897	
CREDITORS: amounts falling due within one year		807628		733414	
NET CURRENT ASSETS			252115		143483
TOTAL ASSETS LESS CURRENT LIABILITIES			269900		157190
CAPITAL AND RESERVES					
Called up Share Capital	3		400		400
RESERVES			269500		156790
			269900		157190

In preparing these modified accounts:

a) We have relied upon the exemptions for individual accounts under Section 247 of the Companies Act 1985.

b) We have done so on the grounds that the company is entitled to the benefit of those exemptions as a small company.

Alan Erasmus

Directors

31 May 1989

27–28 January 1987

New Order play Tokyo, Japan.

29 January 1987

New Order play Festival Hall, Osaka, Japan.

30 January 1987

New Order play Nagoya, Japan.

2 February 1987

New Order play Town Hall, Wellington, New Zealand.

4 February 1987

New Order play the Galaxy, Auckland, New Zealand.

6 February 1987

New Order play the Generator, Surfers Paradise, Gold Coast, Australia.

7 February 1987

New Order play Roxy, Brisbane, Australia.

9 February 1987

New Order play Byron Bay Arts Centre (The Piggery), Byron Bay, Australia.

11 February 1987

New Order play Dee Why Hotel, Sydney, Australia.

12–13 February 1987

New Order play Enmore Theatre, Sydney, Australia.

14 February 1987

New Order play Selina's, Coogee Bay Hotel, Sydney, Australia.

16 February 1987

New Order play the Barton Town Hall, Adelaide, Australia.

17 February 1987

New Order play the Venue, Melbourne, Australia.

18 February 1987

New Order play the Festival Hall, Melbourne, Australia.

20 February 1987

New Order play Canterbury Court, Perth, Australia.

21 February 1987

New Order play Red Parrot, Perth, Australia.

2 April 1987

New Order play Woolwich Coronet, Woolwich.

4 April 1987

New Order play the Academy, Brixton.

May 1987

'Temptation' and 'Confusion' re-recorded for inclusion on *Substance* in Yellow Two, Bamford Street, Stockport, produced by the band.

14 May 1987

New Order play Plaza de Toros, Valencia, Spain.

15 May 1987

New Order play Madrid, Spain.

16 May 1987

New Order play Mollerussa Pabellon, Mollerussa, Spain.

June 1987

'Truth Faith 'and '1963' recorded at Advision Studios, Gosfield Street, London W1 (Stephen Hague producing).

6 June 1987

New Order play Super Tent, Finsbury Park, London, as part of an all-day Factory benefit gig, supported by the Railway Children, Happy Mondays and A Certain Ratio. Mike Pickering is DJ.

> **'It rained, and it rained. It was like being back in Manchester and I remember seeing Knobhead (Happy Mondays' keyboard player) bent over backwards because he'd had so many drugs. He was walking like he was limbo dancing and I said, "What the fuck is wrong with him?" and Shaun Ryder said, "Oh, fucking hell, Hooky. What we do if we get any dodgy gear, we always try it out on Knobhead. He's had some real fucking dodgy acid." I'd never seen anything like it in my life.**
>
> **'We were introduced on stage by Alan Wise. He would always introduce us with some weird shit, like, "Here they are, four girls from Preston, it's Joy D'Odour," or something like that. Nobody**

ever got it, but you can't fight tradition. Tonight it was, "Four girls from Macclesfield, Joy Division." His best or worst moment was at the Tenth Summer gig, when he came on with a girl in a wheelchair and then pretended to push her off the front of the stage by accident. Even we were shocked. I loved him to bits, but he was an absolute nutcase.'

8 June 1987

New Order play the Roxy, Sheffield.

9 June 1987

New Order play Barrowlands, Glasgow.

'The Happy Mondays were supporting us and Shaun was having one of his dark periods. After the gig they had to leave to go home to Manchester, and as they passed our dressing room, he'd said to the others, "Come on, let's fucking ransack it," and they took the whole rider and loaded it in their Salford Van Hire minibus. However, as luck would have it, the owner had spotted them and he made them bring everything back out of the van and put it all back in our room. He was a bit of a Glasgow face, the owner. You didn't mess with him and he really shamed them. Shaun was livid and when he got in the bus, he put his feet up on the windscreen and kicked, and the screen just popped right out, fell on the bonnet and shattered. No matter how they tried they couldn't get anyone to fix it, so they had to drive all the way back to Manchester with no windscreen in the pissing rain.'

10 June 1987

New Order play the Haçienda, Manchester.

July 1987

New Order: '1st John Peel Session' EP
(Strange Fruit)

Track list:

'Truth'	4.13
'Senses'	4.15
'I.C.B.'	5.15
'Dreams Never End'	3.05

Recorded in BBC Studios, Shepherd's Bush, London.
Produced by Tony Wilson.
Recorded 26 January 1981.
Designed by Wyke Studios.

19 June 1987

New Order play CND Festival, Glastonbury.

The concert was recorded for BBC Radio 1, and was the premiere for 'True Faith'.

> **'A great gig, with the first appearance of the Womad stage at the festival. What a spectacle. We were very proud to be there. There was big opposition to Glastonbury this year because of the travellers' presence the previous year. Michael Eavis had to go to court to fight for the licence, with it only being granted if the travellers were controlled. It was very successful, if muddy, and I remember as we were leaving splashing some travellers who then chased us in a car waving hammers out of the windows. When they caught up they hadn't realised the van behind us contained our crew. Ozzy and Eddie made short work of them.'**

27 June 1987

New Order play Stadion, Aarhus Jazz Festival, Denmark, headlined by the Miles Davis Octet.

30 June 1987

New Order play Reading University, Reading.

16 July 1987

New Order were to appear at the Plymouth Rock Festival but the whole thing had to be cancelled.

20 July 1987

New Order: 'True Faith'
(FAC 183)

Seven-inch track list:

'True Faith'	4.02
'1963'	5.32

Twelve-inch track list:

'True Faith'	5.55
'1963'	5.32

Run-out groove one: *Let's go round the roses ...*
Run-out groove two: *... one more time!*

Recorded in Advision Studios, London.
Engineered by David Jacob.
Written by New Order and Stephen Hague.
Produced by New Order and Stephen Hague.
Designed by Peter Saville Associates.
Photography by Trevor Key.
Entered UK chart on 1 August 1987, remaining in the charts for 10 weeks, its peak position was number 4.

New Order: 'True Faith' (remix)
(FAC 183R)
Twelve-inch Remix track list:

'True Faith'	8.59
'1963'	5.32
'True Dub'	10.41

Run-out groove one: *If at first you don't succeed …*
Run-out groove two: *… try try again!*

Remixed by Shep Pettibone.
Designed by Peter Saville Associates.
Photography by Trevor Key.

August 1987

New Order's US tour with Echo and the Bunnymen and Gene Loves Jezebel begins.

13 August 1987

New Order play Northrup Auditorium, University of Minnesota, Minneapolis, Minnesota.

15 August 1987

New Order play Pine Knob Amphitheatre, Clarkston, Michigan (Detroit).

16 August 1987

New Order play Poplar Creek Music Theatre, Hoffman Estates, Illinois (Chicago). This gig had been due to take place on the 14th, but due to adverse weather was rescheduled.

17 August 1987

New Order: *Substance*, double LP, double cassette, double CD (FACT 200)

Track List LP:

'Ceremony'	4.22
'Everything's Gone Green'	5.30
'Temptation' (new version May '87)	6.58
'Blue Monday'	8.12

SUBSTANCE

'Confusion' (new version May '87)	4.41
'Thieves Like Us'	6.36
'The Perfect Kiss'	8.46
'Sub-Culture'	4.47
'Shellshock'	6.27
'State of the Nation'	6.31
'Bizarre Love Triangle'	6.41
'True Faith'	5.53

Run-out groove one: *Goodbye Davy Pils!*
Run-out groove two: *The Pleasure and the Pain …*
Run-out groove three: … *of an Extended Childhood!*
Run-out groove four: *Stephen won't go to Stockport!*

Substance featured the songs' original twelve-inch versions, with the exception of edited versions of: 'The Perfect Kiss', 'Sub-Culture', 'Shellshock' and 'Hurt'.

Also included on the CD is the 1981 re-recorded version of 'Ceremony', and re-recorded versions of 'Temptation' and 'Confusion' plus a bonus disc featuring:

Track List:

'In a Lonely Place'	6.16
'Procession'	4.27
'Cries and Whispers'	3.25
'Hurt'	6.59
'The Beach'	7.19
'Confused Instr.'	7.38
'Lonesome Tonight'	5.11
'Murder'	3.55
'Thieves Like Us Instr.'	6.57
'Kiss of Death'	7.02
'Shame of the Nation'	7.54
'1963'	5.35

Recorded in Advision Studios, Britannia Row Studios, and Jam Studios, London; Strawberry Studios and Yellow Two Studios, Stockport, Manchester.

Engineered by Chris Nagle, Mike Johnson, David Jacob.
Produced by New Order.
Designed by Peter Saville Associates.
Photography by Trevor Key.
Entered UK chart on 29 August 1987, remaining in the charts for 37 weeks, its peak position was number 3.

'After this release things would really start moving for New Order. In total, round-the-world sales would exceed 10 million. We were puzzled. It was the best record we "never" made. Tony was delighted on two counts, he had the CD for his car and the lower deal meant Factory could continue with some impunity in their financial adventures.'

18 August 1987

New Order play Mansfield G.W.A., Boston, Massachusetts.

21 August 1987

New Order play Merriweather Post Pavilion, Columbia.

22 August 1987

New Order play Nautica Stage, Cleveland.

24 August 1987

New Order play Mann Music Center, Philadelphia.

'Much excitement here when the stage collapses while the Bunnymen are playing. I was watching. One minute they were there and the next minute they were all in the orchestra pit with their equipment on top of them. Barney said Mac had been eating too many burgers, but many reckoned it was the weight of his wallet. Our start was delayed while they strengthened the stage to accommodate Barney's wallet.'

25–26 August 1987

New Order play Pier 84, New York.

29 August 1987

New Order play the Palace Theatre, New Haven, Connecticut.

31 August 1987

New Order play Jones Beach Theatre, Wantagh, Long Island.

> **'The highlight of this gig was when I fell flat on my face on "Temptation". Barney was delighted.'**

September 1997

Joy Division: 'Second John Peel Session' EP released.
(Strange Fruit)
Recorded: 26 November 1979.
First transmission: 10 December 1979.

Track List:

'Love Will Tear Us Apart'	3.20
'24 Hours'	4.05
'Colony'	4.00
'Sound of Music'	4.20

Recorded at BBC studio in Maida Vale, London.
Produced by Tony Wilson.
Designed by Wyke Studios.

1 September 1987

New Order play Montreal University, Montreal, Canada.

3 September 1987

New Order play C.N.E. Grandstand, Toronto, Canada.

4 September 1987

New Order play Darien Lakes Amusement Park, Buffalo, New York.

5 September 1987

New Order play Civic Center, Pittsburgh.

8 September 1987

New Order play Red Rocks Amphitheatre, Denver, Colorado.

> **'I play "Anarchy" with the hastily assembled, one-time-only Crew Order.'**

9 September 1987

New Order play Park West Amphitheatre, Salt Lake City.

11 September 1987

New Order play San Diego Sports Arena, San Diego.

12 September 1987

New Order play Irvine Meadows, Irvine, California (Laguna Hills).

> **'Rob asked us to play *Substance* in order, so we did and it was a storming gig, though events beforehand meant it was tinged with great sadness.'**

13 September 1987

New Order play the Forum, Los Angeles.

15 September 1987

New Order play Compton Terrace, Phoenix, Arizona.

18–19 September 1987

New Order play Greek Theatre, Berkeley, California.

December 1987

New Order: 'Touched by the Hand of God'
(FAC 193)

Seven-inch track list:

'Touched by the Hand of God'	3.47
'Touched by the Hand of Dub'	4.11

Twelve-inch track list:

'Touched by the Hand of God' (full length)	7.02
'Touched by the Hand of Dub' (full length)	5.30

Run-out groove one: *I won't be a minute* …
Run-out groove two: … *don't grumble yet!*

Recorded in Pluto Studios, Granby Row, Manchester.
Mixed by Arthur Baker.
Produced by New Order.
Designed by Peter Saville Associates.
Photography by Trevor Key.
Video directed by Kathryn Bigelow.
Entered UK chart on 19 December 1987, remaining in the charts for 7 weeks, its peak position was number 20.

6 December 1987

New Order play Philipshalle, Düsseldorf, West Germany.

8 December 1987

New Order play La Mutualité, Paris.

> 'In all the time New Order Mk I were together we never had a good gig in Paris. This one was no exception.'

10 December 1987

New Order play Wembley Arena, London, supported by Primal Scream.

> 'New Order and Primal Scream ... separated at birth. I had watched their career with great interest since I saw one of their first gigs at the Boardwalk in Manchester. They were fantastic. Bobby is a great frontman. Their road crew were almost as mad as ours, Murray, Stretch, and Fatty Molloy in particular.
>
> 'The best story I ever heard of any road crew member's exploits was Fatty Molloy on an American tour with the Scream, being well refreshed, shall we say, in the crew bus when they ran out of beer, and him saying, "Don't worry, I'll nip to the band bus and get some more." Opening the bus door, he stepped out only to find himself careering down a freeway at 70mph. Not one of them had noticed the bus start moving.
>
> '"I wouldn't have minded, Hooky," he said, "but I nearly grabbed the band bus as it went past. It was right behind."
>
> 'Broken collarbone, broken arms, broken leg, severe case of road rash and concussion, Fatty Molloy was back on tour in a matter of days.
>
> 'This gig sealed a long-lasting friendship between both bands and crews.'

New Order's first job of 1988 was to prepare for a Quincy Jones remix of 'Blue Monday', which was very flattering, to say the least.

To give him the necessary bits and bobs, we decided to record a load of overdubs in Advision. A little too soon for me to be back there after 'True Faith', I'm afraid, but I was outvoted.

Now, the carpet in the studio had the Advision logo woven into it over and over again and after a while it made you feel dizzy, and closing your eyes was no escape. It seemed to be imprinted on your eyelids. Famously, when John Robie was recording there he had banged on about it so much that when he left the studio the owners presented him with a huge framed piece of the carpet, bless him.

I remember bumping into Errol Brown out of Hot Chocolate in the recreation room. I couldn't help but tell him about stealing the guitar line from 'Emma' for 'Thieves Like Us' and again for 'Every Second Counts'.

'Good for you, Peter,' he said.

Nice guy, rumoured to have a love child in Salford round the corner from where I lived in Ordsall; he died in May 2015 of pancreatic cancer, very sad.

Number two, an advertising agency had been on to Rob about using 'Blue Monday' for a Sunkist soft drink advert and they were offering $350,000 for the privilege, but it came with a request to change the lyrics. We were intrigued, as it was a lot of money and they were very persistent, saying they would send their best copywriter over to see us. So there we were doing our Quincy 'Blue Monday' overdubs when this kid from the advertising agency arrived to try and persuade us to record his special vocal version for the Sunkist campaign.

Barney gets it all wrong in his book, which isn't a surprise really, as he got so much wrong. But the truth is we have never been very good with things like this. The incredibly large figures seem ridiculous to you when you haven't much money, which we still hadn't at the time. It wasn't long after this that we turned down $300,000 just to hang a fifteen-foot watch off one side of the stage. We couldn't handle it; it went against our principles. We just pictured the idea of a massive promotional Swatch watch hanging over the stage, hiding our scruples, our punk ethics, so we screwed up our noses and backed away. On the one hand, we'd be moaning about how much of our money Factory were losing, on the other we were spurning dead-easy chances to earn loads of dosh. Work that one out if you can.

So anyway, this kid was being very persistent. Here in the studio, with the alternative lyrics all printed out, and giving us the whole treatment, the big sell, he said, 'This is easy money. You'd be mad to turn it down. Sunkist is a valid product in today's marketplace,' etc., etc., badgering us into submission. He was so enthusiastic that at last we agreed to give it a go, just to get him off our backs.

So then we had this situation where Barney was trying to sing these awful lyrics:

How does it feel
When a new day has begun
And you're drinking in the sunshine,
Then Sunkist is the one
When you need a taste for living
Sunkist is the one.

I mean, it's not like the lyrics to 'Blue Monday' – which were a group effort, remember – were much cop in the first place. But this was taking the piss. They were so awful, and the idea so distasteful, that we went beyond hating them to just laughing at them. It was embarrassing. Barney in particular couldn't sing them without guffawing, and even though we did several takes, including one in which the kid even held up a piece of card with the figure '$350,000' scrawled on it, it didn't help. We said, 'Sorry, mate, it just isn't happening,' and the kid left, shaking his head in dismay. That was the end of that.

Or so we thought. We finished the overdubs and sent the tapes to Quincy, forty-eight tracks' worth of new sound effects, guitar, bass, dentist drills, dustbin lids, choirs of angels and sundry other stuff. But somehow, and God knows how – probably something simple like the engineer at Advision failing to wipe it off the tape – we sent them the Sunkist vocal take as well.

The way Quincy mixed 'Blue Monday' sounded very impressive. He set up three engineers in three different studios, each with the same track, and would then communicate with them by phone, listening to the results, giving them directions, and lastly choosing his favourite mix of the three, sometimes editing bits of all three together later to make one master. It was a very weird way of working but it seemed to get results. 'It works for Michael Jackson,' he said, and you could not argue with that.

He did a very 'safe' job on the 'Blue Monday' remix. We were all very happy with it, and we took the fact that it sounded so similar to the original as a great compliment to our own production skills. Even the great Quincy Jones couldn't improve on it.

Afterwards, what happened was that one of the engineers must have heard the Sunkist vocal tape and for reasons best known to himself – shits and giggles, probably – cobbled together a bootleg, a Sunkist 'Blue Monday' take for fun. He obviously gave it to someone, who gave it to someone ... until eventually it ended up with Sunkist, who grabbed it, put their logo on it, did an edit using some of the 'Touched by the Hand of God' video and issued it as an official advert. We protested and they ended up pulling the ad, but of course by that time the damage had been done and, like it or not, we'd advertised Sunkist. To add insult to injury, we never got paid for it. Not a cent. It's still up on YouTube, check it out.

Not long later came an unusual but very interesting request.

A great fan of ours in California was now managing a nightclub called the Stock Exchange (which was in fact an old stock exchange) in Los Angeles. And was hosting a fashion event called 'UK/LA Week', a series of events meant to strengthen business ties between the United States and Great Britain. This particular event featured the cream of the then up-and-coming young English fashion designers premiering their best designs at a catwalk show. The manager had been given an open budget for entertainment around the show, with strict instructions to put on a very special event, in front of royalty no less, Prince Andrew and a very pregnant Sarah Ferguson being the guests of honour. He booked us.

The idea was that New Order would play live for twenty-five minutes while the models sashayed in front of the stage. This was a one-off and we flew over just for the one gig, business class, all-expenses paid, with $70,000 for our trouble. We just couldn't say no.

We arrived to soundcheck early in the empty club and everything went well and sounded good. The manager had given us his apartment to use as a dressing room, situated in an apartment block right opposite the club on the sixth floor. As he opened the door he pointed to a big bag of white powder on the coffee table, saying, 'Help yourselves, guys.'

We did. What seemed like minutes later we were rudely interrupted by the sound of sirens and then circling helicopters. As we hung out of the window looking down on the club below we could see the road had now been cordoned off by police, with checkpoints at each end and overhead helicopters with spotlights shining down. We were very excited and were all taking pictures when we were lit up by the helicopter's searchlight and told in no uncertain terms over a very loud PA system to, 'GO INSIDE AND SHUT THE WINDOWS ... NOW!'

We retreated back to the coffee table and within minutes our host appeared to take us over to the club. Here the atmosphere had changed considerably, taking on a much more menacing tone, with the secret service very much in charge. Our host waltzed us past a very long and well-dressed queue to a huge portable metal detector, saying, 'This is the band. They must go in now!' He was met with blank looks all round and told in no uncertain terms to go to the back. The officers in charge had no intention of letting a manky Manc Indie band jump in front of the great and gorgeous of Los Angeles.

'Oh shit,' said the manager. He was sweating as much as us by this point and paranoia was definitely creeping in. After what seemed like a lifetime of standing there we were frisked and then ushered into the inner sanctum.

The club had two staircases, one either side of a central space. We were using the left-hand one to get to the stage. Unfortunately, two shaven-headed behemoths had other ideas and stood in our way.

'Hi, we're the band, we need to get to the stage.'

'No one is allowed this way, sir.'

'B-but we have to get to the stage ... T-to play.'

'No one is allowed this way, sir. No one. As I said.'

Getting a little emboldened now, I said, 'How are we supposed to get to the fucking stage then, eh?'

'Listen, motherfucker, I just told you to get lost. So get lost. Try the other staircase, you stupid limey.'

Charming.

Discretion being the best part of valour, me and Barney moved across to the other staircase to be greeted by no security men at all.

One flight of stairs later, we emerged into what appeared to be the models' dressing area and were suddenly surrounded by beautiful women all in various stages of dressing and undressing.

We walked through with the biggest grins ever on our faces; no one even noticed us. Finally at the side of the stage, we prepared to go on. We noticed that Fergie and Andrew were seated on pseudo-throne chairs on our right, but smack in front of the PA system. We walked stiffly on to polite applause and launched into the first number as the models began walking down the runway.

As the intro to 'Bizarre Love Triangle' thundered out, Fergie jumped out of her seat and screamed. God, it must have been loud. Four secret service guys ran forward and started ripping the leads out of the speakers until the noise stopped and the left-hand side of the PA went off. Satisfied their work was done, they sat down, leaving us to soldier on with half the volume and all our carefully planned stereo effects gone. The whole thing was rather bemusing, not only for us but also for the very lukewarm audience, leaving just our host grinning and gurning at the side of the stage, clapping like a demented sea lion.

It went downhill very quickly and after twenty-five shambolic minutes (that seemed like an hour at least), we trooped off stage to a smattering of applause. In the fire curtain we caught up on some drinking (and the other). But it wasn't over yet. Our host grabbed us again and took us round to the front of the club, made us line up then pushed us right in front of Fergie and Andrew for the right royal handshake. We were flabbergasted.

They obviously thought we were designers, asking us questions about the clothes and stuff like that. We desperately tried to hold it together with our frozen throats and running noses, trying not to laugh or cry. We were then ejected into the hall where we got talking – and couldn't stop talking – to the girl running the 'Paul Mitchell Hair Products' stall. She was complaining that no one was taking advantage of any of the free stuff on offer. We soon solved that and dragged bags and bags of the stuff backstage. It lasted me for two years, that lot.

One great upshot of that day was the fact that, according to my mum, we appeared not only on the six o'clock news at home, but also on *News at Ten*, us being trailered as the new wave of young British designers meeting Prince Andrew and his pregnant Princess. If only they knew.

Princess Beatrice was born on 8 August 1988.

'Blue Monday 88', as it was called, came out in April and went to number 8 (ha-ha, not really, it got to number 3) in the UK. It did a lot better than the re-release of Joy Division's 'Atmosphere', which came out in July and, despite Anton Corbijn's video – which I thought was stunning – only went as high as number 34. Ho hum, no accounting for taste.

In the meantime, New Order went on hiatus by mutual and unspoken consent. Barney went off to do Electronic; Steve and Gillian were doing whatever it was that they were doing; and I'd decided to form a band of my own.

I already co-owned Suite 16 studios in Rochdale, so I had the perfect place to record, and what I did was negotiate a deal with Tony, who told me to go away and spend three months writing and recording material.

'Get it out of your system, darling,' he'd say. 'Get it out of your system and then get back to New Order.'

Rob was the same. 'Get on with it and get fucking back to New Order, you daft twats.' Later he'd say, 'If you lot spent as much time on New Order as you did on your solo projects we'd be bigger than them Irish bastards.' He was still obsessed.

I tried working alone, putting together a set-up of DMX and sequencers, then programming basslines to get a groove going. At first it was hard work and most of the time I ended up alone. CJ, the engineer at Suite 16 at the time, was bored senseless, and had taken to wandering off. For a couple of days it went nowhere. I was starting to worry, then at last a breakthrough: I got the synth bassline and drums to 'Jesus I Love You'. Triumphant at last, I turned round to share my good fortune and there was no one there. I went downstairs, no one. Everyone who worked there had gone out.

This working alone was shit. I had to find some musicians, and pronto.

I'd been doing the live sound out front, facing the stage, for Lavolta Lakota, a Factory band who'd made one single, 'Prayer', which I'd produced. I got on well with the singer, Dave Hicks, and doing the sound I came to admire his guitar playing, which was always labelled 'stage left'.

Because he was a mate and because I thought he was a decent guitarist, I asked him to help form the band, but things took a strange turn right away. Dave was a very charismatic guy, good-looking, blessed with the gift of the gab and a real hit with the ladies, but away from Lavolta Lakota he seemed to have lost any talent he had for the guitar. It took me a while to work out that I'd made a catastrophic mistake. The guitar work that I'd admired, labelled 'stage left', did in fact belong to the other guitarist, Ash Major, and Dave, bless his enthusiastic and charismatic cotton socks, couldn't play anywhere near as well as him. Not only that, but he wasn't that great at coming up with ideas either. I say that, but I suppose it would have to be ideas I liked; our tastes turned out to be very different right from the start. He always wanted to do the vocals and only suggested himself doing them. Typically, I had a feeling that I wasn't even out of the blocks and I'd already landed myself with another Gillian. But I liked him as a person and always had, so out of loyalty we soldiered on.

To try and remedy the situation I turned to CJ again. He was Chris Jones from Rhyl in Wales, an engineer I'd poached from Strawberry Studios to come and work at Suite 16 early on. He was a very good engineer, a little bit too direct at times, often getting himself into trouble with clients. He called a spade a spade, shall we say. But a nice guy with a mad infectious laugh, whose speciality was keyboard playing. Add that to Dave's lack of guitar skills and we were already beginning to move away from the harder-rocking band I'd envisioned, where the guitar and bass would be up high.

It threw me, I must admit. I was out of my comfort zone. Trying to nail a signature sound for the new group was difficult. I'm not sure whether or not I was working harder than I was with New Order, but it certainly felt harder because there was no real sense of the material gelling.

I was learning, and I was floundering while I was learning. The sound wasn't really coming together and, looking back, that's because we weren't playing to our strengths, which in my case was the bass. I was famed for my New Order bass sound, but I was sidelining it in order to be the frontman/vocalist, something I'd never really wanted to do and didn't consider myself to be born to; whereas Dave Hicks, who was a great-looking guy, full of charisma and would have made a great frontman, was instead being asked to play the role of writer and guitarist – a role to which he wasn't at all suited.

We weren't just failing to play to our strengths, we were practically thumbing our noses at them.

Meantime, as me, Dave and CJ struggled with the material, trying to find our musical identity, Factory was moaning at me because the bills they were getting from Suite 16 were getting higher and higher and they were seeing nothing for it. No album, no single, not a squeak yet.

I was hardly seeing Iris, seeing very little of Heather too. Truth be told, me and Iris had drifted apart years before, each living our own lives mainly separate from each other. My affair with Jane was in full swing and I was desperately trying to juggle everything. It was, all in all, a fairly crappy period. Indicative of the whole wading-through-mud nature of the enterprise was the difficulty in finding a name.

It's always murder to get a decent name for a band. You've really got to get it right first time, it's got to go with your image, and we didn't have one of those yet either. That was part of the problem. We didn't have anything apart from me, the figurehead, which I suddenly found very frightening. It was one of those times when I could understand and sympathise with what Barney had to put up with.

Then I was watching TV one night and on came George Michael's 'Faith' video. On the back of his jacket was written the word 'Revenge' in studs. It looked great. I thought, *There, that's it, I've got it.* I loved the connotations, the no-nonsense feel of it. Barney wanted to split New Order so this was my Revenge. Bingo. I had the name.

But that was all I had. It was the first time I'd sung and written lyrics alone, and it made me look at songwriting in a completely different way.

Money remained a problem. At this stage the members of New Order were on £200 a week. We still had to mither Rob any time we wanted to do so much as pay a gas bill, and he still made us feel like moaning money-grabbers. At that time – and this before the heyday of the Happy Mondays and the first Electronic album, remember – New Order and Joy Division were the only two bands on Factory that had ever shown a profit. Factory took their half of the split, but New Order's half went straight to the Haçienda. So despite chart success and American tours, the members of New Order still didn't have that much money in their pockets.

We knew we had to do the next New Order record whether we liked it or not. We needed the cash. That said, there was a confidence, maybe even what you might call a devil-may-care attitude, around the group. Like maybe our time away on solo projects meant that we'd seen the light at the end of the tunnel, life after death, that kind of thing.

So we reconvened, against all the odds and – even though we were all convinced it would be our last album together – it wasn't at all a glum, funereal atmosphere. In fact, things were quite the opposite. So much so that while we were rehearsing as New Order in Cheetham Hill and I read an article about what seemed to be an amazing place in San Lorenzo, Ibiza, Mediterraneo Studio, I didn't think twice about being cooped up with the rest of them, and suggested we went to have a look at it.

Sure, they said, go ahead, it will make a change from London. So me and Andy Robinson flew out there, and were shown around a beautiful ten-bedroom villa with its own pool, overlooking a picturesque valley. It was isolated, very isolated. Perfect. To reach it you had to take a long rocky track up from the main road. But it was gorgeous.

Then we saw the studio. And suddenly things were not so good. It had rotting purple carpet on the floor and on the walls. The equipment was old and apart from the live room it was actually very small.

Still, the villa and the location being so beautiful, plus the 24-hour bar staffed by Herman the German, swung it. We decided to go for it, so in June we hired a truck, shoved all our gear in it – including my motorbike and a favourite sofa of Rob's – and a nutty truck driver with the best mullet I've ever seen drove it out to Ibiza.

The group arrived, and as soon as we reached the villa I ran in and used my prior knowledge to grab the best room, one that had a balcony and a spectacular view of the valley beneath. Result.

The first night we all sat round to eat, and after a couple of drinks Mike Johnson and I decided to drive our hire car into San Antonio and take a look around. As we entered the outskirts of the town we had to stop. There was a guy lying in the middle of the road. We checked him out; he was rat-arsed pissed and snoring away. Picking him up, we carried him carefully to the pavement.

'I hope this isn't an omen, Mike?' I said.

It was. Man, when we got into San Antonio it was rocking. I already knew we were going to love it here. Correction, I was going to love it here. We drove home laughing.

The next morning, I threw open the French windows of my room, stepped out onto the balcony to see the valley shrouded in mist below and thought it was one of the most beautiful sights I'd ever seen. I'd brought a Tamiya radio-controlled kit car to build along with my trusty pile of books, thinking I was going to have a lot of time on my hands. There were seven of us, that's Steve and Gillian, Barney, me, Rob, Andy Robinson and Mike Johnson, and to serve us were three staff, a chef, an American engineer and Manuel, who was a general runner and dogsbody – six people to serve seven of us. It was luxury; I'd never known anything like it. This was going to be the best recording session of my life.

I started with the best intentions, even joining a gym miles from the studio, religiously driving there on the bike – a Yamaha IT200, registration number B604 TNF, as you ask – every other day, until one day on the way home, wearing my usual uniform of crash helmet, shorts and Adidas hi-tops, the tick-over screw vibrated out of the bike's carburettor. I was overtaking a busload of Thomson holidaymakers at the time, when all of a sudden the back wheel locked up and I found myself doing a 200-yard power slide down the road, kicking the ailing bike up over and over again, scaring me to bloody death.

When it finally stopped, I collapsed on the grass verge with a mixture of relief and nervous exhaustion. As the bus went past an old lady gave me the Vs. She must have thought I was a local. Turned out the resulting weak mixture of fuel due to the missing screw had caused the piston to melt and stick to the cylinder head. It was a write-off. I would soon be joining it.

One other big problem was the studio. There was no getting around the fact that it was shite. I'm sure the carpet was purple. Barney remembers it being green. He said green and maggoty. Well at least that's one thing we both agreed on, that it was horrible. Them lot couldn't say, 'What have you brought us to?' because I had told them in advance how shit it was. But they still couldn't believe how rank the studio was now they were actually there. It took Mike Johnson a good day and a half just to get the tape machine aligned and serviced so it became usable. I was trying to buck them all up, feeling responsible for them being there. 'Come on, come on, look at the pool. Look at the 24-hour bar and room service. Don't worry about the control room. We'll set up in the live room and bang them out from there.'

Me still thinking like we were a rock band. Them lot probably wondering how they were going to be able to program their 21st-century sequencers in a studio that looked like it had only just entered the previous century.

Still, Mike got it running and we set up the drums in the live room and began working on the few ideas we'd brought over from our practice room in Cheetham Hill. Straight away, we sussed that the live room sounded terrible, another massive drawback. I could sense the storm clouds gathering. Rob had booked for two months. The idea was to record the songs then mix them in the UK, but on any album there are certain hurdles to overcome, and in a way it's how you handle those hurdles that determines the quality of the finished product. A terrible studio was a big hurdle to clear.

That night over dinner, somebody, it might have been Barney or Steve, but I know it wasn't me, said, 'Oh, have you heard about this new drug over here called ecstasy? We should get some. It might help us write.'

It's funny, because I'd never found drugs to help the creative process at all. Give me a drug and the last place I wanted to be was in the studio. I wanted to be in the pub or at a party, not working. Barney used to make me laugh; he'd get off his head and want to do guitar and keyboard overdubs completely off his face. Other people were kings of the minuscule line. They'd chop out a tiny little line like a mouse's whisker and I'd look at it and think, *Fucking hell, that's the stuff I throw away.* My lines were like your finger, the kind that stopped you talking; that felt like a portcullis had slammed down on your tongue. I could never quite understand why anyone would take such small lines, but I suppose it enabled them to combine drugs with work, which is something I never quite mastered.

So me and Andy Robinson took the Ford Escort hire car down the rickety track to the main road and then to a bar we'd spotted, where we ambled inside to discover that we were the only customers. We took a seat and got talking to the owner, Paco.

Andy chickened out, so it was left to me. 'Hey, Paco, I don't suppose you know where we could get some drugs, do you?'

It's always a bit of a risk asking strangers in foreign countries if they can get you drugs, but we weren't that far from San Antonio and, even back then, Ibiza had a reputation as party central, so you might say it was a calculated risk.

It paid off, because Paco, who had been cleaning glasses, looked left and right then leaned forward conspiratorially. There wasn't another soul in the place but, even so, he wasn't taking any chances.

He could get us some coke, he whispered. 'I served up Ronnie Wood, Rollin' Stones, with some beautiful "Flies Wing". Uno gram – Uno line. He eees a monster!' which was a start but ... 'Well, we've heard of this new drug, ecstasy.'

'Eeekstasy. Leave it with me. I know someone ...'

On a promise of getting some of this 'Eeekstasy', Andy and I started going down to the bar after dinner every night, until one evening Paco told us he knew a man who could get us some, a one-armed dealer who was well known on the island. Andy and I arranged to meet this guy, who remarkably had no problem driving a scooter with one arm, and paid him about 50,000 potatoes for nine ecstasies, about £270. Thirty pounds each.

I thought it was a lot of money. Andy thought it was a lot of money. But we'd been waiting to get our hands on it for a while, and expectations were high, so we coughed up and hotfooted it back to the villa with our magic beans. Here they are, everybody, the long-awaited 'Eekstasies'. Let's see the colour of your money.

Except, as soon as they realised how much they had to pay, them lot refused to cough up. Andy was going, 'What do you mean, you're not paying? I've got them. Look, they're here. I need the money. I took fifty thousand potatoes out of the float. Rob's going to kill me when he lands.'

But them lot were like, 'No way, that's too expensive, we're not paying that.'

What a bunch of bastards, after all that effort and it being their idea in the first bloody place.

Me and Andy were fuming. We had a spot where we used to sit on the roof of the villa at night to watch the sun go down, and we perched up there, swatting the mosquitos and moaning about them lot downstairs. Andy was shitting himself because Rob was going to kill him. Don't forget, Rob had had a drug-induced nervous breakdown.

In the end we decided to go for a beer in San Antonio, and good thing we did, because we arrived to find the place absolutely kicking and straight away we brightened up. A couple of beers later and I said to Andy, 'Have you still got that stuff on you?'

He had, so we decided to take a half each, just to see what would happen.

Oh my God. The first thing we felt after sitting there looking at one another and saying, 'Is it working? Can you feel anything yet?' was an irresistible urge to shit. We were running around these bars on the strip in San Antonio, both trying to find a toilet that was hygienic enough to use.

Then with that little bit of business out of the way we went on to have the best night of our lives. Hugging each other. 'I love you, I fucking love you.' Dancing on podiums, friends with everyone, complete strangers, all of us together against the world, off our heads in numerous clubs, hearing music that seemed to reach deep inside our souls, our entire bodies buzzing, each nerve-ending as though it had been dipped in honey, a sensation of absolute and total bliss and well-being, like nothing I'd ever felt before, or would ever feel again. Oh my God. I was reborn. I will never forget that first night, or the first morning, because I came to, with no Andy, on a bench in Ibiza Old Town harbour, watching the sun rise with no idea how the hell I had got there.

As I stared blankly out to sea I saw a little black thing come up out of the water. It looked like a periscope. It was a periscope. Within minutes a submarine rose up and docked. It was beautiful. The sailors all came out, lining up on deck, and then someone blew a whistle and marched them off into Ibiza town right past me. 'Time for home,' said Zebedee.

That was it, me and Andy started going out every night, trooping around town getting to know all the other people on ecstasy, going to the clubs – Eden, KU, Pacha, Amnesia – and having the most amazing adventures. We started bumping into the 18–30 crowd and began bringing them back to the villa for a barbecue every Thursday night, all off us completely off our nuts.

At long last, the other lot overcame their qualms about the cost, and once they got on it too we were all absolutely muntered, all the time. We were going out all night, coming home just before daybreak, lying in bed all day, getting up at four o'clock, sunbathing until the sun went down, having something to eat then going in the studio for an hour or so, getting bored and going out again.

It was absolutely brilliant. I mean, in terms of lifestyle, it was absolutely brilliant. In terms of getting anything done? An absolute disaster.

Apart from the fact that we were up all night, every night, the feeling of coming down off ecstasy the next day is like having had your brain scrubbed smooth with a fine-paper emery board. You're good for nothing. You're staring at the wall. You were as much use as a chocolate fireguard the next day. It's not exactly conducive to productivity or creative endeavour; it's not conducive to anything besides sitting staring at a wall or, in our case, hanging around the villa until we went out again.

I mean, we were definitely inspired, in the sense that the feel and culture of ecstasy-driven Ibiza nightlife was seeping into our DNA and would eventually find its way onto a record that people said was the perfect mix of sun-soaked dance and rock. But in terms of any actual, positive industry – complete disaster.

No, I tell a lie, not a *complete* disaster. One night we'd been off our heads in Amnesia and Barney heard a track he liked and woke Mike Johnson up to try to replicate it, which became 'Fine Time'. That was the only one written while we were there.

The adventures continued: unmentionable, unprintable things involving transvestites, death-defying stunts on motorbikes and hire cars. We kept crashing the cars over and over again until the island ran out and had to import more from the mainland.

One night in San Antonio we actually crashed into one another. We had strange, surreal, dawn encounters with air traffic controllers off their heads in Eden, and one night I was so off my face that I told Steve I loved him. That's how off my face I was. There are many stories of our adventures in the Haçienda book so I won't repeat them here.

Rob should have made us work, of course. But he was preoccupied, smoking dope and drinking, lying in the sun. He wasn't supposed to be smoking dope, but he did. He'd just push his glasses up his nose, say, 'Hey, Andy, what should you be doing?' and Andy would say, 'Skinning up, Rob.'

Meanwhile poor old Mike Johnson was spending hours in the studio by himself doing God knows what. He could have done a solo LP in the time he was there, to be honest. As far as I know, Steve was the only one who ever spent any meaningful time in there and, fair play to him, he did actually do quite a lot of drums in the Mediterraneo.

Because we were having such a great time, we thought, *Why not tell our dear friends the Happy Mondays to come over?*

Sure enough, they arrived with half an ounce of speed to sell on, to pay for the trip, but because everyone was on ecstasy nobody wanted the speed. So they ended up giving the speed away.

From that trip the Mondays and their mate Gordon the chef brought ecstasy back to Manchester. I can only apologise.

My partying ground to a halt for a week while Iris visited. I was so tanned from sunbathing that Heather didn't recognise me at the airport and ran right past me.

Then Iris left and, God forgive me, Jane, now my full-time mistress, came over and the partying continued. After two months we panicked when it suddenly occurred to us that we hadn't got anything done, so Rob booked a third month. We got nothing done then either. We just took ecstasy and partied.

Later on, Tony Wilson would say that New Order's time in Ibiza was the most important holiday we'd ever had, meaning that it was largely because of Ibiza that we created *Technique*, helping bring the madness back to Manchester, the crowds to the Haçienda, kick-starting the whole Madchester era and putting Factory well and truly on the map.

But at the time he felt differently. After a flying visit with a tiny Oliver in tow, during which he'd established how little work we had done, he turned to me at the airport on his way home and said, 'Hooky, this is the most expensive holiday you've ever had.'

Of course, just as the song says, the joy and the fun and the seasons in the sun couldn't last, and we had to return home, where we had a week off before moving into Peter Gabriel's newly opened Real World Studios at Box in Bath, the idea being to knuckle down and finish the album as soon as possible.

Real World, at the time, was the most expensive studio ever built: state-of-the-art recording facilities in luxurious and beautiful surroundings. It had huge live rooms all done out in treated oak, and 'vibe rooms' that looked down on the control rooms. One studio control room was set on a level with the surface of the lake outside, so ducks and swans would go floating serenely past the window as you worked. It was like a recording studio Disneyland.

Luxurious accommodation was included and we lived on the premises, waited on hand and foot by a bevy of the West Country's finest maidens. Everything was home-grown organic with a price tag to match. This would be our most expensive album yet. About £10,000 a week all in. As I left my room for breakfast on the first day, there was Peter Gabriel himself fixing a bulb in one of the wall lights outside my room.

'Bloody murder having a studio, isn't it, mate?' said I. He grinned.

I took my usual position, pile of books at the ready, with Mike Johnson to my right, in the top studio in the mill and, maybe because we were feeling a bit shamefaced having frittered away three months in Ibiza, the group got their heads down and worked. The news from home was that the Haçienda was going bonkers, with queues around the block every night. Suddenly there seemed to be some financial light at the end of the tunnel. The mood was lifting.

Still, the session was not without its difficulties. There was a sense that the three separate parts of New Order were becoming more and more separate: Barney working on Electronic, me making plans with Revenge, Steve and Gillian doing music for a BBC series called *Making Out* (something we were supposed to do together, but which they ended up doing as a duo. So although episode one of *Making Out* featured me and an instrumental version of 'Vanishing Point' over the end credits, by episode two it had been spirited away and was very much the 'Other Two' in their first incarnation), but maybe the most awkward moment came when Mike Johnson inadvertently wiped Barney's main vocal for 'Fine Time'. Barney had been struggling with this one. At first it had a pretty normal type of New Order verse and chorus, with a cute lyric featuring a tramp on a bench, which Rob loved. Barney wasn't keen, wanting something harder. So he had written and recorded another one, taking four or five to nail it down. Later, when overdubbing on it backwards, Mike had miscounted and wiped it.

Uh-oh. It was like that bit in the *Beano* where they say, 'That's torn it.'

If it had been anybody else's work it wouldn't have mattered that much: they would have grumbled a bit, been upset and done it again, putting it down to bad luck, knowing there was no malice intended. But not our lead singer. He was one for simmering and stomping and holding grudges, throwing tantrums like a bowler throws balls. Mike was terrified, waiting for his reaction.

I phoned Rob, who was in his room watching telly. 'We got a problem here,' I told him, 'Mike's only gone and wiped the main vocal.'

'Well, I'm not telling him,' said Rob, and that was the end of that conversation.

In the past, Rob wouldn't have thought twice about telling him. Bring it on. He'd have told Barney about the mishap, and if he'd complained then Rob would have warned him not to be such a moaning twat and to shut up and get on with re-recording the vocal.

I know, I thought. *I'll tell Steve and Gillian, brighten their day.* They were like, 'Oh my God,' faces falling, simpering and recoiling in horror. The next thing I knew, they'd gone home – as in home to Macclesfield, a three-to-four-hour trip.

In the end, we went through it together, me and poor old Mike left to tell Barney. Our illustrious lead singer stomped out, only returning to the studio days later.

Meantime, I worked very hard to squeeze myself onto some of the tracks, mainly the sequencer ones of course, a situation that became even worse when Mike was ousted from mixing the album.

I wasn't sure why, and as Mike was one of the few fans of my bass left in the camp, I was a little worried. Later I found out that that was exactly why he was removed for the mixing. 'The others felt you were too close,' said Rob. He wasn't immune to stirring us all up at times. Mike was moved out and Alan Meyerson was moved in (Mike had done every album since *Closer*; there's loyalty for you).

Alan was American and by that I mean 'very' American, and slightly younger than us. Originally from New York, he now came across as Californian, both in look and attitude. He came highly recommended after recent work with Cameo, Bryan Ferry and Book of Love (a particular favourite of mine). He was a nice guy and I liked him straight away, getting on and working with him very well, much to the annoyance of the others.

He had recently gone through rehab and was now clean, an alien concept to us lot who were right in the midst of our most indulgent phase. He would tell great stories of his time in rehab, in particular one occasion concerning two young ladies. It seemed his rehab was enforced, as in you were locked in for a certain amount of time, completely voluntarily. He told me that the recreation room at the back of the clinic was opposite an apartment block and at night it was easy to see what was happening inside. Pretty soon these two girls in one of the apartments had sussed out the captive audience and were performing nightly, sniffing drugs off each other's naked bodies and performing X-rated scenes. Alan said everyone was hanging off the bars screaming at them, completely freaked out (wouldn't be like that later in the Priory for me, unfortunately).

Alan certainly wasn't against me or pro-Barney/Other Two – he was neutral – but it did mean that I didn't have a natural ally on the team, and Barney began to say that, again, the bass was 'getting in the way of the vocal' on many of the tracks.

I'd be thinking, *Bloody hell, there's hardly any bass on them*, as the Sumner claw strayed to the fader, and unfortunately this fader fucking worked. He'd said it before – that the bass was getting in the way – and to me this was again a way of him establishing his hierarchy, with him and his vocals at the top, dictating how much bass and whatever else would appear on the tracks. You couldn't imagine it the other way round: me nudging down his vocal track.

'Ooh, I think there's a bit too much vocal on this, it's getting in the way of my bass ...'

I've often said that the magic of New Order was all that push-and-pull between the rock and electronic sides of the music, the yin and yang of Barney and me. But if Barney got his own way, the music would have lost that sense of internal conflict that made it so special, and from a purely musical point of view there was much less use of the bass as a counterpoint to the vocal. I had some great basslines on *Technique*: 'All the Way', 'Love Less', 'Guilty Partner', 'Run' and 'Round and Round' all have great parts, but believe me, they were hard-fought and very hard-won. There is a leaked tape of the basslines before the mixing which I did not hear for years, but when I did I had no doubt in my mind that the tracks would have sounded better with more bass. It came up time and time again, and 'don't upset Barney' became the new mantra. And I must admit it was tempting to give in because working under that dark shadow was not very nice at all.

The record followed the usual format of me sitting by the desk next to Mike for the recording and then Alan for the mixing. I am afraid to say that every time I picked up the bass the rest of them would retreat first to the vibe space upstairs then out the studio and then home. I think I could safely say that on all the electronic tracks the others never heard any of the bass parts until we came to mix the tracks months later, generally looking more shocked than delighted.

Once we had finished recording we came up with the idea of having a rave at Real World to say goodbye and wreck the joint. I just remember me and Jane leaving in the morning, party still in full swing at 10 a.m.

The album done, thank God.

Total cost: circa £450,000.

Despite everything *Technique* is a great record and I'm listening to it as I write. I'm very impressed. Just goes to show you don't have to get on at all to write great music.

Time to leave Real World and get back to the real world.

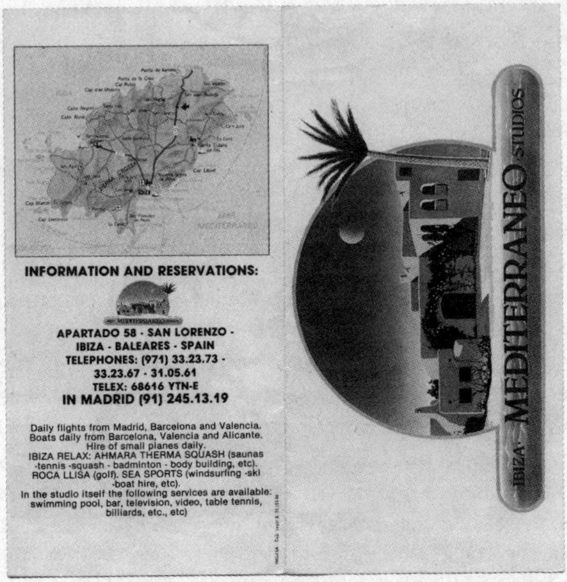
INFORMATION AND RESERVATIONS:
APARTADO 58 · SAN LORENZO ·
IBIZA · BALEARES · SPAIN
TELEPHONES: (971) 33.23.73 ·
33.23.67 · 31.05.61
TELEX: 68616 YTN-E
IN MADRID (91) 245.13.19
Daily flights from Madrid, Barcelona and Valencia.
Boats daily from Barcelona, Valencia and Alicante.
Hire of small planes daily.
IBIZA RELAX: AHMARA THERMA SQUASH (saunas -tennis -squash - badminton - body building, etc).
ROCA LLISA (golf). SEA SPORTS (windsurfing -ski -boat hire, etc).
In the studio itself the following services are available: swimming pool, bar, television, video, table tennis, billiards, etc., etc)
IBIZA · MEDITERRANEO · STUDIOS

IBIZA · MEDITERRANEO · STUDIOS
Home Studio
RECORDING

'Jetlag, Pedro'

The Manchester to which New Order returned was a very different place from the one they had left. During the summer of 1988, acid house had taken the UK by storm and nowhere was it more popular than in the cavernous spaces of the Haçienda, where it provided the soundtrack to the club's sold-out nights: 'Hot', which featured dry ice pumped into the club, dance podiums, and acid music played by the resident DJs Jon DaSilva and Mike Pickering; 'Nude', another acid house night, again with Mike Pickering DJing to an upfront crowd; and 'The Temperance Club', busy forging the indie-dance links that would come to define Madchester. Into this thrilling crucible of rock and dance would come New Order's 'Fine Time' single, the band's declaration of support for the new dance movement, which along with the Happy Mondays' Bummed album, would see indie-guitar-loving students discarding their long coats and scowls and taking to the dancefloor.

I had a couple of weeks to kick back and enjoy family life for a while while listening avidly to tales about the mayhem at the Haçienda before setting off to Brazil with New Order.

There was a great sense of expectation over these gigs. Sad to say, we had been tempted mainly by the money, a guarantee of over half a million pounds, which we needed desperately. All we had to do was keep an eye on the costs and the rest was straight in the coffers. Terry had flown over beforehand on a fact-finding, pre-production visit, and had called me from São Paulo. 'I'm in the biggest whorehouse I've ever seen! And they're all free. It's called Kilt Shows,' he squealed down the phone, excitedly, which pretty much set the whole tone for the tour to come.

The gigs were great. We were pretty big in England by now but here the crowds were huge and going absolutely nuts. I remember during one particular soundcheck changing my bass strings, rolling up the used string and throwing it over my shoulder into the empty auditorium. I heard a scuffling behind me on the floor but, thinking nothing of it, carried on doing the same with another. The noise increased. I turned around to see a crowd of people all fighting over the discarded strings, like they were diamonds. It wasn't because they were fans. They were just poor. There was so much poverty in Brazil, a massive divide between the rich and the poor. Tony used to say that New Order were a bunch of philistines, because when Durutti Column went abroad they'd get out the guidebooks and explore, whereas us lot just hung around hotels, clubs and restaurants with other Brits.

He had a point. We did do a lot of hanging around hotels, clubs and restaurants and not much exploring with guidebooks. But in Brazil you were taking your life in your hands if you went off the beaten track. Even the locals never used to stop at red traffic lights for fear of getting mugged.

I was still with Jane, so I didn't indulge in the hookers, but I did plenty of coke, which was so cheap over there we did it morning, noon and night. Not that there is a morning, noon and night when you're on coke. It all bleeds into one. The record company would be taking us to beautiful restaurants, but we'd get there, have a couple of beers and then the next thing you knew everybody was off snorting in the toilets. Nobody would eat. You can't eat. This beautiful food was coming out and nobody wanted to touch it. All the record company blokes were going, 'What's the matter with you guys? This is beautiful food.'

We were all like, 'Jetlag, Pedro, jetlag,' through gritted teeth.

The fact that the coke was cheap didn't stop the same old beefs from coming up. There were people who bought it, and people who didn't, who used to say, 'No way. When I start paying for it, that's when I'm an addict.' People you couldn't say no to. They'd walk into the crew room to find the crew chopping it out and say, 'Have you got a little one?' and they'd all be thinking, *Get your own, you tight twat*, but they'd have to give it up, and even they'd still end up arguing between themselves with the old 'you've had more than me' at five dollars a gram, like pirates. It really was hideous.

But, God, we were completely off it. Our last three nights in São Paulo were some of the wildest nights of my life. Unmentionable, unprintable things involving hookers hanging out of tenth-floor windows, private strip shows and flashing at the pool. One of the crew, Jerry, brought his to the party room and we watched as she collapsed, banging her head hard on a foot rail in the kitchen, knocking herself out cold.

'Jerry's whore has fell over,' said Rob, from his perch on the couch.

'Oops. Sorry, she's been up all night,' said Jerry.

Various hotel rooms full of coked-up hookers tore born-again Christians off their lofty perches. It was mayhem.

One night, I was laying into the coke while Tom was giving me a lecture about Jane. He started ranting at length about how my relationship with Jane – a 'mere' roadie – was going to be the death of me, the end of the group. As if that was all we had to worry about.

He was saying, 'It's going to cost you, you fucking fucker. You've got to get rid of her. Give her ten grand and tell her to fuck off.'

Tom paused long enough to go to the minibar to fetch another beer but – horror of horrors – the minibar was empty, which meant that – even more horror of horrors – we had to venture downstairs to the bar.

Crippled with paranoia, feeling like we wanted to be locked in a cupboard, we screwed up our courage and took the lift to the bar. About two o'clock in the morning, this was, and it was closed, the guy in the reception taking one look at us and waving his hands: 'No, sorry, señor, ees closed.'

Even though we were off our faces and desperate to return to the security of the room, we were even more desperate for beer. There was nothing else for it but to break into the bar. Doing that meant having to use the stairs or be seen coming out of the lift, so we got the lift back up to our floor then came down via the stairs, where Tom kept lookout while I took my shoes off and then, proper *Mission Impossible* style, slid down the stairs like a snake, then opened the door to the bar, slid along the floor on my belly and made the first of what turned out to be several trips in order to secure a total of – yes! – sixteen beers.

Thus fortified we returned to the hotel room where, without missing a beat, Tom resumed his rant about how I needed to dump Jane.

I didn't take his advice, though. Jane was ace. A real partner in crime.

On the last night in São Paulo, one of the crew, Blacky, had copped off with two hookers who supplied us with twenty grams for a hundred dollars. Everybody chowed down. On the hotel room wall hung a decorative plate with a swirl going round the inside of it, so we took the plate off the wall, laid the coke out on the swirl then passed it round. One of our entourage must have done about twelve inches of this swirl in one snort and, I swear to God, he looked like he was going die. It was really strong. He didn't speak for an hour. He just sat in a corner off his monkey.

One by one the partygoers dropped away until there was just me, Blacky and the two hookers left. We sat up all night, never stopping talking, rambling on and on about all kinds of shit. The hookers just sat there and never said a word. They were doing the stuff just the same as we were, but they never said a thing. We were leaving to fly home at midday, but at nine o'clock in the morning we were still chopping out lines.

'It's all gone,' said Blacky, and upended the envelope just to prove it – only for another five Gs to fall out.

Oh no. We had to do those as well. Which took about another hour. Then Blacky fell over and the two hookers dragged him into the bedroom by his legs, and I traipsed back to my room where I spent a jittery hour before having to leave for the flight home. Oh my God, if I'd had a gun I would have shot myself. I felt that awful. We virtually needed wheelchairs just to get us on the plane we were so fucked.

I suppose, looking back with the benefits of glorious hindsight as I'm now doing, Brazil was where I stopped doing drugs and drugs started doing me. What's the difference? Once, when coke had a hold on me, I went to score rather than have dinner with Quincy Jones and Nastassja Kinski. That's when you know it's got you by the balls – when you'd prefer to be with scuzzy dealers on Hollywood Boulevard than in a mansion with Quincy Jones and Nastassja Kinski. Did the others say anything? No. They sent me.

It was also at least partly responsible for splitting me up with Iris. Coming home from Brazil, our next and last gig of the year was at the G-Mex, supported by the Mondays and A Certain Ratio. The gig earned us £10,010, which was lucky because the party in the Haçienda afterwards, called Disorder, cost us ten grand, so we made a clear profit of ten pounds.

Just as Iris and I were about to leave G-Mex for Disorder, and somewhat ill-advisedly, I asked one of our crew to chop me out a line. Of course, Iris had no idea I was doing drugs and she went mad. I had forgotten. We went to the party, but it was no use. She took one look at everybody else and said, 'We're leaving.' We spent that night in separate rooms in the suite at the Midland Hotel that Rob had booked for us as a treat.

I guess the writing had been on the wall for Iris and me for a long time – our lifestyles were just too different. Just that we hadn't seen it properly until that night.

Mind you, it wasn't all bad. My son Jack was born the following September.

f:Xerox Telecopier 7020 : 1- 3-89 : 1:06PM : TRIAD ARTISTS→61 881 4152 # 2

TRIAD ARTISTS, INC.
TALENT AND LITERARY AGENCY

January 3, 1988

Rob Gretton
NEW ORDER
FAX # 011-4461-881-4152

Dear Rob:

Per our Brazilian discussions, here is a summary of what was agreed upon as it regards to the upcoming New Order U.S. tour.

There will be a maximum of 35 playdates divided into two legs. Leg one will commence approximately April 10-15 and will go until approximately May 7. It will consist of 15 dates starting in Florida and ending up in Seattle/Vancouver. There will then be a five week break, two weeks of which shall be a paid vacation in the B.V.I. for Barney. Vacations for Steven, Gillian and Peter have not been discussed but could be arranged.

The second leg shall consist of 20 dates, shall commence approximately June 15 and will go until July 18.

In regards to support, I believe that taking two support acts (ie. P.I.L. and Sugarcubes) would be extremely beneficial financially in the large outdoor venues. The difference between putting on a three act event similar to last year and a solitary support could be as much as $100,000-$200,000 and this is not an exaggeration. We would be sole star headliner (Unlike 1987).

The first leg, because of the type and size of the venues would need only one support act. If you have any questions or comments, please do not hesitate to call.

Warmest regards,

TRIAD ARTISTS, INC.

Marc Geiger

MG/mio
CC: Tom Atencio

10100 SANTA MONICA BOULEVARD, 16TH FLOOR • LOS ANGELES, CALIFORNIA 90067 • TELEPHONE 213-556-2727 • TELEX 6831753 TRIAD UW • EMAIL TRIAD-LA-US • FACSIMILE 2135570501
NEW YORK • LOS ANGELES

f:Xerox Telecopier 7020 ; 1- 3-89 ; 1:07PM ; TRIAD ARTISTS→61 881 4152 ;# 3

TRIAD ARTISTS, INC.
TALENT AND LITERARY AGENCY

NEW ORDER 1989
U.S TOUR Proposal

DATE	CITY	VENUE	CAP
Apr-08	San Juan PR	Roberto Clemente Coliseum	10000
Apr-11	Miami	Knight Center	5000
Apr-12	Tampa	Bayfront Auditorium	4800
Apr-13	Orlando/fill	Bob Carr Auditorium	4000
Apr-15	Atlanta	Southern Star Amphitheater	12500
Apr-16	Nashville	TPAC/tba	2400
Apr-17	New Orleans	Saenger Theater	3000
Apr-21	Houston	Southern Star Amphitheater	12000
Apr-22	Austin	Palmer Auditorium,Coliseum	tba
Apr-23	Dallas	Starplex Amphitheater	14000
Apr-25	Phoenix	Mesa Amphitheater	3800
Apr 27-28	Los Angeles	Universal Amphitheater	6251*2
May-01	Davis	Freeborn Hall	2200
May-02	Portland	Civic Auditorium	3000
May-03	Seattle	Paramount Theater	2978
May-04	Vancouver	Orpheum	2700
Jun-15	Washington DC	Merriwether/Patriot Ctr	15134
Jun-16	Philadelphia	Mann Center	13149
Jun-18	Long Island	Jones Beach / Nassau Coliseum	10370
Jun-20	New York 7/5-9	Madison Square Garden	15000+
Jun-24	Bristol CT	Lake Compounce	20000
Jun-25	Boston	Great Woods	15000
Jun-27	Montreal	Forum/tba	12134
Jun-28	Ottawa	CCE/tba	18000
Jun-29	Toronto	CNE/Forum	23000
Jul-01	Pittsburgh	Syria Mosque/Palumbo	5800
Jul-02	Cleveland	Nautica Stage	4200
Jul-03	Detroit	Meadowbrook/Pine Knob	15134
Jul-05	Columbus	Vets Memorial Auditorium	3944
Jul-07	Chicago	Poplar Creek/Pavillion	23000
Jul-09	Minneapolis	Northrup Auditorium	4800
Jul-11	Denver	Red Rocks/Fiddlers	18000
Jul-13	Salt Lake City	Park West	10000+
Jul-15	Berkeley	Shoreline Amphitheater	20000
Jul-17	San Diego	Sports Arena	12000
Jul-18	Irvine	Irvine/Meadows	15000

as of 1/3/89

TECHNIQUE TRACK BY TRACK

'Fine Time': 4.42

But I never met a girl with all her own teeth …

Another sequencer *tour de force*. Years later Sarah (Barney's wife) told me it was about her, because she never had a filling until she was twenty-five, and Barney was dead impressed. The Barry White vocal is him slowed down. God knows where his mind was at with that. But it is unique. Post Amnesia morning session, Barney dragging Mike out of bed. Sheep at the end complete our animal-noise fixation.

'All the Way': 3.22

I don't give a damn about what other people say …

Providing a strong contrast to 'Fine Time', but another classic New Order song. Great guitar and strong bassline drive a self-discovery tune. A strong vocal from Barney, now working on them alone, sadly.

'Love Less': 2.58

The keeper of a major key, I lived in a town called Liberty …

Very countrified. Conjuring up a great summer feel. I remember being in Heaton Park with the kids once and some guy walked past with a huge ghetto blaster on his shoulder with this wonderful music blaring out. I had to know who it was. I ran over saying, 'Who's playing, mate? What tune is that?' He went wide-eyed and said, 'Hooky, it's you. It's "Love Less" off *Technique*.'

'Round and Round': 4.29

It's driving me wild, makes me act like child …

NO on a disco trip. I squeeze in on a programming feast, you can practically hear the fader going up and down, down, down. A great dance tune, the Prophet 5 earning its keep. But can anyone sing '*baby*' and make it sound good?

'Guilty Partner': 4.44

Why the sun don't shine in the season …

To me this LP has the best vocal performances of them all, Barney sounding very relaxed and confident. This record gels well with the acoustic tracks balancing the electronic. Considering we were absolutely oblivious to everything and each other, quite an achievement.

'Run': 4.26

So what's the use in complaining when you've got everything you need …

Strong and ballsy, and the obvious choice for the first single. Dreamy middle eight with Barney's strings plucking at your heart. Me and Alan Meyerson created this drop in the studio doing it 'live' – dub style. The whole album has such a summery feel. Thank you, Ibiza. In my more paranoid phases I thought the 'tan for nothing' was about me – he was always taking the piss about how tanned I was.

'Mr Disco': 4.20

Our rendezvous just ended in sorrow, without you there's no tomorrow …

European disco. Lyrically we pay homage to the sun. Bringing nights in San Antonio back to mind. With Yamaha sounds to the fore, Steve's syndrums and percussion breaks make a welcome return, the bass bleats in the distance unsuccessfully begging to be heard.

'Vanishing Point': 5.14

It be like a sleeping demon, listen can you hear him weeping …

In my opinion the best track on the album. Strong musically and lyrically, I had the usual problems but overcame them, getting some great parts. Very dreamlike qualities, the 1980s synths sounding great. My life was a holiday. I went to the point of no return … and returned. Thank God.

'Dream Attack': 5.13

Is it really such a sin, if it is then I'll give in …

My nemesis for this particular album: try as hard as I could, I just could not better the track. I spent days on it. I thought, *He's beaten me, the bastard.*

A sour note to end on, I know.

TIMELINE NINE
FEBRUARY–DECEMBER 1988

February 1988

Salvation! soundtrack released (Les Disques du Crépuscule).
Featuring:

'Salvation Theme'	2.14
'Touched by the Hand of God'	5.02
'Let's Go'	3.44
'Sputnik'	2.31
'Skullcrusher'	2.52

24–27 February 1988

New Order play 'True Faith' at the San Remo Palarock Festival, Italy.

March 1988

New Order performed before the Duke and Duchess of York at the Stock Exchange nightclub, Los Angeles, during UKLA week. UKLA was a week of events meant to strengthen business ties between the USA and Great Britain.

28 April 1988

New Order: 'Blue Monday 1988'
(FAC 73R)
Seven-inch track list:

'Blue Monday 1988'	4.09
'Beach Buggy'	4.18

Twelve-inch track list:

'Blue Monday 1988'	7.09
'Beach Buggy' (full length)	6.52

Run-out groove one: *Years from now …*
Run-out groove two: *we'll laugh about this*

Recorded in Britannia Row and Advision Studios, London.
Written and produced by New Order.
Production supervisor on remix: Quincy Jones.
Additional production and remix by John Potoker for Direct Eject Inc. LA.
Mix engineer by Tokes.
'Beach Buggy' remixed by Michael Johnson.
Entered UK chart on 7 May 1988, remaining in the charts for 11 weeks, its peak position was number 3.

May 1988

Happy sixth birthday, the Haçienda.

May, June and July 1988

New Order decamp to Mediterraneo Studio, Ibiza.

13 June 1988

Joy Division: 'Atmosphere'
(FAC 213)
Seven-inch track list:

'Atmosphere'	4.11
'The Only Mistake'	4.15

Twelve-inch track list:

'Atmosphere'	4.11
'The Only Mistake'	4.15
'The Sound of Music'	3.53

Run-out groove one: *Good men are born in Heaven!*
Run-out groove two: *Great men are born in Hell!*

Recorded at Cargo Studios and Strawberry Studios, Stockport, Manchester.
Mixed at Britannia Row Studios, London.
Engineered by Chris Nagle.
Produced by Martin Hannett.
Art direction by Peter Saville.
Designed by Brett Wickens and Peter Saville Associates.
Photography by Trevor Key.
Entered UK chart on 18 June 1989, remaining in the charts for 5 weeks, its peak position was number 34.

18 July 1988

Joy Division: *Substance*

(FACT 250)

Track list:

'Warsaw'	2.25
'Leaders of Men'	2.35
'Digital'	2.49
'Autosuggestion'	6.07
'Transmission'	3.35
'She's Lost Control'	4.45
'Incubation'	2.51
'Dead Souls'	4.53
'Atmosphere'	4.09
'Love Will Tear Us Apart'	3.25

Appendix track list:

'No Love Lost'	3.43
'Failures'	3.43
'Glass'	3.51
'From Safety to Where'	2.26
'Novelty'	3.59
'Komakino'	3.51
'These Days'	3.25

Run-out groove one: *Why did the chicken?*
Run-out groove two: *Why DID the chicken?*

Recorded in Strawberry Studios, Stockport, Manchester, Britannia Row and Advision Studios, London.
Engineered by Chris Nagle.
Produced by Martin Hannett.
Designed by Brett Wickens and Peter Saville Associates.
Entered UK chart on 23 July 1988, remaining in the charts for 8 weeks, its peak position was number 7.

July 1988

Bright Lights, Big City soundtrack released, featuring New Order's 'True Faith'.

August, September and October 1988

New Order decamp to the Real World studios in Bath to record *Technique*.

October 1988

The Stone Roses: 'Elephant Stone'

Track list:
'Elephant Stone' (12″ version)
'Elephane Stone' (7″ version)
'Full Fathom Five'
'The Hardest Thing in the World'

Produced by Peter Hook.
Mixed by John Leckie.

25 November 1988

New Order play Maracanãzinho, Rio de Janeiro, Brazil.

28 November 1988

New Order: 'Fine Time'
(FAC 223)

Seven-inch track list:

'Fine Time' (edit M. Johnson)	3.08
'Don't Do It'	4.36

Twelve-inch track list:

'Fine Time' (full length)	4.42
'Don't Do It' (full length)	4.36
'Fine Line'	4.43

Run-out groove one: *Read the signs, read the signs!*
Run-out groove two: ... *they tell us everything!*

Recorded at Mediterraneo Studio, Ibiza, and Real World Studios, Box, Bath.
Engineered by Michael Johnson.
Mixed by Alan Meyerson.
Produced by New Order.
Designed by Peter Saville Associates and Trevor Key (after a painting by Richard Bernstein).

Twelve-inch Remix track list:

'Fine Time' (Silk mix)	6.15
'Fine Time' (messed around)	4.35

Recorded at Mediterraneo Studio, Ibiza, and Real World Studios, Box, Bath.
Mixed at Tanglewood Recording Studios, Chicago.
Remixed/engineered by Steve 'Silk' Hurley.
Produced by New Order.
Designed by Peter Saville Associates and Trevor Key (after a painting by Richard Bernstein).
Entered UK chart on 10 December 1988, remaining in the charts for 8 weeks, its peak position was number 11.

The CD single featured the seven-inch edit, both Hurley remixes and 'Don't Do It'.

28 November 1988

New Order play Gigantinho Gym, Porto Alegre, Brazil.

30 November 1988

New Order play Olympia, São Paulo, Brazil.

December 1988

Married to the Mob soundtrack released, featuring New Order's 'Bizarre Love Triangle'.

1–3 December 1988

New Order play Ibirapuera, São Paulo, Brazil.

17 December 1988

New Order play Manchester Exhibition Centre, Manchester, supported by Happy Mondays and A Certain Ratio.

Aftershow Party: 'Disorder' (FAC 208).

'Rob's idea was for a huge Christmas party to end what had been a "*difficult*" year. He spent a fortune doing up the Haçienda's basement, turning it into a Christmas wonderland. There was every kind of drug on offer and our friends and aquaintances turned out in force. Twinny later told me that the toilets overflowed in the basement about midnight, leaving a thick black sludge an inch deep on the floor. The last thing he remembers is his kidneys aching from over-consumption of ecstasy and Barney kicking and punching him in them repeatedly, saying, "It'll make you feel better." Later he woke up at 10 a.m. on Granada TV's steps with no recollection of what had happened before, or how he got there.

'From here on the toilets overflowing would be a regular occurrence, leading to what was known as "The Haçienda Rim", an inch-long black stain around the bottom of clubbers' trousers that no amount of washing could shift.'

'It's a New Order gig, this, not a Revenge gig'

The release of *Technique* in January 1989 was a classic case of good news/bad news.

The good news?

It went to number one.

Not just 'to number one' but straight in at number one. Factory, after years of refusing to do any promotion followed by years of formulating grand plans for it, finally came good and actually did some: 'Advertising *Technique*' was Peter Saville's creation, which you had to admire as a very clever play on words, even if, like me, you weren't that keen on the actual *idea* of advertising *Technique* and thought it was yet another move away from the principles we once held so dear.

Either way, that lovely little cherub that Peter and Trevor Key came up with for the cover soon became a regular sight on billboards and fly-posting sites, not just in Manchester, but all over the country. I remember Tony pricing up the billboards for it. They cost £2,000 each for a week, and he bought 150. 'A great investment,' he said. Never one to do anything by halves, was Tony.

There were also four fifteen-second TV adverts, costing God knows how much. I felt nostalgic for the days when we stuck two fingers up to established music industry models of promotion and marketing; the days when, as members of Joy Division, Factory paid us for gluing sand-paper onto Durutti Column records with the single aim of destroying all the other records in the buyer's collection.

Which leads me on to the bad news. With the success of the album and the outlay on promotion came new ways of doing things.

Specifically: everything was being decided by committee. Even the song titles were being decided that way.

In the old days, mainly me and Rob came up with the titles for songs, but suddenly we were all having to sit round and talk about and decide them collectively; even Gillian had found a voice.

What happened? As well as the interminable meetings, we ended up with these insipid bloodless titles that I just didn't like: 'All the Way', 'Love Less', 'Dream Attack', 'Mr Disco' ... Ugh.

I mean, maybe it's just me. Maybe I'm just being an old fart about it all, but to me they sounded watered down; they actually sounded as though they'd been decided by committee. Same with every other decision we made. We'd have to sit round a huge table, upwards of twenty of us, with representatives from Factory, promotions, press and radio, and whoever was making the tea, and somebody would say, 'Right, what should the next single be?' And everybody would have a different opinion.

I found myself yearning for the days when Rob was his intimidating, bombastic self, when we would have made all the decisions and told everybody to fuck off if they didn't like it. I'd spent most of the late 70s in T. J. Davidson's freezing old warehouse, working on Joy Division songs with Ian, Barney and Steve. Ten years later I was sitting at a boardroom table, having only just survived being written out of the album. Call me a sentimental old bugger, but I knew where I was happiest.

We fucked off to France around the time the album came out. We'd been feeling guilty about concentrating all of our touring efforts on America and latterly Brazil, so we thought we ought to show a bit more love to Europe. After that Rob was making plans for a huge tour of the States, our biggest yet, coming up later in the year, while us lot concentrated mainly on our solo projects.

Meanwhile, I was having a difficult time at home. Iris and I had moved from Moston to Blackley, which wasn't far. Trouble was, the house needed a lot of work and with Iris being pregnant it was decided she should live at her parents while I'd stay in the house. It drove a big wedge between us. I was working every day on Revenge at Suite 16 and the rest of the time was off my head at the Haçienda. My lifestyle was changing too much. My old life was fading fast.

It was around that time that Tony Wilson invited the group on his Granada arts programme, *The Other Side of Midnight*. He'd been listening to the demos for *Technique* and picked out a track he really liked with the provisional title 'The Happy One', a track with one synthesiser sequence and a nice 'Hooky' bassline, and for some reason, even though the song wasn't on the album – and never got an official release – Tony wanted us to play it on *The Other Side of Midnight*.

Them lot wouldn't do it. I can't remember the exact reasons given, but the long and short of it was that they were enjoying being distanced from New Order, even at this stage. The fact that I was prepared to go on was a bit of a miracle in the circumstances.

But anyway, when it became clear that I was expected to do this without my jolly bandmates, I came up with the idea of turning it into a Revenge appearance, our first, and I called up Dave Hicks and CJ and set to work on the bare bones of 'The Happy One'. We stayed up for two nights, writing an intro where Dave played guitar and CJ played keyboards, as well as a load of programmed stuff.

I gave Tony a tape of it. He loved it and said, 'Yes. You're booked, let's do it.' So we got all the equipment together from Suite 16 and trooped over to Granada Studios, only to find Rob waiting for us.

He pushed his glasses up his nose. 'Eh, Hooky, I've been thinking about this, this Revenge thing you're doing.'

'Yeah?'

'Well, it's a New Order gig, this, not a Revenge gig. You can't do it. You can't do it with Revenge.'

'Well, if it's a New Order gig,' I said, 'then where are the other three? I'll tell you where they fucking are. Barney's in the studio with Johnny Marr and Neil Tennant, and Steve and Gillian are scratching their arses in their farmhouse in Macclesfield. Us lot have been up for two nights arranging it, rewriting it, the whole bit. We're going to play it.'

'No,' he said, 'no, look, I can't let you do it, Hooky. You can't do it. I'm not letting you do it.'

The thing about Rob was that he lived and breathed New Order. The group meant everything to him. He was so wound up, so worried that this appearance would add fuel to the rumours that we had split up. He insisted that it was a New Order song and that they should play it; he couldn't let Revenge play it. There was no getting round the fact that the song we were about to play had started life as a New Order composition. It looked as if he was just about to start begging me not to do it.

Meantime, Hicksy and CJ were getting more and more pissed off, while Tony was wondering aloud who was going to play the fucking song. There was an awful lot of shouting in the Granada studio that afternoon, but in the end, what we decided was that Dave Hicks and CJ would have to sit it out while I played the song by myself. We didn't have time to rewrite or edit the material we'd prepared so what was broadcast was the song we'd worked up as Revenge, just without CJ and Dave Hicks playing on it, which sounded and looked odd – as you'll see if you can be arsed to look it up on YouTube.

I felt sorry for Rob. He was prepared to lie down across the studio door rather than let us play this New Order song as Revenge, and you've got to respect that. It broke his heart to see the members of the group going off in separate directions. Mine too in some ways. What used to freak him out was the fact that apart we were never as good as when we were together. We would definitely have been 'as big as them Irish twats' if we'd kept on working the way we had during *Low-Life* and even *Brotherhood*. He was sure of it. Maybe he was right. We will never know.

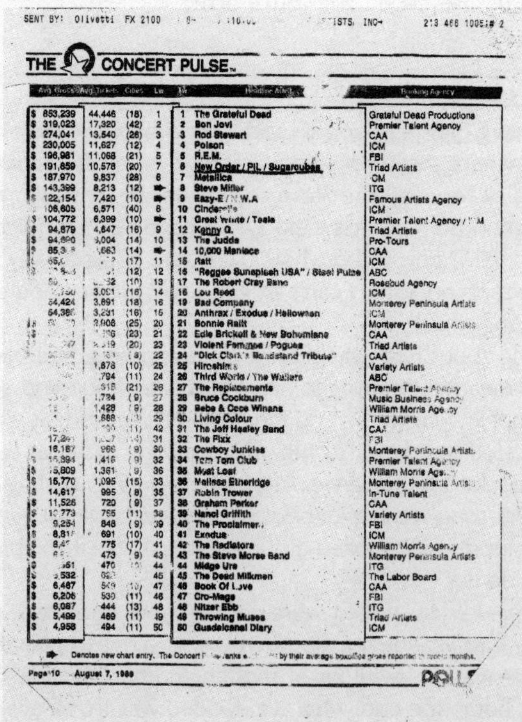

SENT BY: Olivetti FX 2100 [illegible] ISTS, INC- 2:3 466 1005;# 2

THE CONCERT PULSE™

Avg. Gross	Avg. Tickets	Cities	Lw	Tw	Headline Act	Booking Agency
$ 853,239	44,446	(18)	1	1	The Grateful Dead	Grateful Dead Productions
$ 319,023	17,320	(42)	2	2	Bon Jovi	Premier Talent Agency
$ 274,041	13,540	(26)	3	3	Rod Stewart	CAA
$ 230,005	11,627	(12)	4	4	Poison	ICM
$ 196,981	11,068	(21)	5	5	R.E.M.	FBI
$ 191,859	10,578	(20)	7	6	New Order / PIL / Sugarcubes	Triad Artists
$ 187,970	9,837	(28)	6	7	Metallica	ICM
$ 143,399	8,213	(12)	➡	8	Steve Miller	ITG
$ 122,154	7,420	(10)	➡	9	Eazy-E / N.W.A	Famous Artists Agency
$ 106,605	6,571	(40)	8	10	Cinde[illegible]	ICM
$ 104,772	6,399	(10)	➡	11	Great White / Tesla	Premier Talent Agency / [illegible]
$ 94,879	4,647	(16)	9	12	Kenny G.	Triad Artists
$ [illegible]	[illegible]	(14)	10	13	The Judds	Pro-Tours
$ [illegible]	[illegible]	(14)	➡	14	10,000 Maniacs	CAA
[illegible]	[illegible]	(17)	11	15	Ratt	ICM
[illegible]	[illegible]	(12)	12	16	"Reggae Sunsplash USA" / Steel Pulse	ABC
[illegible]	[illegible]	(10)	13	17	The Robert Cray Band	Rosebud Agency
[illegible]	[illegible]	(16)	14	18	Lou Reed	ICM
[illegible]	3,891	(18)	16	19	Bad Company	Monterey Peninsula Artists
[illegible]	[illegible]	(16)	15	20	Anthrax / Exodus / Helloween	ICM
[illegible]	[illegible]	(25)	20	21	Bonnie Raitt	Monterey Peninsula Artists
[illegible]	[illegible]	(23)	21	22	Edie Brickell & New Bohemians	CAA
[illegible]	[illegible]	(20)	23	23	Violent Femmes / Pogues	Triad Artists
[illegible]	[illegible]	(8)	22	24	"Dick Clark's Bandstand Tribute"	CAA
[illegible]	1,678	(10)	25	25	Hiroshima	Variety Artists
[illegible]	[illegible]	(11)	24	26	Third World / The Wailers	ABC
[illegible]	[illegible]	(21)	26	27	The Replacements	Premier Talent Agency
[illegible]	1,724	(9)	27	28	Bruce Cockburn	Music Business Agency
[illegible]	1,428	(9)	28	29	Bebe & Cece Winans	William Morris Agency
[illegible]	[illegible]	[illegible]	29	30	Living Colour	Triad Artists
[illegible]	[illegible]	(11)	42	31	The Jeff Healey Band	CAA
[illegible]	[illegible]	[illegible]	31	32	The Fixx	FBI
$ 16,187	966	(9)	30	33	Cowboy Junkies	Monterey Peninsula Artists
$ [illegible]	1,416	(9)	32	34	Tom Tom Club	Premier Talent Agency
$ [illegible]	1,361	(9)	36	35	Meat Loaf	William Morris Agency
$ 15,770	1,095	(15)	33	36	Melissa Etheridge	Monterey Peninsula Artists
$ 14,617	995	(8)	35	37	Robin Trower	In-Tune Talent
$ 11,526	720	(9)	37	38	Graham Parker	CAA
$ [illegible]	[illegible]	(11)	38	39	Nanci Griffith	Variety Artists
$ 9,254	848	(9)	39	40	The Proclaimers	FBI
$ [illegible]	691	(10)	40	41	Exodus	ICM
$ [illegible]	775	(17)	41	42	The Radiators	William Morris Agency
$ [illegible]	473	(9)	43	43	The Steve Morse Band	Monterey Peninsula Artists
$ [illegible]	470	[illegible]	44	44	Midge Ure	ITG
$ [illegible]	[illegible]	[illegible]	45	45	The Dead Milkmen	The Labor Board
$ 6,467	[illegible]	(10)	47	46	Book Of Love	CAA
$ 6,206	530	(11)	46	47	Cro-Mags	FBI
$ 6,087	444	(13)	48	48	Nitzer Ebb	ITG
$ 5,499	469	(11)	49	49	Throwing Muses	Triad Artists
$ 4,958	494	(11)	50	50	Guadalcanal Diary	ICM

➡ Denotes new chart entry. The Concert [illegible] ranks [illegible] by their average boxoffice gross reported [illegible] months.

Page 10 August 7, 1989

'This was the tour that broke us'

Barney was never a bigger pain in the arse than when we were touring. It was a vicious circle. He was miserable, so nobody wanted to hang out with him, which made him feel isolated, and as a result he got even more miserable, meaning people wanted to hang out with him even less.

He once said to me, 'Do you know what it's like to sit in your room and have nobody phone you?'

'No,' I said, 'I don't, and you shouldn't be such a twat, should you. Then someone might phone you.'

Steve and Gillian had each other. I had the crew. But Barney had nobody. He was and probably still is a creature of the studio; that's where he's happiest, being waited on hand and foot in a five-star prison. So while the idea of a very lucrative 35-date American tour, with the second leg featuring Public Image Ltd and the Sugarcubes, sounded like a bloody good way to spend a significant part of 1989 to me, to Barney it was a lot of a drag. A complete and total interference.

As a result he was even more of a pain in the arse on this tour than he'd ever been before. Factor in the huge amount of drugs we were all doing, and you can see why this was the tour that broke us.

It began in Puerto Rico. Phil Rodrigues was in charge, a promoter we had met in Brazil. To get there we'd been forced to take a cheap airline, Joke Air or whatever from Miami, and, I'm not kidding, there were people on the plane sitting holding chickens on their laps. In addition to that, they were a pretty fiery crowd. Echo and the Bunnymen would have fitted in just fine with this lot, and because the stewardess was taking so long to come down the aisle with drinks, a bunch of guys got up, stole the trolley and started handing them around. When the stewardesses kicked off about it, the guys got a newspaper, balled it up and set fire to it in the aisle. All us lot were sitting at the back of the plane, absolutely terrified, desperate to land, as fights broke out all around us.

Puerto Rico was really good, a proper holiday destination. We were staying in a Marriott hotel by the lakes and for some reason – maybe I was feeling guilty about him being left on his own – me and Barney went on a day trip with Tom Atencio and spent the day whizzing around on jet skis. I was the only one not to fall off. That night, we were taken to one of the most hair-raising gigs I've ever attended. It was a Puerto Rican hip-hop concert. There were a few gangs present, and as a result loads of fighting broke out.

It was a theme that seemed to continue at our own gig, which was a fairly miserable affair. Next thing you know, we were flying back to Miami, where we commenced the tour proper. That night, after our concert at the Knight Center, I ended up back in my room with Frank Callari. John Robie was there too. He and I had patched it up by then. Although I still thought he was a bit annoying, we were friends and, sure enough, that night he was on typical form.

Meanwhile Frank was being his usual hilarious self, spilling the beans, getting all confessional. Coke is a terrible honesty drug, and even though I've dished out some embarrassing truths myself a few times (one such occasion coming up in the next few pages, unfortunately), I've been on the receiving end more times than I care to remember. I'd be begging people to shut up. 'Stop ... telling me this story ... about being abused by your teacher/dog. Please, just stop!'

Gradually I became aware of Frank rustling his wrap. He was rustling it so loudly I'm surprised Ian McCulloch didn't turn up. The reason was we'd run out, and because Frank was off his head he started insisting that with it all gone we should go to bed. 'Come on, Hooky, you go to bed. Me and John are leaving. Come on, Robie, let's fuck off ... now.'

And then, all of a sudden, just as the night looked as though it was grinding to a halt, I discovered I had three ounces in my jacket.

Oh my God. Baggies out on the table, credit cards out, shit everywhere. We were still going at five or six o'clock in the morning when I decided I needed a piss. Now, the thing about charlie is that when you're on it you don't really piss, and then when you do at last go, you're there for ages. So I was standing in my hotel room toilet, marathon-pissing, until after a while I became aware that something wasn't quite right. There was something a bit weird going on, like the floor was moving – as though I'd finally achieved godlike status and was walking on water.

Next thing I knew I looked to my left and saw my case float past the bathroom door. Two seconds later it dawned on me that the place was more than flooded. The room was submerged in about two inches of water.

I ran out into the lounge, trying to tell the other two what was wrong. We came to the conclusion that we must have left a tap on, but no, there was no tap running anywhere.

Just then came a knock at the door. We all looked at each other. There was a lot of coke in a bag on the table, shit everywhere, the room under inches of water and, as far as we were concerned, the police at the door.

'Right,' said Frank, 'don't panic.'

So we immediately started panicking. For some reason, I started opening and closing my case. Frank was jumping on the bed, all twenty stone of him, Robie stood paddling as the blood drained from his face.

Again came the knock. 'Señor, we can hear you in there, please open up.'

Robie tossed me a towel for wiping the table. I hid the remaining coke. All of us sweating like a dyslexic on *Countdown*.

The knocking was more insistent now so I had no choice but to open the door. In the corridor stood about six Mexicans, all clutching big spanners.

'Señor, you have a leak, we must come in, shut water off, stop leak. Four floors flooded.'

Me, Robie and Frank retreated to a corner of the room, standing there wide-eyed and trembling, 'hanging', as we say in Manchester, off our faces and twisted up with paranoia as the Mexicans tore into the room and ripped part of the wall away to get to a stopcock.

Two minutes later they were gone, but by this time I'd had enough. It gets you like that sometimes. You suddenly have a meltdown. Frank had earlier, and now it was my turn.

'No, lads, my head's gone. I've had enough. I've got to get to bed.'

It was Frank who pointed out that there was water on the floor, but I had an idea. I got my bag packed, got the three ounces of Charlie and went down to the bus and knocked on the door. The drivers have to stay on all night, poor sods, and this one opened up, recoiling in horror at the way I looked, all twisted and coked off my face, and then let me in.

And that was the first night of the tour.

'Turns out the chiropodist was a New Order fan'

Right from the word go, there was no doubt whatsoever that we had come to party. We even shipped out a proper flight-cased DJ rig designed by Ozzy all the way from England, with sound system, smoke, dry ice and the works so that every aftershow party turned into a full-on rave.

In Texas we met up with a 21-year-old dealer called Troy, who travelled with us and supplied the entire tour with ecstasy and coke. He was a lovely young boy, round and cuddly and very unaffected by it all. He even used to stroke his face with a little blanket like Linus in *Charlie Brown*. That only changed when Troy went off to do a deal that involved swapping ecstasies, 50,000 of the little buggers, for a De Tomaso Pantera car. Only, when he got there, the guy pulled out a gun and took the tablets, leaving him to return home with nothing. Troy was pissed off but his partner persuaded him to take out a contract on the guy who'd stiffed them, and he ended up trying to employ an undercover DEA agent and got busted. The police raided his house and found enough to put him away for thirty years. And that was the end of that.

He was a great lad, though, Troy was. It was largely thanks to him that we spent the entire US tour with a suitcase full of at least three hundred ecstasies and a fair bit of coke. Me, I went off E in America. I'd developed a bit of tolerance by then and besides, the stuff in the USA was different, much more harsh and not as loved-up. Plus, the coke was on tap. We all had little dispensing bottles, the kind you stick up your nose to deliver a shot without having to chop it out. Terry was disappointed with the amount his dispensed so he ended up boring a bigger hole in order to get more per hit. 'Turbocharged,' he used to say it was. 'Here, have a hit on mine, it's turbocharged!'

Everybody was dead generous when there was heaps of it hanging around; there was none of that hoarding it or drug cliques forming. It was all like, 'Wahey, have some of mine! I got tons!' It's only later when the stuff gets a bit thin on the ground that you start worrying about doling it out.

Throwing Muses were with us at the beginning of that tour and I spent the whole time trying it on with Tanya Donelly, who was gorgeous and (I thought at the time) really flirty with me. Oh, but then, in New Orleans, it came my turn to do the cocaine-truth-drug thing, and in my infinite wisdom I decided to tell her what a flirty prick-tease she was being. I mean, I think I actually used those words as well. Worse, I actually meant it as a compliment.

Oh, how I regretted that the next morning. In fact, I regretted it that very moment, because she got up and ran off in tears, and her boyfriend – yes, there was a boyfriend present – looked like he wanted to chin me. It was only because I was so obviously off my face that he didn't land one on me there and then. I could have shot myself the next day. I felt so bad that I'd upset her. If I ever saw her again I'd die of embarrassment.

The tour rumbled on. We were big by now. A huge touring unit, forty-plus people with a dozen trucks and two buses. There was no driving little vans, no driving at all. We were scooped up, put in a coach, taken to a hotel, scooped into the hotel, scooped out into cars and to the show. And every night after the show would be the big rave, a coked-up, pissed-up orgy, basically.

By now we were selling even more merchandise, and the money we were earning was unbelievable. Don't forget, we were playing stadiums holding between 23,000 and 35,000 people. They did a head count and estimated that the audience was spending an average of $120 per head just on New Order T-shirts. The money was phenomenal. Tom Atencio, who'd spent years trying to persuade us to sell merchandise, only to go against our famous principles – 'It's all self-glorifying bollocks, Tom' – was walking around like a man with two dicks. Some nights he would run into the dressing room to tell us we'd just sold $350,000 worth of merchandise on one gig. You'd be stumbling around a hotel room with all these partially clad women, off your head, knowing you'd just earned a fortune, and you'd think, *Bloody hell*, in the words of the George Best story, *where did it all go wrong?*

The band and management had moved away from the crew. As I recounted earlier, there was no way they could afford to eat or drink in the hotels we stayed in, so they had gone to budget hotel chains. Traditionally I'd always spent more time with the crew than with the other lot, and as the divide grew I took to going on their bus for a while to keep

Jane company. Christ, that was an education – an awful education. The American crew hated the English crew and the English crew hated the American crew. There were all sorts of little cliques and hierarchies going on. The pettiness we inflicted on each other as a group had infected the crew too. In a meeting Barney told me that he thought the crew were 'totally unprofessional', which I thought was hilarious, so I told Terry, who then had T-shirts printed up. 'Neworder Posse Totally Unprofessional', they read. Barney went mad, insisting that if the crew wanted shirts they should pay for them themselves. They were two dollars each. It almost reared into a major incident when Terry went all shop-steward and threatened to strike. Barney relented when I said I'd pay for them, fuck it. On the back Terry had put the crew mantra: 'Pussy pussy pussy on the table table table, get it get it get it while you're able able able', which just about summed up how ridiculous the whole thing was.

We had this one roadie, Jonny Hugo, who's one of the best in the world. One night, at the end of a gig, Barney went to smash yet another guitar, something he was making a habit of on this tour. He launched it high into the air and stalked off without even looking where it was going to land. At the same time Jonny appeared, walking in from the other side of the stage, caught it, turned round, and walked straight back off. It was magic. Absolute perfection.

Best roadie moment ever.

Still, inter-crew relations being what they were, Jonny had an on-going beef with the keyboard roadie, an old mate of ours called Stuart 'Jammer' James, who had actually produced a Joy Division session for Piccadilly Radio in Manchester in 1979. Their beef ended up with Jonny dropping Jammer on his head. Later that evening I came across Jammer in the bus, lying there, dead still and as white as a sheet.

'What's the matter with you?'

'Oh, nothing, I'm all right,' he squeaked.

'Fuck off. You look terrible. What's the matter?'

'Jonny dropped me on me head. But I'll be all right, just leave me here for a bit and I'll be OK.'

'No, mate,' I said, 'you look fucked.' This was me off my face, after four coke ciggies in the shower after the gig, not exactly in the best position to be giving out diagnoses, but believe you me, he looked absolutely terrible, so bad that I went back inside and confronted Jonny.

'What the fuck have you done?'

'Well, he was annoying me, so I dropped him on his head.'

'Well he's out there in the bus looking like he's dead.'

'Oh fuck, really?'

I phoned Jammer an ambulance. Turned out he'd cracked three of his ribs. I'm not saying I saved his life but . . . well, actually, yes, I did save his life, the paramedics said so: if we hadn't phoned an ambulance then in all likelihood one of his broken ribs would have punctured his lung and killed him. Years later, when he was tour-managing the Chemical Brothers, I phoned up Sarge, our security guy who also worked the door at the Apollo, for six guest list places at the Manchester Apollo.

'Jammer says you can have two,' relayed Sarge.

'Put him on the phone, mate,' says I.

Eventually: 'Hello, it's Jammer.'

'It's Hooky,' I said. 'Remember? The one who saved your life?'

'Sorry,' says Jammer. 'Six it is.'

Some people have very short memories, don't they?

There was a strict pecking order on the crew. Another night I joined a despondent-looking Jonny at the bar and asked what was wrong, only for it to turn out that someone had thrown a bottle that had hit him on the side of the head and everyone else just ignored it. The protagonist had been with us for years, right back to the Joy Division era, so naturally he was at the top of the pecking order and could get away with anything. What made it worse for the rest of them was that he was a complete insomniac, a situation made even worse by the fact that he was off his head on coke the whole time. Everybody would be on the bus wanting to get some kip before the next venue, and he'd be playing dub reggae at top volume and God help anyone who told him to turn it down. Apart from me, he wouldn't listen to anyone else.

Right at the bottom of the pecking order was poor old Jane, and I've no doubt that if she hadn't been my girlfriend, things would have been even worse for her. I mean, she could look after herself, but even so, it was pretty horrible the treatment. I found out later they had a daily competition to see who could be the first to make her cry.

Just like Barney's diva strops, it was a situation that should have been handled by management, but although Rob was a dab hand at stopping me debuting Revenge on Tony's show, he was busy being a shadow of his former self when it came to displaying the leadership qualities we needed. The roadies had been with us for so long, you see. They were our friends. This was something the Americans couldn't understand.

One of the American crew said to me, 'Can I just say that I really don't like the way your road crew treat you as a band.'

'What? What the fuck you going on about?'

'They seem to be going out of their way to spend and waste your money. I think you work hard, you should be enjoying the fruits of your labour and success, and not letting them waste it.'

'Fuck off,' I said.

What a bloody cheek, I thought, but familiarity had bred contempt.

Just like if anyone slagged off Gillian or Barney, I leaped to their defence and told whoever it was they should keep their opinions to themselves. But he was right.

Anecdote alert. One night I had to have the night off from partying. It's not very rock'n' roll but I've suffered with ingrowing toenails my entire life and you know what it's like: you have an ingrowing toenail and suddenly everybody finds it a magnet and steps on your feet all the time. So I told Andy that I wouldn't play out that night and booked an appointment with a chiropodist for the next day. We were leaving for the airport about midday, so the idea was that I would meet my appointment and then be picked up and taken to the airport.

So I get my poorly little foot seen to. Turns out the chiropodist was a New Order fan, so we got along famously. When we'd finished, I sat outside the office waiting for the car to arrive.

Only, it didn't come. This was in the days before mobile phones, of course, so I sat there like a lemon, getting more and more worried about missing the flight. In the end the chiropodist took pity on me and gave me a lift.

I hopped to the check-in desk, where I found a boarding pass waiting for me. 'You better hurry up, the flight's about to leave,' said the check-in lady, and, of course, the gate would be the furthest one, wouldn't it? So there I am, hopping through the airport with my foot bandaged, sweating like Jeremy Kyle without his bodyguards.

I got on with literally seconds to spare and all them lot are on the flight going, 'Wahey! He's turned up at last.' Bastards.

I blew up. 'Where was the fucking car, you twat? You were supposed to arrange a car to take me to the airport.'

But, of course, they'd been up the night before, on ecstasies like they were Smarties. Apparently, there was a personal record broken when fourteen girls ended up in a room. Complete mayhem.

'It's funny,' came the reply, 'because when I woke up, the phone was stuck to my head, my ear was all perforated, so it must have been there a while ...'

'That's when I phoned you, you twat, and told you to come and pick me up.'

'Oh dear. Dreadfully sorry about that.'

A sorry tale, but nothing compared to what had happened when the rest of the band were going through security. This was in the days when they hardly used to bother searching you, so we just took all the drugs in a briefcase. They had something like two hundred pills, a whole load of powdered E plus a load of coke in a bag. They were rushing, late as usual, and when the case was slammed on the belt it had opened and a huge puff of white powder exploded from it.

They shit themselves, flicked the catches to close it and then hauled it away, leaving behind a perfect outline of the case in white powder on the belt. How's that for dicing with death? Not only did they nearly leave the bass player, but they wasted a load of drugs at airport security too.

Me and Jane were having a great time. In the first flush of our relationship we'd finish the soundcheck, skip food in favour of a bit of alone time back at the hotel, and then sneak back after the supports. It was very exciting and I was very happy giving up completely on any of my normal aftershow activities.

We decided to drive off for a couple of days. We were still meeting 'in secret', but the fact was, most people knew. We hired a soft-top Mustang and drove to a little town on the Gulf of Mexico called Corpus Christi, then moved on to a small fishing village called Mustang Island. We checked into a motel and had a wonderful time riding horses on the beach, eating the freshest seafood, in this wonderful place. On the last night I woke early while the sun was just rising and shining in through the open blinds. Jane was still asleep. Looking at her, I realised there was something different. I had fallen in love. Bollocks. Almost overnight, things would never be the same again.

*

As the tour went on, Barney's moaning grew worse. Everything pissed him off. The grey wall pissed him off. The fact that it was raining pissed him off. The fact that it was too cold pissed him off. The fact that it was too hot pissed him off. Just being on tour pissed him off.

He used to stomp around the dressing room, moaning, 'I don't want to be here. I want to be at home.' Later on you'd see him off his head and heading back to his room or at the bar, partying with a couple of stunners, and you'd think, *Doesn't look like you hate it now, mate? Doesn't look like you want to be at home at all, funnily enough.* Perhaps he thought all that was just making the best of a bad situation.

One of the other things that pissed him off was the lack of hot food in the dressing room. Everybody else was like, 'Why the fuck does this twat want hot food in the dressing room?' We were on that much drugs we were hardly eating anyway; tumbleweeds would blow through catering, it was so quiet down there. But Barney had insisted on a big rider backstage incorporating hot snacks, not just for the gig but for the soundcheck too.

So what was the first thing Barney did when we got to America? He stopped coming to the soundchecks. 'They're boring, I don't want to do them. They piss me off.'

That was great for us. Any given situation is improved by Barney's absence, so we weren't bothered about that one bit. Everybody had bad memories of soundchecks where twatto would turn up and ruin it by sulking, stamping about, moaning, putting everyone on edge. As the tour wore on he developed a trick of attracting the attention of Charlie, our onstage soundman, by whistling down the microphone. Barney's one of those lucky people who can stick his fingers in his mouth and do a really loud whistle, and on stage it was like someone coming up and slapping you on the head with two dustbin lids. It physically hurt. It made you feel like dropping your instrument and diving for cover. Of course, twatto would cover his ears just before he did it.

The reason he used to do the whistle was he thought there was something wrong with the onstage sound, but of course if he'd come to the soundcheck he might have been able to sort that out. What the bloody hell is the point of saying the onstage sound is bad when you haven't come to the soundcheck?

Charlie ended up quitting mid-tour because he was so fed up. 'I've got to go before I kill him,' he said to me, 'and I'm a devout Christian.'

He broke the news to me at Six Flags, an amusement park we were playing. 'I've had enough of that twat. He's done it to me once too often. I'm leaving.'

Next morning, Charlie came to my room to say goodbye. 'Will you give this to him for me, please?' He was a lovely man, and handed me a laminated ornamental piece of paper. He'd had it done at the amusement arcade, one of those machines where you can print out your own front cover of *Rolling Stone* magazine. 'Peter loves Six Flags', kind of thing, only this one read, 'Charlie says, YOU'RE A CUNT!'

I got a great deal of pleasure giving that to Barney, I can tell you. He just curled his lip and chucked it in a corner of his room. I retrieved it and kept it for years.

Without Charlie, of course, we didn't have a dedicated foldback guy, so the sound onstage was now a complete disaster. It just got worse and worse and, with the foldback getting worse, Barney's moods and moaning got worse.

At least the soundcheck itself was a Barney-free zone. That is until one day when Barney asked Andy how we were getting on at soundcheck without him. The thing about Andy is that even though he's only from Lincoln, he speaks very posh. Rob used to say to him, 'You're a dead affected little twat, you, aren't you?' And he had no feelings filter. He's one of those people who can't help but tell the truth how he sees it. So when Barney asked Andy how we were getting on at soundcheck without him, Andy replied, 'Oh, we have a lovely time actually.'

Barney said, 'You what?'

Andy said, 'Yes, it's really good. There's no stress, no strain. We all muck about, have a great time, eat a meal. It's wonderful, actually, without you there.'

So what happened? Barney started coming back to soundchecks.

Well, at least he'd get to see his beloved hot food. Except not, because what happened then was that with the food plus the paraffin they used in the heaters to keep it warm, the room would stink, and Barney, because he was either hungover (at soundcheck) or off his head (before and after the gig) was just as nauseated as everybody else by the smell, and threw the lot out of the dressing room into the corridor.

Our American management went mad. According to them we were wasting thousands of dollars every night.

Inter-band politics continued being a pain in the arse, so I started taking myself off to the crew room instead of the dressing room. What I'd do was take a load of booze into the crew room. I did that for about six or seven gigs before Barney even noticed, at which point he said to Andy, 'How come Hooky's stopped coming in the dressing room?'

And with his famous no-filter filter on, Andy replied, 'Oh, Bernard, it's because he thinks you're a dick.'

Barney apparently said, 'Oh.'

In my opinion the problem, apart from his natural sense of *joie de vivre*/sarcasm, was the sheer amount of drugs and drink he was consuming. Apart from the night I had my toe done I was off my head every single night of that tour – every single night – and the others were no different. And it was a long tour. There was no having a cup of tea, an early night and a quick look at the porn channel. We were partying all night every night, and of course the next day you felt so dreadful that you had to get back on the horse just to get you through.

Barney constantly complained he was suffering with his tummy. He moaned about everything so it was impossible to know if he was genuinely ill or just whingeing for the sake of it, but I wouldn't be surprised if he really was suffering, because he drank Pernod, which is a fucking dreadful drink, plays havoc with your insides. Add that to the drugs he was taking and it was a recipe for disaster.

'I've got ulcers,' was his most common refrain. I thought it was bollocks; he was just hungover all of the time. And being hungover, and being Barney, he took it out on everybody else.

And when that sort of behaviour continues to go unchecked, you end up with a situation like the one we had in Detroit.

'Off my face – every day – repeat till fade'

During the first leg of the tour we toured with the Throwing Muses. Then halfway through they left and the Sugarcubes and Public Image Ltd came on board for a longer second leg, playing to even bigger out-of-town stadiums and arenas.

I'd been really looking forward to meeting Public Image Ltd. This was around the time of their album *9*, and although it wasn't exactly what you'd call vintage (probably because it was produced by Stephen Hague, ha-ha, only joking), it was still Public Image Ltd. It came with the two Johns, John Lydon – one of my all-time heroes – and John McGeoch, who had played guitar with Magazine and Siouxsie and the Banshees, to name but two.

But they turned out to be a bit of a disappointment. They were wearing hideous, multicoloured costumes, and they had this whole 'band' thing going on, with Johnny Rotten out front and the rest of the band stood behind him like dressed-up turkeys. It was about the most anti-punk thing I could imagine. Plus they were really boring and professional, and they just didn't get us at all. John Lydon in particular was completely perplexed by us. He didn't get the anti-frontman frontman; he didn't get the upstaging bass player; he didn't get the woman that never moved and looked like she was sucking a lemon, and he certainly didn't get the music. It used to drive him mad that we were so anonymous, like I could walk out into the auditorium before a 25,000-capacity gig and not be recognised. John couldn't understand how we not only revelled in that anonymity, but actively encouraged it.

In short, he pretty much hated us on every level possible. We did become friends with the band and crew in particular; PIL's crew still consisted of many of the cockneys from the old days of the Banshees and Killing Joke, people like Stretch, Trigger and Kev the Hammer (who's not so-called because he supports West Ham).

We did get the wrong end of the stick and one night decided to jape them. Me, Ozzy and Jacko, one of the roadies, got a load of banana skins and put them all over the stage while they were playing, carefully placing one on each of John McGeoch's pedals. They did not take it well and got really upset. We had certainly read this lot wrong. From then on Johnny L. would be forever getting up while we were on stage to try and upstage us, appearing in the wings like a pantomime dame shouting, 'They are shit!' to the audience, berating them for enjoying themselves.

In private he'd say to me, 'That fucking lead singer of yours, he's fucking shit, he's got no fucking personality, he's a twat, he can't fucking sing, can't fucking play guitar. And that woman, she's fucking useless.'

I'd go, 'Yeah, but they're mine, and we're still ten times bigger than you.' The legend goes that they had to tell Johnny he was actually headlining but going on before New Order to get him to do the tour. Doesn't sound right to me. John was too savvy, a very bright man. He'd learned the hard way, just like us, and it was certainly not lost on me that my inspiration was now less well known than us, his students.

Which was true. We had *Substance*, which had gone platinum in America, sold three million albums. We were on the crest of a wave and Public Image Ltd were getting further and further away from their major commercial success, which was *Album*. Our bands were going in completely different directions.

Overall, he was bit of a nightmare. Another one to make Barney look like a princess by comparison, even Ian McCulloch was put in the shade by John Lydon. He used to arrive at soundcheck and sit with me, spitting, going fuck this, fuck that, fucking cunts this, fucking cunts that, and I'd go, 'John, there's only me and you here, why can't you just talk normally?'

'Fuck off,' he'd drawl.

It was as though he didn't know any other way. He was just 'Johnny Rotten' all the time, and the thing is that while it's the kind of persona that's obviously very entertaining and colourful, I can tell you from experience that it gets pretty wearing when he keeps it up twenty-four hours a day. One of his idiosyncrasies was that he had to have a particular size of Evian bottle in his dressing room. He had this idea that the big bottles of Evian tasted inferior to the small bottles, so if they only had the big ones backstage he'd refuse to go on.

'You fucking bunch of twats, I'm not going on until you get me the small bottles of Evian,' he'd snarl, leading to a mass panic as various lackeys scrambled to find the right size for him. Don't forget, these gigs were in the middle of nowhere. Trying to find small bottles of Evian for Johnny Rotten wasn't as easy as it sounds, sometimes they'd have to drive for miles.

Still, personally speaking, I got on with him really well, which is why he ended up asking me to play bass on his next album, something I couldn't do. Shame.

So anyway, back to Detroit. The night before the gig at Detroit our mate Lippy decided we should all go to Chicago for a night out, and hired a limo. Unfortunately, when we got there everything was shut so we drove back, getting completely wasted on the drive and again when we arrived at wherever we were staying, and then in the morning we got on the plane to get to the next gig, which was Detroit – a huge, out-of-town venue.

I was nocturnal by this point, staying up all night then getting the flight the next morning, then sleeping and getting up for the soundcheck, doing the gig and spending the rest of the night off my face – every day – repeat till fade.

In Detroit, we were having a grand old time, getting ready for another riotous evening, when a girl came in and said to me, 'There's a phone call for you.'

I followed her to the office.

'Hi, Hooky, it's Tom, I'm at the hospital with Bernard.'

This was the first I'd heard of it. 'You what?'

'Yes, I'm here in the room with him now, and he's really not well. We're going to have to cancel the gig.'

I went, 'You fucking what? You tell that twat to stop fucking around and get his arse back here now.'

'Yes, Hooky, I'll give him your best regards.'

'No, don't give him my best regards, tell him I'm going to fucking batter him, the twat. Tell him I'm going to fucking batter his fucking brains out when I see him. Because I am sick of his "woe is me, please pity me" fucking act.'

'The doctors say Bernard might have an ulcer.'

'Well, tell them they can keep the Bernard and send us the ulcer.'

'Oh, that's very kind of you to be so concerned, Hooky, I'm sure Bernard will be touched.' And he hung up.

I wasn't surprised he might have an ulcer. We'd all been hammering it. Upshot was, we had to cancel the gig, the first time we'd ever done it as New Order.

By the time I got to the dressing room an army of people had arrived and were grabbing everything in sight. The panicking promoter was trying to cash in the rider so his people were stripping out the dressing room while we were still there. Moments before it had been laid out like a maharajah's palace – a haven of delights to come – suddenly it was bare.

Barney turned up the next day feeling better, and of course the tour went ahead, but if you ask me that was a revelatory moment for him. He must have thought, *They need me. They can't do it without me.*

The next gig was Pittsburgh, and for some reason he spent most of it sitting on the drum riser, sighing between delivering the lines of 'Blue Monday'. I spent half the gig watching him thinking, *God, what a twat you are …*

But then I had a change of heart and I thought, *You know what? It really does take guts to do that. I admire that.*

In a way that was the difference between us and Public Image Ltd. If we were pissed off, we showed it to the audience, but if Public Image Ltd were pissed off they hid it. It was like a pantomime with them now, all gloss and surface. But then they walked off and, like every other band, they couldn't stick each other. It's all a big daft act.

So even though Barney was by any normal standards behaving appallingly, sticking two fingers up to the 23,000 people who had paid to see us, I had to admire him for not buying into that whole play-acting thing.

Not that my admiration had any effect on our relationship. By the end of the tour the three component parts of New Order couldn't stand to be in a room with one another. At our end-of-tour party in New Jersey there were three rooms: mine, Bernard's and Gillian and Steve's. Members of the crew moved between them, valiantly trying and failing to bring us together, but it wasn't happening. We had one more date to do. Headline slot at that year's Reading Festival. After that? Nothing.

As far as we all were concerned, New Order was grinding to a halt, it was over, and the sooner the better for all of us, except poor old Rob. He was heartbroken.

Meanwhile, Jane had called my bluff and decided to stay in America. She wouldn't wait for me any more. I returned home and did two things: one, I went cold turkey (well, 'room temperature turkey' – I reverted to nights out and special occasions rather than the tour diet of 'all day, every day'), and two, I came clean about Jane with Iris, who was then seven months' pregnant. She went berserk and kicked me in the bollocks, and we split up. It was one of the hardest things I have ever had to do. But it was either that or suicide, and I even contemplated that ('keep passing the open windows' – thanks to John Irving for that one).

Jane remained in the States while I moved into her flat in a place called Rusholme Gardens, in Rusholme, sharing with her flatmate, a lovely girl called Bernie. The place was really cool and populated mainly by people who worked at the Haçienda. I was in good company. I'd lie in Jane's bed curled in a foetal position for hours, listening to the guy upstairs practise classical piano, all twisted up with cold turkey and the grief of losing Heather, not to mention my unborn child. I thought the pain would kill me. I lived on a diet of Budweiser and Bombay mix for two months. I lost three stone, a proper divorce diet. Bowser, another roadie, took to calling me 'Hooky no arse'.

I remember talking to Barney in the cocktail bar of the Haçienda one night, which in itself was weird because that was something we never did on tour, unless he was off it and apologising. I suppose we must have been off our heads.

He said to me, 'How's it going, now you're back?' and I told him about my shambles of a love life, and he told me, 'Sometimes in life, you have to do something for yourself. Whether you like it or not, Hooky, everything radiates from you, and if you're unhappy then they're going to be unhappy.'

I thought to myself, *Fuck me, he's absolutely right.*

What I had to do for myself, of course, was be with the love of my life – who at that time was Jane.

I pulled myself together. I bought a ticket to America, went and found her and told her it was all over between me and Iris and asked her to return with me. She did, and we ended up setting up house on Circular Road in Withington, a house of six flats I bought for £76,500 and would eventually turn into a home for me, Jane and the kids. I was entering another phase of my life.

When my son Jack was born that September the guilt I felt at leaving my kids was brought home to me. I felt a failure as a man and a father. I didn't get to see him for a while after he was born, and it was a very difficult time for me, Iris, and Jane too. For the American tour I was paid £175,000 and that I gave straight to Iris. Guilt is a useless emotion.

New Order's preparations to play Reading were just as depressing as you'd expect given the circumstances. The circumstances being that there were no New Order plans afterwards, no gigs booked, no studio time pending, nothing. I'd seen Barney's notes for Electronic, remember – how he planned to promote the hell out of it, go dead poppy, the complete antithesis of what he was about in New Order. It was weird but not entirely unsurprising. After all, I had similar plans for Revenge. After ten years of being in a band together we were sick and tired of each other, couldn't wait to get away.

For some reason at Reading, possibly because I was using a radio microphone on my guitar for the first time, I was able to wander around. Listening to the others' sound on stage – the foldback – I became aware that none of them were hearing the whole band. I was the only one who listened to each component part through my foldback. Gillian had Gillian. Barney had Barney. Steve had Steve. They were all just listening to themselves.

That said it all. At the end of the gig Barney smashed his guitar. It was a proper damp squib. It was one of the most miserable gigs I had ever done. We had everything, headlining in front of 100,000 people, but it felt like I had nothing, knowing it was to be the end.

I had watched Jimi Hendrix *Live in Monterey* a few nights before and loved it, especially when he set his guitar alight. *That's it!* I thought, *I'll do that. It will symbolise a new start for Revenge, a phoenix rising from the ashes of New Order.*

Brilliant idea. I bought some lighter fluid and some matches and had it all planned for after 'Fine Time'. At the end I threw the six-string down, sprayed the fluid on it and . . . it wouldn't light. I tried for ages but just couldn't get it to catch, and everyone was laughing at me. Turns out it's the vapour from the fluid that burns. Jimi had obviously benefited from the still Monterey desert evenings. Damn you, Hendrix. In the end I threw down the guitar and stalked off.

In typical fashion, my mates were all there and by the time I came off were all twatted, completely off it, and everything pharmaceutical had gone. I stomped to my room with six warm cans of lager, the only thing I could get my hands on.

The aftershow party was nuts, I heard. I didn't even go; I was in a hotel room opposite and could see it all unfolding from my window, the strangest feeling.

What a life.

International rock star = bollocks.

A few days after Reading, I let myself into the practice rooms in Cheetham Hill intending to get my bass gear and take some keyboards and sequencers back to Suite 16, in order to resume work on Revenge. I got there to find that the others had arrived before me and virtually stripped it bare. Not only had Barney been, but Steve and Gillian had made separate trips. I should have gone mad at them. But let's face it, if I'd got there first, I'd have done exactly the same. I said to Terry, 'I'm slipping.' The only thing left in the whole place apart from my bass rig was Barney's smashed guitars off tour. Jonny Hugo had put all the bits in a big plastic bag and stuck it in a bin in the loading bay. I put them back together and made three Frankenstein guitars.

In the end I retreated to Suite 16 to lick my wounds, and though the next few years with Revenge would be a time of great confusion and not exactly what you'd call a great artistic success – on top of which I had to deal with my split from Iris, then subsequently a painful split from Jane, as well as an increasing consumption of drugs and drink – there was at least one silver lining.

I didn't have to put up with Barney any more.

I remember going to see Echo and the Bunnymen after Mac had left. I got backstage and the atmosphere among the band had palpably changed. Without Mac they were getting on famously, having a laugh, and they were the first to admit, 'Hooky, we know the edge is missing, but it's so much better without him for us.' Talk about suffering for your art.

It was like that with me and him. Even though it was a relief not to have to put up with him, there was no doubt that the edge was missing. It wasn't quite the same without him. The fucker.

In typical fashion, straight after we split we ended up getting back together again, two ideas being mooted. Project number one was very interesting creatively: a long-talked-about collaboration with the famous film director Michael Powell, of *The Red Shoes*. Michael

Shamberg had been pushing this one for a while and it looked as if finally it had come to fruition. We went to meet Michael Powell, then in his mid-eighties, in his offices in London. He was lovely and very enthusiastic about our music. I think the others saw this as an opportunity to feature a new synthesiser dancey track but Michael said, 'No.' He had already chosen the track 'Age of Consent'. I was delighted. His idea was to film a piece based on a poem called 'The Sands of Dee' actually on the sands of the River Dee, which winds its way through Chester and out into the Irish Sea. 'Rugged and wild, much like the song,' he said. I couldn't have been happier when he said that. Stick that in your dancey pipe and smoke it, you cunts. The dramatisation was to star Tilda Swinton.

Project number two couldn't have been more different: a collaboration with the England football squad for the 1990 World Cup. This was purely commercial and could not be turned down. We all wrinkled our noses but had no doubt that for New Order and hence for our solo projects this was indeed great news.

Tony had been at a function and met the man in charge of PR for the Football Association. He was bemoaning the fact that the pop groups who did the World Cup songs were awful and why couldn't a 'good' group do it the way New Order had with 'Best and Marsh'.

Tony simply said, 'Well, why don't you ask them?'

He did: the rest, as they say, is history.

TIMELINE TEN
JANUARY–DECEMBER 1989

© Kevin Cummins

January 1989

New Order: *Technique*
(FACT 275)

Track list:

'Fine Time'	4.42
'All the Way'	3.22
'Love Less'	2.58
'Round and Round'	4.29
'Guilty Partner'	4.44
'Run'	4.26
'Mr Disco'	4.20
'Vanishing Point'	5.14
'Dream Attack'	5.13

Run-out groove one: *What exactly do you mean Peter?*
Run-out groove two: *?reteP naem uoy od yltcaxe tahW*

Recorded at Mediterraneo Studio, Ibiza, and Real World Studios, Box, Bath.
Mixed at Real World Studios.
Assistants at the Box: Aaron Denson, Richard Chappell, Richard Evans.
Recorded by Michael Johnson.
Mixed by Alan Meyerson.
Produced by New Order.
Designed by Peter Saville Associates.
Photography by Trevor Key.
Entered UK chart at number 1 on 11 February 1989, remaining in the charts for 14 weeks, its peak position was number 1.

The Loveless was a 1982 film directed by Kathryn Bigelow, which starred Willem Dafoe. The town in the film is called Liberty and is used in the lyrics.

> **'Another story . . . I had a pool competition on with the young tape-op and was letting the poor kid win. I said, "Fancy a bet?" and he went for it. Now I am sure most of you will know that**

with all the downtime on recording sessions most musicians are pretty good at pool. Me being no exception, I whooped his ass. At the end I was double or quitting him up to £512. Needless to say, he couldn't pay. In the end Rob suggested playing for his leather coat, then his car. I won them both. Then Rob suggested a night with his girlfriend. I was laughing, but the kid phoned her and put it to her, and she agreed, having been assured he would win. I was very flattered but had no intention of going ahead with it. Then Rob said, "Right, one last game. Your car – against all you owe him and double the money?" Rob loved a gamble. Amazingly, the kid went for it. I beat him hands down, he burst out crying, "One thousand and twenty-four pounds. My coat, my bird, my car!"

'I said to Rob, "I'll let him stew, then let him off tomorrow. He's a nice kid."

'Only he never came back. Never rang, never came for his wages. Nothing. A couple of days later I got a message: "Peter Gabriel wants to see you." Oops.'

20 January 1989

New Order play Montpellier Le Zénith, France.

21 January 1989

New Order play Lyon Le Transbordeur, France.

'I went drinking with Ken Niblock in the afternoon, unusual for me but I was annoyed with the others, they were all getting on my nerves. I was really pissed when I got to the gig, so when I got into the dressing room and noticed the key in the lock on the inside of the door, I locked us in, carefully putting the key down my trousers, and sat down going, "Nobody cares. You can fuck off, you twats. Nobody cares!"

'In my mind I was commenting on how being in a successful group meant you could do and act how you wanted. I suppose my aim was to challenge the cliché. In reality I just wouldn't let anyone out of the dressing room. They were going, "Give us the key, Hooky."

'I just kept saying, "Nobody cares. Nobody cares. And you come near me and I'll fucking twat you."

'So Andy Robinson tried to get the key from down my trousers and I twatted him. Rob tried to get it off me, and I twatted him as well. I was really pissed. And then I threw the whole rider out the window and lay on the floor, going, "You're not fucking opening the door, you can all fuck off. We can do whatever we want. It's ridiculous."

'We just sat there for over an hour past stage time and still no one had come to ask us what was going on. Eventually a combination of Rob and Andy shouting and banging on the door brought someone.

'"What eez 'appenin?" he said.

'I was going, "Fuck off, Pedro, you French twat."

'"Help us," they chorused, "He's locked us in and won't let us out!" God, he must have been puzzled.

'Eventually they got three blokes to kick down the door. I was laughing by this point. We were nearly two hours late. The audience were going mental. The crew were crapping it.

'So anyway, we went on stage and we were playing and I thought, *This sounds dreadful.* Every song sounded shit. They finished and walked off and I looked at my set list and I still had one to go. I'd only been playing the wrong bassline to every song. I was playing one behind. I dived about on a flight case on the stage for a while then got bored. I went backstage to find them lot all hiding in the promoter's office. He had put out a line of coke for each of them and I stormed in and went, "What are you doing?"

'They went, "Oh, fucking hell, he's here again," and scarpered, I grabbed the rolled-up note and did all four lines, then went, "See, nobody cares, Mr Promoter."

'Oh man, they were so pissed off, more for that than the bloody gig. Barney was doing a cover picture for a magazine called *Best* and I even muscled in on that. It's one of my favourite pictures that, of me and him. Later the guy said he'd charge me for the door, so I said, "Right! Then I want my door. And I'm not going until you unscrew it and bring it to me."

'I had a terrible hangover the next day, and a lot of apologising to do.

'Thanks, Ken.'

February 1989

New Order: 'Round and Round'
(FAC 263)

Seven-inch track list:

'Round and Round'	3.31
'Best and Marsh'	3.59

Twelve-inch track list:

'Round and Round'	6.40
'Best and Marsh' (full length)	4.25

Run-out groove one: *Shall we tell the Yanks about all this?*
Run-out groove two: *I don't know … what do you think?*
Featuring slightly different mixes by Stephen Hague.

Twelve-inch remix:

'Round and Round' (club mix)	7.07
'Round and Round' (Detroit mix)	6.29

Both mixes by Kevin Saunderson.

CD track list:

'Round and Round'	3.59
'Round and Round' (twelve-inch)	6.50
'Best and Marsh'	3.31
Instrumental *Making Out* mix of 'Vanishing Point'	5.10

Recorded in Mediterraneo Studio, Ibiza, and Real World Studios, Box, Bath.
Recorded by Michael Johnson.
Mixed by Alan Meyerson.
Remixes by Kevin Saunderson.
Co-produced by New Order and Stephen Hague.
'Best and Marsh' produced by New Order.
Designed by Peter Saville Associates.
Photography by Trevor Key.

Entered UK chart on 11 March 1989, remaining in the charts for 7 weeks, its peak position was number 21.

February 1989

New Order's Peter Hook appears on *The Other Side of Midnight* alone, surrounded by technology, playing 'The Happy One'.

13 February 1989

New Order play Armenia Aid, Moscow Stadium, USSR.
CANCELLED.

21 February 1989

New Order were filmed playing live for a new TV show (*Big World Café*) at Brixton Academy.

25 March 1989

New Order play Glasgow SECC, supported by A Guy Called Gerald.

26 March 1989

New Order play Birmingham NEC, supported by the Happy Mondays.

9 April 1989

New Order play Puerto Rico.
New Order embark upon a two-leg, 35-date US tour, the second leg with PIL and the Sugarcubes. The tour programme, *Untitled*, doesn't turn up until the final week.

11 April 1989

New Order play Knight Center, Miami.

12 April 1989

New Order play Bayfront Arena, St Petersburg, Florida.

14 April 1989

New Order play O'Connell Center, Gainesville, Florida.

15 April 1989

New Order play Six Flags Over Georgia (Southern Star Amphitheatre), Atlanta, Georgia.

16 April 1989

New Order play Saenger Theatre, New Orleans, Louisiana.

20 April 1989

New Order play City Coliseum, Austin, Texas.

21 April 1989

New Order play Astroworld, Houston, Texas.

22 April 1989

New Order play Starplex Amphitheatre, Dallas, Texas.

25 April 1989

New Order play Mesa Amphitheatre, Mesa, Arizona.

27–28 April 1989

New Order play Universal Amphitheatre, Los Angeles, California.

30 April 1989

New Order play Santa Barbara County Bowl, Santa Barbara, California.

May 1989

Academy video released. Live video recorded at London Brixton Academy on 4 April 1987.
International Aids Day fundraiser.

Track list:
'Bizarre Love Triangle'
'Perfect Kiss'
'Ceremony'
'Dreams Never End'
'Love Vigilantes'
'Confusion'
'Age of Consent'
'Temptation'
'Temptation (reprise)'

Video produced and directed by Mike Mansfield.
Music produced by New Order.
Designed by Peter Saville Associates.

2 May 1989

New Order play Civic Auditorium, Portland, Oregon.

3 May 1989

New Order play Paramount Theatre, Seattle, Washington.

4 May 1989

New Order play Queen Elizabeth Theatre, Vancouver.

21 May 1989

Tour break. Haçienda's seventh birthday party in Amsterdam, but Hooky misses his flight.

14 June 1989

Pete de Freitas of Echo and the Bunnymen dies in a motorcycle accident.

> **'Pete was a really nice bloke. Sadly missed. I remember Barney telling me he bumped into Pete's ex-girlfriend, Jayne Casey, and said, "Tell me, how is that lovely boyfriend of yours?"**
>
> **'"Not too well," she said, "seeing as how the last time I saw you we were both at his memorial service, you prick."**
>
> **'"I'd forgot," he said.'**

14 June 1989

New Order play Shoreline Amphitheatre, Mountain View, California. The band dedicate their set to Pete de Freitas.

16 June 1989

New Order play Irvine Meadows Amphitheatre, Irvine, California.

17 June 1989

New Order play Aztec Bowl, San Diego, California.

18 June 1989

New Order play Irvine Meadows Amphitheatre, Irvine, California.

21 June 1989

New Order play Park West Amphitheatre, Salt Lake City, Utah.

23 June 1989

New Order play Red Rocks Amphitheatre, Denver, Colorado.

25 June 1989

New Order play Sandstone Amphitheatre, Bonner Springs, Kansas.

> 'It is strange that a lot of these gigs really blend into one. They were very samey. This one I remember because dusk was falling as we went on stage and within seconds it was pitch-black. Then Andy Liddle turned on his amazing light show, and as we looked out into the void all of a sudden it was filled with dive-bombing bugs heading for the lights. We were covered in seconds, in your mouth and every other orifice. My slicked-back hair was crawling as they burrowed under the gel that stuck it down. It was hell.
>
> 'Gillian kept running away screaming. It was the most I'd seen her move in nine years of touring. She had to be persuaded to come back, and just stood there shaking. I have no idea how we got through it and remember at the end Terry Mason turning the keyboards upside down and emptying out a mountain of writhing bugs. As I showered they kept falling out of my hair.
>
> '"I'm a celebrity ... get me out of here!" I cried.'

27 June 1989

New Order play St Paul's Auditorium, Minneapolis, Minnesota.

29 June 1989

New Order play Marcus Amphitheatre, Milwaukee, Wisconsin.

30 June 1989

New Order play Poplar Creek Music Theatre, Hoffman Estates, Illinois, Chicago.

TIMELINE TEN JANUARY–DECEMBER 1989

'A mad night out with Tommy Lipnick, we were at it all night, hope everyone's OK for tomorrow's gig. Not too hungover?'

1 July 1989

New Order play Pine Knob Music Theatre, Detroit, Michigan. Gig cancelled due to Bernard Sumner being ill. Rescheduled for 17 July.

3 July 1989

New Order play Pittsburgh, Pennsylvania.

4 July 1989

New Order play Darien Lakes Theme Park, Buffalo, New York.

5 July 1989

New Order play Blossom Music Center, Cuyahoga Falls (Cleveland), Ohio.

7 July 1989

New Order play CNE Grandstand, Toronto, Ontario.

10 July 1989

New Order play Great Woods, Mansfield, Massachusetts.

11 July 1989

New Order play Lake Compounce Park, Bristol, Connecticut.

12 July 1989

New Order play Jones Beach, Wantaugh, New York.

14 July 1989

New Order play Mann Music Center, Philadelphia, Pennsylvania.

15 July 1989

New Order play Merriweather Post Pavilion, Columbia, Maryland.

'Fifty thousand copies of our tour programme turned up. Titled *Untitled*, they featured photos by Donald Christie. A nice man, Donald, he'd had unfettered access backstage to get the candid shots for the programme. Unfortunately, Peter Saville's lengthy deliberations over the style and content of it had taken so long that it was now too late. We simply did not have time to sell them. It was very arty and told our audience practically nothing about us. It was beautiful but almost useless. Forty-nine thousand were shipped back to England at great cost and languished in a warehouse in Stockport for years, completely forgotten by everyone, until Factory went bust and they were destroyed, because of non-payment of storage charges.'

17 July 1989

New Order play Pine Knob Music Theatre, Detroit, Michigan.

19 July 1989

New Order play Brendan Byrne Arena, Meadowlands, New Jersey.

23 July 1989

Dry 201, owned by Factory, opens in Oldham Street, Manchester.

'We were home for the opening night. I came up from the basement, where the druggies were, to get a bottle of beer from the main bar. I grabbed a bottle of Bud and couldn't find an opener so I thought I'd do the old rock'n'roll trick of banging the cap off on the brand-new bar top. Suddenly I heard a shout. "Hooky, do you know

how much that cost? It's Delabole blue-grey slate, hand-carved, a solid piece," shouted a shocked Ben Kelly. "Thirty-five thousand pounds' worth!"

"'Well done, Ben," said I. "Works perfectly as a bottle opener!'" BANG!

'Pearls before swine, mate, pearls before swine. Luckily it didn't mark.'

25 August 1989

New Order headline Reading Festival, Reading, supported by the Sugarcubes, House of Love, Tackhead, Spacemen 3, Swans, My Bloody Valentine. Compére: John Peel.
It will be four years before New Order play live together again.

September 1989

New Order: *Substance* video
(FAC 225)

Track list:
'Confusion' (directed by Charles Sturridge) 3.58
'The Perfect Kiss' (directed by Jonathan Demme) 5.29
'Shellshock' (directed by Rick Elgood) 3.14
'Bizarre Love Triangle' (directed by Robert Longo) 3.54
'True Faith' (directed by Philippe Decouflé) 4.23
'Touched by the Hand of God' (directed by Kathryn Bigelow) 4.18
'Blue Monday 1988' (directed by Robert Breer & William Wegman) 4.06

Executive producer: Michael Shamberg.
Designed by Peter Saville Associates.
Also includes audio of 'The Happy One' between video clips.

27 September 1989

Jack Robert Lawrence Bates born.

28 September 1989

New Order: 'Run 2'
(FAC 273)

Seven-inch track list:
'Run 2' 3.35
'MTO' 3.43

Twelve-inch track list:
'Run 2' 3.35
'Run 2' (extended) 5.22
'MTO' 3.43
'MTO' (minus mix) 5.24

Run-out groove one: *The Death of Art spells the murder of Artists …*
Run-out groove two: *… so kill me now!*

Recorded in Mediterraneo Studio, Ibiza, and Real World Studios, Box, Bath.
Recorded by Mike Johnson.
Mixed by Alan Meyerson.
Remixed by Scott Litt and Mike (Hitman) Wilson.
Produced by New Order.
'Run 2' remixed by Scott Litt, additional beats on extended version by Afrika Islam.
'MTO' additional production and remix by Mike 'Hitman' Wilson for Real House Productions. Engineered by Chris Andrews.
Designed by Peter Saville, inspired by the packaging for Bold washing powder.

Entered UK chart on 9 September 1989, remaining in the charts for 2 weeks, its peak position was number 49.

John Denver's publishing company filed a suit against the song, claiming that it closely resembled his 'Leaving on a Jet Plane'. The case was settled out of court, and subsequent pressings of the song came with a co-writing credit to Denver.

'Rob fought this so hard. He hired a musicologist in England to analyse the song. It turns out that musicologists use a scale of twelve notes and if eight of those notes are present in both songs, then the accused, us, is deemed guilty. Which we were. Rob wouldn't have it, so he then got an American musicologist to analyse it. He said the same. We lost again. John Denver got his per cent cut and a writer's credit. Warners wanted to take it off the album on any subsequent pressings, but we said no. I still don't hear it now. Denver died in 1997, shortly after it was eventually settled. God, imagine if we did that with all the tunes that sound like us? We'd make a fortune. Humh … there's a thought.'

November 1989

New Order are approached about the England World Cup song.

November 1989

Revenge: '7 Reasons'
(FAC 247)

Seven-inch track list:

'7 Reasons'	4.05
'Jesus, I Love You' (edit)	4.05

Twelve-inch track list:

'7 Reasons'	4.05
'Jesus, I Love You'	6.56
'Love You Too'	5.44

Run-out groove one: *They're being funny with me …*
Run-out groove two: *I've had it now Mam!*

CD track list:

'7 Reasons'	4.05
'Jesus, I Love You' (edit)	4.05
'Bleach Boy'	5.04
'Jesus, I Love You'	6.56

Recorded and mixed in Suite 16, Rochdale, Lancashire.
Engineered by Michael Johnson.
Mixed by Rex Sargeant.
Produced by Revenge.
Designed by Peter Saville Associates.
Photography by Trevor Watson.
Video: Martyn Atkins.

'Me, CJ and Dave Hicks were still working very hard to find our way. But we were desperate to get our record out before Electronic (probably, in truth, it was just me), so we rushed it like mad. Listening now though, I like it. I'd ripped off the Go-Betweens, one of my favourite bands ever, for the track. The first time I'd done lyrics alone, even putting in a reference to the Stone Roses ... "I want to be adored". Factory gave us £5,000 for a video. I was determined not to make the expensive mistakes New Order had on their videos. We roped in Martyn Atkins (who used to work with Peter Saville) to do it. Martyn was a dirt-biker like me so we had a lot in common, mainly a love of thick leather trousers. It turned out OK.'

December 1989

Electronic's 'Getting Away With It' single released.

'Beat him! Yesss!'

PETER HOOK
SUITE 16
16 KENION STREET
OFF DRAKE STREET
ROCHDALE

1st DECEMBER 1989

COPY OF LETTER TO HOME

Gainwest Limited.
11 Hastings Avenue, Chorlton, Manchester M21 1JS. Telephone: 061 861 8403.
Facsimile: 061 881 4152. Telex: 265871 Monref G. Quoting Ref: Dgs 2509. E-Mail: Gainwest UK.
Vat Number: 408 2514 73. Registered Office: Broadhurst, Bury Old Road, Salford M8 6FX.
Directors: G L Gilbert, R L Gretton, P Hook, S P D Morris, B Sumner.

Dear Peter

As you may know I have for some time been considering retiring from the music business, and I have decided that the time has arrived.
Therefore I am hereby resigning as the manager of New Order as of today.

Yours Sincerely

R. Gretton

ROBERT GRETTON

'Gascoigne, will you fuck off!'

With his eye on the prize, Tony had put it to Rob that New Order doing the World Cup song would mean a huge publicity boost for everyone. I seriously doubt whether Rob gave much of a fuck about the publicity, but eventually he put it to us and we agreed. To my mind it was an honour. After this the only way would be up. Eurovision, here we come.

So, at the beginning of 1990, the group reconvened at Real World studios to put something together. Steve and Gillian had been working on a theme tune for the BBC *Reportage* youth programme and put the end-credit theme forward as an idea (credited as New Order on the programme and actually left over from the *Making Out* sessions done together on *Technique*), and although me and Barney thought it was a bit soft, both Rob and Tony loved it. They were always on at us to do a more straightforward 'pop' song, so it ended up being ideal for their needs.

Meanwhile, Keith Allen was drafted in by Tony Wilson to help write the lyrics, a completely inspired choice. A football fanatic, and a firebrand right from the word go, great to work with, we all felt a lot better from the moment he appeared (you always felt safe with Keith around, even though some of the situations he got you in were very, very dangerous). It cut the responsibility and heightened the numbers.

We had a first crack at it in Real World with the producer Roli Mosimann, who had a background in nosebleed industrial music with the likes of Swans and Foetus, and had gone on to produce The The and That Petrol Emotion. We got on quite well with Roli, but it was felt by some that he made a bit of a dog's dinner of the track. Still, at least we'd broken the back of it and made a very good start. (A sad note on the session was the passing of Michael Powell at the age of eighty-five, meaning the 'Age of Consent' art film project died with him. Shame, a lovely man.)

Then a decision was made to employ Stephen Hague to polish it up and turn it into the big chart-bound pop song it would later become.

I was worried. I wondered if I would be treated the same as I was on 'True Faith'. I desperately hoped not.

Against our better judgement, Stephen Hague went to great lengths to completely re-record the whole song. What it needed was just a polish – a remix, some overdubs etc. I did wonder if by re-recording the song Hague was making sure he secured himself that all-important sole-producing credit and thus all the producer's royalties? You might wonder that too. I couldn't possibly comment.

It seemed to cost us a lot of time and money to make sure it sounded exactly the same as Roli's. Relegated (good footballing analogy there) to the B-side, if you listen to his version it does sound unfinished, although it does feature Keith and my mate Richard 'Dickie' Chappell, the tape-op from Real World, on the half rap, a valiant effort.

I would spend a lot of time in the studio with Dickie over the years and would watch him grow from a boy to a man, with him ending up working exclusively for Peter Gabriel and becoming indispensable to him, both in the studio and 'live'. He would phone me up and even called in at my house in Withington once, asking me how much he should be charging Peter.

'Thousands!' I'd laugh. 'He couldn't do it without you, Dickie.'

Anyway, the song now had an almost complete demo and plans were made for the England team to come and sing on the track. We had to accommodate them and so the session was moved to Jimmy Page's Sol Studio in Cookham, Berkshire, which was nearest to their training ground. The studio was an old watermill that straddled a quiet backwater of the River Thames near Maidenhead, deep in the Berkshire countryside. It was lovely and the residential part known as the Wheelhouse floated on its own small island, complete with river flowing underneath. When the studio engineer took us round he thrilled us with tales of Jimmy Page's black magic incantations. 'Often conjuring up the spirit of Aleister Crowley, the Master of Darkness,' he said.

I knew we could bring enough darkness of our own with my old mate Stephen Hague on board. We also now had the Pet Shop Boys' keyboard programmer at a thousand pounds a day. It seemed like Hague was hoping to get rid of all of us and just use our name.

'Don't worry,' he said, 'the money buys him out of any publishing on the track. Whatever he writes is all yours.'

For a thousand pounds a day I'm not surprised! Shame we can't do the same with you! I thought.

The track work went on with most of us just sitting around waiting, but we were due a visit from the England World Cup squad. Naively, we'd assumed that the players would turn out en masse, keen as mustard to record their song with New Order. We couldn't have been more wrong. In fact we were graced by about ten, which included a few hangers-on, who were squeezing us into their tight schedule of a day.

Fortunately we weren't overly bothered at this point. Earlier, Tony had arrived at the session bearing gifts, in this case a huge – and I mean *huge* – bag of coke. Barney, absolutely fucked after a night out with 808 State the night before, was more grateful than most, at last dragging his head out of a sick bucket for a quick trip to the toilet. Stephen Hague and his assistant and programmer didn't partake. The rest of us chowed down. In the toilet I had one of my customary fatties and, what with it being such a huge bag, I took a bit more for later – as you do – so I was absolutely off it when the team arrived.

Tony stood at the door handing each player a brown envelope like it was a party bag. What was in the envelope? Two grand cash each, appearance fee. Despite the fact that we were making this record with the FA's backing, in order to promote their World Cup campaign, the players still needed a cash incentive to take part. Normal practice, we were told.

The drinks started flowing, the team wading into the refreshments on offer, just the alcoholic ones. That was when Paul Gascoigne said to Stephen Hague one of the funniest things I've ever heard. Stephen was giving the lads a sort of verbal tour of the studio gear, with mainly blank looks in return, when all of a sudden Gazza pipes up with, 'Whey aye, man, that's the biggest organ I've ever fucken' seen. Can you play us a tune?' pointing to the mixing desk.

The booze was disappearing fast and, Christ, I've seen some power-drinking in my time but the England World Cup squad took the biscuit. Paul Gascoigne drank three bottles of champagne in fifteen minutes, straight from the bottles. The rest were almost as bad, and it seemed in moments they were all absolutely steaming.

The thing we needed them to do was, firstly, get one player to perform the rap and, secondly, to get them to voice the 'singalonga' bits. Keith had written the rap in Real World but it was decided to extend it here, helped, bizarrely, by Craig Johnston, a South African-born Australian who had ended up playing for England Under-21s in the early 1980s, who the team had in tow. He came up with some great words for the new second half of the rap, with Keith and Barney chipping in (these football analogies are so easy) and tried first by Gazza (hilarious) and Peter Beardsley (beyond funny) and Chris Waddle (wild ... in the biblical sense).

They all had a go at the rap and were shit; Keith was adamant we needed a black guy to do it, insisting, 'White men cannot rap! Period.' John Barnes stepped up and nailed it in one. What a hero.

Then it came to the singalong and it was like herding cats. This lot couldn't concentrate for more than a minute at a time. Hague was panicking. In the meantime Tony had come up with the 'Ing-ger-land' chant, saying, 'This is what the fans will want!' and making matters worse by giving the players more to bloody do.

We gathered in a big circle in the live room around some freestanding microphones and I must say it looked good, with me (twatted), Barney and Keith (not far behind) whipping the boys into a frenzy. I then thought it would be a great idea to get rid of the lyric sheets the lads were holding, and ripped them out of their hands one by one, laughing like a maniac, until I got to Barney. I made a grab. He pulled away, mouthing through clenched teeth, 'Fuck off, you bastard!' I'd gone too far.

Fair play to Stephen Hague, he certainly earned his money here. After half an hour or so of raucous shouting, and just as we were getting warmed up for the proper takes, the players turned round and announced they had to go, promptly turning on their heels and filing out the door and back to the coach.

Everyone was like, 'WHAT THE FUCK?'

I grabbed hold of Steve McMahon. 'Where you going? We've only just started?'

'Gotta go,' he says. 'We're opening a Top Man in Middlesbrough!'

And that was it, they were all gone, leaving alcohol fumes and lots of shellshocked band members, a comedian, a producer, several record company owners and studio engineers behind them.

As we watched the coach depart, we noticed it was closely followed by a big black Mercedes, driven by ... fucking hell, Paul Gascoigne. That was an accident waiting to happen if I ever saw one.

Though we definitely had the rap on tape, Stephen Hague suspected we still didn't have enough for a proper 'singalong' chorus. We were all left a little flat after that, a comedown some might say. With minutes of the session left some bright spark decided it was the perfect time for Hooky to do his bass. Shit. I struggled through but it was the same deal as 'True Faith'. The song was all written. I got a lot of good bits but there was no time to finish them. You can hear it on the track and it sounds better for it, but it's unfinished. Mr Hague's way of working was no good for me at all. I would really be glad to see the back of him, again. Luckily the bass was used much more in the remixes.

We met up later at a small studio in London to mix it and had to replace most of the team's vocals – they just didn't work. We ended up having a great time doing it, though. Even Rob sang along with great gusto. So what you hear on the record isn't the England football team at all. They are there in spirit (or rather spirits, hee-hee). It's us lot pretending to be them. Basically what Tony got for his twenty-grand incentive was John Barnes performing a rap.

The next step was to record the video, to be directed by the Bailey Brothers, great friends of Tony (he spent what felt like years trying to get their co-production of the Factory/Madchester film *The Mad Fuckers* off the ground, sadly to no avail).

First thing they did was film some match footage. The whole of New Order was invited to go along and watch an England friendly against Brazil at Wembley, but I was the only one to take up the offer.

I got to watch the match from the touchline, in a dugout, while the Baileys filmed. This was great. It was freezing, but what an experience being so close to the action, such a thrill, me phoning everyone I knew watching at home, telling them where I was in the ground.

When the match finished, the Bailey boys packed their gear and we made a quick exit via the staff entrance, emerging to see a huge limo parked outside, smoke billowing out of the sunroof, girlies giggling, and the clink of champagne glasses coming from inside. It was Paul Gascoigne's. God only knows how he'd managed it, but he'd got off the pitch, changed and was in that limo in the time it took us to make our way to the staff exit. At least he wasn't driving this time.

He was a complete nutcase, Gascoigne. Another bit of the video involved visiting the players' training ground at Bisham Abbey to film the singalong you see in the video. Watch it and you'll notice I'm the only member of New Order in that gathering, and that's because, yet again, I was the only one to turn up.

As a result of that, though, the kids at Heather's school got it into their heads that I was an England football player. I was suddenly inundated with kids asking me when the next match was and how we were going to do, autographs and everything, brilliant, with me doing nothing to dissuade them.

Back to Gascoigne, and one thing I remember vividly from that day on the training ground was that after most of the players had trooped off, he stayed behind for target practice, standing on the halfway line and punting for goal.

Just outside the hotel on the right of the goal, the manager Bobby Robson was beginning a meeting with a bunch of old-looking FA types. It was a nice day so they'd set up the tables outside. Gascoigne caught sight of this lot, forgot the goal he'd been facing and with a look of intense concentration on his face – not devilment or mischief, just a really serious, concentrated look – started shooting the balls at them.

The first one missed. Not by much, but it missed, hitting the hotel wall, and narrowly missing the conservatory windows, thank God, because if it had hit one of them then it probably would have killed them.

His brow furrowed as though feeling pissed off by the miss, Gascoigne tried again, and this time the ball just missed this group of aged gentlemen by a whisker. Now Bobby Robson looked up, shouted, 'Gascoigne, will you fuck off!' and it was as though Gazza was shaken out of it – like he'd been in a trance and the voice of his manager had roused him. Without a word he went back to target practice on the goal, very weird. Really, it didn't surprise me to hear of him trying to give a chicken sandwich and a fishing rod to Raoul Moat later. The only other thing of note was Peter Beardsley taking the sweaty shirt off his back to give me as a souvenir. I think he felt sorry for me.

The other main part of the video was the bulk of what you see on the screen, which was us lot – all the members of New Order this time – Keith Allen and John Barnes (the only England player present), filmed at Anfield. Which was a mad, mad day, as you can imagine.

Tony was very nervous there. His love/hate relationship with the Scousers was still ongoing. He had to keep a low profile. For some reason Barney turned up dressed as Elvis, complete with wig. He gave his wig to Keith, and the two of them toured around the area in Barney's open-topped Mercedes. The rest of us got pissed; Gillian looked supremely uncomfortable.

A great day was had by all.

We'd wanted to call the song 'E for England', but the FA wouldn't allow it because of the drug reference, so we settled on 'World in Motion', taken from the lyrics.

Of course, the song went straight to number one. Apparently the players didn't think much of it when it was played on the coach for its premiere on the way to the first match (but then again, they all liked Luther Vandross in those days). But after it was a hit John Barnes said that even the ones who weren't on it started bragging about singing the song. Nor did the FA exactly shower us with thanks off the back of it. I suppose it was a bit of a new thing for them, getting serious musicians to do the song, and they didn't know how to handle it. So they handled it by not giving us any tickets, souvenirs, nothing.

After the filming at Wembley I was staying in the Swiss Cottage Marriott and I was the only one in the bar who wasn't inundated with tons of Mars bars and England 'World in Motion' souvenirs.

I had a wonderful reprise with Keith when Tony arranged for us to do some promo on *This Morning with Richard and Judy.* Tony and I had arranged to meet Keith in the Britannia Hotel in Manchester and drive to Liverpool at 8 a.m., but there was no answer from his room. Luckily the desk clerk was a fan and gave us the number, letting us go up. When we got there we could hear loud coupling noises from inside and on the ledge outside the room was a full glass of champagne. We knocked for ages until at last out burst Keith, looking definitely the worse for wear. He promptly necked the champagne and shouted into the room, 'Don't fucking nick anything.'

We set off. Keith and Tony were at it all the way, and when we got there they were twatted. In the make-up room the girl said to Keith, 'Did you have a nice night last night?'

Keith said, 'Yeah, I was up all night with rock stars snorting coke off groupies' tits.'

'Lovely,' she said, without batting an eyelid.

On the way down Keith and Tony wouldn't stop talking, but as soon as we went on they both completely clammed up. It wasn't the best interview ever, let's put it like that. When it was all over, Keith came back to life, winding Richard up by telling him that he'd just caught Judy snogging a cameraman.

In the end I had to drag them both out and we headed back to Manchester. But Keith needed a drink and made us stop at a pub on the outskirts of Liverpool. Tony kept saying, 'It's not safe. It's not safe. We need to go. Scousers hate me.'

'Don't be daft,' we told him. But once inside I looked out of the window to see groups of people in the distance, advancing towards us, like zombies being drawn by some invisible force.

Keith saw it too. 'Fuck!' he shouted, 'let's get out of here. Now.'

We legged it to the car with Tony screeching out of the car park just as the first bricks and bottles landed around us. He was right. The Scousers *did* hate him. The fun didn't stop there. He'd arranged for us to do some promo at Piccadilly 261, then Manchester's biggest radio station, where Keith wouldn't come out of the toilet until we'd all had a line, even telling the managing director of the station to fuck off at one point. It was wild. What a summer.

'But what now for New Order?' I hear you ask.

As in, the future of New Order? Well …

I don't think any of us expected creative sparks to fly when we got together, but the 'World in Motion' turned out great, our first number one. Bloody typical!

By then, I'd released Revenge's '7 Reasons' and Barney's first Electronic single was out. The world would have to wait over a year for the first The Other Two record. In short, we were all into our own thing. As far as we were concerned, we were saying goodbye for the last time. Again.

At this time I was the only one of the group going to the Haçienda. Steve and Gillian had never been regulars there, not since the fateful day they were turned away – turned away from their own nightclub! My heart bled for them. The ignominy being too much to bear, they never set foot in the place again. Not as punters, anyway. Bernard went occasionally on a Saturday, I went most nights including the Friday (Saturday's music was too handbag for me and I usually had the kids all weekend anyway). Barney's attendance at planning and business meetings fell away, too, leaving it to me to fly the flag for New Order. And – as documented elsewhere, of course – I flew it with enough enthusiasm for all of us.

The Dry 201 bar had opened by then, and it was there that we held auditions for Revenge members, to complete the line-up for 'live'. I was still feeling my way, still trying to work out what to do and how to do it – how to be a band without Rob, Steve and Barney. I'm a naturally competitive person, and I'd be lying if I didn't say I was in competition with Barney (and in denial if I didn't admit that he won that particular competition hands down), but the fact was that Barney had gone off to form a supergroup. He was working with Johnny Marr – at that time still fresh from the Smiths split – and Neil Tennant of the Pet Shop Boys. While Revenge didn't exactly start on the bottom rung of the ladder, we were certainly close to the bottom.

Barney would have a taste of that later, when he chanced his arm with a band of beginners, Bad Lieutenant. I bet that gave him something to moan about – when he found himself in the same boat as the rest of us. Up till then, he must have just assumed he had the Midas touch.

At first, it was me, CJ and Dave Hicks who put out the '7 Reasons' single. It came out in December 1989 but, like I say, Barney quite comprehensively won that battle when 'Getting Away With It' went to number one and '7 Reasons' didn't even chart.

Meanwhile we had a new manager in Tony Michaelides, who was then doing a bit of promotion for Factory; he had discovered U2 and was instrumental in getting them signed to Island. He was offered a job there but decided instead to form his own promotions company. He was also a successful and well-regarded DJ on several Manchester radio stations. Revenge had been picked up for a deal by A&M/Capitol in America by an A&R friend of Tom Atencio's, Tim Devine. Tim and Tom between them would give us a huge profile and a massive boost in America.

As a result we did pretty well overall, but in the UK the press didn't have any regard for us. I don't think I've ever had such a slagging as I did with Revenge, not before or since. They just thought we were shit: shit concept, shit music, shit everything else. Perhaps they had a point towards the beginning of our career, when I'd be the first to admit that things were a bit on the fragile side. But they never acknowledged that the quality of the material improved at all, or how good we were live. I had made a conscious decision when I began Revenge that I would not use the bass guitar to write melodies. I would not do it like New Order had done it, and I cannot for the life of me remember why. I threw away my strength to concentrate on my weakness. But I wasn't asking for the same slack as an emerging new band, and after that first batch of bad reviews we were poison to them, no matter what we did.

Still, what adventures we had. I took all my mates with me, running it just like New Order and making the same mistakes, going away for far longer than the gigs dictated, not keeping an eye on the budget or spending within our means. I was investing a fortune that I did not have: Sarge doing security, Bowser selling T-shirts, Andy Liddle along with all the technicians I knew from the New Order days. We spent masses on shipping the gear, security, sound and lighting, monitors guys, money we didn't have to spend on people we didn't really need to employ, not at this level. It just wasn't realistic, but I wanted to have familiar faces and an organisation around me like a security blanket. Jane was our tour manager and I found out later she was paying herself £650 a day (still, she had to put up with sleeping with me, so I guess that has to account for at least £649 of it).

During the years of New Order recording at Cargo Studios in Rochdale I had got friendly with Chris Hewitt, who ran the music shop downstairs. When John Brierley of Cargo decided to retire, Chris suggested we buy into the studio and run it as our own. I had to make that awful visit to Rob's in order to get the money, and we went through with it.

It was Tony's idea to call it 'Suite 16' because when we started we had a sixteen-track Cadey valve multitrack recorder, a lovely machine. It gave you the most wonderful warm, fat sound. ('It also sounds like New York,' said Tony, about the nearest Rochdale could ever get.)

In my opinion a sixteen-track two-inch tape machine is the best recording medium ever. Eight-track two-inch is even better because of the tape width, but you can't get enough instruments on it. A sixteen-track two-inch, on the other hand, gives you the width of tape to get a really good signal – a fat, proper signal – while your sixteen tracks is enough to make a modern pop song, including overdubs and backing vocals. 'Atmosphere', 'Dead Souls', 'Glass' and 'Digital' had all been recorded on that Cadey sixteen-track at Cargo, and they all sounded fantastic.

I suppose one of the major things to happen at Suite 16 was receiving a letter from a lad who wanted to gain experience as a tape operator. This was David Potts. He was nineteen. He explained he was working at a bank in Swinton, Salford, but was desperate to get into the music business and said, 'I do play a little guitar.'

I interviewed him and gave him the job as tape operator/tea brewer. He turned out to be a dab hand on the guitar – started showing Dave Hicks a thing or two very early on – shame he didn't come along sooner – then came on tour with us playing bass, eventually replacing Hicksy in Revenge and later becoming my partner in Monaco.

Meantime, it had quickly become apparent that Chris Hewitt and I had very different ideas for the studio: Chris wanted it to be rough and ready and held together with spit and sawdust – the type of place where bands could kick the skirting board and it didn't matter. I wanted it to be a beautiful, state-of-the-art modern studio. I mean, not *quite* the kind of place where ducks would float past the window, but more in that direction than the other.

We fell out, and then Naru Hira, father of Shan from Stockholm Monsters, was interested and bought out Hewitt. Naru was a very well-respected surgeon at Oldham General Hospital and was the man responsible for pioneering surgical laser use in Britain. By the time of Revenge I was running it with Shan.

Suite 16 was my studio, and I told Factory I'd charge less for Revenge's studio time. What I didn't find out until years later was that, despite the deal, the studio had been billing the full amount of £2,100 a week, not the reduced rate, half that.

Why Factory didn't spot it, I don't know. But as all the Factory history books tell us, the Revenge album took a long time (guilty, your honour), cost a lot of money (not *entirely* guilty, your honour), came in over budget (there was none) and when it came out in May 1990 basically sold fuck all, putting another nail in Factory's coffin.

One day at Suite 16 I got a phone call from Tony: 'I want you to go on a panel at a seminar.'

'What?' I had no idea what he was talking about.

He elaborated, 'It's a music industry conference in New York, loads of industry types, A&R men and record executives all get together and network.'

'Sounds like hell,' says I.

'Well, you're on a panel with Ice-T and Ice Cube. I'll send you the tickets. Keith Allen's coming too.'

Now we were talking. Keith was wild, I had a girlfriend in New York anyway, so it would be a nice weekend. When I arrived and checked into the hotel in downtown Manhattan, I got a bit of a shock. It was a new boutique hotel concept that I had never heard of before. It had no reception or any normal hotel services, just someone in a hole in the foyer who gave you your keys and anything else you asked for, within reason of course.

As I came downstairs for the first trip to the seminar, Tony and Keith were waiting for me, with a rather beautiful young English girl in tow. Tony introduced her quite fondly as Keith's girlfriend and a former Miss England, Yvette Livesey. This seemed odd … Keith had never mentioned her before. But hey-ho.

We set off and, on arriving at the seminar, I was taken to the green room to meet the other panellists. I was amazed that one of them was David Cassidy, the teenage heart-throb himself. David seemed nice and we posed for photos. As we did there was what can only be described as a ruckus in the corridor outside the room, culminating in what sounded like gunshots and then screaming.

As we listened a rather camp and obviously very frightened guy ran in the green room, shut the door behind him, shouted, 'Protect the artists! Protect the artists!' and started running round the room like a headless chicken.

I calmed him down and got the full story. It seems Ice-T and Ice Cube were having a feud and their respective posses had met in the bar, where a fight had escalated into gunfire, the trouble then spilling all round the seminar with people literally running for their lives.

I, of course, by this time well refreshed, grabbed David Cassidy and said, 'Come on, Dave, let's see what's going on.'

As I turned to the door the camp guy threw himself across it, shouting, 'No! Don't go out there.'

'Piss off, mate, I'm from Salford,' said I, as I removed him delicately from the door, then turned and said, 'Come on, David. David? Where's David gone?'

David Cassidy had disappeared, completely disappeared. I looked round the room – no sign, then on hearing a whimpering sound I looked down and under the apron on the table, there he cowered. 'Bloody hell, lead singers. They're all the same.'

By the time I got in the corridor there were various cops running round and it seemed to have calmed down. So the camp guy took me straight to the panel.

I was pretty drunk and as I sat down with this load of strangers, I noticed one empty space with a sign that read 'Ice Cube'. As I looked up, I noticed this huge room was full of people. Weird. The panel started and soon descended into a lot of shouting between people in the audience and various panel members about God knows what. I was just sitting there completely bemused and pissed. Then, in a lull, a journalist stood up and loudly demanded, 'Is Ice Cube coming back?'

I hadn't even spoken until now but thought, *Here's my chance.* I grabbed the mic and bellowed, 'No, mate, he's fucking melted!' laughing uproariously at my own joke. Shit. They all started booing and gesticulating. Obviously someone had done something to really upset them. As I sat back I wondered who.

Then I got a tap on the shoulder and this security guy goes, 'Please come with me, Mr Hook, we are having to remove you for your own safety.'

I flicked 'em all the Vs as I left. In the bar I met up with Tony and Keith, and Keith's new love, which was very strange because Tony had his hand on her arse. There was definitely something wrong here. (It would turn out later, of course, that, having just split from his wife Hilary, this was Tony's first appearance with his new partner Yvette, trying very badly to pass her off as Keith's girlfriend.)

The sad thing was I had bumped into Hilary with Oliver and Isabel, their kids, in Didsbury just before I left. I was walking with Heather and Jack in his buggy and we got talking about kids etc., saying how hard it was, and she said to me, 'You know, I envy you single parents, passing the kids around. At least you get the odd weekend or night off. I'd love that.'

Be careful what you wish for, eh? When he returned from New York Tony moved out of the family home.

But back to our adventures. Tony's panel, 'Wake up, America, You're Dead!' had caused a near riot and almost complete exodus, with all the Americans on the panel leaving disgusted as Nathan McGough (Mondays' manager) told everyone the Mondays were drug dealers first and musicians second. This was a really stupid thing to say but well in keeping with our view at the time that ecstasy was the cure to all the world's problems.

That night me and Keith had been invited to dinner at this new and very exclusive restaurant in Manhattan. The invite had come from Tom Atencio and Larry 'Niceman', our merchandising supremo in America. It seemed that this restaurant was so exclusive you had to be invited to attend. It was unlisted. You couldn't phone up and just book it. This had us written all over it, I must say.

By the time we turned up we were off our heads, and being ushered into this beautiful restaurant full of beautiful people was like a red rag to a bull to Keith, who promptly took off his top and sat at the table berating all the other 'invited guests' and laying lines of coke out for us all.

Dish after dish of wonderful food began arriving on our table, being put down and then removed, completely untouched. By this time me and Keith had taken to crawling round the restaurant on all fours pretending to bite the ankles of all the ladies present, with Keith then joining whoever he fancied at their table for some very intense conversations. Bizarrely the maitre d' and staff loved it, and when we left after getting thoroughly bored or perhaps running out of drugs, there were cries of, 'Oh no, don't leave!' 'Guys stay!' 'You guys are great!' Wow.

We spent the rest of the night at Nell's, a very famous bar in New York that we tried to model Dry 201 on (of course, something getting completely lost in the translation to designer Ben Kelly, as they ended up being completely different). I loved this place and I had actually danced with Madonna here once, just before I got thrown out for harassing her, only to sneak back in then get thrown out again for surreptitiously smoking a coke ciggy in the downstairs bar. I was stood there smoking it behind cupped hands (a trick my dad had taught me so the foreman couldn't see the cigarette end glowing – I still do it now when I DJ, bloody smoking ban!), watching the doorman work his way through the crowded bar like a great white shark, and coming straight up to me saying, 'Right, Peter Hook, you're out!' Turned out he was from Manchester and knew it'd be me.

Anyway, by the time I got back it was about four in the morning and in the foyer was a proper hubbub: the building only had one lift and it was stuck on the fourteenth floor. A very tired crowd of people stood there staring up at the readout. In the end I went to the little hole in the wall and asked the guy behind the counter to run up (I was in no fit state) and see what was going on. He disappeared, and eventually the '14' display started counting down.

'Hooray!' went a great cheer from the crowd, which included this very New Yawk taxi driver who kept shouting, 'Taxi for Allon. Taxi for Allon.'

When the door opened the young man stepped out to a gasp from several waiting people. There in the lift, spreadeagled on the floor, was Keith Allen, sparkled. The receptionist explained that when he'd got there the reason the lift wouldn't move was because Keith had passed out and fallen over with his head between the lift doors. He said the doors were shutting on his head then opening again, over and over.

'How long for?' said I. 'About an hour, sir.'

The taxi driver then let out his usual bellow, 'Taxi for Allon, taxi for

Allon,' whereupon Keith literally jumped up off the floor and, grabbing the guy, yelled, 'Come on, mate, this way, NOW!' and headed off once more into the night. I didn't see him again for two days.

The next day was 18 July, and a Mondays gig at the Sound Factory. This was part of 'The United States of the Haçienda Tour' of America, organised by Angie Matthews, the Haçienda manager. This gig was sold out but was a bit of a miserable affair as the Mondays were not in very good humour.

The venue turned out to be in the meat-packing district, where it really was underdeveloped. It was a grim place, and scary. The venue was also unlicensed, as in no liquor allowed, so there was a big black bin liner backstage you had to ferret around in to get a drink. We weren't well looked after and it was all a bit miserable.

I left early with my girlfriend and after a roll in the hay felt a bit guilty and thought I should go back and keep everyone company. I set off walking, convinced I knew where I was going. It was just getting close to dawn and I was completely lost with no idea where I was in the deep dark Manhattan industrial district. I was just starting to get worried when I stumbled upon the street of the Sound Factory, just as it was getting light.

I started running and when I got to the door it was closed. All locked up. Shit.

I looked down the street. It was deserted. But right at the end I could see the tail lights of a car.

I thought to myself, *You are in the shit here, mate*, and was just about to panic when the car started reversing down the street towards me, the door opened and out stepped Paul, Keith's best mate (he ran a place in Soho called 'Legends' that we would sometimes go to; the only club I've ever known where there would be no one in the club but the toilets would be rammed).

Paul was a lovely man and I was so glad to see him. I leaped into his arms. 'Hooky,' he sang, 'Did you think I would leave you lying, when there's room in the car for two?' We then went off to a dealer's house for another half-day of mayhem. I was glad to get home.

On the plane later, with Tony and (a very happily outed) Yvette, he said, 'Good idea that conference thing ... Manchester could do with one of them!'

*

But come September and Tony Wilson was now a very unhappy man. I was desperate to release an American remix of Revenge's 'Big Bang', which everybody said would be a hit. I really thought this could be the one to save the album. The idea was to talk Tony into releasing it, but I made the mistake of going for a few scoops before the meeting, so when I turned up to see him I was pissed, and, oh my God, he really laid into me. I'll never forget it. On the top floor of the new Factory offices on Charles Street, he destroyed me for about an hour, giving me a no-holds-barred rundown of my various glaring faults – all about how I'd let New Order go, let Rob down, let him down, let Manchester down. How much the Revenge album had cost, how shit it was, how he wasn't releasing the remix because it wasn't representative of the album and he didn't want to be held responsible when people bought it and then bought a shit album off the back of it (which sadly never bothered him with most of the others on the label).

It was a proper roasting, and by the end of it I was in bits. I mean, he was right in one sense, but on the other hand, it wasn't as though I'd taken the money off him with a mask, a brace of pistols and a horse called Black Bess. I'd tell him I needed another few months in the studio and he'd give it to me and let me get on with it.

Yes, Revenge played its part in Factory's eventual downfall, but so did we all, and let's not forget I played a bigger part in Factory's success, which I still had not been paid for. I must say I was delighted to see that in the details of Factory's bankruptcy he had gotten all the money back from our international licensing deals and we were actually in credit. We were owed the mighty sum of £30.26. And never got it.

But Revenge had done brilliantly abroad. If England – with the valiant exception of the Skin Two nightclub – remained immune to our charms, then I only needed to go overseas for confirmation my efforts weren't entirely in vain.

At the end of the year we got offered a tour by my old friend Philippe Rodrigues in Brazil. He had to fulfil a contract he had made with Coca-Cola for one last tour with a foreign band and did I want to do it? He would pay us well but wouldn't be able to promote the gigs as he'd used up his promotion budget.

Being completely off my head, I thought this was a superb idea and we ended up doing five or six gigs in huge arenas all over Brazil to about 400 people in each. We had a great time.

But I had a problem and, to be honest, I was spending more time at Wendy the Chorlton coke dealer's house than I was at my own. By this time I'd had a studio installed at our Circular Road home, and I soldiered on, spending a recording session for Revenge's last EP, 'Gun World Porn', clutching the eight-ball bag I was going through a day.

Sometimes it was difficult; every time I had a mad coke session, the next morning the lads were there all bright and early to record. *Shit.* I swore I would never have a studio in my house again.

Luckily Jane had gone off working with other groups (Inspiral Carpets, the Orb) all over the world, so me and my addiction were left mainly alone. Funnily enough, I really enjoyed making that record, and was very proud of the finished product, even though my drug use was completely out of control. Factory did nothing with it though.

By then, there were rumblings about having to record a new New Order album. 'It's the only thing that can save Factory and the Haçienda,' we were told by Rob and Tony. 'Otherwise, both will go bankrupt and you'll lose your houses.'

The Stone Roses deserve a chapter to themselves, so here we go

I was still with Iris when I met the Roses' manager Gareth Evans, but going to gigs with Jane. We used to spend a lot of time at the International I in Rusholme, which was then one of Manchester's most popular venues (and is now a Greek delicatessen). It was managed by Gareth.

I liked Gareth. As you'll soon hear, he was a complete nutcase, but even so, I liked him. Gareth would always look after you. He had an odd way of doing it, like he'd come up behind you and leave eight cans of beer or, in Barney's case, a bottle of Pernod and some orange juice, and he wouldn't make a big fuss of it, wouldn't want to bother you or bend your ear for hours or get you to do stuff in return. Just left you with your free drinks and scuttled off.

Apart from this one night, when he asked if I'd produce the Stone Roses' next single. Very few people had heard of the Roses at this point, but Gareth was doing his best to change all that, letting them rehearse at the International and telling anyone who'd listen that they were the best band in the world. Actually, what he knew about music you could fit on the back of a postage stamp, so nobody was taking much notice when he said that, but he was loaded so he was well qualified to be a music manager and there was no doubt he was putting his money where his mouth was. He was doing the same as Tony did with the Mondays, part-manager, part-minder, part parent, part-gofer. If the band needed anything, all they had to do was call and he would fetch it for them. New kettle? Hi-fi? Birthday card for the missus? Gareth would go and get it.

At the same time, he was putting gigs on for them and paying people to attend, bribing the audience so it looked like the Roses had a bigger following than they did. Very clever.

He was able to fund this by taking money from the club in cash. Whenever you saw Gareth, his pockets were literally bulging with money. He'd take out a huge wad of notes, peel a few off and pay for everything. This being Manchester, word soon got round that Gareth

Evans walked around with hundreds, maybe even thousands, of pounds of cash in his pockets, so he was always being mugged. 'Oh, bloody hell, I got robbed again last night,' he'd say.

Didn't stop him though; still carried all that cash around with him. I think to him it was a mark of success.

As far as recordings went, the Roses had had a disastrous run-in with Martin Hannett, who'd done their heads in on their first single (good old Martin), and they'd produced their next single, 'Sally Cinnamon', themselves. But that hadn't gone well either, so Gareth wanted someone else. Which was where I came in.

Sure enough, we went into Revolution Studios to record 'Elephant Stone' with Mike Johnson as engineer, and if I'd thought Gareth was a bit of a nutcase before that session, then by the end of it I knew he was completely off his rocker. I remember him coming into the studio one day and saying to me, 'Hooky, what are you doing now?'

'I'm just doing the bass,' I told him.

'Oh, great,' he said. 'Will you be doing the treble next, then?'

Me and Mike fell about laughing. Another time, the Roses were winding up Gareth. Ian Brown came to me and said, 'Hooky, Hooky, Gareth's going to come in disguised as Mani. Just go along with it, will you, mate.'

All right, then. So in comes Gareth, dressed as Mani but looking nothing like Mani, with a scarf around his neck and a hat on, holding Mani's bass and going, in a terrible approximation of Mani's gravelly voice, 'All right, Hooky? Do you want me to do the bass now?'

Inwardly rolling my eyes, I'm going, 'Yeah, Mani, if you would. Do you mind popping in the overdub room and doing the bass?'

'All right, mate,' says Gareth/Mani, brightly, 'I'll go in and do the bass now.'

So Gareth/Mani disappears into this little overdub room at the end of the studio then seconds later reappears, cackling wildly as he whips off the hat to reveal his true self.

'I got you, Hooky!' He was holding his sides he was laughing so hard. 'It's not Mani at all, it's me, Gareth. I got you, didn't I? Come on, admit it. I got you.'

'Yeah, mate, you really had me going there. Bloody hell, how'd you do that? That's brilliant, that is.'

And then they left, and me and Mike were sitting there, looking at each other thinking, *Oh my God.*

But he was actually quite endearing. A bit odd, no doubt about it, but a nice guy. He had a disabled son, and if he saw anyone in a wheelchair he'd stop his car, open the boot and give them T-shirts and CDs, just to brighten their day, he said. For ages in Manchester there were loads of disabled people wearing Stone Roses T-shirts.

Anyway, recording continued and was absolutely fine. We did the bass, we did the treble, and then we got to the vocals, where I had to deal with the only real friction of the session.

Now, Ian Brown's vocals are very distinctive and unique and, to be frank, took some getting used to for me. Although Mike Johnson was a big fan right away, I took a bit of convincing. In time I recognised Ian as not only the leader of the band but also its unique selling point. I'd worked with Barney and Ian Curtis, and they may not have been perfect but they were full of passion, full of heart and soul, and each had an indiscernible quality that made them wonderful.

Matters weren't made any easier by the fact that Reni, the drummer, was convinced he was a better singer. He was, technically, from a pitching point of view, but he lacked the spark, the unique quality that makes someone a frontman.

Reni was always bugging me about it: 'Why don't you let me sing the vocal?'

'Well, because you're the drummer,' I'd tell him. 'You never have a singing drummer, mate. It's the kiss of death to have a singing drummer in the band.'

(One of my group rules, that is: never have a singing drummer or a singing bass player.)

But he was pushy. The others weren't pushy at all, just dead laidback. But Reni was right in your face. He was obviously the ambitious one and made no bones about it; Ian would be in earshot but Reni would be saying, 'I'm a better singer than Ian.'

It's true. He was a better singer – if you're Simon Cowell. But Ian Brown, Ian Curtis, Barney, Shaun Ryder, Captain Beefheart, you name it, were all singers who have something much more valuable, something that can't be learned or tweaked in the studio. Real character.

To shut Reni up I got him to do the backing vocals, along with a nice cannon vocal, which did the trick. But it didn't alter the fact that he wanted to be the frontman. I'm not sure that changed, or ever will.

The session went very well. I helped them write the instrumental middle eight, that I thought the song was lacking, using a dustbin lid we nicked from the studio backyard to give it a really distinctive crash sound. I was happy and looked forward to mixing it at Suite 16.

One night at my home, there was a knock on my door and there, standing on the doorstep, was Gareth.

Like Alan Erasmus, Gareth would never come into your house, didn't like to hang around. He just said what he had to say then buggered off. Can't figure out people like that myself, but there you go.

'I've been thinking,' he said. 'I think you should get paid for doing this record.' The thought had never crossed my mind. Like the rest of New Order, I just did it because I loved music; but, boxing clever, I thought I'd agree.

'Well, OK, I think so as well,' I said. 'Thanks very much, Gareth.'

'How much?' he said.

Oh shit. I hadn't expected that question. I hesitated.

'How about a grand?' he said.

He peeled off a massive wad of cash that he took from his pocket, gave it to me on the doorstep and turned round to leave. As he got to the car he shouted, 'Oh, and points too. Two OK?' He smiled.

'Yes, thanks, mate,' says I, turning immediately to Iris, going, 'What are points, I wonder?'

> Producers' points are the percentage of royalties awarded to a producer for working on a particular song, album or body of work. Generally one point equals 1 per cent of the royalties. The average for a producer is two points per song, or 2 per cent. So if 'Elephant Stone' ended up on an album of, say, twelve songs I would get 2 per cent of one twelfth of the royalties of the album. Bearing in mind that most bands only got 8 or 12 per cent max off their record company, producers can earn a lot of money (e.g. Stephen Hague, 'World in Motion').

Me and Iris were delighted. We were on £200 or something a week at that time, so to be given a grand, just like that, was like winning the pools. (Over the years, because 'Elephant Stone' was reversed and given another name, 'Full Fathom Five', I would get 2 per cent of that too, and since 1987 have earned in excess of £30,000 just for producing that one track.)

The production job rumbled on, and I ended up doing a Christmas rush job and mixing on Christmas Eve in Strawberry Studios as a favour to Gareth.

I had decided 'Elephant Stone' needed a sixteens hi-hat to tie the drum beat together. Without it, it felt just a little too loose. I asked Reni to come and do it on the track for me. When I'd put the idea to him, he'd said, 'No, mate, you don't need it, Hooky, it's great as it is, leave it alone, it's absolutely fine, don't worry about it, in fact ... fuck right off.' I respected that, I must admit.

Reni's an absolutely brilliant drummer. I think him and Steve Morris are the two best-ever Manchester drummers. But I did feel he was wrong on this one.

Gareth had said to me, 'Hooky, the lads won't come, it's Christmas Eve, you'll be on your own.' But the band not being there suited me fine, because I had a great idea. I got Shan, the drummer for Stockholm Monsters, to come into Strawberry and record the new hi-hat pattern.

Fine. Christmas Eve at Strawberry Studios and Shan is in the booth drumming away, brilliant, just what I needed. I'm sitting there with John Dixon, who was the engineer, giving instructions, when all of a sudden this head appears between John and me. 'Merry Christmas.'

It was Reni. And as soon as he'd wished us a Merry Christmas he saw what was going on in the booth and said, 'What's he doing? Is he drumming on my track?'

Shan, meanwhile, saw Reni there and completely went to pieces. And whether by accident, because he realised we had been caught out, or by design, he started playing so badly on the track that Reni went from saying that the track didn't need a new hi-hat pattern to getting frustrated at Shan's crap playing and going, 'Give it here, I'll do it.'

And that was it. Much wiping of brows as Reni went into the booth and finished off the drumming on the track. It was much better.

This wasn't the end of the saga. Oh no. Next thing I knew, I got a message from Gareth. 'Rough Trade want to sign us, can you do a cassette of the mix and send it to Geoff Travis?'

That was Geoff Travis, legendary owner of Rough Trade, which at that time was the Smiths' label. I was more than happy to oblige, and got Shan to send him a cassette.

A few days later, another call, this time from Travis: 'This sounds dreadful, Peter. We can't work under these circumstances. What is going on there? I may have to remix.' Oh, I did not like the sound of that.

I'd checked it in the studio and it sounded fine to me, but I told him I'd get Shan to run off another cassette and, because I was in London myself at the time, play it to him in person.

So that's what I did. Sitting there in the Rough Trade offices, slapping the cassette into the machine, and …

It sounded absolutely bloody awful.

Travis was giving me the evil eye. You could tell he was an ex-teacher. 'Well, Peter, this just won't do, will it?'

Me, wanting the ground to open up and absolutely swallow me. I walked out like a whipped dog, my reputation in tatters.

How had it happened? As it turned out, Shan was being a right cheapskate. I'd always said to him, 'When you get cassettes get proper TDK metal ones, the most expensive you can. It's really important.'

But he had of course ignored every word of it, gone to Shadoos on Wilmslow Road in Manchester and bought a huge job lot of cassettes that worked out to around thruppence each for a thousand. Whenever I was phoning him to do tapes he was putting the mix on one of these and they sounded shit. The studio output was fine, but he wasn't checking the actual cassettes before he sent them out.

So anyway, Travis stayed annoyed with me, and decided he wanted to get the single remixed. Trouble was, the London studio he used for remixing had affiliations with Silvertone, who heard the band and promptly gazumped Rough Trade by getting Gareth to sign a contract.

The first I knew of it was at Suite 16 in Rochdale one afternoon, when Gareth burst in.

'Oh, hi, Gareth, what are you doing?'

'I came to show you the contract,' he said. 'I signed a contract for the Roses and I wanted to come to show it to you because it was your production of "Elephant Stone" that got us the deal.' Not too sure he got that right, but hey-ho.

'Right,' I said, 'great,' and watched as he hauled his briefcase onto the desk – one of those old plastic, hard-sided briefcases that people like Gareth used to cart around in the 80s to make themselves look important.

He looked at me. He opened the briefcase.

'I'm going to show you the contract,' he said to me over the lid of the briefcase.

'Right,' I said.

From the briefcase he took the contract, held it up, waved it for a couple of seconds, then put it back in the briefcase and slammed it shut.

And with that, he left. 'See you.' And roared off.

That's how weird Gareth was.

Why he didn't want to show me, I think, and what I discovered later, was the small print, that he'd signed a ten-album deal for £28,000, and if that wasn't bad enough, the deal didn't include CDs, which at that stage were becoming really big, so the Stone Roses would not be paid for any future CD sales on their next ten albums.

So Gareth was really proud he had done this deal, but it was a shit deal.

Then came the opportunity to produce their album, which I would have loved to do. It was a few months later and we were getting ready to record *Technique*. I was being offered a lot of production work at the time: the Go-Betweens, the Gun Club and the Cramps among them. I literally had to choose between them or New Order, and I agonised. As a producer you are hot one minute and not the next. It's hard work, you're first in, last out, and if the songs don't turn out well it's all your fault. But I liked it, and this was my big chance.

Even so, I chose New Order and the rest is history. Not only that, but Geoff Travis still blames me for Rough Trade losing the Stone Roses.

Later the Roses did the old trick on me, which was to come to Suite 16 and ask if they could make some demos on the cheap, on the assurance that they'd come back and record their second album when they were ready.

So they did: they came in, blew up my hi-fi, blew my studio monitors, smashed my television, stained my settees, basically me cost me a fortune and ... never returned. When it came to recording their record they fucked off to London, just like the Happy Mondays, the

Inspiral Carpets, and the Chameleons did before them. It's all well and good doing your demos in Rochdale, especially when you're getting it nearly free, but not when it comes to recording. Nobody wants to record in Rochdale. The bright lights and streets paved with gold get them every time … including me; I don't blame them at all.

Moral of the story? Never trust a musician. Even me.

Of course, things went wrong for the Roses pretty much straight away, and for the reasons why, we need to look at our friend Gareth Evans. For a start, he compounded the crap Silvertone deal by using the money to buy a fleet of second-hand Range Rovers. This was Gareth all over. These Range Rovers were ex-BT vehicles. BT used them as vans, so Gareth got them for the price of a van, but he'd then remove the metal plate in the rear, replace the windows and turn them back into a car.

A car for the price of a van. Complete Arthur Daley stuff. And Gareth, in his infinite wisdom, thinking he'd struck the bargain of the century, spent all of the band's money on them. Whenever the band needed money, he'd sell one.

Of course, the band thought he was a lunatic. And they were getting more and more pissed off with him because, just like Rob, and just like any other band manager who gets a bit of power and takes control of the band's purse strings, he wasn't giving the individual members any dough. If they wanted something – new gear, a holiday or a birthday present for their missus – they had to ask him for it.

This was just the first advance. With the second one Gareth came up with the brilliant idea of spending all the money on another 'investment': a Lear jet. He actually went to the airport to buy a Lear jet and the band luckily got there first and stopped him.

After that, they really fell out with him. But Gareth had a plan to keep the boys onside: he was going to make them big in America.

He came to me. 'Listen, Hooky, I want to make the lads huge in America. Do you know anyone I could work with to get them huge?'

By this time New Order were with Qwest and we're getting bigger and bigger. The Roses had no profile over there at all, but if anybody could change that then it was our US manager, Tom Atencio.

So I sent Tom the tapes. Next thing I knew, he was ringing me up, talking about how much he loved the band, thought they were absolutely mega. Shortly after that he started negotiating with Gareth to bring them over.

Then I started getting phone calls from Tom. 'This guy's nuts, Hooky.'

'I know, mate, but they're a great band and a bunch of good lads. They've got a superb work ethic. You'll have a great time with them.'

'OK, but I'm finding this guy really difficult to deal with.'

'Don't worry, he's got a brain of mush but a heart of gold,' I told Tom.

(And if you think I was telling Tom white lies, well, I don't think I was, because even though Gareth was nuts – and probably still *is* nuts – I genuinely believe he wanted the best for the Roses. He just had a funny way of showing it, that's all.)

Back then, the way English bands broke America was by doing the college-radio circuit. What you had to do was service local college radio with the record and if they liked it then it would get a lot of airtime and hopefully pass into mainstream radio, at which point the band would go from being a cult college band to a major mainstream success.

Every band broke that way: the Cure, Joy Division, Bow Wow Wow, New Order. All broken the same way.

So that's what Tom started to do. He got the record to college radio and then set up the gigs, twelve dates in all, when Gareth rang him up and said, 'So, the lads are coming over in four weeks, then?'

'Yeah, man,' said Tom, 'it's going to be great, everything's coming together, man, I really have a good feeling about this one.'

'Well, Tom, you know what I'd like. When they arrive at the airport I want them to be greeted like the Beatles when they first went to America.'

Of course, I heard all this later from Tom, so I can only imagine his reaction. I suspect it was the blood draining from his face.

'Well, hey, Gareth, that's a great thought and a wonderful idea. But you know what? When the Beatles came over they were already a huge band. The Roses haven't sold any records over here yet. Nobody over here knows them at all. This tour is the one that's going to establish them.'

'So,' says Gareth, 'you can't guarantee me that there's going to be loads of girls screaming at them when they arrive at the airport?'

'Well, no,' says Tom, 'I can't.'

'Well, we're not coming then.'

That was it. Gareth cancelled it. He cancelled the tour and the band never went.

Now, God knows how the band reacted to all this. For all I know, it might have been the band's idea to have the Beatles' reception, though I very much doubt it. The thing was, everything with Gareth was just getting more and more outlandish. He'd sussed that the Roses were making a huge amount of money on their T-shirt sales so he bought a T-shirt company and printed them himself. Years later, my wife, Becky, and I went to look at a farmhouse he was selling, and in one of the outbuildings was a huge pile of Stone Roses T-shirts. 'You're not still knocking these out, are you?' I asked him.

'No, Hooky, these are left over from when I managed them.' I bet.

I remember being at Spike Island where emotions were running really high, particularly for Gareth. I mean, you had to hand it to him, he'd mentored the Roses from nothing and now here they were headlining this huge rave at Spike Island.

All day Gareth was going, 'This is the Stone Roses' second coming,' which must have been where they got the title of the next album, even though he was ancient history by the time that came out.

But even the occasion of Spike Island couldn't stop Gareth being Gareth. I remember standing with him and his business partner, Matthew, when Reni stormed up with a right face on him. As you know, Reni always wore this painter's hat. It was his trademark.

'Those dirty bootlegging bastards are out there selling copies of my hat,' he raged at Gareth.

Gareth went, 'Oh my God, that's awful. Don't you worry, Reni, I'm going to go out there and stop it immediately.'

Reni went, 'Right, good, great, do it,' and stormed off again, at which point Gareth turned round to Matthew and said, 'You'd better get them hats off the stall, he's going fucking mental.'

That was him all over. Complete nutcase. It was like Rob. Rob had this habit of giving people more money than they were owed. It was a weird trait – one of his weirdest – that he'd say, 'Give him twice what he's asking for, make a twat out of him, and tell him to fuck off.'

We'd say, 'How does giving him twice what he's owed make a twat out of him?'

What Rob was doing was being tight with New Order's money when it came to giving it to us, but ridiculous when it came to other people. Gareth was the same. I did well out of my points for 'Elephant Stone', but you'd have to ask the members of Stone Roses what happened to their money. All I can say is that I remember walking into the Co-op Bank one day and coming across Ian Brown. Just after they'd signed to Geffen, this was. Ian stood there with tears streaming down his face as he stared at bits of paper in his hand.

'You OK, Ian?' I said. 'What's wrong?'

This was in the days when you asked the bank for your balance and the cashier wrote it down on a piece of paper and passed it to you like it was a betting slip.

Ian had three bits of paper for each of the band's three different accounts. He showed them to me. All of them read zero.

Barney tells a great story about Gareth. He had asked to come skiing with him one winter and Barney asked if he'd skied before.

'No,' he said, 'but it can't be that hard.'

On the first day as they arrived they all headed for the slopes, with Barney saying, 'You should be on the nursery slope, Gareth, it can be dangerous.' Gareth ignored him, donning the skis and making for the same slope as them. When they got there he didn't wait, launched himself like a madman straight down the slope, arms flailing behind. They all followed some time after and when they got to the bottom of the slope, which was near a riverbank next to a raging river, Gareth was nowhere to be seen. They stood around for ages and, just as they were getting ready to leave, they heard a voice, 'Hi. I'm up here!'

They looked up at a huge tree next to the riverbank and there, hanging off a branch with both arms, still with both skis on over the raging river … was Gareth.

Mani always says, 'Wish he'd fookin' left him there.'

TIMELINE ELEVEN
JANUARY–DECEMBER 1990

Photographer unknown

25 January 1990

Revenge play Skin Two, London.

26 January 1990

Revenge play La Locomotive, Paris.

Haçienda Temperance Night.

February 1990

New Order record 'World in Motion' at Real World.

19 February 1990

FAC 259. Haçienda Staff Party/Tony Wilson's Birthday at the Green Room, Manchester … then continued at Laser Quest next door.

> **'This was the first time I'd ever played New Order songs on my own, doing a small set of seven songs with Revenge. Afterwards I was sitting backstage with Shaun Ryder berating smackheads. Shaun handed us what I thought was a coke ciggie, which me, Bowz and Neil (Haçienda hairdresser Neil Orange Peel), hungrily devoured, only for Shaun to shout, "That's smack! Now you're all like me now! You fuckers. THE FUCKING LIVING DEAD!" and stormed out. We were terrified for days afterwards.'**

19 February 1990

British film director Michael Powell dies.

24 February 1990

Revenge play the Tegentonen Festival, Paradiso, Amsterdam.

March 1990

Members of the England football squad add vocals to 'World in Motion' at Sol Studio in Cookham.

'If you say so.'

March 1990

Rob Gretton 'resigns'.

'Bit of a weird one. The first I knew of it was when I received the letters. Rob had sent one to me at home and at Suite 16. I didn't take much notice: I wasn't using him for Revenge and as far as I was concerned New Order had split. When I asked him about it later he said nothing . . . denial is a river in Egypt.'

21 May 1990

The Haçienda's eighth birthday party.

18 April 1990

Revenge play King Tuts, Glasgow.

19 April 1990

Revenge play Brighton Zap Club.

20 April 1990

Revenge play Cambridge Junction.

May 1990

The Gallery and the Thunderdome, both central Manchester clubs, are shut by the police.

'This was unfortunate for us. The gangsters were contained in these two clubs and ruled the roost, leaving the Haçienda alone. As soon as the clubs were shut they moved en masse to the Haç and our problems really began.'

27 May 1990

England/New Order: 'World in Motion'
(FAC 293)

Seven-inch track list:
'World in Motion' 4.30
'World in Motion' (B-side) 4.48

Twelve-inch track list:
'World in Motion' 5.54
'World in Motion' (B-side) 4.48

Run-out groove one: *On my head son …*
Run-out groove two: *… not off my head son!*

Twelve-inch remix:
Home side:
'World in Motion' (Subbuteo mix) 5.08
'World in Motion' (Subbuteo dub) 4.14
Recorded and produced by Stephen Hague.
Both mixed by Graeme Park and Mike Pickering.
Away Side:
'World in Motion' (Carabinieri mix) 5.54
'World in Motion' (No alla violenzia mix) 4.12
Recorded by Stephen Hague.
Both mixed by Terry Farley and Andrew Weatherall.

CD single track list:
'World in Motion' seven-inch 4.30
'World in Motion' (No alla violenzia mix) 5.35
'World in Motion' (Subbuteo mix) 5.15

The cassette single (FAC 293c) included versions of the title track from both the seven-inch and twelve-inch.

Written by New Order and Keith Allen.
A-side recorded and produced by Stephen Hague at Sol and Mayfair Studios.
Engineered by Spike.
The Squad: Peter Beardsley, John Barnes, Paul Gascoigne, Steve McMahon, Chris Waddle, Des Walker.
B-side produced by Roli Mosimann at Real World Studios.
Engineered by Felix.
Naff football shouts and JB impersonation by Keith Allen.
Design and art direction by Peter Saville Associates.
Entered UK chart on 2 June 1990, remaining in the charts for 12 weeks, its peak position was number 1.

> **'Factory went completely overboard on the merchandising for "World in Motion", producing hats, balls, shorts, shirts and stickers. Express yourself, indeed.'**

New Order's twentieth single is also their last to be released on Factory Records.

May 1990

Revenge: 'Pineapple Face'
(FAC 267)

Seven-inch track list:

'Pineapple Face'	4.11
'14K'	4.25

Run-out groove one: *We're doomed!*
Run-out groove two: *Weakness is infectious!*

Twelve-inch track list:

'Pineapple Face'	6.05
'14K'	5.52
'Pineapple Face's Last Lunge'	5.10

Run-out groove one: *We're onto something big!*
Run-out groove two: *Don't tell a Soul!*

'Pineapple Face's Big Day'	6.05
(additional production and remix by Graeme Park and Mike Pickering)	
'14K' (full length)	5.52
'Pineapple Face's Last Lunge'	5.04

Recorded and mixed in Suite 16, Rochdale, Lancashire.
Engineered by Michael Johnson.
Mixed by Rex Sargeant and Stuart James.
Produced by Revenge.
Art direction by Peter Saville.
Photographed by Suze Randall assisted by David Hinds.
Styled by Donna Bertolino, hair and make-up by Alexis Vogel.
Revenge girl: Keita.
Designed by Peter Saville Associates.

25 May 1990

Revenge: *One True Passion*
(FAC 230)

Track list:

'Pineapple Face'	5.30
'Big Bang'	5.10
'Kiss the Chrome'	5.45
'Slave'	5.09
'Bleachman'	4.40
'Surf Nazi'	3.50
'Fag Hag'	5.25
'It's Quiet'	3.09

Run-out groove one: *Forty minutes of pleasure …*
Run-out groove two: *… and a lifetime of regret!*

Recorded and mixed in Suite 16, Rochdale, Lancashire.
Engineered by Michael Johnson.

Mixed by Alan Meyerson at Larrabee Sounds using the B.A.S.E.
Produced by Revenge.
Art direction by Peter Saville.
Photographed by Suze Randall assisted by David Hinds.
Styled by Donna Bertolino, hair and make-up by Alexis Vogel.
Revenge girl: Joanne.
Designed by Peter Saville Associates.

June 1990

Haçienda accounts show profit for the first time, £160,663.

16 July 1990

New Music Seminar, Marriott Marquis Hotel in New York.

23 July 1990

George Carman fights the police for the Haçienda's licence and wins.

> **'Also in July, Electronic supported Depeche Mode at two sold-out gigs at the Dodgers Stadium in Los Angeles. I was so jealous, what great exposure. But when the stories filtered back they seemed all too familiar. Barney had ended up completely shitfaced before both gigs and was thoroughly miserable. On one day he'd gone to the lengths of hanging a handwritten notice around his neck saying, 'Do not talk to me!' That's my boy. Roll on my gig in Leeds.'**

26 July 1990

Revenge play the Duchess of York, Leeds.

> **'Back to reality.'**

5 August 1990

Revenge play Metro, Chicago.

10 August 1990

Revenge play Axis, Boston.

18 August 1990

Revenge play I-Beam, San Francisco.

September 1990

New Order: *Peel Sessions*
(SFRLP110)

Track list:

'Truth'	4.13
'Senses'	4.15
'I.C.B.'	5.15
'Dreams Never End'	3.05
'Turn the Heater On'	5.00
'We All Stand'	5.15
'Too Late'	3.35
'5.8.6.'	6.05

A combination of 'Peel Sessions 1981' and 'Peel Sessions 1982'.
Designed by Peter Saville Associates.
Photography by Donald Christie.

September 1990

Joy Division: *Peel Sessions*
(SFRLP111)

Track list:

'Exercise One'	2.30
'Insight'	3.55
'She's Lost Control'	4.10
'Transmission'	3.55
'Love Will Tear Us Apart'	3.20
'24 Hours'	4.05

'Colony'	4.00
'Sound of Music'	4.20

A combination of Peel Sessions from 1979.
Recorded: 31 January 1979, 26 November 1979.
Recorded at BBC studio in Maida Vale, London.
Produced by Bob Sargeant and Tony Wilson.
Designed by Peter Saville Associates.
Photography by Anton Corbijn.

4 September 1990

Revenge play Live Music Hall, Cologne.

19 September 1990

Daytime: Transbordeur, Lyon, Revenge performed for TV.

Charles Street Factory headquarters/edifice, opening-night party

> **'This was a mad night too, I thought it was shit for offices but would make a great club.'**

October 1990

Revenge: 'I'm Not Your Slave'
(FAC 279)

Seven-inch track list:

'I'm Not Your Slave'	4.39
'Amsterdam'	3.42

Run-out groove one: *Give it to me baby!*
Run-out groove two: *Uh huh! Uh huh!*

Twelve-inch track list:

'I'm Not Your Slave'	5.53
'Amsterdam'	3.42

'I'm Not Your Slave II'	5.05

Run-out groove one: *Everything seems brand new …*
Run-out groove two: … *I'm born again!*

CD track list:

'Slave' seven-inch	4.39
'I'm Not Your Slave pt.1'	5.53
'I'm Not Your Slave pt.2'	5.05
'Amsterdam'	3.42

Recorded and mixed in Suite 16, Rochdale, Lancashire.
Engineered by Chris Jones and Rex Sargeant.
Mixed by Daddy-O except 'Amsterdam' mixed by Revenge.
Produced by Revenge.
Written by Revenge except 'Amsterdam' by John Cale.
Art direction by Peter Saville.
Photographed by Suze Randall assisted by David Hinds.
Styled by Donna Bertolino, hair and make-up by Alexis Vogel.
Revenge girls: Joanne and Keita.
Designed by Peter Saville Associates.

4 October 1990

Revenge play Frankfurt.

5 October 1990

Revenge play Hamburg.

7 October 1990

Revenge play Trier.

19 October 1990

Revenge play Düsseldorf.

20 October 1990

Revenge play Freiburg.

22 October 1990

Revenge play Munich.

25 October 1990

Revenge play Daily News, Stockholm.

28 October 1990

Revenge play Gothenburg XL Club.

9 November 1990

Revenge play the International 1, Manchester.

December 1990

Tour of Brazil sponsored by Coca-Cola.

Ten Most Interesting Medical Problems I Got Working in a Band

1. Trapped nerves in neck between fifth and sixth discs. (Playing over a long period of time and the physical weight of the guitar accelerated degenerative spondylotic changes at the C5–C6 level in neck, resulting in existing nerve roots being inflamed and trapped. This has caused muscle weakness called paraesthesia, resulting in pins and needles and numbness in both arms. Neurosurgical advice was that it was inoperable. Normally the weight of the head is balanced on the C-shaped neck. The C-shape acts like a shock absorber, bending with impact rather than a straight neck, which would simply jar. Bending forwards with the neck more parallel with the floor, plus the weight of the guitar (10kg), has massively stressed the neck.)
2. Bent lower spine. (From thrusting the guitar, one love handle sticks out more than the other. Decades of playing bass guitar in my rather distinctive and somewhat unusual style has bent my lumbar spine to one side, and it's become fixed in an antalgic posture.)
3. One arm is longer than the other (guess which one?). (Years of playing has resulted in changes in the morphology of my shoulder girdle so much that one arm now appears permanently longer than the other.)
4. 64db dip at 4K in right ear.
5. Recurrent lumbar spine and pelvic injuries, particularly with my sacroiliac joints, caused by prolonged bending forwards, playing the guitar and years of abuse, sleeping in chairs/cars/floors/weird positions, etc.
6. Alcoholism.
7. Cocaine addiction.
8. Repetitive strain injuries in both elbows.
9. Delusions of grandeur.
10. Various STDs.

'In among all this madness . . .'

On 30 January 1991 the Haçienda closed its doors, some thought for good; in fact, some (mostly members of New Order) *hoped* for good. The escalation of violence in the club (even after winning a reprieve for the liquor licence against the police, orchestrated ably and expensively, by George Carman QC) was shocking and we had no option. Interestingly when Carman walked into our first meeting to discuss saving the Haçienda's licence, the first thing he said was, 'Gentlemen, shut that loudmouth up!' referring to Tony. Greater Manchester Police had taken to referring to Tony as the Timothy Leary of ecstasy and Carman felt it was imperative he keep a low profile, or, as he said, simply . . . shut up.

Sadly, even after all that, we couldn't guarantee anyone's safety inside. It was heartbreaking and terrifying. The resulting fallout was even more bad news for New Order. Insanely, the club cost more to shut than to open and the resulting loss of £270,000 gave us no choice but to record a new album.

I should have been writing and playing on my solo stuff (what would later become Monaco) yet here we were at another emergency meeting being told again that a) Factory was in dire financial trouble, and b) so was the Haçienda.

At that meeting, we were presented with an ultimatum: either New Order do a new record or both Factory and the Haçienda would go to the wall. Of course, nobody wanted either of those two things to happen. If Factory went belly up we'd lose all the money owed to us by the label, which by that time, thanks to the success of *Substance* and *Technique*, was quite a substantial sum. When it came to the Haçienda we had even more at stake. Back in 1982 the group had been persuaded to sign the aforementioned 'personal guarantees' for the bank, the building lessees and the brewery, which made us liable for all the debts, separately and individually.

Rob – who'd signed one too, bless him – had spent years trying to get us out of them, to no avail.

The album has to be made, we were told over and over again, sometimes hysterically: 'If you don't, we'll all lose everything!'

As I said earlier, none of us wanted to come back and be New Order again, especially under these circumstances – Barney in particular was completely against the idea.

However, plans were made to convene and start writing in August. This time the writing would be done for the first time at 'The Farm', Steve and Gillian's house. Cheetham Hill was history. We were all in south Manchester now so it made no sense to venture north any more. I was in Withington, Barney was in Handforth and the other two were in Rainow, Macclesfield. We had become 'soft southern Jessies!' as predicted by Rob Gretton, who saw Chorlton still as deepest, darkest north Manchester. I wondered whether it would change the music. Would we lose our edge?

I think I can safely say, without fear of contradiction, that none of us were looking forward to it at all. So maybe *that* would give us the edge back.

In among all this madness, Martin Hannett died; on 18 April 1991, to be exact. He died of heart failure at home. He had been clean-ish for over four years and was moving house. A very stressful time, as we know, so be warned.

It was Martin who designed my wonderful bass set-up that I was still using (albeit now for Revenge), the Alembic, Amcron, and Gauss system that I used for nigh-on twenty years until it got old and unreliable. I would struggle to replace it. Martin was at least partly responsible for the magic in Joy Division, and wholly responsible for the strange, alien sounds of *Unknown Pleasures* and *Closer*, the foundations on which Factory and New Order had been built. He put all of that into the label, but got hardly anything at all out of it.

Of course, there was a huge turnout – and a huge Factory turnout too – at the funeral, and I remember there being a lot of animosity flying around for what the label had done to him. They'd done what the other members of New Order would do to me years later, exclude me, which is the worst kind of bullying. In my case I can afford to fight them, but Martin could never get the money.

There were loads of musicians at the funeral, ranging from the Stone Roses to Stockholm Monsters, and he got a great send-off, about a thousand people. One of those absent, however, was the New Order frontman. Section 25's Larry Cassidy approached me afterwards. 'Hooky, where's Barney?'

'Oh,' I said, 'Barney doesn't like funerals.'

'Hooky,' growled Larry, 'tell him, no one likes funerals. You come out of respect.' Meanwhile, Alan Wise did a wonderful eulogy at the graveside and the honour of being the first person to throw a flower in his grave went to Hannett's son James, who, on dropping the flower, said loudly, 'Goodbye, Daddy.'

There was a collective wail from most of the audience followed by many, many tears.

I often wonder what would have happened if Martin had got his wish and Factory had bought a studio instead of a nightclub? Who knows? We were such a bunch of fuckheads it probably wouldn't have made a blind bit of difference. He also missed the chance to see Factory go bankrupt, which would happen the following year.

Plenty of reasons were bandied around for Factory going bump: this year the spending by the label had been unbelievable, including the costs of the Happy Mondays' *Yes Please!* (£350,000), Revenge's *One True Passion* (£250,000) and Cath Carroll's band Miaow (£150,000). And, of course, the buildings. This year the Haçienda made a loss of £481,912 (the very thing that Martin had predicted and opposed so vehemently that his whole relationship with Factory broke down). Dry 201 had a £575,478 total cost and was yet to make any profit over running costs and, last but not least, the Charles Street offices cost £750,000, a whopping 50 per cent over budget, the best overspend yet. (Insanely, they had been bidding against me, pushing the price for a nearly derelict building sky-high. I wanted it as a new site for Suite 16, hopefully bringing the studio at last to Manchester. Thank God I didn't get it.) All this, along with the mortgage (or rather the fucked-up bridging loan) we ended up with on the Haçienda building of over a million pounds meant the whole organisation was on very slippery ground. An incoming 'worldwide recession', now running at an interest rate of 23 per cent – that same recession bringing a 25 per cent (at least) reduction in all assets – added to the woes.

Total results: Against, a Factory debt of £2,557,390 (without including all the other debts accrued over years of trading, e.g. unpaid band royalties); For, their only asset, a new New Order LP (as yet unwritten).

We became their only hope. The pressure was unbearable.

Meanwhile, the Haçienda re-opened on 10 May with our new improved door force courtesy of Top Guard Security, fifty men and twelve dogs. The night ended in a riot after a mob of Cheetham Hill gangsters stormed the door at midnight. I was so upset. Even Manchester itself seemed to be against us now.

I had a lot of time off this year and looking at the live dates I wonder what the hell I was up to? Mainly recording and rehearsing with Revenge and swanning round London, I suppose, where me and Jane seemed to be spending most of our time in Groucho's.

Groucho's had been opened in Dean Street, Soho, the bohemian heart of London, on 5 May 1985 by Anthony Mackintosh, who previously had run a members' club called the Zanzibar in Covent Garden. Peter Saville had been a member there and moved to Groucho's as soon as it opened, along with his new partner Brett Wickens. He put New Order up collectively at a membership meeting and we got, amazingly, 'no black balls', he said.

We had been members since 1985 and in the later years had taken to spending more and more time there. Whenever we were in London we would go and it was so expensive, Rob loved it. We were the first 'pop group' or musician members in the club, which had been opened to cater for those working in the publishing industry; for a while we made a hell of a contrast to the ordinary members.

The bar was run on an honour system. You would just tell the waiter whose name it was under: Rob Gretton, etc. This was, of course, open to abuse and as we invited more of our, shall we say, naughtier friends to join us as guests, a lot of drinks would be mistakenly put on other people's bills. Oops.

Rob soon cottoned on to this and insisted we used our own names when we were there on non-New Order business. Sometimes, at the end of the night, you'd be too pissed or whatever and forget to pay and you'd get a postal bill for hundreds of pounds for drinks you couldn't for the life of you remember buying. 'Eight Gin Fizzes!' I'd demand of Jane. 'Who the fuck do we know who drinks Gin Fizzes?' Over the years the place got wilder and wilder as more and more musicians joined. Then came the chefs. Then came the comedians, and they were the worst of the lot, the members becoming a very mixed bunch of reprobates.

The scene soon got druggier and druggier and the basement toilets became the place to meet. Sometimes you didn't need to buy any, you'd just watch a certain member as they nipped to the toilet (very surreptitiously, as it was still frowned upon) to rack them out, follow them down, wait until they came out and, as they went back upstairs to tip off their mates about the buffet downstairs, you'd nip in, do the lot then go back wired and as innocent as you could, and watch the recriminations. It was called 'doing a Groucho', as in 'I've just done a Groucho on them'.

The club became wilder and wilder as the 1980s wore on, culminating in all-night poker parties with people losing thousands. In the early 1990s they added rooms upstairs, which were very small but meant you didn't even have to leave the building for days, getting wrecked then sleeping it off, eating in the restaurant and doing it all again. Groucho's became a bit of a black hole that once you entered you had trouble leaving. Peter Saville used to come into the restaurant every evening just as they were closing at midnight and demand to be fed, which drove the staff wild. 'Just a rare piece of tuna and some vegetables.' They had a pianist in the bar, which led to some of the most bizarre house bands imaginable made up of assorted rockers, comedians, media whores, politicians, trust-fund darlings, you name it ... mostly led by Keith Allen.

In the early days of our membership I remember going in, Jane in tow, and after signing in I held the door for a very upper-class lady closely followed by her drunken husband. On seeing me at the door, with shorts, tattoos and desert boots, he bellowed, 'Oh my God, Natasha, they're letting people like him in now!'

We laughed. The times they certainly were a-changing.

Once I got a phone call at my hotel from the receptionist at the Groucho asking me to come and get my 'lead singer'. It seems Barney had been in the night before and after partying collapsed on the banquette and was snoring and drooling away. One of the staff had heard I was in this particular hotel and presumed we were together. I took great delight in telling them I no longer had anything to do with him and they should phone Barney's Electronic representatives, quoting 'dickhead removal department'.

The adventures here were legion and one in particular stands out: me, Keith, Pet Shop Boys, assorted comedians, Alex James, assorted chefs and drug dealers were partying away in the small upstairs bar (which did become the haven for the heavily addicted) when some very big men came in with their hands in their jackets and started surveying the room. Everyone froze. Having taken a good look around, the heavies left, but it wasn't like they were leaving for good, more like they were biding their time.

'Police raid!' came the call.

Oh my God, it was pandemonium, everyone running, screaming and piling into the toilet almost as one, alternately trying to do it all or flush it away.

Literally we were all shaking in our seats waiting for the bust, when in walked Bill Clinton and bloody Bono grinning from ear to ear. It was the ex-president's security men casing the joint for terrorists.

We gave them loads. 'Watch this,' said Keith, and went up to Bill and asked him if he would sign a napkin as a souvenir, which Clinton duly did with a flourish. Keith then opened the napkin and shoved it in his face; he had already written on it and now the napkin read: 'I love Osama Bin Laden, signed Bill Clinton'.

Bill's face fell and as his security detail closed in Keith legged it, taking great delight in showing everyone in the club, telling them, 'What a bastard that Clinton is. Look at that.'

One night I had got there very refreshed, to find Alex James talking to some older members. We were great friends by then so I thought, my treat, chopped out a hedge for him and then went to get him, grabbing him roughly by the arm. I could hardly speak, 'A-Alex, there's ... there's s-summat ... for you, th-th-there.'

'Later, Hooky,' he said.

Later? I thought. *What!* and walked off, only to reappear seconds later, mithering, 'A-Alex, over th-there, over th-there ...' gesturing.

He then grabbed me and said, 'Fookin' hell, Hooky, these are my grandparents. Go away!' Oops.

Years later, we would witness Stephen Fry's fall from grace and Robbie Williams's downfall too. The boy who once cadged a menthol cigarette off me (and worried he might get in trouble for it) at *Top of the Pops* had now graduated to bigger and not better things, as he stumbled round the club in a daze trying to find the toilet and then being unable to open the door without help from my wife Becky. She drew the line at unbuttoning his flies, she said.

Last Groucho anecdote, promise. Me, my best mate Ken Niblock and Pottsy had been at it all night in one of the rooms after playing pool with Stephen Fry, and as bad luck would have it I had to leave early for a train home. As we checked out at the front desk, dark glasses on, sweating profusely, the receptionist said to us, 'Did you have anything from the minibar?'

Ken, quick as a flash, goes, 'Everything!' Then to me, 'Don't worry, I'll get it, Hooky,' then nearly falling over in shock when presented with the bill for £480 (this was in 1988). He nearly sobered up. The summer flew by.

In August I drove up to Rainow, Macclesfield, to Stephen and Gillian's home and rehearsal studio 'a bag of nerves', my heart in my mouth, for today was the day we would begin writing our new LP, the one being forced upon us by all at Factory and even our own manager.

We were to begin the writing without Barney, who was too busy with Electronic, saying, 'You get some stuff going and I'll come later. You do the music and I'll just do the vocals.' This was great news and would give us the chance to shine. Writing this now, I can't believe I trusted that statement. We were idiots.

However, when I arrived at their place, the Farm, it was to a completely different Steve and Gillian; they seemed confident and relaxed, bullish even. This was definitely their heyday – they came up with some good stuff during these sessions. Why? I reckon because Barney wasn't there with his sharpened elbows shoving everybody out of the way, and us three actually rubbed along together pretty well. We became like friends again instead of some dysfunctional family dragged together at every special occasion or crisis. I marvelled at Gillian's new-found self-confidence. I wondered whether it was artificial or their The Other Two work?

At the time, I must admit, I thought their music was rubbish, much too soft for my taste. On reflection it was a particular brand of New Order-tinged electro-pop that was OK, and Gillian's vocals were rather sweet. I did suspect Steve was mainly responsible for all the music, keyboards and programming etc., but their warm welcome made me feel quite optimistic about the future.

Though you might find this difficult to believe, I'm actually really accommodating when it comes to writing and recording. For me, making a record in a group is a team sport, which is where me and Barney differ. With him, it's all about the song, not about the people, he gets blinkers on and runs away, not caring about anyone or anything: 'Let me try another keyboard line.' 'Let me try a new bassline.' 'You don't mind if I put a low bass on this, do you, Hooky?' He becomes a total control freak and hopefully one day he'll look at his own back catalogue and work out that his best material has all been collaborative.

Anyway, we settled in and began working quite well, jamming and then elaborating on the ideas. On a couple of occasions when I tried to balance 'the other one' with alcohol, unsuccessfully I might add, I couldn't drive home and was actually welcomed into the family home and spent the night. I felt honoured.

Me, Steve and Gillian were getting on the best I had known in ten years and my efforts, be it advice on the music or playing bass and basslines, felt welcomed. This was wonderful after the torment I'd felt on 'True Faith' and 'World in Motion'. I was starting to get a good feeling about this and was quite enjoying this enforced session.

The writing progressed and after a while we had eight pretty good ideas to present to Barney. The planning for the actual recording was a little strained. I was informed that Mike Johnson would no longer be used and a producer was being sought. This I felt was very bad news.

We had produced great music over the years, and the formula (and the angst) of me and Mike producing, with them four – Barney, Steve, Gillian and Rob – executive-producing, had brought fantastic, internationally renowned results. I thought if we changed it we were tempting fate; even *Technique*, our most strained outing yet, had been a great success.

But the others, buoyed by the success of 'True Faith' and 'World in Motion' uppermost in their minds, outvoted me and Rob.

We would have a producer … who? We tried Brian Eno – the first of several unsuccessful approaches we made throughout our career – but he was booked up for two years in advance. As a consolation prize he sent us a set of four Korg Kaoss pads, which we threw in a corner of our rehearsal room. In the end we started off with a Belgian guy called Pascal Gabriel, who was very nice and easy to work with, certainly not as pushy as Stephen Hague from a writing point of view. We were working well at the Farm on one particular track, which would later become 'Regret'. Then Barney turned up, added some great guitar and, hey presto, we not only had the best track on the album, but the one I consider to be the last true New Order track. Why? Because it was a genuine collaboration – in my opinion, the last we would ever do. Barney's input turned it into the wonderful tune it is today. But he didn't like Pascal and afterwards we were informed he did not want to work with him on the LP. There were a few other names in the hat: John Cale, Trevor Horn ... Stephen Hague. *Uh oh.*

TIMELINE TWELVE
JANUARY–DECEMBER 1991

© Suze Randall

TIMELINE TWELVE JANUARY–DECEMBER 1991

30 January 1991

The Haçienda closes.

28 March 1991

Revenge play the Duchess of York, Leeds.

18 April 1991

Producer Martin Hannett dies of heart failure.

10 May 1991

The Haçienda reopens with 'The Healing'.

'Opening another wound in the Haçienda's side.'

August 1991

Compilation: *Martin: The Work of Martin Hannett*, featuring Buzzcocks, Slaughter and the Dogs, John Cooper Clarke, Joy Division, Jilted John, A Certain Ratio, OMD, U2, New Order, Happy Mondays, World of Twist, New Fast Automatic Daffodils, the High.
(FACT 325)

Track list:

'She's Lost Control' (Joy Division)	4.54
'Everything's Gone Green' (New Order)	5.29

4 August 1991

Revenge play Cities in the Park, Manchester. Other acts included Happy Mondays, Electronic, 808 State, A Certain Ratio, Durutti Column, Cath Carroll, the Adventure Babies and the Wendys. DJs: Mike Pickering and Jon da Silva. Promoted by Alan Wise.

'This was a good gig for Revenge. As a group we had been playing regularly and we were very together. It was a nice atmosphere backstage, with anyone who was anyone in Manchester, both past and present, being there. There was a big element of nerves for us as Electronic were also on the bill, but surrounded by friends as I was, I felt very comfortable. The highlight for me was putting my two-year-old son Jack up on the stage and watching him dance his wonderful dance to the acid house playing loudly over the PA as thousands cheered him on. He was quickly scooped up by Iris and dragged off as she took one look at my face and realised I was losing it. As the sun went down there was a discernible change in the vibe. It literally got much, much darker. Backstage we were hearing reports of the fences being stormed and security routed by Salford and Moss Side gangs. It felt like you were under siege. There were loads of drugs about, and I can remember playing, luckily, before things got out of hand. After the show we were using our caravan as a base. We were the nearest to the stage and I was sitting in it with Nidge, an old Salford head, discussing the goings-on outside.

'"They're taxing all the drug dealers outside on the site," says Nidge.

'"Yeah, it's disgusting, isn't it, they are bastards."

'"Beating them up badly, taking their stashes and money," says Nidge.

'"I can't believe it," says I, "it's fucking disgusting."

'"Do you want some of it?" (He'd been given a load it by the Salford lot, his mates.)

'"Yeah," says I, "chop it out."

'There's outrage for you.

'As he was doing the dirty deed Electronic finished and Barney and Johnny came right off stage and crouched down on the outside of our caravan, by the window, doing whatever they were doing, and me and Nidge were on the inside of it, doing the same thing staring out. "Shit!" I said, "it's fucking Barney." We laughed ... small world, how strange.

'Afterwards I end up in a hotel room in the Midland with the assistant manager of Electronic. It nearly ended in a fight as Bowser and the lads were giving them loads about Electronic. I was struck dumb, luckily.'

20 September 1991

Revenge play Norwich Waterfront.

21 September 1991

Revenge play the Venue, London.

9 October 1991

Revenge play Huddersfield Polytechnic Union.

24 October 1991

Revenge play City of London Polytechnic.

31 October 1991

Revenge play Manchester UMIST.

13 December 1991

Revenge play Stoke Polytechnic.

'There was trouble brewing ...'

By 1992 the party was over – thanks to regular outbreaks of violence at the city's clubs, 'Madchester' had become 'Gunchester', and Factory Records was in dire financial trouble. The reasons were manifold. They included all 1990 and 1991's bad luck efforts as well as this year producing various tax issues, added to the expense of opening the FAC281 shop in Affleck's Palace, New Order's new LP and then Happy Mondays' abortive recording in Barbados, as well as expensive and poor-selling releases from Revenge and Miaow. As the year wore on the label was too in debt to release either a proposed Haçienda Classics album (foolishly the record label never capitalised on the success or influence of the club) or a 'new bands' compilation that might have featured Oasis and Pulp. Also Tony's efforts to launch 'In the City' added more financial pressure on the already very stretched label.

New Order-wise, it was pretty good at first, without Barney there. Occasionally we'd drop off a CD or tape for him to listen to and work on, but I doubt he ever bothered to listen. At this time there was no pressure to finish the album. Unfortunately time got away from us, as it has a habit of doing and, before you knew it, the financial deadlines were looming.

Factory was very worried, and in a panic they booked Real World and hired Stephen Hague to produce the album.

There was trouble brewing at Factory, causing more friction. Alan Erasmus was initially shocked when Tony wanted the label to pay £10,000 for development of 'In the City', the Manchester music convention project, but on reflection he thought it was a great idea, and a good investment. Tony used the money, to fly to first New York, then London, seeking sponsors. Then, when funding was finally secured for the project from Manchester City Council (£25,000), Alan found out that all the money had gone into a separate new company, with nothing coming back to Factory. But we had to carry on. It was time to go back to work.

I'll be honest. I wasn't that keen on returning to Real World, especially with Stephen Hague. Still, Barney reckoned we should use him because not only had we proved a chart-busting combination on 'True Faith' and 'World in Motion', but he'd stop us lot from arguing among ourselves.

Anyway, he wanted him, and, if you haven't already got the picture, what Barney wants, Barney gets – especially in the mood he was in. He was livid: 'Having to make an album under such circumstances, making an album purely for financial reasons, is the death of creativity!' he said, and he was dead right. But God bless him and give him his due, he worked really hard on that record. Unfortunately a lot of his hard work involved putting our hard work to the sword.

Because we were so behind, as in, Barney had done no vocals at all, we were running two studios in Real World simultaneously, which meant that we recorded our parts separately in the Big Room – the one where the ducks floated past – for Hague to mould into a nearly finished product. Then it was sent into the Pagoda (a smaller studio, actually Peter Gabriel's personal writing room) for Barney to try vocals. He was basically starting from scratch.

Running two studios meant we needed more engineers than usual, so Owen Morris was brought on board. Owen had been engineering for Electronic. He came in to work for Barney, and spent a lot of time in the Pagoda nodding enthusiastically at Barney's every utterance. I had a feeling he was a bit of a yes-man. (Owen went on to be one of my favourite producers, *Which Bitch?* for the View being a particular favourite. From the stories I heard he went as mad as Hannett, and to me sounded as good.)

So began a process where the material that me, Gillian and Steve had written at their farmhouse, and then subsequently recorded in the Big Room in Real World, underwent a strange metamorphosis once it reached the Pagoda. A record that began as a possible New Order record, slowly became, in my opinion, an Electronic one.

Now, you may be thinking, *Shut the fuck up, Hooky*, because *Republic* is a beloved New Order album and was our best-selling record to date, so I did all right out of it. But to be a hired hand is not why I formed a group. Meantime, it was still the case that the best way to clear a studio was for me to pick up my bass. Gradually the group drifted even further apart than we already were. Much further and we would have been in different postcodes.

How did we cope? By getting off our heads. Before this point we'd all had a bit of a dalliance with crack. You may find this hard to believe, but it wasn't me who got into it the most – although to be fair we'd all had a go and developed a bit of a taste for it. I remember a certain member of our entourage telling me about taking it for the first time. He sucked it back and then, as he exhaled, said, 'If I ever make a million pounds I'm going to spend it all on this.'

The thing with crack is that it's better than coke while you're doing it. It's much smoother, warmer and not as edgy, but really intense. But then afterwards it's like being ripped apart by a team of wild horses. The comedown is that bad, you'd happily slit your own throat. Plus, of course – famously – it really gets its claws into you. I watched a couple of mates of mine do £3,000 worth in one night, then get up in the morning for a taxi to pick up another couple of grands' worth and then do that, too, in one sitting. This guy was telling me how he'd smoked five cars and three apartments before he finally stopped,

'How?' said I.

'Got five years for GBH,' he said. 'Kicked it in the Big House!'

I heard that others had fallen hard too. A hairdresser, who used to deal me up, told me he'd been with some of them once and they were fighting over some white rocks on the carpet that they thought had been dropped. When they put it in the pipe, it turned out to be cheese. Hard cheese. God only knows what they were putting in their sandwiches.

Even so, at Real World we were mainly about the booze and charlie. Some had taken to balancing it out with 'jellies'.

> Benzodiazepines (benzos, temazies, jellies, eggs, moggies, vallies) are used to both counter the effect of 'uppers' like cocaine, speed and E, and 'downers' like heroin and booze. Usually doctor-prescribed drugs for reducing stress and anxiety, they promote calmness, relaxation and sleep, and work as antidepressants. Used as a 'chill-out' drug on the club scene or as a downer, the drug comes in tablet form, although it can be injected. Users can experience forgetfulness, confusion, irritability and drowsiness.

They were little green gels that you'd slit with a razor blade then squeeze a line of the liquid onto your hand, like the trail of a slug, licking it after a line of coke. I stuck with booze. We had barrels sent from Dry 201 and set up our own bar in the studio, so we were able to get pissed as farts at any time. This was the beginning of my proper alcoholism. I was in that boorish power-drinking phase where Stephen Hague would ask for a half-pint of bitter and I'd be, 'Half-pint? You fucking girl! Here y'are ...' and give him three pints and six vodkas. Some evenings I'd drive back to Manchester like a maniac, picking up loads of drugs, then speeding back, them lot waiting for me. We'd stay up until four or five in the morning, sleep, get up about midday, work through until nine, or in Barney's case four in the morning, and then do the same again.

We had people coming down to Real World with drugs for us but I liked to go and get them myself, total addict behaviour: wanting to be in control of the amount I had, so I could be sure I had 'enough', and 'enough' was always more than anyone else – twice as much. I remember Gillian expressing amazement that I had so much of the stuff, a great big phial full of it.

I was getting pissed all the time. Sometimes I'd stay down in Bath for the weekend and bring the Salford lot down and we'd go and blow £500 in a cocktail bar, off our fucking rockers rolling round Bath, which was nice because it was so laid-back. It just didn't have the problems Manchester had. Me and Twinny would go to Moles nightclub in town and there would be no doormen, and the manager, 'the lovely Jan', would say, 'We just don't need them.' We were amazed.

We went to Glastonbury that summer, me, Twinny and Jim Beswick (a mate from Salford), and Jim got set on fire. He'd passed out from too much of everything and we couldn't carry him so we made a careful note of where he was and then left him. When we came back someone had sprayed lighter fluid on him (no wind, obviously) and set him alight. We woke him up, put him out and carried on.

During Glastonbury Peter Gabriel used to invite a lot of musicians to stay at Real World and the studio was full of people for those few days. I'd been on a bender and woke up absolutely starving. I could hear all the voices downstairs but my instinct for survival was too strong, I needed to eat. I crept downstairs in my dressing gown, studiously avoiding eye contact with anyone, and managing to pour out a bowl of cornflakes and add milk before shakily making my way to a seat at the communal table. My hands were shaking like Rob Gretton's in the taxman's office, but I made it, carefully sitting down. As I picked up the spoon I looked up. Sat opposite me was Lou Reed. Bloody Lou Reed, my hero. I went to pieces and had to run back to bed.

At work the massacre continued. We'd give Barney songs that we'd all agreed were more or less finished. All he needed to do was add a vocal, but we'd go in later in the evening to the Pagoda and the track would be unrecognisable. He'd say, 'I couldn't get anything over that verse music, so I rewrote it.'

I'd say, 'Why didn't you tell us? We could have worked on it for you.' Him and Owen would just smirk at each other. He'd put some guitar on, and then it would get to the bridge and of course his new bit didn't fit in with our bridge, so that would have to go, and he'd write another bridge, and then say that the chorus didn't really go with the bridge, so he'd write another chorus, and that was it – elbows at dawn, or in this case, computer programmers.

Owen was so sycophantic he made me sick. Hague just agreed, I think because he wanted to get the record done as quickly as possible. That was what he was being paid to do. I don't blame him for that. He took the path of least resistance. In *Shadowplayers* (James Nice's book on Factory) Barney says our material wasn't good enough. That simply wasn't true. The material had been listened to by all of us, agreed to be good enough for work in progress before we even got to the studio.

Anyway, for me, the drink and the drugs took the edge off what he was doing to our work. For Steve and Gillian, well, I said that the writing at the farmhouse was their heyday and it was. But that meant they took it really badly. They were being dumped on from a great height. I was like, 'Welcome to the club,' but if you ask me, they never really got over it. Steve in particular was very, very quiet and reluctant to work after that, and I bet he still is now.

Siouxsie and the Banshees came in while we were there. Like John Lydon, Siouxsie's one of those characters who's always on. She's always Siouxsie. Whatever time of day you see her, she's dressed and made-up like she's about to go on stage. We got on famously.

One time I got this dealer, a nice guy I knew from Bath, to cycle over and he brought me a load of gear. It wasn't great but, believe you me, there wasn't much knocking round in Bath at that time. It was him or nothing. He was pleased as punch to be doing it with him out of New Order and sat chunnering away until suddenly, without warning, Siouxsie leaned over and chinned him.

'I don't like you. I didn't like him, Hooky,' she explained airily, as she swanned off, leaving the poor guy sparkled on the floor.

Funnily enough, the next time I saw Siouxsie was at the 2005 Brit Awards, when we were making our comeback, presenting the award for Best International Group to the Scissor Sisters. I'd not long come back from rehab, and if you watch it on YouTube you can see that Barney aids my recovery by being completely off his head while I'm as sober as a judge. When we returned to our table after giving the award to the Scissors, we found Siouxsie sitting there with all the other record company folk, and I said, 'Hello, love, how are you?'

She said, 'All right, Hooky, I'm fine, nice to see you.'

And Bernard just said, 'I'd love to fuck you up the arse.' Straight out of the blue.

Oh, Jesus, I could have died. But still, you've got to hand it to him. If you're going to get off your tits and loudly proclaim your desire for anal sex with Siouxsie Sioux, you might as well do it at the Brit Awards. I still cringe when I think of what I said to Tanya out of the Throwing Muses, but that one beat mine into a cocked hat – or should that be a coked wrap. All I can say is that he was bloody lucky she didn't chin him, too; instead, she just stormed off.

The recording continued.

One night, with just me and Barney there, we decided to have a change and go for a meal in town. We assembled assorted tape operators, engineers and Stephen Hague and duly made our way to a lovely little French restaurant in Bath for a nice convivial meal.

At the end when the bill appeared, about £300, I watched as the tape-ops and engineers started raiding their piggy banks, fishing creased chequebooks out of their pockets, searching for their cheque-guarantee cards. So I said, 'Don't worry, lads, I'll get it.' And, grabbing the bill, I headed to the counter to pay. As I was sorting it out Barney appeared at my shoulder and grabbed my arm. 'What did you do that for?'

'What?' says I.

'Offer to pay for their meal. Why?'

'Get out, they work really hard. They deserve a treat.'

'They earn more money than you do,' he spat.

'Yeah, but they don't get anything else, do they?'

'Fuck that,' he said, 'I'd never buy them a meal.' And he walked off.

I carried on and next thing he was back again, grabbing my arm. 'And another thing, I'll never buy you a meal either.' And you know what? He never has.

Gradually, me, Steve and Gillian were written off the album. In the case of 'Ruined in a Day', 'World', 'Spooky', 'Everyone Everywhere' and 'Liar' we were *completely* written off them – as far as I am concerned it was becoming a Bernard Sumner solo album at our joint expense. The only concession made was 'Avalanche'; Barney left that one alone.

But then – right at the end, when all the tracks were written, and all the backing vocals were done – Hague turned to me and said, 'We should put some bass on the tracks now.'

Fuck me, that chat he had with Tom Atencio on 'True Faith' had really paid off. Sure enough, he lined up two 24-track machines to make 48, put a stereo mix of the track on two of them, a sync code on another one, and got me to jam 45 tracks of bass guitar on every song. It took days.

That cleared the studio better than a zombie attack, I can tell you, but the thing was, I got back on the album, and if you listen to *Republic* there's actually quite a lot of bass on it. It's low in places, but it's there. It doesn't really feel like it's 100 per cent me, if that makes sense, because of the way it's recorded, but I am on there, and thank God for that.

Despite that the whole experience of recording and mixing *Republic* was like one long case of good news/bad news. It was great going out and getting trashed with my mates – and at one point I even nicked a girl out from under Robert Plant from Led Zeppelin's nose.

By this time we were mixing in RAK Studios near Regent's Park (the studio was owned by Mickie Most who, impressively, would park his Rolls-Royce right outside and then retire to his office all day). Robert Plant was recording there too, and we were both flirting like mad with the catering girl, who was lovely. I eventually won by inviting her to a Haçienda night at seOne and when we were trollied she ended up staying with me for two days in the hotel. Turns out she used to serve up a *very* famous musician with coke supplied by terrorists. She'd travel around with them on tour all the time with three ounces shoved up her judy (fookin' hell, I was amazed, she was tiny). Anyway, back at the studio after dinner we'd retire to the recreation room for a kiss and a cuddle and we were really going for it when I opened my eyes and stood there outside the window was Robert Plant, alternately pointing at me and making a fist, smashing it into his other hand. I smiled and gave him the Manchester Vs. He was actually a very nice man and, apart from trying to sell me his dodgy old Mercedes, was a real gentleman. We got on well – but sadly, relations with my group were at an all-time low; we were hardly ever together in any of the studios. I was pleased that I'd been brought back into the fold musically, but then I had nothing to do with the mixing of the album, which was something I'd always been involved with in the past.

Hague did everything and, no matter what you said or suggested, mainly that the bass was really quiet, *á la* 'True Faith', nothing ever changed. The whole thing was very unsatisfactory for me, to say the least. Apart from all this it was very difficult to feel involved with an album you were convinced was your last as New Order. Steve and Gillian, in my opinion, were heartbroken. Forgive me for not doing a track by track, but I can't.

Plus, of course, there was the business with Factory . . .

By July of that year a long-gestating deal between Factory and London Records fell through when those negotiating on behalf of London – chairman Tracy Bennett, CEO Roger Ames and general manager Colin Bell – became aware that Factory had little worth buying apart from Joy Division and New Order. As author James Nice says in his account of the Factory Records story, Shadowplayers, *'[Tony Wilson] could no longer hide the fact that Factory had few significant assets to sell, apart from a desirable brand name and a mountain of debt. . . . Viewed objectively, no sane corporate buyer would have purchased Factory as a going concern, and London hit on the idea of allowing the target company to slide into receivership, with the hope and possibility of salvaging certain key assets from the administrators . . .'*

They hoped those assets would include Joy Division and New Order.

Tony had been negotiating with London for so long that it just wasn't funny any more. It was driving both him and Rob crazy. We were starting to have a very bad feeling, a feeling we'd had all along about the attitude of major labels. He was trying to persuade London into signing the entire roster, but London didn't want the Railway Children or Revenge or whoever was on Factory Classical that week, they just wanted the big names – New Order, Joy Division, Happy Mondays – and in the end London decided to wait for Factory to go bump and then swoop in and clear up, like vultures.

Seeing this was the case, Rob referred to our old agreements with Tony where it was stated that the master tapes and copyrights were returned to us six months after delivery. It meant London couldn't buy us from Factory or from the liquidator (if Factory went bust), they had to deal with us direct.

Our new London deal was taking a long time. Their lawyers were a bunch of bastards. Me and Rob used to go to London, guerrilla-style, hang around the Groucho and pounce on Tracy Bennett and Colin Bell to try and get them to hurry it up; Rob was getting more and more desperate for the money. We had some great times with Tracy and Colin, actually; they were a right pair of party animals. But it looked like nothing could stop Factory going bankrupt.

We had to suffer nearly a month of emergency meetings, day after day, with no remedy in sight. Factory's demise was a long, drawn-out process, with London Records and Roger Ames playing a huge part.

At first they offered lifelines only to then withdraw them. Things gradually changed as we removed ourselves from the mess. London began courting New Order and Joy Division and the liquidator, too, so they could get the rest of Factory's assets, a proper harvest.

'Capitalism without bankruptcy is like Christianity without hell,' said Tony. Neither he nor Factory could survive any longer. Rob was relieved and happy that we had extricated ourselves from what looked like a precarious situation. Still having fresh flowers delivered on the last day of trading and leaving the stock cupboard open for the staff to help themselves, Tony was generous to the end. I got a phone call to come down and join A Certain Ratio going through the skip outside the building (containing everything that wasn't nailed down).

The liquidator wasn't very happy either that he'd lost his two biggest assets, New Order and Joy Division, but that's life. And lucky for us. Phew. He did fight legally with London for a couple of years for our return after they signed us independently post-Factory's demise, but didn't succeed.

Meanwhile, me and Rob came up with a great idea to buy the Factory building for ourselves. After all, we had already paid for it. A phone call to the liquidator valued it at £250,000, a third of what Tony had spent. A quick call to our bank NatWest and we were ready with an offer on 25 November, only to be told it had been sold. To whom we could not find out. We were devastated. We later learned it was our greatest copyists, Peter Dalton and Carol Ainscow, who had grabbed it, and we weren't able to table a higher offer. They'd already opened a bar that was a direct rip-off of Dry 201 and now this: they nicked in with a higher offer and bought the Factory building from under our noses, which seemed highly unfair to Factory's creditors. They later opened it as a club, Paradise Factory.

We were devastated to see Factory go, of course. They were our friends and we'd helped to build the label from the start. On the other hand, we were the people who had written the songs on which Factory was built, and the label had repaid us by never paying us – by taking our money and sinking it into a nightclub and a bar and a building for themselves, plus a load of other crap groups – so it's fair to say we had mixed feelings about it. It's hard not to sound callous.

Later, when we moved the mixing of *Republic* to RAK, Colin Bell and Tracy Bennett came to the studio, to 'help', sitting at the back, definitely the worse for wear, making ridiculous suggestions. It was one of the funniest studio sessions I'd ever attended, watching these two wind up Stephen Hague like you wouldn't believe. 'Why don't you put a lion roaring on that track?' 'Let's get a barbershop quartet for this bit.'

In the end Hague lost it completely and chucked us all out. We ended up back at the Groucho where the carnage continued until Tracy grabbed me and said, 'Come on, we're going to Browns.'

We got in this limo outside, and the driver goes, 'Oh, sorry, I'm waiting for Mr Lenny Henry,' but Tracy said, 'I am Lenny Henry, now fucking drive,' and the driver's going, 'No, Mr Henry's a black gentleman,' and Tracy said, 'Just drive. I'm Lenny Henry, Masambula! Fucking drive!'

Meanwhile, with the album near completion, Barney asked for a larger share of the publishing. Apart from 'World in Motion', the publishing had always been split five ways. No matter that Rob never contributed musically, and Gillian only very rarely, they still got an even split and a band vote. I had suspected this was on the horizon. I kept hearing him, 'Johnny says this … Johnny says that …' New Order had always split everything equally. The Smiths famously hadn't.

Barney, meanwhile, would take great delight in dropping in that us three weren't even on 'World' or 'Ruined in a Day', how he'd just written them himself. It certainly did rankle – and it wasn't fucking true, either, as we'll shortly discover.

Rob was terrified. He wanted all this sorted out and he didn't want anything to get in the way of the London deal. He persuaded us to take the cut. Barney wanted 50 per cent of the band's cut, so that left 50 per cent between us three (and Rob got his normal 20 per cent off the top – no pay cut for him).

I saw my chance. Should I suggest Gillian giving over more of her share? In my opinion she had been more than fairly treated on all the other records from *Movement* to *Technique*, getting more than she should have done. Maybe now was the time for her to admit Barney did most if not all of the keyboard work and hand over some, if not all, of her publishing.

But if it was the last New Order record, was it really worth upsetting the fucking applecart so badly? I had got on really well with them at the start of *Republic* and they felt like friends. I thought, *Fuck it*, and we shared the cut, going down to 16.666 recurring (the mark of the devil). Rob was delighted. Nothing could stand in our way now. Could it?

Then Stephen Hague asked for publishing on five songs.

Barney went nuts and wanted to refuse. 'Tell him to fuck off! I did everything,' he cried. But, being all too aware that we really needed to get the album out, Rob persuaded us to agree again. Next thing we knew the publishing had been split six ways.

It was a very, very sour end to a fairly sour recording experience, which haunts me every time I hear the bloody record.

TIMELINE THIRTEEN
JANUARY–DECEMBER 1992

© Kevin Cummins

January 1992

Revenge: 'Gun World Porn'
(FAC 327)

Twelve-inch track list:

'Deadbeat'	4.50
'Cloud Nine'	4.52
'State of Shock' (12" edit)	6.26
'Little Pig'	4.42

Run-out groove one: *Get the handcuffs ...*
Run-out groove two: *The Devil Drives!*

Twelve-inch remix track list:

'Deadbeat' (Gary Clail remix 1)	4.54
'Deadbeat' (Gary Clail Remix 2)	4.37
'State of Shock' (L'Pool edit)	6.01
'State of Shock' (Paralysed mix)	5.16

Run-out groove one: *Up there, Out There!*
Run-out groove two: *Over There Building Site!*

CD single track list:

'Deadbeat'	4.50
'Cloud Nine'	4.52
'State of Shock' (12" edit)	6.26
'Little Pig'	4.42

Recorded and mixed in Circular Road, Withington, Manchester.
Engineered by Mike Johnson.
Mixed by Keith Andrews at Amazon.
Produced by Revenge.
Photograph by Trevor Watson.
Designed by John Macklin.

10 February 1992

New Order: *BBC Radio 1 Live in Concert*
(WinLP011)

Concert recorded 19 June 1987 at Glastonbury. Released on the Windsong International label.

Track list:

'Touched by the Hand of God'	4.57
'Temptation'	8.36
'True Faith'	5.45
'Your Silent Face'	6.05
'Every Second Counts'	4.20
'Bizarre Love Triangle'	4.39
'Perfect Kiss'	10.05
'Age of Consent'	5.20
'Sister Ray'	9.21

Run-out groove one: *Beware my son …*
Run-out groove two: *… your sins will find you out!*

Produced by Pete Ritzema.
Entered UK chart on 22 February 1992, remaining in the charts for 2 weeks, its peak position was number 33.

> **'This was surreal. Rob Gretton had to go to the lengths of releasing a semi-bootleg/live LP on an offshoot of Pinnacle Records for a cash advance and a royalty stream that was not tied to an insolvent label (i.e. Factory).'**

15 February 1992

Revenge play Witchwood, Ashton, for Hooky's 36th birthday party.

> **'Jack Bates's first gig. He loved it. Arranged by our super-fan Fat Alex, who had now become a friend.'**

March 1992

Happy Mondays leave to record their new LP at Eddy Grant's Blue Wave studios in Barbados.

'This could not have happened at a worse time for Factory. As a group the Mondays were getting on very badly and why Tony decided to inflict them on Tina Weymouth and Chris Frantz, who were co-producing, is anyone's guess. Shaun was now a full-blown heroin addict. I cannot for the life of me, after us going to Ibiza and messing it up, see how anyone thought this was a good idea. It was a disaster from start to finish. On arriving at Manchester airport Shaun dropped his supply of Methadone and ended up trying to scoop it up out of the broken bits of glass in the departures lounge. When they arrived in Barbados he was going cold turkey, and soon became completely hooked on the endless supply of crack available (as long as you had money), ruining himself and the record in the process. They eventually returned after six long weeks with twelve vocal-less backing tracks. The stories are legion and have been told at length by the Mondays so let's leave it apart from this one, my favourite ... After stealing all Nathan McGough's clothes, the only thing Shaun could think of to sell was the leather settees out of the control room. The problem he had was getting them to the market to sell, so he stole the studio's golf cart to transport them. After two trips he then sold the golf cart. Eddy Grant was livid.

'Strangely enough, Shaun wasn't the only one to fall foul of this particular hurdle. A friend of mine, let's call him Towser, had gone on holiday and done exactly the same thing, locking himself in the toilet of his villa with some kid popping rocks through the window every so often. He only came out when he ran out of money. When he begged the dealer for more he was offered a deal: if he took these two guys up to the mountains in his rented Mini Moke to visit a friend of theirs, they would give him what he needed to last the holiday. He agreed, and drove them to a shack in the mountains where the two Barbadians said, "Turn round, we won't be long." He turned round. Then the two guys came out of the shack door shooting two revolvers at the interior, letting off

round after round into it. BANG. BANG. BANG. Then jumping into the Mini Moke with a big bag of crack and money.

"You've never seen a Moke move so fast!" he said. "I was terrified."

'Back at the hotel the two guys offered him a huge rock. "No," he stammered.

'He was cured.'

28 March 1992

Revenge play Rock Garden, Dublin.

March 1992

New Order take up residence at Real World in order to record *Republic*, remaining there, off and on, until November.

'Five-star prison. We had so much downtime I went to the local garden centre and bought a plastic sunlounger so I could top up my tan. I spent more time on that than I did in the studio. We were literally never together, everyone took every opportunity they could to disappear, sometimes with the flimsiest of excuses.

'I also ended up having a wonderful fling with one of the lovely kitchen assistants. We tried desperately to keep it quiet, and only met up after dinner. I thought I'd got away with it until I came down one morning and the chef said, "Peter Gabriel's been on the phone. He wants a word." Oh, fuck. Not again.'

20 April 1992

Revenge play Hippodrome, Middleton, Oldham, supported by Oasis, the band's first gig featuring Noel Gallagher.

'I was right in the middle of my heaviest drug phase now, and I wasn't enjoying our gigs, they were getting in the way of my drug-taking. I found out that my brother filmed this gig on Super 8. He called it *Slugfest* because while he was filming it, a slug walked across the table into the ashtray in front of him, and he wrote on

the tapes, "Slugfest". This place was a fucking rat hole. I remember that I went in the dressing room and the rest of them went out for something to eat and I just started on the drugs. I couldn't resist it and ended up completely bollocksed, spending the whole gig watching the clock above the bar tick really slowly. It was horrible. The Salford lot turned up thinking it was a dance night and a huge fight went off at the door. I was so fucked I can't remember what Oasis were like, to be honest. Wish our kid could find the tape. Every time I ask he says, "Oh, it's in the loft. I must get it out!"

'Strangely enough, Pottsy would get an audition to be the bass player in Oasis much later. Jonny Hugo arranged it for him, knowing he knew the songs anyway. Pottsy was a big fan. When he got there they played for a while and then went to the pub. Everything was going well, but Pottsy told me he thought Noel was too loud, drowning everyone out. So, being the first one back from the pub, he just turned Noel's amp down. They started to play again, but almost immediately Noel stopped: "Who's turned my fucking amp down?"

'"I did," said Pottsy, "you're too loud."

'He said Noel looked shocked but just turned it up again. They carried on, then Noel went for a piss. Pottsy seized the opportunity and turned his amp down again. When Noel came back he went absolutely ballistic. Pottsy was sacked before he even got the job.

'When I asked why he did it, he said, "He was too loud. You can't do that, it's not fair."

'Also, they were playing "Wonderwall" and Pottsy suggested some "better chords". You can imagine how that went down with the leader of Oasis.

'David Potts, that's why I love you.'

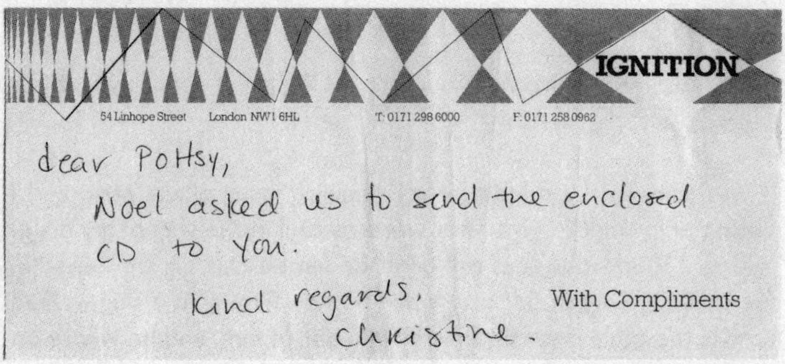
IGNITION

54 Linhope Street London NW1 6HL T: 0171 298 6000 F: 0171 258 0962

dear Pottsy,

Noel asked us to send the enclosed CD to you.

Kind regards,

Christine.

With Compliments

21 May 1992

The Haçienda's tenth birthday party.

> 'As a special tenth celebration the Haçienda booked ten DJs. Unfortunately, no one had worked out a time schedule for the night. There was no way all of them could play. Egos were bruised and battered, leading to many bad-tempered tussles in the DJ booth.'

June 1992

Electronic terminate their contract with Factory and move to Parlophone Records.

> 'Like rats deserting a sinking ship.'

June 1992

The Haçienda accounts show that security was costing £375,000 per annum. This ensured the business could never be sold. All the profit was going on security. Many buyers carried on negotiating, thinking it must be a typing error, Virgin's Richard Branson among them.

July 1992

'The Crow' film project.

> 'This was a comic book story by James O'Barr, first published in 1989. It tells the story of a man brutally murdered who comes back to life as an undead avenger. The comic is littered with Joy Division references. Even the two main characters are called Captain Hook and Sergeant Albrecht. It was to be made into a big-budget feature film and the producer wanted New Order to re-record "Love Will Tear Us Apart" especially for it, the idea being we had come back from the dead. There was a lot of money on offer, £50,000, but because we were recording *Republic*, Barney would not entertain it, saying, "We can only do one thing at once. This is too much. No." The contradiction being he was doing Electronic at the same time

anyway. This was such a great shame. The project was eventually passed to Trent Reznor of Nine Inch Nails, who did a very straight version of "Dead Souls" by Joy Division. This was the first time I had heard this "We can only do one thing at once" mantra. I would hear it a lot from now on though.'

12–16 September 1992

The first 'In the City' music conference, Midland Hotel, Manchester. 'A real music convention in a real music city.'

'This was great. I was the only musician there for the first couple of years and it was very enjoyable. Many industry types used it as an excuse to get completely off their nuts for a couple of days, all expenses paid, and I joined in.'

20 November 1992

Factory Records go bankrupt.

☹

23 December 1992

Joy Division and New Order sign to London Records.

'This was a hard-fought battle, but did signify a new start for both bands. Our lawyer told me that when at last the draft contract had been agreed (even he said it was a tough negotiation) London's lawyers sent over the final copy of the contract for signing last thing on Friday evening. We were meeting him on Monday morning to sign. He said, "I had nothing to do the next day so I got a gin and tonic and sat down to read it, all three hundred pages. It was a good thing I did, Peter, because right at the end they had put in three highly disadvantageous clauses, and when I phoned them they said it was a mistake and sent an amended copy."

'Bloody hell. Major record companies, eh? Well, the big time beckoned ... but could we handle it? Or them? Or could they handle us? Only time would tell.'

'Blink and you miss us'

In January 1993 Revenge played their last two concerts. Me and Jane split up after the first one in London at the New Marquee club. A typical gig for us, everyone had a great time. We were all off our heads afterwards, loading the gear in the back of the van and then all sitting down in the front ready to go home. Only there was no driver.

'Jane, where's the fuckin' driver?' I snapped.

'Hang on?' she said. 'We're all here. Who was supposed to drive?'

No one volunteered any information. The recriminations started, us all screaming at each other, 'You were supposed to drive. You! You! You!' then laughing when we realised the truth. We'd all got plastered with no thought to getting home and now we were stuck in London with no designated driver. Luckily, the support band from Manchester were just leaving. I opened the door of their van and shouted, 'Anyone sober in here?'

'I am,' said one of them. So we press-ganged this poor sober kid into ferrying us back home, driving him mad with the all the 'chunnering' coming from the back.

> Chunnering: when someone keeps going on and on about something that no one else is interested in. Or to grumble, complain or grouse mildly and tediously, often to yourself in a quiet voice.

I got him a taxi home from our house, but only after he'd had to witness the biggest row me and Jane ever had. We had reached the end of our relationship and amazingly it coincided exactly with the end of Revenge too.

Truth was, our ways of life were not compatible. She'd taken to knocking round with all the roadies she'd met doing the gigs at Maine Road while I was off with the dancing gangsters. She'd even been on tour with the Orb for ten days and never phoned me once. I knew the writing was on the wall.

The week before we'd gone to the Haçienda together, again parting once inside, me going in the Salford Corner arms aloft, praising the DJ, and her in the quieter confines of the cocktail bar. She came to get me later, crying.

'I'm having palpitations,' she said. 'I think I'm dying!'

Me, ever the gentleman: 'Can't you hang on a minute, I've just had another pill?'

'I'M DYING, YOU BASTARD!' she screamed at me.

So off to casualty we went.

They put her in a cubicle and I sat in a wheelchair by the door. Unfortunately I was just coming up and within minutes was whizzing up and down the corridors, scattering everyone out of the way, complete with *whee* noises as a running commentary. I got kicked out by security. I was stood outside dancing with the automatic doors when she came out, ashen-faced. 'You fucking idiot,' she said. 'Get home.'

We had grown too far apart. We agreed to split and I moved to Salford to live in Harmsworth Street with Twinny while she stayed in our house and began looking for a flat. Sad days.

I soon recovered and a few weeks later took up with a lovely young lady, who was as mad as a box of frogs.

More or less the first thing we did was take an extensive trip to Mexico, Los Cabos to be exact, where we watched two dolphins appear out of a perfectly still sea right in front of us as we exchanged presents. *Oh my God*, I thought, *this was meant to be*. Then on to America where Tom had me romancing, first the record company in the guise of Jim Swindel, the new manager of Qwest, and then CAA, our agents, headed by Carole Kinzel. They were both important to New Order and Tom was desperate to make a good impression on them. Even though I kept telling him the band was over, he just said, 'Shut up. They're paying for you and your girl's holiday so you'll do as you're motherfucking goddamned told.'

I couldn't argue with that. Tom, like Rob, was in a bit of denial. The meeting with Qwest went well. My girlfriend was jetlagged so she stayed in the Sunset Marquis. Jim Swindel was a wonderful man and I still see him now. The meeting ran over and when I finally got back to the hotel she was very annoyed. 'Come on,' I said, 'we're going for dinner with CAA. Get ready.'

She said, 'What? I've just had four sleeping tablets. I'm knackered.'

Now it was my turn to say, '*What?* Four fucking sleeping tablets … are you mad?'

She got ready under duress. Carole Kinzel and her assistant were waiting for us in this beautiful restaurant, of which Tom said, 'Fuck, even I can't get a table here.'

We took our places in our lovely circular banquette. As soon as the conversation turned to the more technical aspects of touring, as in, 'How can we get them bastards to do gigs?' my girlfriend's eyes started to glaze over. I think it was probably the sleepers. She was still a bit new to the politics, and little by little she started to slip off the seat and slide under the table, to which CAA seemed completely oblivious. The next minute she was gone but the conversation just carried on, with great food and drink, to the sounds of gentle, ladylike snoring from below. By coffee, Carole was demanding some answers to our internal affairs, probing both me and Tom as to future plans. The meeting suddenly turned serious, and just then I noticed a sharp tugging at my fly buttons. Obviously someone had woken in a rather horny morning mood. Fending my girlfriend off, I tried to carry on, but there was a tugging of the tablecloth and when I looked underneath the table a voice demanded, 'I'm hungry.' With barely a blink, Tom got the waiter to bring her dinner back and I spent the rest of the meal feeding her under the table. Carole and her assistant never said a word. Even Tom was laughing by now.

Then she passed out again. Shit. They got the bill and left while I got down on the floor to retrieve my girlfriend, pulling her out by the ankles from under the table in front of this packed and exclusive restaurant. Tom just legged it, leaving a 'fuck you, fucker' behind. I then grabbed her arm and threw her over my shoulder and quickly headed for the door (she had long blonde hair which trailed behind us like a cloak). Just then the maitre d' came flying over to me. 'I trust you had a lovely meal?' he said, wringing his hands.

'Ah, indeed,' said I.

'Hopefully we'll see you again sometime?' he grinned.

'Maybe …'

'When you're next in town? You and your lovely lady. Thank you, sir.' And we left.

Wow, Californians, eh?

My girlfriend then went on to disgrace herself at an aftershow with EMF in the Riot House (Hyatt Hotel on Sunset), listening to all sorts of confessions and asking the drummer his name forty times and going, 'You're unbelievable,' every time he told her. It was great fun.

Coming back home, the Haçienda madness carried on all spring, with me frantically juggling being a single parent and lunatic raver. Which I did badly, I'm afraid, culminating in my arrest for 'conspiracy to supply controlled drugs'.

My mates were dealing, I knew it. I didn't know how much, but I was aware and happy to enjoy its benefits. I was asked to be guarantor on a phone for one of them (they don't usually have bank accounts/credit cards, drug dealers) and again I was happy to, putting both my home address and credit card down. What I didn't know was that they were shifting a million pounds' worth of dope at a time, and were the target of a massive undercover police sting. They all got arrested and remanded to Strangeways.

> Strangeways is a prison, accepting people remanded into custody from the courts in the Greater Manchester area. It opened in June 1868. Following a major disturbance in 1990, the prison had to be completely rebuilt.

This was a strange time. These were some of my closest friends and me and their partners were going down to court to give as much support as we could. By now all our writing and rehearsals were at the Farm in Macclesfield and I'd go to court on my way there.

One day we'd been offering our support and as I left the courtroom I was approached by three police officers, one woman and two blokes, and promptly arrested for being involved with the aforesaid conspiracy. I was cautioned and told I would be taken to the police station at Bootle Street, Manchester, searched and charged.

Luckily one of my mate's solicitors saw what was happening and offered to brief me on my rights, taking me away from the cops to an interview room in the court foyer that had a full-length glass wall, with the coppers waiting patiently outside.

'OK, Peter,' he said, 'don't worry too much. I know the case and they're just pulling everyone in. They'll quiz you then let you go. Is there anything I should know?'

'Yes,' I said. 'I've got a load of drugs in my wallet.'

Like an idiot, I had my week's rations with me: three grams of charlie and two of speed.

Now it was his turn to sweat. You should have seen his face.

Then and now, I do not know how I had the balls to do it, but I squeezed my wallet out of my pocket (luck No. 1: it was in the pocket facing away from the police), got the wraps out, lifted up the Formica table with my knee (luck No. 2: it had a wide round base), dropped them on the floor and with one swift movement swept them under the base. I stood up and walked out to the waiting police, leaving a speechless, ashen-faced solicitor to clear up after me.

I was giving drugs up right now.

I was taken to the station and I must say got on rather well with them all, ending up in the police canteen having tea and doughnuts with the two guys, who were not only trumpet players in the police brass band but also regular visitors to the Haçienda. 'Undercover, you understand,' they whispered.

We got on like a house on fire, me even getting a tour of the station, cells included. 'This is where the naughty boys end up,' they laughed.

I thought, *If only you knew, ociffer, if only you knew.*

I was taken to an interview room and they said, 'No need to search a nice man like yourself, Peter.' I was interviewed and then bailed. Then they escorted me home to search my house. Oops.

My brain was reeling. I didn't live there but Jane was as up it as me. When we arrived, they took one look at it and said, 'It's too big, we'll leave it, Hooky.'

Later I got an almighty bollocking from the superintendent, was told to keep my nose clean from now on, and stay away from gangsters ... fat chance.

Meanwhile, London Records got our first single ready, 'Regret' (rather an apt title for this particular episode, I thought). It would be the first of four single releases that year alone. We had gone from the sublime to the ridiculous, but I loved the song. Pete Saville was struggling a bit with the sleeve for the album, because 'The Committee' now wanted a say in the design. Before, he had been left pretty much to his own devices, but with our new-found independence with our 'solo' projects we all wanted input and control. Interestingly Peter took note of the divergent inputs and decided to include everyone's ideas, showing us photos of stock images and putting them together as our choices, then with his partner Brett Wickens blending the images together on a computer, for the first time, and managing – again for the first time ever – to please all of us ... a bloody miracle.

A video was arranged using the director Peter Care, with filming in Rome. Here we would be introduced to a couple of new concepts.

Firstly, the record company would be in charge of the video instead of Michael Shamberg. Secondly, we would be styled, as in a stylist (not heavy metal) was hired to dress us for the video.

This was quite an alien concept at first but the stylist was a nice woman and we got to keep most of the clothes afterwards – result. Looking back now at some of the press articles and the videos of that London period, there are times when we did look even more uncomfortable and awkward than usual, particularly Steve and Gillian. For the video we were shown a storyboard and, although it didn't make much sense, it seemed the band members would be filmed miming, first in a bedroom and then in the hotel's rather grand ballroom, all separately, no togetherness for this record here either. Then we would walk around various tourist sites, then, via mixed screens, we would be put together, hooray.

The hotel in Rome was beautiful, where I compensated for the boredom (sorry, I know how pampered and spoilt that sounds, but it's true: video shoots are boring, even when they're taking place in Rome) by getting really, really drunk, smashing back glass after glass of champagne. They had a pianist/singer in the bar, and when he sang 'Groovy Kind of Love' (which is one of my favourites, a beauty), I spent the whole time sitting with him, getting pissed on champagne and making him sing it over and over again.

'Sing "Groovy Kind of Love", mate. Come on, mate, one more time, give us "Groovy Kind of Love".'

They had fresh flowers on the tables in the bar and one night I got so pissed I ate them all out of the vase. Just showing off, as you do.

Christ, the video was dull, though. It was dull to make and it was dull to watch and Pete Care seemed dull to me too. During filming we went for a meal and I disgraced myself by calling him a dwarf (sorry, Peter) then telling the rest of the group they were a bunch of useless twats. Proper obnoxious behaviour: scary now to think I'd be behaving that way for the next ten years or so. I'm cringing at the thought.

That night, Rob dragged me back to the hotel, like a naughty schoolboy, where I stormed around for a bit more, eating the flowers again, and shouting the odds in the bar before, at last, deciding to go to bed. Walking along the corridor towards my room, I could see this bloke coming towards me and thought, *Hey up, what's this twat doing?*

Every time I moved to the left, he moved to the left, and every time I moved to the right, he moved to the right.

I was thinking, *He's taking the piss, this twat, he's going to get a battering*, and he was getting nearer and nearer until all of a sudden, *bang*, I walked slap-bang into a mirror.

And that, my friends, is called karma.

We finished, and apart from me getting a right bollocking because the hotel was charging by the glass instead of by the bottle and I had a five-day bill, for champagne alone, of £2,000. We flew home. The cynical me thought Peter Care was just having another holiday at our expense, as he then went to LA to film more backgrounds, the video insanely metamorphosing from Rome to Los Angeles at the end for no reason at all. I have to say 'Regret' looks nice but doesn't say much.

Cost = over £200,000.

We were in a different league now and would soon realise that on a major label making expensive nonsensical videos was a great way to burn money. This would be dwarfed (sorry again, Peter) by the next video, the one that would drive Tom Atencio completely mad: 'World'.

One aside. For our next *Top of the Pops* performance we turned up all ready to mime, having been converted at San Remo, only to be told the singer now had to sing live while the musicians mimed. This was exactly the opposite way round to how it should have been, the vocal always being the most difficult to replicate live. Trust the BBC.

I enjoyed our day, even though Gill Smith (my old 'dominatrix' girlfriend who now worked upstairs in the *Top of the Pops* magazine office) threatened to come down and kick my head in. Having my picture taken in *EastEnders*' Albert Square later was a real highlight. Then drinking the evening away in the bar with Phil and Grant Mitchell.

Republic came out. Remember, we were still in the era of deciding titles by committee, so predictably I hated them all. 'Regret' was OK, but 'World', 'Spooky', 'Liar', 'Special' and 'Chemical' were a long way away from the days when we used to take our titles from novels and arty foreign films and the *Sunday Times*. The more abstract they were, in my opinion, the better. We were now having meetings about the tiniest thing, but what occupied us most was what we should release as the next single, and what the video should be. Here's where Tom Atencio perked up.

'Regret' had done well in America and, with the scent of victory in his nostrils, Tom reiterated his oft-aired point that our next single should be supported by a video that featured the band more prominently. He thought 'World (The Price of Love)' could be a big hit if we had a proper group video for MTV to show.

Man, I fucking hated 'World (The Price of Love)' with a passion. I hated the name, I hated the song, I hated the backing vocals, (I hated the brackets), and sure enough, I would hate the video too.

The crew were out in Cannes for three weeks before we got there, with the band staying for one; we were in the beautiful Carlton Hotel, the very one that Elton John used in his video for 'I'm Still Standing', and God knows why because we were barely in the video. Literally, blink and you miss us, all of us. We hired the jetty of the hotel, which was then dressed and adorned with extras, making it into a real freakshow – ironically the hotel was a freakshow anyway, with some real weirdos we could have filmed for free. Added to that was the fire brigade attending a fake crash and a motorboat filming extra shots from the sea (where intense excitement was caused when the cameraman dropped the fucking £30,000 camera into the ocean; the video had to be suspended while a team of divers were hired to recover it). To me it looked like a Duran Duran video and was as vacuous and stupid as theirs usually were.

Cost = over £300,000.

For that? I was flabbergasted. But the best thing about the video was Tom's reaction, which we'll come to.

God, we did squeeze that album dry when it came to singles. For a while it felt like we did nothing but record videos. Keith Allen heard about the one we did for 'World', and was certain he could do a better job. Fair play to him, he did do a better job. The video he directed for 'Ruined in a Day' was my favourite of the bunch. He had this huge beautiful jungle set built, with specially made hand-carved foam Buddhas (one of which lived with me in Withington for years), hired extras for monks, bought in gold-dust that cost £1,000 an ounce to sprinkle around the camera, and then, just as we were all on set, ready for filming, 'Action!' ... the coke dealer arrived and, before you knew it, we were up to our eyeballs and partying hard.

It did become quite surreal with Barney at one point, convinced they were real monks, cornering two in the toilets to debate reincarnation. A third came to me: 'Excuse me. Your singer's got two of my friends in the toilet and he won't let them out.'

What was most ironic about it is that none of us could stand the sight of each other, and yet this is the video where we looked like we were having the most fun as a group, together like great mates.

But it was a good video, and a great song, one of my favourites (particularly the K-Klass remix). I liked the way that Stephen Hague produced that one, apart from the total absence of me, of course. Ah well, you can't win 'em all. We didn't play it live for long, though. It was one of those songs that Barney found too complicated to play, so it got bumped off the set list along with many others.

Cost = over £200,000.

The *Top of the Pops* performance for 'Ruined in a Day' was a cracker. We had been there all day and were desperate for some artificial stimulation, but kept getting dragged back for take after take. At last the BBC were satisfied and let us go. We went straight back to the dressing room and chopped out a hedge each ... Bam! We were off with the fairies.

Cue popping of champagne corks and smoking of cigarettes. Then a knock on the door. We all froze. It was the floor manager.

'Sorry,' he said. 'Technical issue, we need another performance.'

What then followed was the longest 3.05 minutes of our lives. We were completely paranoid that all these kids in the audience knew what we'd been doing in the dressing room. It was hell, our noses running like fountains. I later got chased off the *EastEnders* set for carving my name in the wet concrete of the newly laid floor in the shop.

Later, as we got ready to rehearse for what would be a very short tour, I asked Dickie at Real World to do me the usual practice tape of the new songs. He would put a stereo mix of the song on the left and the bassline on the right, so I could hear it clearly enough to practise and learn the part. Imagine my surprise when I got the tape and saw

'World' and 'Young Offender' both on it, which was odd because I hardly feature on 'Young Offender', and not at all on 'World'.

So I listened and, lo and behold, there's the bass playing the vocal lines on both songs. My colleagues must have taken the melody I'd written, used it as an idea for the vocal, and then dumped the bass.

In one way I was delighted. At least I'd had more input than I thought. On the other hand, I remembered how much Barney had rubbed it in my face about not being on the tracks. *There's one for the moan bank*, I thought. It could have been worse. Barney told me he'd written 'Liar' about our manager. I was really shocked when I saw the lyrics. Poor Rob.

Republic had been difficult to make, so playing live would seem like a doddle by comparison. Still being a huge fan of gigs, I wanted to play as many as possible, but despite Rob's pleas the other three would commit to no more than thirteen.

I'd said to Barney, only half-joking, 'Thirteen gigs, mate. Unlucky for some, shall we make it fourteen?'

'Twelve then,' he deadpanned, and walked off.

We warmed up in Dublin, which went very well, and in July we found ourselves on the bill of the Montreux Jazz Festival, as special guests of Quincy Jones, which was very nice of him.

Great hotel, too. I remember phoning down for Perrier water and the guy saying, 'Just turn on the tap, monsieur,' his supercilious way of telling me that the lake outside was where it came from, I suppose.

Meanwhile, my old friend Robert Plant was on the same bill, and I was thrilled to discover he was still pissed off about me nicking the girl off him at RAK. That and seeing Quincy (who's one of the nicest and easiest people you could hope to meet – a proper cool cat in a business full of rats) just about made up for the dog's dinner of a gig.

It wasn't that the crowd hated us – if they had, we would have fed off that and lopped their heads off, it was just that they were completely ... *lukewarm*.

The worst kind of reception at a gig.

As a result we gave a pretty crappy performance, only saved from being the worst of the festival by none other than Robert Plant, who came on after us and was even worse. His band looked like extras from the 'Touched by the Hand of God' video and played lousy versions of Led Zeppelin songs.

Later there was a huge party. I was on a promise with this woman who worked for MTV. She was lovely, proper girlfriend material, and I'd been flirting with her on the phone for ages. Now, as soon as we'd got to Montreux, the cry had gone up to get some drugs and, sure enough, we'd managed to score some. Our supplier was warning us to go easy on it because, according to him, it was very strong, but of course we were like, 'Fuck off, we're from Manchester, mate, the coke hasn't been made that can scare us,' and just to prove my point, I had a massive stonking line of it before I set off for the party.

Big mistake. Should have listened to the guy. By the time I arrived, I was hanging. I couldn't even speak. My lovely MTV girl approached me to say hello in the flesh, and I couldn't even talk, let alone be the Terry-Thomas lover boy I'd been hinting at on the phone. It was like I had locked-in syndrome. After two minutes of watching my jaw work up and down and me standing sweating, she said, 'Oh, you're fucking useless,' turned on her heel and went, and that was that. I was so annoyed with myself I stomped off back to the hotel, alone, for another sleepless night. It was shit being single. I missed Jane.

In the midst of all this we embarked on a tour of Europe and America, culminating in what would be our last gig as the classic line-up, when we headlined the Reading Festival again. The European leg of the tour went well. Everyone was pretty well behaved, but the stroppiness started when we moved to America, where it was business as usual.

The first thing on the agenda was to show Tom the new video for 'World (The Price of Love)', the one he had instigated and dearly hoped would break us via MTV to a huge audience.

He was very excited and I for one did not have the heart to break it to him that we were hardly in it . . . again! He had arranged for a VHS video player in his hotel room all set up for a kind of low-key, no red carpet premiere.

Now, as we all know, one of the first rules of rock'n'roll is 'Never have a party in your own room'. If it goes wrong you've got nowhere to run to. Tom had broken this golden rule. We hit the bar and waited for the appointed viewing time, when we all filed down the corridor to Tom's room, giggling nervously as we did so. We knew what was coming. Rob was already in the room, lying on the bed, shoes off, and we all piled in and sat down facing the TV.

Rob handed over the tape, and Tom, spouting various Americanisms – 'This is going to be awesome, we are going to be huge etc. etc.' – put it in the player. We waited. Tom sat on the floor at the end of the bed and stared at the screen for the 4 minutes 38 seconds that it lasted. As the screen faded to black, he got up, turned slowly round and, before any of us could react, jumped on Rob, locked his hands round his throat and screamed, 'Fuck you, fucker!'

Rob did his best to get out of the way, twisting and writhing on the bed, but it took a few of us to pull Tom off, where he collapsed in a heap on the floor, head in hands muttering, 'Fuck … Fuck … Fuck.'

This joke had gone badly wrong and the atmosphere in the room was awful. We did what any self-respecting rock star would do and left them to it, literally running out the door back to the bar. He recovered later and we carried on, Tom trying to make the most of what he considered to be another bad job.

The tour soon settled into the usual routine of divas by day, and monsters by night, but there were a couple of new additions to the strange happenings.

Barney was going to great lengths to make sure no one had a bigger hotel room than he did, mooching round the hotel, knocking on your door and looking over your shoulder, trying to ascertain the square footage. He even went so far as to enquire at reception about the layout of each of our rooms. When I asked Andy Robinson about this he said he'd been doing it for ages. I never knew. He was also still being the last to arrive, so everyone was waiting for him all the time.

Another thing: the set list would never be changed. Barney would learn a certain set of songs and we could not divert from that. He had a computer-operated autocue system for the lyrics delivered. No more learning them; from now on they would be read. Also, a new 16-track Akai digital recorder would be used for the backing track, enabling us to put multiple backing vocals on the tape along with multiple guitar tracks. We were turning into the sort of group we used to hate.

I was absolutely appalled at all this. Not only would he not learn any more songs (and you couldn't make him do it), we were basically miming. Anyway, we set off. Steve and Gillian seemed to spend the majority of their time in their room, while I hung out with the crew, boozing, drugging, dragging my new girlfriend round with me (much to Jane's annoyance – she was still my roadie).

We may have been touring an album made under duress and for the worst possible reasons – an album I didn't like at all – and we may have fallen out as individuals, all our grand dreams and high-minded principles as dead as our former record company. But I for one was going to go out on a high.

Literally – high.

While we were in California we had to record a video for a second *Top of the Pops* performance for 'Regret'. I can't remember why. 'Regret' must have still been high in the charts and *Top of the Pops* had developed a new habit of letting bands on twice if they were in a glamorous location on tour. We fulfilled that easily. Tom Atencio knew one of the assistant directors on *Baywatch* (which was huge on TV at the time) who also did soft-porn movies, and thought it would be funny to combine New Order with *Baywatch* to broadcast it on *Top of the Pops* as an 'as-live' – or should that be 'ass-live'? – performance.

I liked 'Regret'. As I said, to me, *Republic* starts and finishes with 'Regret', the rest of it just sounds and feels like Electronic or the Pet Shop Boys with a bit of my bass thrown in.

Even so, me liking the song didn't necessarily mean I wanted to perform it on a beach. But that's what we did. It was a lovely day, and as soon as we met David Hasselhoff we realised it would be a very interesting one too. He was nuts. Running up and down the beach set screaming and shouting and being, well, a real character. When he had his picture taken with us he insisted on digging a hole in the sand so he was the same height as us. Very thoughtful. The day went very well, with me ending up playing topless in my leather trousers on the beach, surrounded by all these beauties. Weird. A deputation soon stopped that and the top had to go back on. Mine, anyway.

It was a long, hot session and the relief when we were released was palpable.

'That's a wrap everyone!'

Yeah, definitely, we thought, straight in the motor home with our wraps for some artificial stimulation.

Afterwards one of the girls asked me if I wanted to go shopping on Melrose with her, and like a dickhead I refused, preferring to stay in a sweaty caravan doing drugs with a bunch of people I mostly hated. Regret, indeed.

The video crew were telling us they had just filmed at the John Paul Getty Villa in Malibu. The shoot had gone well but then two of them were sent back to the trucks for more equipment. On the way back they rounded a corner to be faced with a full-grown lion just sitting there on its haunches; one guy froze and the other ran and jumped in the truck, closing the door. The frozen one literally pissed himself in fear. He then had to endure the lion slowly sniffing his crotch. He said, 'Then it just turned round and walked away. I have never been so frightened in my life. I only came round when I heard the other guy laughing.'

It seems John Paul Getty actually kept two lions at the Getty Villa for security. People didn't know, but both had their teeth and claws removed. Phew. Our video was a little more sedate.

The American leg of the tour continued. We were huge in the States by then. We could have done 100 dates in America and sold them all out. We landed at the Hollywood Bowl and it was a total sell-out. Backstage we set up what we called a 'bugle room' and all the American crew and venue workers were very puzzled by it. 'What is this bugle room, dude, because you don't have a bugle in your group, do you?'

We were going, 'Oh yeah, we've got the bugle in there, don't you worry about it.'

They'd be dead confused. 'Really? Well, why do you have a room just for your bugle when you don't even have a bugle in the show?'

We'd go, 'Oh, we go in there to practise the bugle.'

'Yeah, but I never hear you blow it, man,' all this lot.

They were absolutely fascinated. Me too. I would go in the bugle room after the gig, and emerge completely off it for the encore. I never used to get out of it before the gigs, honest. I used to save it for just before the encore, so that by the time it was finished I'd be flying.

In other words, backstage was brilliant, and it usually was at the American gigs. It was like a little town back there and, as one of the key figures in the band, you felt like you were mayor of it. Nightmare, in my case, boom-boom.

At the front of house, however, was the same system we'd complained about before. This was the idea that guest-list people and VIP tickets would all get the good positions at the front of the auditorium. Now we just shrugged about it. We found that one as easy to discard as every other principle we began with, and if people wanted to eat chicken-in-a-basket while we played our hits, then who were we to complain? We just wanted it all over with, and the tour chuntered on in a haze of booze and drugs and clearly defined camps backstage.

As a group of people, New Order acted like a divorcing husband and wife: we couldn't even be bothered to hate one another any more. We'd simply stopped caring about each other. We played our guts out most nights – I like to think we didn't let our band politics affect the performances – but as soon as we were offstage all our heart was lost again.

By the time we reached the final gig of the tour at Reading – the gig that, for the record, I consider the last proper New Order gig, we simply couldn't wait to finish and get back to our other lives. Never was it so easy to say goodbye to all that success and hard work, and it certainly wasn't hard to say goodbye to the people involved.

After Reading I didn't see any of New Order for at least three years. Oh, I tell a lie, I think I bumped into Barney once, in Dry 201, when he was off his head, and he came up to me like he always did when he was off it, apologising. 'Sorry for being such a cunt, Hooky, sorry for being so miserable all the time, sorry for being such a twat.'

I'd think, *If you said it when you were sober, it'd make me really happy. You always say it when you're off your head. And it means nothing.*

Anyway, Reading was another one of those gigs where, as usual, by the time we finished there were no drink or drugs left and all my mates were completely trashed, just like the time we finished there in 1990. This one being even more miserable because literally *all* our mates were there, and I think they all had the same sense that the gravy train was pulling into the station, that the happy days were over; and they were planning on partying like it was the end of the world.

Me, I left them to it. There was an unpleasant edge to it all, so I toasted the end of New Order with the obligatory four cans of warm lager and a sleeping pill and went to bed alone.

I'd thought things were at a low then, but they were about to get worse. I met Mrs Merton.

TIMELINE FOURTEEN
JANUARY–DECEMBER 1993

© Kiev. Victor/Shutterstock

22 January 1993

Revenge play London Marquee.

29 January 1993

Revenge play North Staffs Polytechnic, supported by Northside.

> 'A truly miserable concert, everyone feeling very down about it being the last Revenge gig before I went back to New Order. Revenge would never play again.'

12 April 1993

New Order: 'Regret'
(London Records)

Seven-inch track list:

'Regret' 7" version	4.07
'Regret' (New Order mix)	5.10

Twelve-inch track list:

'Regret' (Fire Island mix)	7.15
'Regret' (Junior Dub mix)	7.44
'Regret' (Sabres Slow'n'Low mix)	12.49
'Regret' (Sabres Fast'n'Throb mix)	12.11

Run-out groove one: *Here in the real world …*
Run-out groove two: *… there's no one but me!*

Pre-production by Pascal Gabriel.
Produced by Stephen Hague and New Order.
Engineered by Mike 'Spike' Drake.
Art direction by Peter Saville.
Designed by Pentagram.
Entered UK chart on 17 April 1993, remaining in the charts for 7 weeks, its peak position was number 4.

April 1993

New Order: *Republic*
(London Records)

Track list:

'Regret'	4.07
'World (The Price of Love)'	4.44
'Ruined in a Day'	4.23
'Spooky'	4.44
'Everyone Everywhere'	4.25
'Young Offender'	4.48

'Liar'	4.22
'Chemical'	4.11
'Times Change'	3.53
'Special'	4.51
'Avalanche'	3.14

Run-out groove one: *In space no one …*
Run-out groove two: *… can hear you scream!*

Recorded and mixed in Real World Studios, Box, Bath, and RAK, London.
Written by New Order and Stephen Hague.
Produced by New Order and Stephen Hague.
Pre-production on 'Regret' and 'Young Offender' by Pascal Gabriel.
Engineers: Simon Gogerly, Mike 'Spike' Drake, Owen Morris and Richard Chappell.
Assistant engineers: Ben Findlay and Sam Hardaker.
Additional musicians: Audrey Riley, David Rhodes, Andy Duncan and Dee Lewis.
Art direction by Peter Saville.
Designed by Pentagram.
Entered UK chart on 15 May 1993, remaining in the charts for 13 weeks, its peak position was number 1.

'The cover of *Republic* was reputedly a comment about the decadence in today's society. The cover shows two people playing on the beach in the present day, while a house burns down next to them. The next picture signifies the transformation of the earth, beginning with wave and water, water being the earth's predominant feature four billion years ago. Then we have simple lifeforms in plants and trees, which will inhabit the new terrestrial earth. With the formation of cities, pollution becomes a problem, and man has to inhabit biospheres because the earth will eventually become uninhabitable.

'The images are also supposedly representative of the fall of the republic of Rome, and the belief that our civilisation is heading in the same direction. As Rome edged nearer and nearer its fall, the patricians arranged for circuses to entertain the plebians while the cities declined. Me, I just thought it was a load of old bollocks.'

5 June 1993

New Order play Dublin Point Depot, Dublin, Ireland.

28 June 1993

New Order: 'Ruined in a Day'
(London Records)

CD track list:

'Ruined in a Day' (radio edit)	3.58
'Ruined in a Day' (Booga Bear ambient mix)	5.44
'Reunited in a Day' (K-Klass remix)	6.14
'Vicious Circle' (Mike Haas mix)	3.23

Twelve-inch track list:

'Ruined in a Day' (12" Bogle mix)	4.30
'Ruined in a Day' (Live mix)	4.30
Both mixed by Sly & Robbie and Handel Tucker.	
'World (The Price of Dub)'	6.48
Remixed by Brothers in Rhythm.	
'Reunited in a Day' (K-Klass remix)	6.14

Run-out groove one: *Why did the monk cross the road?*
Run-out groove two: ... *because the New Skete said so!*

Recorded and mixed in Real World Studios, Box, Bath
Produced by Stephen Hague and New Order.
Art direction by Peter Saville.
Designed by Howard Wakefield and James Adams at Icon.
Entered UK chart on 3 July 1993, remaining in the charts for 4 weeks, its peak position was number 22.

2 July 1993

New Order play Montreux Jazz Festival, Montreux, Switzerland.

3 July 1993

New Order play Roskilde Festival, Roskilde, Denmark.

> 'When Barney and I had done the promotion for *Republic* in Denmark earlier in the year, we had ended up vying for the attention of a beautiful A&R girl and fought over her, right to the end of the night. We ended up in a club having a very heated discussion over who was going to cop for her, when I got a tap on the shoulder. Turning round, this kid says to me, "Hi, I'm Def Leppard's bass player."
>
> 'I said, "Fuck off, can't you see we're busy," to my eternal shame, and turned away to carry on arguing with Barney.
>
> 'When we got back to the hotel I had her and we stopped the lift at Barney's floor so he could get out. When I looked at her face she was smiling and I wondered at what? Looking in the mirror I could see Barney in the corridor all sad-faced, imploring her to join him, making a little heart with his two hands and pouting.
>
> 'Luckily for him the doors shut.
>
> 'So anyway, fast-forward to this festival and I met up with her, and went off to her tent in the forest and got completely lost. When I finally arrived backstage them lot had left me. I was stranded in the middle of nowhere for four hours and it cost me a fortune in a taxi. As I got to the hotel, Rex Sargeant was just being arrested for passing fake currency. Porno for Pyros were on the line-up and had been throwing around fake hundred-dollar bills, really bad fakes, and Rex had used one to pay his bar bill so the hotel had called the police. Which was very lucky for me because they'd been planning to leave me there, the bastards. Jane wouldn't even look at me.'

10 July 1993

New Order play Loreley Bizarre Festival, St Goarshausen, Germany.

21 July 1993

New Order play Starplex Amphitheatre, Dallas, Texas.

'Jonny Hugo was obsessed with John Shuttleworth and introduced us all to "What Have I Done with My Life", "Catch the Fox" etc. Those songs became the soundtrack to the tour. It was also the first time we had taken a wardrobe dresser with us, a lad called Greg who had styled us on a couple of occasions in England, and was now responsible for looking after our stage clothes.

'In catering I had met someone who could get us some drugs, but it was nearly show time so the only one free to go was this guy who worked with us, called Jim. When we came off there was no sign of him and after an hour or so, just as we were starting to get worried, we found him wandering round backstage, completely off his face.

'He said, "I got three ounces but the kid's a right nutter and wouldn't let me go ... kept feeding me drugs ... took me ages to lose him."

'Then a cry rang out, "There you are, muthafukker!"

'"Oh shit. It's him," said Jim, and legged it. Then we couldn't get rid of the dealer. We went from club to club in Dallas, trying to dump him at every opportunity, until at the third club he pulled out a silver revolver and shoved it under my chin, snot streaming from both nostrils, saying, "Do that again, man, and you're dead meat."

'Luckily a bouncer saw him and wrestled the gun off him, pinning him down and shouting for the police. I ran straight in the club and on to the dancefloor. Heaven. This place was just like bloody Manchester.'

24 July 1993

New Order play Shoreline Amphitheatre, Mountain View, California. At Tom's insistence, 'World' is filmed here and recorded as an alternative live video for MTV.

26 July 1993

New Order play Hollywood Bowl, Hollywood, California.

29 July 1993

New Order play World Music Theatre, Tinley Park, Illinois.

31 July 1993

New Order play Kingswood Amphitheatre, Toronto.

2 August 1993

New Order play Merriweather Post Pavilion, Columbia, Maryland.

> 'Barney had been joined by Sarah and their baby son, Dylan, for a few gigs. Unfortunately it didn't seem to have much effect on his moods. I have one abiding memory of him running offstage after a gig, straight into a limo and driving off to the hotel. As I waved him off, Sarah shot past me pushing the buggy and shouting. He'd forgotten them. After a few yards the limo stopped and the family were, thankfully, reunited.'

4 August 1993

New Order play Brendan Byrne Arena, East Rutherford, New Jersey.

> 'Tom played a great trick on me here. We were all so pissed off by now that none of us would do any promotion or meetings after the show whatsoever (grip and grins, we called them). He came to me and said, "Hooky, I need a big favour. We have a competition winner here. This girl has won this really difficult competition, beating thousands of people, can you come and say hello to her? For me, please?"
>
> '"What was the competition, Tom?" I asked.
>
> '"I don't know, man, but this girl aced it, she was magnificent. She's your biggest fan."
>
> 'Intrigued, I said, "OK."
>
> 'I really wasn't in the mood but I loved this man. For ages he led me through the bowels of the huge arena until we at last appeared in a room full of gawping people, and as I wiped my nose the young

lady was brought over. She was very nonchalant, nonplussed even, so as I stood there feeling like a spare prick at a wedding, the only thing I could think to say was, "What was the competition you won, love, what was the question?"

'"Oh there was no competition," she shrugged, "I was just the thirteenth caller."

'I turned round. "Tom fucking Atencio!" I bellowed.

'Tom set off running down the corridors with me after him, screaming, "FUCK YOU, FUCKER!"'

5 August 1993

New Order play Great Woods Amphitheater, Mansfield, Massachusetts.

29 August 1993

New Order play Reading Festival, Reading.
Barney changed the lyrics of 'True Faith' here to:

> When I was a very young boy,
> Michael Jackson played with me,
> Now that we've grown up together,
> He's playing with my wi–illy.

Jackson was being investigated for allegations of sexual abuse against minors.

'Our last gig. I felt abused myself.'

30 August 1993

New Order: 'World (The Price of Love)'
(London Records)

Seven-inch track list:

'World' (radio edit)	3.39
'World' (Perfecto edit)	3.39

Twelve-inch track list:

'World (Perfecto mix)'	7.33
'World' (Sexy disco mix)	5.56
Both remixed by Paul Oakenfold and Steve Osborne.	
'World' (Brothers in Rhythm mix)	8.03
'World' (the World in Action mix)	5.51

Run-out groove one: *Chicks = Trouble!*
Run-out groove two: *Trouble = Chicks!*

Recorded and mixed in Real World Studios, Box, Bath.
Produced by Stephen Hague and New Order.
Vocal engineer: Owen Morris.
Art Direction by Peter Saville.
Designed by Howard Wakefield and James Adams at Icon.
Entered UK chart on 4 September 1993, remaining in the charts for 5 weeks, its peak position was number 13.

November 1993

New Order: *Story*
(London Records video)

Track list:
'Transmission'
'Love Will Tear Us Apart'
'Ceremony'
'Temptation'
'Blue Monday'
'Confusion'
'The Perfect Kiss'
'Shellshock'
'Bizarre Love Triangle'
'True Faith'
'Touched by the Hand of God'
'Blue Monday – 88'
'Fine Time'
'Round and Round'

'World in Motion'
'Regret'
'Everyone Everywhere'
'Temptation'
'Ruined in a Day'
'World (The Price of Love)'
'Atmosphere'

13 December 1993

New Order: 'Spooky'
(London Records)

CD track list:

'Spooky' (Minimix)	3.51
'Spooky' (Magimix)	6.56
'Spooky' (Moulimix)	5.49
'Spooky' (album version)	4.44

All remixed by Fluke.

Twelve-inch track list:

'Spooky' (Magimix)	6.56
'Spooky' (Moulimix)	5.49
Mixed by Fluke.	
'Spooky' (album version)	4.44

Run-out groove one: *A sad end, a whimper …*
Run-out groove two: *… not a bang! Onward my friends …*

Recorded and mixed in Real World Studios, Box, Bath.
Produced by Stephen Hague and New Order.
Engineered by Mike 'Spike' Drake.
Art Direction by Peter Saville, FGB West, LA.
Digital imaging by Paul Brown and Brett Wickens, FGB West, LA.
Format design by Howard Wakefield at Thomas Manss & Company.
Entered UK chart on 18 December 1993, remaining in the charts for 4 weeks, its peak position was number 22.

'London Records would not be happy about the split. They felt a little betrayed after all Rob's promises. After the way they acted over Factory, I can only say one word: karma.'

TOP TEN BASS CAB MESSAGES (ACTUALLY SIXTEEN)

1. 'Salford rules'
2. 'Bass how low can u go'
3. 'Free Jeff the Chef!'
4. 'Hello Mum'
5. 'Job wanted, apply within'
6. 'Happy Birthday Jessica'
7. 'Addicted to bass'
8. 'Bye bye The Ox'
9. 'Euphoric recall'
10. 'Wiving wegends' (when we appeared on Jonathan Ross)
11. 'Watch yer handbags'
12. 'God has a DJ' (when John Peel died)
13. 'RIP Valhalla Phil Grubb'
14. 'I'm with stupid'
15. 'CBGB GBFN' (when CBGBs closed down, and we were in New York)
16. 'The end'

'We needed binoculars to see Noel Edmonds'

In February 1994 we were invited to the Brit Awards by London – my first Brits.

The others had been before, of course, in 1988, when New Order received the Best Video Award for 'True Face' (the name on the award) voted for by Radio 1 listeners. The group had been estranged at the time, with me being a very angry young man indeed. I was off negotiating a deal for Revenge so turned down the opportunity, instead watching it on TV. I must say that Barney's crack about Andrew Lloyd Webber's boring speech was spot-on and did make me laugh, even if it resulted in big 'boos' from the audience for New Order.

Somehow I've ended up with the award, complete with one spike missing off Britannia's trident and spelling mistake in the title.

So anyway, back to 1994. The awards were on Valentine's Day but I was single, so it wasn't a problem, and along I went. 'Regret' had been nominated in the Best Single category and Colin Bell and Tracy Bennett were convinced we were going to win. 'We've got inside information,' they said. They had even managed to persuade Barney to come. The evening started well; we were staying at the Halcyon hotel in Holland Park and everyone was very buoyant. A huge limousine arrived and then it started snowing, outside the limo and inside too. There was a massive traffic jam at Alexandra Palace because of the snow, and because of the snow inside we were all gagging for a drink when we did get in.

It was a very grand affair but when we got our table, alarm bells started to ring. We were miles away from the stage, literally *miles* away. If we had won, it would have taken me and Barney at least ten minutes to walk to the stage. Colin and Tracey were panicking – 'It must be a mistake' – and set off running round like headless chickens trying to sort it out. There were normally five nominations but an exception had been made this year, we'd been told, there being six, of which 'Regret' was one. As the evening progressed we ended up messier and messier, and of course no one ate, our table being the only one full of piled-up food.

When it got to our category we were very excited, even though we needed binoculars to see Noel Edmonds, the host, who went through the nominations and … we weren't even nominated.

This caused consternation at the table. Me and Barney were shouting at the London boys, who once more went and did the chicken run. It was so embarrassing. I still don't know what happened. Whether it was a scam by the Brits to sell another table (they cost about £10,000 each even then) or by London Records to show a presence, who knows. We stormed out. Of course, no one noticed. We were then joined by Tom Watkins and two rent boys. Then Barney and a young lady I'd never seen before. The limo was packed. The next stop was Heaven Club, so I bowed out. It was too weird even for me.

Meanwhile …

'Marry in haste, repent at leisure'

I first met Caroline Aherne in the Haçienda. She'd been doing a character called Sister Mary Immaculate on Tony Wilson's TV show that evening, and he had a nice habit (no pun intended) of inviting his guests to the club afterwards. He'd brought her over, introduced us and, with a sly wink, left.

Caroline was obviously drunk and demanded I sing 'Regret' *a capella* for her, over and over again until I complied. But she was unusual and, of course, very, very funny. She certainly made a big impression. I was single at this point but had been rubbing along rather well with a different girl almost every night.

I was very intrigued by her, a career woman no less. Maybe it was because I'd never met anyone like her before. Say what you like – and I'm about to do exactly that – but she's a one-off. I should say, of course, that she *was* a one-off. Caroline sadly died of lung cancer just as I was putting the finishing touches to this book.

She and I got absolutely trashed that first night, setting the tone for the rest of what turned out to be the worst and most tempestuous relationship of a whole lifetime's worth of tempestuous relationships. We ended up back at mine and later, as she was leaving and I asked for her number, she said, 'No. I'm not giving you my number. You've got to find it. If you want me, you'll have to find out my number.'

Even more intriguing.

She got the shock of her life when I phoned her a few days later and we went on our first date to CocAtoos Italian restaurant, opposite the Ritz in town.

It was a great date. She was really easy to get on with, and hilarious company. She was in stitches when I got myself locked in the toilet and had to crawl/limbo out through the gap at the bottom of the door. There was no doubt in either of our minds that this first date would be followed by many more. Sure enough, it wasn't long before we were an item.

I quickly worked out that she was strange. I mean, I knew she was nuts on the first night – and it turned out her whole family was mad as well – but back then being nuts was part of her charm. It often is when you first meet someone; it usually means they're crazy in every other way, too, which she was. When the relationship gets more intense – as ours did, *really* quickly – the nuts stuff becomes a problem. Add the fact that Mrs Merton liked a drink more than most, and you've got a very combustible situation. In comedy they have a big green-room drinking culture; it's a very boozy, incestuous world. They drink together, sleep together, bitch about one another behind their backs, while going out of their way to tell each other how great they are to their faces. They're insecure, paranoid and hypersensitive to criticism.

I met the lot of them. I fitted in perfectly – you name them, the so-called cream of British comedy at the time. I thought they were a right bunch of jerks. And of them all, the worst, most boozy, insecure, paranoid of the lot were the women. I was shocked.

There was a lot of sleeping around in that world. While we were intimate she would delight in telling me who she'd slept with and even where they'd done it, complete with all the gory details, like how she'd make them phone their wives after sex. She loved taking me backstage to mingle with these comedians, with me knowing who she'd slept with. She seemed to have a thing for girls, too. They featured in many of her stories and she loved me taking her to strip clubs abroad, where no one knew her and she could sit transfixed by the girls, getting very close to the action indeed. Put it this way, it came as no surprise when, in 1997, she was pictured kissing Katrina, out of Katrina and the Waves, at some awards ceremony or other. She also went through a phase of wanting me to get a hooker for the two of us, but I told her, 'No way, love, because if I even *looked* at that hooker, never mind touched her, you'd go fucking mad.'

The problem was, she was very, very jealous and possessive, and although she used to work with her ex-boyfriend, who in my opinion is a weapons-grade tool, she was controlling when it came to my female friends. A typical conversation with Mrs Merton on return from a hard day's work, would start with her asking me, 'What did you do today?' all sweetness and light.

'Oh, I was in the studio all day.'

'All day?'

'Yeah, all day.'

'Well, how did you get there?'

'I went on my bike.'

'Did you stop anywhere? Did you see anyone? Did you talk to anyone on the way there?'

'Well no, no, Cara [my pet name for her]. I literally just cycled there.'

She'd go, 'Right, OK. What did you do at lunchtime? Did you go out?'

'Did I go out? I can't remember, love, to be honest.'

'You can't remember? You can't remember if you went out at lunchtime? That's a bit strange, isn't it?'

'Yeah. OK, yeah, I think I might have gone out for a sandwich.'

'Did you see anyone? Did you talk to anyone?'

'No, I don't think so, no.'

'Oh, OK, and then what did you do?'

'Well, then we stayed in the studio until quarter to six and then I left and came home, and here I am …'

'Did you see anyone on the way home? Did you talk to anyone?'

It was like that all the time, like being interrogated by the Gestapo. She'd give me a major grilling every night. And woe betide me if my version of events involved interaction with another woman. That would be it. She'd behave as though I were having a full-blown affair, and the screaming, crying and recriminations would start.

I'd take phone calls and she'd listen in on the extension and then ask me who'd rung. This happened when an ex rang to ask me out, and even though I'd declined I didn't dare tell Mrs Merton, so I made up a story that it was a bloke from Tom's office.

'Well, that's funny,' she said, 'because when I picked up the extension I heard a girl's voice.'

That was it. Mega arguments. Our engagement was off, again. Oh dear, but then it was on again, and like lambs to the slaughter we went and got married in Vegas at the Little White Chapel, with Tom Atencio as my best man.

More than once over those few days he shook me and said, 'Don't marry her, Hooky, she's crazy, too crazy.' (Which if you knew Tom was funny after some of his consorts.)

But love is deaf, dumb, blind and stupid, so I had great company. We'd flown out to LA for a few days to acclimatise, and I went and met with Jim Swindel at Warner Brothers, just to say hello. But she hated it as soon as she saw the girls who worked for the record company.

I had got to know many of them very well over the years, innocently, but she was kicking off all the time.

I remember telling my mother I'd proposed after three months and the only thing she said was, 'Well, our Peter, marry in haste, repent at leisure.' How right she was. We connected to Las Vegas and Caroline left her wedding dress on the shuttle bus at the airport, and it took me ages to get it back. I thought, *Is this a sign?* but it was too late by then and, heart in mouth, we went through with it, being married by a fake Elvis in the Chapel of Love, and we were very happy that night. I remember excitedly phoning our parents to give them the news. They were delighted. Caroline willingly changed her name to Hook even after me telling her it didn't matter, and that she could keep her name for her career.

Now Caroline often spoken about her demons and how she was a very different person when she was drunk, so a lot of what I'm about to say won't come as a surprise. But the fact was she could be *very* demonic, and after the wedding things began to get very weird indeed. We'd go out and get pissed, go to bed, and then she'd wake me up in the middle of the night, perched on the end of the bed, smoking.

I'd go, 'What's up?' and she'd squint through the smoke at me with her evil eyes, and growl, 'Nobody likes you, you know. You're all washed up, your career's over. You've got no friends, not one,' over and over again. I'd swing from anger to fear. It felt like I was being brainwashed.

As it happened, she was right, I didn't have any friends, but the reason was because she'd done such a great job of cutting me off from them. We only mixed with comics or people from her show. Her friends. I'd go, 'Fucking hell, steady on, what's happening here? What's the matter with you?'

I'd go back to sleep and she'd wake me up and do it all over again. 'You're a failure, you are. You're all washed ...'

I had left New Order behind me, and though I was beginning to get Monaco together with Pottsy, I was still a long way off seeing the fruits of that particular labour, so I think her telling me I was a failure started triggering several inherent insecurities of my own.

As a matter of fact, what I saw as her jealousy and paranoia was catching. As far as I was concerned, her ex was still in love with her – no doubt about that in my mind – and he used to ring her up at all times of the evening just to make some lame remark about something he'd be watching on telly. I'd come home from work to find him there, apparently 'writing', spread out on my sofa, shoes off, like he owned the fucking place. It was driving me mad. God help me if Caroline had come home and found me with a woman in the house, ex or not.

I started going everywhere with her very soon. Being on call for her all the time. One time after filming *The Fast Show*, she went to bed while I stayed up partying with some of the cast and crew. We heard a knocking at the door and there was Caroline, pissed and raging at me. Back in our room things got even worse. A lot worse. She attacked me, using her nails to scratch at my neck, tearing off my necklace and ripping my top. It was proper shocking stuff. And although she was really contrite the next morning it marked the beginning of some serious screaming-banshee behaviour – putting cigarettes out on my arm, attacking me with bottles, knives, chairs and other assorted furniture. It would be set off by the slightest thing – talking or looking at another woman was a favourite. She'd come at me like a screaming banshee, and if she was pissed it would be ten times worse.

Like I say, she stopped me seeing my mates, and soon after that she began disapproving of me taking drugs too. Fair enough, I suppose. What wife wants her husband hoofing coke all the time? But the weird thing was she started off by encouraging it, like it amused her that I was taking it. 'Take more, Take more,' she'd say. Then, like so much else about her, the mood suddenly changed and, without warning, she was really, really anti-drugs.

She slapped me round the face in the middle of the British Comedy Awards aftershow party in front of about thirty assorted comedians, accusing me of doing coke with one of them in the toilets (I was, thanks, Vic). We were staying in the Grosvenor Hotel, my first time there, and I ended up on the bathroom floor all night.

Next morning she was again contrite, and very apologetic, but blamed it on me. 'It's because I love you so much,' she said.

Got a funny way of showing it, I thought.

The one thing you'd have to say about her was that she didn't have a private face and a public one. The unpredictable and volatile Caroline I knew was pretty much the same whether she had mates round or was at the British Comedy Awards or it was just the two of us behind closed doors. Years later, when we split up and the comedy community closed ranks tight around her (my first experience of 'Golden Goose

Syndrome', where the least-talented cluster round who they think is the most talented, hanging on for grim life), I used to think to myself, *All you lot know exactly what she's like, you two-faced bastards.*

If anyone came round to ours it would kick off. It wasn't like you could anticipate the exact problem – you just knew there'd be one. It got so it was easier not to have anyone over, my family included, which suited her down to the ground. She used to say her ideal man was an author who stayed at home all day writing alone in his study. It was as though it were her ambition was to cut me off from the rest of society.

We'd bought a beautiful house in Didsbury on Parrs Wood Road, very secluded, and it should have been a dream house, but she made it hell for me, giving me the third-degree every time I got home from work. I'd tell lies to cover up innocuous truths, like the fact that my doctor was female, but she'd find out and I'd be up shit street. It got so that I'd drive home and sit outside in the car for ages, working up the courage to go inside and get a grilling, the fury of which would be determined by how much she'd already had to drink.

Never marry an actress. You never know what role they'll be playing when you get home.

One time we went out to a gig in town. There were loads of people at this gig, loads of Manchester heads. Mark E. Smith was there, the Inspirals, the Roses – it was a big gig and I said to her, 'Right, you stay there, I'll go and get you a drink.' I went to the bar, came back, and she had a right face on. I was like, 'What's the matter with you?'

'Nothing,' she said.

Later I went to get more drinks, came back, she had even more of a face on. 'What's the fucking matter?' I was saying, 'What have I done?'

'Nothing.'

Go to the toilet, come back, fuck me, it was like World War Three. She stormed off, went home. So of course I had to go home too, where I was going, 'What's the matter with you? Will you tell me what's the fucking matter?' until at last she exploded and said to me, 'Every time you went to the bar, Mark E. Smith came over and said, "He's shagging loads of birds behind your back, you know?"'

I thought, *Oh God, you fucking wind-up merchant, Mark. I'll fucking kill you the next time I see you.* That's why she freaked, because, accidentally, he'd found her Achilles heel.

Another time, after a night out with Keith Allen, I returned to the hotel only to discover that she'd been through my briefcase and taken scissors to the contents of my Filofax (hey, it was the 90s), ripping up pictures of my kids, cutting up my clothes, destroying everything she could.

I loved her, though, that was the thing.

She was so funny. God, she was funny. Used to do an amazing impression of me as well, wearing my clothes while she did it, and when she had money she was dead generous, too. She didn't have any at first and I was glad to help her and her family out, even paying for central heating for her mum's house one particularly bad winter. Once, when she'd made it, she caught me looking at a Harley-Davidson and then had it delivered for my birthday. As long as she was sober, she could be really sweet and she was always apologetic after her violent outbursts, ashamed even.

David Walliams had a relationship with her after me, and so much of what he described in his autobiography rang true: the drinking, the weird tormenting abuse, the insecurity.

She used to need complete silence to learn her lines for *Mrs Merton* (she was nearly blind in one eye due to retinoblastoma as a child, and it had heightened her sense of hearing), so I'd carefully retreat to the back bedroom, right at the other end of the house, to do my ironing, and put on the headphones listening to Kiss 102 while I did it.

As a single father I had learned to iron out of strict necessity and my tip to doing it successfully is to buy the most expensive iron you can afford. John Lewis have the best selection. At times I have paid over £350 for one. It really does make life a lot easier. Putting a drop of Olbas Oil in the water will clear your sinuses a treat for the evening too. I mainly did mine in the studio, with the clothes hung all round the control room. Pottsy would say, 'It's like Johnsons the bloody cleaners in here.'

Caroline, who *hated* dance music with a passion, even more so when she realised I had a taste for it, would come storming in, ripping off my headphones, telling me I was disturbing her by tapping my foot.

Now, I doubt I was even tapping my foot. And I'm damn sure she couldn't have heard it if I was. She knew I was in the room listening to dance music, and she was that domineering and controlling she couldn't stand that fact.

I don't think she liked animals, so I guess I should have been suspicious when she offered to look after my cat, Biba, while I was away, to save me putting her in the cattery. When I got home, no cat.

'Where's Biba?' I asked.

'Oh,' she said, like butter wouldn't melt, 'I didn't think you were looking after it properly so I gave it away.'

I'd had that cat for fourteen bloody years – Ian Curtis used to stroke her – but I was so browbeaten by then that I just let the issue drop, my shoulders drooping even further towards the floor. (Years later a bloke came up to me: 'My mum's got your cat, she loves her!' Biba was twenty-one by then so at least I know she went to a good home.)

The Mrs Merton Show would be a huge hit for her and she'd been hearing the music me and Pottsy were writing as Monaco at home, and saying it was great, and that we should have a spot on the show.

She told the producer at Granada, who wouldn't say boo to her goose, 'I'd like Hooky to do a spot. He can play one of his songs every week.' So the guy goes, 'Yeah, that's a good idea,' but was obviously thinking, *Not on your fucking nelly*, because although me and Pottsy were signed up under the impression that we were going to get to play one of our tunes every show (fantastic for us as Monaco, great exposure) we got kicked off for another *popular* band every week. We'd been stitched up completely. All we did was the stings like a bunch of wankers.

> A 'sting' is a short piece of music five to twenty seconds long that has some kind of personal resonance with the guest that, hopefully, the audience will recognise: e.g. for Sylvester Stallone you would play the *Rocky* theme; for George Best you'd play 'Best and Marsh' by New Order. Usually, the cornier the better.

I kept thinking, *How has my world come to this? I've headlined Glastonbury, and here I am doing stings on fucking TV for shitty B-list celebrities* (who, I might add, for the most part were absolutely lovely, particularly Carol Vorderman. I got some shit that night, I tell you).

The money was amazing and we were paid £30,000 a season

between us, with me getting £1,000 extra for being the bandleader. It was money for old rope, it really was.

I will say one thing, though, television is a tough, rotten medium. It makes rock'n'roll look like kindergarten. One foot wrong here, mate, and you're toast, you were out and your career was over too. I witnessed various merciless ostracising of many individuals for the smallest perceived slights. It was absolutely terrifying. Talk about ruled by fear, this lot made ISIS look fair. Luckily for me, my reputation had preceded me and they were terrified of little old Hooky.

Another great thing about being a well-known musician was that I didn't need them and they knew it, they couldn't fuck me about. I could just tell them all to fuck off like a musical Vinnie Jones. There was a strict pecking order and luckily my reputation and Caroline's love put me nearly at the top of it.

So the shows were OK for me, and there were many weird moments with the guests that were quite entertaining. She was a right diva on set and had everyone running around after her, but they all loved it. One night we were out for drinks and someone said, 'What do you think of Caroline when she's dressed as Mrs Merton, Hooky?'

'I think I actually prefer her as Mrs Merton. She's nicer, such a sweet old lady,' I said, only joking (though it was true).

Oh my God, did I get it for that. I nearly got a bottle over the head for saying I preferred her as a nice old lady.

We struggled on for nearly three years. At one point Caroline convinced me I needed therapy and I ended up going to see a very well-known and well-regarded therapist in Manchester. This guy was great. Once I'd poured my heart out he agreed with everything I said. I was flabbergasted. He then told me to bring her in so he could talk to her. The next session was for the two of us and he gave her a right dressing down, telling her she had to change, how it was her behaviour that needed moderating. 'You need to learn some respect, young lady,' he said.

I shit it. Even though I was glad of the back-up I knew the ramifications would be swift and merciless – and so it proved. They started in the car on the way home and continued for days. I was an abused husband and it's embarrassing, and you feel ashamed, and you can't tell anyone. I needed help.

Now I know, reader, that you're thinking, *Hang on, he was the nutter, the tough guy whose reputation preceded him, how had it come to this?*

I did wonder myself. It happened slowly and I was eager, maybe too eager, to please the woman I loved. I'm watching a very close friend go through exactly the same scenario now and it sends shivers down my spine.

Absolutely heartbreaking.

In my opinion her father was like this with her mother. When he got terminal cancer we visited him in the hospice and Caroline became embroiled in an argument with other family members. They took things into the corridor, leaving me alone with the dad, who was very ill by now. I'm sat there looking at this stranger and he's looking at me, and then he does this weird throaty sound that I can only describe as a death rattle, and he dies right in front of my eyes. God forgive me, my first thought was, *Oh no, she's going to fucking kill me for this!* I had to go outside and break up the fight to tell them the poor bastard was dead.

It never got better, and I can remember there being two instances where I felt weird as I was driving around. I thought, *What is this feeling? It's strange?* It was happiness.

I was distressed to realise that I had felt happy only twice in three years, as fleeting as that. For the rest of the time I was walking on egg-shells, absolutely terrified. Then, to cap it all, Iris did an exposé on me for the *Daily Mail*: 'Peter Hook Serial Love Cheat', the headline read. I could just imagine the rest of New Order choking on their fucking cornflakes with that one.

Iris rang me, crying, to tip me off. 'They tricked me, Pete, the reporter was so nice. I didn't even get paid.'

Caroline stayed strangely silent.

Our last night together was at a comedy gig we did with Smug Roberts, me and Pottsy as his punk backing-band. We were sat having a drink afterwards with the landlord and landlady, and I noticed the landlady's trousers had split at the seam halfway down her thigh, and I put my finger in, laughing. Her husband laughed, too, but Caroline's face clouded over, and when we got home we had the worst argument ever. She picked up a chair, threw it at me but I ducked, so she picked up a glass and lunged at me, and then she threw a wine bottle, and then produced a kitchen knife, and that was the moment I thought, *Oh my God, this has gone too far. I'm going to have to defend myself or she's going to stab me.* I knew we'd reached a new low – something from which we weren't going to be able to recover, but she came to her senses, thank God, threw down the knife and ran off in distress.

This was it. I slept in another bedroom and she got up the next morning and left.

Later she phoned from her mum's and said, 'I'm not coming back, Hooky, I'm leaving. I'm going to kill you if I don't.'

Nowadays I look back, and I think things were coming to a head because the whole time I'd been with her I'd been working on Monaco, and it was starting to really click; the stuff we'd recorded was great, and she knew I was going to be out promoting it, gigging, and she just couldn't handle it – not just the jealousy that I'd be outside her control, but the jealousy that I was getting my career back on track.

We split up. But, like everything else with Caroline, it was the worst and messiest split ever. For a start we kept going back to each other. She'd ask me to come and meet her and I'd go into town and we'd slope off somewhere (for sex). It would be nice, but then afterwards she'd start up with the questions and accusations.

One day we were sitting in the car in Wythenshawe Park, near her mum's, and she asked me if I'd done drugs lately and I was like, 'Yeah, I maybe had half an E the other day.' And of course she went absolutely mental. It was madness.

Granada, who produced *The Mrs Merton Show*, issued a statement then edited me out of a programme done about her life. It was suddenly so public. I felt like everyone knew, as if they were all looking at me and laughing. I took to hiding under a hoodie, hood up, head down. Mentally it got worse. Pottsy and Ken did all they could to help, looking after the kids while I lay in bed unable to move, and Andy Fisher came back as a real shoulder to cry on. Thanks, lads.

But eventually I ended up at the doctor's. I was diagnosed with clinical depression. And believe me there is nothing more depressing than being diagnosed with depression. It felt as if I'd fallen in a glass-sided dark hole and could not get out. I just kept sliding back down to the bottom, no matter how much I tried to escape.

Prozac followed for weeks (one more thing me and Barney would have in common). When that didn't work I was prescribed Seroxat.

I'd taken my first Seroxat in the morning at the practice place. We were writing and by the afternoon I was hallucinating. Pottsy had turned into a girl in a shimmering silver dress in front of my eyes (every cloud) but it scared me to death, even more so than the depression.

I threw the tablets away and thought, *Right, that's it. I'm done with that shit now.* Funny how a confirmed addict like me could be so scared of prescription drugs. I thought I was on the road to recovery but then the bloody 'panic attacks' started. These were really frightening and I went back to the doctor for reassurance I wasn't dying.

His answer was to give me a book, 'Panic Attacks for Dummies' sort of thing, which I thought would be no use whatsoever. But, amazingly, once I knew what they were, I could control them. I still get them occasionally now.

After a while I went to see Twinny, then Bowser, and eventually got my life back. Back to drink and illegal drugs for me from now on. One step forward, two steps back, I hear you cry.

Later Caroline moved out of her mother's and bought a house not far away. In fact, a hundred yards away, just further up Parrs Wood Road. I had to drive past her new house every time I went anywhere.

Then she'd be ringing up all the time, asking me to come round. I'd say no but go anyway, and she'd be there, with 'Everybody Hurts' by R.E.M. on repeat and pissed on Bacardi Breezers, blubbing, 'Look at all my Comedy Awards. They mean nothing without you.'

I'd be going, 'Oh fuck off, Caroline, pack it in,' but we'd have a snog or whatever, and she'd go, 'Oh, what's that bruise on your arm? Are those scratches, Peter? Have you been with another woman?'

'We've split up, for fuck's sake. We can do what we want.'

Then she'd say, 'I've been with someone, I've been with a very famous actor – do you want me to tell you who?'

'Listen, I'm going, I've had enough of this. I shouldn't have come round in the first place, because you're a fucking lunatic,' and she'd be shouting the name at me as I was running down the road with my hands over my ears yelling, 'La, la, la!' God, she was a nightmare when she was drunk.

Believe it or not, I did get some work done while I was married to Caroline.

A tour with Durutti Column for a start. Knowing I was at a loose end, and being a bit of a fan too, Vini Reilly got in touch and asked me to come to Portugal with him. Caroline persuaded me, saying, 'I'll come with you.'

I phoned Vini and said, 'I'm delighted, when do you want to rehearse?'

'Do we have to?' he said.

We did one rehearsal and Vini got bored and refused to do any more. It was quite a productive rehearsal as we even jammed a new track that would be known as 'Hooky's Tune', which he would record later. We flew out to Portugal and I fully expected to play some little club gigs for two or three hundred people, only to discover that Durutti were huge there, and we were playing to venues of five thousand or more. You could have knocked me down with a feather. Thanks to his lack of rehearsals it was very loose, shall we say, for the first few performances.

We took wives and girlfriends: in my case, Caroline, in Vini's case this girl he was seeing at the time. Caroline got pissed every night and was really obnoxious, being horrible to this girl for no reason, then starting to accuse me of fancying her.

I remember being in a bar and Vini saying to me, 'Your girlfriend,' and I said, 'Wife,' and he said, 'Your wife. She's very difficult, isn't she?' And I said, 'Yeah,' and he said, 'But she's very funny,' and I went, 'You should try fucking living with her, mate.' He said, 'I'll get you a gin,' and went and got me a double.

Plus, of course, I was working on Monaco. I was getting depressed all the time – that's what the relationship was doing to me – and if it hadn't been for Pottsy and Monaco then God knows what would have happened to me.

She was doing so well, I'd see her everywhere: on TV, in coffee adverts, on billboards, on the sides of bus shelters, and in the *Manchester Evening News* almost every night, out on the town with her new friends and boyfriends. It was hell. She even managed to record a bloody radio trailer for Kiss 102, so I couldn't even listen to that.

For a while I felt like I'd never be rid of her, like she was casting a large and unpleasant shadow over my life, and to try to escape the feeling I started drinking even more heavily. Every day I drank until I passed out, waking up with such bad hangovers that the only way of getting any relief from the pain was to start drinking again.

Caroline and I had split early in 1996, which resulted in me going to live at my mother's for a few weeks, which is definitely what you should always do if you get into big trouble, go home to your mum. She nursed me back to health. I didn't tell her about my depression diagnosis, just plotted up in my old bedroom and had a great time being miserable, being waited on hand and foot by my mam. Terrorising, in turn, the pubs in Little Hulton, then the local girls, leaving as a donkey in 1979 and coming back, maybe not a hero, but certainly a minor celebrity, complete with flash car and everything. It really gave me a chance to reconnect with my mother, who took no delight in telling me how seeing me so unhappy had broken her heart. She also told me that my father had died.

I said, 'What? When?'

'Ages ago. I did mean to tell you.'

They'd split up when I was five. She still hated him after all these years. My Auntie Jean then went on to tell me that my dad knew I had a habit of going into Salford for a drink at the Swan with the lads every Friday night. He would wait for my car, a silver grey XJS, D505 NBU, to pass him on Regent Road and then follow me to the pub and sit and watch me through the window, sometimes drinking at a table nearby. I never knew he was there. The last time I had seen him was when I bumped into him when I was twenty-one. He offered to take me for a drink but I declined; I was scared of what my mam would say. Before that I had no idea what he even looked like. A great shame, and I regret not knowing him now, very much. But that's life and he did treat my mum terribly.

Anyway, I didn't last long in Little Hulton, and when I went back to the Didsbury house it was to the faint smell of Caroline's perfume and four-foot-high grass on the lawn. She told me that because she knew I wasn't there, she would come in and just sit in the house for hours. I had to change the locks. Then I found out she'd been going to the Haçienda in disguise and stalking me. This was getting weirder.

Soon I was out every night, renewing loads of old acquaintances, making my apologies for being such a recluse and shit friend to everyone – and having the time of my life ... again.

One real kick up the arse came in the unlikely form of Pete Wylie, an old mate. I had been invited to take part (£500) in a pilot for a new show called *Never Mind the Buzzcocks* in London. I needed the money badly, so steeled myself and went. When I got there one of Caroline's old boyfriends was running it, but the other guest was good old Pete, who then gave me the best afternoon and evening of my life, listening to my problems and resolving them with his usual mix of Liverpudlian common sense and humour. I can't thank him enough. It marked a real turning point for me. Cheers, la!

One of my other mates was Fran, Francis Carroll, an old friend, who ran a restaurant, the Brasserie St Pierre in Manchester. He and his girlfriend Victoria, who was lovely but as mad as a fish, insisted on setting me up on a blind date.

'She's called Becky,' she said. 'She's had a terrible marriage and moved to Manchester. She's single now and I think you're perfect for each other.'

We made a date to meet in Prague V in the Gay Village but, unbeknown to me, Becky cancelled when she found out I was in a group. Victoria didn't tell me and arranged with Becky's mate Carlos to still bring her to Prague V anyway. It probably explained why she was so surprised to see me when I went over and introduced myself. She was beautiful. For me it was love at first sight.

My first and last time.

Becky and I got on like a house on fire and arranged another date. But when she turned up it was only to tell me that she was going back to her boyfriend. Cursing my rotten luck, I accepted an invitation from Fran and Victoria to join them on holiday in Miami, the plan being to cheer me up. Trouble was, their idea of cheering me up was to spend the entire time at each other's throats. They started bickering in the airport and were still doing it on the plane.

'You two are doing my head in,' I told them. 'I'm putting the headphones on and watching TV.'

What was on? *Mrs fucking Merton.*

So we got there and it was a bloody nightmare. We were staying in the Delano Hotel, which was so hip it hurts. Madonna ran the restaurant. Those two were fighting and I was having a rotten time. I remember on the first night going out to a bar, jetlagged, with them arguing, me falling asleep. When I woke up two hours later they were still at it.

In the end I phoned Becky on the pretext of wanting a chat but really to find out how she was doing, and blow me down, it had all gone tits-up with the boyfriend.

'Come out to Miami,' I told her.

So she did. We had a great week together, and on arriving home she moved in with me and we've been together ever since, and suddenly life was looking good again. Very good – I'd found the love of my life.

Becky was a bit of a party animal when we first got together, which suited me down to the ground. I distinctly remember being in the car one day in the autumn of 1996 and realising that for the first time in almost as long as I could remember, I was actually happy all the time. We have now been together twenty years.

I was with her in November of that year when Bill Wyman opened a branch of his restaurant, Sticky Fingers, in Manchester. We went to the grand opening with Leroy Richardson, who was managing Dry 201 at the time, and his girlfriend Georgina.

Who should be there with her new boyfriend, Matt Bowers, but Caroline? The evening started badly. She saw me with Becky and came over, shouting the odds, drunk as hell. I was going, 'Why don't you just fuck off?' but she just kept screaming at me in front of all the great and good of Manchester, who were gathered to celebrate the opening of this lovely new upmarket burger bar.

Of course, the bit about her screaming at me didn't make its way into the subsequent news reports of the incident. Nor did the fact that she apparently went back to the new boyfriend and started telling him that I was the one who'd started on her.

There were a load of paparazzi there, of course, and for reasons best known to himself, Matt went over and warned them what was about to happen, saying, 'Get your cameras ready, lads.'

What happened was that he came over to me, chest out, wanting to have a go.

We were sitting having drinks at this table and to get to us he had to stand on a step, and he got right in my face.

'Hey, you,' he says. 'You can't talk to her like that now she's with me.'

I went, 'Fuck off, knobhead,' and pushed him off the step. He bounced right back and pushed me and I fell on Fred Talbot, ending up sat on the weatherman's knee (I had a lucky escape; I think I was too old for him) and I thought, *Right, you twat, I'm going to rip your fucking head off.* But by now, Leroy had him and was hammering him, beating the shit out of him. Leroy was head doorman at the Haçienda and you should never mess with a doorman because they don't have any setting other than 'calm' or 'battering', and he was in 'battering' mode.

Me, I was like Scrappy Doo behind him trying to get at this Matt (shouldn't speak ill of the dead, stomach cancer got him in 1997, but he was out of order that night), and at the same time the photographers were clicking away, turning night into day, thinking this is way better than taking endless photographs of the same old faces from *Coronation Street*, when someone grabs me from behind and I swung around, kicking out in the dark and making contact – kicking someone hard in the stomach.

It was Caroline. They were both thrown out for starting the fight.

But the next day, the front page of every fucking newspaper in the United Kingdom had a picture of me holding Mrs Merton by the hair and kicking her in the stomach. Because of the flashes it looked like bright daylight, which made it look even worse for me, but on my honour – and everybody who was there, even Caroline and Matt, accepted this – it was a complete accident.

We had a bender at our house after but finished early; there wasn't much to celebrate. Bowser had asked me if he could put his trail bike in my garage early the next morning, and when the doorbell rang I presumed it was him, storming downstairs in my dressing gown and ripping the door open, hungover to hell, only to be confronted by about fifty journalists and photographers just like that scene in the movie *Notting Hill*.

For the next three days me, Becky and our friends were holed up in my house, the whole lot of us, with the press camped outside offering us stupid money for our story. Little bits of paper would come sailing through the letter box with '£250,000, *Daily Mail*' or £275,000, *News of the World*' or '50p, *Pigeon Fancier's Weekly*'.

Inside we were having a ball. We got drugs and beer delivered. We had a right laugh, reliving the fight, laughing at the photographers outside, occasionally the lads venturing out to shake them up a little, push them off their ladders etc. The manager of Sticky Fingers even thanked me for all the publicity. Whenever I went to Sticky Fingers after that, we got free meals.

What's more, it drew a line under me and Mrs Merton. Or, almost. Me and Becky stayed together, but Matt left Caroline; she moved to London but was still calling me up all the time. One night, she phoned up, three o'clock in the morning as usual, and I was going, 'Caroline, is that you?' and she went, 'I'm so sorry, Hooky.'

'You've got a fucking cheek. Me and Becky are asleep, will you get fucked and grow up?'

She was going, 'I'm so lonely. I just wanted to say goodbye. I wanted to apologise.'

I said, ' How did you get this new number? Oh, fuck off, will you,' and hung up. I said to Becky, 'We're going to have to change this bloody number again.'

The next morning we turned on breakfast TV and there she was, being put in an ambulance after an overdose.

The weird thing was that throughout the whole of that fucked-up and toxic relationship, I never saw Tony Wilson once. It was only after Caroline and I had split up in 1996 that I saw him, when I was doing an interview outside the Haçienda and sitting on chairs on the pavement.

Tony was walking past. He stopped. 'Was she psycho?' he said.

'Yeah,' I said.

'Thought so,' he said, and walked off again.

What a shock it was to hear that she'd died at just fifty-two. The phone rang all day with media wanting a comment – I even got trolled on Twitter, twats saying I should have cancelled that evening's gig out of respect – but I couldn't in all good conscience join those paying tribute. Yes, I loved her. Yes, she could be very funny, and there were times I felt privileged to have a private audience with such a great comic talent. But she was also a very troubled person, and nowhere did that manifest itself more than in our relationship. Perhaps I brought out the worst in her. Maybe we were like chemicals that become volatile when they combine.

Either way, my mum was right.

Luckily, things were looking up on the musical front, too. Musically Pottsy had encouraged me to do something I hadn't done for a while, which was play the bass.

'We need to get it back,' he said. 'We need to use it and write around it. Why did you stop?'

And you know what? I didn't know. I think it was just me trying to distance myself, to put it all behind me.

I went back to the bass and, lo and behold, suddenly it was like a creative dam had burst, and all that had been so effortful before suddenly became easy again. Me and Pottsy worked very hard, taking our time and wanting to get it just right. We were talking about changing the name and the format of the group. Both of us were writing vocal lines and lyrics and singing on certain songs and the talk was whether we should have just one lead singer. I think one lead singer is better for a band, but I liked Pottsy singing and because he was keen to try it we decided, 'Fuck it!' we'd have two lead singers. Let's be different. We decided on the name Monaco and the songs were getting better and better.

We even had a new manager, Steve Harrison, who at that time managed the Charlatans. I had been introduced to him by Caroline the year before. She said, 'He should be your manager.' One thing to thank her for. Steve had his own chain of record shops in the Northwest, and negotiated a great deal with Polydor on our behalf.

We had met Paul Adam, the head of A&R, and he really was an old-fashioned record company man in every sense (he would later go on to judge the first *Pop Idol* TV show). He talked about how he believed in loyalty to the artists and their longevity. 'It's all about the music,' he said, which was very refreshing for me. Revenge had been badly handled and badly managed by everyone, including me, and it was great to be on a label that wasn't staffed by idealists and lunatics. As an artist now, I do believe it's the artists who should be mad not the record company.

Our deal with Polydor was £75,000 on signing, £75,000 on commencement of recording and £75,000 on delivery of the record, all recording and promotional costs to be paid by them and recouped off sales.

So a very generous £225,000 advance to set us up, and a deal with options for four more albums, worth over a million in all. Polydor were very supportive, putting a great deal of money and resources at our disposal, and the record was mixed at Mayfair Studios, Primrose Hill, with Alan Meyerson in charge.

I had got on well with Alan on the New Order sessions and was very impressed by the job he'd done on *Technique*, which Pottsy loved too. It was a complete no-brainer. The one slight hiccup was the record company insisting we live together for the duration of the mixing in an apartment they booked for us in Kensington. Alan was a recovering alcoholic and now I sympathise, I really do – how he must have felt watching us three party constantly hurts me now. (I would suffer from this in 2004:

karma, as we say.) He didn't last long and soon moved out to a hotel, but bore us no malice and turned in a great performance in the studio.

We were very excited and felt very happy about the plans made for the first single release, 'What Do You Want from Me?', and accompanying video. It came out and if it hadn't been Mother's Day that week and the bloody Spice Girls hadn't released 'Mama' at the same time, we would have got into the top ten.

As it was we went in at number 11, played the song on *Top of the Pops* and it felt like I was back. From the opening bass motif – Pottsy's idea, to signal that it was very much me – onwards, it was a Peter Hook moment, and bloody hell, I felt like a drowning man suddenly breaking the surface of the water and gasping at the air. I was driving with Becky the first time I heard it on the car radio, a sublime moment.

Then our recording was interrupted.

Rob had been heartbroken by the end of New Order in 1990 and sad all the way through *Republic*, knowing it would be over in 1993 for good. For us to spend ages writing, then seven months in the studio, and come out to do a paltry thirteen live dates – and *then* break up – was like a dagger in his heart. The only thing he loved as much as New Order was the Haçienda, and he always felt that if we'd pushed our advantage on the back of *Republic* and rinsed the arse out of the album, then not only would we have been 'as big as them Irish twats', but we could have earned enough to buy the Haçienda building and keep the club in business and have financial security for the rest of our lives. He did actually get me, Steve and Gillian together for a meeting suggesting we employ a new singer and carry on as New Order without Barney.

'No. It would not be New Order without Barney, no chance. He started it with me that night at the Lesser Free Trade Hall. No! That's it,' said I.

In my opinion, Steve and Gillian didn't deserve it.

As it was, me and Rob were the only two representatives of the band still maintaining an interest in the club, so while I never saw or heard from the others, Rob and I stayed in close touch running the club together, with me at one point nearly giving up music and going full-time at the Haçienda.

Regarding the club his great mantra was, 'If only New Order would tour. If New Order would tour then everything would be all right. I wouldn't mind but Electronic owe me £75,000 and I can't get that either.' (Rob had managed Electronic since their inception and for the first single, before getting passed over for Marcus Russell.) This as we staggered from meeting to meeting – with the police, with the gangsters, with the bank managers, with prospective buyers, with the licensing committee.

Rob and I even went cap in hand to Barney, who was in London doing Electronic with Johnny Marr. We wanted money to rebuild the basement to turn it into a smaller club, but we were laughed at and told to 'fuck off'. In no uncertain terms.

In the end it was left to me, and for over a year I paid £7,000 a month to keep the club open and pay its mortgage.

That same year, 1997, Becky and I got married, and I had to tell Rob I couldn't afford to keep paying it any more. I was nearly skint. In the end it came down to either I had to stop putting money in, or Becky and I were going to lose our house.

Rob came to the wedding-night party. It was one of the wildest, greatest parties I've ever been to. We catered for seventy-five people and only two people ate. Paul Carroll, our Haçienda doorman, said to me, 'As a present I'm going to bring all the booze for everyone.' I was very flattered. Then early on in the evening I phoned him, worried about where the booze was, to be told, 'I'll be there as soon as I can. I've got Roger Cook and the *Cook Report* team camped on my drive. Don't worry,' he said, 'the lads are coming round to shift them.'

A couple of hours later he turned up with a van full of every kind of booze. I didn't ask.

Later Rob took me out in our garden, walking me round, begging me to keep pumping money into the Haçienda, which was dying on its arse. One expensive problem after another, drive-by shootings, disputes with the brewery, accountancy problems and so on and so on. All the gory details are in the Haçienda book, so read away. Becky had to come and rescue me. Later I caught Rob smoking coke ciggies with our gay friends, Steve and John, who were really upset when I told them it could kill him. I got Rob a taxi and sent him home.

In the end I had to go to the office to tell him I was pulling out.

He called me Judas. 'It's always you, isn't it?' he said, seemingly forgetting that I'd been the one who'd stayed loyal for the last six years, the only one who visited him when he was ill with his thyroid and heart problems later, while them lot had been off collecting tanks and annoying Johnny Marr.

Anyway, in June 1997, the club shut. In October that year we sold Dry 201 to Hale Leisure. Rob and I ended up buying the Haçienda name. Which, as we're on the subject, is something that has caused untold amounts of bad feeling among my former bandmates. They even used it as the main reason why they re-formed New Order without me.

Here is the truth: having spent a decade or so, quite publicly, distancing themselves from the club, those three now claim I stole the name from under their noses, when in fact Rob bought it fair and square from a public auction at the liquidators, after the club had gone bankrupt. Also in the bidding were Cream nightclub and Gio-Goi. To be honest, I really wasn't bothered at the time, but Rob begged me to lend him £5,000 to buy the names, which I did, and when he couldn't repay me he gave me a 50 per cent share. That deal must be on a par with Jack and the Beanstalk, pay for it all but only get half.

And please don't forget that Steve and Barney turned down the opportunity to own the other half-stake in 2010. If they'd taken up the offer, they would have owned 50 per cent of everything to do with the Haçienda, could have stopped me in my tracks, and they would have nothing to moan about.

Afterwards, Rebecca Boulton, their manager, told me they simply didn't know what to do with it and that's why they turned it down. Perhaps they think Rob should have given them a heads-up in 1997, but why he'd do that when they spent years denigrating and refusing to support the club *when it was actually open* is beyond me. They had made his life a misery for what they'd felt he'd done to them. Otherwise, it was another chapter of my life that was over.

Now, after the Haçienda shut, Rob called another meeting in the spring of 1998.

At this point I'd not seen anyone in New Order for a long time. No, I tell a lie. There was that time I'd bumped into Barney in Dry 201 and there was also a strange and awkward evening when a pissed Mrs Merton insisted I introduce her to Steve and Gillian, and we'd driven round to their house. That was the only interaction in over three years.

In the meantime, Barney, Steve and Gillian had had a nasty public falling-out. In interviews to promote the Other Two, Steve and Gillian claimed they'd written most of *Republic*. Barney was furious (even though they had; it had just been dumped by him). Steve even told me they'd seen Barney in Manchester and he'd crossed the road and run away rather than face them.

However, all this aside, Rob was at the end of his tether not knowing the status of the group. We'd been telling him for years, 'There is no New Order,' so maybe this was his last throw of the dice, a means of trying to pin us down to a decision once and for all or try to persuade us otherwise. 'I keep getting these huge offers for you to play,' he moaned.

It was difficult and very frustrating for him, I understood that, and maybe he just needed to hear it from the horse's mouth again, perhaps to shake hands and walk away. I don't know. Point is, the meeting was called and we all trundled along to the Haçienda to see what he had to say for himself.

Personally, I was enjoying my work with Monaco very much. It was creatively fulfilling and OK financially; me and Pottsy were getting along very well. We had toured and had a great time doing it; Becky was with me all the time and she got on great with him too. With the exception of the various shit flying around the Haçienda, my working life was in pretty good shape. I had no desire to get back with New Order at all. But at this meeting in spring 1998, the funniest thing happened. We all got on.

I mean, talk about time being a great healer, it was actually quite nice to see them all again.

So when Rob pushed his glasses up his nose and said something along the lines of, 'Right, you lot, what are we doing? Is it over or what?' it didn't actually seem that weird for Barney to suggest maybe getting back together. He definitely seemed the most enthusiastic; maybe he was feeling guilty about putting an end to it in the first place.

I don't know, maybe the sun was shining that day. Maybe Rob had put something in the tea. Perhaps I thought that the happiness I'd found elsewhere would somehow follow me to a revitalised New Order, but all of a sudden we were talking like we were going to be a unit again.

'Let's see how it goes,' said Barney. 'Let's see if the magic is still there. Let's do some gigs and if it goes well maybe we could record again?'

Fucking hell, Barney asking to do gigs? This was double weird. I wondered if he'd fallen out with Johnny. Was he skint? What on earth could have made Barney want to come back and, even stranger still, want to do gigs?

We all went off to think about it and later I sat with Pottsy talking about how bad it had been on *Republic* and what if it got back to that again? Pottsy simply said that I should go back and capitalise on the success we'd created; that I'd be crazy not to. I owed it to myself.

By now, we were used to the solo projects working alongside New

Order and there was no doubt the extra money would be great. Me and Bex talked about it at length and she agreed it was the right thing to do. I was still apprehensive.

I wonder now if Pottsy had been dead set against me going back and asked me not to, what might have happened. I will never know. We all agreed to give it another go.

So, given the remit to look into live dates, Rob took the bit firmly

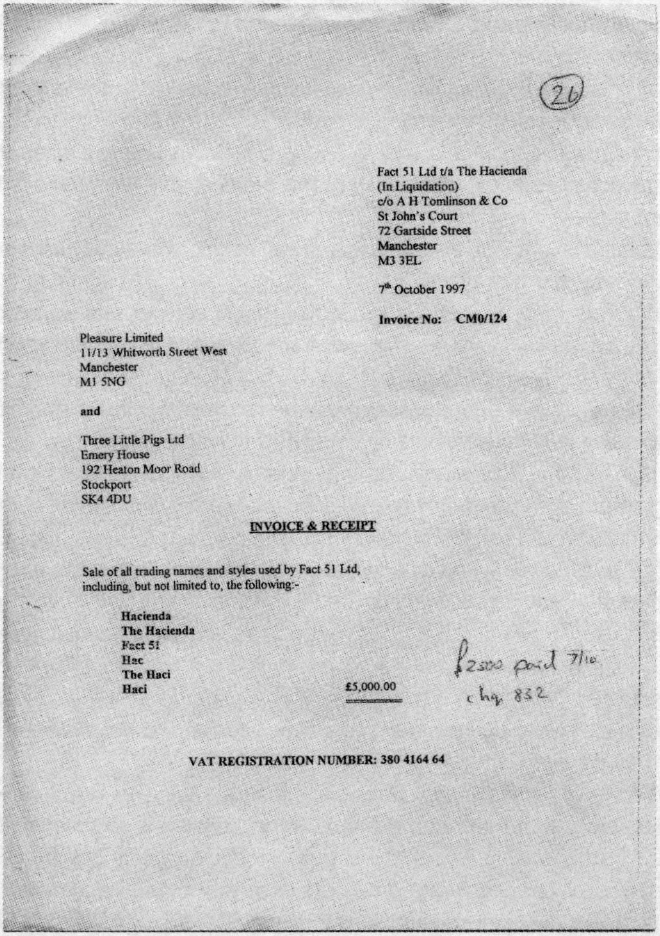

(26)

Fact 51 Ltd t/a The Hacienda
(In Liquidation)
c/o A H Tomlinson & Co
St John's Court
72 Gartside Street
Manchester
M3 3EL

7th October 1997

Invoice No: CM0/124

Pleasure Limited
11/13 Whitworth Street West
Manchester
M1 5NG

and

Three Little Pigs Ltd
Emery House
192 Heaton Moor Road
Stockport
SK4 4DU

INVOICE & RECEIPT

Sale of all trading names and styles used by Fact 51 Ltd, including, but not limited to, the following:-

Hacienda
The Hacienda
Fact 51
Hac
The Haci
Haci — **£5,000.00**

£2500 paid 7/10
chq 832

VAT REGISTRATION NUMBER: 380 4164 64

between his teeth. Soon he was dangling various enticing pay packets in front of us. Did we want to do Glastonbury? Did we want to play Reading? A rejuvenated New Order was suddenly a big draw and Rob was talking about getting a quarter of a million quid just to play one gig at Reading Festival. Even split five ways that was a damn sight more than I was ever paid in Monaco.

I went to Pottsy for his opinion again. To be honest, I expected him to kick off, and was sort of hoping he would, then I might well have been tempted to plant my flag in Monaco for good. Instead, he was really encouraging, again. He knew the amount of money at stake and his philosophy still was that I should see some more return on the hard work of all those years.

'You owe it to yourself and your family to go back, Hooky, you really do.'

At the same time, it was as though Barney was unveiling a new sunny-side-up personality. The man who used to hate touring – famously kicking the furniture backstage, shrieking, 'I don't want to be here, I don't want to be here' – was suggesting all kinds of new live arrangements. 'We'll do a new record and then we'll tour here, tour there,' he was saying. He must have been keen to get back together because he knew playing live would be a big carrot for me.

Before I knew it, we'd arranged the comeback gigs, the first one for Manchester's Apollo.

And feck me if I wasn't a member of New Order again.

'I wish I could thank that cleaner'

It's murder to try and combine two bands at once, but for a while that's what I did. In the summer of 1998 I was gigging both Monaco and New Order. Pottsy was writing while I was away and there was that little friction when I'd come back and suggest changes, me telling him rather tersely, 'I told you not to get precious. You should have waited for me.'

At that year's Reading Festival I played in both bands on the same day, lower down the bill with Monaco, headlining as New Order.

Meanwhile, at the end of 1998, Becky and I were parents, Jessica Scarlett Hook making her first appearance. I was over the moon. Another absolutely gorgeous redhead.

At the Alexandra Palace gig in December, I kissed Bernard on stage, and you know why? Because I was a very happy man – I was a father again, my daughter had just recovered from a very dangerous illness, bronchiolitis, and I was as happy as Larry to be playing with New Order again. This band had been my life. At that moment my life seemed pretty good.

This was the honeymoon period, if you like. The pressure was off. We were earning good money. We'd all proved ourselves outside of the group, no longer feeling simultaneously responsible for and shafted by our record company, no Haçienda to worry about any more.

We rehearsed a lot but we weren't living in each other's pockets so it wasn't as though I'd rediscovered what I didn't like about Barney or vice versa.

So the gigs went well, and at the beginning of 1999 it was decided to reconvene again to write a new record at the farmhouse. It had worked well for *Republic* (apart from the obvious).

So we were at the farmhouse trying to write again, jamming and recording ideas, then the interminable bit of listening to the hours of jams and picking out the good bits to work on.

Here it soon became pretty apparent that Gillian's heart didn't seem to be totally in it. She seemed very distracted. Every chance she got she'd run over to the house, often disappearing for hours. It was fine, though. Obviously by now you've got the picture that in my opinion she'd never been the most active participant in the writing. But at least she was usually in the room; she'd be 'available for work', let's say, and this was supposed to be a new start.

By this time, Steve and Gillian were leading a different sort of life. They'd turned their backs on partying and had two daughters, Tilly and Grace, so I guess Gillian was off doing mum stuff, probably loving the change of pace, and fair play to her for that. Grace had been very ill. God bless her, I knew exactly how that hurt.

The strange thing was, Gillian never said anything. She'd just disappear. Me and Barney would look at Steve and say, 'Is Gillian coming back over today?' and he'd leg it out and we'd be looking at each other going, 'He's still as mad as a fish, isn't he?' and you'd see him scuttle past the windows of the studio into the house, and we'd carry on until he came scuttling out, ten minutes, half an hour later, only to go, 'No, no, I don't think so,' and we'd go, 'Oh, right, OK,' and carry on without her.

I understood completely. Jessica had been ill over the Christmas before and as she lay there in intensive care in Pendlebury Children's Hospital, both Bex and I were convinced we'd lose her. I can safely say it was the worst thing I had ever been through. Heather had suffered with lactose intolerance when she was six months old, and Jack with a peanut allergy, but what Jessica went through was in a different league. As we sat round the ventilator with the machine breathing for her, I would have happily died for her to live.

We would watch children in the ward pass away around us and break our hearts with their grieving parents. It was awful. Then you had the contradiction of the relief and guilt you felt as your child fought on. I remember when she got ill, Becky as a mother knew straight away – men only catch on much later. She was diagnosed with a cold three times and sent home, but Becky kept on pushing until she was finally diagnosed properly and taken to the children's hospital in Withington, where they couldn't treat her because they didn't have a ventilator to keep her breathing.

'We should have a portable one somewhere?' the doctor told me, 'but we can't find it.'

It ended with me grabbing him by the lapels and screaming, 'I'll buy two, where do you get them from?'

'Mr Hook, it's nine-thirty at night, everywhere is closed.'

In the end the doctor phoned Wythenshawe hospital and spoke to a cleaner there who, when the doctor described it, found one and put it in a taxi to Withington. We got it just in time to save Jessica's life. I wish I could thank that cleaner, I really do: she saved my daughter's life without even knowing it.

But I had never felt as useless in my entire life as I did that night. Jess was transferred to Pendlebury Children's Hospital, and her life hung in the balance for weeks. They were fantastic in the hospital, every single one of them, and watching Father Christmas visit her on Christmas Day was surreal.

So I completely understood if Gillian didn't want to be there, and as the writing went on and 'Mr Elbows' started to make an appearance, I understood even more. There were tracks that Steve and Gillian would work on when Barney and I were away, doing our other bands, which progressed well but would fall to the sword when we made it to Real World to begin the recording.

So, Gillian simply faded away. It wasn't like we could go and tell the HR department or even snitch to Rob. So in true New Order fashion we just carried on. Barney and I were used to it. I must say that this time we were both hoping it would be different. Maybe I understood more than Barney how Steve and Gillian could have been affected by *Republic*, but along with the below-par live performances we'd suffered for so many years, we had hoped that this time it would be different.

'Fingers of God'

Rob died on 15 May 1999. He'd had heart problems for a while, so maybe it wasn't entirely unexpected. But even so, it came as a shock.

The funny thing was, Rob had actually resigned from New Order in 1989, in fact, he wrote, 'from the music business'. It was a depressing time. He had obviously, like the rest of us, had enough and sent the letters announcing he was leaving. Personally, I think it was a reaction to Barney calling it a day at that meeting in California. He didn't resign from either in the end. He carried on and also concentrated on his label, Rob's Records. He'd been doing well with it. A better talent-spotter than Tony Wilson ever was, and always more of a gambler, Rob had had hits with the Beat Club and Sub Sub and was turning the label into a very successful Manchester cottage industry.

When Ian died I was a lot younger and I made the mistake of not saying goodbye. I realise now that saying goodbye is very important to the grieving process, and not saying it to Ian remains one of my big regrets.

Thankfully I didn't make that mistake with Rob. I wasn't as close to him as I was to Ian, and I'm not sure I would have said he was a 'friend', because we'd butted heads so much and he could be a vindictive bastard when he put his mind to it. But we'd worked together on the Haçienda a lot, and I had the greatest respect for him. He was a genuine one-off and, whatever else you had to say about him, he loved New Order and fought hard for the group, even when the members couldn't be arsed; he loved the Haçienda just the same, and he loved Manchester most of all.

His funeral marked a big reunion of the Haçienda and Dry 201 staff. They all loved Rob. At the church it was packed, with a huge crowd of people spilling into the road outside. I remember 'Abraham, Martin and John' by Marvin Gaye being his last song in the church. The service continued at Southern Cemetery where it began to rain but then, as it reached the stage where you throw the soil on top of the casket, the sun came out, and rays of light – fingers of God, I believe they're called – shone through a canopy of nearby trees. It was beautiful, awe-inspiring.

At the wake in the Midland Lesley looked shellshocked. We had never been close, but even so, I have to say that out of everybody, she must have suffered with Rob the most. He was not a man to do anything by halves, whether it was football, cocaine, managing a band or opening a nightclub, and I can only imagine what a nightmare he had been to live with at times. I remember lots of people being really shocked they had to pay for their drinks. 'A Rob Gretton do without free drinks?' they moaned. The times they really were a-changing.

In the meantime, Rebecca Boulton, Rob's secretary, proposed herself as the new manager alongside our very own Andy Robinson, the idea being that she would manage the admin/financial booking side and Andy would handle the recording and touring side. They proposed a 10 per cent charge on back catalogue and a normal 20 per cent on future catalogue, touring etc. The only thing we didn't take into account was still having to pay Rob's estate in perpetuity, so our commission payments jumped to 30 per cent.

Having two managers, each with their own responsibilities, made sense, but even so, I thought we should have a proven, professional, experienced manager to knock us into shape at this point in our career, for this new start. Peter Saville felt very strongly too and actually arranged for me to meet a few more experienced managers in London. At the time I must admit I thought it made great sense to go with some big-group manager; the time for working with friends, I felt, had passed with the Haçienda. I was outvoted. The others, being as averse to change as ever, thought we should go with Rebecca and Andy: Prime Management. I wish I'd put my foot down about that more, as it turned out.

'Thick as Thieves (Like Us)'

As we returned to write, Barney's new mantra, the small bee in his bonnet shall we say, about only doing one thing at once, and therefore doing it properly, became the law. I had heard it before with regard to *The Crow* and a few other great missed opportunities. This worried me a little more. Basically what he was saying was, 'If we're recording we shouldn't gig, and if we're gigging we shouldn't record.'

Doing the two didn't bother me at all. In fact it made sense, because one offset the expense of the other and I thrived on it. Obviously the contradiction here was that Barney was still recording with Electronic, but I was used to his many contradictions. (Electronic would fizzle out after the release of the *Twisted Tenderness* LP in 1999. They had never gigged since 1992.)

Anyway, once we had about ten good ideas together, Bernard said he would go off home to write the vocals, which meant everything ground to a halt for a long time.

'Uh-oh,' the devil in my right ear said, 'déjà vu, Peter.' Bernard was insisting on writing his own lyrics and doing the vocal lines himself; Bernard was calling the shots, possibly changing everything, closing us all down on a whim; Bernard was forgetting he's a member of a group, and not solo?

The angel in my left ear said, 'At least you've got the escape of Monaco.'

True.

So when you looked at it that way, they weren't especially auspicious beginnings: Steve and Gillian were clearly distracted (for very good reasons, I'm sure, but still . . .) and I was hoping Barney wasn't laying the groundwork for another creative and publishing takeover.

On the other hand, he and I were getting on very well, and we soldiered on. We even started to socialise together with our partners in tow. This really was special. We did a few local openings together, a couple in Manchester, Bar Cuba in Macclesfield, Brasingamens in Alderley Edge.

Me and Barney were a power couple, as thick as thieves (like us). We went out for dinner one night and at the end Barney said, 'Sorry, I've left my wallet at home, Hooky.' There I am, Dolly Dimple, pleased as punch we were getting on so well. 'Don't you worry about it, mate, I'll get it.'

The next time we went out, blow me down, he'd done it again. The third time it happened Bex got up from the table, walked off and returned with his coat. 'Right, you, Mr Sumner, I've got a taxi, let's go back to your house and fetch your wallet.'

Me and Sarah pissed ourselves as off he went like a shamed little boy to fetch it, Bex accompanying him all the way in the cab. What a woman.

Barney hadn't changed, even after his Electronic days, and I know he was just as tight then, because him and Johnny Marr used to go out with a couple of ticket tout friends of mine. One of them, Mikey Williams, was telling me that Electronic would never put their hands in their pockets. Barney and Johnny must have thought that them hanging out with rock stars was payment enough. But this was Manchester, and in the end these guys got so pissed off that one particular night they ordered loads of Cristal champagne and foie gras and filet mignon, filled up, then sneaked out of the restaurant toilet window, leaving the two freeloaders to pay the bill.

In January I got a nasty shock. On the Millennium Eve my mother was dancing on the tables in the Dun Mare in Little Hulton. Two days later she died of a massive pulmonary aneurysm. That was definitely how she would have wanted to go. She would always say to me, in her more morbid moments, scrunching her hand into a tiny fist and waving it in my face, 'Don't you ever let them put me in a home, our Peter. Promise me you'll kill me first or I will haunt you forever.'

This wonderful woman, who had brought up three fine strapping sons, more or less alone, and given us everything she could, was gone. She had never understood my job, or calling, or whatever. She was always much more proud of Paul, my younger brother, who was a policeman, and of my other brother Chris, a mechanic.

'Proper jobs,' she'd say. 'Can't you get a proper job, our Peter?' she'd ask me, even after I bought her the house, the car, telling her that now she could have whatever she wanted in the world. Her answer? 'I'd love a new shopping basket with wheels.' I got one for her, the most expensive one you could get, all bright, shiny and new, and it was stolen in Little Hulton, the same day. Someone left a crappy old one in its place. She never told me it had gone, not wanting another.

I remember one time arriving late for Sunday lunch in 1989, an institution every fortnight in the Hook household; she would cook for about twelve of us, refusing any help, even at seventy-four years of age. When I got there she was very annoyed.

'Sorry, mam, I had to go for a really important interview.'

She turned to me, her face lighting up. 'An interview?' she said. 'Hooray! Our Peter's getting a proper job at last, everyone!'

'No,' I said, 'it was for a music paper.' Her face fell and she clouted me round the ear, telling me not to be late again.

I was devastated, of course, so Becky suggested Twinny take me out to drown my sorrows. 'I know where we can go,' said Twinny, and off we went to Cheetham Hill, where Jan De Koning was having a party for his fairground workers. There Twinny got talking to a guy whose girlfriend he'd tried to steal years ago. He was a bit weird, this bloke, and alarm bells should have rung when he bought us a drink, but they didn't, and within minutes of necking it we were as high as kites; it was spiked with acid. I spent the rest of the night thinking I was on a plane and shouting at an imaginary stewardness who was refusing to offer me drinks.

The next morning I was still tripping and had to go straight to the funeral parlour and meet my brothers, including Paul, the copper. The meeting didn't start well when the funeral director informed us the boss was absent due to a bereavement. I piped up with, 'Does he get a discount?'

Things went from bad to worse, me acting like a loon. Thankfully, everybody put it down to grief. As we were leaving I decided to say goodbye to my mum, who lay in an open coffin in the chapel of rest. I went in, only to discover that she had ginger hair – she'd been dyeing her hair all these years. It was a mystery solved: I'd often wondered where my daughters' ginger hair and my own ginger beard came from.

I bent to give her a kiss but leaned forward too far and knocked the coffin off the stand. I reacted by grabbing it to steady it and then, because the combined weight of body and coffin was so much lighter than I'd expected, I found myself doing a crazy dance around the room, clutching mother and coffin – all to the bemusement of the rest of my family who stood watching me.

No one from New Order came to the funeral, which didn't bother me at all. I knew what they were like. For the funeral she had insisted she was driven at normal speed to the crematorium, which was nice. We scattered her ashes where my step-dad was scattered, as instructed. I wish I'd kept them now, I really do. I miss her every day.

'Back to the Real World'

In June 2000, Becky and I moved to Alderley Edge. Funnily enough, it was at Barney's suggestion. His philosophy is that you should move to the best area you can afford so you can send your kids to the local state school and save on private education fees. To this day me and Barney still live there, and I occasionally see him on the high street, when we'll stop, chat and reminisce over old times, slapping each other's backs with great gusto, all our many differences forgotten (in your dreams).

It was also around that time that I went to a specialist for my irritable bowel syndrome. Nasty business, IBS. It had started in around 1997 and tended to get worse in times of stress with the group, as in all the time. Really suffering with it, I went to the best specialist in the North, who funnily enough also lived in Alderley Edge, where I was told I'd have to have a colonoscopy. I mentioned I was nervous. 'Don't worry,' they said, 'we'll give you a shot, you won't remember anything.'

That seemed odd to me – 'you won't *remember* anything'? – but I submitted all the same. Just before the shot, the nurse said to me, 'I'm glad you're here. He's got a full set of New Order now.'

They were right, I didn't remember anything afterwards – apart from that comment. But the funny thing about the IBS was that when the group split in 2007, my IBS went for good. In one fell swoop, I'd lost two major pains in the arse.

Anyway, back to 2000, and the album was announced at the beginning of the year. In short order we decamped to the studio – back to the Real World. We'd be there for a long time.

Steve Osborne was producing; he was well known by now as half of the Perfecto Records production team with Paul Oakenfold. He'd got our gig by doing a great job of producing the track that was to be New Order's comeback song, 'Brutal', on the soundtrack of *The Beach*. I had read the book in 1996 and loved it.

We recorded the track first with Rollo out of Faithless and it sounded good, but as Rollo spun more of his magic on it he lost us, and in the end we didn't like his version at all. Steve Osborne was brought in to save the day. We were well into recording *Get Ready* by the time the film came out in 2000, and we rolled up to the premiere along with every other band on the Pete Tong-produced soundtrack.

The Beach director Danny Boyle had done *Shallow Grave* and *Trainspotting*, both of them famed for their innovative use of music, so we were dead excited to see how the song had been used, thinking it would be different from the usual case of hearing it on a radio in the background. How was it used? It was featured on a radio playing in the background, in a shack with a tin roof, during a monsoon. You can't trust film-makers, you really can't.

Which was again proved by our next foray into film, *Mission: Impossible II*. We had been told Tom Cruise was a huge New Order fan and that supplying the track beforehand was just a formality. It was fun to record, turning out a lot better than I expected. I was able to really let rip on the bass sound. Unfortunately we lost out to Limp Bizkit, who were huge at the time.

Back to *Get Ready*. Alan Wise called up. Would we like Jerry Lee Lewis to provide piano for a track? Alan was promoting him at the time and Barney *really* liked the idea – that was, until the subject of money came up. What did the 'Great Balls of Fire' hit-maker want to play on our track? He said he'd do it for the same money he got for his first-ever session in the early 1950s, which was with Elvis. We thought, *Great, it'll be peanuts*, but he must have been adjusting for inflation and then some, because the price he quoted was $50,000. Balls of fire? Balls of brass, more like. We told him to sling his hook.

As ever the producer of the album was an issue. I liked Steve Osborne, but I was still of the opinion the group should produce the album. Again Barney said, 'I don't want to argue with you, Hooky. I want things to be different. A new session, a new start ...'

'But it's better when we argue, because we produce better music,' said I.

He wouldn't have it, and what Barney wants Barney gets, even when we're getting along, and, hey, at least his reasoning here was sound and I did understand. He was at least paying lip service to the idea of the greater good. In the past and future, Barney's interpretation of compromise was that it was something that *you* did and sometimes he would wait very patiently until you capitulated.

At Real World Steve and Gillian hardly ever came. They were still working on other versions at home then sending them to us in Bath. They developed a habit of arriving late on a Thursday afternoon, poncing round for a bit, having something to eat at seven and then going home again. The tracks they sent were the kind of thing they'd been doing as the Other Two, not New Order songs at all. Me and Barney opened the window and let them fly away.

This being the case, we ended up having to close ranks, aware that we would not finish it otherwise, and ended up writing most of the album with Steve Osborne in Real World, who contributed to making it one of the best New Order recording experiences I'd had for a long, long time. As with *Republic* we were writing with a producer, only now I was included. I remember being asked to work on '60 Miles an Hour' on my own while Barney worked on the vocals. Recording it with Pottsy, Barney was delighted that I wrote the keyboard-based ending. I was laying bass on all the tracks and people were actually staying in the studio. There weren't many of us there: me, Barney, Steve, a keyboard programmer (£1,000 a day, no publishing) and Andy Robinson, who looked after us really well. Barney was giving me encouragement all the time, suggesting improvement after improvement for the bass. It was a very happy, harmonious period for both of us.

Some of Barney's old tricks were still apparent – doing his own backing vocals and his awful timekeeping. Back in the days of *Low-Life* and *Brotherhood*, Barney used to say that the early hours were when the ideas came to him, like the ideas were pixies or something (Jesus, you can see why we never really got on, can't you?). Being nocturnal was normal for him, a point of pride. The odd hours, always starting after lunchtime and working until 11 p.m-ish. I alternated five-mile walks in the morning, accompanied by my faithful spaniel Mia, with long gym sessions in the Lucknam Park hotel nearby, working off the booze from the night before. It wasn't a problem yet, but I was drinking a fair bit, starting with cocktail hour at 6 p.m., a double Bloody Mary, then getting through a bottle of wine while the others did a glass, finishing off another two before I'd stagger to bed. There was also hardly any drugs, only on high days and holidays. It felt almost healthy.

For a couple of weeks we recorded at Monnow Valley in Wales, which was very isolated and quiet, nowhere here to get into any trouble. The owner took great delight in showing us the piano Freddie Mercury played on 'Bohemian Rhapsody' and told us great stories about Queen's roadies.

It seems that when they recorded here, they turned up driving sports cars, full of drugs, with pretty blondes on their arms and this guy was talking to them asking, 'When are your roadies arriving with the gear?'

'We are the roadies,' they said, 'but we have our own roadies doing the gear. Don't tell the band, will ya!'

Duly, the 'other' roadies arrived, set up the gear and then disappeared, leaving the glamour roadies to take all the glory when the band finally turned up.

Steve Osborne was great here and he took Barney's 'Crystal' and changed the soft electronic backing track completely, even waking me up at some godawful hour to put some lead bass on, turning it into the *tour de force* it became. To be honest, I didn't mind being woken up, in fact I was delighted. We'd worked on the track together, and it was a great one, and being woken up in the middle of the night to play bass was much better than arriving in the morning to find that your work has been wiped and replaced. It was definitely another step forward.

Sometimes Barney would get absorbed, as always. The thing about him is that he's incredibly lazy unless he's in the studio, where he's happy spending hours, days and millions of pounds, redoing synth and guitar parts ad infinitum as long as he's waited on hand and foot. I've said it before, but he's a real creature of the studio.

So, you know how it goes. One door opens, another one closes, and although the Monaco bit of my life was on permanent hiatus, I was still very excited about what lay in store for New Order. An album that had begun life slowly and tentatively in Steve and Gillian's farmhouse at the tail-end of 1998 was, by the end of 2000, beginning to look like it might actually come out soon. We moved to Hook End Studios, near Checkendon in Oxfordshire, to mix the tracks. Originally owned by Alvin Lee of Ten Years After, then sold to Dave Gilmour of Pink Floyd, it had ended up in the hands of Trevor Horn, who brought it under his Sarm West umbrella. This place was fantastic and, looking back, I can see that this was where my drinking went into another gear. I was regaling everyone at dinner with drunken stories night after night, getting louder and louder as the session went on. I thought it was the highlight of their day. I'm sure the others thought otherwise.

One night, after a bender with Ken Niblock, we nearly got an album title when Barney declared, 'Houston, we have a problem!' at the sight of my face. It was shelved later – the title, not my face.

In a big change for us we decided to bring in some special guests, with Billy Corgan (guitar and vocals) and Bobby Gillespie (vocals) working on the tracks 'Turn My Way' and 'Rock the Shack' respectively. Bobby was a pussycat, of course, and it was a really enjoyable afternoon, but Billy was something else entirely.

I knew he had a reputation as being a little difficult but even I wasn't prepared for what went on. He'd played some wild guitar for the break, and it was apparently fantastic, but unfortunately our engineer, Bruno, didn't press save on the computer, so it was lost.

Now, I've lost umpteen thousands of words of this very book by making the same mistake Bruno did, and I know that once something is wiped, it ain't coming back: you can either beat yourself up about it from now until kingdom come, or just get on with it, or ...

There's a third way. Let's call it the Billy Corgan Method. I was in the main house when one of the engineers ran over to say there was a problem in the studio and when I got there it was pandemonium. Billy was going berserk at poor, apologetic Bruno, and I have never seen anybody moan, whine and threaten as much as he did that afternoon. He was following Bruno around the studio, screaming blue murder at him until he'd reduced the poor bloke to tears.

Truth is, Billy's a great bloke. We'll come to how he saved my bacon and put up with me being a total tosspot shortly, and fair play, as soon as I pointed out that he was being a twat, and that Bruno was my mate and he couldn't talk to him like that, he stopped behaving like one immediately.

Meanwhile, Barney would fall out with Steve Osborne over production and mixing problems but leave me alone. I was 'good cop' at long last. The only blemishes of the whole session came at the end. The first was when the record company sent 'Crystal' to Mark 'Spike' Stent for remixing and instead of coming back sounding £10,000 and two points different, his version was almost exactly the same. Steve O was delighted, of course.

The second was when the Chemical Brothers were employed to produce 'Here to Stay'. I am a huge fan of the Chems musically and personally, Ed and Tom are a lovely pair of blokes and great musicians, and the suggestion to use them to produce this in-between-album song I thought was a great idea. Intended as an extra track for the *24 Hour Party People* soundtrack album, it had been recorded by Steve Osborne on the *Get Ready* sessions and left over. I spent ages with Andy Robinson, recording the bass in Real World, coming up with loads of slightly different bass riffs all through the song. Normally I would have picked the best out and wiped the others but Andy suggested leaving it to the Chems. The song was sent off and when the mix came back my bass was all over it, literally all over it, all the riffs. Barney said, 'We can't have that.'

When I asked why they'd left all the riffs in, Tom said, 'It was weird, Hooky, we couldn't decide and neither of us could press the delete button on any of them. So we left them all in. It was you, we love your bass.'

Strangely, Barney had no such qualms and when we went down to the lads' studio in London it turned into one of our biggest tussles, with Barney trying to persuade me it should just come in halfway through the second chorus and giving me a long list of reasons why, mainly, 'It's getting in the way of the vocal.'

'Good,' I said, and this time stuck to my guns. While I didn't get the intro, I come in halfway through the first verse. Still, it was all getting a bit too *déjà vu*. (PS: I did think this would have made as good a football tune as 'World in Motion' and should have been released as such but . . .)

That November we went to the Q Awards. Hosted by my old mate Davina McCall, it was a particularly wild event, with the Oasis–Robbie feud kicking off in style and yours truly driving people mad by being so off my head, shouting out 'New Order' at the top of my lungs as they announced every award. In fact, I was such a pain that Barney asked one of our handlers to give me a line of coke to help straighten me out, only it turned out to be such a huge line I could hardly speak and had to resort to starting a food fight instead.

Up on stage to receive our award, Barney quipped that I couldn't speak because I'd had one Viagra too many – the funny bugger – and then Davina was mortified when I found my tongue and used the opportunity to try and remind her of an occasion she'd no doubt rather forget involving my hotel-room coffee table. All in all, not one of my finest moments.

Back to *Get Ready*, and a really good album experience was ending on a positive note. I know that *Get Ready* isn't considered a New Order classic but personally it's one of my favourites, much better for me than the dreaded *Republic*. Not only that, but a buoyant Barney was again saying things that were like music to my ears. 'This is great record …' he'd say, sitting at the control desk.

It was!

'And we've had a great time making it …'

We had! I mean, it had taken a long time, but for one reason or another – clicking with the producer, the diversion of other projects – we'd had a good time recording it.

'And you know what we need to do? We need to tour the arse off it. Really get out there and play it to people. Really show them what a great album this is.'

Yes!

Oh my God, this was like heaven to hear. For Andy Robinson as well. We danced round the studio. Andy was saying to me, 'Did he really just say that?' and I was like, 'Yeah, he definitely said it,' because Barney wasn't talking about doing thirteen dates this time. He was talking about doing thirteen *countries*. We were going to get out there and tour the arse off this album and, maybe for Rob, we'd even be as big as them Irish twats. This was going to be absolutely wild. I couldn't wait.

GET READY TRACK BY TRACK

'Crystal': 6.51

I'm a man in a rage, with a girl I betrayed ...

The dreamy start is soon destroyed by the best comeback since Ricky Hatton. Steve Osborne turned this track on its head, proving him to be one of the greatest producers we had ever worked with, taking our strengths and putting them right to the fore. Keep it coming, man.

'60 Miles an Hour': 4.34

Why don't you run over here and rescue me ...

A great second single that should have been a hit. Catchy themes, aggressive and anthemic in equal measures. Great guitar work from Barney all the way through leads to a wonderful crescendo ending.

'Turn My Way': 5.05

Don't wanna have to work, don't wanna wash my car ...

Billy's vocal is great, plaintively telling us he's free of the normal world, and his and Barney's voices complement each other very well, they make a lovely couple. The Neil Young-sounding guitars made both Billy and Barney happy. Needed a lead solo at the end. I blame the studio engineer.

'Vicious Streak': 5.40

You've got a vicious streak, for someone so young ...

An older-sounding New Order track. Very melancholy with a classic bassline, a quite daring order musically, experimental almost. Highly

Kraftwerk-influenced. A lovely contrast to the rocky side so evident on the rest of the record.

'Primitive Notion': 5.43

It doesn't take a lot to confuse me …

A great bassline leads into a monster of a rock track, the programmed drums being the only thing holding it back. Reminds me of Golden Earring. A simpler order would have made a lot more sense but, hey, I wasn't in charge.

'Slow Jam': 4.53

The sea was very rough, it made me feel sick …

Taking its name from the original slow jam written at the start of the session, this mean and menacing song sounds young and cocky. Barney's yachting metaphors inspire a tale of never giving in, despite what happens.

'Rock the Shack': 4.12

My hand laid on my beating breast …

My least-favourite track. The punkiness sounds badly wrong, too cock-rocky for me. Looking back, if there was ever a B-side it was this, the best thing about it being Bobby's vocal.

'Someone Like You': 5.42

You're everything to me, the sweetest symphony …

The lack of drummer on these tracks is so apparent now. The programming cannot make up for it. We missed Steve very much, personally and professionally. This track would have rocked live. Sadly, we never got it there.

'Close Range': 4.13

There on the floor, thirty years or more …

A sophisticated rock tune, starting out electronically then getting more and more acoustic by the second. The bass steals the end … rightly so.

'Run Wild': 3.57

If Jesus comes to take your hand I won't let go …

This felt personal to Barney from the word go, very close-up and intimate. It came in as a more or less finished demo. I worked hard on the verses, which didn't make the final cut, but I did get the two middle eights. The 'good times around the corner' ends the record on a very positive note. We hoped …

TIMELINE FIFTEEN
JULY 1994–NOVEMBER 2000

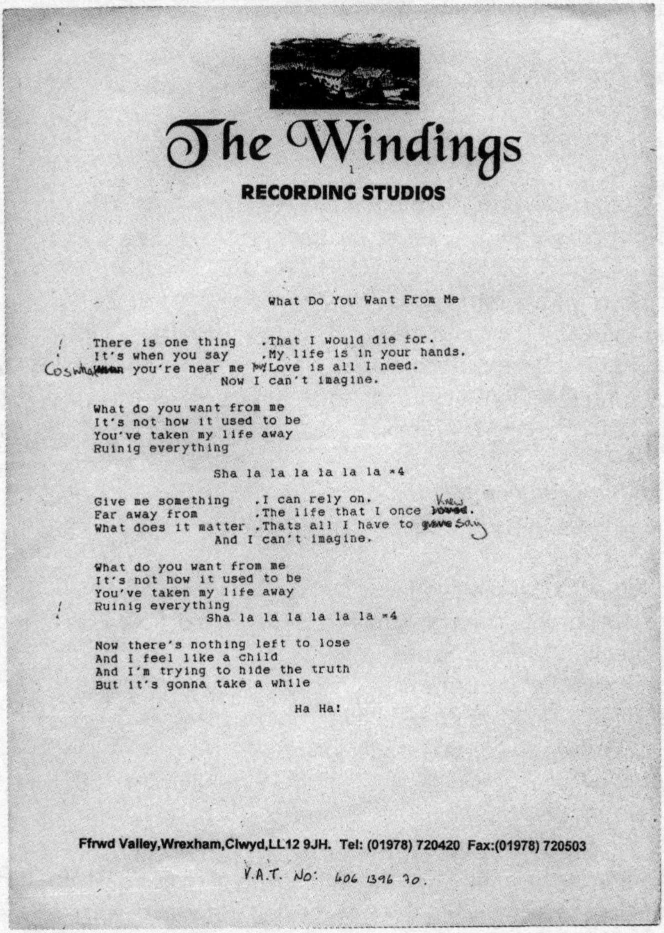

The Windings
RECORDING STUDIOS

What Do You Want From Me

There is one thing .That I would die for.
It's when you say .My life is in your hands.
Cos what ~~When~~ you're near me ~~my~~ Love is all I need.
Now I can't imagine.

What do you want from me
It's not how it used to be
You've taken my life away
Ruinig everything

Sha la la la la la la ×4

Give me something .I can rely on.
Far away from .The life that I once ~~loved~~ knew.
What does it matter .Thats all I have to ~~gave~~ say
And I can't imagine.

What do you want from me
It's not how it used to be
You've taken my life away
Ruinig everything
Sha la la la la la la ×4

Now there's nothing left to lose
And I feel like a child
And I'm trying to hide the truth
But it's gonna take a while

Ha Ha!

Ffrwd Valley,Wrexham,Clwyd,LL12 9JH. Tel: (01978) 720420 Fax:(01978) 720503

V.A.T. No: 406 1396 70.

July 1994

Peter Hook marries Caroline Aherne at the Little White Chapel in Las Vegas.

31 October 1994

New Order: 'True Faith -94'
(London Records)

Seven-inch track list:

'True Faith -94'	5.34
'True Faith -94' (radio mix)	4.28

Run-out groove one: *Will the first one in …*
Run-out groove two: … *please put up a fight!*

Twelve-inch track list:

'True Faith -94' (Perfecto mix)	6.23
'True Faith -94' (Sexy disco dub)	5.48
'True Faith -94' (TWA Grim up north mix)	6.11
'True Faith -94' (the '94 remix)	5.34

Run-out groove one: *Will the last one out …*
Run-out groove two: … *please turn out the light!*

Written and originally produced by Stephen Hague and New Order.
Additional production and remix by P. Oakenfold, S. Osborne, TWA.
Art direction by Peter Saville.
Photography by Trevor Key.
Designed by Howard Wakefield at Thomas Manss & Company.
Digital imaging by Martin Orpen, Idea.
Entered UK chart on 19 November 1994, remaining in the charts for 8 weeks, its peak position was number 9.

'London were in the habit of ordering a lot of remixes, which must have cost a fortune, but this was the first instance of what we can call an *obvious* record company cash-in, to be put on *The Best of*…

along with several other remixes. We had sold out to the devil and now we had to dance to his tune. We weren't the first and we certainly won't be the last. They had the freedom to do it, so they did. Saying all that – contradictory statement alert – I love it. It's a powerful mix, with the bass louder and much more prominent, and it sounds great in a club. So fair play. Well done, London.'

20 November 1994

The Durutti Column featuring Peter Hook play the Royal Exchange, Manchester.

'We used to end with a track called "Hooky's Tune". Despite the fact that I'd co-written it and it was called "Hooky's Tune", Vini wouldn't give me publishing on it. Classic. I love him.'

21 November 1994

New Order: *The Best of ...*
(London Records)

Track List:

'True Faith -94'	5.36
'1963 -94'	3.47
'Regret'	4.10
'Fine Time'	3.10
'Bizarre Love Triangle -94'	3.54
'Thieves Like Us'	3.58
'The Perfect Kiss'	4.48
'Shellshock'	4.25
'Round and Round -94'	4.00
'World (The Price of Love)'	3.40
'Vanishing Point'	5.17
'Run 2'	4.31
'Blue Monday -88'	4.05
'Touched by the Hand of God'	3.46
'Ruined in a Day'	4.00
'World in Motion'	4.31

Run-out groove one: *Let us celebrate …*
Run-out groove two: *… and hail our best!*

Track List US version:

'Let's Go'	4.02
'Dreams Never End'	3.11
'Age of Consent'	5.13
'Love Vigilantes'	4.18
'True Faith -94'	4.27
'Bizarre Love Triangle -94'	3.54
'1963 -95'	4.02
'Fine Time'	3.08
'Vanishing Point'	5.14
'Run'	4.28
'Round and Round -94'	4.00
'Regret'	4.08
'World (The Price of Love)'	3.38
'Ruined in a Day'	4.22
'Touched by the Hand of God'	3.41
'Blue Monday-88'	4.07
'World in Motion'	4.29

Design consultant: Peter Saville.
Designed by Howard Wakefield, Thomas Manss & Company.
Original photography by Trevor Key.
Digital imaging by Martin Orpen, Idea.
With thanks to Sammy Farrington for the original.
Entered UK chart on 3 December 1994, remaining in the charts for 17 weeks, its peak position was number 4.

23 November 1994

The Durutti Column featuring Peter Hook play the Queen Elizabeth Hall, London.

December 1994

New Order: *The Best of . . .* video
(London Records)

Track list:

'True Faith -94'	4.23
'Regret'	4.06
'Run'	3.38
'Bizarre Love Triangle'	3.47
'Fine Time'	3.06
'The Perfect Kiss'	9.10
'Shellshock'	3.12
'Confusion'	3.55
'Blue Monday -88'	4.03
'Round and Round -94'	3.46
'World (The Price of Love)'	3.47
'Ruined in a Day'	3.50
'State of the Nation'	3.30
'Touched by the Hand of God'	3.40
'World in Motion'	3.56
'Spooky'	3.44
'True Faith'	4.14
'Round and Round' (Patti edit)	3.43

9 January 1995

New Order: '1963 -95'
(London Records)

Seven-inch track list:

'1963 -95' (Arthur Baker radio remix)	4.04
'1963 -94' (album mix)	3.47

Twelve-inch track list:

'1963' (Joe T. Vanelli dubby mix)	7.13
'1963' (Joe T. Vanelli light mix)	7.13
'1963' (Lionrock full throttle mix)	7.50

'1963' (Lionrock M6 Sunday morning mix)	7.50

Run-out groove one: *Let the strings hum …*
Run-out groove two: *… their merry tune!*

CDS track list:

'1963 -95' (Arthur Baker remix)	5:05
'Let's Go'	3.56
'Spooky' (night tripper mix)	7.03
'True Faith' (Shep Pettibone '87 mix)	9.02

'Let's Go' was originally recorded during the 'Touched by the Hand of God' era, but was never completely finished. Rediscovered recently by Arthur Baker and Bernard Sumner, the two got together to re-record and finish the track, adding completely new vocals.

Written by New Order and Stephen Hague.
Produced by New Order and Stephen Hague.
Remix and additional production by Joe T. Vanelli, Justin Robertson, Arthur Baker.
Art direction by Peter Saville.
Photography by Trevor Key.
Designed by Howard Wakefield.
Digital imaging by Martin Orpen, Idea.
Entered UK chart on 21 January 1995, remaining in the charts for 4 weeks, its peak position was number 21.

'Again the bass was featured much more prominently and I thought it sounded pretty good. Using all these remixers would become a London Records trademark.'

10 February 1995

The Mrs Merton Show Series One begins.

6 April 1995

The Durutti Column featuring Peter Hook play the Coliseu dos Recreios, Lisboa, Portugal.

> **'Here I got the shock of my life. Vini was huge, he was mobbed. Touring with these boys was very laid-back and nice and I really hated inflicting the missus on them. Bruce had brought a collapsible bike with him and would spend his time cycling round all the places we played. Very refined.'**

7 April 1995

The Durutti Column featuring Peter Hook play the Teatro Académico de Gil Vicente, Coimbra.

8 April 1995

The Durutti Column featuring Peter Hook play Coliseu do Porto, Porto.

3 May 1995

The Durutti Column featuring Peter Hook play Clapham Grand, London, with intro by Mrs Merton.

12 May 1995

The Durutti Column featuring Peter Hook play Espace Européen, Paris.

12 June 1995

Joy Division: 'Love Will Tear Us Apart -95'
(London Records)

Seven-inch track list:

'Love Will Tear Us Apart -95' (radio version)	3.40
'Love Will Tear Us Apart -95' (original version)	3.27

Run-out groove one: *No-one cares any more …*
Run-out groove two: *… what you two say … War & Lore!*

Twelve-inch track list:

'Love Will Tear Us Apart -95' (original version)	3.27
'Love Will Tear Us Apart -95' (radio version)	3.40
'Love Will Tear Us Apart -95' (Arthur Baker remix)	4.20
'Atmosphere' (original Hannett twelve-inch)	4.11

Recorded in Strawberry Studios, Stockport, Manchester.
Engineered by Chris Nagle and One-eyed John.
Produced by Martin Hannett.
Art direction by Peter Saville.
Designed by Howard Wakefield.
Digital imaging by Martin Orpen, Idea.
Photographic images by John Holden.
Entered UK chart on 17 June 1995, remaining in the charts for 3 weeks, its peak position was number 19.

The single was released in May 95 on the fifteenth anniversary of Ian's death.

26 June 1995

Joy Division: *Permanent-95*
(London Records)

Track list:

'Love Will Tear Us Apart'	3.11
'Transmission'	3.34
'She's Lost Control'	3.58
'Shadowplay'	3.53
'Day of the Lords'	4.45
'Isolation'	2.53
'Passover'	4.44
'Heart and Soul'	5.48
'Twenty Four Hours'	4.26
'These Days'	3.27

'Novelty'	4.00
'Dead Souls'	4.53
'The Only Mistake'	4.13
'Something Must Break'	2.52
'Atmosphere'	4.10
'Love Will Tear Us Apart' (Permanent mix)	3.37

Produced by Martin Hannett.
Art direction by Peter Saville.
Designed by Howard Wakefield.
Digital imaging by Martin Orpen, Idea.
Photographic images by John Holden.
Entered UK chart on 1 July 1995, remaining in the charts for 3 weeks, its peak position was number 16.

31 July 1995

New Order: 'Blue Monday-95'
(London Records)

Seven-inch track list:

'Blue Monday' (Hardfloor radio edit)	4.14
'Blue Monday' (original radio edit)	4.07

Run-out groove one: *No-one cares any more …*
Run-out groove two: … *what you two say … War & Lore!*

Twelve-inch track list:

'Blue Monday' (Hardfloor mix)	8.34
'Blue Monday' (Andrea mix)	8.23
'Blue Monday' (Manuella mix)	7.29
'Blue Monday' (original mix)	7.23

Run-out groove one: *We're in the desert …*
Run-out groove two: … *where nothing grows!*

Written and produced by New Order.
Additional production and remix by Oliver Bordizo, Ramon Zenker,

Jam & Spoon.
Art direction by Peter Saville.
Designed by Howard Wakefield.
Digital imaging by Martin Orpen, Idea.
Entered UK chart on 5 August 1995, remaining in the charts for 4 weeks, its peak position was number 17.

> **'Pete Tong was our A&R man and, as well as being dead laid-back, he knew what he was talking about, inspired confidence and was able to take advantage of the dance-culture side of New Order. Later mixes would feature the bass but in the beginning (with the glorious exception of Arthur Baker's "1963") it would always come off first. Them lot thought it was hilarious. Not only was I excluded by the band, I was excluded by the remixers, and paying for the privilege. Thanks a lot, lads.**
>
> **'Who'd be a bass player, eh?**
>
> **'Answers on a postcard please to Peter Hook, Suite 169, Court Hill House, 60 Water Lane, Wilmslow, SK9 5AJ.'**

August 1995

New Order: *The Rest of . . .*
(London Records)

Two-LP track list:

'Blue Monday (Hardfloor mix)'	8.35
'Age of Consent' (Howie B. remix)	5.23
'Bizarre Love Triangle' (Armand Van Helden mix)	8.59
'Everything's Gone Green' (Dave Clarke mix)	5.31
'Touched by the Hand of God' (Biff and Memphis mix)	10.00
'Temptation' (C.J. Bolland mix)	7.41
'World' (Perfecto mix)	7.28
'True Faith' (Shep Pettibone mix)	9.02
'Confusion' (Pump panel recon mix)	10.12
'Ruined in a Day' (K-Klass remix)	6.13
'Regret' (Fire Island mix)	7.07
'Spooky' (Magimix)	6.58

Run-out groove one: *As the DJ takes a bow …*
Run-out groove two: *… take me by the hand, I need you now!*

Art direction by Peter Saville.
Designed by Howard Wakefield.
Original photography by Trevor Key.
Digital Imaging by Martin Orpen, Idea.

'London's frustration with our lack of activity was becoming evident. They wanted their money back, and who could blame them?'

12 November 1995

The Mrs Merton Show Series Two begins.

1996

No New Order releases, and no gigs for a whole year.

'For the first time since 29 May 1977, when Warsaw played the Electric Circus, the world was temporarily a Peter Hook-free zone.'

15 June 1996

Peter Hook meets Rebecca Jones.

'My search for love was over; I'd found "the one".'

13 November 1996

Sticky Fingers: celebrity deathmatch.

3 March 1997

Monaco: 'What Do You Want from Me?'
(Polydor Records)

Seven-inch track list:

'What Do You Want from Me?'	3.54
'Bicycle Thief'	3.59

Run-out groove one: *Back ...*
Run-out groove two: ... *to what we do best!*

CD track list:

'What Do You Want from Me?'	3.54
'Bicycle Thief'	3.59
'Ultra'	7.54
'What Do You Want from Me?' (Instr)	4.36

Recorded in the Windings Studio, Wrexham, and Chapel Studios, Lincoln.
Engineered by John Grey.
Produced by Monaco.
Cover picture: Lawrence Watson.
Designed by Peter Saville Associates.
Entered UK chart on 15 March 1997, remaining in the charts for 6 weeks, its peak position was number 11.

> **'I had noticed TV football shows doing their own instrumental edit of "Regret" for the highlights programme. I thought, *That's a good idea!* and from then on we always tried to do instrumental versions of every song. For a break-up song, it was very flattering that it would be used so extensively: by Dom Jolly in *Trigger Happy TV*, the MTV cartoon series *Daria* and even by the fans of Irish football team Shelbourne FC as a terrace chant.'**

28 April 1997

Monaco play the Grand Hall, Dundee, supporting the Charlatans.

> **'These gigs as support were a great way to start our musical rebirth. All the fun, none of the responsibility.'**

29 April 1997

Monaco play Newcastle Mayfair supporting the Charlatans.

19 May 1997

Monaco: 'Sweet Lips'
(Polydor Records)

Seven-inch track list:

'Sweet Lips'	3.43
'Shattered'	3.59

Run-out groove one: *Get yer smackers …*
Run-out groove two: *… round me Knackers!*

Twelve-inch track list:

'Sweet Lips'	4.10
'Sweet Lips' (Joey Negro Main Slice)	8.13
'Shattered'	6.17
'Sweet Lips' (Fire Island vocal)	9.20

CD track list:

'Sweet Lips'	3.43
'Shattered'	6.16
'Sweet Lips' (Fire Island mix)	9.20
'Sweet Lips' (Tony de Vit trade mix)	5.37

Recorded in the Windings Studio, Wrexham, and Chapel Studios, Lincoln.
Engineered by John Grey.
Produced by Monaco.
Mixed by Alan Meyerson.
Art direction by Peter Saville.
Cover picture: Lawrence Watson.
Designed by Howard Wakefield at the apartment.
Entered UK chart on 31 May 1997, remaining in the charts for 4 weeks, its peak position was number 18.

'The storyboard for this video looked fantastic. Buoyed by the success of the first single the record company upped our video budget to £50,000. A giant lighted monolith complete with attached waterway was built, gorgeous female twins were hired, and Pottsy and I sang, swam and hammed it up as much as we could. Looks OK, but, you may well ask, what does it all mean? I have no idea. The record went to number 18 in the English charts, followed by a *Top of the Pops* appearance that was different in one very sad respect: I wasn't there. Family emergency.'

1 May 1997

Monaco play Liverpool Royal Court, supporting the Charlatans.

2 May 1997

Monaco play Gloucester Leisure Centre, supporting the Charlatans.

3 May 1997

Monaco play Leicester De Montfort Hall, supporting the Charlatans.

5 May 1997

Monaco play Portsmouth Guildhall, supporting the Charlatans.

6 May 1997

Monaco play Exeter University, supporting the Charlatans.

7 May 1997

Monaco play Reading Rivermead, supporting the Charlatans.

9–10 May 1997

Monaco play Manchester Apollo, supporting the Charlatans.

11 May 1997

Monaco play Cambridge Corn Exchange, supporting the Charlatans.

13 May 1997

Monaco play Wolverhampton Civic Hall, supporting the Charlatans.

14 May 1997

Monaco play Doncaster Dome, supporting the Charlatans.

16 May 1997

Monaco play Brixton Academy, supporting the Charlatans.

24–25 May 1997

Monaco play Brighton Stanmer Park, Indie day, Essential Music Festival.

26 May 1997

Monaco play Manchester University supported by Travis (first ever gig) and Hurricane No.1.

> **'This was a very good gig and boded very well for the future. We had about 600 people, quite a success.'**

June 1997

Monaco: *Music for Pleasure*
(Polydor Records)

Track list:

'What Do You Want from Me?'	4.07
'Shine'	3.59
'Sweet Lips'	4.10
'Buzz Gum'	6.04

'Blue'	2.39
'Junk'	9.14
'Billy Bones'	4.58
'Happy Jack'	4.14
'Tender'	4.33
'Under the Stars'	3.51
'Sedona'	6.52

Run-out groove one: *One small step for Monaco …*
Run-out groove two: *… a huge step for Mankind!*

Recorded in the Windings Studio, Wrexham, and Chapel Studios, Lincoln.
Engineered by John Grey.
Produced by Monaco.
Mixed by Alan Meyerson.
Art direction by Peter Saville.
Cover image: Sam Taylor-Wood.
Designed by Howard Wakefield at the apartment.
Entered UK chart on 21 June 1997, remaining in the charts for 3 weeks, its peak position was number 11.

'I was now happy beyond belief. Pottsy and Becky had helped me find myself again and I could not be more grateful. I could not stop smiling. New Order was a dim and distant memory.'

28 June 1997

After a run of fifteen years, during which it helped change youth culture, acted as a springboard for the global dance-music business, launched dozens of careers, was the crucible for the whole Madchester scene and put its parent city firmly on the international music map … the Haçienda closes.

'A very, very sad day, but we tried, we really did. I'm not sure Rob ever recovered.'

July 1997

New Order: 'Video 5.8.6.'
(Touch)

Twelve-inch track list:

'Video 5.8.6.' (New Order)	22.25
'As You Said' (Joy Division)	2.01

CDS track list:

'Video 5.8.6.'	22.25

13 July 1997

Monaco play T in the Park.

> **'Life goes on.'**

2 August 1997

Monaco play the Guvernment, Toronto, Canada.

4 August 1997

Monaco play the Axis Club, Boston.

5 August 1997

Monaco play the 9:30 Club, Washington DC.

> **'We have great fun here watching all the rats in the alley, hundreds of them. The security guy had an air rifle and it was like being at the fair. No prizes though.'**

6 August 1997

Monaco play Irving Plaza, New York.

8 August 1997

Monaco play Metro, Chicago.

9 August 1997

Monaco play Cotton Club, Atlanta.

11 August 1997

Monaco play the Fillmore, San Francisco.

> **'A great gig, five hundred people in attendance. When I sing the song "Tender", the line "in my mind I live in California", the whole audience sings along, a wonderful moment. Afterwards we all get ratted in a pool hall and Pottsy would not go to bed.'**

12 August 1997

Monaco play El Rey Theatre, Los Angeles.

16 August 1997

Monaco play V97 Festival, Chelmsford (NME stage).

23 August 1997

Monaco play Festival, Free Show, Cincinnati.

September 1997

Monaco: 'Shine'
(Polydor Records)

Seven-inch track list:

'Shine' (single edit)	4.10
'Comin' Around Again'	5.04

Run-out groove one: *Fly into my arms ...*
Run-out groove two: *... make me happy once again!*

CD track list:

'Shine' (single edit)	4.10
'Comin' Around Again'	5.04
'Tender'	4.29
'Shine' (Instr)	4.10

Recorded in the Windings Studio, Wrexham, and Chapel Studios, Lincoln.
Engineered by John Grey.
Produced by Monaco.
Cover picture: Sam Taylor-Wood.
Designed by Peter Saville Associates.
Entered UK chart on 20 September 1997, remaining in the charts for 1 week, its peak position was number 55.

> **'This third single release, which I thought was pushing it, only got to number 55 in the charts. The record company refused to do a supporting video. This song was described by Peter Saville as "the best New Order song New Order never wrote". Compliments aside, my favourite song from the album. Strangely we got offered to appear on *This Morning* to play it, my first appearance after the "World in Motion" debacle with Keith Allen. When I get there I realised why. An old girlfriend is now the producer. She used to go out with a photographer in Manchester, and we'd had a dalliance in the late 1980s just before they moved to London. It was lovely to see her, and Richard and Judy.'**

10 September 1997

Monaco play the Garage, Glasgow.

> **'We were amazed at the amount of used Durex outside the back doors. They know how to party in Glasgow, safely.'**

11 September 1997

Monaco play Riverside, Newcastle.

12 September 1997

Monaco play L2, Liverpool.

15 September 1997

Monaco play Wulfrun Hall, Wolverhampton.

15 September 1997

Monaco play Wedgewood Rooms, Plymouth.

20 September 1997

Monaco play Astoria, London.

December 1997

Joy Division: *Heart and Soul*, 4CD boxset
(London Records)

Disc one:

'Digital'	2.52
'Glass'	3.56
'Disorder'	3.31
'Day of the Lords'	4.50
'Candidate'	3.04
'Insight'	4.28
'New Dawn Fades'	4.47
'She's Lost Control'	3.57
'Shadowplay'	3.55
'Wilderness'	2.38
'Interzone'	2.16
'I Remember Nothing'	5.56
'Ice Age'	2.25

'Exercise One'	3.08
'Transmission'	3.37
'Novelty'	4.01
'The Kill'	2.16
'The Only Mistake'	4.19
'Something Must Break'	2.53
'Autosuggestion'	6.10
'From Safety to Where ...?'	2.27

All tracks produced by Martin Hannett, 1 & 2 recorded at Cargo Studios, Rochdale, 3–18 & 20–21 at Strawberry Studios, Stockport, Manchester, 19 at Central Sound, Manchester.

Disc two:

'She's Lost Control' (12")	4.56
'Sounds and Music'	3.56
'Atmosphere'	4.11
'Dead Souls'	4.57
'Komakino'	3.54
'Incubation'	2.52
'Atrocity Exhibition'	6.05
'Isolation'	2.53
'Passover'	4.46
'Colony'	3.55
'A Means to an End'	4.07
'Heart and Soul'	5.51
'Twenty Four Hours'	4.26
'The Eternal'	6.07
'Decades'	6.13
'Love Will Tear Us Apart'	3.27
'These Days'	3.26

All tracks produced by Martin Hannett. 1 & 16 recorded at Strawberry Studios, Stockport, Manchester, 2 & 17 at Pennine Sound Studios, Oldham, 3 & 4 at Cargo Studios, Rochdale, 5–15 at Britannia Row, London.

Disc three:

'Warsaw'	2.26

'No Love Lost'	3.42
'Leaders of Men'	2.34
'Failures'	3.44
'The Drawback'	1.46
'Interzone'	2.11
'Shadowplay'	4.10
'Exercise One'	2.28
'Insight'	4.05
'Glass'	3.28
'Transmission'	3.51
'Dead Souls'	4.55
'Something Must Break'	2.54
'Ice Age'	2.36
'Walked in Line'	2.47
'These Days'	3.27
'Candidate'	1.57
'The Only Mistake'	3.43
'Chance (Atmosphere)'	4.54
'Love Will Tear Us Apart'	3.22
'Colony'	4.03
'As You Said'	2.01
'Ceremony'	4.21
'In a Lonely Place' (detail)	2.26

1–4 produced by Warsaw, 5–7 by John Anderson, Bob Auger, Richard Searling and Joy Division, 8 by Bob Sargeant, 9–11 & 14 by Martin Rushent, 12, 13, 15 & 22–24 by Martin Hannett, 16–19 by Stuart James, 20 & 21 by Tony Wilson.
1–4 & 16–19 recorded at Pennine Sound Studios, Oldham, 5–7 at Arrow Studios, Manchester, 8, 20 & 21 at BBC Studios, London, 9–11 & 14 at Eden Studios, London, 15 at Strawberry Studios, Stockport, Manchester, 12 & 13 at Central Sound, Manchester, 22 at Britannia Row, London, 23 & 24 at Graveyard Studios, Prestwich.

Disc four:

'Dead Souls'	4.15
'The Only Mistake'	4.05

'Insight'	3.46
'Candidate'	2.03
'Wilderness'	2.27
'She's Lost Control'	3.40
'Disorder'	3.12
'Interzone'	2.04
'Atrocity Exhibition'	5.57
'Novelty'	4.21
'Autosuggestion'	4.05
'I Remember Nothing'	5.32
'Colony'	3.53
'These Days'	3.50
'Incubation'	3.38
'The Eternal'	6.32
'Heart and Soul'	4.43
'Isolation'	3.14
'She's Lost Control'	5.26

1–10 recorded live at the Factory, Hulme, 11 at the Prince of Wales Conference Centre, YMCA, London, 12–14 at the Winter Gardens, Bournemouth, 15–19 at the Lyceum Ballroom, London.

Designed by Peter Saville, Jon Wozencroft and Howard Wakefield.
Abstract photography and video stills by Jon Wozencroft.
Booklet edited by Jon Savage and Jon Wozencroft.
Entered the UK chart 7 Feb 1998 and stayed for one week, peak position, number 70.
Entered UK chart on 7 February 1998, remaining in the charts for 1 week, its peak position was number 70.

February 1998

The members of New Order meet to talk about re-forming.

> **'If I knew then what I know now, eh?'**

1 June 1998

Monaco play Sankey's Soap, Manchester.

24 June 1998

Monaco play Aberystwyth University.

27 June 1998

Monaco play the Glastonbury Festival.

16 July 1998

New Order play Apollo Theatre, Manchester.

> **'Our first comeback gig on home turf and, as with every other home-town gig, it was a guest-list nightmare. We actually lost money, with two days' pre-production and a guest list of over a thousand – the biggest of all time, according to the Apollo – taking £40,000 out of the revenue. Talk about business as usual. It was nice to be back.'**

26 August 1998

Monaco play the Stage, Hanley, Stoke-on-Trent, a warm-up gig before the Reading Festival.

30 August 1998

Monaco play the Reading Festival.

> **'This was weird, playing with my boys and seeing tape with "Barney" written on it on the stage. We had a great time here, although doing both bands was very stressful and a bit odd. I felt like I was betraying both bands simultaneously.'**

30 August 1998

New Order play the Reading Festival.

> **'Keith Allen appeared in a cage lowered from the gantry. As it came down it was apparent he was naked. Much was made of the handshake between me and Barney at the end of "True Faith". At that point I thought everything was going very well.'**

21 September 1998

Official handover of the Commonwealth Games from Kuala Lumpur to Manchester. This event took place in Manchester's Albert Square. New Order played 'Temptation' and James played 'Sit Down' live to an audience of nearly 400 million people during a ten-minute BBC1 TV broadcast.

12 October 1998

Jessica Scarlett Hook born.

> **'A wonderful, beyond-words moment. Now there were five.'**

12 October 1998

Bee Gees Tribute Album: *Gotta Get a Message to You*
(Polydor)

Track list:
'You Should Be Dancing' (Monaco) 5.26

29 December 1998

New Order play Manchester Evening News Arena, Manchester.

> **'This miserable gig wasn't very well attended and was very cold. It was done to appease the Mean Fiddler organisation, run by Vince Power. We were embroiled in a highly political situation because we'd done our other gigs with SJM. We had become**

involved in a sort of North/South power struggle. SJM would eventually win.'

31 December 1998

New Order play Alexandra Palace, London.

> **'What a fantastic line-up. I drove straight home after the gig, my first time ever, because Jessica was still very, very ill. Kim from Bournemouth was there with Andy Robinson, which was puzzling; Noel Gallagher was in the dressing room with his missus, and Bez joined us on stage for "Fine Time" and "Blue Monday", where he just repeated "Manchester, 061" over and over. It was hilarious.'**

January/February 1999

New Order convene at the Farm to start writing.

15 May 1999

Rob Gretton, manager of Joy Division/New Order, a director of Factory Records and a tireless supporter of the Haçienda and Manchester City, dies in his sleep at home, of a heart attack, aged forty-six.

June 1999

Joy Division: 'Preston 28 February 1980'
(FACD 2.60 / NMC)

Track list:	
'Incubation'	3.06
'Wilderness'	3.02
'Twenty Four Hours'	4.39
'The Eternal'	8.39
'Heart and Soul'	4.46
'Shadowplay'	3.50
'Transmission'	3.23

'Disorder'	3.23
'Warsaw'	2.48
'Colony'	4.16
'Interzone'	2.28
'She's Lost Control'	5.02

Recorded live at the Warehouse, Preston, 28 February 1980.
Designed by Howard Wakefield and Paul Hetherington.
Art direction by Peter Saville.
Photograph by Daniel Meadows.

23 July 1999

Monaco play Castlefield Arena, Manchester.

25 July 1999

Monaco play Guildford Live 1999 Festival, Main Stage.

12 August 1999

Monaco play the Eclipse 1999 Festival, Cornwall.

30 October 1999

The *Q* Inspiration Award is won by New Order, presented to Peter Hook and Bernard Sumner, and joined by Keith Allen at Grosvenor House in London.

January 2000

Monaco dropped by Polydor Records.
New Order begin recording *Get Ready* at Real World.

2 January 2000

Peter Hook's mother, Irene, dies.

February 2000

Release of *The Beach* soundtrack featuring 'Brutal' by New Order, the band's first new material since the release of *Republic* in 1993.

Produced by Rollo and New Order.
Engineered by Crippa.
Backing vocals by Pauline Taylor.
Additional production and mix by Steve Osborne.
Programmed by Andy Gray.
Assistant engineer: Bruno Ellingham.

> **'We had gone back to basics to write this track – me, Barney and Steve jamming. It ended up mean and moody, with loads of bass, a real rock track. It was great to be back.'**

26 June 2000

New Order: *BBC Radio 1 Live in Concert*
(Strange Fruit / Fuel Records)

Reissue album featuring new artwork and sleeve notes. Concert recorded 19 June 1987 at Glastonbury.

Track List:

'Touched by the Hand of God'	4.57
'Temptation'	8.36
'True Faith'	5.45
'Your Silent Face'	6.05
'Every Second Counts'	4.20
'Bizarre Love Triangle'	4.39
'Perfect Kiss'	10.05
'Age of Consent'	5.20
'Sister Ray'	9.21

Produced by Pete Ritzema.
Designed by the Peter Saville Studio.
Photography by Jon Wozencroft.

21 August 2000

Monaco: *Monaco*
(Papillon Records)

Track list:

'I've Got a Feeling'	4.33
'A Life Apart'	6.18
'Kashmere'	5.08
'Bert's Theme'	4.45
'Ballroom'	5.37
'See-Saw'	5.45
'Black Rain'	4.02
'It's a Boy'	5.06
'End of the World'	4.51
'Marine'	6.21

Run-out groove one: *Can you feel . . .*
Run-out groove two: *. . . it slipping away?*

Recorded at Chapel Studios, Lincoln, and Mayfair Studios, Primrose Hill, London.
Engineered by Mike Hunter.
Mixed by Alan Meyerson, assisted by Ricky Graham.
Produced by Monaco.
Concept and design by Peacock.

> **'I thought there were some great tracks here. It was a shame about the timing. We couldn't agree on a title for the record. I wanted "Be Careful What You Wish For" and Pottsy wanted "The World of . . ." I suggested we use both. He said, "No. It's one or none." So it was none. With hindsight, a great mistake, typical of the time. We could no longer agree.'**

7 August 2000

Joy Division: *The Complete BBC Recordings*
(Strange Fruit / Fuel Records)

Track list:
'Exercise One' (recorded for the John Peel show 31 January 1979) 2.32
'Insight' (recorded for the John Peel show 31 January 1979) 3.53
'She's Lost Control' (recorded for the John Peel show 31 January 1979) 4.11
'Transmission' (recorded for the John Peel show 31 January 1979) 3.58
'Love Will Tear Us Apart' (recorded for the John Peel show 26 November 1979) 3.25
'Twenty Four Hours' (recorded for the John Peel show 26 November 1979) 4.10
'Colony' (recorded for the John Peel show 26 November 1979) 4.05
'Sound of Music' (recorded for the John Peel show 26 November 1979) 4.27
'Transmission' (recorded live for *Something Else* 1 September 1979) 3.18
'She's Lost Control' (recorded live for *Something Else* 1 September 1979) 3.44
Ian Curtis and Stephen Morris interviewed by Richard Skinner 3.32

Designed by the Peter Saville Studio.
Photography by Jon Wozencroft.

9 August 2000

Monaco play Milky Way, Amsterdam.

29 August 2000

Monaco play University, Manchester.

> **'This was a good gig. I was grabbed at the door by my first ever girlfriend, Christine from Salford in 1970; she was now a New Order fan, small world. Later Rebecca Boulton would tell me how much she enjoyed our new songs, praise indeed.'**

31 August 2000

Monaco play the Scala, London.

> **'Our last show as Monaco. My lyric book with new songs in it was stolen, gone forever. It seemed strangely prophetic. Weird how both Revenge and Monaco would finish forever at gigs in London.'**

13 November 2000

New Order: *The John Peel Sessions*
(Strange Fruit / Fuel Records)

Reissue album featuring new artwork and sleeve notes. A combination of *Peel Sessions 1981* and *Peel Sessions 1982*.

Track list:

'Truth'	4.13
'Senses'	4.15
'I.C.B.'	5.15
'Dreams Never End'	3.05
'Turn the Heater On'	5.00
'We All Stand'	5.15
'Too Late'	3.35
'5.8.6.'	6.05

Designed by the Peter Saville Studio.
Photography by Jon Wozencroft.

25 November 2000

Fixtures and fittings from the seminal Haçienda nightclub went under the hammer prior to the building being demolished for luxury flats. The DJ booth, dancefloor, light fittings, bar, stage and telephones were among the items sold at the auction.

'A crowd of adoring Goths'

At the beginning of 2001, with *Get Ready* completed and plans for New Order to resume touring in hand, Gillian decided not to play live. We'd been trying to sort out publishing for the new record – the bane in the life of any group, an issue almost guaranteed to drive a wedge between you and everybody else – when during a meeting Andy and Rebecca told us that she wouldn't be joining us for the live dates. It hardly came as a surprise, considering her parental responsibilities. I understood why she wouldn't want to join the group on a gruelling tour, never mind the gruelling rehearsals.

We were desperate to keep Steve, of course. Despite him not having done much on this album, he was an integral part of the band's history and sound, 'live' especially, but we were happy to let Gillian go. Very happy, in fact.

Picture this: me and Barney dancing around the studio, arms round each other, over the moon that there was no more having to carry someone who I thought was a bit of a passenger; no more having the world think that someone brought something of value to New Order when they didn't. (Disclaimer: Now, I know it sounds a bit heartless. But, I'm relating it to you from my point of view, and from that perspective – and that perspective only.)

Get Ready cost so much to make – £505,000 – that after two years of making it we got just £15,000 each in wages at the end, money left over from the advance. However, the publishing for *Get Ready* actually ended up being quite easy to sort out. Me and Barney splitting 80 per cent: fifty to him, thirty to me, Steve getting fifteen and Gillian getting five, which we felt was fair.

As part of the using-different-producers doctrine, our old friend Flood was enlisted to re-record and remix 'Rock the Shack'. We first met Flood, a.k.a. Mark Ellis, you might remember, when we were mixing *Movement* with Martin Hannett in Sarm West in London. He had just joined as assistant engineer/tea boy and was very nice and enthusiastic. Over the years he would become very famous because of his work with artists such as U2, Nine Inch Nails and Depeche Mode, among many others.

Again, while I hated the idea of all the producers the thought of a few days in Dublin really appealed. Ever since our time there recording *Brotherhood* the city has an uncanny knack of feeling very much like a second home. At the same time, though, our radio promotion people had identified a problem with the single 'Crystal'. It seemed it was heading for the playlist of Radio 2 only (presumably because of the band's age?). For us this was thought of as the kiss of death and plans were made to do a bit of major arse-licking to get it back on the Radio 1 playlist.

But how? Easy, we invited the head programmer of Radio 1 for a weekend jolly with us in Dublin, all expenses paid, staying at U2's Clarence Hotel for good measure.

This seemed like a good idea until he turned up and, as Twinny would say, 'He's not one of us, Hooky!' The guy was an absolute turkey and was outspoken and annoying right from when we took him for dinner in the Clarence and then on to Nells nightclub after. I hated him with a vengeance and, once I was obnoxiously pissed, decided to get me and him right off our heads. I turned into a right cokehound, badgering everyone I came across for charlie, but it was proving to be very difficult indeed, with everyone from the punters on the dancefloor to the cloakroom girl being unable to help. Then, just as I was beginning to lose all hope, a guy sidles up to me and whispers out of the side of his mouth, the true time-honoured druggy greeting, 'You want some action?' We retired to the toilets where he relieved me of a hundred quid and gave me five magic beans ... well tablets, rhubarb and custard capsules.

'Ecstasy,' he said. 'Be careful, they're very strong.'

'Yeah, I bet they are,' says I, necking one. 'Don't worry, mate, I'm from Manchester. We invented the bloody stuff.'

Going back into the club I spied my mate from Radio 1 and smarmily said, 'Shall I get you another drink, Tarquin?'

'Yes please, Hookah, old boy,' he says.

I got the drink and seized the opportunity to empty two of the capsules' contents into it, then, sniggering to myself like Muttley off *Wacky Races*, I started to walk across the club. I thought I looked normal but Andy Robinson tells me later I looked and walked like a *Thunderbirds* puppet right across the dancefloor. Turns out Andy had been keeping an eye on me and grabbed me just before I got to Tarquin. 'What the fuck are you doing? You trying to kill him?'

He then tries to grab the very cloudy and weirdly foaming half of lager from me, attempting to wrestle it from my grasp. I thought, *Hey up!* kicked him in the shin then necked it in one.

Fuck me, then I am off my nut completely and disgrace myself absolutely, ending up getting kicked out of the club and on my own in the closed bar at the Clarence, dancing in a dark corner.

The next day I was wrecked and crawled into the studio in tatters about three in the afternoon. Barney told me the session wasn't working – another producer bites the dust – so we decided to have a brainstorming session on a title for the LP.

We'd not had much luck or inspiration and basically had a long, long list of crap titles. I said, 'I always liked how the titles made sense in the way they ran: *Unknown Pleasures*; *Closer*; *Still*; *Movement*; *Power, Corruption & Lies*; *Low-Life*; *Brotherhood*; *Substance*; *Technique*; *Republic* (which I have to admit I felt was the joker in the pack); and here we are getting ready for a comeback and can't think of one to save our lives!'

'Hang on,' says Barney. 'Getting ready ... *Get Ready*. How about that?'

Fuck me, we'd done it again. I went out that night and got absolutely hammered again to celebrate, ending up alone in a restaurant with no idea how I'd got there, what it was called or where it was and being so pissed I couldn't even make it to the door. So I did what every other non-self-respecting alkie would have done and carried on drinking until I was the last one in the restauarant, then paid up and crashed out, staggering round Dublin for what seemed like hours until I found the bloody hotel. Shit, this drinking was becoming a real problem.

Preparing for live, Barney didn't waste any time in suggesting a guitarist he had worked with in Electronic, Phil Cunningham, also from Macclesfield, who used to play with the group Marillion.

We'd also invited Billy Corgan to play with us on the tour, to ease our way back in. It seemed a nice idea to share the load with someone we respected and admired and vice versa, a sharing of the limelight. We were a little worried how our comeback would be perceived. The idea was that Billy would play the warm-up, then Fuji, then the North

American dates – Moby's travelling Area: One Festival, which featured Moby, us and Outkast – and then for a couple of the European shows.

It was a good thing he was only on a few of the dates, because although he attracted a crowd of adoring Goths wherever we went, he was costing us a fortune. Whereas we'd fly business he'd insist on first class (double ours), then he insisted on staying at some of the best hotels in certain places, the one in Paris costing £3,000 a night, whereas we'd be in one down the road for £300. No problem, it was just how he worked and we didn't have to use him if we didn't want to. Different people have different survival techniques. After all, we were forewarned.

Phil Cunningham came in as a session man, who as I said used to be in Marillion (he didn't; actually it was Manchester's own Marion, of course. I used to say it just to piss him off: 'Oi! Where's that Fish when you need him?' I'd bellow after a few drinks) and who would play with us full-time from then on.

Phil seemed like a great guy. He brought a lot of confidence to the band, which gave Barney confidence, and – more importantly – he actually played very well. And you know what? We never played a bad gig after he joined. It was like someone had fixed the table with the wonky leg and all of a sudden it was just ... better. Even Steve seemed much more relaxed.

Musically we were lifting off. Gillian still used to come to gigs occasionally and she'd be at the side of the stage in tears because she missed the old life.

The first date of our 35-gig, year-long tour was a warm-up at the Olympia in Liverpool, promoted by our old mate Alan Wise.

I'd recommended a foldback guy to the band. We'd used him in Monaco, an Irish bloke called Gerry Colclough who was, hands-down, *the* best foldback engineer I'd ever met, and a lovely man to boot. As you know, the sound on stage had been a major bone of contention throughout the history of New Order, so to finally get the foldback ninja on our team was bliss, and every gig with him was an absolute pleasure, even for Barney.

In Fuji we actually scored some of the best drugs ever too. It had always been notoriously difficult to score in Japan, the Japanese themselves being very anti-drugs. We were told an English guy was selling it in the backstage area.

'How will we recognise him?' we asked, only to be told, 'You'll recognise him. Don't worry!'

We did, easily. He was completely off his nut, obligatory towel round his neck to mop up the rivers of snot pouring from both nostrils. 'Aren't you worried about getting caught?' I asked. 'No, man, them Japanese don't know anything about drugs, they just think I've got a cold.'

In Fuji you stay right next to the festival in the old Naeba Ski hotel, which isn't great, so we stayed up all night as a protest, ending up in a party room with Hothouse Flowers (where I was giving Liam daggers because in 1992 he'd stolen a girlfriend off me in Manchester – luckily, I couldn't speak).

We gave up at dawn and sloped off to our rooms. The road crew carried on, off their nuts, each and every one of them, and when Andy Robinson looked out of the window and saw a load of people raving in a field, hands in the air, they decided they needed a bit more action. Later Coatesy, my bass roadie, told me what happened: they'd set off in search of this rave, absolutely off their faces, but urging each other on like intrepid explorers. After an hour's walk, they finally got to the field – only to discover it was a load of Japanese doing early morning Tai Chi. They had to backtrack like drugged-up Keystone Kops, turn round and come straight back.

We got up later that day and I felt awful. I thought it was just a hangover but it turned out I'd contracted a virus that Western men are susceptible to in rural Japan (the same one Slim caught in 1985). Because I was so hungover my immune system was low, so I was the perfect host. I travelled with this flu-like virus to San Francisco (and thank God Becky was there to look after me, otherwise I think I would have died, for sure). As it was, I lost two stone in four days, just sweating it out. I couldn't get warm, that was the thing. Added to that, I was scared I wasn't going to be able to play.

After checking into the hotel I would go straight to bed, where I would be sweating that much the mattress was soaked, Bex would turn it over for me and when that soaked through she'd have to phone down for another one. The doctor wouldn't give me anything for it. 'There is nothing,' they said.

I'd been really looking forward to our dates with Moby and Outkast, both of whom I loved; on top of which, I've never had to pull a gig in my life.

Who should come to the rescue? Billy Corgan. Being a man with a Jedi-like pharmaceutical knowledge, he knew of a flu medicine containing an upper that helps you pull through, Theraflu. Sure enough, he had some of this stuff; it did the trick and I played the gig. I was a mess in the dressing room beforehand though. I couldn't stand up, and Tom Atencio took to grabbing me by the shirt and slapping me, trying to bring me round. Post-Theraflu I was running round like a nutter, only to collapse again in a heap straight after playing the gig.

I repaid Billy in true Peter Hook style (2001 version): by getting steaming drunk and taking the piss out of him the following night. We were out having a Chinese and I was at my big-mouthed drunken obnoxious best, so bad that even Sarge gave up on me that night. Everyone disowned me, in fact, and I spent the next two days making grovelling apologies for my behaviour and crying for my mum – one of my first alcoholic breakdowns, that was, the first of many.

The problem was that I was becoming a very gobby, physical drunk. I used to do a lot of exercise and weights so I could be a right handful when I was pissed. I was the one who used to start all the food fights.

Our comeback in 2000 was accompanied by a lot of invitations to awards ceremonies. Before, I could literally count the number I had been to on one hand (cue: 'in our day we had to make our own entertainment'-like comments), but now there seemed to be one every week – *NME*, *Q* Awards, the Brits, *FHM*, *Razzle*, you name it – and if you were at an awards ceremony and a bread roll bounced off your head, you could bet your bottom dollar it was me who threw it. Bono, Bruce Springsteen, Iggy Pop, Cher – I've aimed bread rolls at them all.

Years later when I got sober I was at another awards do and this young lad comes up and introduces himself, saying, 'You've been sober a while now, haven't you?'

I said, 'Yeah, about six or eight months or something.'

He went, 'Well done, but we don't half miss your food fights. I was sat next to Bono once when a bread roll hit him on the back of the head and when he turned round you gave him the Vs. I pissed myself. We miss moments like that.'

Ah well.

Anyway, on we went with the tour, and by the time we'd reached Seattle a dark cloud had descended. We were five gigs into a tour of more than thirty dates and Barney had had enough already. He was in the worst mood you could possibly imagine, not helped by the fact that Moby and, in particular, Outkast were going down a storm, while we were being met with young indifference and treated like dinosaurs. At Seattle one kid stood giving me the middle finger throughout our entire set. Meantime, on stage, Barney had a paddy at Roger Lyons, who was doing his autocue and operating the sequencers, and fired him during the gig – actually *during* the gig, over the microphone. I can't remember what the problem was, but Barney said something well snarky, fired him, and then Roger came backstage and there was all kinds of screaming and shouting.

At the next gig Barney got so off his rocker that he didn't even remember we'd all gone back on to play 'New Dawn Fades' with Moby – including Gillian and her sister.

By now I had the family on tour with me: Becky, Jessica, Jack and Heather. I was hardly what you'd call clean and sober but I was trying to keep a bit of a lid on it. We moved on to Cologne, Germany, where we supported Robbie Williams on one date of his 'Weddings, Barmitzvahs and Stadiums Tour'. (We even got to see Robbie's famous mobile laundry into the bargain, so it wasn't all bad.)

We shared the same agent. Robbie needed something cool and we needed the exposure. I was still suffering from the virus at this point and the crowd showed absolutely no sympathy. Fuck me, they hated us, all 70,000 of them. Barney, in his infinite wisdom, decided to start slagging them off, introducing 'Blue Monday' by saying, 'Here you are, here's a good marching song, 'cos I heard you Germans like to march.' Cue 70,000 people booing from start to finish.

We weren't victimised though – JJ72, the other support, were treated exactly the same. This had not worked and Barney was waiting for Ian Huffan from X-Ray Agency backstage, and as soon as he appeared called him every name under the sun. Strange, as he had been the first to agree when we were told the fee for the show, £75,000 plus expenses.

Robbie came up to me afterwards, slapped me on the back and said, 'Well done for getting through that.'

Barney's mood stayed black. He'd taken again to complaining that my bass was too loud. We had talked about it, me saying, 'Just let me know and I'll turn it down. You don't have to shout it over the mic.'

By the time of Barrowlands he'd forgotten and during 'Temptation' starting shouting, 'Gerry, the bass is too loud, turn the bass down.'

This was something he was *always* doing – and probably still is now – ruining songs by yelling out instructions. If he wasn't whistling, yelping or whooping then he was giving some poor technician a public dressing-down over the microphone. Didn't matter what the song was – he seemed to delight in spoiling 'Atmosphere' by whooping over the top of it. I mean, who the fuck *whoops* during a song like 'Atmosphere'? My mate said to me once, 'Why does he scream, "COME ON!" during "Love Will Tear Us Apart"? It's the only song that doesn't need it.' A backhanded compliment, Stefan, but noted. I know for a fact that no one has ever asked Barney why he does something as crass as that. Let's hope he reads this book, eh?

Anyway, the thing was, by addressing Gerry, who as you'll recall was our foldback guy, Barney was complaining about the sound mix on stage. In other words, only the sound *he* could hear, as we each had our own foldback. He felt my bass was too loud for him, and fair enough wanted it turned down. But what normal people do, if you want a change in your sound mix, is you signal to the foldback guy. You get his attention, you indicate a player and you point up or down to get the level changed. By doing it over the mic, Barney was doing it in such a way that you, the audience, could hear him – and there was no need to. He knew it didn't affect the sound mix for the venue.

Basically, it's a twat's trick. It's just for effect. Maybe it makes him feel better, maybe he wants you all to suffer like him and get some hate going for the big bad loud bass player. Maybe he thought it made him look like the big chief, not caring that it pisses off everybody in the process: the crew who think he's being a condescending prick, and the audience who'd rather hear him sing than yell instructions at technicians.

I went over to him. Perhaps I should have done his trick and remonstrated with him publicly over the mic. But no, I went over to him. 'Listen, if you've got a problem with the volume, signal to Gerry or tell me, don't fucking mouth off over the mic, yeah?' And then I started seething about it, storming off at the end of the gig. Then I went and did what every good rock'n'roller does and smashed up the dressing room.

Phil Cunningham arrived, and what do you know? He joined in, unveiling an appetite for destruction that was to rear its ugly head many times later on. If I recall, the whole entourage joined in smashing up the dressing room. Even Barney.

Oasis were on the next night. When they complained about the state of the dressing room they were told that Peter Hook had smashed it up. The lads were most impressed.

So I suppose you could say that relations between Barney and me began to deteriorate once again. Like I say, for much of the tour I'd had my family with me, so I'd kept the drinking and drugging to a minimum, but whether they weren't there at Brixton or I got pissed anyway, I can't remember. The fact was I was pissed and on the first night I stayed on stage long after the band had left, playing the intro to 'Dreams Never End' over and over again.

Of course, the crowd went bananas, thinking my intro heralded the return of the band and an encore of 'Dreams Never End', but after about six or seven minutes of this, I finished and then departed, leaving a bewildered audience behind me, me thinking I'd made a proper protest.

Then, on the second night, we were playing 'Blue Monday', the band walked off and I continued playing the outro. Only this time, as Barney walked past my amp, he unplugged me, the miserable bastard – funny though.

One of the good things about being back in New Order meant you got a lot of time off. Which, I have to say, at this point I was enjoying very much. I was reaping the only benefit of Barney's mantra of 'only doing one thing at once'.

At the end of the year we were offered the 'Big Day Out' or, as most groups called it, the 'Big Day Off' because of the amount of downtime on this particular tour, looked after by our old friends Ken West and Vivien Lees.

Big Day Out had become a winning formula and was the biggest of all the Australian festivals. Only problem was, we had an unwilling participant. Now I know what you're thinking – only Barney could turn down a great gig like that. But you're wrong … on this particular occasion it was Steve, saying, 'I don't want to go away for three weeks.' Me and Barney talked about it, what a great opportunity it was etc. Then Barney pipes up, 'I know, why don't we ask the drummer who did Electronic to do it, and me and you will go.'

Blow me down. It really was getting like dog eat dog around here. He'd be getting rid of me next. The management cleared it and negotiations were begun with said drummer, who was available. Then suddenly Steve changed his mind, turned out he could stand three weeks away after all.

The saga continued.

TIMELINE SIXTEEN
APRIL–DECEMBER 2001

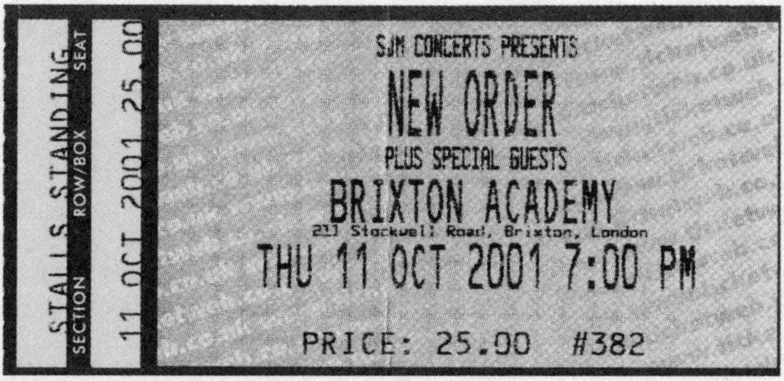

April 2001

Joy Division: *Les Bains Douches 18 December 1979*
(FACD 2.61 / NMC)

Track list:	
'Disorder'	3.21
'Love Will Tear Us Apart'	3.17
'Insight'	3.25
'Shadowplay'	3.46
'Transmission'	3.19
'Day of the Lords'	4.39
'Twenty Four Hours'	4.12

'These Days'	3.42
'A Means to an End'	4.17
'Passover'	2.18
'New Dawn Fades'	4.40
'Atrocity Exhibition'	6.56
'Digital'	3.39
'Dead Souls'	4.46
'Autosuggestion'	4.13
'Atmosphere'	4.47

1–9 recorded live at Les Bains Douches, Paris, 18 December 1979, 10–12 recorded live at Amsterdam, 11 January 1980, 13–16 recorded live at Eindhoven, 18 January 1980.

Designed by Howard Wakefield and Paul Hetherington.
Art direction by Peter Saville.

April 2001

New Order: *3:16* video
(London Records)
Featuring performances from New York on 18 November 1981, Reading Festival on 30 August 1998.

New York 18 November 1981 track list:
'I.C.B.'
'Dreams Never End'
'Everything's Gone Green'
'Truth'
'Senses'
'Procession'
'Ceremony'
'Denial'
'Temptation'

Reading Festival 30 August 1998 track list:
'Regret'
'Touched by the Hand of God'

'Isolation'
'Atmosphere'
'Heart and Soul'
'Paradise'
'Bizarre Love Triangle'
'True Faith'
'Temptation'
'Blue Monday'
'World in Motion'

'Temptation' (filmed for the 2002 Commonwealth Games / Manchester bid) 'and in conversation' documentary filmed on 5 September 2000 with footage from the Ampersand Club, Manchester, 27 March 2000. Interview filmed at Ampersand Club by Michael Shamberg and Jamie Matson.

Produced by New Order.
Designed by Peter Saville Associates.

So called, *3:16*, because of the three Joy Division tracks and the sixteen New Order.

2 July 2001

New Order: 'Crystal'
(East West Japan)

Track list:

'Crystal'	4:21
'True Faith' (recorded live at Reading Festival 30 August 1998)	5:40
'Temptation' (recorded live at Reading Festival 30 August 1998)	7:27
'Atmosphere' (recorded live at Reading Festival 30 August 1998)	4:17
'Isolation' (recorded live at Reading Festival 30 August 1998)	3:01

Art Direction: Peter Saville
Design: Peter Saville Studio
Unique Japan release CDS to promote Fuji Rock festival.

18 July 2001

New Order play the Olympia, Liverpool, supported by Hanky Panky and Elbow.

'It was lovely to see Mike Johnson here. He'd moved and opened a studio in Liverpool. We ended up completely trashed afterwards in the Marriott hotel in a room with Bobby Gillespie and an American designer of Xboxes who I'd picked up in the bar. The most hilarious thing I've ever seen was Bobby trying to talk to this geezer in a very drunken broad Scottish accent. The guy didn't understand a word and Bobby ended up chasing him out of the room and down the corridor. Shame. I'd been hoping for a free Xbox.'

28 July 2001

New Order play Fuji Rock Festival, Japan.

'When we arrived we were mobbed and it was great to be back. On the bus from the airport to Tokyo everyone was buzzing with tiredness and excitement, an almost hysterical atmosphere. Then after a while someone went, "Where's Barney?" We then noticed he wasn't aboard. Shit. We drove back to the airport and there he was sat on a bench outside, face like thunder. The door opened and he got on and sat down without a word. For the whole of the two-hour trip to Tokyo no one spoke. Turned out he'd wandered off for a piss, not told anyone, and we'd left without him.

'Neil Young was on the same bill on the bigger stage. He started playing before us in front of a huge audience, but as soon as we went on they all deserted him and came running down to us. It was a wonderful moment to see, all these people fucking bombing down the hill to see us. It was, "Wow, we're back. Sorry, Neil." We had actually seen him on the bullet train on the way and Barney tried to get me to say hello, but I was too starstruck. He is one of my all-time musical heroes, and it's a bubble I do not want to burst.'

31 July 2001

New Order play Shoreline Amphitheatre, Mountain View, San Francisco, with Moby and Outkast.

'Billy Corgan had got me through my virus, and on "Your Silent Face" where I don't come in for about two minutes I started wobbling, so I thought, *I'll just have a walk off stage and have a sit down for a minute*. That was when I came into my "walking about in the audience" phase. Barney didn't notice. He never noticed anything. You could have died onstage and he wouldn't have noticed – I just walked back onstage for when the bass came in. I was getting to be a bit of a nomad.'

2 August 2001

New Order play Thunderbird Stadium, Vancouver, with Moby and Outkast.

3 August 2001

New Order play Gorge Amphitheatre, Gorge, Seattle, with Moby and Outkast.

'This was quite a trip and only possible by small private plane. Barney was so late we went without him and he came much later, saying, "It's too early to go to a gig."

'We arrived at this tiny airport in the middle of nowhere but it still had a customs post and we were taken in to meet this grizzled old customs guy in his office. On the wall he had a noticeboard full of pictures of Mexicans in some amazing hiding places in cars and vans, next to piles of drugs, obviously some of his many captures, but at the bottom in the corner was a picture of him with Mother Teresa. Seeing this, Coatesy pipes up with, "Blooming hell, how much drugs was she carrying?" resulting in a resounding silence in the room, broken only by the sound of this customs guy unclipping his gun and putting his hand on the handle. "Sorry," gulped Coatesy, to this obviously very religious man. "Get the hell out of my office," he growled in response.

'A beautiful location for this gig, but we were again blown off stage by Outkast. Barney managed to upset Roger Lyons before saying to Andy Robinson, "Why didn't we get here earlier? This place is beautiful."'

5 August 2001

New Order play Glen Helen Blockbuster Pavilion, Devore, Los Angeles, with Moby and Outkast.

'Before this gig we were invited to the Adidas store in LA. I was getting grief off Becky, who wanted me to come back to the hotel, but the Adidas PR woman kept grabbing me and asking me to choose something from their wonderful new range. In a hurry, and very exasperated, I said, "Listen, love, why don't you just get me the most expensive thing in the shop?" thinking, *That will get rid of her!* But thirty seconds later she appeared again saying, "Here, Mr Hook, it's a limited-edition Adidas watch, one of only fifty made, $2000!" I just grabbed it off her like the spoilt, obnoxious rock star I was and legged it.'

11 August 2001

New Order play Müngersdorfer Stadium, Cologne, supporting Robbie Williams.

13 August 2001

New Order: 'Crystal'
(London Records)

Twelve-inch track list (I):
'Crystal' (bedrock remix) 12.52
'Crystal' (bedrock dub) 10.33
Additional production and remix: John Digweed and Nick Muir.

Twelve-inch track list (II):
'Crystal' (Lee Coombs remix) 8.44
'Crystal' (Lee Coombs dub) 7.05
Remixed by Lee Combs.

Twelve-inch track list (III):
'Crystal' (Creamer K intro remix) 3.21
'Crystal' (Creamer K main remix) 11.24
Remixed by John Creamer and Stephane K.

Run-out groove one: *Don't shut the stable door …*
Run-out groove two: … *after the horse has bolted!*

CDS track list:
'Crystal' (Mark Stent Remix) 4.19
'Behind Closed Doors' 5.24
'Crystal' (Digweed & Muir bedrock mix edit) 10.06

Recorded at Real World Studios, Box, Bath, and Monnow Valley Studios, Monmouth, Wales.
Written by New Order.
Produced by Steve Osborne for 140DB.
Engineered by Bruno Ellingham and Andrew Robinson.
Programmed by Pete Davis.
Mixed by Mark 'Spike' Stent.
Mix engineer and protools: Jan 'Stan' Kybert, assisted by Matt Fields.
Backing vocals by Dawn Zee.
Cover art direction by Peter Saville.
Designed by Howard Wakefield and Sam Roberts.
Entered UK chart on 25 August 2001, remaining in the charts for 4 weeks, its peak position was number 8.

'In the video the fake band were called the Killers, which a young Brandon Flowers from Las Vegas thought very appropriate for his new group. I must admit I didn't know that Barney had already released a version of the song with Corvin Dalek via Mark Reeder on a German label called Mastermind for Success. I was very surprised. I had no idea. We went to the video shoot

and I suggested to Alan Parkes from London Records, "What if we go on and pull their instruments off them? Wouldn't that be a better ending?"

'"No," he said.'

27 August 2001

New Order: *Get Ready*
(London Records)

Track list:

'Crystal'	6.52
'60 Miles an Hour'	4.34
'Turn My Way'	5.04
'Vicious Streak'	5.39
'Primitive Notion'	5.42
'Slow Jam'	4.51
'Rock the Shack'	4.11
'Someone Like You'	5.41
'Close Range'	4.12
'Run Wild'	3.55

Run-out groove one: *I have a feeling of . . .*
Run-out groove two: . . . *Deja Deja Deja vu!*

Recorded in Real World Studios, Box, Bath.
Produced by Steve Osborne except 'Rock the Shack' produced by New Order.
Mixed by Steve Osborne, Mark 'Spike' Stent and Flood.
Special guest vocals Billy Corgan 'Turn my Way'.
Special guest vocals Bobby Gillespie and guitar Andrew Innes 'Rock the Shack'.
Cover art direction by Peter Saville.
Photography by Juergen Teller.
Designed by Howard Wakefield and Sam Roberts.
Entered UK chart on 8 September 2001, remaining in the charts for 4 weeks, its peak position was number 6.

'We dedicated the album to Rob, it seemed only fitting. It had been his idea to get back together, and it was strange doing an album without him. Peter Saville was fascinated that the model he'd picked for the cover was actually a film-maker herself, and a very talented one at that, Nicolette (Coco) Krebitz. We were very careful with the review copies for the album, and each one was watermarked with an audio serial number by Warners. They had a computer program that analysed the audio sample and could tell you who had been sent that particular piece of music. The power of the internet and illegal downloading was becoming a huge problem and this was thought to be an ideal deterrent. It wasn't. Our record was uploaded on the internet a long time before the release date, losing us unknown amounts of sales. Warners tracked it and found it was a *Rolling Stone* journalist's listening copy. They even had his name. Barney was livid, wanting to prosecute the guy immediately, but on reflection Warners thought better of it. I guess they needed *Rolling Stone*. Our sales on *Get Ready* would be about 300,000 worldwide. *Republic* sold three million. Warners reckoned that drop was entirely due to illegal file-sharing.'

4–5 October 2001

New Order play Apollo Theatre, Manchester.

7–8 October 2001

New Order play Barrowlands, Glasgow.

10–12 October 2001

New Order play Brixton Academy, London.

11 October 2001

The *Muzik* magazine Dance Award for outstanding contribution this year was New Order, presented to Peter Hook and Bernard Sumner at the Arches in London.

19 October 2001

New Order appear on *The Jools Holland Show.*

Track list:
'Crystal'
'60 Miles an Hour'
'Love Will Tear Us Apart'

> **'A very spirited performance, this one, very confident, and one of our best TV appearances in my estimation. Bizarrely, Ryan Adams was on the show and just as we were about to start a number shouted, "I lost my virginity listening to Peter Hook's Revenge album." Well, Ryan, I'm glad it helped.**
>
> **'This was one of our best TV sessions. We sounded absolutely mega that night.'**

11 November 2001

New Order play Olympia, Paris, supported by Experience and the Music.

12 November 2001

New Order play Olympia, Paris, supported by Bosco and Benjamin Biolay.

15 November 2001

New Order play Columbiahalle, Berlin.

16 November 2001

New Order play Palladium, Cologne.

> **'I had "Salford Rules" sprayed on my cab at this one. Bernard offered roadie Phil Murphy fifty pounds to spray "Alderley Edge Rules" on my cab but he declined.'**

18 November 2001

New Order play Cirkus, Stockholm, Sweden.

19 November 2001

New Order: '60 Miles an Hour'
(London Records)

CD track list:

'60 Miles an Hour' (radio edit)	3.47
'Sabotage'	4.48
'Someone Like You' (Funk D'Void remix)	9.55

Recorded in Real World Studios, Box, Bath.
Produced by Steve Osborne.
Designed by Peter Saville Associates.
Entered UK chart on 1 December 2001, remaining in the charts for 2 weeks, its peak position was number 29.

24 December 2001

New Order: 'Someone Like You'
(London Records)

12" (I) track list:

'Someone Like You' (Futureshock vocal remix)	8.04
'Someone Like You' (Gabriel & Dresden 911 vox mix)	11.13
'Someone Like You' (Futureshock stripdown mix)	9.55
'Someone Like You' (Gabriel & Dresden voco-tech dub)	11.10

Run-out groove one: *Recorded 9/11/01 and dedicated ...*
Run-out groove two: *... to the men, women and children ...*

Twelve-inch (II) track list:

'Someone Like You' (James Holden heavy dub)	9.55
'Someone Like You' (Gabriel & Dresden voco-tech dub)	11.10

Run-out groove one: ... *who senselessly ...*
Run-out groove two: ... *lost their lives that day*

Written by New Order.
Produced and mixed by Steve Osborne for 140DB.
Engineered by Bruno Ellingham and Andrew Robinson.
Programmed by Pete Davis.
Mix engineer and protools: Adrian Bushby.
Cover art direction by Peter Saville.
Designed by Howard Wakefield and Sam Roberts.

'Grandmaster Flash being marched out by a copper with a machine gun'

At the airport leaving for Australia all our problems seemed to be forgotten. It looked like we were going to have a great time on this tour right from the moment we arrived.

Sadly, before long, things got a bit lairy. Phil Cunningham had settled in and started to show the rock'n'roll side of his character again, getting absolutely ratted, partaking in 'high octane furniture arranging' and playing up on his girlfriend who had joined us for this tour. Me and him took to smashing things up together for a while, and had a sort of 'Clouseau and Cato' thing going on from the *Pink Panther* films, where we'd be attacking one another, trying to take each other by surprise.

At the time it was great to have a new playmate. That aside, most of that particular tour's wildness can be laid at the feet of one of our crew members, who because he was having a bit of trouble at home was on a mission to get as wrecked as possible every single night. And he did. From the moment we arrived in Auckland he was necking it like it was on special offer, and me and Phil were happy to keep him company. In Sydney he took great delight in telling us he'd gobbled five different types of ecstasy in one night. We were staying in the Ritz-Carlton in Sydney, the hotel where Michael Hutchence had killed himself, and since Andy Liddle was in the actual room, number 524, we had to honour the occasion by throwing a massive party. Arriving a little later, Phil Cunningham walked straight in and chucked a chair out of the window into the courtyard below. It wasn't late and shouldn't have been that big a problem apart from the stuff we had laid out on nearly every surface in the room. Phil was very happy about it and only stopped when I threatened to throw him over the balcony – asking nicely having failed to work.

The next morning I came across our resident ecstasy-gobbler as he arrived back at the hotel in a taxi. He was accompanied by a little old man – or at least I thought it was a little old man until I looked closer and realised it was actually my guitar roadie, Coatesy, all twisted up with a massive comedown. As soon as he saw me he legged it, running dangerously across a busy road to get away from the boss, me, who wasn't bothered at all.

Bear in mind this was at the beginning of the tour. Things were about to get worse.

In Melbourne we were asked to do a signing session at a local record shop, so we trooped along to that. I hadn't seen much of Barney (I was with Phil and the crew most of the time), but I'd heard he'd been in a terrible mood all day, and was as miserable as sin. When we arrived there were hundreds of fans queuing up to get their stuff signed. We sat in a row on a raised stage, with Mr Happy at the end. At first we were having a bit of a natter and a laugh with the fans, but misery-guts soon became impatient. 'Come on, come on,' he began saying, 'move it, move it,' changing quickly to, 'Hand it over, let me sign. Come on, time's money, time's money.'

Jesus. It was so embarrassing. I have no idea why he agreed in the first place or just didn't walk off. There was no need for this very public show. I knew very well that nobody could sour a happy atmosphere more quickly and effectively than Barney, he was an expert at it, and our jolly little meet-and-greet was instantly transformed into a nervy production line, with the man at the end snapping at anyone who dared to so much as ask when the next album was out.

'Time's money, time's money,' he'd repeat, like he'd only just discovered the phrase. And if someone dawdled, 'Next!'

I mean, you've got to give it to him. He was a one-off. We used to go to group meetings at his house and sit there dumbfounded as he appeared from the kitchen with a cup of tea and chicken leg for himself, offering his guests nothing. *This man just does not give a fuck*, I thought. I alternated between being proud of his attitude and being appalled by it.

One of his big complaints on that tour was that he didn't like starting the gig in daylight. It is tough going on in daylight, I will admit, but let's face it, it's not the end of the world, and it was dark when we finished. I can't really see what difference it made, since as soon as he got his in-ear monitors in he went to another world, seemingly shut off from the whole experience anyway. But that was his complaint – his new complaint, I should say, since you just added them to a long list.

In-ear monitors:

(IEMs) are devices used by musicians to hear a personal (i.e. individual) mix of vocals and stage instrumentation mainly for live performance. Custom-fitted to an individual's ears to provide comfort and a high level of noise reduction in ambient sound. They sometimes can give an isolating or distant feeling to the wearer, a sense of being cut off from your surroundings.

The gigs were OK – not great, because the Prodigy were blowing us off stage every night. They had tons of hits, were a more current band and the audience were going mad for them. They had one roadie who was the dirtiest dog you can possibly imagine, an absolute hound. One night he managed to talk this couple into bed for a threesome but the woman put her back out, so they had to call an ambulance and cart her off on a stretcher. Us lot in reception were cheering as she was carried out with her arse in the air, screaming in agony, husband trailing sheepishly behind her.

On this particular tour, I had started on my own with Phil as my escort, then after a few dates I'd been joined by Becky and Jess. So I had been Mr Hyde for the first part and then Dr Jekyll in the middle, then back to Mr Hyde for the end. Now, I can be a bit of a git if my rest is interrupted. 'That's a bit hypocritical, Hooky' you might say, and maybe you'd be right, but if there's one thing all of us hate it's having our sleep disturbed, and I am also very conscious of it happening to other people around me. Paranoid, you might say. So every time we partied in my room, or house for that matter, I was always turning the music down and shushing everyone. Do unto others etc.

Years back, in Switzerland, the crew were partying with Grandmaster Flash. I phoned the room and said, 'Listen, lads, I'm really tired, I need to get some sleep, can you turn it down?'

They went, 'Fuck off, you miserable twat. Hey, it's Hooky, he wants us to turn it down. Turn it up,' and all that.

'Listen, if you don't turn it down, I'm going to call hotel security.'

They went, 'Fuck off, you knob.'

Security couldn't do anything. So I called the police. The Swiss police came in and busted the whole party and kicked them all out – including Grandmaster Flash.

Rob was like, 'I've never been so embarrassed. Grandmaster Flash being marched out by a copper with a machine gun, all because of you, you twat.'

Another time in Canada, same thing. Politely, I tried to get our lot to turn down the noise but they refused, so I said, 'Right, I'll call the Mounties!'

'Fucking call 'em!' they replied. So I did. Called the Mounties and told them there was a riot going on in a room or whatever. Not long after the cops came steaming in mob-handed, and our lot had to chuck all their drugs down the toilet. From then on they were very careful.

So anyway, back in Australia, and Jake, one of our entourage, was having this mad party in Melbourne. Now the girls were here, I was even less keen on being kept awake. That night I stormed up there and threw everybody out of the room; it was getting out of hand, and I'm sure I would have had to call the police the following night, except that night, Jake completely lost it.

By now he'd been up for three nights straight doing all kinds of different things. Tottering around the hotel foyer after the gig his phone rang and he answered, said a few daft comments and instead of hanging up he handed it to the nearest person and headed straight for the toilet. It was his wife, and the phone was passed around the room, juggled like it was a hot potato, with her screeching, 'Where is that twat? Where's he gone?' until it reached me and I put it to my ear – just in time to hear her say, 'Tell him I'm divorcing him.'

That was it, end of conversation, and perfectly understandable, because when you're off your nut in Australia and your wife's at home dealing with the kids, the bills etc., the least you can do is take her call. Or else …

I remember when phones were just introduced on aeroplanes and we were flying home from America, 1993 I reckon, Jonny said to me, 'I'm going to phone the missus. She'll love it.'

The rest of us weren't so sure. He dialled, it took him ages and then there was no answer at home, and on phoning his mother to check everything was all right he was duly informed, 'What's going on, our Jonny? Your clothes are all over my front lawn in black bin liners.' He'd been bin-bagged and, worse still, she'd run off with one of his mates, that old one. Then he got so pissed, upset and disruptive they had to cable-tie him to his seat on the plane and the last we saw of him was when two security guards escorted him from his seat to his connecting flight to Leeds Bradford airport. Bizarrely, he had on his head a deely bopper complete with flashing heart lights. Nowadays they would have thrown away the key.

On the subject of phoning home, Bruce Mitchell of Durutti Column had a very staunch opinion on this very delicate of matters. 'Peter,' he'd say, 'phoning home is very difficult. What I do is, do it religiously once every two weeks, whether she likes it or not.'

However much they love you, what wonderful woman, stuck at home with the shitty kids and/or shitty weather, wants to hear what a great time you're having in some wonderful foreign clime with your mates, all expenses paid? Let that be a warning.

Back to Melbourne. 'Right,' I said to Sarge, 'we need to break the news his wife wants a divorce.'

But Jake didn't come back from the toilet. After a while we started to worry and went in. From a cubicle we could hear the sounds of obvious sexual pleasure, someone going, 'Oh yeah, baby, yeah, baby,' all this lot. Except we were positive there was nobody else in with him. When he failed to respond yet again, Sarge kicked the door in, and there he was, in the throes of ecstasy – all on his own. The poor sod was so off his head he seemed to be hallucinating getting a blow job in the toilet cubicle. The news from his wife didn't help at all.

After that, he had a complete screaming nervous breakdown. We had to put him to bed, where he wept like a child. I'd never seen anyone lose it quite that badly, apart from me. Fair play, though, he gave up everything because of it. Only trouble was, with him teetotal there was nobody to get drugs for us, so were cursing him for being a selfish bastard the rest of the tour. He was a great guy, sober and pissed. I can highly recommend having him around.

On we went to Paris. The camaraderie we had enjoyed on making *Get Ready* seemed to have very much evaporated. At Finsbury Park I was as pissed as a fart by the time John Simm came on for the encore. We were in the eye of the storm by then: the film *24 Hour Party People* in which John had played Barney was due to come out that month and Factory Records were all over the media again.

Michael Winterbottom and his production partner Andrew Eaton were big Factory Records fans and desperate to tell the story of the label and its groups and achievements. It began with the scriptwriter Frank Cottrell Boyce taking me out to lunch and pumping me for all the anecdotes he could get, aided by numerous bottles of wine. It was a pleasure. Then he did the same to a few other Factory survivors and put all the anecdotes together to produce the wonderful comedic script, a real light-hearted and very funny look at our history. I loved it. They even did something Factory couldn't give us . . . a Haçienda closing party.

Me and Tony Wilson had been on television in early 2002, starting the digger that demolished the real Haçienda, and then three weeks later we got a phone call saying that it was being rebuilt, typical. The film company, in a fit of post-Factory irony, had decided to rebuild it for a scene where everyone got together, the living and the dead. Steve Coogan was to play Tony Wilson, an event I dubbed 'the second biggest twat in Manchester playing the first' and was delighted to find that Coogan himself began using the quote. In another twist of fate Ralf Little was to play me, Ralf of course having just found fame working with Caroline on *The Royle Family*. I did wonder what insights to my character he might have gained, but on seeing the film realised he'd learned, or been told, precious little. I was drafted in for a scene, the one where the Mondays spiked the pigeons on the roof. I was supposed to drive a car down Piccadilly Approach in Manchester and do an emergency stop as a pigeon hit the windscreen. I was summoned to a huge costume department in a mill near the Manchester Evening News Arena, put in costume and dragged about for hours, then told they couldn't get insurance for me and sent home, bastards.

Now I thought Michael Winterbottom missed a trick in the scene on the rooftop where Coogan as Tony is looking to the heavens and Coogan as God appears. Wouldn't that have been perfect if it was Tony playing God?

Come to think of it, Tony was always playing God, maybe God should have played Tony.

When Tony did his book I asked him why he based it on the film.

'Darling, Peter,' he said, 'you must remember fiction is more powerful than fact.'

'Tony,' I said, 'in this case you're absolutely wrong.'

It was a very good film and surprised me with its huge international popularity. I've lost count how many times I get in a taxi in some exotic place to be asked where I come from and be regaled with the only two things that taxi drivers know about Manchester, *24 Hour Party People* and United (sadly these days it's three, with our noisy neighbours, City, getting many a mention).

There was an advance screening in London and we were all mortified by the Ian Curtis scenes. The first time any of us had been confronted by what happened to our erstwhile lead singer on the big screen, and we were shocked.

I thought Michael Winterbottom did a great job. In a bizarre turn my mate, a big dealer in Heaton Norris, ended up working on the film and would regale me with tales of the excessive consumption while it was being made. Art imitating life, there.

It has always seemed to me that most actors are desperate to be musicians, so maybe it was that so-called 'research' they always claim they have to do. As the film was wrapping Andrew Eaton proposed that the last night of the 'fake' Haçienda should be a combination of real people, actors and extras, liaising with us on a 'special invite list' of people we considered important to the club's history. These invites soon became like Willy Wonka's golden tickets. The location was a huge old warehouse in Ancoats, and on the evening I was delighted to see the Salford Lot and Moss Side had turned out for old times' sake and were storming the gates. The police had to be called to restore order. Andrew Eaton was shocked, saying to me, 'How on earth did you put up with this?'

'Mate, you've only got one night. We had ten feckin' years,' said I.

As I entered the warehouse you could only see the back of the set and I wasn't too impressed, but on opening the door, as you see in the film, it was breathtaking. I freaked out straight away. Paul Mason, my friend and our former club manager, grabbed me, saying, 'Come and see the cocktail bar, it's amazing!'

'Oh my God, they've even done the cocktail bar downstairs?' I garbled, only to burst through the doors and be back in the empty warehouse, little devil.

Back inside, and even Alan Erasmus had made an appearance. I wandered round, open-mouthed, bumping into people like Barney doing exactly the same thing. I said to him, 'All this place needs is Rob Gretton?' He pointed: 'Look,' and there was Rob, ably played by Paddy Considine, then joined by Martin Hannett and then, fuck me, Ian Curtis. It was like a surreal dream.

I legged it to my favourite spot, the corner of the main bar by the stairs, where I'd spent so many great hours, to find bar manager Leroy and Ange Matthews already there in tears. I joined in helplessly. Twinny came running up and shoved a little fella in my mouth; 'For old times' sake,' he laughed, charging back into the dancing crowd. It was a great night and I only ruined it a few hours later, in the lighting booth, by having a big fat line and going immediately paranoid and freaking out, having to leave, going to the bar in the Malmaison hotel where everyone else soon joined me. It was simply too weird for most of us and we commiserated by sitting there, getting completely wasted.

The next day I got a phone call from the production manager asking me if I wanted to buy the set for £250,000. I said no, I didn't have anywhere near that much money to buy a film set. 'Right,' he said, 'we'll sell it to Mantos then.'

Turns out Carol Ainscow and Peter Dalton had put in a bid, only to be told we would be offered it first.

I was aghast. I couldn't bear the thought of them two finally getting their hands on the Haçienda, even in kit form. As it turned out I had nothing to worry about because a couple of garbled messages to the crew in the warehouse resulted in it being completely destroyed. They'd heard 'smash' instead of 'save'.

Karma? Maybe there is a God.

Needless to say, New Order were going to capitalise on our increased profile by playing just two more shows and then disappearing into a studio for the next three years. That's the New Order way, kids.

We finished the tour with a gig at Old Trafford cricket ground which, on the one hand, was great because all our family and friends were there, and for once it wasn't a guest-list bunfight, but on the other was tinged with sadness because it meant the end of the gigs.

Since the split at Reading Festival in 1993, we had played a grand total of forty gigs in over nine years and, instead of carrying on touring and continuing to recoup on what had been a very expensive record, it was decided to have a few months off and then reconvene to make what would turn out to be an even more expensive record.

Little did I know it then, but that's what I'd be doing for the next three years. I'd be making *Waiting for the Sirens' Call*, slowly running out of money and turning into a full-blown drink and drug addict. As you can imagine, readers, things start to get a bit grim from here on in. Bear with me.

'The idea was that I'd hide in the bushes'

Picture the scene: me with my spaniel, Mia, hiding in the bushes in the park (like an old perv) opposite Brasingamens in Alderley Edge.

Brasingamens was a bar and restaurant that later changed its name to Panacea and then got burned down in a door-security dispute, about two years ago. But that day, in 2002, it was the scene of a New Order meeting. The group were going to talk about reconvening to write a new album. However, Barney and I had decided that if Gillian was involved we were going to leave the band.

We informed Rebecca and Andy and the blank looks on their faces told us all we needed to know: that they were completely out of their depth. As I lived nearer, the idea was that I'd hide in the bushes, wait to see if Steve turned up with Gillian and then either warn Barney off or give him the all-clear.

In the event, Steve turned up alone, we all went into the meeting and decided to start writing again.

You never learn, do you?

We decamped to the farmhouse and started getting ideas together. Musically, we reverted back to how we did it for Joy Division, with me, Steve and Barney jamming and refining ideas. After a couple of months we got some good ones together, about seven, and then Barney unilaterally decided he was going home to write lyrics and vocal melodies. That meant me and Steve were surplus to requirements. This wasn't too bad and it certainly got all your DIY done, but it didn't bode well for how long the project was going to take.

Months later, Steve and I were still twiddling our thumbs so I suggested bringing in Phil to help. Our destructive ex-Marillion mate had been a boon on tour, so why not try him out in the studio?

In he came, and for a while, we were motoring. Jamming as a three-piece allowed us to develop even more song ideas. However, one weird thing I noticed was that Steve was reluctant to elaborate on his ideas. I reckoned it was because Barney would just change everything anyway and Steve thought it wasn't worth the effort. I must add, though, that as soon as Steve got in with the producer he was happy to do anything and suggested lots of ideas.

This incarnation of the group worked decent hours, ten until six. I'd leave the Farm, buy my two bottles of wine from the village shop in Prestbury, go home, cane the wine, racing Becky to get the most, and return in the morning.

I was ringing up Barney, going, 'We've got loads of ideas here, mate.' And he was saying, 'Great. This is more like it.'

Knowing Barney, he was just sat around watching the History Channel, drinking tea and eating chicken legs and chocolate digestives, but it was nice to hear.

Having Phil onboard as an extra player really helped. I was delighted. Being this prolific was fantastic and my head was filled with thoughts of double LPs.

At this point we had managed to turn out around eighteen strong 'A' ideas and another thirteen 'B' ones. Then a worried-looking Andy Robinson came in. He said Barney was getting irate about so many ideas, getting swamped, and we must stop. We had enough to make two albums already.

Oh dear. Luckily we had been asked by Pete Saville to contribute some music for an exhibition he was doing. He wanted a thirty-minute piece of music to play, half an hour being the length of time he reckoned that a person would need to go round his exhibition at London's Design Museum.

Barney refused, quite rightly saying he had enough to do. Me, Phil and Steve were delighted to do it alone, with Steve even writing the drums for it.

There are two main reasons that *Waiting for the Sirens' Call* is a more guitar-based album than *Get Ready*. One is the writing process using Phil, and the other is because I stood my ground. There's one other reason why, despite the guitars, it still sounds weak, but we'll get to that later.

Still, it took a long time and we were into 2003 before we knew it and we felt it was time to start recording proper. Our A&R guy at Warners was a bloke called Paul Brown, who was a bit vague but nice with it. Him and Barney came up with an idea to use a number of different producers, matching the producer to the style of the track. Yours truly felt the band should produce the album – I was envisaging all kinds of problems with not just one but a series of different producers clogging up the place – and I was dead right, it turned out to be a nightmare. It didn't work at all.

Back into the wonderful privileged world of Real World (still nothing like the real world) I took my drinking to the next level. The six o'clock cocktail had crept forward to four, sometimes three. I had a lot of time on my hands, rattling around Real World, getting more and more frustrated with the producers and more and more pissed.

The first producer was Tore Johansson. He came and went. He had actually managed to lose the bass I had spent days doing on 'Sugarcane', something Barney took great delight in throwing in my face in his book, saying I never finished it. In fact, I never had the opportunity to redo it after the split in 2007. Tore still got a credit on *Lost Sirens*, though.

Steve Osborne was next to come and go. He didn't get a credit at all, even though Barney brought him back in later for another attempt. As he left the second time he said to me, 'I must be the only producer in the history of music to be sacked off the same session twice.' I hugged him goodbye.

Then came John Leckie. They were dropping like flies. In my opinion most of them were not as good producers as we were; we were definitely selling ourselves short. After a few drinks I'd corner Barney and suggest we went back to our old way of working, and beg him to stop listening to the record company. It was always the same answer: 'I don't want to argue with you, Hooky. No.'

In the end we decided to give more of the tracks to Stephen Street and produce some ourselves with Jim Spencer, Barney's engineer from Electronic. I was never impressed with Jim's ability and, fuelled mainly by the booze, christened him 'cloth ears', giving him a hard time whenever I could. I apologise, Jim. It's not a sin to have different ideas, after all. It does boil down to taste.

I think I was taking my frustration out where and when I could, again, sorry. We put him down as producer on some tracks to make amends.

Stephen Street used an engineer called Cenzo Townshend, who was excellent. They would turn out to be a great team. Stephen had a very good manner and was easy to work with and for the recording of his songs arranged a recording set-up to be installed in the actress Jane Seymour's house near Bath.

The set-up was in the main house with accommodation scattered between the old house, which was quite spooky, and a newer extension. Robbie Williams and many others had recorded there before us. The rest of the producers would use Real World for their recording, meaning that at one point we were running two of the country's most expensive studios simultaneously.

We started the sessions in Bath with the best intentions but soon crept back to the old way of working, with Barney going on until all hours. I'd go to bed pissed about 11 p.m., closely followed by Steve. At least we could work with Stephen and Cenzo early in the morning with Nosferatu surfacing around lunchtime. Things went quite well for a while, until Barney went on holiday.

Coming back newly inspired, he decided he wanted to write some more tracks from scratch on the computer. I brought up his statement about us having enough songs, only to be met by a blank look. Now, Barney had an equation for writing and recording. He reckoned that each track took a month from start to finish, which for New Order wasn't far wrong. So by adding three more he was lengthening the session by another three months at least.

'So?' he said.

That was it. As we know, readers, it's not do as I do, it's do as I say. And if you're wondering which three songs I'm talking about:

1. 'I Told You So'
2. 'Scott Walker', which became 'Recoil'
3. I've Got a Feeling'

Back in Real World it was still chaos. Barney enlisted even more help, bringing in Mac Quayle (another Electronic find) from New York, to re-program 'Guilt Is a Useless Emotion' and 'Shake It Up'. The studio was full of people I hardly knew. The record company would come down and tell us they didn't like where it was going and go off to think of someone else to bring in. It was really going from the sublime to the ridiculous.

But against all the odds we got all the songs finished and adjourned to Olympic Studios in Barnes, to do our mixing or await mixes from the various producers. At last the end was in sight. It was summer 2003.

*

Over the years, Rebecca and Andy were coming in with offers of tours for all round the world, and I was busting for the group to take a break and earn a bit of money, but all the way through New (New) Order or New Order II, Barney's mantra that you can't do two things at once stuck. For some reason it was OK to take a holiday for a few weeks and make an album, but you can't gig once or go on tour for a week and make an album.

Besides, he still loved being in the studio. For most bands it's a case of wanting to get the recording done, because it's so bloody expensive and they can't wait to get out of there and gig. I felt that for Barney it was a case of, 'Let's string this out for as long as we can, so we *don't* have to gig.' It used to drive me mad, and it certainly drove me to drink.

Luckily, salvation arrived in the form of a second career. Thanks to the advice of Mani, I was going to become a DJ.

'Refuelling the whole time'

My first DJ gig was with Mani in Barcelona in late summer 2003. Up until then I'd thought DJs were a bunch of overpaid, overblown, egotistical twats. So why it took me so long to decide to have a crack at it, I'll never know, because as soon as I became one ... you know the rest.

Anyway, Mani had been let down by someone and suggested I have a go, and that was it. Barcelona Razzmatazz Club was the venue, with a three-night stay for two in a four-star hotel, plus 500 euros on offer. I was pretty skint and very tempted, and when Mani told me all I had to do was stand there, look pretty and tell people why New Order won't gig, I said yes, never thinking for one minute this would cause as much trouble as it did, nailing the coffin lid down once and for all.

How could it, you say? Barney had been DJing off and on since 1990 and was always telling me, 'It's the best way to get pissed for nothing in the world. You should do it.'

I had never fancied it, but now needs must, so off I went. Great trip, great hotel, come the evening after dinner with Juan the owner and we were all very well refreshed and flying by the time we got to the club.

In the DJ booth our wives were dancing on podiums, which Imelda (Mani's wife) kept falling off. Mani was DJing away with me just stood drinking and boogieing. Then I noticed him scratching away furiously at a record he had on the deck that didn't seemed to be switched on. There was no sound. I tried to get his attention but he really was absorbed. Finally he turned round and as he did the other record stopped. So me and him were chatting away off our heads and the club was in complete silence.

Soon the Spanish got annoyed and we were victims of a rain of plastic bottles and glasses, some full, some empty. Without missing a beat, Mani reached down, took the record off the deck and flung it like a Frisbee at the crowd, then reached into his record box and threw another one, before finally deciding to play one.

Blimey, I thought, *I could do that!* and my DJ career was born.

We came down with a bump later that night when we got a call from our full-time nanny. Jessica was three, nearly four, at the time, and we were due to stay another day, but the nanny called from the hospital saying she wasn't well.

She had a really sore neck, couldn't turn, and when you put the light on it was blinding her. Of course we both thought 'meningitis', panicked and got the first available flight back – only to arrive home and find she was absolutely fine, nothing wrong with her at all, bloody kids.

Apart from that blip, though, DJing was great. Here was something I could do that was independent from the group that could earn me a bit of money. I liked it, too. I've met so many more people DJing than I ever did in a band, because the band sticks together, well protected and cut off from everyone; you act like a gang too, whereas when you're DJing you're alone, you have to mix. There's a much nicer social aspect to it. All the DJs really support each other.

For the first year or so I'd be drinking and doing drugs as well, so I'd be absolutely blotto. It was great. I just didn't care, really going for it and doing everything in my power to piss off the audience, playing some really mad stuff, really mixing it up. If anyone complained I'd tell them to fuck off. I can safely say I did not learn to DJ properly until after I got sober. I treated the audiences the same way as I treated everyone and everything – terribly.

The gigs started to come thick and fast, and I was soon getting the full beady-eye treatment off the lead singer, who seemed to be keeping an eye on everything I did. Pretty soon an edict was passed down from on high that when I was DJing I had to put a clause in my contract stipulating that the promoters were not allowed to use the New Order or Joy Division names to promote my shows.

It caused all kinds of headaches. A promoter wants as many people through the door as possible, and a lot of them simply ignored or 'accidentally' missed that particular clause in the contract. But if Barney got to see it then he'd be on the blower to Rebecca or Andy and in turn they'd have to give me grief about it. I had been in the bands for twenty-seven years and I was being told I could not use the name of the group to promote anything I did outside of it. Worse, I agreed. What a sap. Barney had me as well trained as Mrs Merton.

Either way, I was able to work the DJing around the recording sessions, and it certainly took the pressure off financially. It didn't help with my drink and drug consumption though. You're probably not supposed to get completely twatted before, during and after your DJ gigs, but I did, without fail. I was also drinking more at Real World, too, where I was abusive to pretty much anybody who happened to be within earshot.

I'd be going to bed pissed, wake up in the middle of the night unable to get back to sleep, so I'd sneak down to the kitchen and have a double vodka to knock me out again, and then in the morning I'd feel so rough, I'd go straight to the gym. When that didn't work I'd snatch a glass of wine, just to make me feel better, classic hangover cure, more alcohol.

When I got home, I didn't drink during the night because Becky would have noticed, so what I did was drink fairly normally in the evening and then get up and have a sneaky glass of wine in the morning, another at lunchtime and then, when I picked Jessica up from school, I'd nip into the Brasingamens on the way. Becky would say, 'Isn't it a bit early to go for Jess?' and I'd go, 'No, no, I'll take the dog for a walk.' The dog should have been fit as a fiddle, but, of course, I'd tie her up outside, have a massive glass of red wine and then go and pick Jess up, pissed, all over her with affection, taking the mick out of her and stuff. Fun Dad. (Sadly there were always a couple of other dads in there, too.)

I was refuelling the whole time, just topping up, and at Real World I was even worse than I was at home. Except, I was No Fun Hooky.

Things came to a sort of head one Friday night when I was talking to Andy Robinson about what was happening with the three tracks Bernard had written by himself. Once again exercising his world-famous tact, Andy said, 'Well, to be honest, he doesn't want you to play on them.' And left it there.

'Oh,' I said. Barney had already left and as I drove home I started to dwell on what he'd said.

I had a DJ gig in Glasgow on the Sunday night so off I went to it still fuming. Got completely fucked at the gig. There was a big fight and the promoter kept saying sorry by chopping out more and more. I stayed up all night then went straight to the airport in the morning and then straight to the bar for the first of a series of double vodkas before the plane, then drank all the way home. I arrived home pissed and fuming and determined to have it out with him, and though Becky tried to stop me, I'm ashamed to say

I drove to Bath – not my finest hour, this – arriving ready to knock Barney's fucking block off.

He wasn't there, thank God, or I'd probably be writing this from Strangeways. Instead it was Phil who got the brunt of my rage. I was ranting, saying why didn't he save this kind of shit for his solo album? Who did he think he was, stopping the group from writing and then rolling in with new ideas of his own? He promised me it would never go back to how it was on *Republic*, blah, blah, blah.

Poor Phil could only think of one thing to do – get me another drink.

A huge glass of white wine. Time? One in the afternoon.

'El Brimmo, Hooky, just how you like it,' he said, trying bravely to calm me down. I finished the bottle. In the meantime, Barney arrived back and to his eternal credit met the situation head-on.

'What's going on here?' he said.

Drunk and emotional, but thankfully no longer violent, I raged at him, 'When we got back together, I swore I'd never let it get back to how it was on *Republic*, and so did you, but it's happened again. You've fucking ring-fenced these three tracks. You don't want me to play on them because you don't want it to be New Order.'

'Hooky,' he said, 'I never said that.'

I was like, 'You what? Eh? Andy told me ...'

'I never said that to Andy,' he said. 'Of course you're free to play on the tracks. When Andy gets here, we'll sort it out.'

I proceeded to get even more pissed, and eventually passed out in my room at Real World.

When I woke up, Andy was sitting on the floor at the foot of my bed, waiting for me to surface. Don't forget, Andy was my mate. I got him both his jobs. We'd roomed together, had a million and one adventures together, and I couldn't for the life of me understand why he'd say that to me.

'I don't know why,' he said, dead shamefaced. 'It was just a feeling I got.'

In the end, I went, 'Oh, fuck off, Andy.'

Now I wonder if he was doing the same thing at other times. Did Barney really turn down an offer for us to remix 'Crazy' by Gnarls Barkley? Paul Brown had arranged it, saying, 'They want a New Order-y remix.' According to Andy, Barney said, 'Why would they want that?

It'll ruin it!' and turned it down. He also turned down a Killers remix on our behalf as well, the 'I've got soul but I'm not a soldier' track, which I managed to bag separately for myself (that was a story in itself, too), but Barney went mad when he found out I'd done it alone, so Andy said. Did he also really turn down the chance to play with Ennio Morricone? Another of his heroes.

These were things that frustrated and infuriated me at the time. I thought Barney had no right to be making decisions on behalf of the whole group – especially when they were so short-sighted and shit.

I wonder now if any of these decisions had gained or lost something in translation. Andy had no agenda I can think of. It certainly wasn't in his interests to drive a wedge between us. But, my God, he had an uncanny habit of doing it.

We moved to Olympic Studios in Barnes to mix some of the tracks, and I was drinking like a fish. A wine shop next to Olympic had a sampling hour, so of course I'd pop in, and the guy would go, 'This is a Cabernet from South America and it's a lovely little wine,' and I'd say, 'Put a bit more in, mate,' and he'd go, 'Well . . .' And I'd say, 'Come on, mate, put a bit more in,' so he'd give me half a glass and I'd neck it and then say, 'Go on, give us a bit more, I couldn't really taste that,' and he's going, 'No, no, this isn't what wine tasting's all about,' but I'm going, 'Come on, mate, fucking pack it in.' In the end, he threw me out, so I'd go to the pub, where I'd buy two for myself and neck one at the bar before taking the order to the table.

All of which would mean that by the time I got back into the studio, I was absolutely steaming – poor old Jim Spencer, the enginneer, usually getting it in the neck again.

I was still drinking when me and Barney were invited to guest on Gwen Stefani's *Love.Angel.Music.Baby.* album, on a track called 'The Real Thing'. We'd been offered $20,000 each. Barney had one go at the backing vocals then declared that he wasn't 'feeling' the track and refused to do any more. Meanwhile, I'd worked out a bunch of bass riffs for the whole song, and they sounded great. Sending them off, I was dead excited, only to be asked by the dreaded Mark (Spike) Stent, the producer, to come and have another go.

I turned up to be asked just to double-up the guitar riff they already had, finding all my ideas had been dumped. I tried it but it felt crap, was really annoyed and told him so, which must have got back to Gwen, who very magnanimously rang me to explain. I was so starstruck my annoyance completely disappeared; lovely lady.

Meanwhile, Paul Brown had brought in a load of dance mix albums to the studio and I responded to his generosity by slagging them all off. They were crap. He responded, 'You do a better one, smartarse – a Haçienda one.' I had never thought about it.

Putting the wheels in motion for that kept me busy. I set to work with my mate Phil Beckett, collating a wishlist of tunes for a three-CD set that Paul had arranged for me to release on New State Records.

Remember I said that me and Rob buying the Haçienda name in 1997 became a massive bone of contention with Barney, Steve and Gillian ... Well, they never turned a hair when I was putting that album together, and I talked about it often in Olympic as we mixed, even discussing it in interviews we did together. Couldn't have cared less, never said a word. Which is strange, isn't it, considering they were apparently so cross with me for 'stealing' the name from under their noses?

Or am I being too suspicious? In his book, Barney accuses me of telling him about buying the name while we were recording in 2004, and refusing to reveal how much I had paid for it. That, I can assure you on my children's lives, is not true. I think it's just how he has chosen to justify his taking of the New Order name to you, the fans. I'd be happy to take a Jeremy Kyle lie-detector test on that one and you're all invited. In fact, I may do that ... my mate knows him.

Fact is, they weren't interested in the club when it was open and losing money; they weren't interested in the Haçienda mix-CD. They weren't interested in the Haçienda name at all ... not until things started getting really nasty.

The album sold well, something like 175,000 copies, which made me realise there was still an appetite for the Haç. Tony's son, Oliver, had already staged a successful reunion club night at the Academy 1 (not a peep from Barney or Steve about that either), but when he made a hash of a second night, a New Year's Eve extravaganza, me and my DJ agent, Paul Fletcher, had to step in to sort it out. From there, we started doing our own nights.

With the New Order album almost done, we started thinking about the cover. I say 'we' but I was way too pissed by then, so stayed out of the resulting fracas. We'd already had a massive row about the title:

Barney had suggested sharing it with one of the songs on the album, him saying, 'They did it all the time in the sixties.' My answer to that being, 'It was shit then an' all.' Very constructive, I know. I lost.

At the sleeve meeting I could see Peter Saville was getting a bit fed up of Barney calling the shots, and the last straw came when Barney picked a 1970s image by Eliot Elisofon of naked Tahitian girls bathing for the LP cover. You could see his thinking. She looked like the sort to lure sailors onto rocks.

Pete didn't like it but Barney was insistent. Like I say, I was way too pissed to get involved. I was legless when we turned up for the meeting, couldn't even focus, I did think it was corny, but Barney got his own way, which in my opinion infuriated Pete.

Now, this meeting would have taken place in mid-to-late 2004, over two years after we started recording, and a lot happened between that summit and the album coming out. One of them was that terrible tsunami in Indonesia on Boxing Day. Because of that, the record company got cold feet on Barney's cover image, fearing a possible media backlash, and Alan Parkes from Warners had to go to Pete's studio, pleading with him to do another sleeve.

Pete was insistent. 'No, I don't want to do one. I don't want to do it,' but Alan was just as persistent, until at last Pete got fed up and wrote 'NO' on a piece of paper, gave it to Alan and said, 'There's my answer,' and Alan went, 'That'll do,' and took it.

I like it. I think it's one of his best sleeves.

The other thing to happen in between that meeting and the album being finished (we had one week left to go) was that I went into rehab.

We were staying in a lovely, old-fashioned hotel in Wimbledon called Cannizaro House and even now if I see a picture of it I get a nasty shiver down my spine. I was still drinking like a storm drain. In Phil I had an excellent partner-in-crime. The ex-Marillion man wasn't as far gone as I was and he wasn't nearly as obnoxious with it; he was like a young pup, as keen in the studio as he was out on the lash. He could certainly be relied upon to go in search of extra fun.

This one night we'd finished at the studio and gone for a Thai in Wimbledon, one of those evenings where I had a bottle of wine to myself while everybody else was sharing one. Then they shared another one and I had another one to myself. By the end of that I was desperate for some drugs so I was nagging Phil, 'Come on, Phil, let's go to the Groucho. We can meet up with Keith Allen, get some bugle, come on, mate.'

Later, back at the hotel, I was still mithering, 'Come on, Phil. Let's go to the Groucho.'

'Hooky, mate,' said Phil, 'we've just been.'

Oh dear. That moment turned out to be one of the major stepping-stones on my path to the Priory. I'd had an alcoholic blackout, not my first, but my longest, losing completely the hours during which Phil and I had taken a cab from Wimbledon into the centre of town, gone to the Groucho, threatened one of Caroline's ex-boyfriends, met Keith in the Café de Paris, done a load of drugs then hours later returned to Wimbledon. And here we were, in the hotel bar for a nightcap, before turning in. I grabbed a half-bottle of champagne and went to bed. The next morning I was dry-heaving for England. This was bad. I was sweating and shaking much more than the normal I was used to.

That night we went out again, to Arthur Baker's restaurant in Notting Hill, and I was off it quickly, making a real nuisance of myself and pissing everybody off. At least I had the sense this time to leave early with Steve. The next morning, as I got out of the car at Olympic

Studios, in a terrible state, Andy Robinson grabbed my arm. 'Hooky,' he said, 'I think you're drinking too much.'

It hit me like a thunderbolt. I knew it and now everyone else seemed to know it. I was embarrassed and ashamed. Normally I would have told him to fuck off, but something in me had changed.

My friends had given up trying to tell me I was drinking too much. I couldn't get drugs because I'd been too rude to all the dealers I knew (God bless those sensitive drug dealers, eh?) and, worst of all, Becky had just about cut me loose. She's scarily bright, and she's tough, and she's a mother. She knew the way things were going; she knew that if I didn't help myself then nobody would, and she knew that I shouldn't be anywhere near our daughter. On one visit to Wimbledon she saw me at my worst and took Jess home, leaving me to stew in my own juice.

To everybody I'd protest, 'I'm not that bad,' but by then I was regularly taking a bottle of champagne for when I woke up in the middle of the night. Drinker's dawn, they call it. The only way to get back to sleep was to down more booze. In my room was a sherry decanter and I was tanning that every day. Who the fuck drinks a decanter of sherry every day? I did. The staff must have thought I was mental.

Thing is, I was mental. One thing you learn in recovery is Albert Einstein's quote about how the definition of insanity is doing the same thing over and over again and expecting a different result, and that's exactly what I was doing. Every day I'd promise myself I was going to rein it in. Every first drink was 'just to sort myself out' or 'just the one'. But every day turned out the same: that first drink eroded my good intentions, the second made me feel like a hero and before I knew it – oblivion. I'd be startlingly awake at some godawful hour of the morning, drinking myself back to sleep, waking later, polluted with hangover and twisted up with shame and regret and recrimination, deciding today would be different. No way was I going to get in that state again, but I was still having that first drink, expecting a different result but getting the same one. Ironic, considering the album we were trying to finish, but I was like one of those sailors lured to the rocks. Every day the sirens were calling and every day I answered, obedient as a dog.

A great man once said to me, 'One drink's not enough and two's too many.'

Thanks for that, Barney.

I felt low the whole time. I realised that I didn't even like being drunk very much, and was overjoyed when I just couldn't get pissed any more. I was drunk but not pissed. In the past I'd always taken cocaine to straighten out the booze – on it you can keep on drinking but not be pissed – but now I couldn't get hold of any I was just a shambling, obnoxious drunk the whole time, a parody of the boorish 'Hooky' of the music press. I used to think back to the early days of Joy Division, when I was driving the van, humping the gear and living for the thrill of being in a band and playing my music. Back then I'd thought of myself as a Viking, not because I was behaving like a drunken thug but because I was a daft twat from Salford surging into unexplored territory. But something had got corrupted along the way, some wires crossed.

Gradually it dawned on me that something had to give; that I was either going to die or lose everything. Living with alcohol terrified me but living without it terrified me even more. I couldn't spend the rest of my life dry-heaving every morning. After all, it wasn't like I was using alcohol to escape my awful life – having a mardy-arsed lead singer hardly compares to some of the horror stories I heard later in recovery. In fact, my life was fucking great. I was a successful rock star (albeit nearly skint) with a gorgeous wife and kids. I wasn't using alcohol to dull the pain. Alcohol was the pain.

So it had to go.

Which of course is easier said than done. The day I decided to stop I was out in the West End and already rattling so I decided to have a drink. My drunk voice was singing its familiar tune, 'Just one more drink, and then give up,' and I was about to heed its call when the phone rang and who should it be but my old mate Keith Allen.

I didn't realise who it was at first. I didn't recognise the number when it came up, but as soon as I did, oh my God, it was like the devil himself was calling.

'All right, Hooky,' he growled. 'I realise I've been somewhat remiss in failing to visit you in your Olympic-sized studio, and seeing as it's your last week how's about I come down there and we go out and get absolutely fucking arseholed?'

Of course, my drunk voice was yelling, 'Yes, yes, yes!' at me. My whole being was lit up at the thought of larging it with Keith. It was an instinctive, Pavlovian reaction – and it scared the life out of me. The dreadful knowledge that I had no control over myself, that I was a helpless passenger on a train about to plummet over a cliff, just freaked me out and gave me enough of that extra push to turn it all around.

I told Keith I'd see him next week, ended the call, and phoned Becky to come and get me. She came to Wimbledon and I phoned the Priory and they told me to come in for an assessment tomorrow, 27 November 2004. I stopped drinking that day.

The group were due to spend one more week finishing the album for 4 December, but I left. I went home. The next day I was very nervous at the meeting but the counsellor told me I was showing the typical signs of alcohol and drug addiction, and not to worry, they could help. He booked me in for admission to the secure mental hospital, the Priory in Hale, for a month from Monday morning.

I'd stopped drinking by then, two days spent climbing the walls, but I went in sober, which turned out to be a big mistake. You're advised not to give up because on the comedown you might lose your resolve. No one told me. The rest of the day's intake were all off their heads, having the last drink or snort or whatever they were in for in the car park outside. They were coked-up, smacked-up, drunk as lords, all of them having much more fun than I was. I felt cheated. Bollocks.

I was checked in and put in a room and I remember sitting staring out of the rain-streaked window, thinking, *What the fuck am I doing? I can't drink. My life's over! I'm a rock star who can't drink.*

In reality, of course, my life was just beginning. I was taking the first steps to prising it back from addiction.

There was some fun in the Priory, though. It was a living *One Flew Over the Cuckoo's Nest*. It has a reputation as a celebrity hangout but most people in there were regular Joes and not all minted – the majority of people in there were paid for by the government – and I'll say this for it, there was never a dull moment.

As an alcoholic you go through a 'dry drunk' stage, which is when you've come off the booze but you still act like a twat. I went through it myself (still am). On our first outing, after ten days inside, we were taken to Tatton Park in Knutsford and somehow ended up alone, as in, our handlers had disappeared. We convened in the café to wait, and suddenly one of the other inmates goes, 'Christmas cake. It's got brandy in it.' And they descended on it. I'm not kidding, some of them were sat there with six pieces each, cramming it in their mouths as fast as they could before our handlers reappeared. It was hilariously desperate. I used to get on the minibus for outings to the local AA meetings (you see? How *Cuckoo's Nest* is that?), shouting, 'Stringfellows, driver, and don't spare the horses!' and I got in trouble for that. There was a poster up for a co-dependency meeting. I wrote on it, 'Bring a friend.' I got in trouble for that too.

Luckily for me an old mate of mine, Big Stu, was in there at the same time as me. He used to roadie for Theatre of Hate and was in for depression, alcohol really, but if you had medical insurance you could claim for depression but not for alcoholism (I bit the bullet, borrowing the £15,000 to pay for the month). Alcoholism is still not recognised in England as an illness, so you aren't covered. It's a different treatment for depression, all pottery-making and weaving, and he did make me a couple of lovely trinket boxes.

Stu helped me a great deal in there. I cried on his big, big, broad shoulders many times. He's a great mate now, even though, sadly, he started drinking again.

Meanwhile, the smackheads were all getting dead aggressive. I've no doubt they were meek little kittens when they were on the stuff but as soon as they got off it they were like raving lunatics – always trying to escape and start a fight.

I must admit I treated it a bit like school. I mean, I took the recovery seriously – out of my group of twelve there were only four of us that didn't fall off the straight and narrow in the first two weeks – but what used to annoy me was how po-faced they could be about it. Having a bit of a laugh was really frowned upon. It got even worse when I left the Priory and had to go to AA meetings. They didn't work for me at all. *Christ*, I thought, *this is a forum for windbags.* Someone puts up a hand 'to share' and my heart would sink. I heard the same people telling the same old stories time and time again: 'I had three pints of Cinzano and then I was up dancing like Elvis,' for forty minutes. Forty minutes! I suggested we have one of those clocks like they do in chess to keep the speeches to a decent two-minute length. That went down like a lead balloon.

One time I was sitting there listening to someone's sad story about getting wrecked at the Reading Festival when it slowly dawned on me that we'd headlined that year. *Oh my God*, I was thinking, *this is it. My life really is over.*

Me, I never really shared. The idea of talking about disgracing myself in the Groucho with Keith Allen or naughtiness on tour in the US didn't really appeal. 'I stood up Quincy Jones. I called Robert Plant a twat.' No thanks. Besides, even though I'd arrived at a bad place, I was able to acknowledge that I'd had an awful lot of fun getting there. It seemed to me that AA wasn't really set up for that. You had to disown your former self/life completely and I wasn't able to do that.

Meanwhile, the group-therapy sessions worked for me. For the first one I walked in timid as a mouse and the guy running it came straight over to me, saying, 'Hooky, nice to see you again.'

Again? I had absolutely no idea who this geezer was.

'Sorry I, I don't r-remember,' I stuttered.

'It's me, Travis ... I used to serve you up with Es in the Haçienda.'

He was now a counsellor, and one thing I must say was how good they all were. All of the counsellors were fantastic. They were all ex-addicts and knew exactly what we were going through and needed. It was very tough at times and there was nowhere to hide from these people. Thank you all.

It was hard in there but I felt safe. I had two weeks alone to sit and think and face myself. Twinny, Fran, Bowser and Ken Niblock came down to spring me. None of them believed I wanted to be there or could ever get sober and they all said the same thing, 'I've come to rescue you.'

God bless them. I did the course, said goodbye to my former self, cried a lot, prayed for forgiveness, heard some awful stories, saw people much worse than me. Went to both NA (Narcotics Anonymous) and AA. It was just before Christmas and everyone in the meeting was panicking about Auntie Nora with her eggnog and Uncle Frank with his sherry. How will they get through Christmas Day without everyone finding out they're an alkie?

Then I had another idea and, springing to my feet, I said, 'Hey, seeing as how everyone's so upset about Christmas Day, how about we have it off and start again on Boxing Day? Three hundred and sixty-four days sober has to be a great achievement, hasn't it? What do you say?'

I got asked to leave, again.

I did get an answer to one mighty conundrum that I had been suffering from for years: when I got low and wanted to sack the charlie, when I'd really had enough. I would go out with the best of intentions, as in: I'm only drinking tonight. No powder. Then as soon as I'd had a couple of drinks I was on the blower to every bloody dealer I knew, desperate to score. Why?

Cocaine is composed of many chemicals (and a lot that aren't supposed to be there); some give you the rush but wear off quickly, others stay in your blood and become inert. But when you mix that inert compound with alcohol it changes to another compound that craves the rush compound, the one that disappears quickly. That's why when you go out you're Dr Jekyll and then after a couple of drinks you end up as Mr Hyde. I was told these inert compounds stay in your blood for six months after any cocaine use. Thank God for that. I thought I was just being a weak-willed twat.

Inside, the nights were tough, just you and your guilt. You were given your medication before bed and then checked every hour through the night (it was a hospital). So everyone was knackered. Slowly, the combination of not drinking, sleeping (a little), and good food did have a remarkable effect. We all got very bright, very quickly. I had damaged my liver but the doctor reckoned it would recover if I didn't drink again. Things were looking pretty good.

Then the counsellors would remind us what we'd left on the outside, the deceit and the lack of trust that we'd earned; the damaged friends and family, the upset children. How you wouldn't be trusted for a long time, at least two years, they reckoned, before anyone would start to even think of trusting you, how your loved ones would get their own back. *Surely not*, we thought.

But it was true. We would have to work very hard to be trusted again and it would be an ongoing situation – forever. We might be able to say goodbye to our evil twins and start again. But they would be very fresh in our injured loved ones' memories.

I'm pretty sure Barney phoned me once while I was in, unless I was dreaming. Steve hadn't contacted me at all. I phoned Andy Robinson and got an acoustic bass brought in and it made me feel a lot better. All too soon it was time to leave and face the world. I was terrified.

I came out of the Priory just before Christmas 2004, knowing that while I still had a long way to go, I'd done something truly positive for change – something to get my life back on track. As I say, I'm not one to do things by halves, and while on the one hand, that was how I'd got myself in such a mess in the first place, on the other, it was going to help me take my recovery just as seriously. It was a quiet Christmas.

'The clarity can be blinding'

It was Andy Liddle who said to me, 'Be very careful when you get sober. The clarity can be blinding.'

Bloody hell, he wasn't kidding. Sitting in my room in the Priory I'd had ample time to think – and I was wondering why I'd put up with Barney's bullshit for so long. It dawned on me that for thirty years he'd tried, and sometimes succeeded, to make my life a misery and the only thing that had kept a lid on it was the drink and drugs. How would I respond to him without that safety valve? Was his talent worth it? I was soon to find out. (Clue: look at New Order's current line-up.)

While I was inside the album was deemed finished. Total cost, in excess of £700,000. There would be nothing left to share after this one.

Then a slight change of direction resulted in a load of tracks being remixed to make them more radio-friendly (i.e. 'radio-friendly in America') as well as adding vocals from Ana Matronic out of the Scissor Sisters on 'Jetstream'.

I didn't like the song much anyway but have to say I preferred Ana's vocal; I would have liked her to sing the whole thing. I also thought Stuart Price did nothing for it and giving them both publishing on it was ridiculous. To me it still sounded mediocre, and I was sure everyone was taking advantage of my time in the Priory to smooth the record over, bland it out even more. What had started out lively and edgy had ended up sounding bland and yacht-rock. When I complained, I was told it was my own fault for missing so much of the recording process.

A week, I'd missed. Out of three fucking years. A week. (He would never let me forget that.)

It's not like I expected much support from my bandmates – after all, I'd been awful before I went into rehab – but that was lucky, because there wasn't any forthcoming. I have to be honest and say that even Becky wasn't much help in those first few months. She just didn't believe I'd stay sober. As I said, they had warned us in the Priory that your other half may be unconsciously (or maybe even deliberately) getting their own back on you for all the shit you've put them through.

No, all the adjusting to a sober life I was going to have to do alone.

That became starkly apparent on New Year's Eve. Barney and I had a DJing gig booked months before, at the Zap Club in Brighton, (strangely, on this occasion, they were allowed to use the New Order name in the promotion). Barney insisted on being paid more than me (£4,500 for him, £3,500 for me) but I was on expenses, and he wasn't, so it worked out the same.

We arrived to discover that we'd been booked into the Hotel Pelirocco, which is Brighton's most rock'n'roll, 24-hour hotel, the sort of place where you can get dildos on room service.

So there I land, newly sober, in party central on New Year's Eve in Brighton, my first sober gig. I remember coming out of the hotel on the way to the gig and there was a car parked outside with the number plate A8 EVY, only it had been put together so it looked like 'a bevy'. I couldn't believe it. I was being mocked at every turn. Barney turned up and he'd been out the night before, so not only was he shedded but he was demanding stuff to keep him going. None was forthcoming but that didn't stop him complaining about the lack of it all night. Midnight came and went as we made our way to the club, and I noticed that nobody was saying 'Happy New Year' to each other, like they would in Manchester; they were very cold, which added to my sense of unreality about the whole thing. I went to play, I was on first, and thankfully it went well. About an hour in I cued up 'Bizarre Love Triangle', when Bernard appeared and, seeing what I was about to do, tried to stop me. 'What are you doing?' he said.

'What do you mean, what am I doing? I'm about to put one of our tracks on.'

'You can't play New Order, you'll look like a right twat.'

It gave me pause for thought. Everything did then. Six weeks sober, and I'd never been less sure of myself. If he'd told me my name wasn't Peter Hook I'd have probably believed him. But I found the courage of my convictions and played the tune, then a few more New Order, and then he whispered into my ear, 'They sound really good, don't they, play some more.'

Contradictory to the end. Good man.

Anyway, we played the gig and as I picked up all the money from the rather lovely young lady who ran the club, she grabbed my arm and said, 'This should be the other way round, Hooky, he was shit.' Bless. We went back to the hotel, where Barney stumbled to bed and I found Becky propping up the bar with our PR woman. Fed up by now, I retired to bed. They'd put us in the vodka room, loads of vodka posters around the walls, empty bottles hanging from the ceiling as decorations. Still I was being mocked. Then a party started in the room above. Then another one in the room below. Then the one next door. Our PR woman came in, off her tits and crying because of a recent bereavement. She left. Then Becky came in, off her tits, saying I should come down to the bar. 'It's great. Everyone's twatted.' It was like I'd died and gone to hell.

That was it. I told her to get in the car. I'd had enough. We were going home. She screamed at me, called me a bastard, saying she'd been watching me get pissed for the last eight years, and now I was ruining her New Year's Eve. And even though she was dead right, my mind was made up. I wasn't staying another second. Still arguing, we piled into the car and I set off. The roads were so clear it was unbelievable. It was a pleasure to drive. And then at a service station we came across a girl who'd put petrol in her car and none of her credit cards would work. She had no way to pay and was crying. I pulled the wad out of my pocket, peeled off £100 and gave it to her – 'Here y'go, love, Happy New Year. When you're flush, stick it in the poor box,' then fucked off home.

And that was it. Welcome to sobriety, eh?

It didn't get any easier. We played the *NME* Awards in the February of 2005 – and I remember I couldn't get in the dressing room because various comedians were in there, doing all sorts.

Next year, at the same awards, I found myself at a table with Princess Beatrice (thankfully unaffected by hearing 'Bizarre Love Triangle' at full volume while still in her mother's womb), Princess Eugenie, Pixie Geldof, Noel Fielding and Shaun Ryder. The two princesses were just sixteen and seventeen. I don't know what Noel was doing in the toilets, but he was off his nut. I was presenting an award for best live act and Russell Brand was in charge.

Now, I hate it when you go up to present an award and the group aren't there and the dopey video comes on. As bad luck would have it, that's what happened here. Franz Ferdinand won and on came the dopey video, so I walked off the stage and gave the award to the Kaiser

Chiefs, who in turn gave it to the Cribs, where one of them got so excited he jumped on the table, landed on a wine bottle and nearly cut his own liver out. It was pandemonium. There was claret everywhere. They had to call an ambulance, and he nearly died. They let him keep the award though. As I sat down Bex said to me, 'You're still causing trouble bloody sober.'

That night we were staying in the K West, London's famously rock'n'roll hotel (a modern version of the Columbia), and I was kept awake by the bands running around the corridors all night. I was thinking, *This is karma. This is rough fucking justice.* There'd been an incident, years ago, at the Brit Awards, when I'd taken the piss out of Marti Pellow out of Wet Wet Wet, who'd just got out of rehab. This was divine retribution for that. (I met him not too long ago, actually, and he was very nice, a real gentleman; forgiveness is a wonderful thing.)

It went on. The album came out and we started gigging, and after shows Barney would say, 'Are you coming to the bar for a drink?' and I'd go, 'No, I'm going to bed,' and he'd grin and say, 'I'll get you a water.' Yeah, fucking tap water, knowing you. But I couldn't really complain about that because I'd been guilty of doing just the same when I was drinking. After all, it wasn't so long ago that I'd been calling Jake a selfish bastard for getting straight in Australia.

What began to gnaw at me was that feeling that had first reared its ugly head in my room at the Priory. A sense of not wanting to put up with it any more – of not having to.

Backstage I'd look around the room and see all these familiar faces and think: *They're all working for Barney; they have to be here and it's in their interests to keep him happy. But I don't work* for *him, I work* with *him, and I don't have to be here.*

I'd end up getting a car with Steve, dissecting his behaviour on the way home. Or at least, I would be. Steve was a closed book. He started off in 1978 odd and detached, almost to the point of being a shut-in, and stayed that way. Although he did agree, who could tell what he was thinking?

Meantime, we had to perform our new single, 'Jetstream', on the Jonathan Ross show. I liked Ana Matronic but thought it was a weak choice for a single and hated the awful performance video they made for it. If ever a song was not about a performance it was that one and I couldn't figure out what the hell we were thinking.

I knew Jonathan well, I had worked with him a couple of times before, and as we were waiting to perform he was doing an interview with Kelly Osbourne, but what they didn't show on telly was that he was, in my opinion, a bit tough on her, and made her cry.

To be honest, I was a bit surprised to see him being so hard; I was thinking, *Tell him to fuck off, Kelly.* By my side, Ana Matronic was getting more and more agitated and defensive of Kelly, and then, when Jonathan was trying to record our intro, she started mouthing off over the mic at him. That hacked him right off and he came over, arguing. Then Barney chipped in. Unfortunately, he'd got in a bit of a state as usual, gurning and stammering like a twat, and Jonathan squared up to him. Barney cowered as Jonathan held his gaze and reached to the guitar head, twiddled the tuning pegs and put it right out of tune. Returning to his desk to record the intro, Jonathan said, 'Here's New Order, with their frankly mediocre new single.'

I thought, *This is going to be interesting.*

We launched into the track and the combination of Barney's out-of-tune guitar and Ana's wound-up vocals meant we had to stop, retune and start again. Jonathan was pissing himself.

Afterwards I asked him about Kelly. 'Listen, Hooky, these kids put themselves out there, they're getting paid. Call it a life lesson, eh?'

I didn't agree with that, but you know what? He was dead right about the song. It was mediocre. And apart from that show of solidarity with Kelly Osbourne, there was never an ounce of chemistry between Barney and Ana Matronic. He wouldn't even look at her when we played it live. She was gracious enough to join us on a number of TV shows and gigs on that tour, but despite her best efforts it remained a low point of the show. It was always a pleasure to see her though. She's a lovely girl.

On the DJ front I soon got used to travelling alone, and my next gig was for *Vogue* magazine on a boat sailing from Punta del Este in Uruguay, $20,000 just for the afternoon. It was a great gig but a hell of a journey. I'd flown out business class courtesy of a free upgrade by David Sultan, who worked for Air France. But on the way back I got middled in economy between a load of pissed-up Argentinians who kept passing me an open bottle of brandy and going on about the Falklands for sixteen hours. I had two panic attacks, the bastards. Apart from that it was fantastic.

Then came a booking for a full DJ tour of Brazil. My career was certainly taking off. I was delighted.

Unfortunately someone had booked New Order gigs without informing me, expecting me to cancel my pre-arranged DJ appearances because the New Order gigs were more money. I said, 'I don't work like that.' It was a mess. The penalties for New Order cancelling were more, so my tour bit the dust. They had to compensate the Brazilian promoter to the tune of £5,000. I was livid. They would do exactly the same thing again later when we played in Liverpool.

The first tour was America, where a very prestigious slot playing on *Jimmy Kimmel Live!* had been won. This would give us huge exposure and promotion for our tour.

We arrived early in Los Angeles to prepare for the appearance on Jimmy's show. The sun was shining and it was great to be back. I had noticed that Phil had been caning it a lot with Barney recently (in my opinion it had been affecting both their performances), so I told Phil to make sure Barney took it easy before the show. Afterwards, fine. Just not before. The reason? To be honest, he ended up in a fucking mess otherwise. It was a long afternoon and after soundcheck and a few drinks and, obviously, a lot of mithering on Barney's part, Phil's resolve slipped and by the time it came to the performance our lead singer was gurning like a bastard. I gave Phil a right bollocking but it was just too late. Barney sang OK but in-between performances he looked absolutely ridiculous. Even Jessica said to me, 'What's wrong with Barney's mouth, Dad?' She was seven. Out of the mouths of babes, eh?

Things just carried on degenerating, and I got a hell of an education in Hamburg the night before our gig. I had decided to join everyone for dinner. I was still feeling very fragile but made an effort.

As we sat down, Barney late as usual, it came home to me how there were some things I didn't miss about drinking, like choosing the wine. This now seemed like a right load of old bollocks. Hey, believe me, in the past I was just as guilty as everybody else. 'Is it from the south side of the vineyard? Has it been trod by an Albanian virgin?' All that crap! Basically just showing off, because believe you me, and you know I would not lie to you, a couple of glasses in, and I'm sure no one, not even Barney, could have told the difference between the finest Chablis and donkey piss.

He became rude to the waiters, something I must admit I'd noticed before on many occasions, maybe not so clearly, but then exceptionally rude to poor old me, and Andy Liddle.

Before long we were getting a right sarky 'tongue lashing', which only stopped when him and Phil decided to go to the red-light district accompanied by Sarge and Andy Robinson (I thought he was joking).

I turned to Andy Liddle and said, 'Fucking hell, was I like that?'

'No,' he said, then, as I breathed a sigh of relief, 'you were worse.'

Oh shit, I'll never drink again.

The next morning it turned out they had been recognised to boot, with fans coming up to them all the time they were trawling the red-light district.

These were the reasons why I called the meeting in Japan. I was very concerned about the future, the future of the group, the management agreeing I had a point. In Barney's book he makes me out to be an ungrateful lunatic. The truth was his and Phil's constant partying before gigs and its effect on our performance was becoming a real worry to me. It was very frustrating to witness and awful to listen to. I did wonder if it was because I was sober? Was I just jealous? Either way, I had a feeling if we didn't address it we would soon become a laughing stock. *Jimmy Kimmel Live!* was a prime example. We had so few gigs booked it seemed criminal to ruin any of them. I know it may seem I was getting a bit preachy here, and hypocritical coming from King Caner, but one thing I tried not to do when I was off it was let it affect a performance for the band or audience. Once, you were allowed, that's human. This was getting to be every gig.

I was very nervous. We were having the meeting in the bar on the top floor of the Park Hyatt Tokyo hotel, the Peak Bar where Sofia Coppola filmed her great film *Lost in Translation*. Steve wouldn't come, just agreeing with everything I had said as per usual, ending with, 'I don't like heights.'

The bar was on the 52nd floor and came with beautiful views of the glittering city lights below.

I remember Rebecca Boulton saying, 'You watch when Barney comes in. I bet it's minutes before he goes for a wee, then once he starts he can't stop.' Sure enough, when Barney deigned to join us – fashionably late, of course – it wasn't long before he was getting up for an endless series of wees. I was getting more and more frustrated by the constant interruptions, and in the end I exploded. 'For fuck's sake!' I apologise for that particular outburst but overall, I was right: they were out of order (not the toilets – Barney and Phil).

And guess what? Nothing came of the meeting.

Off we went, touring again. Barney had a face on him, as we say, the whole of the UK leg – apart from Glastonbury. The presence of Kate Moss and Gwyneth Paltrow in the dressing room seemed to perk him up. At T in the Park he sang most of one song in a strange baby voice and when I asked him what the hell he was playing at, he said it was because my bass was too loud. To sacrifice the song for something that could have been sorted with Gerry or, better still, just got the fuck on with the job and left? I couldn't understand it. What a twat.

At the gig there were two stages side by side and I went and played on the other one for a couple of numbers on my own, which was nice. This was a sad occasion; the gig was supposed to be an all-nighter but some poor kid died of an overdose early in the morning. The police shut the festival down and discovered the kid was the son of the mayor, who had given permission for the festival.

We did a benefit gig for a special-needs school in Salford. It was something Barney had asked us to do, and he went to great lengths to make it very special, even arranging Damien Hirst to come and do an installation of his famous circle paintings, very generously gifting the kids one each. He was nice with the kids.

Now, on this English tour, there began the whole business with the onstage decibel meter that Barney insisted on using to monitor the stage sound levels, he said to try and combat his tinnitus.

He had been complaining about the noise onstage for years, starting with Steve's monitors and then working his way to the front and the rest of us. He seemed to need an excuse to limit everybody else's foldback levels while he stood there using his custom-fitted, noise-limiting earphones that should have prevented him being affected by our levels anyway. It was just a control thing for him. As soon as the gig started we turned back up to our preferred levels, and because of the earphones Barney was none the wiser.

But still, it was a pain in the arse. The £1,000 dB meter was set up right in the middle of the stage, but didn't seem to get the results he wanted so he sent Andy out for another one to monitor each side. It was then Gerry's job to write down the readings for each song to be analysed later.

Now, most musicians, especially those with a few years' experience, know that the sound level changes every night, on different songs, depending on whether they are acoustic or use a backing track (usually naturally going louder for the chorus and breaks), and with each different venue. It is mainly uncontrollable. You just have to work round it. In venues it typically depends on the size of the stage, are there curtains or not, the size of the venue, is the back wall straight or angled, how far it is from the stage to the back wall ... hundreds of things.

Later, for the gig, it changes completely again. As the audience come in, soaking up the volume and echoes, it usually improves. The backline volume and foldback levels are controlled by us and, with an expert like Gerry in control, rarely changed.

But what Barney wants he gets. You either stand up to him or simmer in silence. The trouble with the standing-up option is that if you wear your heart on your sleeve (as I do) and you've not long kicked drink and drugs (as I had) then you run the risk of looking like a loose cannon (which I often did). If you simmer then it's all got to go off sooner or later (which it did).

In Blackpool he stormed off after the gig, leaving me to do a prearranged interview with Phil Jupitus alone. Not that I minded, I felt sorry for Phil (an old mate). He had come all the way from London, but – worse – we were doing the gig with our old friends Section 25. Barney had produced their first album. It should have been a great get-together. I'll never forget poor Larry Cassidy's face when he came looking for Barney after, only to find he'd already left.

I've read his book. I know he says the problem's me and professes to be bemused by my antipathy towards him, and it's true that I came out of rehab without that safety valve of drink and drugs, no 'off' button. I was more assertive than before. But he was behaving like the life of a rock star was the worst kind of life there was, and in my opinion he was taking it out on the group, the management, the technicians, and now the audience, and there was one person – one, me – who wasn't prepared to let him get away with it.

On the night we played Glasgow Academy he cleared the dressing room with his misery and I got the impression he had something on his mind. He was banging about the place, getting more and more agitated, until at last he blurted out, 'I shouldn't be here. I shouldn't be in fucking Glasgow on a Wednesday night. I should be at home with my kids. This is fucking ridiculous.'

He was always kicking off with that. 'I don't want to be here ...' all his favourite moans rolled into one, usually accompanied by him putting the boot into whatever unlucky bit of furniture happened to be nearby. Prior to coming on the tour – before we even started planning the gigs, in fact – I'd said to him, 'Listen, if you don't want to do any gigs, let's not do any, we could be Manchester's Blue Nile.' Of course, I would have been in a right hole if he'd taken me up on my offer, which he didn't, thank God. Instead he said, 'What are you talking about?'

I said, 'You act so badly on tour. Like you're really not enjoying it.'

'No, not all the time,' he said. 'I'll be all right, don't you worry.'

But then here he was in Glasgow, again complaining that he wanted to be anywhere but here.

'You shouldn't be DJing,' was his next thing. 'You shouldn't be DJing and using the New Order name. It's just a PA, a personal appearance.'

I started shouting at him, saying why didn't he just fuck off home if he was that miserable and leave my DJing out of this. I was nearly skint, mainly thanks to him. The DJing was a necessity for me. The situation calmed down after that, but I realised it was the first time we'd spoken in three weeks.

I suppose that before we'd at least had drink and drugs in common, but by now I was sober and married, so all we had in common was the group, and we had wildly differing ideas about how that should be run, never mind the music.

When I DJed that night in Glasgow all the rest of the band turned up like they always did, Phil, even Steve, Andy and some of the crew, even Barney's new cabin boy Tin Tin (a tour DJ for New Order) turned up, full of praise. Everyone else seemed to like me DJing, using the night as a very social occasion, with Phil often using/abusing his position to rustle up some female company.

I thought we were already broken beyond repair by then. What finished us off completely was the *Control* soundtrack, never mind South America.

'The rift widened ...'

The first time *Control* came up was way before Anton Corbijn came on board to direct. Two American journalists, Orian Williams and Todd Eckert, old friends of ours, had already bought the rights to Debbie Curtis's book and were trying to get backers for a film version. We met them in Prestbury at the restaurant Steve and Gillian had their wedding breakfast in. ('They were horrible to us,' said Steve.) It was there I suggested that Joy Division or what was left of them should do the incidental music for the film, and later the others had taken up my idea that we give a quarter of the publishing to Natalie, Ian's daughter, so that the credits on the new songs for the soundtrack would read 'Curtis, Hook, Morris, Sumner' again.

When Anton came on board, which of course we were delighted about, him being an old mucker of ours, it felt that now it was bound to happen and that was very exciting. They were having difficulty finding financial backing for the film, and Anton ended up re-mortgaging his house to fund the film to the tune of a million pounds, he believed in the project that much.

Andy Robinson went to meet him to talk about the soundtrack, which was our first mistake, because we all knew Anton and should have sat down with him ourselves. Having it done through an intermediary – especially when that intermediary was Andy, whose track record for passing accurate messages wasn't exactly unblemished – ended up making things much more difficult. He came back and announced, 'Anton doesn't want any drums on the tracks.' I went off on one.

'Hang on a minute,' I told Andy, 'you're supposed to be Joy Division and New Order's manager. Steve is in Joy Division and New Order, and someone has said to you, they don't want his drums. Andy, what makes Joy Division unique?'

He said, 'Er, what do you mean?'

I said, 'It's the fucking drums, you knob. Why would you agree to not have the fucking drums on? You should have said, "No, Anton,

Steve's drums define Joy Division," not go stabbing him in the back. Steve, have you seen what this twat's done? He's just fucking dumped you from the fucking soundtrack of the film ...'

I went ape. I probably went too ape. On a scale of ape from *Curious George* to *King Kong*, I was scaling the Empire State Building and swiping at passing biplanes. But the fact was that neither a frame of film, nor a note of music had been created. It was obvious that what Anton wanted was a more textured, ambient sound for the soundtrack, but how we achieved that was up to us, not him. He had no right to issue an edict restricting us from using drums – it was like us telling him he had to direct the film with one eye closed – and when the group in question is Joy Division, and the drummer is Steve Morris, famed for his innovative drum playing, it's just plain daft. Andy should have said, 'Tell you what, Anton, let them get on with it and see what you think of the results. If you don't like it, then we'll talk ...' not meekly agree to send Steve home. Not that anybody – including Steve – gave a shit, to be honest. Apart from me.

I have lived with the death of Ian Curtis for over thirty years and I didn't need anyone to tell me how the music for that particular scene should sound.

It was obvious this film wasn't called *Control* for nothing.

In the end what happened was that we wrote the music with drums, me and Steve started it at the Farm and then the tracks went to Bernard at his house where he added the keyboards, then it was mixed. I think they have a prominent Joy Division sound to them. They are very good. They were mixed low in the film, which usually happens. But had we obediently agreed with Anton's initial decree then we wouldn't have achieved the sound we did – the sound that everyone was delighted with.

Getting there was another story. Once again there was a difference of opinion as to how we should write. I wanted to jam songs, just as we had in the old days (when, in my opinion, we'd written our best material); Barney wanted to work on ideas alone at home (just as he had been doing in latter years).

Nevertheless, I wasn't exactly dogmatic about it – I'd long since given up on my cherished vision of us as an actual band, playing together, enjoying each other's musicianship or company. That was an ideal I'd had to abandon over a decade ago, when out went the practice of a bunch of musicians trying, often failing but just as often succeeding, to catch lightning in a bottle, and in came watching someone piss about on a computer for hours and hours.

However, Andy had somehow given Barney the impression that I was digging in my heels about the jamming issue, even though it simply wasn't true. I didn't care how we did it as long as we did it. Barney made some sarky comments about it after the Wolverhampton gig – the last gig of the English leg of the tour – like I was a dinosaur for even suggesting we do things the old way. I drove home and left him to it.

In his book he says I refused to work on it because I was DJing, simply not true ... kids, prepare yourselves – I swear on your lives that it wasn't true. Can you imagine Mr Bernard Sumner sitting there and going, 'Oh, we can't possibly do anything because Hooky's not here'? He never fucking noticed half the time when I was there.

Personally I think he was jealous of a leather coat I'd just been given by Gary Aspden at Adidas. I was wearing it that night for the first time and he couldn't stop looking at it, echoes of the All Saints split. The end result was I felt even more isolated, and the rift widened.

I had a huge phone argument with Andy about all this after the tour. He interrupted the argument to say, 'I have to go. I've got an important meeting about future Joy Division releases.'

'More important than talking to one of Joy Division?' I asked.

'Yes,' he said.

'You're sacked,' said I.

Rebecca said, 'Don't worry, I'll manage you on my own.' By now we had six gigs left to see us out to the end of the tour, but I'd decided I'd had enough. I was sick of having my heart broken. I was sick of trying to play music and being told to turn it down, or having it ruined by whistles and whoops and whinges at the soundman; I was sick of having the touring experience spoiled by someone who by his own frequent admission didn't want to be there; and I was sick of being dictated to in the studio sessions.

I was just fucking sick of Bernard Sumner. I told Prime I didn't want to go to Brazil – I'd had enough. As far as I was concerned this group was over. I could see the pain in Rebecca's eyes. 'But we're getting £600,000,' she said. 'You can't not do it.'

Then she announced, 'Oh, Bernard's having a year off after these six gigs anyway,' which in one sense infuriated me, because yet again he was dictating the terms, but in another sense I welcomed because it gave me some breathing space. By now he was definitely managing the band. I'd been talking to Rebecca and Andy and Tom Atencio about wanting the group to split for ages and they all said to give it time, let things cool down a bit, and of course I knew that time is a great healer, and I remember how well we'd got on making *Get Ready* – so I agreed to go on the tour. This year off afterwards seemed like a light at the end of a long dark tunnel.

At the airport, ready to fly out, he grabbed me by the arm and said, 'Don't forget I'm only doing this for you, because you need the money.' Jesus, I nearly chinned him.

Here we go, another moan. The fucker had kept us waiting so long to agree on the gigs that we'd lost our brilliant foldback guy Gerry to Primal Scream, so we'd got a replacement, a guy called Big Tiny, who we were told was very good. Of course, he wasn't good enough for our frontman. Cue yelling instructions at him mid-song, time and time again.

Meanwhile in Rio he dealt us another blow. We'd been trying hard to get 'Jetstream' to work; he just wasn't happy with it, and Phil, Steve and I had at last worked out some better parts for it, trying to make it swing more, to make up for Ana Matronic not being there and to make it sound more confident. He listened then dismissed it out of hand. 'We just won't play it any more,' he said. The next day we were delayed at the airport for about six hours. He went mad at Andy, as if it was his fault. We decamped to the business lounge but there he was acting like a spoilt child, kicking the furniture, throwing cushions and complaining he didn't want to be there.

Phil said, 'Come on, we'll go for a walk.'

'Can't,' said our petulant lead singer, 'the Vikings are down there and they keep bugging me.'

Our staunchest fans, travelling with us all round South America, had earned no goodwill either. He was making such a show of himself that me and Phil sacrificed the comfort of this executive palace for the plastic seats of the departure lounge.

I was DJing after nearly every gig, and was looking forward to that more than playing. Brasilia is a fantastic place and I must admit not pacing the favelas looking for drugs has a lot going for it. I got to see the city. It is Romanesque and beautiful. Them lot were moaning because it always used to be me that sourced the drugs. Left to their own devices they were useless.

I remember at one of my first DJ gigs in Rio we had gone for a meal and my guide was carefully leading me round the streets to avoid the favelas. Jokingly I said, 'Shall we go in?'

'No, signor,' he said. 'There are only two kinds of people that can go in the favela and survive, the Federales and English road crew.' At least that made me laugh. It was nice to be appreciated for something.

In Argentina for the last gig we stayed in a beautiful hotel, the 'F', and Tom Atencio turned up for a visit. My room was gorgeous and I didn't want to leave. But Barney demanded we soundcheck in the afternoon. We weren't due one here. As it was a festival we had to agree to pay for the extra time and men needed, and were given a very strict schedule. After a long hot drive to the site, when we arrived there was no sign of twatto.

'Where is he?' I enquired of Andy Robinson.

'Oh, he's gone shopping with Tom.'

'What about the soundcheck?' I asked. 'The soundcheck that only he wanted.'

'Don't know,' he said.

Barney eventually turned up five minutes before the end of our allotted time. He was just putting his in-ears in as the stage manager said, 'Finish now,' and ushered us all off. I was fuming.

Tom took me to one side, muttering, 'The traffic, man. The traffic.'

'Fuck off, Tom.'

I stormed off to a car.

The only bright note was later that evening, when they arrived back at the hotel to party on in the bar round the swimming pool, Phil Cunningham picked up a nearby chair and threw it in the drink – can't imagine what he's got against chairs – and, thinking no more of it, got absolutely hammered with the others. As they checked out the next day, dreadfully hungover, he was presented with a $2,000 bill for the chair, which turned out was a limited edition Philippe Starck. That'll teach him.

You're terribly unforgiving when you get sober. You can be a bit self-righteous, and want everyone to be like you, right on it. I have to say, I was as guilty as anyone for that. But I was ill with it. I was all torn up by a sense that it shouldn't be this way. That it didn't need to be this way. In the bus after the gigs on the way to the hotels, I'd been talking to Steve about it as usual, not expecting much, but there seemed to be a shift in opinion. Steve was agreeing it was too much as well, agreeing it was over.

In São Paulo I had sprayed on my cabs the words, 'Two boys formed a band.'

Then, second date in São Paulo, 'It all went wrong.'

Then in Rio. 'They split.'

And for that last gig in Argentina. 'The end.'

That was it. My message to the world, my departing words, my cry for help.

No fucker even noticed.

And after the last show in Argentina I was to DJ with Andy Rourke in a marquee on the site. I was feeling very miserable when I arrived. There were only a few people there, a couple of hundred, and the festival held about 115,000.

Ah well, I thought, *better get used to this now New Order have split*, when suddenly a gate opened on my right and about 10,000 people ran in. *Hello,* I thought, *there is life after death.*

'I should have smelled a rat'

I returned home with mixed feelings. I felt guilty taking £130,000 for five gigs that I'd hated playing. Somehow it felt like dirty money (but on the other hand, not *that* dirty), and I felt very sad that the band had wheezed its last, after twenty-six years.

But also optimistic.

By then I had a decent second career as a DJ, we were doing exciting things with the Haçienda name, plus I was in the throes of forming a new band, Freebass, with Mani and Andy Rourke. (Didn't work out, but that's another story.)

The main thing, though, was that I felt released from the tyranny of the band. I had a meeting with Rebecca soon after we'd got back and told her the group was finished; it was over. Rebecca did what any manager would do, she implored me to think it over, take some time to cool off and so on. In the meantime, with remastered versions of Joy Division and New Order albums on the way, I was asked to keep my trap shut and pretend everything was hunky-dory for the good of the group. Say nothing. See how you feel in a year.

Trouble was, I didn't get my year's cool-off to think about it. In February 2007, via Alan Wise, we had an invitation to play the Manchester International Festival. Suddenly Barney was keen to play this gig, Rebecca told me. 'The offer is £125,000 plus production. Barney says we should just nip down the road and pick the money up.'

'What happened to the year off he wanted?' said I.

'What do I tell Barney?' she said.

I said, 'Tell Barney I don't want to work with him any more. I told you when we got back from South America. The band is over.'

She said, 'Can't you tell him?'

I said, 'No. That's what I pay you to do.' To be honest I didn't feel I knew him any more. We certainly had nothing in common.

So she did. Not word for word, I don't think, but the message got through and Barney did the equivalent of shrugging his shoulders, which confirmed my suspicions that he didn't care.

In May 2007 I was interviewed by Clint Boon on *XFM*. Clint asked if we'd split and I replied that I wasn't working with Barney any more, which became 'New Order have split', which in turn created all sorts of problems, although I'm not sure why. After all, we had split. We were the two major songwriters, and we hated each other. How much more split do you want to be? Without us two writing together it was Bad Lieutenant or Electronic or Monaco. It wasn't New Order.

Barney was furious about the interview. Shortly after that came the premiere of *Control* in Cannes, and he didn't speak to me the whole time we were there. I stayed in the same hotel as Steve and Gillian and we got on just fine, travelling everywhere together.

The premiere of *Control* was in a huge theatre holding over 2,000 people, a really wacky bunch. It reminded me of our 'What Do You Want from Me?' video. Anton had changed the ending of the film and when I heard Debbie scream my heart was in my mouth. 'Atmosphere' again stole the show. I couldn't believe the audience clapped at the end; I thought a dignified silence would have been much more apt. They always say that you can tell how good a film is by how many people go for a piss while it's showing. Out of 2,000 people there were two, an old lady of about eighty and Barney. At the end even I was desperate for the toilet and when I unzipped at the urinal and looked round (as you do), next to me were Ian (Sam Riley), Steve (Harry Treadaway) and Barney (James Anthony Pearson), all staring at me. I said, 'Where's Joe?' (Joe Anderson, who played me).

'In Hollywood,' they chorused.

'Ha!' said I, 'if you'd have played me you'd have ended up in fucking Hollywood.' *Zip.*

We even went to a party after the premiere and I was sat with all of them, but Barney wouldn't look at me or talk to me. After that, we were due to attend a couple of award ceremonies, but we avoided one another. I went to the first with Steve and he went to the second one with Steve. Poor old Steve, eh?

Meanwhile, the group, as in just the three of us, had a couple of bad-tempered meetings, where we all called each other twats – well, me and Barney did, Steve just sat there – then a very good-tempered meeting where we all shook hands and agreed to go our separate ways. (It was actually quite tearful; we reminisced about the old days, agreed it was all over and even wished each other well for the future.)

'I should have smelled a rat'

The band split was definite. I should have smelled a rat when them two left together and were chatting away in the car park afterwards. Was Golden Goose syndrome snaring Steve?

Meeting four was another bad-tempered affair, this time with managers present, again at the Alderley Edge hotel in Cheshire about two minutes up the road from my house and not that far from Barney either (we're practically neighbours, remember, even today).

This one, coming after the Clint Boon interview, nearly ended up in a fight. It happened at a time when I was trying to buy Lesley Gretton out of her co-ownership of the Haçienda name, and with this happening in the background I arrived at the meeting to be greeted by a strange atmosphere.

Barney flew at me. 'You've taken the Haçienda off us,' he said. 'You've stolen it off us.'

That caught me off guard. After all, I'd bought the Haçienda name a whole decade previously and nobody had turned a hair. Suddenly it was a big issue.

I said, 'You never had anything to do with the Haçienda for ten fucking years. You'd not been to a meeting for seven before it closed, and I was funding it on my own for a year.'

He said, 'That's got nothing to do with it, you went behind our backs and bought the trademark.'

'I did no such thing.'

'Anyway, Lesley's offered us her share. And we're going to buy it.'

She was asking £8,000.

Imagine getting out of prison but then being told there was a mistake and they wanted you to serve another ten years. You'd go berserk, wouldn't you? Well, one thing about being sober is that you are more in control (no pun intended). Which is what I did, I stayed in control and left. I slammed the door on the way out, mind you. I'm not perfect. I stormed home, furious at them and worrying that my hard-won precious freedom was about to be snatched away from me. Like Al Pacino snarled in *Godfather III*, 'Just when I thought I was out, they pulled me back in!'

The thing was, I was immensely proud of what we'd achieved in Joy Division and New Order and with the Haçienda brand – and I consider myself a custodian of the back catalogue – but staying within the organisation was out of the question. The push and pull of me and Bernard had created some great music; as a musician I've untold respect for him. He's a brilliant guitarist and a great producer. But I couldn't spend any more time with him, not another second; I wanted nothing more to do with him. It was like a series of doors were clanging down and this was the final one.

Rebecca phoned me, full of apologies, saying she didn't know they were going to do that and they'd discussed what happened after I left and decided they weren't going to go through with buying out Lesley.

I said, 'Why?'

'Because they don't know what to do with it,' she said. I was very relieved.

Things went quiet for a while, and then in July came the statement. I was abroad DJing at the time. This would become a habit for most of their actions from now on. I heard about it at the same time as everybody else:

'After thirty years in a band together we are very disappointed that Hooky has decided to go to the press and announce unilaterally that New Order have split up. We would have hoped that he could have approached us personally first. He does not speak for all the band, therefore we can only assume he no longer wants to be a part of New Order.'

I don't believe that for one second. Both of them knew the group was over. Steve had done since the end of 2006 after our conversations on the Brazil tour, and Barney had from February 2007.

I phoned our press officer (supposedly still working for me at the time) and asked why I hadn't been told about it before release. She said, 'Oh, I forgot.'

'You're sacked,' said I.

I phoned Steve Morris from Los Angeles. 'What the hell is this, Steve? You knew exactly what was happening, about the group splitting. What's going on?'

'You know me, Hooky, whichever way the wind blows.'

So that was the end of that.

And you know what? Life got good again. There would be some terrible legal tussles but they were in the future. Meanwhile I could spend time with my family, as well as DJing and making music with Freebass. Plus I'd started to work on a book about my time with *The Haçienda: How Not to Run A Club*.

Eventually, like the sucker for punishment I promised myself I wouldn't be, I opened a new club of my own, FAC 251, with my partner Aaron Mellor, which is in the old Factory Records building at One Charles Street in town.

Ben Kelly redesigned it for us. Like I say, sucker for punishment. (Rob and Tony always told us how important it was to keep the circle going, give and take.)

As with drink and drugs, the further I moved from the New Order personnel, the happier I was. I began to look back on the work with an even greater sense of pride, a process that eventually found me forming my new band, the Light, in 2010, to celebrate the thirtieth anniversary of Ian Curtis's life. It had struck me that very few people had heard Joy Divison live, so this was a great opportunity to remedy that. Plus, I had come to greatly appreciate Martin Hannett's input and saw the chance to replicate the otherworldly sound of the records in a live setting.

At first there was a negative reaction to the announcement on the internet – those keyboard warriors who make all our lives a misery – which scared off the three people I had lined up to sing. It was Rowetta from the Mondays who said to me, 'Hooky, stop fucking about. You're going to have to sing,' in more or less those words. Me, I wanted to play bass, not sing. Ian's are very big shoes to fill. But I agreed. Which meant we needed a new bass player. My son Jack had been playing bass since he was fourteen and, having played a couple of charity gigs with Monaco, was the obvious choice. He's almost as good as me. Weirdly, he's the same age as I was when I began and has been as we've moved through the albums, which leads to some very stange *déjà vu* moments on stage. As the Light has moved on to performing New Order songs (slightly smaller shoes to fill) it's driven the others crazy. Again, another story.

Meanwhile, I began work on a second book, *Unknown Pleasures: Inside Joy Division*, which came out in 2013 and, I'm happy to say, did very well indeed. Shortly after that, I started work on the book you now hold, the one I knew would be the most difficult to write. I've agonised over every word and it's taken me a while, but I've put my heart and soul into what was the most important thirty-one years of my life, the idea being to bring you the most complete and truthful record of life inside New Order as is humanly possible. I hope you enjoyed it. And if you didn't, you know what you can do!

TIMELINE SEVENTEEN
JANUARY 2002–OCTOBER 2007

18 January 2002

New Order play Big Day Out at Ericsson Stadium, Auckland, New Zealand, featuring the Prodigy, Garbage, Basement Jaxx, the Crystal Method, NOFX, Jurassic 5, Dave Clarke, System of a Down, Kosheen and many others.

20 January 2002

New Order play Big Day Out at Gold Coast Parklands, Gold Coast, Australia.

23 January 2002

New Order play Big Day Out at Hordern Pavilion, Sydney.

26 January 2002

New Order play Big Day Out at Sydney RAS Showgrounds.

28 January 2002

New Order play Big Day Out at Melbourne Showgrounds.

30 January 2002

New Order play Big Day Out at Metro, Melbourne.

1 February 2002

New Order play Big Day Out at Adelaide RA&HS Showgrounds.

3 February 2002

New Order play Big Day Out at Claremont Showgrounds, Perth.

13 February 2002

Release of *24 Hour Party People*, directed by Michael Winterbottom, starring (among others) Ralf Little as Peter Hook.

8 April 2002

Release of *24 Hour Party People* soundtrack, featuring Sex Pistols, Happy Mondays, Joy Division, Buzzcocks, the Clash, New Order, Durutti Column, A Guy Called Gerald, 808 State and Marshall Jefferson.

Joy Division track list:

'Transmission'	3.37
'Atmosphere'	4.10
'Love Will Tear Us Apart'	3.25
'She's Lost Control'	4.45

New Order track list:

'New Dawn Fades' featuring Moby	4.53
'Temptation'	5.44
'Blue Monday'	7.30
'Here to Stay'	4.58

Executive soundtrack album producers: Pete Tong and Anthony Wilson.
Designed by Howard Wakefield at Peter Saville Studio.

15 April 2002

New Order: 'Here to Stay'
(London Records)

Twelve-inch track list:

'Here to Stay' (Full-length vocal)	5.00
'Crystal'	6.49
'Here to Stay' (Felix Da Housecat – the Extended Glitz mix)	8.00
'Here to Stay' (The Scumfrog Dub mix)	8.01

CD1 track list:

'Here to Stay' (Radio edit)	3.55
'Here to Stay' (Full-length vocal)	5.00
'Player in the League'	5.35

CD2 track list:

'Here to Stay' (Radio edit)	3.55
'Here to Stay' (Felix Da Housecat – the Extended Glitz mix)	8.08
'Here to Stay' (The Scumfrog Dub mix)	7.47

DVD track list:

'Here to Stay' (Radio edit)	3.55
'Here to Stay' (Felix Da Housecat – the Extended Glitz mix)	8.08
'Here to Stay' [Video]	
'24 Hour Party People' (4x30 seconds clip) [Video]	

Recorded in Real World Studios, Box, Bath.
'Here to Stay' produced by the Chemical Brothers and New Order.

Engineered by Steve Dub.
'Crystal' produced by Steve Osborne for 140DB.
Engineered by Bruno Ellingham and Andrew Robinson.
Programmed by Pete Davis.
Mixed by Mark 'Spike' Stent.
Engineer and pro-tools by Jan 'Stan' Kybert.
Assisted by Matt Fields.
Backing vocals by Dawn Zee.
Designed by Peter Saville Associates.
Entered UK chart on 27 April 2002, remaining in the charts for 3 weeks, its peak position was number 15.

21 May 2002

New Order: 'World in Motion '02'
(London Records)

CD track list:

'World in Motion' (radio mix)	4.30
'Such a Good Thing'	4.11
'World in Motion' (No alla violenza mix)	5.31

Entered UK chart on 15 June 2002, remaining in the charts for 2 weeks, its peak position was number 43.

> **'Done to cash in on the 2002 World Cup in South Korea and Japan, to make it a bit more interesting we had David Beckham lined up to redo the John Barnes rap, and then at the last minute he was blocked by the Football Association. A great shame, Tony Wilson was particularly upset. England went out in the quarter-finals.**
>
> **'In a strange twist of fate the previously unreleased track "Such a Good Thing" would be declared the BBC Radio 5 Live World Cup theme tune for all their coverage of this summer's key sporting event. Thanks, kids.'**

26 May 2002

New Order play Le Zénith, Paris.

9 June 2002

New Order play Finsbury Park Festival, London, supported by Hanky Park, Arthur Baker DJ, the Cooper Temple Clause, Echo and the Bunnymen, Super Furry Animals and Air.

15 June 2002

New Order play Hultsfred Festival, Hultsfred, Sweden.

22 June 2002

New Order play Southside Festival, Germany.

> **'Our first of two concerts, with our old friend Scumeck Sabottka, who started out with us as a runner and now ran these huge festivals in Germany, as well as managing Kraftwerk (our heroes). It absolutely pissed down here all day and when we went on stage everyone and everything was soaked through, the conditions were intolerable and, spying Scumeck in the wings, I went over to remonstrate with him.**
>
> **'"Scumeck, this is ridiculous, we need to stop."**
>
> **'"Stop? Stop? You fucking English arsehole! Are the fucking people stopping? Look at their faces, you fucking idiot! You're getting paid a fucking fortune and they are paying a fortune. You will fucking play until they tell you to stop!"**
>
> **'I thought, *Well you can't argue with that*.**
>
> **'I went to the front of the stage in the rain and played my little heart out. He was absolutely right. Eventually the hollow body of the guitar filled up with water until it started coming out of the f-holes and shorted out. I was free.**
>
> **'Ein Volk, Ein Reich, Ein Scumeck!'**

23 June 2002

New Order play Hurricane Festival, Hamburg.

25 June 2002

New Order play Lansdowne Road, Dublin.

29 June 2002

New Order play Roskilde Festival, Roskilde, Denmark.

13 July 2002

New Order play Old Trafford cricket ground, Manchester, with support from Doves, Echo and the Bunnymen (who replaced Shaun Ryder prior to the event), Elbow, Alfie and Hanky Park.

3 September 2002

The Muso award for best bassist this year is awarded to Peter Hook at a charity music award ceremony held in London.

29 October 2002

New Order: *International*
(London Records)

Best-of compilation for territories other than UK.
Track list:

'Ceremony'	4.25
'Blue Monday'	7.26
'Confusion -87'	4.43
'Thieves Like Us'	6.39
'The Perfect Kiss'	4.51
'Shellshock'	6.31
'Bizarre Love Triangle'	6.44
'True Faith'	5.52
'Touched by the Hand of God'	7.05
'Round and Round'	4.01
'Regret'	4.11
'Crystal	6.52

'60 Miles an Hour'	4.36
'Here to Stay'	3.59

Art direction by Peter Saville.
Cover illustration by Victoria Sawdon.
Designed by Saville Associates.

> **'It was very hard to get used to the sheer volume of releases sanctioned by London Records.'**

16 November 2002

NME staff voted the 100 greatest singles of all times:
Joy Division 'Love Will Tear Us Apart' was number 1.
New Order 'Blue Monday' was number 20.

25 November 2002

Arthur Baker vs New Order: 'Confusion '02'
(Whacked Records)

Twelve-inch track list:

'Confusion -02' (Koma and Bones Old Vox)	6.00
'Confusion -02' (Larry Tees Electroclash mix)	5.30
'Confusion -02' (Acapella Old Vox)	6.09

Run-out groove one: *It aint over . . . til it's over!*
Run-out groove two: *. . . it aint done . . . til its Fun!*

Recorded and mixed in Planet City Studios, Lancaster.
Remixed at Shakedown Laptop.
Produced by Arthur Baker and New Order.
Designed by Arthur Baker.

> Arthur Baker & Whacked Records have – In Honour of the 20th Anniversary of 'New Order's electro-rock classic "Confusion"' – commissioned an outstanding/eclectic set of remixes for the floors of 2002 – including interpretations from 'Koma & Bones', 'Junior Sanchez', 'Asto' & 'Arthur Baker'.

LTM recordings, http://www.ltmrecordings.com/one_true_passion_v2_ltmcd2375.html

Entered UK chart on 30 November 2002, remaining in the charts for 1 week, its peak position was number 64.

December 2002

NEW ORDER: *511*
(London Video)

Live from Finsbury Park, 9 June 2002.
Track list:
'Crystal'
'She's Lost Control'
'Transmission'
'Bizarre Love Triangle'
'Regret'
'True Faith'
'Ceremony'
'Temptation'
'60 Miles an Hour'
'Love Will Tear Us Apart Again'
'Atmosphere'
'Digital' (featuring John Simm)
'Brutal'
'Blue Monday'
'Close Range'
'Your Silent Face'
'NewOrder 9802' (live excerpts and interviews)

Produced by Geoff Foulkes.
Art direction by Peter Saville.
Designed by Howard Wakefield and Paul Barnes for PSA.

9 December 2002

New Order: *Retro* box set
(London Records)

Disc 1: 'Pop' – Compiled by Miranda Sawyer

'Fine Time'	4.42
'Temptation'	8.42
'True Faith'	5.53
'The Perfect Kiss'	4.49
'Ceremony'	4.24
'Regret'	4.08
'Crystal'	6.49
'Bizarre Love Triangle'	4.21
'Confusion'	8.13
'Round and Round'	4.31
'Blue Monday'	7.28
'Brutal'	4.49
'Slow Jam'	4.52
'Everyone Everywhere'	4.25

Disc 2: 'Fan' – Compiled by John Mccready

'Elegia'	4.55
'In a Lonely Place'	6.15
'Procession'	4.28
'Your Silent Face'	5.59
'Sunrise'	6.00
'Let's Go'	3.53
'Broken Promise'	3.45
'Dreams Never End'	3.12
'Cries and Whispers'	3.25
'All Day Long'	5.10
'Sooner Than You Think'	5.12
'Leave Me Alone'	4.40
'Lonesome Tonight'	5.11
'Every Little Counts'	4.28
'Run Wild'	3.56

Disc 3: 'Club' – Compiled by Mike Pickering.

'Confusion' (Koma and Bones mix)	6.01
'Paradise' (Robert Racic mix)	6.40
'Regret' (Sabres Slow 'N' Low mix)	6.41
'Bizarre Love Triangle' (Shep Pettibone mix)	6.42

'Shellshock' (John Robie mix)	6.28
'Fine Time' (Steve 'Silk' Hurley mix)	6.16
'1963' (Arthur Baker mix)	5.04
'Touched by the Hand of God' (original version)	3.42
'Everything's Gone Green' (original version)	5.31
'Blue Monday' (Jam & Spoon Manuela mix)	6.39
'World in Motion' (Subbuteo mix)	5.08
'Here to Stay' (extended instrumental)	5.55
'Crystal' (Lee Coombs Remix)	7.03

Disc 4: 'Live' – Compiled by Bobby Gillespie.

'Ceremony' (Barcelona, 7 July 1984)	4.49
'Procession' (London, 6 December 1985)	3.39
'Everything's Gone Green' (London, 12 March 1983)	5.14
'In a Lonely Place' (Glastonbury Festival, 20 June 1981)	5.32
'Age of Consent' (Warrington, 1 March 1986)	5.02
'Elegia' (Glastonbury Festival, 19 June 1987)	4.46
'The Perfect Kiss' (Glastonbury Festival, 19 June 1987)	9.43
'Fine Time' (Chicago, 30 June 1989)	5.02
'World' (Dallas, 21 July 1993)	4.48
'Regret' (Reading Festival, 29 August 1993)	4.01
'As It Is When It Was' (Reading Festival, 29 August 1993)	3.47
'Intermission by Alan Wise' (Paris, 12 November 2001)	1.20
'Crystal' (Gold Coast, 20 January 2002)	6.51
'Turn My Way' (Liverpool, 18 July 2001)	4.57
'Temptation' (Gold Coast, 20 January 2002)	7.47

Disc 5: Bonus limited edition

'Temptation -98'	4.08
'Transmission' (Live at Gold Coast, 20 January 2002)	3.59
'Such a Good Thing'	4.05
'Theme from *Best and Marsh*'	4.27
'Let's Go' (extract from instrumental)	2.01
'True Faith' (Pink Noise Morel edit)	4.29
'Run Wild' (Steve Osborne original mix)	4.11
'The Perfect Kiss' (recorded live at video shoot)	9.55
'Elegia' (full version)	17.31

'This was our idea to try and at last give the fans something of artistic value. Four different ways of looking at the group: "Popular", "Purist", "Remixed" and "Live". Each section curated by an appointed expert. The planning sessions got off to a surreal start when Barney, in a meeting at the Lowry Hotel in Salford, suddenly questioned a track.

'"What's that song?" he said.

'"Procession," said I.

'"Pro what? I've never heard that before."

'"Eh?"

'"I have definitely, never heard that song before in my fucking life!" he went on.

'"But it's you singing."

'"Definitely not! I have never heard it before and definitely didn't sing it!" he said, banging the desk then leaving. This was going to be harder than I thought.'

21 April 2003

Release of *Hope* (compilation), a War Child compilation for the benefit of the children in Iraq, featuring 'Vietnam' by New Order.

Written by Jimmy Cliff.
Produced by New Order.
Engineered by Merv de Peyer.
Backing vocals by Dawn Zee.

June 2003

New Order produce *The Peter Saville Show* soundtrack '30.13' for Peter's exhibition at London's Design Museum.

Written by New Order.
Produced by New Order
Mixed by Merv De Peyer.

1 Mar 2004

Revenge: *One True Passion V2.0*
(LTM Records)

Disc 1:
'Televive'
'The Wilding'
'Deadbeat'
'State of Shock'
'Little Pig'
'Cloud 9'
'Jesus I Love You'
'Pineapple Face'
'Big Bang'
'Slave'
'14K'
'Bleachman'
'Surf Nazi'
'7 Reasons'
'Amsterdam'
'It's Quiet'

Disc 2:
'Underworld'
'Deadbeat' (Gary Clail dub)
'State of Shock' (US edit)
'Pineapple Face's Big Day' (US remix)
'The Trouble with Girls'
'Wende'
'Slave' (bonus beats)
'I'm Not Your Slave'
'Hot Nights / Cool City'
'Surf Bass'
'Bleach Boy'
'Soul'
'Kiss the Chrome'
'Fag Hag'
'Precious Moments'
'Pumpkin'

Produced by Revenge.

Art direction by Peter Saville
Photography by Suze Randall.

From the sleeve notes:
One True Passion has been remastered and reconfigured by Peter Hook, and includes new recordings of the late-period unreleased tracks 'The Wilding' and 'Televive'. The 2xCD set also includes a full-length bonus disc, *Be Careful What You Wish For*, featuring rare remixes and unreleased songs in demo form.

April 2004

New Order: *The Radio 1 Sessions*
(London Records)

Track list:

'True Faith' (John Peel Sessions 1998)	5.35
'Isolation' (John Peel Sessions 1998)	2.44
'Touched by the Hand of God' (John Peel Sessions 1998)	4.39
'Atmosphere' (John Peel Sessions 1998)	4.30
'Paradise' (John Peel Sessions 1998)	4.08
'Slow Jam' (BBC Evening Sessions 2001)	5.22
'Your Silent Face' (BBC Evening Sessions 2001)	6.01
'Close Range' (BBC Evening Sessions 2001)	5.01
'Rock the Shack' (BBC Evening Sessions 2001)	5.24
'Transmission' (video from John Peel Sessions 2002)	

Designed by Peter Saville.
Photography by Jon Wozencroft.
Filmed by Miles Prowse.

23 May 2004

A memorial event for Rob Gretton: 'And you forgotten'.
The event was at the Ritz, Manchester, and all proceeds were for local charities.

This event was introduced by Tony Wilson. Bernard Sumner joined Doves for an acoustic version of 'Bizarre Love Triangle'. A Certain Ratio played 'Heart and Soul' by Joy Divison and were joined by Peter Hook on bass (of course).

25 October 2004

John Peel dies.

> **'John Peel was such an inspiration to – and true friend of – the group. He gave us our first commercial airing, our first "In Session". He was one of our first media fans, and a lovely man.**
>
> **'After a gig at Manchester University John was given a lift in a crappy old Morris Marina by Julz, the guitarist of Delta 5. I happened to come up behind them in my old Mk10 Jaguar 420G, KFR 666F. This car was so solid, it weighed two and a half tons, and so powerful, 265bhp, a lot then. I used to take great delight in creeping up to people's bumpers, touching them and then pushing them along. Most cars could not hold it. As I started to push Julz and John in the Marina, fully expecting them to look behind and tell me to eff off, they just shrank down in their seats and sat there as I pushed them right through the lights and onto Oxford Road, towards the oncoming traffic. Then the lights changed and Julz accelerated away. Always felt bad about that.'**

27 November 2004

Peter Hook goes into rehab.

> God, grant me the serenity to accept the things I cannot change, the courage to change the things I can, and the wisdom to know the difference.

> **'Amen to that!'**

15 January 2005

Joy Division's 'Love Will Tear Us Apart' is nominated for a Brit Award in the category 'Best Song of the Past 25 Years'.

15 January 2005

New Order win the Lifetime Award at the DMA (Dance Music Award) in Germany. Presented to Stephen Morris, Peter Hook, Bernard Sumner and Phil Cunningham. New Order perform 'Krafty' and 'Blue Monday' at the end of the show.

7 February 2005

Revenge: *No Pain No Gain Live 1991*
(LTM Records)

Track list:

'Intro Jam'	1.18
'Jesus I Love You'	6.41
'Slave'	5.05
'Deadbeat'	4.50
'Bleachman'	5.01
'Cloud 9'	5.23
'State of Shock'	6.12
'Dreams Never End'	3.48
'7 Reasons'	3.34
'The Trouble with Girls'	4.54
'Citadel'	5.33
'Kiss the Chrome'	4.52
'Pineapple Face'	5.38
'White Light / White Heat'	8.36

Designed by Julien Potter @ the Boxroom.

The first eight tracks are an entire performance at Manchester's Cities in the Park festival in August 1991. The remainder is from a show in Kawasaki, Japan, several months later.

17 February 2005

New Order are presented with the 2005 *NME* Godlike Genius award at Hammersmith Palais, London.

Presented to Stephen Morris, Peter Hook, Bernard Sumner, Gillian Gilbert (even Alan Wise came along), introduced by Pet Shop Boys. The band followed their acceptance speech with a live performance of 'Krafty', 'Love Will Tear Us Apart' and 'Blue Monday' – the first time the Godlike Geniuses had performed live at the *NME* Awards.

> **'This was a tough gig. Playing to an audience of your peers and musicians you've inspired and been inspired by was very strange, especially sober. It really was a baptism of fire. I was terrified. One good thing I soon noticed was that a lot of people around me, who I had just assumed were as off it as me, were actually sober. I never noticed. As time went on it would become apparent that most people were sober.**
>
> **'It would take me about four years of sobriety before I didn't feel threatened on occasions like these. After that I could watch anyone do whatever and it didn't bother me at all. I was shocked to find that most DJs are sober. I never expected that in a million years. Still, whenever I am out with my mates and it starts getting a bit leery, I usually get an attack of the heebie-jeebies and have to go home. It's too close.'**

7 March 2005

New Order: 'Krafty'
(London Records)

CD track list:

'Krafty' (single edit)	3.47
'Krafty' (album version)	4.33

Twelve-inch track list:

'Krafty' (single edit)	3.47
'Krafty' (The Glimmers twelve-inch extended mix)	6.52
'Krafty' (Phones Reality mix)	7.05
'Krafty' (The Glimmers dub mix)	5.53

Run-out groove one: *Forgive me father . . .*
Run-out groove two: *. . . for I have sinned!*

Recorded at the Farm, Rainow, and Real World Studios, Box, Bath.

Produced by John Leckie.
Remixed by Rich Costey, Paul Epworth and the Glimmers.
Art direction by Peter Saville
Designed by Howard Wakefield, Peter Saville Associates.
Photography by Mike Slack (from OK OK OK).
Entered UK chart on 19 March 2005, remaining in the charts for 4 weeks, its peak position was number 8.

'The first single off our new LP and I wasn't happy. In my absence Rich Costey had done a remix which to me sounded worse, more radio-friendly maybe, but when did we ever get anywhere being friendly to the radio? A weird video by Johan Renck to go with it and we were off . . . course. A great bass riff, though, one of my best. Some of the mixes were good.

'I started out hating remixes. I never thought anybody could do a better version than we did but with age I've mellowed and there were a couple of remixes, "Bizarre Love Triangle" by the Crystal Method and "Krafty", Morel's Pink Noise vocal mix, that I thought were actually better than the originals; same with that "Fine Time" mix by . . . Now who was that?'

28 March 2005

New Order: *Waiting for the Sirens' Call*
(London Records)

Track list:

'Who's Joe?' (produced by Jim Spencer)	5.41
'Hey Now What You Doing' (produced by Stephen Street)	5.16
'Waiting for the Sirens' Call' (produced by Jim Spencer)	5.42
'Krafty' (produced by John Leckie)	4.33
'I Told You So' (produced by Jim Spencer)	6.00
'Morning Night and Day' (produced by Stephen Street)	5.12
'Dracula's Castle' (produced by John Leckie)	5.40
'Jetstream' (produced by Stuart Price)	5.23
'Guilt Is a Useless Emotion' (produced by Stuart Price)	5.39
'Turn' (produced by Stephen Street)	4.35
'Working Overtime' (produced by Stephen Street)	3.26

Recorded at the Farm, Rainow, and Real World Studios, Box, Bath.
Executive producer: New Order.
Written by New Order except 'Jetstream' by New Order, A. Lynch, S. Price.
Keyboard and additional programming by Mac Quayle.
Special guest on 'Jetstream': Ana Matronic.
Art direction by Peter Saville.
Photography by Peter Saville and Anna Blessman.
Designed by Howard Wakefield, Saville Associates.
Entered UK chart on 8 April 2005, remaining in the charts for 4 weeks, its peak position was number 5.

New Order: *Lost Sirens*
(London Records)

Track list:

'I'll Stay with You' (produced by Stephen Street)	4.22
'Sugarcane' (produced by Tore Johannsen)	4.50
'Recoil' (produced by Jim Spencer)	5.09
'California Grass' (produced by Stephen Street)	4.35
'Hellbent' (produced by Stephen Street)	4.27
'Shake It Up' (produced by Mac Quayle)	5.23
'I've Got a Feeling' (produced by Stephen Street)	4.29
'I Told You So' (Crazy World mix) (produced by Stuart Price)	5.06

Art Direction and design by Studio Parris Wakefield.
Entered UK chart on 19 January 2013, remaining in the charts for 1 week, its peak position was number 23.

'I've put these two together because they were all from the same recording session. After we had finished and put out *Waiting for the Sirens' Call* the idea was to finish and release another LP very quickly. Unfortunately it then fell foul of Barney's one thing at a time regime, so was on hold for the gigs and then put on a backburner by the split. Andy Robinson, in late 2007, sent me the stems (i.e. the component parts of the track) to re-record the bass on "Sugarcane". Then it was shelved again while Barney did Bad Lieutenant. I suggested putting the three tracks we had

done for *Control* together with what was left over to form a full-length LP. This was ignored. Then Warners came up with the idea for *Total*, one record showing the dance progression of both bands, Joy Division and New Order. I thought this was a great idea and agreed to put "Hellbent" on it. Sadly, it just became another greatest hits package, and kick-started our feud in the press.

'The others then tried to release *Lost Sirens* without my permission, going straight to Warners without including me. Luckily, the most minority shareholder power you have is when a song has not been released before. I was able to stop them and we came to a compromise and at last it was released. Bands, eh? Who'd be in one? Answers on a postcard to ...'

21 March 2005

New Order play Canal+ Décalé.

27 April 2005

New Order play on *Jimmy Kimmel Live!*
'Krafty'
'Love Will Tear Us Apart' (dedicated to Ian Curtis)
'Waiting for the Sirens' Call'
'Crystal'
'Temptation'
'Waiting for the Sirens' Call' (retake)
'Transmission'

Only the first two songs were aired on ABC.

29 April 2005

New Order co-headline with the Chemical Brothers at the Henry J. Kaiser Convention Center, Oakland, California.

16 May 2005

New Order: 'Jetstream'
(London Records)

CD track list:

'Jetstream' (radio edit)	3.47
'Jetstream' (Richard X remix edit)	3.38

Twelve-inch track list:

'Jetstream' (Jacques Lu Cont remix)	8.19
'Jetstream' (radio edit)	3.47
'Jetstream' (Richard X remix)	7.42
'Jetstream' (Tom Neville remix)	7.35

Run-out groove one: *Ten Hail Marys ...*
Run-out groove two: *... and four Bloody Marys!*

Recorded at the Farm, Rainow, and Real World Studios, Box, Bath.
Additional vocals: Ana Matronic.
Remixed by Stuart Price.
Produced by New Order.
Designed by Peter Saville.
Entered UK chart on 28 May 2005, remaining in the charts for 2 weeks, its peak position was number 20.

1 May 2005

New Order play Coachella Valley Music and Arts Festival, Indio, California.

> **'This is a beautiful festival site. I started by DJing in the afternoon at a private party for DKNY. They didn't even seem to mind me blowing the PA up immediately. It was a great gig and I was given four wonderful goodie bags, one for each member of the band. When we arrived at the gig, Barney's huffiness about me DJing seemed to evaporate as he opened his, oohing and aaahing at the delights therein, even wearing his new DKNY watch straight**

away. It seemed to be the day for freebies, with us each getting a free pair of Converse shoes off the battle wagon and then being visited by a gentleman who proclaimed himself "the Black Santa", who, as you've asked, was black and had a huge sack of free Fox gear for anyone who wanted it. We tucked in like we'd never seen clothes before: socks, tops, trousers, jackets, everything. The gig was very good with good moods and smiles all round. Oh, why couldn't gigs be like this more? I saw one person drunk the whole weekend. As if we could ever say that about an English festival.'

3 May 2005

New Order play Aragon Ballroom, Chicago, Illinois.

5 May 2005

New Order play Hammerstein Ballroom, New York.

27 May 2005

New Order play Primavera Festival, Barcelona, Spain.

28 May 2005

New Order play Parque Tejo (Super Bock, Super Rock) Festival, Lisbon, Portugal.

3 June 2005

New Order play on *Later with Jools Holland*: 'Krafty', 'Waiting for the Sirens' Call' and 'Transmission'.

10 June 2005

New Order play Southside Festival, Germany.

12 June 2005

New Order play Hurricane Festival, Hamburg.

24 June 2005

New Order play Hyde Park, London.

25 June 2005

New Order play Glastonbury Festival.

30 June 2005

New Order play Rock Werchter Festival, Belgium.

2 July 2005

New Order play Traffic Festival, Turin, supported by 808 State and a Shaun Ryder DJ set.

9 July 2005

New Order play T in the Park, Balado, Scotland.

10 July 2005

New Order play Oxegen Festival, Punchestown Racecourse, Ireland.

14 July 2005

New Order play Arvikafestivalen, Sweden.

22 July 2005

New Order play Les Vieilles Charrues (Old Ploughs Festival), Brittany, France.

31 July 2005

New Order play Fuji Rock Festival, Japan.

21 September 2005

New Order: *A Collection*
(London Video)

Disc 1 track list:
'Confusion'
'The Perfect Kiss'
'Shellshock'
'State of the Nation'
'Bizarre Love Triangle'
'True Faith'
'Touched by the Hand of God'
'Blue Monday -88'
'Run'
'World in Motion'
'Regret'
'Ruined in a Day'
'World'
'Spooky'
'1963'
'Crystal'
'60 Miles an Hour'
'Here to Stay'
'Krafty'
'Jetstream'
'Waiting for the Sirens' Call'

Disc 2 Alternates:
'Round and Round' (USA/Patty)
'Regret' (Baywatch)
'Crystal' (Gina Birch version)

Paris/Beijing:

'Ceremony'
'Temptation'

Live 1981:
'Temptation' from *316*

26 September 2005

New Order: 'Waiting for the Sirens' Call'
(London Records)

CD track list:
'Waiting for the Sirens' Call' (Rich Costey radio edit) 5.39
'Waiting for the Sirens' Call' (Jacknife Lee remix edit) 6.10

Seven-inch track list (I):
'Waiting for the Sirens' Call' (Rich Costey radio edit) 3.52
'Temptation' (Secret Machines remix edit) 4.37

Seven-inch track list (II):
'Waiting for the Sirens' Call' (Band mix) 3.53
'Everything's Gone Green' (Cicada remix) 4.33

Seven-inch track list (III):
'Waiting for the Sirens' Call' (Jacknife Lee remix edit) 4.11
'Bizarre Love Triangle' (Richard X remix edit) 4.19

Run-out groove one: *All this scratching …*
Run-out groove two: … *is making me atch!*

Recorded at the Farm, Rainow, and Real World Studios, Box, Bath.
Remixed by Rich Costey.
Produced by John Leckie.
Designed by Peter Saville.

'Barney did say WFTC was his favourite New Order song ever. A lovely song, and a great bass riff, thank you, god of riffs. Released as a triple seven-inch vinyl single by London, each single featuring

as the B-side of a brand new remix of an old classic single of ours, interesting.'

October 2005

New Order: *Singles*
(London Records)

CD Track List:

Disc 1:

'Ceremony'	4.39
'Procession'	4.29
'Everything's Gone Green'	4.10
'Temptation'	5.24
'Blue Monday'	7.26
'Confusion'	4.56
'Thieves Like Us'	3.57
'The Perfect Kiss'	4.51
'Sub-Culture'	3.26
'Shellshock'	4.24
'State of the Nation'	3.32
'Bizarre Love Triangle'	4.22
'True Faith'	5.54
'1963'	4.21
'Touched by the Hand of God'	3.43

Disc 2:

'Blue Monday -88'	4.09
'Fine Time'	3.10
'Round and Round'	4.00
'Run 2'	4.31
'World in Motion'	4.32
'Regret'	4.10
'Ruined in a Day'	3.58
'World (The Price of Love)'	3.40
'Spooky'	3.45
'Crystal'	4.21

'60 Miles an Hour'	3.50
'Here to Stay'	3.57
'Krafty'	3.47
'Jetstream'	3.44
'Waiting for the Sirens' Call'	3.52
'Turn'	4.13

Entered UK chart on 15 October 2005, remaining in the charts for 5 weeks, its peak position was number 14.

10 October 2005

The *Q* Legend Award this year is Joy Division, presented to Stephen Morris, Peter Hook and Natalie Curtis at Grosvenor House in London, England.

12 October 2005
New Order play John Peel Tribute Night at Queen Elizabeth Hall, London.
It is the first time the surviving members of Joy Division have perform 'Shadowplay' and 'Warsaw' since the death of Ian Curtis.

10 November 2005
New Order play the Academy, Brixton, London.

14 November 2005
New Order play the Apollo, Manchester.

16 November 2005

Joy Division / New Order are inducted into the UK Music Hall of Fame at Alexandra Palace, London.
Joy Division / New Order were honoured as were Bob Dylan, Eurythmics, Pink Floyd, Aretha Franklin, Jimi Hendrix, the Kinks, Ozzy Osbourne and Black Sabbath, the Who and honorary member John Peel.
Presented to Stephen Morris, Peter Hook, Bernard Sumner, Gillian

Gilbert and Phil Cunningham, introduced by John Simm. They performed live 'Regret' and 'Love Will Tear Us Apart' (without Gillian Gilbert).

18 November 2005

New Order play Oakwood High School, Salford.

28 January 2006

New Order play Manchester vs Cancer, Manchester Evening News Arena.

25 May 2006

New Order are among the winners at the Ivor Novello Awards in London. The 51st annual ceremony took place at London's Grosvenor House Hotel. New Order are honoured in the Outstanding Song Collection category and are at the ceremony to claim their award.

> 'At this event I discovered that the PRS has over 500,000 songwriting members but only 2,000 of them make a full-time living from it.'

3 June 2006

New Order play Ejekt Festival, Athens.

8 July 2006

New Order play Summer Pops, Liverpool.

> 'Anton brought the actors from *Control* to meet us. Which was quite interesting, but my actor never made it. The others did, but mine was busy. At the gig a bunch of Vikings were being hassled by security – for the crime of dancing, would you believe. Every time someone danced a security guy would beckon them over and when they came near the bouncer – out of natural curiosity, I suppose – the security guy would open the fire door and push

them out. It was causing uproar. I stopped the gig to sort it out. A big fat security guard got hold of me afterwards and said, "You're a fucking troublemaker." I said, "No, mate. I'm a fucking troublemaker from Salford. Fuck off.'"

14 July 2006

New Order play Summercase Festival, Boadilla del Monte, Madrid.

15 July 2006

New Order play Summercase Festival, Parc del Forum, Barcelona.

2 September 2006

New Order play Stradbally Hall Estate, Stradbally, Ireland.

9 October 2006

New Order play Bournemouth International Centre, Bournemouth.

11 October 2006

New Order play Newcastle Academy, Newcastle.

16 October 2006

New Order play Empress Ballroom, Blackpool.

18–19 October 2006

New Order play Glasgow Carling Academy, Glasgow.

28 October 2006

New Order play Wembley Arena, London.

29 October 2006

New Order play Civic Hall, Wolverhampton.

> **'My back guy Scott Middleton, Wilmslow Chiropractors, 01625 531164 (mention my name for discount), fixes my back, thank God.'**

10 November 2006

New Order play Ginásio Nilson Nelson, Brasilia, Brazil.

11 November 2006

New Order play Mineirão Stadium, Belo Horizonte Brazil.

13 November 2006

New Order play Via Funchal, São Paulo, Brazil.

14 November 2006

New Order play Via Funchal, São Paulo, Brazil.

16 November 2006

New Order play Vivo Rio, Rio de Janeiro, Brazil.

18 November 2006

New Order play Club Ciudad, Buenos Aires, Argentina.

'The End.'

May 2007

The premiere of *Control* (a biopic of Joy Division frontman Ian Curtis directed by Anton Corbijn) in Cannes follows an *XFM* interview with

Clint Boon, during which Peter Hook reveals he and Bernard Sumner are no longer working together.

18 June 2007

Joy Division are among the winners at the 2007 MOJO Awards in London, honoured in the Outstanding Contribution to Music category. Presented to Stephen Morris and Peter Hook, introduced by John Simm.

10 August 2007

Tony Wilson dies of a heart attack in hospital.

7 September 2007

The premiere of *Joy Division* documentary at Toronto film festival.

1 October 2007

Control soundtrack album
(OST)

Track list:

'Exit' – New Order	1.14
'What Goes On' – The Velvet Underground	5.07
'Shadowplay' – The Killers	4.11
'Boredom' (live) – The Buzzcocks	3.07
'Dead Souls' – Joy Division	4.51
'She Was Naked' – Supersister	3.53
'Sister Midnight' – Iggy Pop	4.18
'Love Will Tear Us Apart' – Joy Division	3.26
'Problems' (live) – Sex Pistols	4.18
'Hypnosis' – New Order	1.35
'Drive-In Saturday' – David Bowie	4.31
'Evidently Chicken Town' (live) – John Cooper Clarke	0.31
'2HB' – Roxy Music	4.29
'Transmission' – *Control* Cast	3.02

'Autobahn' – Kraftwerk	11.23
'Atmosphere' – Joy Division	4.33
'Warszawa' – David Bowie	6.21
'Get Out' – New Order	2.44

'In the film Anton had made the actors learn to play their designated instrument, then got them to chronologically play the songs. So they played "Digital" early, as they were learning, then moved on to the later songs. This gave a very subtle progression in the music, the early stuff was a bit rougher, less polished, and as they became more proficient at their instruments the power emerged. He wanted all the Joy Division songs on the album to be played by the cast. Warners came back with an emphatic 'No', fearing it would decrease sales. Such a shame, that was as mad as most of my ideas, that one. Brilliant.'

EPILOGUE

I have no idea what Tony Wilson would have thought of New Order's public feuding. He hated the private feuding when we split up, so I can hazard a guess. I think it would just have saddened him more. Maybe he would have seen the Situationist side. I never got to hear his opinion and to be honest I doubt he was overly concerned anyway. He was too busy dying. Stephen Lea (our solicitor) was telling me about his appeal for medicine. He was denied the medicine Sutent in what's known in England as a postcode lottery. This meant he could only pay for the drug privately.

He'd been suffering from renal cancer, and earlier that year had one of his kidneys removed. Unfortunately, this was one of those times when he would regret giving his three most popular bands back their master tapes, because he was skint.

Stephen set up a fighting fund to buy him the drug he so badly needed, and the music community round the world, for the most part, responded positively. Stephen said they used to have an opening session every Monday morning, reviewing the donations, where Tony would, hilariously, praise and damn the contributors in equal measure. Tony steeled himself to go to the Coachella Festival for the Happy Mondays re-formation gig (non-original line-up), to support Shaun, and with the aid of a walking cane introduced them. It was the last time he would travel abroad. It took him weeks afterwards to recover.

In July 2007, Bernard had finally married Sarah. I waited in vain for my invitation, must have got lost in the post, just like the invite to his first wedding, but Tom Atencio came over and, having lost his bag on the flight, borrowed my coat, so my coat went to Barney's wedding even if I didn't. Tom and I had lunch with Tony that day, which was wonderful. Even in his advanced state of illness he was witty and sanguine. Tony managed to turn up for Barney's wedding, too, but not for too long, with him being so ill.

Having a kidney out hadn't stopped the cancer progressing, and he died of a heart attack in the Christie hospital on 10 August 2007. I had been to see him the week before, taking my great mate Dave Dee with me for support. Dave had just been treated there for his prostate cancer, and when we got to the ward he went to pieces, saying, 'Shit, Tony's in the same room I was.'

When I went in Tony was with Oliver and Isabel, his children, but he was so ill he couldn't speak. It broke my heart. It was the last time I saw him.

I enjoyed Tony's presence in my life. I liked him, and I knew I'd miss him, which I do – just like I miss Ian and Rob. On a personal note, it was as though Tony's death drew that chapter of my life to a close, just as Ian's had opened it. The story ended the same way it began, with a fond farewell.

They played 'Atmosphere' at Tony's funeral. I know from painful experience that it's a very popular song at funerals, but he had more claim to it than most. Tony had moved heaven and earth to bring Joy Division and New Order into the world, so it was only right we played him out.

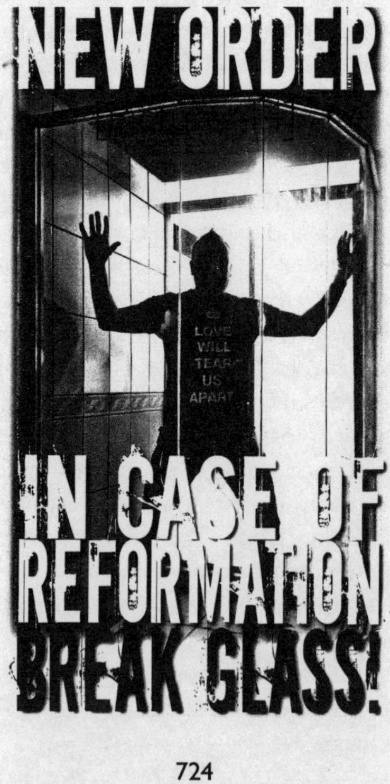

ACKNOWLEDGEMENTS

Thanks to Rebecca Hook, Irene and William Hook, Jack Woodhead, Heather Bates, Jack Bates, Jessica Scarlett Hook, Paul and Jayne Hook, Christopher and Diane Hook and families, Twinny, Andrew Holmes, David Sultan, Claude Flowers, Kerry Jaggers and Saxon, Tom Atencio, Joe Shanahan, James Masters, Stephen Lea, Mike Hall, Big Stu, Mr & Mrs Manley, James Roochove, Sandra and Anthony Addis, all at Intangible, Gwilym Harbottle, Mark Wyeth, Aaron Mellor, Tokyo Industries, David Potts, Phil Murphy, Steve Jones, Andy Poole, Paul Kehoe, Diane Bourne, Sarah Walters, Aaron and Jessica at Kill the 8, Eamonn Clarke, Lesley Thorne and all at Aitken Alexander, Pete Byrne and Peasey (Oxygen Management), Hector Morangues, Heitor from Brazil, Karen Donald, Andrew Lamb and all at OJK Ltd, Kate King at JMC, James Nice and *Shadowplayers*, Alistair Rawlence at Novagraaf, Andrew Clear and Martin, Scott Middleton and all at Wilmslow Chiropractic Clinic, Geoffrey Power, Dave Simpson, Tony Michaelides, Judy Riha, Wendy Fonarow, Marc Tilli, Bart Plooij, Matt Holyoak, Geoff Power, Suze Randall at suze.net, Trevor Watson, Peter Saville, Kevin Cummins, Keith Allen, Les Johnson, Kerri Sharp, Ian Allen, Mike Jones and all at Simon & Schuster. Carrie Thornton, Dey Street Books, Clint and Charlie Boon and family, Mike Sweeney, Mani and Imedla and the twins, Ange Matthews, Leroy Richardson, Alan Erasmus, Bruce Mitchell, and the rest of you can fuck right off.

Graffiti artist unknown

PICTURE CREDITS

The images reproduced in this book span decades, and some photographs were taken before the existence of the internet. The author and publishers have made all reasonable efforts to identify copyright-holders, and apologise for any omissions or errors in the form of credits given. Corrections may be made to future printings.

Front endpaper: © Kevin Cummins
Back endpaper: © Roger Lyons
Author shot: © Julien Lachaussée, www.julienlachaussee.com

Plate section 1

All photographs Peter Hook's Private Collection except 4, 5, 12, 14, 15 – photographers unknown
13 Courtesy of Judy Riha
16 © Kevin Cummins
25, 26 Taken from an unknown Brazilian magazine, 1985 – photographer unknown

Plate section 2

All photographs Peter Hook's Private Collection except 2, 5, 7 – photographers unknown
8 © Martyn Goodacre/Getty Images
9 © Donald Christie
10 Photographer unknown
11 © Tom Sheehan
12, 13, 14, 15, 16, 17 © Eamonn & James Clarke
18, 19 Photographers unknown

Plate Section 3

All photographs Peter Hook's Private Collection except 5, 9 © Eamonn & James Clarke
15 © Mark L Hill
18, 21 © Al de Perez, www.aldeperez.com

19 © David Sultan, worldinmotion.net
20 © Shaun Gordon, www.shaungordon.photography
22 © Shaun Gordon, www.shaungordon.photography

BIBLIOGRAPHY

Primary source: the memories, recollections, exaggerations and opinions of Peter Hook, various friends, family and enemies.

Secondary sources:

From Heaven to Heaven – New Order Live: The Early Years (1981–1984) at Close Quarters by Dec Hickey.

New Order + Joy Division: Dreams Never End by Claude Flowers.

The Blue Monday Diaries by Michael Butterworth.

Chapter and Verse by Bernard Sumner.

From Joy Division to New Order by Mick Middles.

Shadowplayers by James Nice.

True Faith: An Armchair Guide to New Order by Dave Thompson.

Vintagesynth.com

Soundonsound.com

Neworderonline.com

David Sultan, Worldinmotion.net FAC 441, factoryrecords.net FAC 421

Factoryrecords.org

Factoryrecords.net

mdmarchive.co.uk

Kinoteca.net

http://www.niagara.edu/neworder/

INDEX

Index

Index

Index

The Beach Club, Shude Hill. Where it all began. 30 July, 1980. If I knew then what I know now, eh readers?

My second brand-new car – an Audi Coupe, a beauty, outside my house on Minton Street, Moston. The house was £9995, the car £8010

Barney's second car – a Mercedes 200. He seems to have borrowed Steve's chin!

Jonathan Demme directed, filming on the roof and through the skylights, which drew rather a lot of unwanted attention. We were robbed for months afterwards

Filming 'The Perfect Kiss' video, Cheetham Hill, 1985. I certainly didn't dress for the occasion

Nordoff Robbins Charity Motocross, sponsored by Pinnacle. Both of us loved motocross. He was always much more careful than me. I came second to Eddie Kidd . . . saying that, he was a mile in front

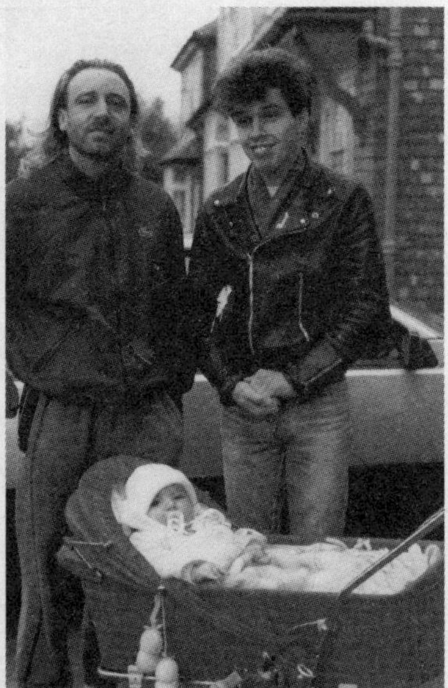

Me and Dave Pils with a very young Heather outside Tyndall Avenue, Moston. Just off on tour. . . again!

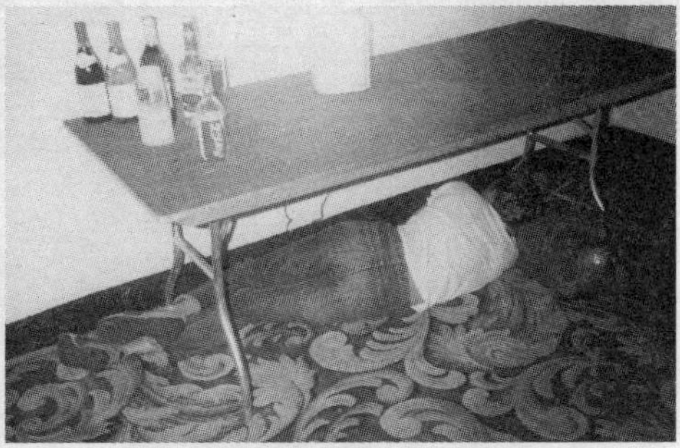

Sleeping it off in Washington. Someone shoved me under the table. Notice the second course above

'TBTHOG' video styling in Cheetham Hill. Sadly it felt dead right. No wonder it was banned!

Producing the Inspiral Carpets in Suite 16 Recording Studios. Great session! I played on one song too . . . Happy Days ;)

A lighter moment. Paris, late 80s. Great photo bomb, Barney

Lancaster University, 1985. I was always very serious on stage. Kill 'em all! Let God sort them out! Simmons pads and drum rack to my left

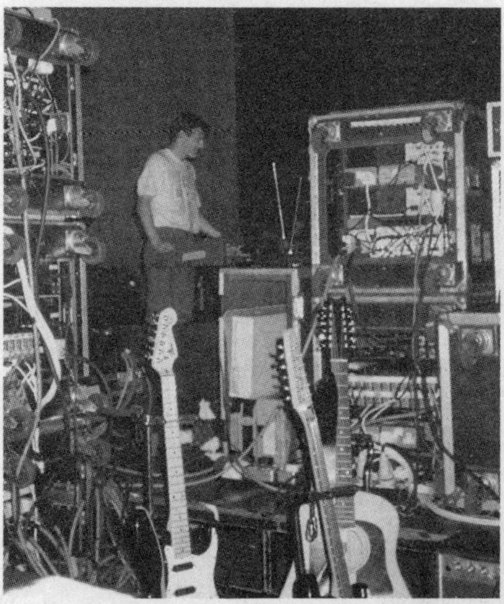

LA, 1988. Bloody Hell! Look at that lot! No wonder it broke down all the time and our sound checks took forever. We must have been mad

Smash Hits picture, the morning after. Note Barney's smug grin. Sylvia Patterson was fuming. I can't believe we didn't make it into her book

If looks could kill! I think someone walked past with a bottle of wine

On stage soundcheck, Paradise Garage, New York, 1983. Great club with a superb sound system. We filmed the 'Confusion' video after the gig

Me and the godfather of music, Quincey Jones, a lovely man. At the Montreux Jazz Festival – awful gig, even he couldn't stop that

With Tom Atencio backstage pre-gig. Digging the stereo black leather trousers. Ah, the '80s, I love you

Me and Keith Allen at the 'invite only' restaurant, 1990. Note absence of food

Ounce of coke, was supposed to last the whole tour, but three days later we were scrabbling for more.

Complete with a load of transvestites filming the 'Play at Home' video in New York New York, Manchester. Great suit. But now I have no idea why I did it

Me and another load of old trannies at 'Play at Home', the quiz show. Only joking! Pete Saville, Paul Morley, Tony Wilson, Ben Kelly and Keith Allen. A very funny day

Bobby Gillespie doing his impression of me, The Zap Club, Brighton, April 1990. He started out as a bass player in The Wake, a Factory Records band

The people you bump into at Real World Studios. One of my heroes, John Paul Jones. I was too shy to go and say hello, so said it to his Fairlight computer and flightcase

Me and Jane and my bass rig in Rio de Janeiro. Look at the rack on that! As my mam used to say, 'If you can't fight, wear a big hat, our Peter!'

Japan 1985. Now, what were we doing? Oh yes! Telling the story of New Order

Rob Gretton on tour mid-90s, doing what he loved best, skinning up and eating

Singing with Revenge at Alan Wise's Heaton Park Festival

At my heaviest weight, early '90s, a really bloated 15st. *Melody Maker* interview with Stuart Maconie, Graham Massey 808 State, Miles from The Wonderstuff

Inspecting the van crash, Revenge, Germany. With Murray and Sarge

Revenge Mk.1, 1989. CJ, Ash, David Potts, the youngest at 19, Dave Hicks

Dave Hicks takes over for the Charity Motocross. I am still a great supporter of Nordoff Robbins

Skin Two gig, London, 1990. I just loved the fashions . . . honest!

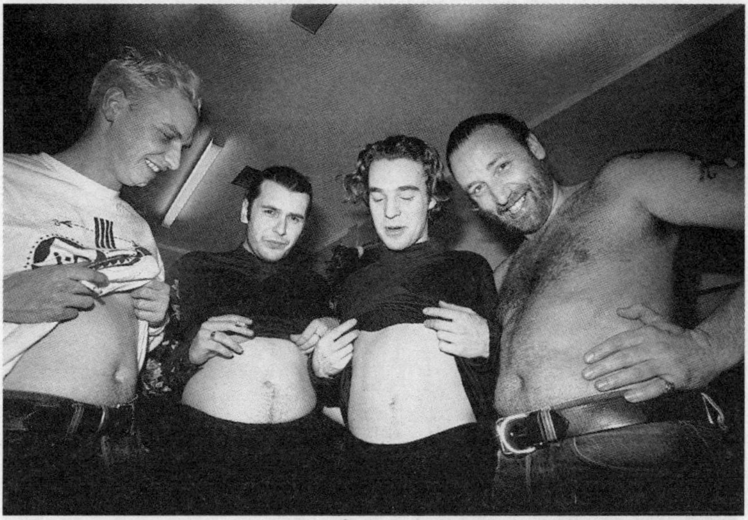

One of my favourite photos. Revenge seemed so 'light' after New Order. We really had a laugh. Just how it should be

Still biker-influenced but Dave Hicks on his way out sadly . . . we were on our way to Monaco

'I'm going to wash that band right out of my hair!'

Pottsy and I are Monaco. One of the first publicity shots, 1997

My great mates Clint Boon and his wife Charlie

Perfectly safe behind Sarge, complete with dodgy outfit outside Leroy Richardson's No.1 Club, post New Order Apollo appearance

With Tony W. for *Granada Reports* as they start the digger to demolish the Haçienda, early 2002. He was in tears

The Sticky Fingers fracas, November 1996. Caroline started it and Matt Bowers prepared the photographers, saying, 'He's going to get a beating!'

It was pitch black but the flash photography made it look quite barbaric. Leroy Richardson battered him. I was like Scrappy Doo stuck behind him

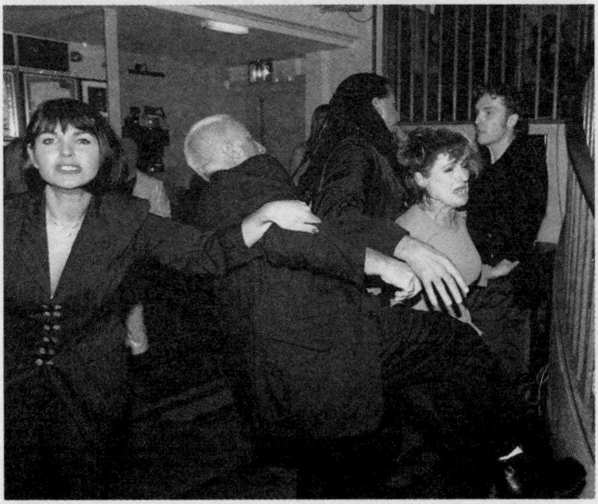

Oops! These photos were on the front page of every newspaper in Great Britain and Ireland. I was amazed. Becky makes her first public appearance

Bex went on to fit in very easily. Backstage Paris, 2002

A young Jessica with Alan Wise, R.I.P. I loved Alan but he was a total nutcase. Very well educated and erudite

Barney with Pascal Gabriel, the first of many sacked Producers. Regret? He had none. Rainow, Macclesfield, 1993

Paris Promotion and we meet our No.1 Superfan, David Sultan. Now my great friend and Pilot. Congratulations, David. Rosbeef!

Now as I was saying . . . 'Back to the story!'

With Pottsy and Bex on Sunset Boulevard, Los Angeles, 1997. We stumbled across this billboard above the Whiskey A Go Go. A fantastic moment

Jack and Heather with Robbie Williams, Cologne, 2002. I was still recovering from the Japanese virus. After the gig he grabbed me and said, 'Well done for getting through that!' Tough crowd

Heather and Jack in my bachelor pad bathroom. I decorated every inch of it myself

Jack is a great mate

Our wedding day, Brasserie St. Pierre, Manchester, December 1997. We catered a three-course meal for seventy-five people and three ate!

With Jessica at opening of Cirque De Soliel, Trafford Centre, Manchester. She was terrified, bless her

At Chad and Marita's wedding. Lovely day. How beautiful are them two? Royton, Manchester

My mother with Jessica and her cousin Terran. This one's for you too, Mam. I miss you so much xxx

All four kids together at Disneyland, 2000

This woman saved my life, over and over again. Thank you, Darling. I am so proud. I love you xxx

Prom night, King's School Macclesfield, 2015. Where do the years go?

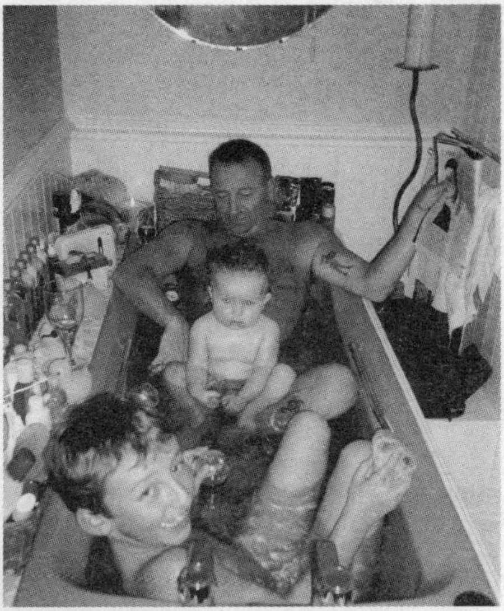

Bit out of sync these, but I like them. Bath time at Parr's Wood Road, Didsbury. I can't believe I had the time to read

Jack with three dummies, refusing to sleep. I am knackered

Rowetta, Imelda Mounfield (Mani's Missus), Bex and Jess. Two great Aunties and mentors

One of my first DJ gigs after New Order split in 2007. Punte Del Este, for Vogue Argentina. Free at Last!

Summer 2015. Jack has grown into a great man. One proud dad. Soon to join the Smashing Pumpkins

They always said I had a big ego, Ha Ha!

It's always nice to see your name in lights. Another 'sell out' show. Thank you, America

'This is how you play it, Son.' 'No it isn't. This is how you play it right, Dad.'

Rowetta looking gorgeous and me like a sweaty tramp. First gig by The Light, Factory 251

Tim Crooks up a storm, Factory Classical, Bridgewater Hall, Manchester, February 2016

Rocking the cockneys at Koko, Camden

Happy Birthday to me. Haçienda Classical, February 2016